D1736397

A Rebel Wife in Texas

A Rebel Wife in Texas

The Diary and Letters of Elizabeth Scott Neblett

1852–1864

EDITED BY

Erika L. Murr

Louisiana State University Press   Baton Rouge

Copyright © 2001 by Louisiana State University Press
All rights reserved
Manufactured in the United States of America
First printing
10   09   08   07   06   05   04   03   02   01
5   4   3   2   1

Designer: Barbara Neely Bourgoyne
Typeface: Adobe Caslon (text) and Centaur (display)
Typesetter: Coghill Composition, Inc.
Printer and binder: Thomson-Shore, Inc.

Library of Congress Cataloging-in-Publication Data

Neblett, Elizabeth Scott.
    A rebel wife in Texas : the diary and letters of Elizabeth Scott Neblett, 1852–1864 /
edited by Erika L. Murr.
       p. cm.
    Includes bibliographical references (p.) and index.
    ISBN 0-8071-2702-7 (cloth : alk. paper)
    1. Neblett, Elizabeth Scott—Diaries. 2. Neblett, Elizabeth Scott—Correspondence. 3.
Texas—History—Civil War, 1861–1865—Personal narratives. 4. Texas—History—Civil
War, 1861–1865—Social aspects. 5. United States—History—Civil War,
1861–1865—Personal narratives, Confederate. 6. United States—History—Civil War,
1861–1865—Social aspects. 7. Army spouses—Texas—Diaries. 8. Army
spouses—Texas—Correspondence. 9. Neblett, William—Correspondence. 10.
Soldiers—Texas—Correspondence. I. Murr, Erika L. II. Title.

E605 .N34 2001
973.7'82—dc21

                                                                            2001029664

The author is grateful to the Center for American History at the University of Texas at Austin
for granting permission to publish the letters and diary of Elizabeth Scott Neblett.

The paper in this book meets the guidelines for permanence and durability of the Committee on
Production Guidelines for Book Longevity of the Council on Library Resources. ⊗

For Chris, Regan, and Olivia

CONTENTS

ILLUSTRATIONS

PREFACE

The Elizabeth Scott Neblett Papers at the Center for American History is a rich collection that includes twenty-eight boxes of scrapbooks, postcards, a diary, photographs, legal documents, clippings, and numerous other items spanning the years 1849 to 1935. Eight of the boxes contain Elizabeth Neblett's letters, as well as those of some of her descendants. To narrow the scope of study, I have focused on the period between 1852 and 1864. Elizabeth Neblett sporadically wrote in her diary from 1852 to 1863. The Civil War letters of Elizabeth (or Lizzie, as she was called) and her husband, Will, then pick up the narrative between April 1863 and July 1864.

I have tried to keep my editing to a minimum in order to faithfully transcribe the diary and letters of Lizzie and Will Neblett. The original spelling has been reproduced, but I did take some liberties with the punctuation. Lizzie was exceedingly fond of the comma, which makes reading her writing disjointed and difficult. As a result, I removed unnecessary commas for the sake of clarity. I also erred on the side of good grammar whenever Lizzie's or Will's handwriting created doubt about their spelling, capitalization, or punctuation. In addition, because many of the letters went on for several pages without breaks, paragraph indents were added for ease of reading.

I would like to thank Victoria Bynum, whose insight, guidance, and support made this book possible. Her assistance and encouragement were invaluable. Also, my thanks to Sylvia Frank and Andrea Blair for guiding me through the editorial process. My appreciation also goes to the staff at the Center for American History and the Texas State Archives for their aid in the research phase of this endeavor, and to David Ringberg for his search of military records. I would like to thank my family for their enthusiasm and support. And a special thanks to my husband, Chris, for his encouragement and faith.

Abbreviations

LN	Lizzie Neblett
WN	Will Neblett
CAH	Center for American History, University of Texas at Austin
LND	Lizzie Neblett Diary, Neblett (Lizzie Scott) Papers
NFB	Neblett Family Bible, Neblett (Lizzie Scott) Papers
NP	Neblett (Lizzie Scott) Papers
Memoir	"A memoir of the Life, Death, and character of my dearly beloved husband William H. Neblett" by Lizzie Scott, Neblett (Lizzie Scott) Papers
TX Census 1850	Federal Manuscript Census, Seventh Census, 1850, Texas
TX Census 1860	Federal Manuscript Census, Eighth Census, 1860, Texas
TX Census 1870	Federal Manuscript Census, Ninth Census, 1870, Texas

A Rebel Wife in Texas

NEBLETT FAMILY TREE

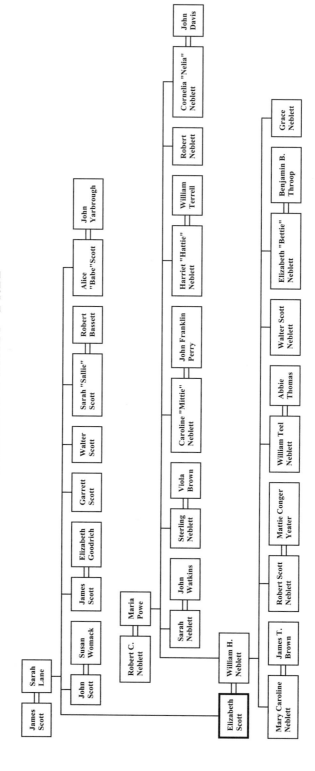

Introduction

I am so sick of trying to do a man's business when I am nothing but a poor contempt-ible piece of multiplying human flesh tied to the house by a crying young one, looked upon as belonging to a race of inferior beings as Swift says scarcely a degree above a monkey.

—Lizzie Neblett, August 25, 1863

In the midst of the nation's Civil War, Elizabeth (Lizzie) Scott Neblett wrote the above words to her husband, Will. Her words of anger and frustration give the reader pause. Like many southern women, Lizzie faced unanticipated hardships during the disruptive years of war; at the same time, her words speak to broader issues of gender that transcend the effects of war.

Many readers will remember Lizzie from Drew Gilpin Faust's ground-breaking study *Mothers of Invention: Women of the Slaveholding South in the American Civil War*, in which Faust analyzed the dramatic impact of the Civil War on southern women of the planter class. Lizzie's letters were among the many that enabled Faust to illustrate how the war ripped through the social and cultural fabric of white southern women's worlds. Lizzie emerged as a woman frustrated not only by the war's disruption of her domestic sphere, but one unprepared to "do a man's business." As Faust concluded, Lizzie expressed her anger and despair both inwardly, by continually castigating herself, and outwardly, by abusing her children.[1]

---

1. Drew Gilpin Faust, *Mothers of Invention: Women of the Slaveholding South in the American Civil War* (Chapel Hill: University of North Carolina Press, 1996), 47–48, 64–70, 124–26, 132, 139–40, 248–49.

In addition to revealing the impact of the war on one woman's life, Lizzie's diary and her Civil War letters illuminate many aspects of southern life, including plantation economics, master-slave relations, gender conventions, and the cultural norms of white southern elites. It is the related themes of marriage, childbearing, and child rearing, however, that recur most frequently, particularly because Lizzie struggled throughout her life to reconcile her individual needs and desires with society's expectations of her as a woman.

Unable to find happiness within the narrow sphere of the plantation mistress, Lizzie was unnerved by the increased responsibilities brought by the war. Performing Will's work satisfied her no more than performing her own. She may have wished for a creative respite from her wifely sphere, but she was unprepared and ill-equipped to handle the "manly" tasks required of her as a result of Will's absence. Rather, she felt betrayed by a society that assigned her one role, then forced her to fill another for which she had no training. There was no escaping her fate, however. Frustrated by her growing sense of powerlessness and inadequacy, Lizzie frequently railed in anger at her husband, herself, and her children.

Although Lizzie's wartime letters reveal a deepening level of discontent, it is important to recognize that inner doubts and contradictory impulses were not new to her, particularly in regard to marriage. When she first began keeping a diary in 1852, she was a young woman on the verge of matrimony. A rather naive and pampered southern belle, her vision of happiness would change over time. She began her marriage in an optimistic frame of mind, only to find herself caught in a cycle of domestic duties, childbearing, and child rearing. As the years progressed, she grew ever more dissatisfied with marriage and motherhood. To understand the significance of Lizzie's wartime letters we must therefore first examine the early years of her life.

Elizabeth Scott Neblett was born January 17, 1833, in Raymond, Hines County, Mississippi, the second of James and Sarah Lane Scott's seven living children. James and Sarah achieved financial and social success after several moves West. James Scott, born in 1799 in Milledgeville, Georgia, had moved to Tennessee by 1820, where in October of that year he married Sarah Lane, born on May 25, 1803, in Hickman County, Tennessee. Some time after 1825 the couple moved their family to Mississippi, where James built a successful career in law and politics. In 1839, when Lizzie was six, the family moved to Texas, where they spent their first winter in the village of Houston. The following year they settled permanently in Fanthorp Springs in Grimes County, three miles east of Anderson. By 1850 the Scotts were a well-to-do family who owned sixty-five slaves. In 1845 James Scott was elected a delegate to Texas's first constitutional convention, where he helped to frame the state's constitution. In 1846, after attending one session at a school in Houston, Lizzie continued her education in a log schoolhouse in Anderson, where education and literature quickly became important elements of her life.[2]

On May 25, 1852, at the age of nineteen, Lizzie married William Henry Neblett. Will Neblett was born March 2, 1826, in Winchester, Mississippi, the first of seven children born to Dr. Robert Caldwell and Maria Powe Neblett. Robert Neblett, a physician and veteran of the War of 1812, brought his family to Texas in 1839, the same year the Scotts arrived. There, he practiced medicine, farmed, and served in the Texas legislature from 1855 to 1856. His son Will met Lizzie Scott when he was twenty and she thirteen years old. At the time, both attended M. A. Montrose's male and female school in Anderson. After finishing his schooling, Will studied law with Lizzie's father and often came by the Scott home to borrow law books.[3]

Lizzie's early relationship with Will faithfully followed the courtship rituals appropriate for a southern belle. She strove to be attractive, enchanting, and flirtatious, and she married for love. Like a true belle, however, Lizzie could be fickle in her affections. For example, she broke her engagement to Will twice in three years. "Since I first loved Will," she wrote in April 1852, "I have grown cold some what in my affection three times, but every time have returned to my old love." Just one month earlier, she had expressed concern that Will had begun "to feel certain of the prize" in regard to her affections. Three days later, on March 20, 1852, she angrily lamented that she would never be loved by Will as much as she loved him. By the time she returned to her diary, that very evening, she was filled with regret for having criticized Will so harshly, especially since the diary was a gift from him. She blithely announced that they would be married in May, her pique apparently forgotten.[4]

2. *Memorial: Judge R. S. Neblett* (Texas, n.p., 1918); Irene Taylor Allen, *Saga of Anderson: The Proud Story of a Historic Texas Community* (New York: Greenwich Book Publishers, 1957), 254–55, 264–65; Drew Gilpin Faust, *Southern Stories: Slaveholders in Peace and War* (Columbia: University of Missouri Press, 1992).

3. Dorothy Neblett Perkins, *Some Nebletts in America* (San Diego, Calif.: Neblett Press, 1994) 83–89.

4. LND, March 20, 1852; April 19, 1852; March 17, 1852. For more information on courtship see Carol Bleser and Frederick M. Heath, "The Clays of Alabama: The Impact of the Civil War on a Southern Marriage," in *In Joy and in Sorrow: Women, Family, and Marriage in the Victorian South, 1830–1900*, ed. Carol Bleser (New York: Oxford University Press, 1991), 135;

In her quest for romantic love, Lizzie recorded tender moments between her and Will as well as coquettish doubts about their relationship. On May 4, 1852, she wrote: "To day he was leaning his head on my shoulder, we were both silent, he raised his head, and his eyes were over flowed with tears[;] I could not tell the ray of divine joy that shot through my soul, as those happy tears met my eye betraying his love." Yet her feelings for Will remained ambiguous. At one point she came to the unromantic conclusion that "I can never be rid of him as a lover untill I convert him into a husband." She then expressed confidence that after two broken engagements, this time they would actually exchange vows.[5]

There are no records that document Lizzie's early relationship with her parents, but in her diary she expressed fear that they would give her nothing after she left home because they disapproved of her impending marriage to Will. Relations apparently warmed after the marriage, however, for Lizzie frequently visited her parents and spent all of her "confinements" (deliveries of children) at the home of her mother. Nonetheless, it is true that her father only reluctantly consented to the marriage. Both parents predicted that the marriage would not last because of Lizzie's fickleness, and because they believed Lizzie thought herself smarter than Will and was "marrying him to rule him." According to Lizzie, they ridiculed Will in front of her, making fun of his red hair, his limited intelligence, and his limited financial resources.[6]

Lizzie's parents may well have feared that Will would not properly support their daughter. Despite society's emphasis on romantic love, parents knew only too well that the marital contract was an economic one. Lizzie, in contrast, expressed confidence that love would conquer all, writing that "I have nothing to give him but myself and my whole heart, and, I know ours will be a life of toil, yet a life I hope where love will abound." She defiantly declared that she would "*suffer & die first!*" before asking her parents for anything. Even if she and Will did separate, she vowed, she would not return to her parents' home, but would support herself.[7]

Despite her bravado, Lizzie knew that marriage required more than ro-

---

Ellen K. Rothman, *Hands and Hearts: A History of Courtship in America* (New York: Basic Books, 1984); and Catherine Clinton, *The Plantation Mistress: Woman's World in the Old South* (New York: Pantheon Books, 1982), 59–68.

5. LND, May 4, 1852; April 19, 1852.

6. LND, May 10, 1852.

7. LND, April 3, 1852; May 25, 1852; May 10, 1852.

mantic passion to survive. Her diary entries in the months surrounding her wedding day are testimony to the enormous effort it took for a young bride to keep romantic ideals alive and pragmatic fears at bay. As her wedding day approached, Lizzie's defiance of her parents' wishes gave way to frequent bouts of depression. In one of her "blue" moods she lamented that "the dark side of everything should always present itself to me. I seem to be the aim and butt of ill fortune." About her upcoming marriage, she wrote: "I have a thousand fears, and missgivings whether I should marry or not. Will is a new begginner in the Law business, and may not get practice, and I must have something to live on. Oh the stern realities of life!"[8]

Lizzie also worried about her impending role as household mistress. She was intensely gender conscious, ever mindful of the role women played in society. Like any "true woman" she knew she was expected to bury her own ambition in favor of her husband's. Thus, only weeks before her wedding day, Lizzie worried, "My identity, my legal existence will be swallowed up in my husband," but assured herself that "I have no cause to murmur [for] I love, and am beloved!" She strove to act accordingly. When Will announced he wanted to move to Marlin, a small town near Waco that contained no more than a dozen houses, Lizzie acted the dutiful wife: "to ensure him success," she wrote, "[I] would submit to any privation of taste or society." Yet try as she might, Lizzie never succeeded in completely submerging her own ambitions. In letters peppered with literary quotations and discussions of various authors, she made clear that she held her education in high esteem. She dared express hope that she might parlay it into a career. Specifically, she wished to obtain a teaching post at Marlin but, anticipating Will's objection, declared, "I won't listen to any thing Will says about it." Displaying faith in her ability to convince him, she decided, nevertheless, to wait until after their marriage to tell Will of her plans to teach. By then, she hoped, he would be more receptive to the idea, for she intended to "try every means to persuade him." Despite her dreams, Lizzie never taught school. Will's opinion on the subject was never revealed in the letters, but like most women of her time, she soon became immersed in the daily rituals of running a household. The birth of the couple's first baby within the first year of their marriage probably laid to rest any thoughts she had of becoming a teacher.[9]

8. LND, April 12, 1852; April 14, 1852.
9. LND, May 3, 1852; April 23, 1852; May 15, 1852; May 9, 1852. On the nineteenth-century "true woman" see Barbara Welter, "The Cult of True Womanhood, 1820–1860," *American Quarterly* 18 (summer 1966), 151–74.

Lizzie was well aware of the gendered barriers that prevented her from achieving her goals, and tried to accept them. On April 14, 1852, she wrote in her diary, "Heaven in her wisdom has placed insurmountable barriers between me and my individual ambition. I can never gain worldly honors. Fame can never be mine. I am a *woman!* a woman! I can hardly teach my heart to be content with my lot," she admitted, because that ambition was "the ruling passion of my life, in all things save love." She realized these "opposite passions" required that she subordinate her ambitions to Will's. And, as any "true woman" should, Lizzie believed she had no choice but to place the love of a husband above worldly success. Although she mourned the sacrifice of her ambitions, she expressed cautious hope that her future life as Will's wife would compensate for her loss: "I will have much to do, and I hope much happiness," she wrote, "if not, miserable will be my exchange."[10]

Like many young women of her class, Lizzie was not trained for life after marriage. Her instruction in sexual relations, for example, came not from her mother, but from Will's cousin Nelia. "Nelia," wrote Lizzie shortly before her wedding, "came to see me this evening, and led me into some of the mysteries of wedded life. Told me much more I am convinced than she would tell any one else. She told me in order that I might avoid several errors she ran into unknowingly." Perhaps because of Nelia's counsel, on May 27 Lizzie wrote of her wedding night that "I was not frightened the night I was married much; Will was not much either, but more than I was, his arm trembled *slightly*."[11]

The newlyweds lived with Will's parents during the first six months of their marriage. On the surface Lizzie's earlier doubts and fears seemed to vanish, and she looked to the future with joy and optimism. Less than two weeks after their wedding, she wrote, "I am so deeply happy. . . . I think it will last, always. . . . I find Will better than I thought he was." Not all had gone smoothly, however. Will had fallen ill shortly after their wedding day, giving Lizzie wifely duties that she had not anticipated: "I little thought I should have to begin *nursing* so soon after marriage," she wrote. Will's illness also made her wonder what she would do if he died. She insisted that she would not again

---

10. LND, April 14, 1852; May 7, 1852.

11. LND, May 12, 1852; May 27, 1852. On southern women's lack of training for marriage see Clinton, *The Plantation Mistress,* 59–86; Elizabeth Fox-Genovese, *Within the Plantation Household: Black and White Women of the Old South* (Chapel Hill: University of North Carolina Press, 1988), 207–10; Brenda E. Stevenson, *Life in Black and White: Family and Community in the Slave South* (New York: Oxford University Press, 1996), 68–72, 76–77.

love as she loved Will, but she did concede that she might remarry, and she mused over whether her father would allow her in the interim to move back home.[12]

In view of Lizzie's earlier defiance of her parents' wishes, it seems odd that she would consider so soon the possibility of moving back to their home. Apparently, she depended far more on their advice and company than she cared to admit. Only one week after she and Will married, the couple returned to her parents' home for a visit. Only Will's illness prevented her from visiting more frequently. She claimed to be primarily visiting her siblings, and complained of the cold reception her parents gave them. Nevertheless, she and Will visited her parents six times in the first four months of marriage. Even after Lizzie herself fell ill, and despite Will's nursing her, she visited her parents' home as soon as she was able.

Like many women in the antebellum South, Lizzie found it difficult to break girlhood ties. Certainly, she was aware that marriage would greatly alter her life, and that she would have new responsibilities. She noted in her diary, "My life will be entirely changed, all my cherished recreations, of mind & body must in part be abolished." Nonetheless, she found it difficult to meet the demands of being a wife. She confessed, for example, to having read a novel when she should have been working: "I can hardly do anything but read it, and think of it."[13]

Lizzie's transition from belle to household mistress was no doubt hindered by not living in her own home. In essence, she had traded one set of parents for another. Clearly anxious, she wrote, "Yet I fear all the time that I won't please them, that they will not like me." Predictably, she became jealous of Will's relationship with his mother: "He vexes me . . . and never commences a conversation with me, no more than if I had no ears to hear. But frequently goes where Ma is, and will talk for hours with her. . . . He thinks more of Ma any how than he does me."[14]

Lizzie's insecurities about whether Will loved her were not new. Even before their wedding she worried, "As long as love lasts I shall feel no fears, but

---

12. LND, June 7, 1852; June 13, 1852; June 16, 1852.

13. LND, May 7, 1852; September 1852. On southern belles' adjustment to marriage see Anne Firor Scott, *The Southern Lady: From Pedestal to Politics, 1830–1930* (Chicago: University of Chicago Press, 1970), 3–27. On their reading novels to escape household chores see Fox-Genovese, *Within the Plantation Household*, 261.

14. LND, July 13, 1852; June 16, 1852; September 1852.

alas! when love *dies*, 'There's the rub' to prevent love dying." Ever mercurial in her emotions, she reported with delight two days after their marriage that "he seems to have such respect *for my feelings!*" A month later, she searched for signs that their love was fading, concluding that "our love as yet has not become [an] old song to us, and I hope never may." Two months after their marriage, she expressed fear that her "sad melancholy disposition" would make Will unhappy and eventually destroy his love for her.[15]

In the fall of 1852 Lizzie's father provided the couple with a new home in west Anderson. Finally, Lizzie could set up her own housekeeping and be the mistress of her own home. Her new home and new status did not alleviate her problems, however. Lizzie soon claimed to be so occupied with "sewing & fixing" for the home that she did not have time to sew for her coming child.[16]

Mary Caroline, the first of the couple's six children, was born on April 7, 1853. Filled with anticipation and happiness during her first pregnancy, Lizzie wrote in November 1852 that "my joy is not yet replete, that my cup of happiness is not yet quite full the time is not yet come, when I hope to feel a Mothers joy, a mothers love. The life of my dear Babe, that I have implored Heaven to bless me with." She wholeheartedly embraced society's view of motherhood as her most "sacred occupation." She wrote, "Before a half year rolls round I will be a Mother—and feel all a mothers love, the holiest passion in the human breast." She thought giving birth so worthy an endeavor that it might help her to reach heaven: "[O]h! will it be spared, by a merciful Father to glad my pathway here, and perhaps lead me to Heaven at last."[17]

For Lizzie, however, the contradictions between lofty ideals and fearful realities proved as great in regard to motherhood as they had marriage. Despite her joy over impending motherhood, she frequently expressed anxiety about her coming confinement and childbirth: "How I do dread it, and wish it was all over with, and the baby and myself doing well. I know I have no conception of the pain nor can have none, until I feel and experience it." At the same

15. LND, April 10, 1852; May 27, 1852; June 13, 1852; July 13, 1852. On the importance of love and marriage in southern women's lives see Elizabeth Fox-Genovese, "Family and Female Identity in the Antebellum South: Sarah Gayle and Her Family," in Bleser, ed., *In Joy and Sorrow*, 15–31; and Clinton, *Plantation Mistress*, 70–76.

16. LND, December 19, 1852. Lizzie's parents' views of Will seemed to undergo a drastic change. In 1856 Mary Haynie, a friend of Lizzie's, wrote, "Will your Ma said, was the *best husband in the world*," Mary C. Haynie to LN, June 17, 1856, NP.

17. LND, November 11, 1852; January 2, 1853; November 11, 1852.

time, she worried that if she died, "My Babe could never know a mothers love kindness and protection."[18]

Death in childbirth was all too real a possibility for women of the nineteenth-century South. Whereas the average size of northern families declined as industrialization increased, the South remained overwhelmingly rural and families correspondingly large. Climate and settlement patterns increased the risk of certain diseases and decreased the availability of midwives and doctors. As a result, in 1850 one in twenty-five southern women died in childbirth, twice as many as in the Northeast. In Lizzie's state of Texas, 4.99 percent of white women's deaths in 1850 were a result of childbirth, one of the highest percentages in the nation. Women who did not die during childbirth faced the possibility of debilitating ailments afterward. During childbirth, many women suffered from puerperal fever, prolapsed uteruses, seizures, or hemorrhaging as a result of doctors' sometimes dangerous and unsanitary practices and because pregnancy weakened women's immune systems.[19]

Not only did nineteenth-century women fear death during childbirth, they feared the deaths of their infants. Lizzie shuddered at the thought, writing that "I cannot associate death with my Babe—no[,] death is cold and inanimate and my Babe is warm & full of life." She comforted herself by embracing motherly martyrdom. "[E]ven if Heaven has ordained that I shall purchase the life of my babe, by the sacrifice of my own," she wrote, "I should be content."[20]

Like many elite women of the nineteenth-century South, Lizzie spent her confinements at her parents' home, where she was tended by her mother. So essential was a mother's care deemed for an adult daughter's delivery of a child that when Lizzie stated she intended to remain home with Will during her first pregnancy, her father and brother convinced her instead to return to the family home.

18. LND, April 4, 1853; March 31, 1853.

19. U.S. Bureau of the Census, *Mortality Statistics of the Seventh Census of the United States, 1850* (Washington, D.C.: A. O. P. Nicholson, Printer, 1855). On the dangers of childbirth for nineteenth-century southern women, see Sally G. McMillen, *Motherhood in the Old South: Pregnancy, Childbirth, and Infant Rearing* (Baton Rouge: Louisiana State University Press, 1990), 81. On childbirth in the nineteenth century, see also Judith Walzer Leavitt, *Brought to Bed: Childbearing in America, 1750–1950* (New York: Oxford University Press, 1986); Richard W. Wertz and Dorothy C. Wertz, *Lying-In: A History of Childbirth in America* (New Haven: Yale University Press, 1989), 109–31.

20. LND, January 2, 1853; March 31, 1853. In 1850, 9 percent of the 6,194 children in Texas under the age of one died: U.S. Bureau of the Census, *Mortality Statistics of the Seventh Census.*

Although doctors had begun to replace midwives in the birthing chamber by the mid-nineteenth century, Lizzie was attended by the same midwife who had delivered her mother's last three babies. She did not engage doctors in any of her subsequent pregnancies either, although a note that she wrote during her labor with her first child may indicate that Will's father, a physician, served as her doctor. In that note, she informed Will, "Well I have been in labor since morning, [so] bring your Pa with you to night." Considering the times, however, her father-in-law was likely on hand in case of an emergency, rather than actually assisting in the birth of his own grandchild. Lizzie was particularly anxious about possible complications during her first childbirth because she had been exposed to measles.[21]

By mid-1853, Lizzie was mistress of her own household and the mother of a new baby. Her domestic responsibilities had rapidly increased in the space of only a year. In addition to caring for her new child, she oversaw household spinning and weaving and tended the garden and the chickens. Despite owning slaves, she struggled to learn to cook. While pregnant with Mary, she moaned to her diary about having ruined Will's supper by burning the meat and spilling the milk. To make matters worse, Will did not hand her anything, but sat there silently eating "as if it was the last he expected to eat this side of Jordan." Despite problems in their first year, Lizzie nonetheless remained positive about her marriage. In her diary, she wrote: "The current of our Matrimonial life so far has been smoothe, and unruffled[;] occasionally a harsh word, or harsher thought would for a while disturb the sunshine of our home, but angry feelings were not permitted to be inhabitants of our bosoms long."[22]

21. Fragment [presumably to WN from LN, ca. April 7, 1853], NP. On the growing preference for doctors over midwives during the nineteenth century see Leavitt, *Brought to Bed*, especially 37–63; McMillen, *Motherhood in the Old South*, 67, 72–75. For references to midwifery in Lizzie's letters see LN to WN, April 26, 1860; May 24, 1863; May 6, 1863, NP. It is interesting that in the May 6 letter, Lizzie mentioned that her mother wanted to find a white midwife. Slaves were engaged by whites as midwives before the Civil War. The war, however, raised fears among many white southerners about this practice.

22. LND, December 19, 1852; March 31, 1853. It is difficult to determine the extent to which Lizzie participated in household chores. She wrote about her garden and her hens, but mentioned very little about her actual involvement with them. She had one slave, Sarah, who appeared to have been her primary domestic help. It does not appear that Lizzie did much of her own weaving and spinning until the war, and even then it is clear that these were tasks she disliked: "I have come to the conclusion which has been forced on me, I will have to spin or weave one or the other myself, and have been doubly anxious to get a wheel, to find out which I can

By 1860, however, Lizzie's rosy picture of marital bliss had begun to unravel. By then she had given birth to four children. Mary Caroline, the couple's first child, had been joined by Robert Scott, born March 16, 1855; William Teel, born April 10, 1857; and Walter Scott, born May 14, 1860. In summer 1855, shortly after the birth of Robert, the family moved to Corsicana in Navarro County, where Will established himself as a planter, a lawyer, and in 1860 as the editor of the *Navarro Express,* a weekly secessionist newspaper. Financially, the couple thrived. By 1860 they had eleven slaves, real estate valued at $12,500, and a personal estate worth $14,500. Their main crops were cotton and corn. In the meantime, in spring of both 1857 and 1860, Lizzie traveled back to her parents' home in Grimes County to give birth, first to William and then to Walter.[23]

During the years 1853–1860, many of Lizzie's diary entries and letters described a "true woman," devoted to motherhood. When Mary suffered a bout with measles shortly after her birth, Lizzie remarked, "She has been a very healthy child since, as smart and pert as a wicket, she can sit alone now, and almost crawl." In March 1858 she wrote to Will that their third child, William, was "as good natured as Bob, always smiling, and when he cant smile he forces a smile which is only a grin and he looks so funny *grinning.*" In 1860 Lizzie provided a doting description of her fourth child, Walter, to her sister Babe. "I wish you could see little Walter, Babe," she wrote, "he is the sweetest little fellow; any one naturally fond of Baby's could not help being very fond of him he is such a good quiet babe, and so good natured laughs and crows, everytime you notice him."[24]

Still, despite the family's economic success and Lizzie's loving words, by 1860 domestic responsibilities had clearly taken their toll. On January 22, 1860, while pregnant with Walter, she entered a passage in her diary titled "A Review of the past eight years." Her words revealed fading optimism and self pity: "Eight years of checkered good and ill, and yet thro' all it seems the most of the ill has fallen to my lot." Although only twenty-seven years old, she felt that the years had not been kind to her: "The 17th of this month I was 27 years old—and I think my face looks older than that, perhaps I'll never see an

---

stand to do best, spin or weave." LN to WN, April 5, 1864; LN to WN, April 27, 1864; NFB; Memoir.

23. NP; TX Census 1860.

24. LND, November 1, 1853; LN to WN, March 6, 1858; LN to Babe [Alice] Scott, August 20, 1860, NP.

other birthday and I don't grieve at the idea." Her days as a young belle had passed. In fact, by the age of twenty-five, Lizzie already looked back to her days as a belle with longing. In April 1858 she admonished her younger sister Sallie to remember, "You know not how precious the present years of your life will be regarded by you, if you live to number my years, and how you will sigh as I do now and have often done, that they were not better improved."[25]

In her diary and letters, Lizzie continued to express fear that Will's affection for her was dwindling, and she also expressed her growing dread of childbirth. As ever, she struggled to accept her womanly fate, assuring Will during her pregnancy with Walter that "more meekly & humbly do I bow to the bitter cup of suffering ahead of me than I ever thought to do." She apparently had not felt the same way earlier in her pregnancy when she threatened suicide to her cousin Jannie. Jannie responded by writing, "Now I know I was and would be again miserable if I was so as you are[;] still I do not think I could meditate *suicide*." Jannie advised Lizzie on how to prevent pregnancy in the future: "Lizzie, I know that 'the Sponge' *will prevent conception* and tho I deem that a sin, still it is not so bad as killing one's self—so after you are over this trouble remember, if you get so again 'tis your own fault. I know the sponge is a safe and sure preventive—but I do not use it—I am not *in a fix* thank fortune, but I know not when I may be." The sponge was not a commonly used birth-control device during the nineteenth century, although it appeared to be one of the more effective ones. There is no evidence to suggest that Lizzie took her cousin's advice in regard to using the sponge. During the war, however, her letters reveal that she eagerly sought to obtain birth-control devices.[26]

Lizzie never reconciled the tensions between her personal ambitions and society's expectations of her as a woman. Despite her growing sense that she had failed to be a "true woman," she continued to advocate its tenets. On the one hand, she urged her sisters to study hard and get a good education, "so when you get married you will be as smart as your husbands and not ashamed

25. LND, January 22, 1860; LN to Sallie Scott, April 9, 1858, NP.

26. LN to WN, April 26, 1860; Jannie Teel to LN, January 2, 1860, NP. On birth-control practices see Janet Brodie, *Contraception and Abortion in Nineteenth-Century America* (Ithaca, N.Y.: Cornell University Press, 1994); Linda Gordon, *Woman's Body, Woman's Right: A Social History of Birth Control in America* (New York: Grossman Publishers, 1976); James Reed, *From Private Vice to Public Virtue: The Birth Control Movement and American Society since 1830* (New York: Basic Books, 1978).

to go in any company." Yet, although she praised her daughter Mary for being a good scholar, she feared that Mary "won't be smart about other things that women has to perform—she never minds getting a lesson but she don't like to sweep the house." Although many of her earlier ambitions for herself had been swallowed up in the day-to-day routine of being a wife and mother, she made use of her education by writing articles for newspapers under various pseudonyms. Nevertheless, in 1860 she reminded her younger sister, Babe, that "*mutual forbearance* towards each others faults and concession is the strong hold of domestic happiness," and that the wife was able to "concede with more grace than the husband [and] consequently should practice that virtue more than the husband." In 1864 Lizzie would simply proclaim education to be useless for girls. "Foolish women are the happiest," she wrote, and later, "better [to] be a fool than educated."[27]

Unhappy with living so far from relatives, Lizzie persuaded Will in late 1861 to move from Corsicana to Lake Creek, in Grimes County, where her family lived. Despite the move, she found neither the closer family ties she sought nor satisfaction with her life. While she became closer to her widowed mother, relations with her sisters, brothers, and sisters-in-law deteriorated. Apparently, Lizzie's siblings believed that she had cozied up to their mother in order to gain a larger share of the family inheritance. Lizzie vehemently denied this in a letter to Will. After telling him that her siblings believed she had moved back to Anderson in order to "rule" her mother and "see how she spent her money," she declared, "I don't want any larger share than the others of her property God knows no such notions influences me."[28]

By the time of the Civil War, Lizzie Neblett was a restless young wife who suffered from a number of conflicted relationships. Then came Will's enlistment in the Confederate Army. Although he was ardently prosecession, he sat out the first two years of the war for reasons not entirely clear. He did suffer from a variety of physical maladies, including rheumatism, headaches, and neuralgia, which, along with farm and family responsibilities, may have caused him to delay enlistment. On March 9, 1863, however, Will enlisted in the Twentieth Texas Infantry. His company, stationed at Galveston, never left the

27. LN to Sallie Scott, October 8, 1857; LN to Sallie Scott, January 27, 1861; LN Scrapbooks, NP (According to Faust, *Southern Stories,* 242, "Agnes Lyle" and "Meg Merrilies" were two of Lizzie's pseudonyms). LN to Babe [Alice] Scott, August 20, 1860, NP; LN to WN, March 28, 1864; LN to WN, January 3, 1864, NP.

28. LN to WN, January 21, 1864, NP.

state, and consisted mostly of middle-aged men. Although he initially served as a guard for the gunboat *Bayou City,* Will obtained a position as a clerk in a government office on grounds of poor health, through the intervention of a well-placed friend. In the meantime, Lizzie was left to manage the plantation and slaves; worse, she was pregnant with the couple's fifth child, Bettie (later called Lizzie), to whom she gave birth on May 26, 1863.[29]

Lizzie tried to reassure Will about her pregnancy, displaying her usual flair for the dramatic by insisting that "the three or four, or even eight hours of intense suffering that I will have to go through, will be as nothing when compared with my anxiety about you." Yet her apprehensions about bearing another child were evident when she remarked that "as to myself I know I will suffer terribly but, I have no idea that I'll die." She assumed the role of martyred mother, assuring Will that "if the babe can only be saved, & I not ruined for life, I will try and not mind the suffering." Of course, Lizzie *did* mind the suffering she endured during her fifth pregnancy, which was compounded by her husband's absence.[30]

A comparison of Lizzie's diary and letters over the years reveals how dramatically her attitudes toward motherhood changed. On April 5, 1853, as she awaited the birth of her first child, she had written: "It seems to me, if I live, and it dies I cannot possibly get over its death. I do love it so much, it feels so near me it don't seem to me I could ever love another as I love it." Contrast those words with these written to Will on August 13, 1863, three months after the birth of Bettie: "God knows her suffering after she grows to be a woman will be great enough to exempt her from all pain during infancy & childhood[.] I declare I sometimes think I had rather bury my daughters now then to live to see them mothers." Although she blamed Bettie for her misery, her antipathy was not limited to this daughter. She expressed discontent and aversion for her other children as well: "Above all things," she wrote on March 20, 1864, "I regret that I have lost all pride in the children, and view them more as a curse then a blessing." She would rather be locked in a penitentiary for thirty-five years, she told Will, than have one more child added to the five they already had.[31]

The Nebletts' wartime letters reveal deepening problems in their marriage,

29. WN served in Company I, Captain Stephenson's company. Military Records of William Neblett, Company I, Twentieth Infantry (Elmore's Regiment), from Compiled Service Records of Confederate Soldiers Who Served in Organizations from the State of Texas, M323, roll 400, National Archives, Washington, D.C.

30. LN to WN, April 26, 1863; LN to WN, May 6, 1863.

31. LND, April 5, 1853. LN to WN, August 13, 1863; March 20, 1864; May 24, 1864, NP.

particularly for Lizzie, who was forced to fulfill both male and female spheres of work. Dissatisfied in the role of the "true woman," yet frightened by the prospect of filling her husband's shoes, Lizzie moved haltingly between two opposing and contradictory spheres. Feeling comfortable in neither, she became frustrated and depressed, often lapsing into self hatred and disdain for the female sex. One of the ways in which she confronted her wartime fears was through the practice of spiritualism, especially mesmerism, which enjoyed great popularity during this era. Engagement in spiritualism convinced her that there was a special link between her and Will's minds. This in turn seemed to assure her that she could maintain his love and monitor his safety, despite the distance between them. In her letters she would inquire if he had been ill or thinking of home the night before, because, she explained, she had a strong "sense" of his feelings, which she believed emanated from him to her.[32]

Lizzie's ongoing quest for assurance of Will's love only intensified under the strain of war. On one occasion she complained that her brother John's letters to his wife were more "lover" like than Will's to her. In other letters, she openly accused him of not loving her and the children and of not wanting to return home. In contrast to Lizzie's letters, Will's were more practical than romantic. When Lizzie complained about their unromantic tone, he wrote: "I am sorry Lizzie that you cannot take my love for you on trust without frequent renewals of the pledge. . . . My mind I think is of the matter of fact & reflective cast and of course dictates the style of my letters."[33]

Will could in fact be romantic, however brief the moment. On March 27, 1864, he wrote, "I dreamed of seeing you so vividly in *dishabille* (in your night gown) sitting up in the bed in the act of getting out, one foot and leg bare up to the knee. I thought I admired your foot so much, and perhaps this was not

---

32. For an example of Lizzie's belief in mesmerism see LN to WN, May 3, 1864, NP. On mesmerism see Peter McCandless, "Mesmerism and Phrenology in Antebellum Charleston: 'Enough of the Marvellous,' " in *Journal of Southern History*, 2008 (1992): 199–230. On the popularity of mesmerism and related "treatments" among nineteenth-century Texans, see Gene Fowler, ed., *Mystic Healers and Medicine Shows: Blazing Trails to Wellness in the Old West and Beyond* (Santa Fe: Ancient City Press, 1997). Lively accounts of the popularity of spiritualism are provided in two recent biographies of feminist Victoria Woodhull: Mary Gabriel, *Notorious Victoria: The Life of Victoria Woodhull, Uncensored* (Chapel Hill, N.C.: Algonquin Books of Chapel Hill, 1998), and Barbara Goldsmith, *Other Powers: The Age of Suffrage, Spiritualism, and the Scandalous Victoria Woodhull* (New York: Alfred A. Knopf, 1998), as well as Gregg Andrews, *Insane Sisters, or The Price Paid for Challenging a Company Town* (Columbia: University of Missouri Press, 1999).

33. LN to WN, April 26, 1860; May 14, 1863; WN to LN, August 25, 1863, NP.

singular. For I always thought you had the prettiest foot & waist I ever saw." As though suddenly awakened from a reverie, he quickly added: "Well speaking of feet puts me in mind of shoes," and went on to ask Lizzie if she had gotten shoes made for the children.[34]

Perhaps if Lizzie had had closer relationships with female friends and relatives, she would have adjusted more easily to Will's wartime absence. The structure of plantation life in the nineteenth-century Southwest often isolated women from one another, hindering their ability to form close bonds. Since she did not get along well with either her sisters or sisters-in-law, she looked to Will for all her emotional sustenance. Her fear that his love would grow cold was surely exacerbated by this dependence, as was her related fear that he might be unfaithful to her. After Will contracted hydrocele, a swelling of the scrotum that was sometimes mistaken for a venereal disease, she felt compelled to deliver him a lecture on the sanctity of marital fidelity.[35]

Combined with Lizzie's fears of losing Will's love was her fear of losing him through death—her own, not his. In December 1863 she brooded over whether Will might take a second wife if she should die, since there were plenty of examples of men who quickly remarried after their wives' deaths. Although she advised Will to remarry in the event of her death, she warned him that he would not find a woman who loved him as much as she did. Her letters show that she was ready, nevertheless, to try to find him a replacement before she died, although she had been so "deceived" by women that she doubted her ability to find a suitable one.[36]

As Will's absence stretched into 1864, Lizzie's letters displayed ever more anger and frustration with her plight. Ultimately, she castigated herself for failing to live up to society's ideal of womanhood. "I again, unlike women generally," she wrote, "have given up all hopes of happiness." Increasingly, she wrote of considering suicide. Will's responses to such talk varied. He often did not address Lizzie's remarks directly, or occasionally he offered a mild rebuke, such as when he wrote on December 4, 1864, that "[your letter] had as usual a deep tinge of meluncholy and despondency pervading it . . . if it is a wish for sympathy it has the contrary effect on me."[37]

34. WN to LN, March 27, 1864, NP.

35. See LN to WN, June 19, 1864, and LN to WN, July 3, 1864, NP for Lizzie's discussions of marital fidelity. Also see Joan E. Cashin, *A Family Venture: Men and Women on the Southern Frontier* (Baltimore: Johns Hopkins University Press, 1991).

36. For examples of Lizzie's fears about Will taking a new wife see LN to WN, April 26, 1863; December 6, 1863; and LND, March 31, 1853, NP.

37. LN to WN, March 28, 1864; WN to LN, December 4, 1864, NP.

Although Lizzie had long expressed frustration over the constraints of a woman's sphere, being forced to assume male responsibilities during the war made her even more miserable. She had little agricultural knowledge, and worried that she lacked the ability to supervise the slaves. Ill-equipped to manage the farm, her failures only exacerbated her contempt for her own sex. Trapped within the female domestic sphere, she quickly came to feel helpless outside it. Overwhelmed by fears of failure, she constantly urged Will to return home. Ultimately, she was forced to rely on a male overseer to control the slaves but had difficulty finding one whom she could trust. She became disenchanted with the first one, a man named Rivers, and replaced him with a man named Myers. Myers, however, could only work at the Neblett plantation three days a week. The rest of the time Lizzie managed alone, convinced that the slaves did little work and would desert the plantation at the first opportunity. Because of the ravages of war and Lizzie's poor management skills, the plantation suffered declining profits. This left her feeling that she only "pretend[ed] to be chief of affairs" and prompted her to complain frequently to Will about her "poverty."[38]

The crisis of the Civil War strained many southern marriages to the breaking point, and it would appear from the Nebletts' letters that theirs was no exception. Lizzie's fears for Will's safety diminished as it became increasingly doubtful he would see any field service. Instead, she focused her anger on the additional burdens thrust on her and increased her efforts to get Will to return home. She complained bitterly about being left to manage the house, children, fields, and slaves, while he, in her opinion, had few responsibilities. When a neighbor called Will lazy, perhaps out of resentment for his easy position in Galveston, Lizzie repeated the neighbor's words to Will. She warned him that he might indeed become lazy because "if you have the good fortune to out live the war and come home, it will go hard with the most of the men, to go to work after living such an idle [life] for so long a time."[39]

---

38. LN to WN, October 25, 1863, NP. Lizzie's reaction to being a slave manager conforms to Fox-Genovese's assertion that plantation mistresses had only limited authority and management skills (Fox-Genovese, *Within the Plantation Household*, 110–17). For a contrary image see Clinton, *Plantation Mistress*, 29–35.

39. LN to WN, March 18, 1864, NP. On the Civil War's stressful effects on families, see George C. Rable, *Civil Wars: Women and the Crisis of Southern Nationalism* (Urbana: University of Illinois Press, 1989), 50–72; Victoria E. Bynum, *Unruly Women: The Politics of Sexual and Social Control in the Old South* (Chapel Hill: University of North Carolina Press, 1992), 119–29; Catherine Clinton and Nina Silber, eds., *Divided Houses: Gender and the Civil War* (New York: Oxford University Press, 1992); and Lee Ann Whites, *The Civil War as a Crisis in Gender: Augusta, Georgia, 1860–1890* (Athens: University of Georgia Press, 1995).

Despite their marital tensions, Lizzie and Will continued to express love for one another. Although Lizzie's letters to Will were filled with words of anger and frustration, it was motherhood that caused her greatest anguish. She was at times both verbally and physically abusive to her children, and they could not help but be aware of Lizzie's dissatisfaction with domestic life. When Mary asked her if she would like to be a little girl again, Lizzie replied that she would not live her life over. Mary responded by telling her mother that if she did, perhaps she would not marry this time. Lizzie petulantly wrote to Will that "I fear . . . my unfortunate views of marriage & children will cause my children to love and respect me less than I deserve."[40]

Although Lizzie had her hands full with five children, she also had borrowed a female slave, Polly, from her brother, to assist her with childcare. Lizzie, however, did not believe that Polly, who was perhaps seven or eight years old, relieved her of many motherly duties. In November 1863 she complained to Will that "Polly is too small to do anything for the baby but hold her & consequently my attention to the baby takes up so much time." In truth Polly did provide Lizzie with some respite from her children. A week later Lizzie admitted that when Bettie sometimes woke her up at 4 A.M., she would dress the baby, hand her to Polly or another female slave, and return to bed, where she might sleep "till daylight, sun up & often after sun up."[41]

Lizzie's wartime letters indicate that during Will's absence her physical punishment of the children shaded into abuse. Apparently, the children themselves physically abused one another and, at times, animals, suggesting a disturbing cycle of violence in the Neblett household. In part this violence reflected the culture of southern slave society. For example, the audacious behavior of one Neblett slave, Joe, so infuriated Lizzie that she contemplated shooting his mule. In another instance, when her overseer informed her that he might have to kill a few slaves in order to keep discipline among them, Lizzie counseled him not to kill them, but conceded that, if necessary, he could shoot at their legs. Lizzie herself was raised in a family that enforced discipline through the threat of whippings. At the advanced age of nineteen, while already engaged to Will, she complained in her diary that her father had "cursed me and told mother he had a great mind to *cow hide* me. Such expressions for a *father*."[42]

40. LN to WN, January 19, 1864, NP.
41. LN to WN, November 4, 1863; November 29, 1863, NP.
42. LN to WN, March 18, 1864; LND, May 10, 1852.

Although one might argue that Lizzie's discipline of her older children remained within the boundaries of nineteenth-century southern society, that was clearly not the case in regard to her daughter Bettie. Lizzie's letters reveal that she began whipping Bettie when she was only ten months old. Despite her Aunt Cinda's scolding her for such behavior, Lizzie defended her actions to Will on grounds that Bettie was so "bad."[43] At this point Lizzie's only gratification from motherhood seemed to come from treating the sicknesses of her children. Her letters to Will are filled with descriptions of their various illnesses and her care of them. Clearly, when her children were sick, Lizzie was a caring and devoted nurse. Her concern and devotion for her sick children, however, contrasted with her distaste for them when they were healthy. She herself remarked on this inconsistency when she wrote, "My conduct, & my words about my children do contradict each other." The children's illnesses apparently allowed her to feel important as a mother and powerful as a "doctor." She could better control passive, ill children than active, well ones. Once the children recovered, however, her special position was gone and they once again became noisy burdens.[44]

Despite Lizzie's aversion to motherhood, she knew she had no other recourse. In despair, she wrote the following words to Will on January 3, 1864: "God knows I wish you could raise & educate the children, and I could be allowed the delightful privilege of dying," and "I constantly wish that I had no one in the world to care for but myself." Realizing how this would sound to a husband, she conscientiously tacked on "no child I mean." As an upper-class southern lady, she was supposed to find fulfillment in her role as mother; instead she only longed for escape. A few months later she expressed her despair with the bitter remark, "If I could purchase a life of 80 years with 25 cts confederate money I would spurn the offer."[45]

As Lizzie contemplated Will's return from war, her thoughts turned to

43. For evidence of Lizzie's physical abuse of her children, see especially LN to WN, October 25, 1863; January 3, 1864; March 12, 1864; April 5 , 1864, NP. For more on nineteenth-century discipline see Jane Turner Censer, *North Carolina Planters and Their Children, 1800–1860* (Baton Rouge: Louisiana State University Press, 1984), 40–41; Kenneth Greenberg, *Honor and Slavery* (Princeton, N.J.: Princeton University Press, 1996); Steven M. Stowe, *Intimacy and Power in the Old South: Ritual in the Lives of the Planters* (Baltimore, Md.: Johns Hopkins University Press, 1987), 128–32, 138–39, 109–14; Bertram Wyatt-Brown, *Southern Honor: Ethics and Behavior in the Old South* (Oxford: Oxford University Press, 1982) 141, 145, 150–52, 158, 244.

44. LN to WN, May 9, 1864, NP.

45. LN to WN, January 3, 1864; fragment March 20, 1864, NP.

finding a method of birth control. In September 1863, Will assured Lizzie that he would cooperate in limiting the size of their family, writing that he was "willing to make sacrifices for your happiness or peace even if it results in unhappiness for me. But that is a subject better to talk of than to write about." Will's words imply that he would agree to abstinence, if that was what Lizzie wanted. In April 1864, however, she wrote to Will of her intention to find a "sure & certain preventive." In several letters she demanded that he obtain the necessary devices and supplies before returning home. The letters exchanged between Lizzie and Will in the ensuing months provide readers with one of the frankest exchanges on the topic of birth control recorded by a nineteenth-century southern couple. Although there is no concrete evidence that he provided Lizzie with the birth-control goods she requested, she did manage to avoid pregnancy for almost seven years.[46]

Although her demand for birth-control devices indicated defiance of social norms, Lizzie's determination to limit the size of her family was not unique among southern women. Her husband's willingness to consider practicing birth control may have reflected its growing acceptance in the South. And, of course, the mere fact that the South had a higher birthrate than the North does not preclude southerners' use of contraceptives—Lizzie's failed attempts at birth control attest to this.

Lizzie regularly expressed dissatisfaction with her gender role, but ultimately accepted her position. In March 1864 she wrote, "You speak of my self sacrifices, I admit, my life has been full of such, but don't make a virtue of what was a necessity. Woman was made for such things, and when she tries to evade them is only kicking against the thorns." Her letters provide us a tantalizing glimpse into the private world of one southern marriage.[47]

---

46. WN to LN, September 3, 1863, NP. For similar discussions of childbirth and birth control see William W. Hassler, ed., *The General to His Lady: The Civil War Letters of William Dorsey Pender to Fanny Pender* (Chapel Hill: University of North Carolina Press, 1988), 22, 52, 57–58, 68, 118–19, 216, 225–28.

47. LN to WN, March 18, 1864, NP.

I
THE DIARY

I

Love Will Unite Us!

1852–1863

Introduction

As learning holds the key to earthly distinction, and so many are wending (slowly it is true[)] their way up the rugged Hill of Science; I have thought to benefit myself by writing down occasionally such thoughts as may occur, in any particular form, in my chaotic mind.

I intend this book as a faithful repository of my inmost thoughts, my hopes, my sorrows, my joys. I have ever found relief from sorrow, by recording my grief, and in joy have reaped a double harvest. I find in writing[,] my thoughts assume a tangibility that I can never arrive at by mere thinking. My heart is now young full of hope, life, and animation. [R]easoning from the regular course of nature, I may have many years yet to live, and as it is wisdom to prepare for the wintry season, not only of the year, but of Human Nature, I think it may perhaps afford me some pleasure in those dark hours, when perhaps every earthly tie may be sundered, to read over the thoughts, the feelings of my youth "when life seemed formed of sunny hours." The knowledge that I have had my share of the joys of Earth may afford consolation for the griefs that are the portion of all Earthly travelers. I know that my sorrows will be many if I live out the sum of Human life, and the knowledge makes me humble in my gayest moments. I do not know that any other eye than mine will ever rest on these pages, as I have not the vanity to think any one would be interested in my secret thoughts that of course will relate almost entirely to myself.

This book may yet bring me sorrow, for it shall certainly hold my most secret thoughts of every thing. Yet I hardly suppose any one will have curiosity sufficient to prompt them to search into its pages.

Yet if any one should ever read this I hope they will be benefited by my trials and experience, and that I will not be judged too harshly, if occasionally I err slightly in both precept and example.

Tuesday March 16th/52[1]

Near Anderson Tex

Grimes Co Texas

Wednesday night

March 17th/52

I have been thinking to night, that Will did me great service the last time I saw him (which will be a week tomorrow). He made some remark about my writing to every body, or answering every letter I rec^{ed}, whether I knew to whom I was writing or not. The remark was provoked by my speaking of answering an anonamos letter I had rec^{ed}[;] he did not like my wishing to do so, and such was his method of expressing disapprobation. His remark was not just, and he partly confessed that he was in the wrong. I told him that I would write to him no more, which of course he did not believe, neither did I. [Y]et I feel convinced that I can never write with the same freedom that I have hither to writen to him. It has partly cured me of my inordinate degree of love for him; that is I do not feel it so sensibly, and can bear absence with a much better grace.

I do not suppose he intended wounding my feelings[.] I can not think so. His conduct, when I last saw him, was it seemed to me somewhat different from what it had been. He appeared more indifferent and careless than I had ever noticed before. I suppose he begins to feel certain of the prize. Well I find I do not take his indifference at all to heart. Pa[2] told him last Thursday that

1. The following words were added to this entry in pencil at a later date: "R. S. [Robert Scott] Neblett was born March 16th 1855." Robert Scott was the couple's second child.

2. Lizzie's father, James Scott, was born in 1799 in Milledgeville, Georgia. He married Sarah Lane in October 1820. He moved his family to Mississippi, where he practiced law, became a member of the Mississippi legislature, and served as a district judge. In 1839 the family moved to Texas, settling in Grimes County. James Scott was elected to the first state constitutional convention and helped frame the Texas constitution in 1845. He died aboard the *Nautilus* when it sank off the Gulf of Mexico on August 10, 1856. Memoir; Allen, *Saga of Anderson*, 264–65.

he had no particular objection to our union, mother[3] has yet to be consulted by him, tho' she knows how matters stand with us. It has been quite cool to day and my wits don't flow very rapidly.

It is quite early for my bed time, yet I am so sleepy I must stop.

Saturday night
March 20th 1852

I am feeling so sad, so despairing. When I think how full of hope, how happy I was only two weeks ago, I can hardly recognize that it is one and the same spirit that inhabits my bosom. Now I feel joyless, alone, unappreciated; and bitter feelings are continually rising and engulfing the few stray beams of light, and hopeful aspirations, that occasionally struggle for the ascendency in my darkened soul.

My feelings are deeply, painfully acute, and here even among those who I know love me better than any one else does I am often pained and wounded, beyond the power of expression, and for my own happiness I strive to persuade myself that the wound was not intentional[.] I cannot check my heart with such reasoning; too well, too feelingly, is the knowledge taught, that I am *bound to be unloved,* or with Mad^e De Stael[4] I can feelingly say, and with the conviction deeply rooted "Never never, will I be loved as I love," and Nature seems to have assigned my heart for loving ardently truly & has implanted the longing[,] I may say holy desire[,] to be loved. Oh! I have sometimes cheated myself with the belief that my wish is realized, that I am loved to the fullest extent of Earthly passion. Then I am happy, life seems not a burden, all Nature sings in echo to the delightful, hymning praises of my greatful soul; and a life composed of an eternity could not utter half of my praises, nor gratitude;

3. Lizzie's mother, Sarah Lane Scott, was born May 25, 1803, in Tennessee. James and Sarah Scott had seven children who lived to maturity: John, Elizabeth, James, Garrett, Walter, Sarah, and Alice. After the death of her husband in 1856, Sarah Scott took over the family farm. The 1860 census reported she had personal property valued at $70,000 and real estate valued at $52,344. She died February 17, 1880. Sarah Scott's granddaughter Elizabeth Neblett Throop (Lizzie and William Neblett's fifth child, born during the Civil War) contributed an article on her grandmother for Annie Doom Pickrell's book *Pioneer Women in Texas* (Austin, Tex.: F. L. Steck Co., 1929). NFB; TX Census 1860.

4. Baronne Anne Louise Germaine Necker de Staël-Holstein (1766–1817) was a Swiss-French writer whose principal work, *On Germany* (1810), helped introduce German romanticism to French literature. Her other works also include two novels, *Delphine* (1802) and *Corinne* (1807).

no even tho' the tongue of an angle [*sic*] were loaned me to utter those praises. The sunniest day has its shades, and dark shades soon fall on the sunniest, the greenest spots in the garden of my heart. Why do I complain? What charms, mental or personal, have I to enlist the love I crave? No it is too true [that] Nature has not been lavish with her gifts to me, yet is it wisdom to weep over what I have not; I will strive to improve the few and scanty talents I have, and fit my immortal soul for the abode of the 'just made perfect.' "To whom much is given much shall be required"⁵ is the words of holy writ, and perhaps if I had talents they would not be employed, in a manner to benefit either myself or the world. What aid will quarreling with existence bring me? The boon of life has been bestowed, and now it needs only that I "work out my own salvation with fear and trembling."⁶ In no case, and mine more than this, does it affect any good, to "whine put finger in the eye and sob," and still more to snarl and snap like "dog distract or monkey sick." Yes! I feel and know this; philosophy, or rather reason, teaches me this, yet can reason can philosophy teach my heart not to feel? No, tis this principle of feeling in the heart, that that [*sic*] gives us a place above the brute creation, or rather as some one has beautifully said "the *mute* creation." At times I am almost ready to curse my heart for feeling, but in calmer moments, when possessed of reason, I feel greatful for this only spark of divinity in man.

I am a selfish creature, and I fear am fostering that passion daily. Two weeks ago, I was very happy and hopeful, but for the last week [clouds] have been gathering in my internal world.

To night, Brother James⁷ brought me a letter from the office, and I found on examining it that it was from Ben.⁸ It is a very feeling letter and I now think that I have done him much injustice. Many and hard were the accusations I made against the poor fellow; and tears in spite of me rolled down my cheeks, for I am pained that I should wound the finer feelings of any soul on Earth. [A]nd Ben, that I once loved, and to listen to his story still loves me,

5. Luke 12:48.

6. Phil. 2:12.

7. James Lane Scott was Lizzie Neblett's brother. He was born in 1835 in Hinds County, Mississippi. He married Elizabeth Briggs Goodrich in Grimes County, Texas, in 1858. Grimes County Historical Commission, comp. and ed., *History of Grimes County: Land of Heritage and Progress* (Navasota, Tex.: Grimes County Historical Commission, 1982), 507.

8. Ben Smith was apparently a former beau of Lizzie Neblett's. Lizzie writes again of him in her entry of November 1, 1853.

how could I deride the sacred feelings of his heart in the manner I did? I was stung by his conduct, and vented it in firery reproaches, against him who I believe has been "more sinned against than sinning."[9]

I have scarcely thought of Will, without being in connection with his late unkind, unjust remark. How did every fibre of my heart cling round him, and every secret thought no less mine than his. [N]ow, how can I go to him for advise [*sic*], to be made strong? [H]e cares not to bear the burden and advise [*sic*], he will instead of showing me any error, if there be one, mock at my wishes, or else say nothing. Oh! Will[,] you certainly did not think or you would not have made that remark. I wish I could forget it. I do not know that he ever said anything that wounded me more deeply, except once he wrote these lines to me, or for me so said

It were all one, that I should *have* loved a bright particular star, and *thought* to wed it

I am sorry that these pages should have opened with complaints against Will. I do love him, in spite of all, and in May I am to become his wife. Pa has yielded a rather reluctant consent, and Will has not yet said anything to Mother about it[.] I feel confident that we will be married this time after being twice engaged to him before.

I wrote a note to him and sent it to the office on Friday, telling him of my intended visit to Bro John's[10] on Tuesday. He had expressed a wish to go with me when I went. I do not much expect him and truth to tell do not much care whether he comes or not. He got this book and sent it to me on last Monday. I expect he thought I would write a great many nice things about him in it,

9. *King Lear*, act 3, scene 3.

10. Lizzie's oldest brother, John Newton Scott, was born August 15, 1825, in Hickman County, Tennessee. He attended Columbia College in Tennessee until April 1841. Rejoining the family in Texas, he married Susan E. Womack September 24, 1844, and they had thirteen children. In the census of 1860 he is listed as a farmer with real estate valued at $1,370 and a personal estate of $12,880. Along with Will Neblett he served in the Twentieth Texas Infantry in Captain J. B. Stevenson's Company I. He spent most of the war near Galveston. John Scott became the first postmaster at Longstreet, Montgomery County, during Ulysses S. Grant's administration and held that position for thirty-five years. In the census of 1870 his occupation is listed as merchant with real estate valuing $10,000 and a personal estate valued at $9,000. He died on March 15, 1913. Lizzie Neblett wrote his obituary. "Scott, John Newton," vertical file, CAH; TX Census 1860.

and so I will if he does nice, and don't say unkind things to me again. He is a
good boy, and I do love him truly. It is raining to night, and the 'patter' on
the roof is rendering me sleepy. I do love to hear it rain and sometimes I love
to be awake at night in a storm. I wish Will was with me to night, my hand
in his, I feel that I could think better, and I know I should feel better.

Anderson Grimes CoTexas

Ten Oclock at night

March 20th/52

April 3rd 1852.

Tis night; a high wind is revelling among the leaves and branches of the
trees around my lowly habitation. The moon occasionally shows her face, from
behind a cloud, and is then quickly obscured again. This night makes me think
of life. [O]ccasionally, a stray moon beam will throw its light across our path,
and reflect on our heart its own bright hue, and then, a dark cloud will obscure
the brightness, just as we have began to hope. And so all the happiness we
have here, is snatched away just as we begin to appreciate it, as we begin to
feel the blessing we enjoy, and so I have learned to bear joy with humility, and
hail it as a "harbinger of woe."

The frailty of human hopes, of human joys! Yet "hope springs eternal in the
human breast"[11] and divine is the ordinance, for deprived of hope life would be
dark indeed. The future has ever some bright spot, around which, and for the
attainment of which, we struggle on, hope on, and die with our bright hopes,
unrealized[.] And I with the weakness of human nature have built me a lovely
arbor, in the bright deceitful future, to which my thoughts ever turn to find
there the rest and peace for my weary soul. Yet when I look at this bright this
lovely arbor [and] down the vista of coming years, when I think seriously,
aided by my knowledge of what has been, I know that if ever attained, many
very many dark clouds and many storms must intervene before that Earthly
paradise be mine. This spot is a *home*, where love esteem and happiness are
ever attendant spirits, where sorrow is ever soothed, where joy is shared by one
whom I love infinitely better than life. This is the *home* of *my heart*, where
every virtue will grow and flourish, nurtured by love, and esteem. To day, I felt
almost like this spot was unattainable, and I was almost ready to despair. Will

11. Alexander Pope, *Essay on Man.*

is poor, so am I.[12] I have nothing to give him but myself and my whole heart, and, I know ours will be a life of toil, yet a life I hope where love will abound. Pa and Mother seem to have a great many fears that we will come to them, to be supported by them. But no, I would suffer in penury and want all my life before I would implore their aid. Will can support me, I know, or he would never have sought to wed me, and poverty were better with him him [*sic*] than riches with another. No, Will and myself will never implore aid of my parents. I have told him that I would not bring him any property, and that I never expected any thing from Pa nor Mother before their death, and it was more than probable not then. Riches and worldly honors are nothing to me, nor am I any too good to suffer poverty with one I love. I shall hope. In May I shall marry with as little display and noise as possible. Will has or is going in three or four days up the country, near Waco and around there, to look out a location for practicing Law. I think he will locate up there, and I am exceedingly anxious that he should. We will stay down here till fall I expect, tho not at my home, for Mother has told me that I should not stay around her and faith to tell the truth I would not for pay, and Will would not I know.

I half expect I will stay at his Pa's[13] until we go up the country. Tho' I don't know that his Pa will want us around him either. I know my parents would not have either a son in law or a daughter in law around them. But all Parents are not alike. I am willing to go any where, put up with any thing do anything for Will, and with him.

My friends have all deserted me.

Sallie and Amanda Noble[14] have not writen in four or five months, so our correspondence has entirely ceased, and 'twill never again be renewed, for I would not answer a letter from either of them now.

---

12. The 1850 census reports William H. Neblett as a lawyer living with his parents and owning $600 in personal property. TX Census 1850.

13. Will's father, Robert Caldwell Neblett, was born October 28, 1795, in Roanoke, Virginia. He married Maria Powe on March 22, 1825. As a youth he served in the War of 1812. Robert Neblett received his medical training at the University of Pennsylvania and practiced medicine in Tennessee and Louisiana before moving his family to Texas in 1839. He was a member of the Texas legislature from 1855 to 1856. Robert Neblett died December 21, 1871. Perkins, *Some Nebletts in America*, 83–89. Robert Neblett is featured in Mrs. George Plunkett Red, *The Medicine Man in Texas* (Houston, Tex.: Standard Printing and Lithographing Co., 1930).

14. Sallie and Amanda Noble were friends of Lizzie Neblett. Both are also featured in Lizzie's letters. Sallie Noble married John Kennard March 22, 1855, and Amanda Noble married Henry White March 4, 1856. Marion Day Mullins, copyist, *Grimes County, Texas, Marriage Record, 1848–1879* (n.p., 1962).

I have been much deceived in those girls[;] they I do not believe were ever my friends and were ever making remarks about me. I cannot for my life say what caused them to cease writing, and have some curiosity to know, and have a great will to write to Mrs Noble.[15] They were kind to me during my stay in Houston and I believe did not wish me any particular harm. [Name crossed out] writes to me yet, tho' I do not care very much about her letters, as I cannot believe much she says. I rec^ed one this week I did not much like. I believe I will write to Mrs Noble whether I rec^e an answer or not. I owe them gratitude at least. About half after 9 Oclock at night

Saturday night
April 10th/52

I am feeling in the humor for communing to night. I have just finished reading a No. of the "Saturday evening Post," which has a most beautiful and absorbing story, I might say stories for there are two. Their perusal has awakened some of my dormant feelings and energy, and there is an inward prompting of the heart, to ease my soul, by giving heed unto its inward workings.

It has been some time since I was etherealized, transported, in extasies. Yet I have been elan, and I hope viewed things in their true and natural light. I feel hopeful, resigned, and full of trust, and love.

My future has many bright colors, tho' I know there must be shades. I have every confidence in Will, and distrust myself more than I do him. I have so many faults and fear I have not power sufficient to overcome them. Will must practice forbearance. He too must have faults. Tho' now I may see them as "through a glass darkly"[16] yet I know human nature is is [sic] a mass of imperfections. As long as love lasts I shall feel no fears, but alas! when love *dies*, 'There's the rub'[17] to prevent love dying.

If it was the nature of my heart to desire evil to others, I should not wish my most deadly enemy a worse evil than to be united [to] a person they did not love. To me this would certainly be a hell on earth.

It strikes me that I had some plan of writing in view when I commenced to night, if so it has all vanished.

---

15. Marianne Noble (age 38, spelled Nobles in the 1850 census) lived in Houston with her husband, E. B. (45), a wharfmaster with personal and real property valued at $4,000. They had five children: Sarah (16), Amanda (14), Mary (11), Louisa (5), and Stephen (3). TX Census 1850.

16. 1 Cor. 13:12.

17. *Hamlet*, act 3, scene 1.

To day I had a letter from Will, a kind affectionate and truly welcome one. I am better pleased with it than any one I have rec^{ed} from him in a long time. 'Tis so honest so candid so good, so like Will, that I could not help feeling happy and pleased to get it—it bears [the] date the 7th of April.[18] He tells me, he started up the country on last Thursday and will be back on the 19th or 20th and that I will see him the day after he gets home. I hope he will get home safe and well, and be pleased with the country. He will write me from Leona, and at Waco. Tis at Waco I half suspect we will live[.] Will is many miles from me to night, and how blest am I in knowing and feeling that to night, he has over and again thought of me, and I doubt not if he is not asleep (for tis 10 oclock) he [is] thinking of me now, and he may be dreaming of me. I may be smiling on him, and Heaven knows I would ever bring him smiles. Tho' it would not be expedient as yet to utter the wish of the poet, yet, my heart utters it loudly

> "Would my form possessed the magic power
> To follow where my heavy heart would be
> Would I were with thee *eternally*"

I know Will is happy, and his heart exalts as the time approaches which is to crown with sucess the dearest wish of his heart. The love of his boyhood, and the love his manhood, the one love of his life, is to be his, beyond all doubts. "Tis more blessed to give than to receive,"[19] says holy writ, and in this instance 'tis doubly blessed, for by giving I receive, and by receiving increase ten fold the value of my gift—and here tis blessed to receive. And "the debt immense of endless gratitude"[20] should ever warm my heart towards the the [*sic*] giver— but "the loan for love is love only"[21] and tis love, in its warmest purest state without spot or blemish.

It will not be long before "the consumation devoutly to be wished"[22] by our hearts will be realized, and then we are "no longer twain but one flesh"[23] and

18. An interlineation added later reads: "just one year after, on the same day of the same month Mary was born."

19. Acts 20:35.

20. John Milton, *Paradise Lost*, book 4.

21. Epigraph to Sarah Josepha Hale's 1849, *Woodbine Cottage* ("love only, is the loan for love").

22. *Hamlet*, act 3, scene 1.

23. Matt. 19:3–6.

as one flesh has the same interests. I look to this time with more calmnesss than I imagined I should feel. I hesitate not, nor falter. I am determined, and know the consequences, 'tis not a step taken rashly and *unadvisedly*.

We have had a good deal of rain to night but it has ceased altogether now, and the never ceasing tick of the clock admonishes me that time is passing, and that it is less than half an hour to 11. I saw Mr Banton last Wednesday, and he came to the 'point' and so did I. I told him on being asked that I was engaged, he did not seem to mind his bluff in the least. [H]e cared very little about me[.] I saw Josephine McGown on Thursday. I told her of our marriage. I am too communicative on some subjects. Night April 10/52 Anderson

Sunday night
April 11th

Yesterday evening I sent Mary Haynie[24] some papers and a note, and she sent me the April No of Graham's magazine, and a No' of the Post, and a most delicious, beautiful bouquet and it is of this I have been thinking the fresh beautiful flowers. Every time I see them I think of Mary. Flowers are such soul speaking such appropriate gifts. I have been learning the song by Mrs Hemans 'Bring flowers young flowers &c." The words are beautiful, and the air is good. Will sent me a bouquet by Mittie[25] to s[c]hool, and Sarah[26] brought it home, on last Wednesday. I did not know it was from Will, for I thought he was gone, but every time the wind wafted their fragrance to me, it was as a message from Will, thrilling my bosom with a feeling I can not describe, and throwing a spell over all thoughts, and I was almost ready to caress the beautiful offering of flowers. Unfortunately they were greatly spoiled by

24. Mary Haynie (age 20 in 1850) was one of Lizzie Neblett's closest friends. During the Civil War she was still unmarried and living with her mother, Dealthea C. Haynie. TX Census 1850.

25. "Mittie" was the nickname for William Neblett's sister Caroline Eliza. She was born January 1, 1835. She married John Franklin Perry November 12, 1856. The couple had four children. Caroline Perry died August 5, 1920. Grimes County Historical Commission, *History of Grimes County*, 469–70; Perkins, *Some Nebletts in America*, 113.

26. Sarah "Sallie" Scott was Lizzie Neblett's younger sister. She was born April 9, 1843, in Texas. She married Robert Houston Bassett in 1862. The couple had one child who survived to adulthood, Barbara "Belle" Bassett Blackley. Sallie died on October 20, 1915, at the home of her daughter in Washington, D.C. The relationship between the sisters soured during the Civil War, but the letters they exchanged later in life indicate that the relationship improved over time. NP.

being exposed so much to the sun, and did not retain their color and fragrance longer than two days[.] I have wrapped them up and put them away[.] I do thank Will for his gift. I love flowers as I love almost every thing for the associations which cluster round them. Some of my favorites are not rare, or beautiful, but the associations that cluster round them are more beautiful to my soul than the richest rarest flower to the eye of an Amateur Botanist. [A]nd truly their associations come o'er my heart, "like the sweet south breathing o'er a bank of violets Stealing and giving order."[27] I love the violet. The little blue Houstonia, the rose and bright Heart's ease.

Will likes the rose the best I believe. Flowers, they are the dew drops from the garden of Paradise the only thing that was not polluted by the fall of man. They certainly retain their original sweetness and beauty, and Milton must have been mistaken in making his Eve say 'oh flowers that never will in other climates grow &c"[28] for they the garden flowers of Eden grow and flourish as I believe in this beautiful land. Oh! I wish I knew where Will was may God bless him where ever he is! Sweet be thy dreams dearest. Pa started up the country to day. night

Monday night
April 12th

I am feeling so sad to night. I view every thing to night on the dark side, and alas! that the dark side of every thing should always present itself to me. I seem to be the aim and butt of ill fortune. That I was "born for bad luck," and I fear me, [I] am likely to answer my calling through the length and breadth of my entire life.

Oh! I am not worthy even to share the thorns of life, to sip its bitter. I *am* unfortunate! My temper my disposition is truly an unfortunate one. On every side unfortune!

I am not calculated [to] render any one any thing else than unhappy, and imbiter my own life. I say so many things that I mean not and which the moment after I would give any thing to recall, but this monster pride in my bosom swell[s] up, and repels every effort I make to solicit pardon for the offence, that should tinge forever my cheek with shame. I say such angry sinful,

27. *Twelfth Night*, act 1, scene 1 ("O! it came o'er my ear like the sweet sound / That breathes upon a bank of violets, / Stealing and giving odor!").

28. John Milton, *Paradise Lost*, book 11.

wicked and ungreateful words to my mother, and all because I am mad to as-
sert my *independence my pride*. But she is too to be blamed, for such harsh such
bitter such unjust remarks as she makes about me. I would not stain the paper
with the taunts she throws out. She says she is done with me the day I marry
Bill Neblett. She thinks I love him not, but am bent upon marrying some one
and that I made the first advances towards him that I courted him. Alas! alas!
what is to become of me when those who should by natures very law be most
lenient, most partial towards me, turn thus, and reproach me, with what they
say is my disposition. Who is there that such words would not sting? and who,
beside Our Savior, that "man of sorrows and acquainted with grief"[29] would
not make angry replies, even tho' it were to a parent. Oh how often tho' it is
sinful, do I earnestly desire death, as an end of grief, sorrow, and trouble and
wish that the boon of life had never been bestowed on me. Oh God! we know
not thy designs, and should not murmur. [O]h! help my unbelief! I will I am
determined by Gods assistance to lead a better and a happier life, for I believe
with some writer that our happiness is a sacred deposit, for which we must
render an account! at the final day. My unfortunate temper leads me ever
astray, and in passion I lose all reason, and care not, know not, think not what
I say, and if by a word of mine, I could do such a thing would send in a moment my soul to hell—and alas! wo is me! my sins will yet sink me there.
[A]nd am I to be bound thus by my temper, be sent to Hell, live miserable,
die unwept, be hated? No, no, by the divine power within me, by the few good
qualities of my soul, I *will reform*. Oh merciful God assist me. I would not be
vain and puffed up with pride—but meek lowly and deserving as far as 'tis in
my power. My conduct, the events of my life have been strange, & fickle—and
it seems in all things I have proved unworthy. Have "been weighed in the balance and found wanting"[30] yes wanting in a large degree. Mother don't believe
I love Will, or says she don't, and she says if any one else should come along I
would soon fancy him. Fickle! fickle! But she don't know the silent the hidden
workings of my heart. 'Tis all corrupt, full of deciet, and inconstancy to her.
Yet is there any good there? Oh! I hope 'tis not all wicked. There are some
good qualities. I have a heart a soul that can that does feel—that can be greatful, that can love. 'What am I that the Son of Man art mindful of me.'[31] I

29. Isa. 53:2.
30. Dan. 5:27.
31. Possibly Heb. 2:6. ("What is man, that thou art mindful of him? Or the son of man that thou visitest him?")

am humbled—low—and altho' Jesus says "Are not five Sparrows sold for two farthings, and not one of them is forgotten before God?—Fear not therefore ye are of more value than many Sparrows."[32] I feel that in worth, in good deeds [I] sink below the Sparrows. My heart needs puryfing making strong. Next sunday I think I will join the Methodist church on probation. And see if that will aid me any in my reformation, it will do me no harm I know. Will is absent, yet that need not deter me, he will not care, and if he does I do not deem it my duty to yield to his pleasure in this matter. I have gained some peace from this resolution. I will say nothing to anyone.

I have thought the 'pearl of great price'[33] was mine, and may have been, but I have fallen from grace. I always felt doubtful concerning my religion, and to very few did I ever breathe my dark, and doubtful hopes. I do not wish to be hypocrite, and will not.

Wednesday night
April 14th

Ambition! Who is there that have not had dreams of ambition? What hearts have remained dull and sluggish, always pulsating with the same even slow throbs? Every heart it seems to me, must have some kind of ambition, and tho' it may not have been of a very laudable nature, yet it was ambition. It has been the ruling passion of my life, in all things save love. There a weakness is ever manifest, and ambition is drowned in the play of stronger, and opposite passions. But when my heart is enlisted I am ambitious for *him*, to a painful degree. Heaven in her wisdom has placed insurmountable barriers between me and my individual ambition. I can never gain worldly honors. Fame can never be mine. I am a *woman!* a woman! I can hardly teach my heart to be content with my lot. Old Keefer (the dutchman)[34] has been entertaining me to night with a relation of facts that clearly in his eye established Will's dullness. He says he has put himself up for a lawyer and is no lawyer, knows nothing about it. That Old Ed Bower says he is not a smart man, and I know not what else. I felt and feel so indignant at the two old fools, that I could it seems to me endowed by Heaven with strength in a just cause, whip both of

32. Luke 12:6–7.
33. Luke 13:46.
34. According to the 1850 census, Conrad Kifer was a 38-year-old tanner from Germany. In the 1860 census he is listed as a farmer with real and personal property valued at $1,250. He had no family. TX Census 1850; TX Census 1860.

them. He asked Will to see something about a case of his, and he permitted it to be thrown out of court, when if he had been a smart man, he would have had it in the fall courts. I intend telling Will all he said. He talked it at table, and Mother and Jim enjoyed it vastly, to hear old Keefer abuse Will, both laughed heartily and looked at me, and I could have choked the old dutch to death.

I have a thousand fears, and missgivings whether I should marry or not. Will is a new begginner in the Law business, and may not get practice, and I must have something to live on. Oh the stern realities of life! How imagination with her throng, ambition with her dreams, love with her romance, flee before the touch of reality. And 'tis necessary we should view things in their true and proper light. I am determined while there is strength in my arm, and a little sense in my head that I will not be dependent on my parents. never! never!

Thursday night
April 15th
    Somewhere in the course of my life I have seen this couplet.

> "Of all afflictions taught a lover yet
> 'Tis sure the hardest science to forget"[35]

and in the fullness of my heart, and from the deepest conviction I will and can render it thus.

> "Of all afflictions taught a *bile*[36] yet
> Tis sure the hardest science to forget."

And as Job of old, I have labored, and am at present laboring under this dire affliction[.] I could weep at the idea of what I am yet to undergo, if weeping could reverse my doom. But the bile is here, and here it will remain until it sees cause to leave, which I awfully fear will not be soon. Alas! poor me! And in such a bad place, (but tis always a bad place wherever they come)—mine is immediately under my right arm. It is with some pain that I write, but it is pain any way and I fear in another day my arm will be perfectly useless. So I

---

35. Alexander Pope, *Eloisa to Abelard.*
36. Bile here refers to a boil.

seized the passing moment to record my affliction, not that I will forget it no, no who would ever forget the feeling of a bile? No letter from Will. I will expect one Monday sure.

Friday night
April 16th

I have been thinking of the 'stern realities' of life. How it is regarded by mankind, and its end and aim its chief good in their minds. When, we look at life in its true colors, it seems to me, that it is as Byron[37] says 'making reality too real,' robbing it of its romance, and disclosing nothing which is greatful to the soul. The world, the opinion of the world is worth [more] to the mass of men, than their own individual happiness. What does it matter if they are miserable so the world know it not. Their holiest and best affections are prevented, by contact with this same world, for whose applause they would and do barter their souls. Its end its aim among them is riches. 'Defraud whomsoever thou canst' is their motto followed verbatim. Alas! man formed in the image of his God! Thus to prevent, and drown all the godlike attributes of his soul.

I could write longer but my arm is getting so painful I must stop.

Will I have not forgotten you.

Monday night
April 19th

I am reading Rasselas[38] for the second time in my life, and it will admit of many more readings even if my days are short. The stile is so beautiful, and the sentiment so worthy of imbibing and retaining. I wish my memory was more retentive.

I am disappointed to night, and the disappointment has saddened. I had fondly hoped that to days mail would bring me a letter from Will, but my hopes have been blasted. I fear Will is sick or something has happened [to] him. He wrote me before he left that he expected to get home to day or to-morrow, yet I fear to indulge in the hope. Tho' I know I should be very happy to see him tomorrow. He said he would be certain and come up to see me the next day after he got home. Some how I can not believe that I will be married.

---

37. George Gordon, Lord Byron, "The Dream" (1816).
38. *Rasselas, The Prince of Abyssynia: A Tale*, by Samuel Johnson (1759).

Tho' if I am not, it will not be my fault. My Bile is getting well, tho' is not entirely well as yet.

What changes a few years will effect. I recollect distinctly this day four years ago. It was the day after Nannie[39] was married. We came up from Mr Green's. Mrs & Mr Barnes, Sarah Neblett[40] & Fletcher Stockdale[41] Will & myself. Four years have passed, and two of that company are silent in their last resting place. Nannie died in Feb/50 and Sarah soon after. We were all young and expect[ed] little thought of death. Will and I were lovers then and thought then that we would be married ere this. Tomorrow the 20th of Apr will be 6 years since I first saw Will to know him, and July will be 5 years since he told me he loved me. And last January was three years since we were first engaged. "The course of true love never yet run smooth"[42] nor never will while the world exists. Since I first loved Will (July 1847) I have grown cold some what in my affection three times, but every time have returned to my old love true as the magnet to the pole. So as I told Will, "after all I will have to marry Bill Neblett[";] it seems I can never be rid of him as a lover untill I convert him into a husband. I wonder how we will get along. I know I will be loved well enough. I feel many fears about Will. I will not look for him much untill Thursday and friday.
Nearly 9 Oclock night.

Wednesday night
April 21st
Wednesday has passed, and no news of Will, what can be the matter? I know if he was able he wrote while at Leona, and the letter should have

39. Nannie Bowin was a friend and schoolmate of Lizzie Neblett's. In the 1850 census she is listed as living in the home of James and Caroline Barnes along with F. S. Stockdale, a 22-year-old lawyer. On April 18, 1848, she married Jas. Lawrance. TX Census 1850, NP.

40. Sarah Neblett was Will Neblett's sister, the second child of Robert and Maria Neblett. She was born January 1, 1828, in Wayne County, Mississippi. She married John Watkins September 20, 1848, and died with her husband in a yellow fever epidemic in Texas on January 23, 1850. Perkins, *Some Nebletts in America*, 113.

41. In 1850 Fletcher S. Stockdale was living in the home of James and Caroline Barnes. He was a 22-year-old lawyer with personal property valued at $300. As a member of the Secession Convention in 1861, he helped draft the Ordinance of Secession. He served as lieutenant governor of Texas from November 1863 to June 1865, and briefly as governor until August 1865, when a Reconstruction governor was appointed by President Andrew Johnson. He died February 4, 1890. TX Census 1850; Marcus J. Wright, comp., and Harold B. Simpson, ed., *Texas in the War, 1861–1865* (Hillsboro, Tex.: Hill Junior College Press, 1965), 139–40.

42. *A Midsummer-Nights' Dream*, act 1, scene 1.

reached here long since. Then he wrote me he expected to get back by the 19th or 20th of Apr, but this is only the 21st. I cannot help feeling some uneasiness about him, April has ever been my most unfortunate month, and tho' it has been superstitious, I have dreaded this month in this year for two years back, why I could not tell. I was sorry Will had to go up the country this month. I will look some for him tomorrow, and next day, and untill I see him I do want to see him, it has been three weeks to day since I saw him, and I begin to feel quite anxious to see him, and I doubt not that he wants to see me too. I wish I was as good as Will thinks I am. He tells me I will go to Heaven any how. My virtues are few, and my foibles, their name is legion. Will for your sake I would and do wish I was better and more worthy. I dreamed of Will last night but thought it was Ben & I called him Will.

Thursday night
April 22nd

Another day has passed, and no news of Will. A thousand fears occupy my mind, and render me heart sick. All day long, I have watched and hoped that he would come, but nature moves on in her accostomed course, heedless alike of others happiness, and my weary watching. The sun set, amid all her accostomed splendor the gloryious canopy of clouds gilded with gold. The twilight, the hour of love, drew her veil over the earth, and all things were at rest and in peace but me—night with her sable robes drew on, and all without was gloom, save a few spots, in which the moon's smile rested, and her radiance is dim to night. The wind breathes o'er all and whispers tales of all countries & climes. Yet I listen, and no tale does it whisper me of Will. Oh Will! why tarriest thou? Our affections tho' they afford us much pleasure, yet often fill our hearts with fear, doubting and grief. Disarm us of all our strength, and render us weak languishing creatures ready to start at every alarm, and yet ever ready to listen to the voice of hope.

I cannot work with any zest, and nothing affords me more than momentary pleasure.

> "To weep yet scarce know why,
> To sigh yet feel no pain"[43]

I thought I would go and practice this morning but soon I was wearied, and closed the Piano and left the house, and Flora[44] and I went over the woods

---

43. Thomas Moore, *The Bluestocking: A Comic Opera* (1811).
44. Flora was most likely a slave owned by Lizzie's father.

and prairie, looking for I knew not nor cared not what; found some berries, and a Tarapin, and came home much wearried. I do think I will see Will tomorrow[.]

Tis Friday evening, and I am alone, after having company all day[.] Mrs Whiting in the morning and Eloisa, Mary & Leonadus Graves[45] in the evening, and I write with a load of uneasiness removed, with a happy heart[.] Will yesterday evening reached home sound & well, and surely tomorrow he will make his appearance[.] I am glad, and feel at ease. Pa this morning reached home also, looking well. I will expect Will tomorrow. I want to see him so bad, and hear his plans. Waco Pa says is a perfect grave yard, so I know Will, will not locate there. Some how I think, but I am mistaken the mail comes from Huntsville today and I won't get Will's letter. Apr 23rd

Yes, but I did get a letter from Will. [T]he greater part of it written while he was in a little town called Marlin, and a page on Thursday night, (last night) and mailed to day, and he says tomorrow he is coming to see me. I do want to see him, & he knows it too. He says he was sorely disappointed on finding no letter for him at Wheelock and he did not ask me to write in his last. But fool he don't care, and neither do I. And if I am willing Marlin will be our home[.] He says it has only about a dozen houses, and is 8 or 9 months old. I will go of course if he thinks he can do best there, and shall not murmur at the privation of society he tells me of, so he does well. I am so ambitious for him, and to ensure him success would submit to any privation of taste or society, and if he does succeed in his practice, and acquits himself worthy of the praise of the wise & good I shall feel too supremely happy to murmur at anything that I will have to submit to for his sake. I fear I feel too acutely on this subject—for myself I care not, for being a woman I can never arrive at any greatness & fame, and all the ambition of my soul is centered on him. Friday night April 23rd 1852

Sunday morning
April 25th/52

Unheard of calamity! And strange, instead of provoking my regret anger or sorrow, only inspires me with mirth. Will has not come yet. Yesterday it rained

---

45. In 1850 Leonidus (age 17), Eloisa (15), and Mary (12) Graves lived with their parents, John (53) and Mary (46). John Graves was a farmer with $4,500 in real and personal property. TX Census 1850.

until after twelve oclock, and consequently the boy did not present himself in person.

I know he is well, at home &c, and I do not feel much disappointed in not seeing him yesterday. A cousin of mothers Dr Alfred Patton from Raymond Miss[issippi] has been at our house since Friday night, quite an intelligent gentleman, has a wife and two children. He has been telling me much about cousin Bettie Lane. I must write to her soon. Pa and cousin Alfred have gone to church to day, my unfortunate bile has risen again and is as painful as it was at first. I tried my muse yesterday in making some verses to Nelia,[46] they do not please me much, Nelia asked me to write something in her Album and if Will thinks my verses good enough I'll write them for her.

I declare I don't know what to think about going to Marlin with Will. It is such a little out of the way place, but I suppose I need not care. I am feeling so indifferent about every thing that I'll stop.

Sunday
Apr 25th

Shades of evening are closing o'er us. There is scarcely a breath of wind stirring, a perfect calm in nature, but not a calm in my heart. I hear the birds singing in every bush, the hen clucking to her chickens, the cow lowing to her young. All nature seems to be endowed with the desire to have something to care for, something to protect, and that desire has been granted to all.

To day has passed away, without scarcely anything to enliven the ennui of my lonely moments. I thought Will would come to day, but he came not, and I care not. Garret[47] brought me a letter from him to day writen while he was at Springfield, and writen because he knew he could never convince me that he was right in not writing, as so he wrote to escape my upbraiding. Truly a laudable reason for writing when he first asked if he might write. I am so glad

46. Cornelia McCaskill Kerr was Will Neblett's cousin. She married James Kerr, a physician, February 18, 1852. NP; Mullins, *Grimes County, Texas, Marriage Records*.

47. Garret [at times spelled Garrett] Scott was Lizzie Neblett's brother, the fourth child of James and Sarah Scott. In the 1860 census he is listed as 22 years of age and living with his mother and two sisters, Sarah and Alice. His occupation is listed as farmer. Garret Scott died in the battle of Sharpsburg on September 17, 1862. Lizzie was never satisfied with what little information she received regarding his death. She felt there was evidence that he survived the actual battle and would later write in a memorial to her husband, "My brother Garret was killed *after* the battle of *Sharpsburge* in Maryland, on wednesday evening the 17th day of September 1862." TX Census 1860; Memoir.

I did not write to him while he was gone. I expect he will be coming over tomorrow, and tell me he wanted to see me so badly, that days were as years! I expect he does want to see me, worse than I want to see him. I believe he does. Sunday evening Apr 25th

The new house
Thursday night Apr 29th

"Man proposes but God disposes"[48] and how true & wise is the decree. We make plan after plan build up cherished hopes, which an angry wind can frustrate or a gentle rain entirely overthrow, and we pine, sigh & shed tears, and yet '*God disposes.*' We know not what a day may bring forth, and are we not as the grass of the field, to day is and tomorrow is not? How humble we should feel, & how greatful! All true wisdom tends to make [us] humble, contented & happy—and true wisdom comes from God alone. "We spend our years as a tale that is told"[49] and at the appointed time die. Others fill our place, and we are forgotten—perhaps in a few hearts our memory may be live[s], but with them it dies. Let me strive to do all the good in my power, while here, and never knowingly cause another sorrow. I am contented to live, and would that I was ever under the control of my better angle [*sic*]. But angry passions sometimes arise, and overthrow all my good thoughts, and laudable ambition. What weak what frail creatures we all are, and I most of all "Woman thy name is frailty."[50] Alas! alas!

As I expected Will came on Monday the 26. He was looking very well, and seemed quite glad to see me, and remind me that our marriage was not quite three weeks off. I had not thought of it being so close at hand. I dont know how we will arrive at the day. Pa and mother must be consulted by Will when he next comes. I begin to feel sad about it, not so much about it as Mother 'taking on' so. She can't speak to me in a good humor, calls me a fool if I say anything to her, and looks at me with vengance in her eye. Really I don't expect she will give me [a] rag when I leave—and would to God Will was rich enough to do without it—but if she murmurs, I will leave all. I feel myself an intruder. Mother rails at the family, and Pa curses them all as [the] worse family in existence. I wish I was married and gone, and I am sure I would not

48. Thomas à Kempis, *Imitation of Christ*, book 1, chapter 19.
49. Ps. 90:9.
50. *Hamlet*, act 1, scene 2.

come back soon, unless I change very much. Will is coming back, on next Teusday, tho' I told him I did not want to see him, he said he would come. [A]nd then if Pa says so, we will be married in about two weeks, and in June Will is going up to Marlin and we will board until he can build. We moved yesterday up here. Thursday night Apr 29th

Monday night
May 3rd

The moon is shining beautifully bright, to the almost total obscurity of the stars. The sweet breathe [*sic*] of the south, comes laden with the cool fresh breeze of the ocean. A few moments ago, the song of the Whip poor Will, broke on the stillness of the air, and I hear now the cricket singing his merry song. I am tranquil and happy why should I not be? I have no cause to murmur[.] I love, and am beloved! I have all that needs insure happiness. A few more weeks will pass away and I will become a wife—a great responsibility. My identity, my legal existence will be swallowed up in my husband. I wish the trouble excitement &c was over, and I was married and quietly settled down, in that remote corner of the earth (Marlin) "teaching the young idea how to shoot"[51] for such will be [my] occupation for awhile if Will will let me, and if he comes to morrow I will ask him. I think it is an excellent idea. I could teach a session at least, which would be some assistance to poor folks. I am getting sleepy, and must read my chapt in John, say my prayers and sleep. night May 3rd/52

Teusday night
May 4th/52[52]

According to his word Will came to day, and I was glad to see him. He seemed in fine spirits, & to be truly happy. To day he was leaning his head on my shoulder, we were both silent, he raised his head, and his eyes were over flowed with tears[;] I could not tell the ray of divine joy that shot through my soul, as those happy tears met my eye betraying his love, his happiness, his truth, and the divinity of his soul. I could have shouted with joy, I was never

---

51. James Thomson, *The Seasons, Spring* (1728).

52. Written in pencil at the top of this entry are the following words: "On the 4th May 1871 just 19 years after this was writen Will, the best and dearest friend I ever had or will ever have in life, breathed his last on earth. His death was the worst stroke I ever had, or can ever sustain during this life. Sept 11th 1882."

more purely divinely happy in my life and I clasped my arms 'round his neck, & on his bosom shed tears of joy. What an inestimable gift I am possessed of, a loving noble, truthful heart. Oh what love did those tears of his speak. How proud do I feel of his love. He is coming again next week, on Teusday, and then the day will be agreed on and other things arranged, and the next week we will be married. Will wants it to day two weeks. I wish it was over with. It makes my heart throb to think of it. Mr Gillette[53] I suppose will marry us. I hope Pa & Mother will invite Will's family. It is growing late, and I cannot write for thinking. May 4th 1852/Night

Friday night
May 7th 1852

Tis raining, the clouds are thick and heavy. Sometimes I think really that I cannot marry so soon, that it is impossible. I am not ready. Have a good deal of sewing to do yet, but I think tis no use in delaying it longer, and I had better get married at once and have it over with. I told Cousin Alfred this evening after much importunity that I would be married in about two weeks. My life will be entirely changed, all my cherished recreations of mind & body must in part be abolished. I will have much to do, and I hope much happiness, if not, miserable will be my exchange. I can better in no degree my perplexity now so I'll let it rest. I'll see Will Teusday certain. I wrote him a famous epistle on last wednesday night[.] I feel ashamed of it now. I should be ashamed to let such little things trouble my mind as some now do. I can't help it. I expect I will go to see Eloisa & Mary Graves tomorrow. It is raining some yet. I wrote to Bettie this evening, to send by cousin Alfred tomorrow morning. Oh! Will dearest I wish you were with me. I wish I was married and the excitement over with.

Sunday morning
May 9th/52

Yes! tis Sunday morning every thing calm still & pleasant. Some clouds are visible, but the sun occasionally peeps forth & is then obscured.

God watches over all! What need then to fear? Tho' I feel my deep unworthyness, yet if I strive to do good, my endeavors will not be lost. I do feel that

---

53. Roswell Gillett (age 41 in 1850) was an Episcopal minister. He and his wife, Martha (35), had twelve children. TX Census 1850.

God pitys & loves me. I feel a thousand anxieties & fears about Will, if I could feel that each of us were at peace with God, my cup would be full. Oh! Earth it does not seem to me would hold my happy soul! I will talk [to] Will, I will win him over. I'll plead with him with tears in my eyes. I will not despair. Oh! God do thou assist me, crown my efforts with success.

The Martins are singing all around the house, every thing seems contented & happy. And I am happy. I have cast care away. I hope years of happiness are in store for Will and myself. My earnest endeavour will be to render him happy, and if he is happy I can be neither else than happy blest. We will have to toil I expect all our lives for the support of Nature, but love will unite us!

Sunday night
May 9th

I am happier than I have been for a good many days. The future begins to smile and the past is not so gloomy as it has hitherto appeared. I will write to Nelia to night in answer to her kind note last week.

She is a pure hearted loving and loved creature. I love her very much, perhaps 'tis because she is Will's cousin. I hope Dr Kerr[54] and she will do well, live happily, and find a better home in Heaven! She wishes Will & myself much happiness & prosperity. Will's parents, I am so glad that they are willing for him to marry me. Will is a great deal better than I am. I don't believe I could keep any thing from him should I try ever so hard, it is so natural to tell him every thing, every thought, and purpose.

There is one purpose I have not told him—that of teaching school at Marlin, I fear he will oppose it now, and I'll wait until the knot is tied and then maybe he won't oppose it. I will try every means to persuade him to let me do so. I'll write to Nelia.

Monday night
May 10th/1852

Pa asked me to day if I intended having that affair over with, I told him yes, and he the[n] asked me if I was not ashamed of myself? and that he knew I did not love that man, and I saw what a hell it was, if love was absent, mean-

---

54. Dr. James Kerr (30) was a physician married to Will Neblett's cousin Cornelia C. Mc-Caskill. TX Census 1850.

ing himself and mother. I told him he did not know what I thought or anything about me, in answer to his saying that I did not love Will, and he said
"the hell & devil I don't.["] [M]other said I could not love one man more than
a week and would be so all my life, and if I did marry *'that man'* I would not
live long with him, and I was marrying him to rule him that I thought I was
smarter, and that I would make him do all I wished—a good deal more was
said—he cursed me and told mother he had a great mind to *cow hide* me. Such
expressions for a *father*, and it was because Mother was & is too busy to make
him some pantaloons, and I will not do it, let him get the taylor to make them.
I am so proud that my days are nearly at end here, that I am done being cursed
and threatened to be *cow hided*. I'll warrant I'll never trouble him much with
my company when I am married. I want nothing from him, even if he wished
to give me anything—no I'll work my finger nails off before I'll be dependent
on him and if Will and I do sepperate, I'll never come back to him. I'll support
myself. Tomorrow is the day Will is to come and make some definite arrangement about the event, and let Pa into the secret.

Will says he is going to bring a buggy for me, and we will go to his Pa's the
next day after we are married. I told him (Pa) to day that if I was not happy it
would be nobodys look out but my own.

Well now, even if I did not love Will, I should be tempted to marry him,
if I had the chance to get away from here. Mother does not see a moment of
happiness, he curses her on all occasions, and thinks he [is] so much smarter
than she is, & I told him so to day—he did not deny it. Nobody on Earth
could get along with him. What has he not done to mar married happiness,
his vows have been broken on all occasions! Night May 10th

Wednesday night
May 12th

On yesterday, Will came to have some definite arrangement about our
marriage. He went to Pa something about it, and learned to our astonishment
that [Pa] was going to Houston the last of this week, so he would be absent
on next Teusday the 18th the day we had fixed upon to consumate our marriage, and of course we are obliged to delay it a week, to have him at home[.]
Of course I would not think of marrying during his absence. Will was sorely
disappointed, and I had rather it was over with, and who knows that he will
not go on from Houston some where else? It will be on the 25th certain—even
if he does not come back, if Will can get [a] license. Mother & Will did not
speak on Teusday, he is wrong there he ought have spoken any how. She dont

like him at all, calls him a fool says I am marrying a fool to rule him. Oh! I won't be here long, and my back is broad enough to hold all her rebukes &c.

Oh Nelia came to see me this evening, and led me into some of the mysteries of wedded life. Told me much more I am convinced than she would tell any one else. She told me in order that I might avoid several errors she ran into unknowingly, and I take item therefrom. Will is good, and I do sincerely think he is as moral as any *man* in the world, unless 'tis a *really pious minister*. I do not believe he indulges in illicit love. I believe he has been guilty, but I don't think it has been often—and I love him better ten thousand times for this character. Unless both conform strictly to their marriage vow in this instance, I think there can be but little happiness. Here is where my father is at fault. He cares not with whom he indulges this passion, and Great Heaven! what misery has he brought on his family! The picture is too dark to put in paper.

> "I could a tale to thee unfold
> Whose lightest word would,
> Harrow up thy soul!"[55]

I am sorry our marriage has been deferred[.] Nelia says her Aunt says she is glad I am coming down there to stay with them. I am glad they are pleased with me. Night May 12th.

Saturday night
May 15th

Pa starts I believe for Houston in the morning, and Mother thinks now that he will return immediately. I hope so. To day he put the note to the clerk in the office for Will. I suppose he did. He wrote him a short letter on last Thursday telling him that he considered it his duty to make to him a few confidential disclosures & there told him that he & mother did not get along happily and for their mutual peace of mind a separation would have to take place—& that it was for him to consider the propriety of uniting his destiny in any degree with such a family. He went down to Bro Johns that evening (Thursday) and next morning came back completely changed, and I see he tore the sheet containing the letter to Will off and left it in his drawer. They

---

55. *Hamlet*, act 1, scene 5.

blow out about every two months, and a separation is all they will hear too [*sic*] for a day, and then tis all made up, and every thing goes on as usual. I hope he will come back immediately & let me have my marriage over with on next Teusday. I wrote to Will on Thursday night, and told him to come as soon as he rec^ed my letter, and we would come to some conclusion. If he got it to day I expect he will come tomorrow.

He says he wants to go up to Marlin about the 20th of June. We will have to board until Will can have a house built. That will not be very pleasant but we must put up with it. I tell you they are not going to let me take any thing from here I see it, not even my bed. I'll have to leave all, but I know one thing I can do. I will sell my watch (it cost 50$ in N[ew] York) and I reckon I can get at least 70$ for it here & that will get a bed stand, bed & clothes. That is all I will have worth a farthing & that shall be sold to assist Will. And if I can get a school at Marlin I will certainly do so, I won't listen to any thing Will says about it. We will be poor and I can not be contented to do nothing and see him toil. Saturday night May 15th.

Saturday night
May 22nd

Will has been here all day just left a few minutes ago. The last evening I will spend with him as Lizzie Scott. He is happy and so am I—why should we not be, loving & beloved. Pa gave him a line to the clerk for issuing License this evening, and on Teusday evening he & Mr Gillette will come out, only three days off. I don't feel at all excited or frightened, as calm & collected as I ever felt. Pa returned from Houston on last Thursday in a very good humor. Says Mrs Noble asked him at the supper table if the report was true about Neblett & myself marrying & he told her he reckoned it was true, so they know it is so. He says the girls were writing, but he did not go back any more after he went first to get the letters but the Judge said they could send by mail[.] Let them write or I'll never answer their letters certain. He heard nothing said of their getting married. Mr Richardson & Mr Grimes were here this morning.

Monday evening
May 24th 1852

Tomorrow is my wedding day. It will be a very quiet wedding I fancy, no one stranger but Will & Mr Gillette.

I have not even let Bro John into the secret. Susan[56] & her little family were up here on Friday last, and in consequence of Susan going over to her Fathers I did not tell her, she would have told it certain. Enough are aware of it now. I don't feel at all frightened, as calm as I ever felt. Mary Haynie came by for me yesterday evening & I went home with her and returned home this morning. They are perfectly in the dark there, dont seem to suspect any thing. On Wednesday we will go down to my Dr Pa's—and in a month or so Will will go up to Marlin, I dont know whether I will go or not yet. It has been raining nearly all day, and only stopped about a half an hour ago. Will said he would get his license to day, but I don't think he will. It is about sunset I guess.

My Wedding Day.
Teusday after 12 Oclock
May 25th 1852

It does seem to me I have more trials, more to contend with than any one ever had before. Mother blusters around bauls about things that no one else would ever say a word about, in fact has no respect at least for my feelings. She says she is so glad I am going to leave she don't know what to do, and God in Heaven knows I rejoice, tho' troubles come in leigons, 'tis better than this. John came up yesterday evening and this morning he found out I was to be married to night, and he & mother set up and made all sorts of sport about Will's red head, and as they said white eyes, as if I cared for their mockery, and then John asked me if I was not affraid of *starving*, said he thought Neblett was one of the kind to let any body *starve*, I told I did not reckon we would come any nearer starving than he did. For him to talk when if it had not been for Pa's assistance what would he have been? They amused themselves vastly about Will & myself. If a single one of them of any age has respected my feelings in the least degree except Jim (I don't recollect that he ever said anything) I don't know. And I do hope to rid myself of the whole of them. And I do most solemnly declare, that never will I even tho' despair wretchedness and disease is staring me in the *face* apply to them for a *farthing*, no for a drink for sympathy, or assistance in any degree. No I'll *suffer & die first!* And if Will cannot support me, and disease will not let me make an effort

---

56. Susan Womack Scott was the wife of John Newton Scott, Lizzie Neblett's older brother. John and Susan were married September 24, 1844, and lived in both Grimes County and neighboring Montgomery County. They had 13 children, 12 of whom grew to maturity (6 boys and 6 girls). Susan died August 27, 1905. "Scott, John Newton," vertical file, CAH.

to support myself I'll die with their charity unsought, and die blaming Will, if he makes the first advance towards asking or hinting at them for charity! Now on *this I am resolved!* and the thunders of mighty Heaven may shake the whole earth, but my resolution will remain *unshaken!* Pa says nothing. When I woke this morning it was raining very hard, and continued to rain *floods* until about a half an hour ago it stopped, a bad beggining—but let the wrath of Heaven be poured out on my head for amply as I deserve it, but it causes not my heart to *faulter* or weaken. I know what I am doing, and if I suffer, what is it to mankind as long as their *charity is not taxed.* I am sorry that on my wedding day such bitter feelings should be stirring in my bosom. Mother has caused it all. The creeks I expect are all full and Will, will have some difficulty in getting here. Mother told John all about it this morning, about my being intoxicated about the love & sociability in Dr Neblett's family. She accounted for it by Dr Nebletts *Blarney* &c. Oh! I'll almost *shout* for joy when I leave *tomorrow!* And I dont think now I'll ever write I know I won't first, if they write me I'll answer as briefly as possible. Will shall not write either. (*shall not* is not a pretty sentence for me to use, yet in this case 'tis admissible I think) I reckon John will not go home this evening, I don't care whether he stays or goes. Six hours to be Lizzie Scott. It still thunders and is cloudy. Teusday 1 Oclock May 25th

Thursday morning
May 27th 1852

I am married! I do not as yet feel any difference. I am happy, happy as I ever thought to be, and I believe Will too is happy.

Yesterday we came down to Dr Neblett's[.] They all received me very kindly, and seem pleased that Will has married me. I do hope they will continue to be pleased with me. I do hope we will do well. Oh! I do love Will so much, better than I did before we were married *he is so good! So good!* and seems to have such respect *for my feelings!* Oh I do love him *so much.* I was not frightened the night I was married much, Will was not much either, but more than I was, his arm trembled *slightly.* Mr Gillette made a mistake in the ceremony asked me "if I would take this man as my lawful and wedded *wife.*" I noticed it but Will did not. Bro John stayed[,] Mr Baumgardner[57] also was present. I don't feel much like I was married no difference. I can hardly realize it. We got here yesterday for dinner. I am happy, *so happy.* May 27th 1852

57. In 1850 F. A. Bumgertner (age 30) was a cabinetmaker from Germany. He and his wife, Yugina (25), had one child. TX Census 1850.

At Dr Neblett's
Monday evening June 7th

The happiness still lasts. I am so deeply happy. Will is such a good, kind husband and I feel loves me devotedly. I think it will last, always. We have been married now two weeks tommorrow, and really it seems scarcely a week. I have been so happy. A great deal better than I had expected. I find Will better than I thought he was, and I love him ten times better than I did before we were married, and I believe he loves me better.

He has concluded not to move to Marlin, before fall at least. We fear the place will prove sickly, as there has been a good deal of sickness so far in the country. Will and I have some rare times, and I am getting mighty lazy. I wrote to Mrs Cochran & Jane on yesterday. I have not been to church yet. Will went home with me on last Wednesday, I don't think Pa wanted to see us, nor Mother much. I don't know as yet what Will, will do. His Pa is anxious for him to stay down here at his house. I am perfectly willing to do so. I find the family very agreeable, and I am rendered very agreeable here. The family seem to have so much affection for each other and every member seems to almost worship Ma,[58] and she is certainly very worthy all the love that is lavished upon her. Pa (Dr) is very fond of his children, and will assist Will considerably. My Pa, we do not expect the least assistance from. I will feel very thankful indeed if we can always be beyond the necessity of his assistance. Dr Pa stayed all night with him Saturday, and he was to start up the country to day to be gone some ten or twelve days, and I want to go home during his absence.

Will is so good he will go with me any time I want to go. I don't know how long it will last. Pa still talks to Will about partnership with him but he will never practice I think but I know it would benefit Will greatly, but Pa is so fickle. There is no reliance to be placed on what he says. Monday evening June 7th 1852

Sunday night
June 13th 1852

Nearly *three* weeks has now passed since I was married. Half of the "honey moon" and my husband has been dangerously sick. On last Thursday, the 3rd

---

58. Maria Powe Neblett, mother of Will Neblett, was born December 13, 1807, in Chesterfield County, South Carolina. She married Robert Caldwell Neblett March 22, 1825. The couple had seven children who lived to maturity: William Henry, Sarah Elizabeth, Sterling Powe, Caro-

the day we returned from Pa's, went up on Wednesday, Will commenced taking cold, and for several days kept stirring round with slight fevers until Teusday night, he had considerable fever and sensation of choking, difficulty in breathing, and from Wednesday until Saturday he was confined to his bed quite sick. [O]n Wednesday night I was very much alarmed about him, and indeed he was bad off. Pa gave him something (Tartar)[59] which caused him to throw up, and kind and dilligent nursing has at length got the old fellow on his feet again tho' he is as yet quite weak. I was very much alarmed. He looks quite thin now, but in three or four days I hope he will be entirely recovered. I little thought I should have to begin *nursing* so soon after marriage.

[O]ur love as yet has not become a old song to us, and I hope never may. I know I love him better than I did before we were married, and this also is [his] state of feeling to believe him.

Last night I had fret, because he blew the candle out before I came in the room to go to bed, and like not to have slept with him. He is better than I bargained for in a husband, and I am completely happy and contented. I expect Pa has not yet returned from the up country and if Will had been well enough, I would have went home last week, or the first of this. I am perfectly satisfied here. I have [been] no where except home and Cousin Eliza Demarets[60] since I was married. I have not yet seen Nelia. She cant leave the Doct. long enough to come down to see us. I have many fears for Cousin Nelia. Will must write in here for the benefit [of] the little Neblett's who are to follow. He has not read all this, none that I have writen since our marriage. I'm sleepy. June 13th/52

Wednesday evening
June 16th 1852

Will is yet confined to his bed. He had a slight fever on Monday night, and again last night, but I do hope so sincerely that to day is to be the last day he is to be sick. He is so weak. It is now nearly two weeks since he was first taken. I did not think when I was married, that the first weeks of my married life

---

line Eliza, Harriet Maria, Robert McCaskill, and Cornelia Love. Maria Neblett died March 22, 1879. NFB; Perkins, *Some Nebletts in America*, 83.

59. Tartar was a poisonous compound used as a purgative or to treat parasitic infections like schistosomiasis. Will was apparently suffering from pneumonia. Memoir.

60. Eliza Demaret [spelled Demerrit in the 1860 census] was married to Edgar Demerrit, a farmer with real and personal property valued at $70,600. TX Census 1860.

were to be spent in a sick chamber nursing my husband. But I feel that I can do this better than any one else—and tis a task lightly felt, for tis for one infinitely dearer than life that I am laboring. I have nursed him as faithfully as I know how since his sickness and he seems satisfied with the degree of attention I have bestowed. I have not heard from home since Pa (Dr) stayed up home. I would have been up to see them this week if Will had been sufficiently well to go with me, and I did think of going with out him but I am so glad I did not. I thought he was getting well, he got up on Saturday, and continued to rise of a morning and remain up all day until yesterday morning.

I love Will better ten times better than I did before we were married. I have thought since his sickness what I would do if he should die. I could not cannot bear the idea I almost

> "forget when by his side,
> That he can mortal be"[61]

I could never love again, as I love him, tho' I might marry again. I don't know whether Pa would take me home or not. I rather suspect not. I wish Will had not neglected this cold so long, he would now be well I know. They are exceedingly kind to Will here. Pa nurses him so good—and Ma is kind to every one. Yet I fear all the time that I won't please them, that they will not like me.

Oh! I do wish Will was well. He is so tired of being sick, of being so weak, and confined to his bed. The sun is almost down. Yesterday was *three* weeks since I was married, it does not seem so long to me. Will has been sick nearly two weeks of the time. Poor Will! he has suffered much. I wrote Mother a note this morning, but the girls[62] did not go to school, so I did not send it.

I am tired, and sleepy. Will has slept a good deal to day. Near Sunset June 16th 1852.

Friday evening
June 25th/52

It is almost sunset. Thick clouds veil the west, and the Sun's last fading ray cannot gladen our hearts this evening. A gentle breeze is apparent among the branches of the trees, waving the long moss to and fro, and giving a somber

---

61. Charles Wolfe, "To Mary" ("But I forgot, when by thy side,/That thou couldst mortal be").

62. Will's younger sisters, Caroline Eliza (16) and Harriet Maria (14). TX Census 1850.

hue to the scene without. There the clock strikes six! I am peaceful and happy. Will sits not far from me, deeply absorbed in some of the mysteries of Law. He looks pale[.] I gaze at him, he looks thin yet, and seems at this moment lost to all else on Earth save the subject occupying his attention. He has been up a nearly a week.

We did intend going up home this morning but it looked so cloudy, I feared for Will to go. We will go tomorrow if it [is] a fair day. I don't suppose they want to see me but I want to see the children, and don't suppose I'll torment them much being there a few days. Will don't wish to be about them at all—and I don't blame him at all. I think I am welcome here. June 25th

Monday morning
June 28th/52

Tis morning, in every bush the Birds are warbling their notes. Tis cloudy, but occasionally the sun shines out, and gladdens every thing with his presence. It rained very hard last night, and Will and I returning from Pa's came very near getting a good ducking, I was very much affraid that he would get wet, and it would make him sick again. He has gone to town this morning, and I am feeling very dull, and can do nothing with any kind of zest.

We went up [to the] house, or to Pa's on last Saturday, they seemed very indifferent to our coming, or going. Mother especially manifested no concern respecting our movements, and of course I told her nothing. Pa likes me better than she does I am convinced, and he cares very little I am certain.

Mother is a strange compound—and really it seems to me she is not invested with the feeling of a mother, especially towards me. I don't think I will go back there soon. I have no idea that they wish to see me, but I can live very well without their love, or assistance in any degree. I got a little wet yesterday evening coming home and feel dull and sleepy to day.

Will wont go up to Marlin this year, but will practice in Town. Pa said something to him about letting us have White's house, but he may have changed his mind before this. I rec^{ed} a letter from Mary Haynie last night, a long and in[t]eresting one containing some very good verses. ["]On hearing of my marriage." Some I think are very good. I am so sleepy.

Thursday evening
July 8th 1852

It is excessively warm this evening, and I have dispensed with my dress and donned my sack. It has been some time since I wrote in here. I went up to

Anderson on Saturday the 3rd to a celebration of the fourth. I enjoyed myself very well[;] it was very warm riding up there. Mr McAlpine delivered an oration, and did himself much credit. A great number of persons were present. After dinner they all returned home or to some friends house. Will had business in Town and I went down to Fanthorps[63] and stayed until late and went up to see Mrs Taylor, and came home, about dusk. Will was very attentive to me on the day of the dinner, I had some conversation with Jake Grimes[,] Patrick, and John Kennard. Wm Patrick made me mad, confound him! On monday night Mittie Hattie[64] Will and myself went up to Town to the grand "Star state circus." They did very well[;] the horses were quite poor. The lady rode very well. The married life so far goes very well. Will makes me cry some times, and vexes me too, but it is over in a moment. He has promised me to write here, this evening.

Thursday night

July 8th

According to promise and promises are easily and often rashly made but to perform—there's the rub as a justly celebrated writer once said about death "To die and know not where we are *going* theres the rub."[65] [T]o promise and know not what we are going to do there's the rub. I have promised to write. There is no doubt of that but what to write is the question, and one to be solved only by trial. I have been married only about six weeks, to the object of my dearest and strongest affection to one whom imagination and memory have long conspired to render immortal in my memory at least, and surely thou wouldst say I could not want for a words to express such an idea in the sense of a [unction] but a feeling[.]

63. Henry Fanthorp (59) was a farmer and hotel keeper. He built Fanthorp Inn in 1828 in Anderson. The inn housed the post office, and Fanthorp served as first postmaster. In 1850 his household included his wife, Rachel (36), son John (9), and daughter Mary (5). His real and personal property was valued at $6,800. TX Census 1850; Grimes County Historical Commission, *History of Grimes County*, 56.

64. Harriet (Hattie) Maria Neblett Terrell was born February 12, 1838, in Calcasieu Parish, Louisiana. She was the fifth child of Robert and Maria Neblett. Harriet Neblett Terrell married William Joseph Terrell July 7, 1858, and died October, 20, 1914, in Navasota, Texas. Perkins, *Some Nebletts in America*, 114.

65. *Hamlet*, act 3, scene 1 ("To die, to sleep;/To sleep: perchance to dream: ay, there's the rub:/For in that sleep of death what dreams may come").

Teusday evening
July 13th 1852

Yesterday and to day I have had the blues. I have felt so depressed. Indeed I seem bound for distinction! I am doomed to be unhappy, and am rendered ten times more so by the knowledge that my sad melancholy disposition is not one calculated to render Will happy. I have been so depressed yesterday, and to day, and Will asked me if it was not because I did not love him. I could not help loving him for my life, he is so kind and good to me, he gets vexed at me sometimes, but I do not blame him. 'Tis my fault. I am not truly worthy of any one's love, so full of faults. He is in Town to day and was there yesterday. I am so poor and worthless, have nothing but myself, and he too is poor, and will have to work so hard. I do not intend to spend[,] only what I absolutely stand in need of, if I had brought anything with me, I would feel better, but no, I'd suffer the misery of ages, before I would lead them my parents to suspect for a moment that I was trying to wheedle in with them, to give me something. I had no saddle, and Pa declared to Mother that he would not give me any, and Will bought me one in Town, about two weeks since. I don't feel right for him to buy me any thing. I don't know when I will go back to Pa's, not soon I reckon, but I have some things left there I should like to have, and know no way to get them unless I go up after them.

I am treated as one of the family down here and am perfectly contented. No, not contented for I had rather have a home of our own, as it is, I can not call a single place on Earth *home*. I have no home. No one loves me except Will, and he should not love me[.] I feel desolate. I believe it will rain this evening. I am writing a love story for my own amusement, but consider it decidedly a failure. It won't do.
Teusday evening July 13th/52

Monday evening
Aug 2nd 1852

I commence writing with a full weight and sense of my deep unworthiness and Will's worth and honor. I feel degraded in my own eyes, I feel my unworthiness of all that's good and noble—and that I have grieved Will and that he thinks less of me, that I do not appear as good and as worthy his love as I have heretofore, and how the believe [*sic*] wounds me; tears every moment are ready to start to my eyes when the recollections comes over me. And he good kind heart, waited this morning to tell me good bye and kiss me, and looked affectionately at me and kissed me with as much fervor as usual, yet my jealous heart made and makes me believe that he looked [at] me as if he pittied me. Poor me how undeserving! and yet his love, the share I do have in it, will make me a better being. Oh Will! how I do love you cannot conceive, more than I ever did, as you know that I am unworthy [four lines have been crossed out and are illegible]

I am so sad. Will has gone to Groce's retreat[66] about 12 miles distant, to cast his vote in the county elections, he said he would be back to night and I fear he will come back with the sick headache, which he is subject to when exposed to the sun for any length of time and as he will be today. I was at Pa's two weeks ago. Pa saw Will in town and asked him to come up the next day and we went. They were more friendly. On Saturday, I went with her (Mother) to see Mary Haynie, enjoyed myself very well, I like Mary very much. She is very intelligent, about 20 years old. I wrote to her last week. I have not heard from Jane[67] yet. I wrote the week after I was married. The first part of June. I think I'll write a short note this evening to her—perhaps she did not get my letter. I wrote to Mrs Cochran at the same time, and she has not answered me yet, is [it] because I am married? I don't care[.] I am not bad off to write to any one. Aug 2nd/52

Monday morning
Aug 16th 1852

I am feeling very badly. Rather depressed in spirits. On last Thursday week the 4th of the month, Will and myself went up to Pa's, while there I went to the Springs[68] and stayed with Mrs Noble and her Mother two days and one night. She says she does not know the reason Sallie and Amanda have not written to me, and that she knows they are not mad at me. On last Friday evening I came home[.] And since that time I have felt so sick and bad, I

66. Groce's Retreat was named after Jared Ellison Groce II. George Childress was said to have written the Declaration of Texas Independence at the Groce homestead. In 1851 Groce's Retreat became the site for the Houston-Springfield stagecoach stop. Grimes County Historical Commission, *History of Grimes County*, 62, 84–85.

67. Jane Nix Teel was Lizzie Neblett's cousin. She was born in 1835 in Hickman County, Tennessee, the daughter of Lizzie's maternal aunt Lucinda Lane Nix McClure and her first husband, John Nix. Jane married Robert Teel in 1853. NP.

68. Piedmont Springs was seven miles west of Anderson. The sulfur springs were visited by many for supposed health benefits. In 1861 Alonzo Cannon bought land and built a four-story, one-hundred-room building near the springs. Some time in 1863 Cannon went broke and a Mrs. Alsbrook took over the springs. Allen, *Saga of Anderson*, 149.

hardly know what to do with myself. I *think my future prospects are beginning to break*. I feel so listless. I cannot write longer. Will is in Town to day.

Teusday morning
Aug 31st 1852

This is the last day of the month. The weeks and months glide away, and I hardly know, or think that time passes, not that time passes with velvet tread through my little internal world, but every thing appears indistinct undefined, and dreamy. I know that I am eternally launched on the shores of Matrimony, that in a few more years nay *year*, my very feelings pursuits & thoughts will be changed. That a new feeling, something I can scarce conceive now, will fill my bosom, and from thence forth, will be a tie which even death cannot sunder. I say I know this yet, it appears like a dream. I feel like I had wandered out alone by the clear stream, winding through beautiful groves of timber, clothed in their garb of green, bearing on their spreading branches thick clusters of grapes purple and black, and seemingly inviting the traveller to partake and on a bench of grass, bedecked with flowers, I had reclined, and lulled by the babling of the brook, and the songs of the birds, I had fallen to sleep, and many and pleasant dreams had hau[n]ted my mind, telling of one (in whom I did not recognize myself) who dressed in a simple white dress without ornament or jewel. Her dark hair put back over her ears, and fastened behind with a shell comb[, she] was led to the Altar by a young man of high open brow, with happy look. [A]nd then, in the presence of the assembled brothers and sisters [they] made the fitting vows, and were pronounced by the minister "husband & wife." The bride left her home, and went with him to his home. I saw them again, he was prostrate on a bed of sickness, the feverish and aching brow was his, and his young wife wore an anxious face, he was sick very sick, and often she knelt in prayer for him. Death passed, he was once more well and happy. I saw them once more, she was gazing in his face with happy yet anxious look, and with joyful exulting look [he] clasped her to his bosom, while she whispered something low in his ear, that I could not hear. I was awakened from this pleasant dream by the hideous frightful rattle of the snake, and starting up I fled with light steps, and fainted not nor tired until I was safe within the enclosure of my home, where naught shall disturb my peace and happiness.[69]

---

69. For interpretation of other southern women's dreams see Jean E. Friedman, *The Enclosed Garden: Women and Community in the Evangelical South, 1830–1900* (Chapel Hill: University of North Carolina Press, 1985), 39–53.

I think I will go up to Pa's this week sometime if Will will go with me. About every three weeks or so, I get restless and want to leave and go some where, and having a once called home, I go there. Will has gone some where this morning to be back for dinner I suppose, he went away somewhat mad at me, and I at him. But I suppose it is as much my fault as his.

He is as loving and kind as he was the day we were first married—and I think will remain so if [I] do not wear him by my bad temper. I expect we will not go to housekeeping before November sometime[.] I wish I could do so tomorrow. August 31st

—September—

"Procrastination is the thief of Time"[70] is an old Copy I used to write when I was a school girl, but I thought little then of its truth & sense, after years have taught me that the sentence is replete with truth and that procrastination is one of my greatest evils. September past and I did not write a single line in this book, that I intended writing every week in any how when I commenced it. Last month [I] was very sick. I went up home the first of the month, returned on Thursday the 9th with a fever on me. [W]ent to bed, and was not out of bed again until the 24th of the same month a day over two weeks. I was Salivated[71] from the 15th and I was so weak when I got up I could hardly stand alone a minute with[out] assistance, I was never so weak before in my life, and was never before Salivated, and I do not think I [ever] will be again, as long as I possess a grain of rationality. Oh! tis so disagreeable, cant eat anything cant talk, cant sleep, cant do anything, but rail, grumble and cry at the old Colonel.

When I was up home on the First of the month, old Mrs Noble, Judge Noble's Mother was at our house[.] Pa brought her from the Springs, where she had been staying for a month to be cured of the Dropsy.[72] Poor old Lady,

---

70. Edward Young, *Night Thoughts* (1741).

71. Salivated most likely refers to a painful nineteenth-century "cure" that took place over several days. On the first day, mercurial ointment was rubbed into the patient's feet and in subsequent days into the legs, thighs, arms, shoulders, and trunk. The name probably originated from the fact that the mercury induced heavy salivation, and the patient's salivary glands, gums, and tongue would become raw and inflamed.

72. "Dropsy" was the name given for any condition that produced swelling in the limbs. Possible causes could include diabetes, emphysema, and heart or kidney disease.

she was a perfect sight, swolen so much, perfectly helpless, had to be turned over in her bed. I had no conversation with her upon either religion or death. I never heard her mention either of the subjects. She died about 2 weeks after she reached Houston. I felt when I told her good bye that I was shaking hands with one just on the verge of Eternity. I thought of her dying, but never once of my dying, and when I reached Dr N[eblett]'s I had a high fever on me, and came nearer dying than perhaps She did at the same time. How uncertain is life! how full of pain and evil, yet how short. "The pains, the ills that flesh is heir too."[73] Will watched, and nursed me so kindly and attentively I shall ever feel greatful for his patience and kindness during my illness. I went up home on the 25th of Sept. the day after I was out of bed and stayed 3 weeks, during the time Mother had a Cancer on her nose which she had began to doctor and she suffered greatly for near two weeks—the time it took to kill it[;] she cured it entirely by her own application, and a very simple one at that. She got the common sorrel[74] called by some sheep sorrel, bruised it well, and [put] it in a thin cloth and squeezed the juice out in a pewter vessel, and put another pewter plate over it, and dried it in the sun, and it made a gluey stuff which she put on a small piece of cloth and applied to the place affected. It was very painful, but most assuredly produced a cure, the piece of flesh, the half of her nose, came out, it was almost entirely well when I left, yesterday was a week ago. She speaks of going up to Limestone County Fairfield to visit an Aunt of hers, Grand Pa's sister—Ann Patton and she wishes me to come and keep house for her while she is gone which I promised to do. She expects to start in a week from this time if she goes, which is doubtful.

I was to see Mrs Haynes, on Friday the 15th of Oct. She had been expected to die every day & night for nearly a week then, and two weeks now—with the Dropsy. She is a smaller woman naturally than Mrs Noble was, but I think was swolen as much as Mrs N. I would not mind dying if I thought on my death bed I would have her faith, her hope, and joy[;] she longs and prays for death. I would give all I ever expect to own during life, if on my death, I could and will have her feelings and hopes. This is the 25th of Oct, I have been married 5 months to day. The 25th of every month I have to tell Will that it

73. *Hamlet*, act 3, scene 1 ("The heartache and the thousand natural shocks/That flesh is heir to").

74. "Sorrel" is the name for several plants that have a pungent juice containing oxalic acid. Sorrel was used for a variety of medicinal purposes including scurvy, ringworm, jaundice, to cool a fever, and to remove tumors or boils.

is our marriage day. He never thinks of it, unless I tell him of it. It has been raining this morning but I believe it will clear off now, the sun has come out. Will sits before me [in] the rocking chair that Ma gave me last Saturday, with a paper in his hand and never hears a word I say to him unless I ask him do you hear me? He vexes me so much about that[.] I talk and talk to him, and he never hears me, and never commences a conversation with me, no more than if I had no ears to hear. But frequently goes where Ma is, and will talk for hours with her if she'll stay to listen, and never talks to me unless I begin to talk to him & ask him questions, which he'll answer in the shortest manner. I get so vexed at myself for talking to him. He thinks more of Ma any how than he does of me. He had a fever last Teusday, which lasted until Wednesday morning. He took a large dose of Blue Mass[75] on Teusday night, and Quinine[76] since, and is almost well, had only the one fever. I am getting so lazy. I must go to work this morning, and work like fury. I am reading a novel by James, called the Step Mother,[77] and [it] facinates me so. I can hardly do anything but read it, and think of it.

Mr McCaskill,[78] arrived at Demaret's on last Friday night. Nelia is there sick again, threatened with miscarriage. I was to see her yesterday evening, she was some better, she is so thoughtless and imprudent. I am sorry for her she has suffered so much. Monday morning Oct 25th/52

Thursday night
Nov 11th 1852

Time swiftly glides! how trite the sentence yet how true. Time changes the face [of] Nature continually and often, often, the heart of man. Tis an old and true proverb that "a wise man changes his mind often, a fool never." [I]t shows man's rationality that he is governed by reason, to change when circumstances convince him of his error. Tis sad to think that all things change and most sad

75. Blue Mass was a common medicine containing mercury and chalk. It was most likely used as a laxative.

76. Quinine is an alkaloid derived from the bark of various species of Cinchona trees. It was most commonly used in the treatment of malaria, but was often used as a remedy for fevers in general.

77. G. P. R. (George Payne Rainsford) James published *The Step-Mother* in 1846.

78. Will Neblett's maternal aunt was Caroline McCaskill, mother of Nelia McCaskill Kerr. Mr. McCaskill most likely refers to Nelia's father, but there is no record of him in the census. NP.

to think, to know that warm friends by time will grow cold, loved ones scorn the warm pure offering of your heart, and learn to smile at what has been, when the very recollection with you causes the tears to start.

But since it is ordained of Heaven that Nature should be continually, and at stated times changing her outward dress, let it be so, the green and velvet leaf change into "the sear and yellow leaf"[79] of Autumn[;] let the beautiful rose crumble into nothing, the mild and balmy air of Spring give place to the cold cutting one of heavy winter: but oh! save me from the blightning of the affections, let me meet the warm embrace, feel the tear of sympathy on my cheek and the answering throb of love in the breast of one good and true soul, and oh God! let that one soul ever remain as at present my husband! and I will feel ever as now that I am blessed of Heaven. Tis the purest most refined joy on Earth, the knowledge that you are loved truly singly, and sincerely by one on whom the richest portion of your love is centered. Oh! my dearest husband, my own Will, should I ever repine or fail to thank Heaven for the riches of thy good and true heart?

I feel that my joy is not yet replete, that my cup of happiness is not yet quite full the time is not yet come, when I hope to feel a Mothers joy, a mothers love. The life of my dear Babe, that I have implored Heaven to bless me with oh! will it be spared, by a merciful Father to glad my pathway here, and perhaps lead me to Heaven at last. God, grant it may! Nov 11th/52

Sunday night
Dec 19th 1852

I am feeling in an ill humour with myself, & every body to night. I have just finished supper where there was nothing right—every thing wrong, exactly as I did not wish it. I felt vexed in the first place about my chickens. Some of my neighbor Mrs Owney's chickens have taken up here, and some of my hens [are] gone. The chickens always mixing, tis vexatious, I don't think now that I'll try to raise [a] single foul. [A]nd then at table, I had to put so many things on that had been left off, found the meat fly blown, turned the milk over on the table indeed every thing went wrong. Will sat and ate as complacently as if there was no one on Earth saving and excepting himself, never handed me a potatoe nor the milk, nor meat, which were all beyond my reach, finished his supper with as much zeal and dispatch, and as silently as if it was the last

---

79. *Macbeth*, act 5, scene 3.

he expected to eat this side of Jordan. Well let it be so, since there is no remedy I can better it none by grumbling whining or crying—so I will strive and be content, tho' contentment is a blessing not easily taught. I have been house-keeping now about three weeks, we came here on the last day of November.[80]

I felt, and feel a great deal more contented than I did before. Yet I am not contented yet, nothing seems to be fixed right and as I wish it. Pa sent me my Bureau and Mother sent my Baby's Box, to put his little clothes in. The things came safe enough. Do flee from me unpleasant thoughts let me rest a little while. I expect to be confined about the middle of April.

This coming event occupies my mind continually, tis the one great thought of my brain the one joy of my heart. I have, and do wish so fervently for it to be a boy, that I can not think of it as anything else. I felt it move, or quicken on the night of the 26th of last month, Nov, nearly a month ago. I have not sewn one stich for the little fellow yet, but I must, and will make him some little clothes soon as christmas and New years is over.

I have been quite busy sewing & fixing since I came here, and for some time before. So my little sweet child had to be put off, but not much longer. I have some curtains to make and put up around my bed, a dress to make for myself and a cape for Ma. I believe [that] is all the urgent work on hand—and then Ma's little man shall be attended to.

Last Friday I went up Town, and bought some little articles, and got a letter and two numbers of the Evening Post from Mary Haynie. She is the only regular correspondent I have, all the rest seem to have dropped me. I have had only one letter from Jane since I was married. I don't know what is the matter.

I answered Amanda's letter, but have received no answer as yet. Jim my Brother is in the Post Office at Houston, has been since Oct. I hope he will do well. Nelia is in about 4 weeks of her confinement, like to have miscarried about two weeks ago.

I'll go to bed and try and sleep off my bad humour. I guess about half after 8.
Dec 19th 1852

Sunday night
January 2nd 1853

Christmas and new year's day have both passed. It was a bad rainy Christmas, but when did that ever fail to happen. It is almost invariably the case that

---

80. Lizzie's father bought the couple a house in the "western part of the town of Anderson." Memoir.

we have bad rainy weather about Christmas. Pa was here the evening before Christmas, and asked us if we would not go out to his house the next day, and promised to send the carriage after me, but it was so bad he thought I would not come if he sent, and did not send, but I made up my mind to go, and go I must, so I borrowed Franklin Webb's[81] buggy & horse & Will drove me out. I enjoyed myself very well. Played some on the Piano[.] I don't believe Pa intends giving me my Piano. I wish he would, it would be so much company for me. On the 31st of Dec we borrowed Uncle McCaskill's buggy or surrey from Nelia & Kerr, and Ma sent us a horse and we went down there to spend New Year's day with them which is Mittie['s] birth day also. She is 18 years old. We had a very nice dinner and came home on yesterday which was the 1st. I was anxious to attend church to day for the last time, but there was none in the fore noon, and we did not hear that Mr Gillette preached this evening until sunset, we passed Mrs Webbs walking and she told us he preached this evening. Now I must hear no sermon until my little man comes, and gets large enough for Ma to leave him. I have not done up the work I intend doing before I work any for him yet. My dress is about half done, and the lining of Ma's cape is cut out. Oh I am so anxious to sew for him to make his sweet little clothes, he is beginning to kick ma right hard, but it only makes her feel happy to feel the little sweet one move, and feel certain that it is no delusion, that before a half year rolls round I will be a Mother—and feel all a mothers love, the holiest passion in the human breast. I am too full of hope to despond. I cannot associate death with my Babe—no[,] death is cold and inanimate and my Babe is warm & full of life. About 7 Oclock.

At Pa's
March 31st 1853

This is the last day of March, and perhaps the last day before my confinement, for I am looking every day now—and will be until the 9th of April when the last day of my nine months will be out.

I came up here to Pa's on the 18th of March intending to remain until after my confinement. I had made up my mind to stay at home, until Pa come, and told me I had better come, and that Mother thought so also, and John wrote

81. In 1860 Franklin Webb (age 34) was a farmer married to Amanda Webb (31), with real and personal property valued at $3,000. Robert and Maria Neblett adopted a son, Franklin X. Webb, from a Catholic orphanage in New Orleans. TX Census 1860; "Neblett, Robert Caldwell," vertical file, CAH; Perkins, *Some Nebletts in America*, 83–84.

me a note, telling me I had better come home, that he thought, or knew, I would do better at home where Mother could attend to [me] better, so I packed up and am here with the old midwife Mrs Ford or as some call her Mrs Hill who came here last sunday the 27th, she was with Mother when she had Walter[82] and Babe[83] and Mother praises her very much, I had rather trust myself in her hands, and Mothers, than any doctor I know of.

I have been exceedingly low spirited, for the last month until within the last two or three days. I have thought I would die, and have been very badly frightened and would almost have the histericks, in fact, did have them at times.

But now, I feel that my chance for living is as good as most women's, and that I will get over it, and even if Heaven has ordained that I shall purchase the life of my babe, by the sacrifice of my own, I should be content, for I believe God to be all wise, merciful and good, and have sufficient faith to think & believe that "he doeth all things well."[84] I know it seems hard, that I should have to die and leave my babe and husband in the world alone. My Babe could never know a mothers love kindness and protection, but Will would and will love it better if I am gone, and who knows, beside He to whom all mysteries are open, that my death would not cause Will to repent of his sins, and become an heir to the Kingdom of Heaven. God grant that it may be so, even tho' I die not. Will has a susceptible tender & loving soul which harbors honor and honesty as its chief ornaments.

And should I live or die, I have no complaint to make of Will's neglect or coldness towards me since we were married, no woman, I am convinced ever had a more faithful loving and confiding husband than I have, and no wife ever loved her husband better than I do mine, and in all things have I striven to be to him the "help mate" Heaven designed woman to be; how far I [*sic*] my efforts have been crowned with success, is not for me to say.

The current of our Matrimonial life so far has been smoothe, and unruffled, occasionally a harsh word, or harsher thought would for a while disturb the

82. Walter Scott was the brother of Lizzie Neblett. He died March 20, 1859, while attending school in Clarksville, Red River County. Memoir.

83. "Babe" was the nickname of Lizzie Neblett's sister Alice. She was the youngest child of James and Sarah Scott. In 1860 she was 14 years old, living with her mother, and attending school. She married John Yarbrough on August 24, 1864. TX Census 1860; Mullins, *Grimes County, Texas, Marriage Records.*

84. Probably Mark 7:37 ("he hath done all things well").

sunshine of our home, but angry feelings were not permitted to be inhabitants of our bosoms long. If I should die I don't think Will, will ever find another wife who will please him as well as I do, or who will love him as well, or whom he will love as well.

I am willing he should marry again if I die first, if he can find one he loves well enough to marry, my child or children as the case may be, are not better than other womens children, that they should not be subjected to the control of a Step Mother. Will suffers a good deal of anxiety on my account and that of the babys I know, and I have many fears also.

Walter is just getting well of the measles and unfortunately, I went where he was the day before they broke out on him and I have never had them, tho' I have repeatedly been with them.

I am very fearful I will have them, and the baby too if it lives, and it would go very hard with both of us, I am wearing garlic in my bosom, to keep them off, and as soon as the baby is born I intend having garlic put round its neck. I am surprised at myself for being in such good spirits, I have hitherto been so dejected [*sic*], and sorrowful. I had a letter from Jane just before I left home. She was married some where near the 20th of January last to a young man living in Lockhart named Robert E. Teel and they are now living at his Fathers in Lockhart, his Father is a Dr; Bob is either a merchant on his own hook, or a clerk for some one I think. Jane don't tell me any thing so Earthly about him as that. Aunt Lucinda[85] has an other babe, a boy [who] sits alone named Bob after his Father I guess. Little Ella her first child by McClure[86] died about 4 months ago, I don't know what was the matter with it. I am very much in hopes that Jane has done well, and that her husband may succeed in life well. I wrote to her a short time before I left home, and told her my secret that a little stranger was expected shortly. I rec[ed] a letter this week from Mrs Cochran, and she tells me she had heard that I was expect[ing] a babe, I don't know how she heard it. I wrote to Sallie Noble, about a month ago, rec[ed] no answer yet, and wrote to Amanda near two months ago, no answer, yet.

---

85. Lucinda Lane Nix McClure was the sister of Lizzie Neblett's mother, Sarah Lane Scott. She was born around 1809 in Hickman County, Tennessee. She married John Nix about 1827, and they had three children: James, John, and Jane (Teel). John Nix died around 1842, and Lucinda married Mark McClure. The couple had two children, Robert and Kate. Lucinda McClure died in 1867. Lizzie refers to her as Aunt Cinda throughout her letters. NP.

86. In 1860 Mark McClure was a forty-six-year-old farmer with personal property valued at $70. During the Civil War he assisted Susan Womack Scott, and the family lived on her and John Scott's land. Lizzie refers to him in her letters as Uncle Mc. TX Census 1860.

Nelia had her baby a little girl named Mary on the 12th day of January last—done very well, did not have a hard time at all, the baby was small, but has grown a good deal[;] she dont give milk enough for it, and she has to feed it on cows milk which gives it the cholic.[87] Nelia was out to see me, at home, when the baby was 6 weeks old brought it with her. Will brought me a letter this evening from Brother Jim, he seems quite anxious to hear from home and to come home. I am fearful he is not doing very well down there.

If he does come home, I am in hopes he can get employment in Town, and board with us. I don't think Pa wants him here[.] I have been laughing a good deal about my babe coming tomorrow, and then it would be an April fool—it will be quite funny if it should happen so. I have felt quite well all day to day no pain, or any disagreeable feeling and, and [*sic*] those who know tell me they always feel better two or three days before hand than they felt for some time.

Will says if Mary comes tomorrow he will call her his little *April Flower.*

This I suspect will be the last I'll write in here, before my confinement, and perhaps the last I'll ever write, who can tell save God himself? Thursday night March 31st/53

Monday night
April 4th 1853

I am alive, and navigating yet. Five more days, and I will be to the last notch. How I do dread it, and wish it was all over with, and the baby and myself doing well. I know I have no conception of the pain nor can have none, until I feel and experience it. I feel so sleepy I cannot write any more to night, and perhaps this may be the last time I'll ever write, either in here or any where.

Teusday night
April 5th

Well to night I think I have the measels, have little or no doubts of its being so, and have been drinking tea for it ever since dinner. Saffron and Composition[88] to drive it out. So I have very little doubts, so many *many* fears, that my

87. Colic is a condition typically found in infants. It is characterized by chronic severe abdominal pain. Modern medicine has yet to fully understand the causes of colic.

88. Saffron, a flowering plant of the iris family, was often used as a sedative and cathartic. Composition may refer to a tea made from Compositae or composite, the largest family of flowering plants. Some of the plants in the composite family include the sunflower, artichoke, lettuce, and wormwood. Many of the plants within the family were used as tonics, also as a diaphoretic, vermifuge, cough remedy, flea treatment, as well as other uses.

poor little Babe will die with them and how sad, sad, and grieved it makes me feel. It seems to me, if I live, and it dies I cannot possibly get over its death. I do love it so much, it feels so near to me it don't seem to me I could ever love an other as I love it. But I must think "all things are for the best,["][89] and if it dies, it will be I doubt not for the best tho' I can not see wherefore, and if I die, it will be for the best; tho' I do feel sorry for Will, I know it will grieve him almost to death for I do know he loves me, even as well as he loves himself, but Will, do not grieve as one who has no hope, and remember that I am not dead but gone before, where, I do hope, to see you after death.

Wednesday night
April 6th.
    Up all day again cant tell whether I have the measels or not[.] I think I had a good deal of fever last night have been drinking warm tea all day, and have been almost constantly in a perspiration all day—and have been led to hope it was not the measels, but a bad cold I took last Sunday evening. There blew up a north wind in the evening, and I was suffering so all day from a pain [in] the back that I could not be still.

Teusday morning
Nov 1st/53
    My last date I notice in this was April 6th, a long time, nearly 7 months. I have been so lazy I have not writen one word in this since—and what changes have taken place, in me, and in the world. On the next morning Thursday after writing in here I was taken in labor, and at 7 oclock that night was born, (not my little man) but, my little lady Mary Caroline Neblett she weighed 6 pounds and three quarters, a sweet little babe. But as I expected and feared, on the night of her birth, the measels broke out on me, and on the third day after her birth, they made their appearance on little Mary. At two weeks old she was smaller than at her birth, and had such a cough that I despaired of her life, she would almost loose her breath and foam at the mouth, and then poor little thing she could not spit up what she coughed. When she was two weeks old, Mrs Haynie came to see Mother and I, and began giving her Lobelia,[90] or I do not think she could have lived and then I did not much believe she

---

89. Possibly from John Milton, *Samson Agonistes*, or Francois Voltaire, *Candide*, chapter 1.
90. *Lobelia* is a genus of plant. It was commonly used as an emetic.

would live. I would get up in the night and give her Lobelia, and make her throw up, and it would relieve her. I did much better than she did, tho' it is almost a miracle that we both had not died. When she was 5 weeks old we returned home. She has been a very healthy child since, as smart and pert as a wicket, she can sit alone now, and almost crawl. Nelia's baby is never well. Carrie Demaret is larger than either Mary Eliza Kerr, or Mary C. Neblett. Mary N. weighed only 13 pounds at six months old. Mrs Noble had one on the 4th day of Oct and it weighed 12 pounds. By the bye Judge Noble has bought a place near me and has moved up, Sallie and Amanda seem the same as ever.

I had a letter from Beck Wallace a month or more ago, informing me of the birth of her son, James Westwood Wallace, he is over ten months old now and Jane Nix, Jane Teel, expects a little stranger in Nov, next month. The Yellow fever[91] has been raging very bad in Galveston and Houston this summer— the week ending the 19th of Oct there were 37 enterments in Houston[;] among the number on the 16th of Oct was buried Benjamin Smith.

Oh it seems so strange to think that Ben is dead. I can hardly realize it[.] I am sorry and deplore his early death yet I expect he is infinitely better off than if he was alive. His lot in life was poor—an orphan cheated out of his property, cast from post to pillar in in [*sic*] his infancy, without the love of a Mother or Father, and then nipped in his early manhood by deaths untimely, unrelenting hand[;] he has gone, I hope, to a brighter and a better world. I do not like his conduct to me much, and feel at a loss what course to pursue. He has been asked, and solicited repeatedly by me to send me the letters, and my likeness he has had in his possession, and has always promised to do so, and has never done it, now they will be exposed to the gaze of the world, if at large if Amelia and Mrs Hadley get hold of them. [A]nd no telling into whose hands they will fall. I feel troubled about it.

I got Sallie Nobel to write to him, and ask him to send them to her through the mail, and they were not sent neither was her letter answered. I'll hope for the best any how. I believe I'll go and see Sallie and Amanda this evening. I saw his death announced in the "Galveston news" as Benjamin Smith an

---

91. Yellow fever is a disease carried by mosquitoes that produces flu-like symptoms and can lead to death. It derives its name from the fact that victims of the disease often become jaundiced. The 1853 epidemic in Galveston and Houston was typical of outbreaks in southern seaport towns during the nineteenth century.

American. I know of no other Ben Smith in Houston. I hope there may be some mistake about it.

I went to see Bro John on Saturday, found John and nearly every one of the children sick they all look badly. I dont think they will raise the baby she looks so bad. I think there is something the matter with her head it is so large, and she looks so dull and heavy out of her eyes. Nov 1st/53

Monday 2 Oclock
Dec 12th 1853

How time changes all things! how time has changed me. My pursuits, my tastes, my feelings have all changed. And when I think how I once felt, and thought, I could weep that those feelings are forever fled. I look sometimes at Mary, and can hardly credit the tale that she is mine, "bone of my [bones] and flesh of my flesh."[92] I sigh unconciously, as I gaze at her fair face, that trustful look as she gazes in my face. That innocence of which she is a perfect type. I think of what the future may have in store for her, what her lot may be, and I feel sad. Oh my daughter I would that you had been a boy, for "womans lot is hard to bear,["] and I would save you from what I have endured, and should life be prolonged must still endure.

Cares even now crowd on cares for thy welfare, now and in after years. Oh! would to God you may prove to be what my proud heart would have you. I think of you now my daughter, as I hope you to be, when childish ways will have passed away; and you [are] reading this record of your Mothers thoughts. My almost every thought is for my little Mary.

I feel very anxious about Jannie Teel[;] she wrote me, about two months ago, that she expected to be confined about the middle of Nov, which has been almost one month ago. I have not heard one word from her yet. I hope she is well by this time.

The last time I wrote, I thought Ben Smith was dead, but have since found out it was a mistake, it was a German. Mary can crawl every where, could crawl at 7 months, has one tooth, can get up by a chair, she was 8 months old the 7th of this month. Sallie and Amanda were to see me, on yesterday. They do not visit me often, and I do not go there often. They are better satisfied than they were when they first moved up.

Sometimes I think Sallie and Len Cox will marry yet. She corresponds with him regularly.

92. Gen. 2:23.

Monday night
Jan 24th 1854

On yesterday I received a letter from some of Jane's kin folks, written at Jannies request. She has a little daughter, born the 27th of Nov/53, calls it Anna. Has blue eyes light auburn hair and very fair skin. Jannie's breast has rose three different times and she has suffered greatly I know[.] I feel sorry for her. I am glad it is a girl for I am even with her now.

I do not like the name she has given it. All three of us cousin's have little ones now. Beck the youngest, [has] a boy nearly or quite a year old, and my Mary [is] 9 months old, and Jannie's nearly two months old. It seems only a few years and we were all children, and now, the child has given place to the woman and mother and a few more years will mature our young hopeful's, and they will be heads of families, and so the world goes on and will continue to move on till it ceases to be.

Anderson
May 16th 1854

Tis night "calm night that breedest thought,["] occasionally the melancholly note of the Whipowill breaks upon my ear mingled with the bark of distant dogs, and the drowsy bell of the herd, which sounds some how serve to make me more lonely. Tis a dark and sad looking night. I peer through the darkness and afar, a faint glimmering star meets my eye. There! a flash of the quick playing lightning has darted across the sky startling me by its suddeness.

I see three stars close together, they look lonely to me, as if their glory was departed, and their luster shorn. The noise of the boys in Town comes to my ear now, but not joyously as the voice of childhood wanted does. Methinks twas amid scenes and sounds like these, that Gray must have conceived and writen that beautiful poem "Elegy written in a country church yard"[93]

> "Now fades the glimmering landscape on the sight,
> And all the air a solemn stillness holds,
> Save when the beetle wheels his droning flight,
> And drowsy tinklings lull the distant folds.["]

Amidst these different confused sounds, which come to the ear softened and subdued by distance, I seem to be alone, the solitary listner. [A]nd thought

---

93. Thomas Gray, "Elegy Written in a Country Churchyard" (1751).

courses on, unheeding the flight of moments, and from the silent chambers of
the past, memory comes forth, bringing with her the forms of the loved and
gone—those, now mouldered into silent dust, once like unto myself. I see
them all—and their memory is bedimed with a tear—friends of my childhood,
in sunny hours, ere the dark form of death had presented itself to my childish
thoughts. I knew and loved thee. My Teacher! I love thy memory, and mind
me, of many a word of praise, that gladened and made proud my heart and
many a saddened reproof, that caused my tears to flow in the silent watches of
the night, to wound one I knew was laboring for my good. I remember with
saddened tenderness, the scene of the reward of my first great ambition, to
excel. I had toiled day after day for two months & a half, to excell my class in
spelling, toiled late and early, and sobbed many a night on my pillow at the
mere supposition and fear that a boy, older than my self by a year, would gain
the coveted prize. The time at length came to award the prize, a 50 cent piece,
and, well, well do I remember the exultant pride with which I arose, and then
in the presence of the school and a few friends, received the 50 cents from the
hand of my honored Teacher. How light exultant & happy was [my] step, as
I gaily triped it home that evening, and in the hands of my father placed the
glittering gift, feeling as proud as a Boneparte at any of his greatest victories.
I turn the leaf, and the twin sister of my soul is before me, how are my bitter,
wrangling feelings hushed in her presence, the cold sod has long lain upon her
bosom, and the colder white marble slab received the pelting rains and gentle
dews of Heaven.[94] Oh! death how unmerciful art thou! How many, many
times have I sobbed away the childish griefs of my heart on that dear, loving
bosom, and felt my right to be pillowed there as the dearest friend—now I
mind me of the plum grove in front of the little old log school house, where
we would go at recess hours, and there tell each other our every joy and sorrow
and wonder, over and over again what we should do when vacation would separate us—years have fled. She the loved and lost makes one of the ["]Spirits
of the just made perfect"[95] in that large assembly of the just & Holy. [W]hile
I, where am I? let me pause and think, alas! I fear years have not brought wisdom, and I am not as worthy as in childhoods hours. Oh! ye old friends where
are ye this night. "Some at the bridal and some at the Tomb."

Fond memories of thee ye old friends crowd upon me this night, and were

---

94. This presumably refers to Lizzie Neblett's deceased childhood friend Nannie Bowin.
95. Heb. 12:23 ("The spirits of just men made perfect").

it possible I would fain know where ye are. Death has filled many I know—the form of one arrises before me. Young hopeful and energetic, a young man of some promise, & many hopes, who inlisted as a volunteer in the war between Texas & Mexico was captured cast in a lonely dark prison in Mexico, where he died of disease tis said, but I think me of a broken heart—sad sad fate to die thus, away from home, without a single cheering smile or beaming look from a friend, prized and loved for many years. Oh! ye thronging memories that keep swelling up from buried recollections—saddening and subduing all restless & turbulent feelings, I feel better by your presence. The old spring down under that rocky hill, with mint growing all around the watter, how I would prize one leaf of that mint now, methinks it could whisper many tales to my heart. The Spring house is before me where we used to bury our bottles of milk in the sand under the water, to have it cool at dinner, our old swing in the woods, where every trouble was swung away ere their impress was left upon our brows. The little foot path we traveled night and morning, the the [*sic*] creek, where we used to sit and rest under those large forest trees, listening to the little warblers above us, or watching the tiny fish gliding so swiftly about in the water at our feet until the hooting owl with her loud and melancholly noise has startled us, while each, looking in the others face, have risen and and [*sic*] hastened quickly on our way.

Years have fled but these memories live, fresh and green, and while writing[,] one memory has been displaced to find an other there, until my time and paper is spent.

The Power of Association

A sound, a scent, a tone, a shade, what a tumult of feeling can they at times excite, thrilling our inmost being and causing the tear of chastened sadness to glisten in our eye. The past with its hopes & fears, its joys & tears is before us, its shadow resteth on our hearts and causeth it to bound again with the same feeling it did perhaps years ago. The association may be of a mother, who has nursed us on a bed of pain, hung over us day after day while we lay in her lap, and gazed into her tearful eyes and frale face, until unto our little hearts was added an other pang, the knowledge that our mother grieved and for us. She has stilled her grief and sang lulaby, by which we have closed our eyes in sleep. In maturitys hour in a strange land among strangers that song sung by some mother to her infant falls upon our ear, and oh what a flood of feeling rushes over us! That mother was long since numbered with the dead, the sunny hours [of] childhood are past, and, tho cares and duties of life press daily upon us—that old song we shall ever remember and love.

Jan 22nd 1860[96]

A Review of the past eight years.

It has now been almost eight years since I became a married woman. Eight years of checkered good and ill, and yet thro' all it seems the most of the ill has fallen to my lot, until now my poor weak cowardly heart sighs only for its final resting place, where sorrow grief nor pain can never reach it more. Through these eight years I must say that you my husband have been kind to me much kinder than I perhaps deserved, but you will have the approving conscience to sustain you when I am no more.

I feel that I have faithfully discharged my duty towards you and my children, but for this I know that I deserve no credit nor aspire to none; my affection has been my prompter, and the task has proven a labor of love. You have not rightly understood me at all times, and being naturally very hopeful you could in no measure sympathize with me during my seasons of gloom and despondency—and your conduct which may have been only indifferent, has appeared to my excited imagination harsh, and caused a thrill of anguish in my bosom, that I hope yours may never feel. I know I am full of faults, and feel that you are much better than the most of men to have borne with [my] many faults as kindly and leniently as you have, for which I pray God that you may have your reward both here and hereafter. And here above all other thoughts arises the conviction that I have not made you as happy as some other woman, combining a happier disposition with a better mind than I have, could have done, and that often this truth forces itself upon you. But marriage is a lotery and that your draw proved an unfortunate one on your part is not less a subject of regret with me than you, and Heaven send that your next trial may prove fortunate, in every respect. I do not wish you to remain single when I am gone, a widowed life is a lonely one, and you need the tongue of a sensible woman to occasionaly awake you from a revery, that if indulged in continually might lead to we don't know where, certainly not to happiness. I think

96. In May 1855 Lizzie and Will moved to Corsicana in Navarro County, Texas. Here, Will practiced law, farmed, and became editor of the *Navarro Express*. By the date of this entry Lizzie had given birth to two more children, Robert Scott (March 16, 1855) and William Teel (April 10, 1857), and was expecting her fourth child, Walter Scott, born May 14, 1860.

you have undergone a gradual change and that the present finds you a far different man from what you were eight years ago. It seems to me that you regard all things that approach towards sentiment or sentimentality as beneath your notice, and that the wife of [to]day is a far different creature from the bride of eight years ago, that she has not the same call upon your love and sympathy that she had then. If she has proven herself unworthy, surely the thought that she is the mother of your children [who] has suffered greatly in giving them to your arms should at least encircle her name with thoughts of tenderness and feelings of sympathy.

You never tell your feelings, and if subject to spells of mental depression I never know it and you often seem very indifferent, about me in particular. It seems to me that could we change places, I would feel great solicitude and anxiety about you.

It is useless to say that during these eight years I have suffered ten times more than you have and ten times more than I can begin to make you conceive of, but of course you can not help the past, nor by knowing my suffering relieve it, but it might induce you to look with more kindness upon [my] faults. I feel different and am more afflicted now than ever before, and think it probable, (tho' I fear not,) that my desire to die will be gratified, but oh the suffering that lies between me and the port of death, and who knows I may suffer it all, and yet live to go thro' with the same again in [a] few years? No, my hand shall be raised to take my own life first. I will never dread death as much as I dread the suffering of my coming confinement, for deaths pangs are, methinks, as nothing compared with the pains of labor, and I look forward to a very tedious one and painful one, more than an ordinary degree. But let me banish the thought[.] I can benefit it in no way by thinking of it, and God knows the suffering will be sufficient when I reach it. The 17th of this month I was 27 years old—and I think my face looks older than that, perhaps I'll never see an other birth day and I don't grieve at the idea.
Corsicana Navarro Co Texas,
Jan 22nd 1860[97]

April 2nd 1862[98]

I open this book to record another calamity, which came upon me like a clap of thunder. Our home, or house rather that we left rented in Corsicana

97. Two sheets (four pages) between this entry and the next have been cut out of the diary.
98. In December 1861 the Nebletts moved back to Grimes County. They lived in houses owned by Lizzie's sister Sallie until June 1862, when they moved to their farm on Lake Creek.

to Mr Tom Oakes, was burned down on the 25th of March, through the most culpable neglect I think. Mr Oakes joined a company in Waco, went to the latter place & sent wagon's to move his household furniture and family to Waco. The negros it seems had entire control of things, and after loading up their wagons, they say they made a fire in the east room, which was my room, to bake some bread or sweet cakes to eat on the road. Their excuse for cooking in the house was that the kitchen door was down, and the wind blew in there so they could do nothing. They built a fire out of cedar & dry wood, and they (the negros) say the roof must have caught fire from sparks out of the chimney. The beds, in the wagon by the dining room door, caught first, and they put that out, next the roof of the dining room, the well bucket broke off in the well, and after that I suppose they just folded their hands & looked on, and by the time the alarm of fire had been given and the people from the square had reached the place, it was too far gone to be possibly saved. So perished 15 hundred dollars, at the lowest calculation, tho' the house cost us at least $2,000. It will be our entire loss, I doubt not, tho' I think Oakes ought to be responsible, to go off so and leave the house in charge of negros, to do as they please, and every body know what careless don't care creatures they are. Not a building now stands upon the place except the old crib, which never was worth more than $5.00. It makes me feel so sad, to think of the destruction. I always heard that places rented out went to decay & ruin, but ours went in a galop, no slow decay. I am trying to suspend my judgement, but I can not help thinking that the house was purposely set on fire. Mr Duren[99] writes that nothing was burnt in the house—it seems strange that the burning should take place just as they got every thing out the wagon's loaded up. For a few in town it was a glorious spectacle, Mrs Croom[100] the Jester family, and old Elsie—and perhaps a dozen more. Altho' we never know how to number our enemies, we know less how to number our friends. I feel like the Indian burning at the stake. I see the flames which will devour me & mine without power to avert or defer the doom. We are the butt of misfortune, at whom she hurls shaft after shaft, and not until the last shaft has been spent will the merciless foe

99. In the 1860 census an A. Duren was listed as living in Corsicana, Navarro County. He was the county clerk with a wife and six children and real and personal property valued at $1,350. TX Census 1860.

100. In 1860 James Croom (age 35) was a doctor in Corsicana, Navarro County, with real and personal property valued at $5,500. He lived with his wife, M. E. Croom, and four children. The Crooms are also featured in the Neblett letters.

desist. Poor blind creatures we can't see an inch before our nose. Had we remained in Navarro Co our house would now by standing, our Briar Creek
farm all planted in small grain, wheat & oats, which would have brought a
good price during these war times. As it is we have a most clear and delightful
prospect of starving and going unclad. Cotton cannot be sold, corn will be so
abundant if seasons prove good that it will not be worth ten cts per bushel next
year. We have no house to call our own (are living in Sallie's houses) new land,
building to do, and now comes the draft and Will of course is subject to it,
and just as sure as the draft comes, he will be drafted I feel it so, and when he
starts, I will feel that misfortunes arrows are almost spent for he will never
return to me a living man. If he does not fall a victim to bullets he will to
disease. He can't stand the hardship and exposures of camp life. And I what
will become of me? I can't stay here, the negros will have to go free, not earn
their living. I feel like it will be impossible to get any one to stay with them. I
would feel so insecure of my life, that I feel I could not stay. My heart fails
me, my courage sinks. [A]nd [I] feel that I would be willing if it was not for
my helpless dependant children to lie down and die, to avoid all the anxiety
and bodily suffering that lies spread before me in imagination. I have felt so
secure, so certain that the south would be victorious, so hopeful, and now the
picture has changed, all looks cloudy, g[l]oomy and distressing. I try not to
despair utterly but the faint spark of hope is almost gone. As to the house
burning, I can summon Philosophy to my aid, and bear heroically what I know
cannot be mended, and what touches the purse alone. [B]ut, Oh God! if the
strong holds of my heart are to be destroyed, my hearth made desolate, and
my bosom filled with mourning, 'tis to thee only that I can look for aid! And
such calamaties I now expect. Two brothers Garrett and Jim both in the army
another subject to the draft, and my husband also. The enlistments are all for
three years or the war. A long, long time to be gone even if we prove successful
in arms. And how many, many will never return.

May 1st 1863

Just one month ago, to day, Will left me for Galveston—he having joined
Capt Step[h]enson's Co (I) Col Elmore's Regt.[101] The first day of April 63

---

101. Henry M. Elmore commanded the Twentieth Texas Infantry Regiment. J. B. Stephenson commanded Company I in that regiment. On March 9, 1863, Will Neblett enlisted as a private in Company I of the Twentieth Texas Infantry. Company I served as guard for the gunboat
Bayou City in Galveston. Military Records of William Neblett, Compiled Service Records.

will long long be remembered by me. I felt when he bid me good bye that he was lost to me forever—and [I] never felt more desolate and bereaved in my life than I did all that day. My being left in my present situation no doubt makes me feel worse.[102] I expect to be confined in three weeks from this time perhaps earlier, and when that event takes place, my dear husband may be far beyond the borders of this state. All the terrors of my own situation have fled before the harassing fears I feel for Will's welfare. Oh! God, am I to be taught, to feel more plainly than I do at present that there are worse things in this world than childbearing? I have thought foolishly and rashly that no worse calamity could befall me, than to be doomed to have an other child. Now I feel that I would be willing to bear as many more, to be assured that Will would be safely returned to me, even if it is a year off.

102. Lizzie Neblett was pregnant with her fifth child, Elizabeth "Bettie" Neblett. Bettie was born May 26, 1863.

II
THE LETTERS

2

The Coming Pains of Labor

April 6, 1863–June 9, 1863

Galveston Texas Apr 6th/63
Mrs L S Neblett

Dear Lizzie

I have postponed writing for a day or two for the purpose of getting this to Anderson on Wednesday night when you or Susan can send on Thursday and get letters and papers at the same time. We arrived here on Friday about 2 O'clock and are quartered in the city. We sleep (that is our mess) on the 3rd story of a large brick building formerly the printing office of the Christian Advocate, and find things fully as comfortable as could reasonably be expected. We were on guard yesterday and last night. I did not sleep more than three hours but feel no bad effect from it. Guard duty here is a mere matter of form that is the part performed by our Regiment. Before we arrived here we heard that the soldiers were put to work on the breastworks and consequently felt a little uneasy on the subject but on arriving I learn that volunteers were called for and thirty dollars per month allowed which was responded to by a sufficient number to meet the call.

This is certainly the laziest and most monotonous life that can well be imagined we are restricted to very narrow limits and cannot go through the city without a permit and only two of those can be granted a day in each Co. John and I procured one and walked over town on Saturday but saw little worth the walk. Since arriving here I find that it will be very difficult to get a furlough for a long time perhaps three or four months if not longer if the present rules on the subject is adhered to. The rule is to grant furloughs to four in each Co at a time for twelve days. I will try very hard to get home about the last of May but feel not very confident of success. If you had passed through your ordeal I should not be so anxious on the subject because I know one man has no better right to go home than another. I feel very anxious about the health of the children this summer. For I expect a great deal of sickness up the creeks in May and June. There is nothing new here except a rumor that a Co of our Reg is to be put on a steam boat which is to lye [*sic*] in the bay all day & watch the blockaders.[1] Some think our Co will be detailed for this business & all dislike it very much as it will exhile us from the world, although we will get our letters & papers. I am well. Write soon.

Yours affectionately
Wm H. Neblett

Galveston Apr 9th/63

Dear Lizzie

Having an opportunity of sending this by Mr. Carson I write although it was but three days ago since I wrote by the mail. I have nothing worth saying but judging you by myself concluded it would be a pleasure for you as it would be for me to hear from you every day. I have been in good health and fine appetite until to day. I am now a little unwell from Diarrhea. This is quite common in camp. I think eating fish is one of the causes of it with me. I catch some and buy some. I caught a mess a few days since and always think of you whenever I see or eat fish. If it was possible to send some I would do so but am informed that they would be certain to spoil unless preserved by ice. This is an extremely monotonous and tiresome life. We do not drill any and have nothing to do but answer to our name at roll call which is done at morning and evening and go on a dress parade in the evening. I have been to the book store here but find nothing but a few school books. I pick up something to read however and manage to pass superabundant time between reading talking and doing nothing. I will get me some spanish books if I can and go to study-

---

1. On Union blockades of Confederate ports see James M. McPherson, *Battle Cry of Freedom: The Civil War Era* (New York: Ballantine Books, 1988), 378–82. On the blockade of Galveston see Edward T. Cotham Jr., *Battle on the Bay: The Civil War Struggle for Galveston* (Austin: University of Texas Press, 1998), 168–75; Gary Cartwright, *Galveston: A History of the Island* (Fort Worth: Texas Christian University Press, 1991), 108–15.

ing spanish in a few days if no order comes changing our way of living or we are not sent to some other post. Our room is almost directly on the bay. The water comes within ten feet of the house and from where I now sit the Porpoise and everlasting sea gull are seen through the day. This water scenery is extremely tiresome to the eye and much more monotonous than a prairie.

Five negroes ran away from the island night before last and it is not known whether they went to the blockaders or home. John Scott's boy [S]quire[2] left this place on the Teusday before we started & is probably at home now. Write me how the farm is getting along &c. Do not let Walter[3] forget me. Kiss the children for me.

Yours affectionately
Wm H. Neblett

At Mothers Grimes Co
April 13th 1863

Dear Will—

Your letter of Apr 6th reached me on Friday after it was written. Tis needless to say that I was glad to hear from you, & rejoiced to hear you were well, you know this without my saying so. God grant that you may keep so, & have no fighting nor hardships to undergo during your term of service, and when the Confederate states split & civil war is again upon us, I'll offer up this unborn *warrior* upon the Altar of his country, for that country's good. But if on the contrary the warrior turns to a maiden, must I admonish her to "multiply & replenish the earth"[4] with boy's, to fight their country's battles? But I did not intend to write any such stuff (as I know you call it) as the last, but it came to mind & was scribbled down before I thought. You want a stern matter of fact letter free of sentimentalism or any thing a kin to it. The negro's finished planting cotton on Saturday after you left the 4th Apr, & next monday commenced running round the corn, and replanting where it was missing— they will finish plowing the corn in a few days, tomorrow if last nights rain

---

2. Squire was a slave of John Scott's.

3. Walter Scott Neblett was born May 14, 1860, the fourth child of Lizzie and William Neblett. NFB.

4. Gen. 1:28.

did not make it too wet. Thornton[5] replanted that wet place where the stand was so bad, and planted me a roasting ear patch where the rice is, and planted the water mellon patch last week. He says the rice is coming up very well in the wet places particularly. I had Sarah's[6] tobacco patch checked off, as you are to have part of the crop, and this morning she will set out cabbage & Tobacco plants. We had a very good season last night & will be of benefit to the crops, it is cloudy, & threatening rain to day, tho' I hardly think it will rain. Coleman[7] came down to Lake Creek, *pretending* to come expressly to see Susan's and *my* crop, rode over your field, says tis a very good stand of corn, cotton just beginning to come up. Says the new ground corn is fine, much more advanced & better corn than the old field.[8] Coleman was going to John's to see old Mangum[9] about the tanning of *his* and mothers leather. After he tried in vain all around to get his hides tanned by the neighbors, he then sent to the mill for the lumber to make mothers vat, and is flying round mightily about it because he wants *his own hides tanned.* Mangum will attend to mothers hides for her—& I think I'll get one in also. [T]hat yearling that was put up to keep

---

5. Thornton was a slave of Lizzie and William Neblett's. He was married to another of the Neblett slaves, Nancy (or Nance). Lizzie recorded in her diary the births of their children as follows: Levi, July 23, 1857; Margaret, March 28, 1859 (died at one month); Henry, October 3, 1860; Harrison, March 9, 1863; Jack Hamelin, September 1865. LND.

6. Sarah was primarily used as a house slave by Lizzie Neblett. Of all the slaves, Lizzie had the closest relationship with Sarah and would often go to her for information and advice on the other slaves.

7. Alex Coleman (spelled Coalman in the 1860 census) was the overseer for Sarah Lane Scott, Lizzie Neblett's mother. In 1860 he was age 33 and living with his wife, Mary (31), and their four children. His personal and real property was valued at $3,800. TX Census 1860. On November 4, 1863, Lizzie wrote that Coleman had begun courting, indicating the death of his wife, Mary.

8. In 1860, William Neblett owned eleven slaves and 5,859 acres of land, 92 acres of which were improved. His farm was valued at $12,500 and his farming implements and machinery at $150. His livestock was worth $1,460 and included 4 horses, 25 milch cows, 8 working oxen, 120 cattle, and 30 swine. His year's production was 500 bushels of corn and 19¼ bales of cotton (1 bale = 400 pounds). 1860 agricultural census. For more on southern agriculture see Richard G. Lowe and Randolph B. Campbell, *Planters and Plain Folk: Agriculture in Antebellum Texas* (Dallas, Tex.: Southern Methodist University Press, 1987), and John Solomon Otto, *Southern Agriculture during the Civil War Era, 1860–1880* (Westport, Conn.: Greenwood Press, 1994).

9. This was probably Joseph Mangum. There is some confusion in the census. The 1850 census lists a Joseph Mangum (age 48), a tanner. In the 1860 census, however, there is only a Joseph Mangrum (age 54); his occupation is listed as a fisherman. TX Census 1850; TX Census 1860.

it from sucking the cow, died a few days ago. Joe[10] skinned it, says it was fat, but its entrals were rotten. We have up five cows with young calves, since you left, making 7 with the two you got up. They all came from this side the creek, & lost only a half a day in getting them up. I hired Bill & Randle[11] to get up two on Sunday.

Susan got old man Mangum to go to the Penitentiary for her, and she furnished the horses, & I the buggy, which came back safely but brought no cloth—Mangum says he talked his best, but to no avail. Says old Besser[12] said we would have to appear personally before the Chief Justice of the Co, & make affidavit ourselves before he would let the cloth go. The commitey appointed to inspect the Penitentiary met the day before Mangum went & I suppose altered things somewhat. I came up here yesterday (sunday) and will send for Dr Patrick,[13] and make [an] affidavit before him, & enclose it in a letter to Parson Fullenwider[14] and when he succeeds in getting the cloth I will send for it myself. I don't know what Susan will do. I suppose she will have to go to Montgomery to make her affidavit. I don't know whether she will do that or not. I think I will get my twenty yards wove by the first of May, & will make you two pair of pants, and a coat if I think the cloth will do for a coat, and send them to you as soon as I can. Spinning goes on slowly, for Sarah help[s] plant all the cotton. I feel uneasy about your leather, old Mangum has been sick since he returned from Huntsville and has not been over to see it. I had two pots of strong ooze[15] poured in the trough, & left word for another pot full to be boiled & put in. Joe will get Bark this week, and I'll try & do the

10. Joe was another of Lizzie and William Neblett's slaves. His family did not live on the Neblett farm, and to Lizzie's consternation he would often disappear to go visit them. He owned his own mule, a fact that caused a great deal of conflict with Lizzie during the war.

11. Bill and Randle were two other Neblett slaves who were apparently in their mid- to late teens and were unmarried.

12. John S. Besser (age 57 in 1860) was an agent at the Texas Penitentiary at Huntsville in Walker County, Texas. His real and personal property was valued at $7,950. TX Census 1860.

13. Dr. George Moffett Patrick was born September 30, 1801. He moved to Grimes County in 1837. In 1848 he was elected chief justice of the county. By 1860 he was married to Augusta Patrick (age 40) and had real and personal property valued at $27,987. George Patrick died in 1889. TX Census 1860; Allen, *Saga of Anderson*, 259.

14. Peter H. Fullenwider (age 62, spelled Fuldenwider in the 1860 census) was married to Belinda (48), and his occupation was clergyman. His real and personal property was valued at $7,200. TX Census 1860.

15. Ooze refers to the vegetable matter (usually oak bark) that was boiled and used in tanning.

best I can with the hides. I gave old Mangum a bottle [of] our wine, and he was more *delighted* with it than any one you ever saw, said he just considered that I had made him a present of $10—& Coleman says he took a tea spoonful at a time, often through the day when Susan was giving him medicine, and that it done him more good than any thing he ever took, says the bottle of wine was worth 100 dollars to him—the best wine he ever drank in his life. The old man is very weak & frail don't think he will live long. He was mightily troubled that he did not get the cloth for us.

The children all well. Bob[16] was complaining, but 4 of those Bundle's pills[17] set him right again. Walter talks often about you, & always consoles me & himself by saying, "Ma he will come back again." He may see you again, and I may not, tho' I made up my mind to be reconciled to look my last on you when you left. I felt so desolate & heartbroken when that wagon rolled off, as it seems to me I would were I left a widow by death & not by absence. I was sick both mentally & physically for four or five days after you left. Getting in & out our old buggy nearly used me up, I could scarcely walk across the floor—worse than I ever was in my life, no comfort day nor night. I am now much better than I was then. I had no hopes when you left home that you could get a furlough the last of May. You could do me no good—& it would do you no good to see me die, as I hope & trust I shall. I will remain here until next sunday, then return home, & try & dye the filling for my cloth. I see no other alternative than to come up here to pass through my ordeal as you say. I rec'ed a letter with yours from Mrs Henderson. She was fixing Col Henderson[18] up to join his Bros in Miss & Tenn, no news of importance. I suppose from what she wrote that Charley Van Horn[19] has returned home to Corsicana or else he has writen some bad tale on me [to] home—for she says that Charly Van Horn told a bad tale on me, & that I can guess what it is— tho' she don't believe it & writes to know whether it is so or not. He is a nice

16. Robert Scott Neblett was born March 16, 1855, the second of Lizzie and William Neblett's children. NFB.

17. Medicines of the time often took the names of the "doctors" who created them. They often contained alcohol or a narcotic and some agent to act as a purgative or laxative.

18. William F. (age 42 in 1860) and M. L. (28) Henderson lived in Corsicana, Navarro County. William Henderson was a lawyer with real and personal property valued at $32,000 who had been law partners with William Neblett in Corsicana. TX Census 1860; Memoir.

19. Charles E. Van Horn (24) is listed in the 1860 census as a printer living with his brother Richard and his family in Corsicana, Navarro County. TX Census 1860.

young man ain't he, to be talking about married women. I never dreamed of his noticing anything when he saw me in Jan. I reckon Dick[20] will corroborate the "bad tale" and the secret will be out, tho' I will deny it, without lying about [it]. There are two things I think I will always feel reb[el]lious about, the bringing forth of this child and poor Garrett's death, the later I know I will[;] after the other comes, and I be forced to live I may grow in a manner reconciled to it. I have never found it in my heart to blame you. I only detest myself and think that death should be my portion—and if I desired to live, I might die—death like sleep shun's the wretched.

Mother had Irish Potatoes for dinner yesterday—the frost did not hurt hers. Walter ate like a longing woman of them and this morning asked for the Peaches at breakfast—he would not believe they were potatoes, as he was used only to sweet potatoes. Dick Van Horn has not come back to mothers yet, don't know whether he has returned home or not. Mrs Henderson heard from her Mother up to Nov, she had not been molested by the Yankees, had managed to keep all her negros & was in good spirits & health. She writes that several have applied to her to know if I would sell my Piano, thinks like Duren that it will be ruined if 'tis not removed. Mrs Halbert[21] has an other daughter, all mightily disappointed that it was not a boy. Write soon & often, and try and not get tired reading my long letters. Perhaps you won't be troubled with many more. Please write soon & often. Do you ever think of me when you are eating fish? I think of you everytime I eat anything I know you would enjoy. Since I commenced writing[,] a splendid shower has fallen, and the sun is now shining brightly.

Yours affectionately
Lizzie N.

[Letter fragment ca. April 13, 1863][22]

My cloth is wove out. Will make your pants as soon as I can & send them the first chance—I wish you had them now.

---

20. In 1860 Richard A. Van Horn (30) was a printer living in Corsicana, Navarro County, with his wife, Ellen (22), his brother Charles Van Horn (24), and a child, Franklin (2). His real and personal property was valued at $2,700. Richard Van Horn was the publisher and proprietor of the *Navarro Express,* the newspaper Will Neblett became editor of in 1860. TX Census 1860.

21. In 1860 Fanny Halbert (18) and her husband, J. L. Halbert (27), a lawyer, were living in Corsicana, Navarro County, with William F. Henderson and his family. TX Census 1860.

22. This and all other letter fragments are given the date in the collection supplied by the Center for American History, University of Texas at Austin.

When I came up I brought six pounds of butter saved after I sent yours off, and 8 dozen eggs, and Jim carried them to town monday, got $4.75 for them, which is my Postage money. I now feel independent as long as my paper lasts, & as soon as I get able to return home I can make more butter, get eggs, & chickens & buy my paper. I sent two dollars to town by Babe to day for stamps[;] if she gets them I'll send you one dollars worth to pay the postage on what you write to me and I don't want you to stand on postage. I know it is more gratification to me to receive letters from you & write to you than any thing else in the world, & I want to pay for the gratification in my own earnings, a foolish whim I know you will smileingly think, but it is one I want gratified. If Babe don't get them to day I'll send them next letter—& when they give out I'll send more. I'll write every week, now 'till I can tell you of my fate and the little one's. Good bye, forgive all my faults & all the pain & trouble I have cost you.

Galveston Apr 17th/63
L S Neblett

Dear Lizzie

This is the third letter I have written to you since I arrived here and have received none from you. I wrote you one on the 6th and another on the 9th. The latter I sent by Mr Carson who is a brother in law of Mrs Jim Rogers,[23] and was written just as I was taken with a Diarrheah which prevails as an epidemic in camps. I was quite sick on the day that was written[;] after finishing the letter I was sick only one day in bed and confined two days to my room. I did not have any fever but pains in the head back and bowels. It has been gradually getting well for five or six days and I find myself now quite well again. John has had it very slightly. With this exception the health of the Reg is good. We are still situated exactly as when I wrote you last. There has been a good deal of complaint among the soldiers of a late order of Col De Bray[24]

23. Possibly Martha Rogers (age 27), who was living in Grimes County in 1860 with her husband, James (30), a farmer with personal property valued at $200. TX Census 1860.

24. Xavier Blanchard Debray was born in France in 1819. A graduate of the French Military Academy at St. Cyr, he moved to Texas in 1852. During the Civil War, after serving as Governor Edward Clark's aide-de-camp, he assumed command of the Military Subdistrict of Houston in 1862. On May 30, 1863, he was given command of the troops on Galveston Island. He took part in the Red River campaign in April 1864. On March 24, 1865, he discharged his brigade. He died January 6, 1895. Wright and Simpson, *Texas in the War*, 76–77.

stopping all furloughs. This will be temporary I think & I understand already it is to be countermanded. To give you an idea how home sick some of the men are of camp I will state a little circumstance that occurred a few days ago. A young man got a promise of Gen Scurry[25] some time ago that he should have a 60 days furlough to go & see his mother near Alexandria and received it after De Brays order came out stoping all furloughs. One man offered him three hundred dollars for it and another three head of horses. Neither of them got it. This Company still feel[s] quite uneasy about the prospect of being placed on a boat to guard the channel during the night and camp on Pelican Island during the day. For several reasons I feel certain that we will go. It will be a most lonely and dreary life. From some cause there has been some apprehension of an attack on this place but for my part I cannot see anything of the sort. Ed Carrington whose mother lives near Bill Dodd[26] died last night of Typhoid fever.[27] He had the Consumption[28] also.

As this is my third without any answer you may readily believe that I can scarcely find material to fill this, so barren of every thing is our monotonous life here. When I wrote you before I thought it extremely doubtful whether I could get to come home before July or August. I think now that I will be able to do so by the first part of June if De Brays order is countermanded and the old rule is reestablished. For I have lately ascertained that the married men go first and the single men last. You can say to your Mother that I find out from

25. William Read Scurry was born February 10, 1821, in Tennessee. He received his law degree, and by 1840 he was living in Texas. He enlisted as a private in the Mexican War and rose through the ranks to major. Scurry represented De Witt County in the Secession Convention in 1861. He began the Civil War as a lieutenant colonel, and in 1862 was promoted to brigadier general. Scurry fought in the New Mexico campaign in 1862, participated in the recapture of Galveston in January 1863, took part in the Red River campaign in 1864, and fought in the Battles of Mansfield and Pleasant Hill in 1864. He died at the battle of Jenkin's Ferry in Arkansas April 30, 1864. Scurry County, Texas, was named for him. Wright and Simpson, *Texas in the War*, 92–93.

26. William H. Dodd (age 36) was a farmer married to Mary Ann Dodd (36). He had real and personal property valued at $990. TX Census 1860.

27. Typhoid fever is a highly infectious disease characterized by high fever, rose-colored spots, and intestinal hemorrhage. It is conveyed by water, milk, or food contaminated with *Salmonella typhosa*.

28. Consumption, or pulmonary tuberculosis, is an infectious disease caused by the tubercle bacillus. It is characterized by the progressive "wasting away" of body tissue. In the nineteenth century there was no known cure; the victim experienced fever, poor appetite, coughing of mucus and sputum, and eventually death.

John that I cannot make any arrangement about the cotton I wished to sell to pay taxes with. He cannot gin until after his crop is laid by and it will be too late then. I will have to call on her now for my state taxes and after a while for money for Confederate tax. I do not recollect the amt of my state taxes but the Assessment was made last Feb or March. I will write to Carley[29] the tax collector to call on her for the amt. I understand cotton has advanced five cents within the last ten days. Oliver[30] I understand is going home to day & I therefore wrote sooner than I otherwise would. I bought a little book a few days ago on the ear for you hoping that you may find something in it of benefit. I have read but little in it & will send by Lt Oliver.

Write me when you expect to be confined and I will try to be with you. Furloughs are granted only for 12 days now. Kiss the children for me and tell them to be good children and mind what their mother tells them.

Yours affectionately
Wm H. Neblett

PS. John Scott & I have sent by Lt Oliver a bucket which will contain about 8 or 10 lbs which we wish filled with butter. A man by the name of Neal who lives at Dodds & who started with the remains of E. Carrington yesterday with a seven days furlough will bring it down.

Hawthorn Cottage, Sunday
April 26th, 1863.

Dear Will,

I have this morning attended to my dairy, every part of it, rummaged over my trunks, and other old plunder. [G]athered up next weeks washing, after which I rested awhile on the bed reading Irving's Alhambra,[31] until I grew tired of even the gifted Irving's thoughts, and his descriptings of romantic

29. William Carley (age 49 in the 1860 census) was the county assessor in Grimes County. He had personal property valued at $2,500. TX Census 1860.

30. In 1860 William Oliver (33) was a farmer living in Anderson, Grimes County, with real and personal property valued at $16,500. He was a lieutenant in Will Neblett's company, Company I of the Twentieth Texas Infantry. He and his wife, Margret (28), figure prominently in the letters. The couple had four children: John, Hannah, Ellen, and William. TX Census 1860.

31. Washington Irving's The Alhambra (1832) was a collection of sketches written while Irving was a diplomat in Madrid.

Spain, and the faithful portrayal of the character of the proud hardy & frugal Spaniard. Growing tired of all this what could I do better, or more congenial to my taste, than write to you. Like some harum skarum preachers I will say in the begining that I do not expect to confine myself to any particular subject but shall treat of the present past & future just as fancy dictates. I do not expect this to cost me anything for I will send it, with much that lies yet unwriten in the future[,] by Mr Oliver & it will only cost you the trouble of reading. Mr Oliver sent me a note by Bob saying when he would return to camps, & that he would with Mrs Oliver come over & see me in a few days. You don't know how I dread his visit, I look so unsightly, & feel that I do, so sensibley that a man is a horror to me. I often awake in the night and think, does Will ever think of me during the night, or does he care so little, & know so little of my feelings that thoughts of me never banish sleep from his eyelids one single moment. & then I think, 'tis better even so, if I made the sacrifice of my feelings & fears for his pleasure, & because I loved him, let the sacrifice be an entire and complete one, & may he pass his time as pleasantly as possible, as far from pain, & suffering, as it can be, and may he never be a prey to this gloomy, desponding, hopless feeling that almost kills me at times. I know I act very selfish in betraying a sorrow that I might hide, and that on a subject that I know makes you feel badly, but "the sorrow that speaks not whispers the overfraght heart & bids it break,"[32] so with me it must have words. Tis a desire of sympathy that prompts us to tell our troubles, and, & [*sic*] to whom else could I go, with such a trouble, and expect sympathy as readily as from you, & altho' your sympathy cannot relieve me of one single bodily pain, yet the knowledge that I suffer for a tender feeling and loving husband, is a balm to my heart, and makes me feel, that amid all my misfortunes & what has seemed to me the curses of Heaven, I have one blessing yet left to me, & in that one particular have been truly fortunate & for which I can never feel sufficiently thankful. I know that I have a true loving tender and noble husband.

I have seen Mary Haynie lately and while listening to her recital of her troubles and wrongs, her grief at the idea of her mother dying and leaving her homeless upon the cold charity of the world, her brothers, seeking to defraud her of what any court of justice would say were her rights, I felt that my lot, tho' full of physical pain and drugery, yet it was preferable to her's. But in one particular we are alike. [H]er peculure mental organization makes her lot ap-

---

32. *Macbeth*, act 4, scene 3.

pear harder than I think I or many others would regard it. She can make a living by teaching, but the idea of a home troubles her. She wants a place to call her own place where she will be surrounded by the social ties of home and regrets so much that she did not marry years ago, and have now children of her own to raise instead of looking around for a place where she could be of assistance in helping others raise their children, & finding a home with them. She could select no place where she thought she could do good in this way & be happy, so she says she would *marry for a home*, but she says the silly part of it is she has no one to marry[.] I told her I thought it would be very foolish in her to marry the most advantageous offer at her age. She says every body tells her so, yet she says she has marrying in her head to get a home. I feel sorry for her. Now if you want a chance to marry, when I am gone, think of her. [B]ut always think that I would never be willing for you to marry her, so long as one of my children are alive, and under age. I know she would not suit you, for a wife. Would cause you more trouble than even I do. She would never do for a step mother.

Last Friday evening after dark, Babe[,] Mary Scott[33] and Sallie, came down, Babe bringing Mary[34] behind her. They left Mary here and Sallie stopped out in the road, & I did not see her, and did not know until next day that she came down with them. Babe told Mary not to tell me that Sallie was along, that I would not let one of the negro's go with them over to Aunt Cinda's & John's if I knew Sallie was along. So it was all kept secret from me, till I found it out by accident. They have grand notions of my character don't they? She has lived with a low down revengful creature 'till she judges every body by him. Don't you think it is ridiculous the way she and Babe talk before Mary. Why Mary says "it is in every body's mouth that aunt Sallie is going to have a baby, that aunt Sallie says she wants everybody to know it, don't want to surprise anybody." Then she knows where and how she is going to get her baby clothes and all about it. She says Aunt Babe told her not to tell me she knew anything about Sallie's going to have a baby. And Mary told me yesterday that Aunt Sallie asked her the strangest question she could not think why she asked it. She asked her if I was not going to have a baby, and what she wanted it to be. Mary says she told her no I was not but if I ever had one she

---

33. Mary Scott (age 11 in 1860) was the daughter of John and Susan Scott, Lizzie Neblett's niece. TX Census 1860.

34. Lizzie and Will Neblett's daughter Mary Caroline Neblett.

wanted it to be a girl. Did you ever hear of such talk to a child ten years old? All the innocence that beauty of childhood will soon be gone departed from her if she is tutored much longer by Sallie & Babe. I believe they do it on purpose to trouble me, they know I would not like such talk at all. Mother says she don't believe Sallie and Babe have good sense, I think they make mighty little use of it. Mary says they talk about her grandma & me all the time how mean we are &c. And Mary can give the whole history of Bassett,[35] as told by Sallie to Babe, what a great man he is and how he achieved his splendid education by his own extraordinary exertions. [A]nd tells Mary that he is so much smarter than her Pa, *that every body says so* 'till I reckon the poor child thinks her Pa is & must be a mere pigmy beside the renowned & far famed Capt Bassett. Don't you reckon she will hear us abused and made little until the poor child will indeed think we must be as they describe us to her, or before her. I would not seek to deprive the meanest man I know of & that is Bassett, of the respect of his child for nothing. When before his offspring his faults & failings would not be spoken of by me. When a child ceases to respect & reverence their parents, I think they are then on the broad road to ruin. Mary will render herself hateful I fear in the eyes of mature persons, by letting them know how wise she is in matters that children should be kept ignorant of, and the blame of course will fall on me. I have neglected my duty. Babe goes by Mr Fanthorps nearly every morning Mary says, to supply Sallies longings out of her bucket, that Sallie takes the bucket, Babe gets down & walks with Sallie nearly to the school house, and she ride the horse. It is impossible to keep Mary away you see.

Frank[36] came over to day to spay those wild hogs in the pen spayed one, & left the other alone (two,) says they will have pigs in about two weeks, I dont know what we will do with such a host of piges as we will have soon. We have now, from three sows—17 pigs, and 4 more to have pigs I believe. I fear they will all die, for we don't get more milk than the negros can drink, I give out 4

35. Robert Houston Bassett married Lizzie Neblett's sister Sallie on March 13, 1862. In the 1860 census he is listed as a 24-year-old bookkeeper. Robert Bassett joined Company G of the Fourth Texas Infantry Regiment, known as the "Grimes County Grays." He was made captain of the company at the death of J. W. Hutcheson at the Battle of Gaines' Mill, Virginia, in June 1862. Bassett was wounded during the Battle of Chickamauga, Tennessee, on September 20, 1863. He returned to Texas and practiced law after the war. Robert Bassett died in 1870, leaving his wife and daughter. NP; TX Census 1860; Allen, *Saga of Anderson*, 155–56.

36. A slave who belonged to Lizzie Neblett's brother, John.

pounds of meat a day, which does them amply with the milk.[37] We have up seven cows I think. Joe went to day to see about the cows Mrs Dalford had up—says she has none up now, but Mr Mills has one up that run over here all last year, with Sarah's cow, that we killed her yearling, and he thinks she must have been driven from over this side the creek. They told him they got her off salt creek. I am mistaken it was a man living near Mill's that has this cow up, and Mill's has one of those Mrs Dalford turned out we suppose. Joe can't go to count them until it rains so the plows cant run, and that may not be before I leave and I can't leave either one of the horses here, so I reckon the cows will have to go. I had my garden plowed Saturday, I saw if something was not done soon I would have no garden. [A]nd if I live, I see no other plan than to shoulder the burden of doing my best towards making the negros support themselves, and having some thing at home—being independent. So if I live at home I must try & have some thing to live on. My chickens are doing finely—think I will have fully 2 hundred when all my hen's now setting hatch. Oh Will you don't know how heavily the burden & responsibility rests upon me of having things done which are highly necessary outside of the farm, and my fear that the negros will not support themselves, and I know so little about farming.[38] If I thought you would have to serve in the army another year I would insist upon a different arrangement somehow. God grant that we may have peace, during this year at least. Oh what joy it would bring to me. Tis true my poor brother would not return to me, his face I'll never see again upon earth, but it would return me you, if it comes speedily. For god's sake Will, hire a substitute[39] if the war continues this winter, even if it takes half we have, what would the world full of money be to me if you were dead. Oh I cant stand the thought I believe it would kill me. I think it is time to stop writing now, and wait for more material to unfold itself. I expect the men who see you reading this will think you have a strange wife, & wonder what she can find

37. On slave rations see Eugene Genovese, *Roll, Jordan, Roll: The World the Slaves Made* (New York: Vintage Books, 1972), 62–63, 540–49.

38. On women and slave management see Faust, *Mothers of Invention*, 53–79; Whites, *The Civil War as a Crisis in Gender*, 115–16, 120–22.

39. By September 1862 the Confederacy had imposed a national conscription on all men ages 18 to 45. A man could be exempted from service if he worked an occupation considered important to the war effort, such as miner, railroad worker, teacher, etc. Also exempted were landowners possessing twenty or more slaves. In addition, those who could afford it could pay someone to take their place, termed a substitute. The "20 nigger law" and the hiring of substitutes caused morale problems and resentment among those who had not the wealth to elude the draft.

to fill so many sheets of paper. I know you will never read this over but once—
but when you have no other employment (and you say you have ample time
to spend any way you please) if you read this over, you will find some things
in it that you missed the first reading. I don't say they will be worth anything
but, it will serve to pass away time.

Monday night Apr 27th. Oh how different I feel to night from what I did
last night, if I would give way to my feelings, I could make myself intensely
miserable. God knows with all my self battling and all my courage called forth,
I feel bad enough. To day I heard from Jack Oliver,[40] and from Sam[41] this
morning, that Mr Oliver said he had been sent for, & would go earlier then
he expected to. Jack told me that the Regt has been ordered to L[ouisian]a,
where we met with that defeat[42] I suppose, and I suppose you are to go immediately, & will not come this way. I did not know 'till now what a hold the
hope that I would see you[,] if I lived[,] in two or three months any how had
upon me. [N]ow God only knows when if ever I will see you, and my heart
sickens at the idea of what hardships you will have to undergo that long, long
march ahead of you, and then you have no summer clothes, oh I feel like dying
in despair almost like you were gone forever. Oh God will it be my lot to live
to see you dead. Oh I can't nor won't think so, the idea is too terrible. When
I think of the misery & unutterable woe your death would cause me[,] I can't
help thinking about how badly you must feel, to hear me wish so ardently to
die and leave you. If you love me as much as I do you[,] I know it must make
you feel badly. It is a selfish cowardly desire that I have to die. The terrors of
my situation are fast loosing [*sic*] their power when I think of the dangers that
will soon surround you. I feel like the three or four, or even eight hours of
intense suffering that I will have to go through, will be as nothing when compared with my anxiety about you—even if you escape death. I think of poor
Garrett, and his sad fate, & feel the more anxious for you. I feel if my prayers
could avail anything that I would be willing to spend a life time in humble

40. William and Margret Oliver's son, John.

41. Sam was a middle-aged slave of Lizzie and Will Neblett's. He, like Joe, had family belonging to another slave owner.

42. There were various skirmishes in Louisiana during the month of April; Lizzie could be
referring to any of a number of engagements. She might, however, be alluding to Union general
Nathaniel P. Banks's occupation of Fort Bisland and Franklin, Louisiana, on April 14 and 15,
respectively. E. B. Long, *The Civil War Day by Day: An Almanac, 1861–1865* (New York: Da
Capo Press, 1971), 338.

penitential prayers, to save you from death, either by sickness or the enemy's bullets. Oh do Will take care of your self, & do not, for my sake and the children expose yourself to *unnessary dangers.* You will have to go in to battle I know and may Almighty God preserve you through such dangers, and return you safely home!

Teusday morning Apr 28th. This morning, Mr Oliver sent a boy by here to say if I wanted to write I must do it to day as he would leave tomorrow. I have nothing new to write but like we do when we part with those we love I linger over this letter, my heart filled [with] grief & fear and my eyes filled with tears, and [I] feel loth to quit, for while I write it seems there is [a] link which yet binds me to you. Last night, or rather this morning about day, I found myself sitting bolt upright in bed, listening with terror to what I thought at the moment was the noise & roar of cannon. I thought you were engaged in the battle then going on, & for the moment I felt awful, but I soon grew sufficiently awake to know that it was only *thunder,* and that we were having a nice shower of rain. This morning they are all setting out potatoe slips & I hope will finish setting out the patch.

You know Joe's propensity for running about at night & on Sundays—well two weeks ago I asked for him one night to give him some directions & he was missing, next morning at breakfast he reported himself to me to hear what I had to say. After telling him what I wanted to, I asked him where he was the night before, he denied being gone off the place, & I then told him, he would have to receive an other lesson, similar to the one he got last year, about being out of his place &c. Well, it was hardly a week after before, sure enough, he was over at Alstynes or Alstons,[43] and, he says doing nothing but talking to a negro woman, when Alston shot at him, (not intending to hit I think only to frighten him) he ran, hard as he could tear for John's, and as he passed Martins at the top of his spread Martin shot at him. Susan says he was the worst scared negro she ever saw, begged her for a pass & came home. The beauty of it is he has never said one word to me about his shooting scrape and [I] never knew it 'till yesterday, Aunt Cinda was here & told me. That accounts for Joe wanting to hunt cows last Sunday & trying to make himself useful to me. He would not come to me about it because I had talked to him about it & told

43. There is some confusion in the census records. The 1850 census lists a Nathaniel Alston (age 40), a farmer living with his wife, Winford (36), and five children in Grimes County. The 1860 census, however, does not have anyone of that name, spelled either Alstyne or Alston, listed in Grimes County.

him he would get into another scrape. I am glad of it, I have no idea that either Martin or Alston tried to hit him, only wanted to scare him—tho I will let on to Joe that I believe they were trying to kill him. I think I will go up to mothers next Sunday the 3rd [of] May, I am afraid to put it off any longer, if am going—and I may be sick in less than two weeks after reaching Mothers tho' I do not much expect before the last days in May—but if I go that long the child will have been moving six mo, which is or will be very uncommon.

Frank is coming over again to spay this last fall pigs, Joe is putting them up as he catches them, turned out those wild shotes.[44] I'll try and have things attended to the best I can. Van Horn bought Jim's Black horse, and mother is to pay Jim the money & keep Van Horn's mare. I expect she saved money enough to pay our taxes for I heard her speak of a conversation you had with her about it, so don't trouble about that, I'll manage some how to fix that matter up. Don't feel any more uneasiness about home matters than you can help, we will get along. The negros seem to be mightily stirred up now, about making a good crop. Sarah is worth a team of negro's with her tongue, & she has been working out, & talking to them. They say River's[45] praised their last week's work mightily. I know you will have your fears about me & the children but, rest assured, that the children will be well attended to & watched over, & if my best endeavors can save this poor little unborn innocent, it shall be done to delight your eyes when you return. As to myself I know I will suffer teribly but, I have no idea that I'll die. Oh if you were only safely quartered in Galveston, I would feel so much better. Write to me, every chance you have don't regard postage, for each one of your letters will be worth more than dollars to me. I'll write often, & I know you won't think of postage when you get my letters. I fear so much for your health. Oh! this war, this terrible war when will it end? Walter poor little fellow, has had his hope deffered so long, that he now sometimes says, "Ma, Pa, won't come back no more." Bob is troubled about you. Billy[46] don't say anything. Oh that I could see you I would say ten thousand things that this letter wont contain—tho' it is a complete book now. Do write soon, & often, and may the good Lord bless, comfort and protect

44. By "shote" Lizzie means shoat—a young pig just after weaning.

45. Rivers was Lizzie Neblett's part-time overseer. He was also the overseer of the Neblett's neighbors, the Hursts. The Hursts, with Rivers, apparently came from Florida shortly after 1860. There is no record of Rivers in the 1860 or 1870 census.

46. William Teel Neblett was Lizzie and Will Neblett's third child, born April 10, 1857. NFB.

you, is & will be the constant prayer of one who would freely lay down her life to save yours.

Yours affectionately Lizzie S Neblett
(This was writen with our homemade ink)

Pelican Spit Apr 28th/63
Mrs L S Neblett

Dear Lizzie

Yours of the 22nd just reached me last night about 8 O clock on board the Bayou City[47] (a cotton clad gun boat) just as I and fourteen others were going on guard on the boat for the night. It is now about a week since we left Galveston City and have since then been encamped on Pelican Spit which is a portion of Pelican Island and comprises an area of about one hundred acres of low sandy soil detached from Pelican Island by about half mile of shallow water. Our Co is here alone. We stay on the Spit except what goes on guard on the boat during the night. Our guard duty is light and it is intended to prevent the enemy (about five miles off) from surprising us or firing the boat, and also to guard the channel from the approach of the enemy through it. We are about 2 1/2 miles from Galveston whence we get our rations of beef daily and also our mails. We are comfortably situated in good houses and having but little to do are put to our wits ends to pass the time. I am particularly as I do not play cards. Most of my mess including John spend about six hours a day on card playing. No money is bet in our mess. I have spent several of my morning and evening in walking around the Spit selecting shells to send home. None of them are very rare but afford me some pleasure in gathering them as it connects my thoughts with the "loved ones at home," and will please the children for a while. I do not know when I can send or bring them as there has been a recent order prohibiting all furloughs and an order commanding privates and officers off on furlough to be back by the 1st of May. This will bring Oliver back sooner than he expected and looks like putting things on a war footing.

47. The *Bayou City* was a steamer armored with cotton bales. On January 1, 1863, it took part in the Battle of Galveston and was instrumental in retaking the city from the Federals. By May 1864 the ship was considered no longer seaworthy. Cotham, *Battle on the Bay*, 121–28.

You need not send me a coat. The two I have with my heavy one are sufficient. The pants I would like to get. I would have written to you before this
but have been expecting a letter in answer to mine of the 17th every day for a
week and from a feeling vascillating between annoyance and fair sense of neglect have been in no enviable state of mind. And to add to this I feared some
accident might have befallen you. I am so much grieved at your helpless and
unfortunate state of body. I hoped that it would not get worse but it seems
that it has. I am in excellent health and have been since I got well of that attack
of Diarrhea. The life we lead here could hardly be considered camp life at all
except for the galling and damnable military restraint which calls all a mans
patriotism in to reconsile him to it; though I am well pleased with our Co
officers. We are so comfortably situated here that for my own part I would
prefer to fight and board a Yankee boat rather than foot it out the state. Your
letters are so full and satisfactory that no room is left me to ask questions or
give directions. Continue to write in the same style. Susan Scott sent that
bucket about full of butter. If you can send some by Oliver do so for it may be
a long time before you will have another chance. Start the negroes to using the
oats for the horses and oxen as soon as possible and cane the corn. Did my
fresh potato seed come up? I noticed in the paper that our neighbour Hurst[48]
was mortally wounded in the fight in La. I feel very uneasy about Mittie. The
Yankees have overrun that country and from what I notice in the papers a battle took place at Perrys Bridge where they were living. I expect Texas to come
in for her share of battles if Banks[49] is not badly whiped in La soon. I think
next spring will find us enjoying peace unless some unexpected reverses of fortune should overtake the Confederacy. I stated in my last that I would or had
sent by Oliver a small book on the ear. I forgot to give it to him with the letter.

Yours affectionately
Wm H. Neblett

48. The Hursts apparently came to Texas from Florida after 1860. There was an Isaac Hurst
(age 23) living with his wife, Emma (19), and a child in Grimes County in 1870. He was a farmer
with personal and real property valued at $350. He may have been related to the Hursts men-
tioned in Lizzie and Will Neblett's letters, but there is no record of any Hursts of a more appropriate age living in Grimes County in 1860 or 1870. TX Census 1860; TX Census 1870.

49. Union general Nathaniel P. Banks was born January 30, 1816, in Waltham, Massachu-
sets. Before the war he served in the House of Representatives, was governor of Massachusetts,
and was president of the Illinois Central Railroad. In his capacity of general, Banks served primarily in Virginia until the fall of 1862, when he was placed in command of the Gulf Department.

Pelican Spit May 2nd/63
Mrs L S Neblett

Dear Lizzie

Yours of the 28th by Oliver was handed me last evening by him. I notice that you have heard the report that this Rgt has been ordered to La and have been making yourself uneasy in consequence. We had the same report here some time ago, but it has blown over. This Reg has no orders to go to La and I feel almost satisfied now since we hear that Pyrons Reg[50] now has tow of Baylores Rgts[51] and Gurleys[52] and Phillips[53] are ordered to La that this Reg will hardly go out the state during the war. For after the above five have left it is hardly possible that any more will ever be sent out the state. I recd your letter after sun set and read until it was too dark and adjourned the balance until I went on the boat where I had to stand guard and finished it. I appreciate it according to its length.

I hasten to correct the report about the Reg going to La and as there will be no mail from this place to Galveston tomorrow (Sunday) and the boat leaves in a few minutes I must bring this to a short close. We are situated now exactly as when I last wrote you (on the 28th)[.] In a few days I will write you again. My health is very good. So is John Scotts. When I wrote you last I stated that one of those fights in La was at Perrys Bridge & feared for Mittie & Family but have learned from a man whose mother lives in Vermillion that the bridge spoken of is 30 or 40 miles above.

Yours affectionately
Wm H Neblett

He led the Red River campaign in 1863 and again in 1864. After the failure of his campaign he was replaced by General Edward Canby. After the war he served several more terms in Congress and died September 1, 1894. Mark Mayo Boatner III, *The Civil War Dictionary* (New York: David McKay Company, 1959), 42.

50. Charles L. Pyron commanded the Second Texas Cavalry Regiment. Wright and Simpson, *Texas in the War,* 111.

51. Presumably George Wythe Baylor, who commanded the Second Cavalry Regiment, Arizona Brigade. Ibid., 30.

52. Edward Jeremiah Gurley commanded the Thirtieth Texas Cavalry Regiment. Ibid., 29.

53. Presumably Joseph Phillips, who commanded the Third Cavalry Regiment, Arizona Brigade. Ibid., 30.

At Mother's May 6th 1863
Wm H Neblett

Dear Will—your letter of Apr 28th which reached me Sunday 3rd inst[54] afforded me great relief, for it inspired me with the hope that Elmore's Regt. would not be sent to La and, I feel that I can content myself and feel comparatively easy about you, so long as I know you are on Galveston Island leading the monotenous life you so often speak of. And if you are only allowed to remain there until the war closes and keep well, I feel that I should always return daily thanks to God. I am an exceedingly selfish person, so long as no danger real or imaginary threatens the object, or objects of my love, but soon as danger threatens those I love, all selfishness is lost to the winds and I then feel strong to suffer and endure anything to save them. So I feel about you now. Since I loved you as well when you were with me, but I felt you were safe, and in gloom, terror, and almost insanity I regarded my own unfortunate & painful situation. [N]ow strange to tell you, I feel less fear, and dread the closing scene less than I ever did before for, in a slight measure it has been taught me that there is something worse than bearing children. I only pray that no more may be added to that lesson. You see by date of this that I came up to mothers as I expected the 3rd of May. I got along coming up very well, except one place; that bad crossing close to Hursts negro cabins, it had rained the night before was very slippery, and I got out, and got about half way up the bank when I gave out, Jim[55] was out of the carriage driving the horses, and saw my fix, offered to help me up, and almost slipped down himself, when he said Miss Lizzie you just get in, and I'll push up against the side of the carriage so it can't turn over. No choice being left me, with Jim's assistance I got in, and he drove up safely. After I got in and thought of you, that I knew would have assisted me so willingly and from whom I would so much rather have received help than anyone in the wide world, and you were far away. I could not help crying. I had to receive from a negro what I felt was a duty you owed me under the circumstances and I felt so gri[e]ved at what I could not help, nor you either. Oh! I do feel so utterly wretched & hopeless at times, when I think that you may never return and my being left a widow with five little helpless dependent children, to raise & educate. If it was not for them, I might end my own life, I believe my exceeding wretchedness would be a pardoning plea

---

54. Inst. is the abbreviation for instant, meaning the current month.
55. A slave borrowed from Lizzie Neblett's mother, Sarah Scott.

with God for the act of suicide, but when I have children, to live & struggle for, God would not forgive the act. I am drinking the Squaw vine[56] tea, and that or something else has made me much better than I have been for months. I can turn over in bed very well now, and can walk with much more ease. I know you will be glad to know this, is why I tell you. Altho' you could not help my unfortunate situation any more than I could, I believe you much oftener reproach yourself for it than I do, & it makes you feel badly to hear of my suffering on account of it. I never have reproached you, never felt mad at you but oh how I have hated myself, now I feel that such feelings are too late, and in calmness, and in a much better frame of mind I strive to fit myself for an abode with the spirits of the just made perfect, if it pleases God to call me, hence.

Mother went to Town Monday had a Power of Atorney made out in John Nix's[57] name, for him to draw what money is coming to Garrett in Va from the Government, had it enclosed in a letter to John, & sent it by Wm Raines who is just going back to Va. Bassett wrote to Dr Patrick that he & the Quarter Master had had some words about the 43 dollars he drew of Garrett's, for which Bassett would not give him a receipt, & wrote back for Mother to pay 43 dollars to Sallie, that he had given the Quarter Master 43 dollars back, & mother thinks that he only wanted her to send him the Power of drawing all Garrett's money, as it is customary for the capt to do such things for the soldiers, but she said the Government might burn it before she would place that power in his hands. After she done that, she went around & hunted old Mrs Boney up, and she would make no promise. Says she is under promise to Mrs Christian, (dutch) to stay in town the whole month of May, to wait on her, but she half way promised that if Mrs Christian got down before I did, she would after that was over come out here tho' she said old Bennet, and Tom Walker, had both been after her, & she would not promise either of them. Mother is more concerned about it than I am. She says she believes that if I will drink this vine tea freely, and have the Rasberry, and No 6[58] when I am

---

56. Squaw vine is a perennial evergreen that was thought to be beneficial in childbirth. It is a natural sedative.

57. John Nix was Lizzie Neblett's cousin, son of Lucinda Lane Nix McClure and John Nix. In the 1850 census he was an 18-year-old farmer living with his mother and stepfather, Mark McClure. There is no record of him in the 1860 census. TX Census 1850.

58. Raspberry was often used in conjunction with squaw vine as a way to lessen the pain of childbirth and strengthen the uterus. No. 6 was one of Samuel Thomson's remedies. Thomson

taken that I will have a quick and easy time but, she feels like she wants a white woman here, for fear of some accident[.] I made up my mind long ago that I would leave, to be alone this time, and the idea dont frighten me, if the babe can only be saved, & I not ruined for life, I will try and not mind the suffering—tho' it hangs a mighty weight upon my mind. In three weeks more I think it will all be over with, and I won't be so cruel as I once thought I would be, I'll write the next hour or two after wards, if tis daylight. I know I'll be so glad & relieved that it will give me more joy to write it, than it will you to hear it. Try and make yourself easy as possible about it. I am in good hands, and no doubt will fare much better than I deserve.

Well I have occupied more of your time & more of my paper than the subject deserved, and I will no doubt to your relief stop and tell you of what I know will interest you vastly more; the farm, how they are all doing &c. They had been doing finely I think for some time before I left home—done so well, that Rivers gave them half of last Saturday, and told Sam (so he says) that he could spare him this next sat. to go to see his wife if I said so, of course I thought it best to give my consent for him to go.[59] They have finished plowing the cotton, & are now going over the corn, want to lay some by this week. Have a good stand of cotton so they say. I had the hide lifted and found the ooze so full of large white worms that contrary to Mr Mangums directings, I had it thrown away and the bark beat and put in, and then the hides covered with strong ooze, which I had boiled. Joe & Nancy[60] worked faithfully all day long before I left home with the hides, I had the ooze boiled very strong and made Joe go in the evening and get another lot of bark, which will be enough to finish tanning I think. Mangum says there was a great deal of leather worked on last fall which was not half as good as ours is now, but I knew we were in no hurry for it & wanted it well tanned, never heard of worms getting in the ooze before.

Thornton was mistaken about the Rice coming up, and I had it plowed up and planted in corn some time ago, and that Hungarian graf did not come up either, and monday last I left word for it to be plowed up and planted in peas, which I suppose they have done. I can't tell whether they set out any potatoe

---

founded the Thomsonian or natural therapeutic medicine of the nineteenth century and had a variety of herbal and vegetable tonics and emetics.

59. On slave broad wives see Genovese, *Roll, Jordan, Roll,* 462, 472–73.

60. Nancy (or Nance) was one of Lizzie and Will Neblett's slaves. She was married to another Neblett slave, Thornton.

slips or not. The rain that fell just before Mr Oliver left, did not wet the ground deep enough to set out slips. I feel so anxious to make a good crop of Potatoes. Your Irish Potatoe seed did not come up, neither did mothers. A few of the Peach seed have come up. I am now dining finely almost eat myself sick on Beans, Peas & Irish Potatoes. Plums have just begun to ripen a little. I never set down a nice vegetable dinner that I do not wish you had some. I left some Bundel's Pills with Sarah, & some Lonie ones, with directions how to give them, some one of them will be sent here every Saturday night or Sunday to let me know how they are getting on. I left Kate[61] to work in the field, and Sarah to work a part of this week. I had my pea patch planted where the watermellons are, last week, the watermellons are up finely Thornton says, & will be worked out this week. I left all that Joe could get of the young sows up in the pen for Frank to spay the day I left[.] Joe said there was five. Those wild hogs have not been seen since they were turned out but Joe said he [would] look for them. I left word if he could by any means catch the sows & put them in our garden place at the house, to do so, and perhaps after they have their pigs they will become gentle & stay at home. Bob drove up a cow we milked last year with a young calf the day before we left. Tell John that I heard from Susan the day I left home the 3rd inst she was getting well, had nursed her fever & was clear of pain in her head & side, all the rest well. On the 3rd inst Poor Mrs John King died with typhoid fever, sick about one month, had Brown & Foster[62] with her. Carley presented your Taxes, or asked mother to pay them when she was in town, gave her a recpt for sixty three dollars for state & county tax she is to send the money in by Coleman—so rest easy about the Taxes.

The children are all well. Mary learns very well I think. Frank[63] & Mittie reached home a week since, all well, I hear. Frank says (so I hear) that the yankees destroyed every thing they could in that country, he was within six

61. Kate was one of Lizzie and Will Neblett's slaves.

62. George Washington Brown was a doctor in Grimes County. He was born in 1826 in Mecklenberg County, Virginia. He received his medical degree in 1846 from the University of Pennsylvania Medical School. With his wife, Louisa Jane Scott, and five children, he moved to Texas in 1860. Foster was another doctor in the area but is not listed in the 1860 census. Grimes County Historical Commission, *History of Grimes County*, 243.

63. John Franklin Perry was born March 9, 1833, in Perry's Bridge, Lafayette Parish, Louisiana, to Robert Samuel and Ezemily Booth Perry. He married Will Neblett's sister Caroline (or Mittie) on November 12, 1856. He died in 1869. Ibid., 469–70.

mile of the battle when it was going on—am glad Mittie is at home. I haven't heard from Ma, nor none of them only through others. Franklin Webb has been home, some three weeks. They have had no news, only through the papers from Hurst, I fear he is dead. Bettie[64] has heard from Jim twice[;] he found all thing right when he got there, expects to sell out at whole sale & return home soon. Think of me with pity & sympathy, and pray for me. Write soon & often. Mother payed Bettie $400 for the Black horse and she keeps Van Horn's mare. I recd John's letter last night, was glad to get it and glad of the news it contained. I have not heard a word from Huntsville won't till the tyth is got. Babe got the stamps but forgot to bring them home, I'll send them next time. All well Thursday morn May 7th. Garrett[65] is here, says his Ma & all are well, tell John.

Yours most affectionatly
Lizzie S.N.

Pelican Spit May 8th 1863
Mrs L S Neblett

Dear Lizzie

Your very long and most welcome letter was handed by Oliver and a few hasty lines written on return to correct the report you had heard of this Reg going to La. Well I intended to write more at length before this but John Scott wrote several days ago to you and that caused me to defer for a while. I have nothing new to say[,] for you must recollect that here one day is so much alike another that it is really difficult to keep the days of the week in the month. When I say that I am here—and well and expect to stay here for a good while I have said all. I have read your letter more than once and I must confess not without some surprise each time, that Babe and Sallie should condescend to us as mean a thing as to talk to Mary as they have done. I regret that Mary has been exposed to the influence of such bad company and we must see to it that Mary must change her school companion the next session. She shall stay

---

64. Elizabeth (Bettie) Briggs Goodrich was married to Lizzie Neblett's brother James Lane Scott. In the 1860 census she is listed as a 17-year-old living with her parents, Benjamin and Serena Crothers Goodrich. Ibid., 507; TX Census 1860.

65. Garrett Scott (age 13) was Lizzie Neblett's nephew, the son of John and Susan Scott. TX Census 1860.

at home or board out in preference. I would prefer that she should never be thrown in company with her aunt Sally again during life. I suppose from what you said Sally has at last concluded to visit Susan Scott. I suppose by this time you are at your mothers awaiting your time of trial. I would like to be with you but it is doubtful whether I can possibly do so or not. No furloughs have been granted for the last two weeks but I hope that the order will be relaxed before long and it certainly will be unless some new demonstration is made towards Texas by the Yankees. You say that if the cows and calves are not gathered before you go to your mothers that it will have to go undone I do not think this will do. We will loose [*sic*] too much by it. You had better send Joe & some one to help him when he can be spared out the crop. Oliver tells me that he saw two of my cows with young calves near his house. These might be got up with little trouble. I tried to buy that thread from Gravy but without success. He was to start home on a sick furlough yesterday. He has been in the hospital at Galveston since I arrived in camps. I recd a letter a few days since from Nelia[66] and was relieved to hear that Mittie & Frank were at home. She did not say what Frank Perry intended doing. Nelia says he is still spitting blood but looks very well. Mittie was in good health. She says Terrell[67] was examined by the conscript surgeon some time ago and a 60 days furlough granted him. This looks as if he would have to try it again. Nelia also says she had recd a letter from Robert[68] at Pine Bluff Ark. He was well. Also one from Sterling[69] then at Victoria. He had been sick with the fever and when he wrote had a fever on him. I think it probabl[e] the Reg he is in will go to La. Nelia says she had heard that Elmores Regt was ordered to La and wrote to me ex-

66. Cornelia Love Neblett was born on September 20, 1847, the youngest child of Robert and Maria Neblett. She married John W. H. Davis December 21, 1870, and died December 3, 1921. Perkins, *Some Nebletts in America,* 113.

67. William J. Terrell married Will Neblett's sister, Harriet (Hattie), July 7, 1858. In 1860 he was a 31-year-old farmer with personal and real property valued at $11,000. Perkins, *Some Nebletts in America,* 113; TX Census 1860.

68. Robert McCaskill Neblett was the sixth child of Robert and Maria Neblett. He was born January 30, 1844. During the Civil War he enlisted in Company D, the Twelfth Texas Infantry. He died in the Battle of Pleasant Hill on April 9, 1864, near Mansfield, Louisiana. Perkins, *Some Nebletts in America,* 113.

69. Sterling Powe Neblett was the third child of Robert and Maria Neblett. He was born February 12, 1830. In 1860 he was living with his parents and working as a farmer. His real and personal property was valued at $9,000. He married Viola Brown on August 14, 1862. He died June 2, 1909. TX Census 1860; Perkins, *Some Nebletts in America,* 112.

pecially to know wheth. it was true. We drew clothing yesterday. I got a pr of pants which are too short for me and I will have to sell them. I also drew a pr of shoes and two thin unbleached domestic shirts which are so badly made that I may not wear them until I can have them fixed. I believe I told you in one of my letters that the two coats you made me would be sufficient in that line. I would like to get the pants but am in no hurry for this is certainly the coolest place I have ever found. The Gulf waves break upon the East side of this island about one hundred yards distant while a strong south wind blows like a gale most of the time damp with salt water. Almost every one is still wearing worsted cloth. John and I have worn our thin coats only about one third of the time. The North wind which has been blowing for three days is causing me some uneasiness, for the wheat crop as well as the corn up country.

Within the last ten days we have been living better than heretofore. We get about four meals of flour & wheat the same of peas. We get plenty of beef and molases and corn bread. Occasionally we buy a mess of cabbage, and have had dew berry & sugar once and one large dew berry pie[.] The berrys were gathered on Pelican Island about a mile distant. They are all gone now but we anticipate some diversion some in the way of gathering and eating Gull egs. I think we will be without bacon before long[.] Jack[70] is very wastful and I think he would like very much to be sent home after more, John will not say any thing to him about his wastfulness, and I shall not do so again. John eats more bacon & butter than any of the men and less beef and if he cannot make Jack more economical I can stand it as well as he. Our bacon may last us until we get furlough, but I doubt it. I was somewhat amused at what you wrote me about M[ary] H[aynie], and at the same time sympathetic with her. She has the feeling of friendship stronger than any of the family but is naturally cold hearted I think. You need not have given me any warning on that subject. Perhaps she expected you to offer her a home if she should need it. If you did I feel sure she would tire of it very soon and perhaps as soon [as] you would. You must not let Babe read my letters. Tell the children I will be home one of these times for a short time, and that they must be good children and obey you & their Grand Ma.

yours affectionately
Wm H. Neblett

70. Jack was a slave John Scott brought with him while stationed at Galveston.

At Mothers,
May 14th 1863
W H Neblett

Dear Will,

Your letter of 8th inst was read yesterday. My uneasiness and great fear that you would have to take that long & arduous march to that unhealthy state La. & incur also, the danger of battle having subsided, I began to look around me, and view a few other matters & through a different medium, from any that has presented itself to me for years, in fact since I was a girl, and having made myself very miserable on the subject, I must make a clean breast of it, expose the whole difficulty no matter how useless it may be to you. If you were not my husband, & worthy the love I have so fully expressed in all my letters, I would feel ashamed of what I have writen, when the crumbs in return have been so scanty. This should have been plain to me before, but I never thought of it and I do not now think of it to reproach you, by words or in thought, it is only a source of great mortification to me that I have failed to inspire even one fourth of the love that I feel. I feel & know that tis my fault, & with your memory I have attached no thought or word of blame. Let me briefly state how this thing has at last forced itself upon me. I thought of my *anxiety,* and how it would find expression in my letters, when I thought you were about to leave the state & become exposed to so many dangers & hardships, & even before that, how my heart went out for you, when you were gone, how absence made my heart grow fonder, and that I always gave expression to it in my letters. I began to think of the manner & matter of your letters as contrasted with mine, of your conversation & acts when at home, & the humiliating truth was forced upon me that you felt no more than you wrote, nor wrote no more than you felt. Whenever I grew gloomy & intensely miserable at home, & I gave vent to it in words, you immediately grew taciturn, closed your eyes, & no doubt your ears, & wandered off amid the realms of thought, the subject was not diverting nor entertaining consequently you put it far from you. And now, when I am standing on the brink of a great suffering, attended with some danger, a suffering that claims you as the unintending originator you never by word disclose or evince any anxiety about how it ends. You say, "I would like to be with you, but it is very doubtful whether I can or not &c[.]" You said that no doubt with a view of pleasing me. If you are at heart really as cold as you seem to me, I had rather you were miles away from me at that time, so that you might not see what suffering a poor weak minded woman had brought upon herself, through her love for you. You have been always uni-

his Buggy at Chatfield point lived a few days & died happened over a month ago. She [Molly] says Flour sold in town a few days before she wrote at $18 per hundred. The prospect for wheat in the up country was never better she says—the worms are eating up the crops & gardens then in C[orsicana]. Mrs White has a Bro W L Means in Pyron's Regt. was in the Battle of Gal[ves-ton], slightly wounded in the head with a piece of shell—was also in the battle at the mouth of the Sabine. Mr White wrote a few lines saying that he had heard that you offered your place where your house once stood for sale, and he had concluded to offer you $300.00 says if that will do send him the deed & he will send the money. You can do as you please but I would not sell the place for confederate money & that is a low price it seems to me. Bettie don't look for Jim now under two months, has concluded to stay their [*sic*] until he sells his goods. The ladies of Anderson will have a fair the 3rd of June for the bene-fit of the soldiers wives—great preparation making—I guess I shall not be able to attend. The Plums are in their prime now. Walter is fretful like he was feel-ing bad, I fear he will be sick from eating too many plums. Sallie did not go to see Susan, stopped at Aunt Cinda's & Mary Scott & Babe went on to John's. If I should happen to the good luck die, you had better come up as soon as you can and make whatever disposition of the children you please, I need express no desire about it, for dead people, wishes are seldom regarded. I shall leave a few directions & wishes with mother which as they relate en-tirely to myself & are simple & not troublesome I hope will be reagarded—one of these is that Babe is not to handle my letters & papers, nor search into any thing I leave, so make yourself easy about your letters. Coleman carried the Tax money to town the other day. I will have your pants done in a few days. Write me if you get the stamps I send in this. Mother sent two negros, Sol & Wash. Frank Briggance[73] is the overseer.

yours affectionately
Lizzie S Neblett.

[Fragment 16 May 1863]

All well here at mothers on this Morning Saturday May 16th Garrett was up yesterday passed by our house thinks all were well, and all were well at his

---

73. Franklin Briggance (age 41) was the district clerk in 1860. He was married to Susan Rog-ers Briggance and had real and personal property valued at $6,200. He also served as the first tax assessor-collector for Grimes County. He died June 17, 1900. TX Census 1860; Grimes County Historical Commission, *History of Grimes County,* 239.

house. Tell John this. One of Mr Kings little boys has Typhoid fever & is expected to die, two negros down with the same disease. I heard from Mrs Oliver yesterday the 15th the boy said all were well, at least he said Mrs O was
well. She was sick when I left home[.]

Pelican Spit,
May 15th/63
Mrs L S Neblett

Dear Lizzie

I rec'd yours of the 6th inst several days since and would have answered it
before this but mine to you was on the 5th and caused me to defer writing in
the expectation that I would get another from you by this time. You have
probably done the same thing that I did. You must recollect that I *now* look
with great anxiety for news from home and any unusual delay or failure in getting a letter causes me great uneasiness. More so than I ever felt in my life. It
is very trying on one to be placed as I am. Furloughs are not granted now to
either officers or soldiers, even sick furloughs are now refused by Debray. I
cannot see the reason for such an unusual strictness. There appears to be no
more indications of an attack on this place by the Yankees than there has been
for months past. There is now on the Island Cook Reg,[74] three Cos of Debrays
Reg and Elmores. Just as few as can be got along with. Texas it seems is to be
stripped very close of her soldiers to assist in La. The Yankees undoubtedly
will soon know this and then Texas may come in for her share of invasions.
All these things must press upon our mind the importance of military rule and
discipline but it requires all the patriotism as well as love of home and family
and liberty to make one submit as he should. I have dispared of getting to see
you before or be with you in your sickness. The thought of the danger usual
at such times and the thought that I may never see you again is almost intoler-
able. I shall look with a painful interest the arrival of every mail until I hear of
your safe delivery. It is unfortunate that you cannot get old Mrs Boney to stay
with you. But I cannot see how it can be helped. Do take care of yourself you
must recollect that your life is now of more importance to your children than
in times of peace.

74. Joseph J. Cook commanded the First Texas Heavy Artillery Regiment. His regiment
defended the Texas coast between Sabine Pass and Velasco. Wright and Simpson, *Texas in the
War,* 130.

Just as I finished that sentence the whistle of the cars as they cross the bridge from Va Pt to Galveston so distinctly heard about for miles off. It may bring me a letter from you is the hope it suggests. Since I wrote to you I have had a troublesome bowel affection and yesterday and to day Rhumatism[75] in my shoulder. I am still going about with but little inconvenience and feel better to day than yesterday. John Scott has had Rhumatism slightly in his knees and ankle for about a week past. This is the first time he ever had it[.] When we were staying in Galveston John went to see Shackelford.[76] He found him confined to his room with Rhumatism. He says this is the worst country in the world for it. Oliver told me yesterday that Mrs O writes that the pressing officer has demanded a hand to work on the fortifications here & that she had told or sent him word that he might take one but she would not send any. I suppose they have been at my house for the same purpose before this. There has been the worst mismanagement of the negros sent here last winter or the work would long since have been done. So far as I have been able to see & hear they do not perform more than half as much work as they should. The only danger is that the negroes may not receive proper attention when sick. If as many negroes are had as would be furnished by a just quota it does seem to me that all the work could be done in a month. I understand that two hundred negroes are to be sent on this place to build fortifications. Some work of that kind was commenced here before the war but not completed. There are four large wooden cannon painted black mounted here to deceive the Yankees. I have no doubt the Yankees have ascertained their mettle before this. A few days since we were all looking on what we then supposed a naval engagement. Seven or eight vessels about ten miles off were practicing at a target as we since learned. The smoke and report were very distinct.

Saturday morn 16th May 1863. The mail has arrived but no letter from you. I get one from Nelia, and one a few days ago from Sterling. His Reg was not ordered to La but two others in same Brigade were. He writes as if he would like to be in this Co. We are having an easy time of it but there is no telling when we may be called upon for hard work and hard fighting.

yours affectionately
Wm H. Neblett

---

75. "Rheumatism" was the name given for any of numerous disorders characterized by discomfort or inflammation in the muscles, joints, bones, or nerves.

76. In 1860 there was a J. Shackleford (age 45) living in Galveston. He was a merchant with no wife or personal or real property listed. TX Census 1860.

At Mother's
May 24th 1863
W H Neblett

Dear Will,

Your letter of 15th inst came to hand three days since, and rather surprised me in a few items of its contents. I am grieved & at the same time gratified that you should at last have awakened to the idea that I am to suffer & perhaps die. I do not doubt what you say relative to your anxiety & fear because I know you are above deceit of any kind, & now since I believe you feel anxious about me, I feel sorry for you. I know it would be so much better for you to be indifferent. I was being foolish, in my last letter, when I thought you were perfectly easy about me. I lost sight of our children, who certainly have a hold upon your affection, even if I have forfeited all title to it, and their interest would prompt a desire in your heart for my life to be spared for their benefit. I have just been reviewing the past—the 24th May 1852, 11 years ago, I stood on the brink of a new existence, from a maiden, was about about [*sic*] to assume the responsibility of a wife & mother. How bright and joyful seemed the future that day. I knew their [*sic*] would be grief & pain, but the idea could not dampen my happiness. My trust & confidence in you was unbounded, & I have not been deceived. Now, to day what lies before me in that same future? I stand perhaps upon the brink of a new existence again, a bright a glorious one which will indeed be free from care, pain & sorrow. The constant cry of my soul is "Lord save or I perish" and "have mercy upon my soul."[77] I do not dread the idea of death. If God will's that I go, I am ready & willing. I have during our wedded life been very little satisfaction to you, and after this, were we both spared, I know I will be less & God knows I cannot help it. I may be, perhaps am, a monomaniac on a certain subject, but I feel that I am an incurable one, & when thought dwells upon this subject, in connection with the future, it seems dark as midnight unillumined by a single ray of hope—then I think what a blessing death would be. It seems to me that no martyr bound to the stake ever dreaded the devouring flames worse or more than I do the coming pains of labor. A few weeks ago I felt brave & strong to suffer now, but I cannot, & should not if I could make you know how I feel. When it is over with I will feel so happy, so easy, & relieved that I will not know how to con-

77. Ps. 86:16.

tain myself. I have been unwell, sick physically & mentally for a day & night, took cold some how & have suffered so much, every motion of the child (& it seems to me it has been turning up side down ever since) is so painful I can hardly stand it. I have to hold my breath while it lasts, this keeps me constantly in mind of what is coming. Will I know you are tired, the subject is or ought to be worn thread bare to you, but the feeling, the pain is as acute as ever for me. I don't think I can hold up longer than an other week. Mrs Christian has been confined & mother (who has seemed quite anxious & uneasy all the time) will send in this evening & try and get Old Mrs Boney to come out— perhaps she will, but the dutch never mind a broken promise you know. But don't feel any more uneasiness than you can help. No doubt I'll live, tho' the suffering be piled a mountain high. I mentally ask, live to go through this again? The very thought is madness—consequently it would be a blessed thing to die. I am sorry you began to expect, or feel anxious, about my confinement so soon, you know I always go over the time, I drink tea & creep about so easy, hardly dare take a long breath, for fear of bringing on the dreaded time, that the time is deferred as long as nature will permit. I hope to be relieved of my present suffering soon, for it [is] almost as hard as labor. I sometimes think the child is wrong & it is an effort of Nature to turn it right, before labor begins. Oh that I could drown thought and have courage to sustain me at the trying time! I'll relieve your anxiety as soon as my trial is over with. I'll write every three or four days until the time has passed.

Mother has three right sick negros, one whose recovery is doubtful. Mima, Big Bob's child nearly grown, she has, mother & I both think, the Typhoid fever, has been sick now nearly three weeks. The other two are small children, have the Remittant fever,[78] may terminate in Typhoid fever. Bob went down to our house yesterday to get me some squaw vine, reports all well there. Sarah has been at work in the field this week, I sent Rivers word if he need[ed] help to take her until the pinch of crop time was over. I have not heard a word from Parson Fullenwider yet. I will write to him to know whether he rec'ed the money or not. Bob says another one of the little guilt's[79] have pigs lost all but two. The blue pig as the children call her lost all her pigs. As soon as Rivers can spare Joe & Bill out of the crop they will hunt up the cows & calves. I

---

78. Malaria was often called remittent or intermittent fever because of the cyclical nature of the sufferer's chills and fever. The disease is transmitted by mosquitoes. It was often a recurrent ailment that was treated with quinine.

79. A gilt is a young sow that has not farrowed.

have your Pants done finish last monday. I was greatly grieved & shocked last Teusday by a false report. Negro Jim came in & told me that Mr Chandler had just left the gate inquiring the way to Dr Browns & said he was going from there to our place. Jim says he told him I was here, he then said to tell me that my mother-in-law was *very low,* he just left there that morning. That put me on my head, I just thought Ma was going to die certain that Pa had sent to the nearest house for help & Chandler volunteered to go after Brown, & Pa had accepted his services as being more prompt & certain than a negro and that he was sending for all the Drs far & near, & they not knowing my situation had sent for me also. I wanted to go, & felt so badly that I had not gone there long ago, on Ma's account, but Mother told me, & I knew it would not do for me to start, I would have been in labor before I reached town I knew—so, I tried to send a negro boy down immediately, to see how she was, the horse got out, & did not get him ready until night then I was affraid as none of the young negro's knew the way, that he would get lost in the night, so I had him up & off an hour before day next morning. I dreaded his coming so much, I feared she was dead—when I read the note, was joyfully relieved by knowing that she was as well as usual, up & about. It was William Terrell who sent me word Ma had [a] sick headache, & he was on his way seven or 8 miles below Brown's. The children all well. I am going to doctor *promptly* & watch closely so as to nip this dreadful Typhoid in the bud when any of them get sick. The Typhoid cases at Mr Kings getting well. Remember me as kindly as the nature of my faults will permit and be as happy as you [can]. We had a good season here the 21st. Coleman thinks the corn is now safe. Bob says all our potatoe slips were set out.

Yours affectionately
Lizzie S Neblett

At mother's Wednesday morn,
May 27th 1863

Dear Will,

The mountain of anxiety & dread has been removed, the time of exquisite suffering has been passed, and I this morning lie on a bed of ease a free unshackled woman once more! Tho' all undeserving I have been dealt with most mercifully & if any poor frail suffering creature ever felt greatful, I do. I thought I should never get through shouting when it was over. Yes the dutch gal has come, but she is not dutch like in her proportions. A perfect Amazon, her face is dutch like, is so ugly. No physical deformity, but if she unfortunately inherits her mothers mental conformation, her peculiar idiosincracys she will be a most miserable woman. But let us hope for the best. At this time she has a better forehead, her intellectual organs seem better developed than any baby I have ever had at her age. Mother has just weighed her, 9¾ lb. The fattest little thing you ever saw, but oh Will I am so sorry, so grieved that it was not a boy—that was a great damper to my joy after it was over with. Old Mrs Boney came out Sunday eve 24th inst and the babe was born last night the 26th May about 8 O clock. I was in labor about three hours, bore it very well, had what is called an easy time up to the last pinch, then had greater difficulty, & suffered more than ever before. She was so long in the birth, had to be attend some. Oh god! What pain I felt—her face was bruised in the birth. I shall not get well as quickly as heretofore, because I have lost more blood than ever before, 4 times as much. I feel very weak this morning. The children are all delighted, except Walter, he dont like it taking his place in my bed. He says he will sleep with Pa. If you could just step in now my cup of joy would run over. Oh I do so long to see you once more. You were never so long from me before since we were married. I havent heard from home since I wrote the 24th. Mother has now 5 sick negros in the cabin, the three first still linger on, not much difference to be seen. Wm Taylor of Givens Regt Sybley's Brig[80] stopped here yesterday first from La. Reinforcement had arrived, from Texas Ark & La, Banks was reported to be at Ft Hudson,[81] as to the intended movements of our army he could tell nothing. He was on sick furlough. Hurst was taken prisoner at Franklin, he dont know whether he is dead or alive. Write often to me,

yours affectionately
Lizzie S Neblett

---

80. Henry Hopkins Sibley was born in 1816. In 1861–1862 he was in command of the Department of New Mexico. By 1863 he was in Louisiana, where he was court-martialed for his conduct during the battles at Irish Bend and Fort Bisland. He was acquitted of the charges and remained attached to the Department of the Trans-Mississippi. He died in 1886. Boatner, *Civil War Dictionary*, 759.

81. Lizzie was likely referring to Union general Nathaniel Banks's siege of Port Hudson, which began on May 21, 1863. Long, *Civil War Day by Day*, 356.

At Mother's
May 30th 1863
W H Neblett,

Dear Will,

Your letter of dates 21st and 24th inst was read a few days ago, and altho'
you make no self defense as you say neither own nor disown any thing I attributed to you, in my self made unhappiness I feel now that I was in fault, &
unlike you, I always feel irresistably compelled to acknowledge an error when
it is proven to be one to my satisfaction. And unlike you again, I must say a
few words in self defense, and if my plea is not a good one, try & banish all
memory of that letter from your mind and think as leneiently of my foibles, &
transgressions, as your nature will permit. I know I was more intensely miserable while the ideas in that letter were in force in my mind, & that was a good
many days than the letter made you. After I commenced drinking that Squaw
vine my general health was much better, and that female disease I had 10
months before the birth of my babe was also a great deal better. I felt more
hopeful than I had done for many long months. From some cause, a few days
before I wrote that letter, the disease returned worse than ever, and my mind
soon became tinctured with despair, and all its attendent evils, & you with
your hopeful disposition can never know how injurious a despairing mind can
become in inflicting torture, by warping all our just & true ideas. And this
gloom instead of bettering made me worse & then, from cold or some other
cause, I became so sore over my bowels that I could hardly move, and the motions of the child were exceedingly painful. During this season of suffering,
that letter had its emanation from my mind & pain. Had your letter of the
15th reached me before that was writen, you would never have read that letter.
In that letter of the 15th inst you did express much anxiety about me, &
throughout was very kind & affectionate. Any one suffering always desire the
sympathy of those they love, and I was pining for evidences of your love &
sympathy, & when your letter came & you seemed so unconcerned about me,
my unhappiness was complete, and my thoughts supped at the banquet of
gall & wormwood. I defered writing three or four days, on account of this
morbid state of the mind, for my good sense told me tho' faintly that I was
wrong. I knew I ought to write, and as no anger flowed from my heart, I
thought it my duty to give you the pleasure of hearing from your farm and
children intending to say nothing about myself, but "from the abundance of

the heart the mouth speaketh,"[82] and what I suffered, & wherein I considered you remiss became the theme of my letter. But I feel now like another & new woman. I feel as I imagine Noah & his children felt when they stepped from the Arc, on dry land, & saw the waters of the flood retreating, and the rainbow of promise on its clouds. What to them were the storms they had weathered, the dangers they had overcome. They were all past. And let me hope that no such season of suffering & despair as the last nine months has been, will ever again be my portion. I now bury that part of the past, & will try & think of it no more.

I have not been doing as well as I usually do since my confinement. The flooding caused me to be weaker than common, & less milk in my breasts. I gave the baby the breast as usual, and there being no milk made my nipples sore. I now suffer awfully whenever she sucks I never had my nipples so sore before, & fear I will have to suffer with them some time. The baby has been sick, is now better. I think she had fever the first two days and then her bowels seemed to pain her so much, like Bob was when he was a baby. It is an ugly little thing. Has a forehead like Mary's, except 'tis fuller over the eyes than Mary's, mouth and chin like Bob—the wide & expanded nostrils indicative of fine blood, a wide dutch face, & at present dark blue eyes. You will never love her if you never see her. I find myself loving her better & better every day, no one can withstand the sweet winning ways of their own innocent babe. Bill came up Thursday evening reporting Sarah sick & wanting more medicine, and wanted a horse to get up some cattle which were breaking in the field. John's old fence breaker, another one of his cows & an ox of his, beside other cattle. Rivers is sick so Bob was told by one of Hurst negro's on Friday. I fear the negros will let the cattle eat up all the corn. You know how careless and neglectful they are. Thornton has yoked John's old fence breaker. Joe will come up to night I reckon—and perhaps I can give you a better account of things tomorrow. Old Mr Buck Walker's daughter Mrs Randal died this week very suddenly—it looks like nearly every letter I write, I have to report the death of some grown woman.

Sunday eve May 31st—Joe came up this morning, says the cattle only broke in once in the old field, broke in through Martin's part of the fence, had sent Martin word to fix his fence, supposed he would do so tomorrow, says they did not eat much of the corn before they found them out. Have put two large

82. Luke 7:34.

yokes, made of that old broken ox yoke, on two of John's cows, have'nt got the ox yet. Tell John that if his cattle broke our fence & let in other cattle & eat up all our corn, I'll have to charge him for damages. Joe says the corn is suffering very much for rain, the oldest corn is in silk, that fine rain we had here on the 21st inst (I think it was) did not extend to our house, rained on the other side of the creek, but only sprinkled at our house, rained none at Brown's nor Hurst's. I do hope it will rain there soon. Many of the last Potatoe slips have died, only a little over half of the patch doing well—the watermellon patch suffering for rain. I suppose every thing is down there. They have finished running round the cotton, will commence breaking out the middles tomorrow & will finish by that night, and get nearly through hoeing it, & next week Joe & Bill will gather up the cattle & pen them in the old potatoe patch by the house. I told him to be certain & get the cows that are at Mill's and Mrs Dalford's, if he don't we will loose the calves certain. Bill Dodd thinks it was Mill's trade to drive up other peoples cows & then steal the calves. Joe has Ranger down there & says he goes round the field every evening & drives the cattle all up to the old Gilmore house, & they don't go back to the field before morning. The calves are watered every day, & Bob says look well. They churn at night, and have meat only once a day, have only used three shoulders since I left which is doing remarkably well. They have 10 shoulders yet, & never touched the middlings. Joe has put up the guilts with their pigs in the old potatoe patch & feeds them with some of that old corn & some milk I suppose. He has seen that bunch of wild hogs down in the bottom by our field, but they run when they saw him, don't know whether they have pigs or not. Rivers is not sick, Joe says he was at our place last night. I asked him through a note I wrote him before I left home to visit our cabins occasionally at night to see if every thing was going on right. Poor Hurst is dead, his negro reached home yesterday Joe says. Says his master only lived three days after he was taken prisoner, and he was with the Yankee's three week before he made his escape. I feel so sorry for poor Mrs Hurst. I do hope & pray that your Regt may not be ordered to Nacadoches. Oh Will, it would almost kill me for you to go off, and not get to see you. But I feel hopeful that you will stay where you are. I'll learn whether you will or not in your next letter and feel so anxious to get it. Mother's sick negro's still linger on, the two little ones are better but Mima is not much if any, had the fever over 3 weeks now. Sarah is well Joe says. I hope we won't have any bad cases before I get home. All well at John's yesterday.

Yours most affectionately
Lizzie S Neblett.

[Fragment, June 1, 1863]

This letter has been on hand two days writen little at a time no other lying in woman in the Co would have writen such a lengthy epistle but me, but you know how untiring I am when I undertake any thing in earnest. I got up this morning & walked (very toteringly) in to mothers room, Mother thinks if I had not been brim full of strong rasberry tea & No 6, I would have flooded to death. I suffered more than I did in giving Billy birth with after pains. I never knew what after pains were before. I think my flooding was caused by the way the old woman managed me, I can't recommend her—& I think notwithstanding what she says that my child was born feet foremost or double, can't tell which. Oh I never suffered such agony, and it was three times as long as that period ever was before, & she was working for life & death all the time. I had an uncommon amount of water, & a very large after birth. I tell you I was a sight to behold. The baby weighed 10 pounds and mother thinks some over, as her stilyards [aren't] exactly correct, don't weigh enough. The children are on their head to have the baby named. Have you a new name picked out? She has your thumb and ears, is growing prettier every day. Walter sleeps on a pallet by himself. Oh I do want to see you, so badly. I dream of you so often, & I am always in distress calling for you.

I wrote you first that the baby weighed 9¾ lbs, mother afterwards said her stilyards were not right & she knew it was 10, & perhaps over 10 pounds.

Do send me word how I will get your Pants to you I want you [to] have them so much, every warm day it makes me feel much warmer when I think of you without your summer pants. I am by you like I am my baby's. I dress them according to my feelings. Nelia wrote me that she saw a man belonging to your Comp on the 19th inst & if I had known who it was or anything about [him] I would have tried to send them by him. I ate Roasting ears for dinner to day—Irish potatoes & Beans—how I wish you were here, I thought of it at table. Oh shall I ever see you again?

At Mothers
June 9th/63

Dear Will—

Jack has just this moment arrived on his way to Galveston, and is in a hurry to be getting on towards the Depot. I hardly expected him so soon, and have been promising myself the pleasure of writing a long letter to send by him, &

now must write briefly, confining myself to facts, & indulge in no revelation of feelings. My letters to you are my safety valves. I must have some one to tell my troubles too [*sic*], no matter if you don't want to hear them. I must tell you, or seek a patient listner some where else. Jack can tell you how John is, I don't think he will be able to return at the end of the 20 days. I have given out all hope of your coming soon, I don't expect to get a glimpse of you under 10 or 12 months if I do then. It seems very hard to me, but, I must make up my mind to bear it as well as I can, no doubt it seems & will be fully as hard to you, but we both know there is no help for it. My baby is cross, & consequently a great deal of trouble to me. Oh I do deplore her coming so much, and shed a bitter tears over the work of last August as I ever did. Would to God I had never seen last August. It was awful enough for her to be a girl, but to be as she now is, is more than I can well bear, I can take no pleasure in her, the very sight of her is a pain to me. It is only when asleep that it is off my mind. I cant play with her, & fondle her as I did my other babes. Altho, I cant wish her dead and could not neglect one iota of my duty to her, yet I can't help feeling that her death would be a blessing, to me & her. There was 5 baby's born in about 2 weeks of each other and all of them were boy's but mine. If mine had been a boy, I could feel that all my suffering had not been in vain, that my boy might prove a prop to my old age, & be a source of pride & honor to me, but this poor little, dependent, diseased or unnatural girl, may prove a greater source of *shame* & *grief* than any thing else that could befall me. I think sometimes that I *can't stand* it, but I know I must. Sterling's wife had a boy born 3 days after mine. But Jack waits & all the tears that I must weep, & all that I must write cannot now change what is unalterable. We are all well, I am getting along better than when I last wrote. I go all about now & improve in strength every day—but oh life is the greatest burden I have.

I send your Pants by Jack, one pair is rather light colored for camp life, but I have not had time to dye them over since I came up to mothers, if you can get home on furlough I can dye them over then. The negro's at our place finished laying by the cotton last week, and are getting up the cows. The cattle have broke in only that one time Joe says. The corn & every thing is needing rain very much. I fear the corn crops will be cut off very much if it don't rain soon. The ladies made over 2000 dollars at the fair, & had 1000 donated before hand. I have been looking for a letter from you several days. I fear you are going to become indifferent about writing now that I have passed through that awful, awful suffering. But tho' the dread, & it was a mighty one, [and] physical pain has been removed, I am more unhappy now than before for I had some hopes of having a boy, now that hope is ruin. I did not find out the condition of my child until she was nearly a week old, mother would not tell me, hoping it would get better. I am trying simple remedies, but see no good results as yet. She was born with the disease I had one time, as much a drop of blood passed. The changes that disease has made, or else tis natural, is what grieves me. I am almost affraid to write to you about her, so fearful that you will drop the letter & some one will pick it up & read it. I had several little items of news to write you, but am so hurried I can't write this morning. Bob Bookman, I ought to say J M Bookman,[83] & his scouts were captured about the time of those fights in Va. John Nix is among them they were unharmed we hear, but are in the hands of the Yanks. Bob Bassett was taken with Hemorage of the Lungs, just before their fight came off & is now in Richmond. Much sympathy is being arroused for the poor fellow by his friends here. I'll write again soon, that is, if I find you have not dropped me. I'll govern my letters by yours.

Yours affectionately
Lizzie

The next letter in the collection is dated July 28, 1863. During this break in correspondence, Will Neblett gained a sixty-day furlough because of ill health and went home to recover from what Lizzie described as an illness resembling break-bone or dengue fever.

---

83. There was a J. M. Bookman (age 26) living in Grimes County in 1860. He was a lawyer and had personal property valued at $325. He served as second sergeant in Company G, Fourth Texas Infantry Regiment. He was killed at Chickamagua on September 20, 1863. TX Census 1860; Wright and Simpson, *Texas in the War*, 211.

3

Tied to the House by a Crying Young One

July 28, 1863–October 25, 1863

Harrisburg Texas
July 28/63
Mrs L S Neblett

Dear Lizzie,

We are still at this place and will remain here until the first when we will start for Pelican Spit and remain there fifteen days. John Scott is here—did not succeed in getting his substitute in for the reason that the surgeon found that the cut on his ankle would lame him on a march. John got a transfer into Dickies company[1] in order to get his substitute in but the transfer being informal he is here still & will probably remain here a few days more. He is still making efforts to get another substitute. There is a great deal of bitter prejudice against getting substitutes arising from the envy of those who are unable to do so or are so opposed to being in the service. I have heard nothing about this Reg going to La, but the severe drilling the troops on the Island undergo leads me to believe that active service is expected some where—perhaps in La perhaps here. I am strongly in the notion of getting into cavalry and if we march I shall certainly make the effort to do so. I notice in a late Telegraph that Magruder[2] notifies the owners of runaway negroes that if they do not re-

1. J. C. Dickie commanded Company H of the Twentieth Texas Infantry Regiment.
2. John Bankhead Magruder was born August 15, 1810, in Winchester, Virginia. During the Civil War, he made major general October 7, 1861, and in October 1862 he was given command of the District of Texas. He was instrumental in retaking Galveston in January 1863. After the war he left Texas for a time to serve as a major general under Emperor Maximilian in Mexico.

turn them that double the number will be pressed. This is an outrage in my case and I want you to tell them to take [to] the bottom if the impressing officers come. If they come to you while the negroes are in the field send some one to them to tell them. Randal was gone 49 days. When he was taken they said he would be wanted only three weeks.

I stopped all night at Mrs Cochrans when I came down—found Owen quite sick with the fever. I found all well at Pa's. I want you to save me some butter as soon as the weather will permit. I could not sell any cotton the evening I was in Houston for the reason that most of the cotton buyers were afraid of the Gov impressing it. Consequently I did not buy any salt. I will try it again soon. Has Bettie[3] got any better of her cholic. I dreamed of seeing her last night. Kiss the children for me. I send you some stamps for it is more convenient for me to buy than you.

yours affectionately
Wm H. Neblett

Pelican Spit
Aug 3rd/63
Mrs L S Neblett

Dear Lizzie

I was somewhat disappointed in not getting a letter from you to day but console myself by hoping for one in a few days. I am writing now on board the boat on her way from Galveston back to the Spit and if you find any words illegible place it to that account for the boat shakes badly. Our Reg is now on the "qui vive" on the subject of its departure for La two companies left on the 1st for Nebletts Bluff and it is said three more are under orders to leave in a day or two. This will leave but half of our Reg here and the supposition is that the whole Reg will go before long. I think it probable that all the troops here except Cooks Reg will go to La as soon as the Militia can get here if not

---

John Magruder died February 19, 1871. Jon L. Wakelyn, *Biographical Dictionary of the Confederacy,* with Frank E. Vandiver, advisory ed. (Westport, Conn.: Greenwood Press, 1977), 305–306. On Magruder and Galveston see Paul D. Casdorph, *Prince John Magruder: His Life and Campaigns* (New York: John Wiley & Sons, 1996), 211–364.

3. Elizabeth Neblett was Lizzie and Will Neblett's fifth child, born May 26, 1863. At first the family called her Bettie, but after she turned two, they began calling her Lizzie, after her mother. NFB.

sooner. You need not make yourself uneasy about me. My health is improving every day. It is said that there are 14 Yankee vessels in sight or near the Island. I doubt this but it may be true. Texas in my opinion will have to depend on the Militia for her defense. John got his transfer completed yesterday and went to his Co (Dickie's) to day. He has no substitute yet. An old fellow in Galveston whose business is to find them & furnish them offers him one for $4600.00 John has not made up his mind what to give.

When I was in Houston (on the 30th) I sold my cotton five bales to a man by the name of Winn for 45 cts and he furnish bagging & rope. He also promised to advance 300 or 400 lbs of salt and send them all to Navasota. If your Ma's waggons go there get them to haul them. I saw Bagby and instructed him to send your Ma 1000 lbs salt.

I did not get any money for the cotton and if I go to La you will have to get it. I promised to have the cotton at Navosota by the 1st of Sept at furtherest. So that as soon as you get the bagging & rope send it to McCunes[4] Gin.

I wish you would send to the post office on next Saturday & if I wish any thing I will write so that you can get it by that time. Tell Mary I will write to her the next time I write to you. Kiss the baby for me & let me know how she is getting along.

yours affectionately
Wm H. Neblett

At Mothers
Aug 5th 1863

Dear Will,

I fear you will grow impatient before this reaches you, and perhaps feel a little hurt at me, but I had little or nothing to write, and my pen and ink were so bad at home that I dreaded to undertake to write with them. I expect you are surprised at my being here so soon after you left, to explain, Mother sent me word to come up and bring Kate, and she would let Betsy[5] help out & dry me some peaches, as she was not weaving. [S]o, I came up this morning and

---

4. In 1860 James McCune (age 40) was a farmer with real and personal property valued at $15,300. He and his wife, Nancy (28), had four children. TX Census 1860.

5. Betsy presumably was one of Sarah Scott's slaves.

now have Betsy Jim & Kate cutting & drying for me, tho mother says I was too late about coming as most of the good peaches have been used up. I read your letter of July 28th yesterday. I did not send to the office myself & no one brought my letters & papers until I asked Mr Collins to do so on Election day.

We have all been tolerably well since you left, I came nearer having the fever than I have done before in a long time, but nature made a cure without the aid of Esculapius.[6] The children Walter Billy & your Bettie have all had sore eyes. Did you remark that pronoun before Bettie's name. I always think of her as your baby and not mine. I reckon that is because she was so unwelcome to me. I cured her sore eyes in two days. She still has the Cholic but has been better of it for two days now and I am in hopes that she will be entirely over it by the time she is three months old. She grows fast, and is more interesting every day. I am so sorry that you will miss all the pleasure of her baby days. The time passes very slowly with me at home, and I do so long to have you with me. So many things are constantly occuring that I want to talk to you about. Bro Jim came up to mothers, a few days after you left, and asked me what I was going to do when the yankee's came—of course I was not prepared with an answer at that time. Jim is mightily in the blues about the war, and I hear from several sources that he is not as much so as Dr Dickson[7] and some others about town. Coleman told me I had better send my wagon up and get it fixed ready to roll out when they come. Mrs Benjamin from town says that is all the talk in town, what they are going to do when the yankees come. I am in a bad fix to get out of their way, & must hide before they come, and when I find my cave, I'll let you know where it is. I can't explain the why & wherefore, in fact I have no reason only a presentiment that the war will not last much longer and the presentiment clings to me all the time. I am not hopeful one day and depressed the next, so I expect & hope you will be at home this winter or next spring. I feel about this like I did about your going to La.

Now about the wagon, dont know what you wanted Coleman to have done to it, but I know tis broken now and I'll tell you how it happened. You loaned

6. Aesculapius was the Greco-Roman god of medicine and healing.

7. Dr. David Catchings Dickson (age 42) was born in Georgetown, Mississippi, February 25, 1815. He moved to Texas in 1841 and served as a representative in the Texas legislature. He had personal and real property valued at $18,000. He was married to Nancy Ann Magee (35) and had seven children. Allen, *Saga of Anderson,* 218–20; TX Census 1860.

the wagon to Joe Collins[8] & he smashed the tongue & wraped it with raw hide, and last week he borrowed it from me to haul a load of lumber to town and broke the tongue clear out, but is having a new tongue put in it. Don't say I ought not to have loaned it for I did not know how to refuse—and now when they wanted the wagon to haul up the cotton house logs, they could not get it, but let me tell you, they ain't a going to hurry about any thing for they have determined not to get that piece of land cleared up ready to cultivate next year. I can see very little that they have done since you left. Joe & Thornton have perhaps six stacks of fodder and about as many corn tops (I reckon) as we had last year & they got the basket timber & made 8 large baskets and 4 small pi[t]ch baskets, just finished last night. Sam & the three boys have been cutting burr's and got out the logs for the cotton house—got other logs next to Sallie's field, in the strip of timber between your field and Sallie's. Rivers put them there so they say. I don't think Rivers sees to them much. Randle Bill & Tom are picking cotton. Thornton & Sam started to day to get out boards for the cotton house, borrowed a saw from Collins. Sam went down there yesterday morning to get a saw and to see if we could not use Collins wagon to haul logs, and if not to tell him we wanted ours, and last night he did not come home, and reached there this morning after break fast, with a dog lie in his mouth about his going to his work and [arriving too late he remained] over where he was going to get out boards. I don't think he did any thing yesterday evening and never said a word to Collins about our wanting our wagon, or to get one of his. Sam has run out. He started to see his wife last Sat after dinner, and returned late Monday evening. He is determined not to clear up that land, and no doubt expects to be a free man before another year. I don't know when I have been fretted so with a negro as I was him this morning. Failed to do the very thing he went to find out at the mill—says he he [*sic*] sharpened the saw & I reckon that was all he done yesterday evening. But if the Yankees come along & take both negro's and crop it don't matter much. It is a task to get them to water & feed the hogs. I told them how much corn to feed, but I have no idea that they bring half what I told them to. I will return in a few days. I don't bother Mother so much now. Babe has been at Plantersville

8. Most likely J. W. Collins (age 27 in 1860), who made his living through steam saw milling and had real and personal property valued at $2,000. His wife's name was Adaline (24). John (45) and James (32) Collins, presumably J. W.'s brothers, also listed their occupations as steam saw milling and had $6,500 and $2,000 in personal and real property, respectively. John was married to Elisa (32) and had two children, and James was a bachelor living with J. W. TX Census 1860.

(went home with Sue Baker⁹) over a week & will remain a week longer. No more of the hogs have died, but that sow & shotes over at Hurst's were dugged out of their Potatoe patch and have worms in them. Joe has had them up twice. She had three shotes & but two can be found, and only one little pig. Jim Scott started yesterday or to day for La in company with Tom Rogers and some body else, we suppose to buy negros or wagons & team. So he put Coleman to hunting John's Substitute—don't want John's cotton. I told the negros to take the bottom as soon as I heard of Magruders order. They have not come to our house yet, but the negros told me [they] were at Yarbores,¹⁰ & handcuffed and took three out of the field—our negros have been panic striken about the "*conscripts*" as they st[y]le the impressing officers.

Pelican Spit Galveston Bay Texas
Aug 11th/63
Mrs L S Neblett

Dear Lizzie

Yours of the 5th & 6th inst was rec'd last Saturday. I suppose you have recd my second letter written last Monday on board the Bayou city. Well the next day two more Companies of this Reg took up the line of march for Orange. This Co I understand would have gone[,] being the next largest Co but for the protest of Gen Debray, who seems to being opposed to sending off troops from this place. John Scott got his transfer completed on monday and the next day his Co left for Orange before he had time to get his substitute and he went with it. He is in Capt Dickie's Co in same Reg. He wrote me a note stating that he would leave his mattress at Mrs Cochran's where I could get it if I wished. Two weeks ago two Co of this Reg went to Nebletts Bluff to guard the Gov property there captured at Brashear city [Louisiana]. It is said the two last Co have gone to Orange to also guard Gov property. I think the Companys which have gone will not remain there for a great length of time by themselves. They will either be ordered back to the Reg or the Reg will go

9. In 1860 Susan Baker was 15 and living with her parents, Issac (60) and Aurelia (56) Baker. TX Census 1860.

10. In 1860 J. Q. Yarborough (spelled Yarborro in the 1860 census) was a 35-year-old farmer living with his son Parham (8). He had personal and real property valued at $50,000. He figures later in the letters as a romantic interest and eventual husband of Babe, Lizzie Neblett's sister. TX Census 1860.

there; the latter most probably if we need reinforcements in La. I am glad that you do not take as gloomy a view of the prospect of the war as as [*sic*] some do. We are not whiped yet by a great deal and will not be unless the demoralization of our army does it. We have more to fear from that source than all others, and I am not alarmed at that, though there is a good deal of it in the Reg here, produced probably more for the want of active service than any other cause.

In regard to home matters I will say that I spoke to Coleman about having the tyres cut on the hind wheels of the wagon, and when that is done it would be as well to have some irons shortened that go through the end of the tongue. I think Rivers ought to put all hands to clearing as soon as that cotton house is done for I do not suppose the cotton is sufficiently open to do good picking. Have you had any rain since I left. A good rain fell here on the 6th or 7th. In my last I wrote to you what disposition I had made of my cotton. While at Harrisburg I got John to write home and instruct Susan to get me 50 lbs of sugar of Mrs Biggsby when he got his. The understanding is that she sells the sugar at 75 cts pr lb and take it in corn, at its market price this Fall. John says she has a first rate article of La sugar. Such an article is worth in Houston $1.00 pr lb. I am glad to hear that *my* Bettie is getting over the cholic but think I will hardly have the pleasure of seeing her before this Winter or Fall even if we remain here. I have just recd a letter from Owen Cochran who has been sick for some time with the fever. He says he intends to make a visit to Grimes soon & will call on you while up there.

> yours affectionately
> Wm H. Neblett

At mothers
Aug 11th 1863

Dear Will—

I sent Smith in town this morning hoping that I would get a letter from you but was disappointed. I feel very sorry about John having to go and not being able to find a substitute. The fact of my feeling so badly about it astonishes me, for it proves to me what I have recently doubted—that I yet have [a] heart capable of feeling much. I have sometimes felt like my heart was seared, incapable of feeling as it once did. Oh Will, I don't know what will become of me. Mr Coleman has been riding now four or five days to find a substitute for John. Thought he had one for $5000, but before he got to see the man, some one else offered him $6000 and he went for it. Coleman is now after a man he thinks he can get for $4,000 in money and a negro woman, mother is going to furnish the money. John wrote very gloomy to Susan just as he was leaving. It is the general opinion that as soon as the Militia is organized it will be sent to Galveston & that then the remaining Co's of Elmore's Regt will be ordered off. I hope and pray that you may be left, tho' I fear you will have to go. The militia was drafted in town last week, and glorious news, Jeff Haynie[11] drew to go. McCune came clear, Coleman is exempt because he served as Col awhile. There is a big meeting going on down on Lake Creek, raking in the sinners by the whole sale—been going on now over a week & still continues with unabating interest. Uncle McClure has professed and joined, Ben Langum[12] professed—so did Martin, and a number of others. Garrett has been up to the mourners bench several times.

I am going home this evening if it don't rain, (which it is threatening to do) and am going to try and go to church to night, leave the baby with Sarah—let Nancey suckle her if she cries. She is better of the cholic now, hasent taken any cholic medicine for four days now, had no bad spell of cholic in that time. Oh Will she is so much like you, every body says she is more like you than any child we have. Charley Van Horn says he would know she was a Neblett any where he saw her. I went to Anderson yesterday went to Betties to get my teeth plugged, both dentists gone, and they have no gold if they had been at home, but expect to have some soon.[13] I fear it will be too late when I get a chance to have mine plugged. I remained up here longer than I would have done, in order to get my teeth worked on. Bettie don't look for Jim back under a month. She thinks he is more apt to get wagons & teams & may buy drivers and after, or if the impressment act about cotton is done away with, buy cotton and haul it to mexico. I went to see Amanda White[14] she looks wretchedly bad. The worse looking person I ever saw, to be up going about

---

11. The 1860 census lists Thomas J. Haynie (age 38) as a farmer with real and personal property valued at $19,600 and married to Euny J. Haynie (28); his sister, Mary, was Lizzie Neblett's close friend. TX Census 1860.

12. Probably B. B. Langham (38), a farmer with a wife, Caroline (29), and four children. He had real and personal property valued at $6,570. TX Census 1860.

13. Gold foil was the preferred material for filling teeth in the nineteenth century.

14. Amanda Noble White, Lizzie Neblett's childhood friend. She was married to Henry White.

visiting &c, don't see how she can live long. Henry made it all when he bought these negros—one man the war will enrich greatly if the Yanks don't invade us and destroy all he has. Babe has returned from Plantersville—delighted with her visit. Charley Van H is still in the neighborhood—is now at mothers, has been spending several days at Piedmont Springs. Old Magruder has a crowd there, he being the chief attraction—dancing and flirting going on. Miss Robinson from the Brazos [is] his favorite. I hear he wanted to bring his ladies to the Springs with him but Cannon[15] told him no they could not come on his place, one vile woman came & Cannon gave her a half hour to leave in—she cursed & snorted around at an awful rate but left. I hear Bettie Scott is going to the Springs this week, tho' she did not say one word about such a thing to me. She cuts a dash, feels herself richer than any body else, & I fear, will make herself a fool about old Magruder. I know Voilaite[16] would if she did not have that baby to tie her at home. I cant tell you any thing about home affairs did not get many peaches dried, because it rained two days here. Coleman tells me that there was a good rain down at the school house & Hursts last week, hope we got some of it[;] the last setting of potatoe vines were dying before I left. I have no idea the negros have worked any. They don't when I am at home, I put Sarah overseer over the hogs, they they [sic] will attend to them so as to let them starve for food & water. There is a lot of La negros near town, in fact, in town to hire for their vituals & clothes—run from the Yankees. The impressing officers are taking negros in Montgomery Co, those that run away. They all tell me to tell the negros not to run, and let them take half of our negros if they want to. I told them to run soon after you left & won't countermand the order unless you say so. I don't expect [to] have a negro six months from this time or a house to cover my head, and if you can take all you have & get a substitute with it would it not be a great deal better, you could take us, and flee to an other county with us and as long as we both remain in good health we certainly could support our family.

Bettie & Amanda talked to me yesterday about the risk I was running by sleeping with my doors open—what do you think about it? I don't believe

---

15. In 1861 Alonzo Cannon bought land and built a four-story, one-hundred-room building near the springs as a type of health resort. General Magruder stayed there during the summer of 1863 and 1864. Allen, *Saga of Anderson*, 149.

16. Violaite (Viola) Brown Neblett was 17 and living with her parents, Oven and Cinthia Brown, in 1860. She married Will Neblett's brother Sterling on August 14, 1862. TX Census 1860; Mullins, *Grimes County, Texas, Marriage Records*.

much if any of this good news that is coming, only a trick to elevate the spirits of the people. I don't believe any thing after The taking of Washington City turned out to be such a humbug. I will write soon after I reach home. The ink is so bad here and at home that I can hardly write with it so I used a pencil this morning and am affraid you can't read it all. Do write to me often, and tell me what I must do when the yankees come, every body even the most hopeful believe Texas will be invaded this fall & winter[;] news comes now that they have landed at Sabine City and Matagorda.[17] I don't credit that tale. News has reached here that Bassett is very low in Richmond hasen't been able to be in the Co since he left here—this is to prepare the people for his coming in Sept. Mrs Haynie[18] told me she heard Garrett left a will, and gave all he had to his sisters. Mrs Lee told mother & we think she got her information from Mrs McDaniel who boards at Howards (her son in laws) that Bassett urged Sallie to have Garretts will opened last winter, wanted her to bring forward the matter and have the will *opened*. He seems so positive about Garrett's death, that I haven't hope that we will ever see him on earth again. Please write often and tell me about what I ought to have done at home &c. I will do the best I can at home but it will be so lonely there, that I expect I cant stay very long at a time. I see no one when I am there and hear no news. Good bye.

yours affectionately
Lizzie S Neblett

Hawthorn cottage Grimes Co
Aug 13th 1863
Wm H Neblett

Dear Will—

Altho I have writen twice since I recd your first and only letter yet as I have or will have an oportunity of sending a letter up tomorrow I have concluded to write. I am feeding myself on the hope that I will get a letter from you to night when I go to church. Mr Wessen the preacher brings down the Lake Creek mail when he come down to preach. I will be so disappointed if I don't

---

17. The Battle of Sabine Pass took place in September 1863, resulting in a Confederate victory. The landing of Union troops in that area could have been a preliminary to that battle.

18. Dealthea C. Haynie (60) was a farmer living with her daughter, Mary Haynie, in 1860. She had real and personal property valued at $22,000. TX Census 1860.

hear from you—it has been over two weeks now since I heard from you. I fear you are sick. I would torment myself to death about you if I did not exert a strong will to the contrary. Oh the future is all gloom for me, and my heart is continually asking oh why was I created, & if created why was I not permitted to die long ago. My unhappiness is so great when I think of the direful calamities that might & may befall me, that I wish only for death never thinking of what you would suffer were I to die & leave you, but when I think of your suffering in that case I always look upon it like we do when a painful opperation or duty has to be performed for our children[;] we deplore the pain inflicted, but never hesitate when we know 'tis for the *good* of the child. You are too good a man to have been tied to such a woman as I am who will under all circumstances persist in being unhappy, & sometimes very miserable. Was peace established & you at home, you know the *horrible* nightmare which would always frighten away any little happiness that might occasionally cross my path. So I am a doomed creature any how, and my only hope is a speedy death. I am too truly unhappy to be willing to suffer thus, during the allotted space of woman's life for the sake of my children. I am not a true mother—in some things am wanting & God ought never to have given me a child. A year has wrought a great change in me. I am a much worse woman now than I was one year ago—and another child would make a *demon* of me, provided I did not end my days before the nine months expired. But this is my crazy subject and I never think of it that a ball does not rise up in my throat & threaten to choke me—but I know you are tired of this & disgusted at my egotism—but pity me when you know that I have no one to talk to, & that I am one who must give vent to my feelings in some way. I went to church last night, the baby was right good while I was gone. Sarah stayed in the house with her. She had the cholic worse yesterday evening & again this morning than she has had it for over a week. I do hope she will be well of it soon, she suffers so much. God knows her suffering after she grows to be a woman will be great enough to exempt her from all pain during infancy & childhood[.] I declare I sometimes think I had rather bury my daughters now then to live to see them mothers, & know that they felt on certain subjects like I do, for their sakes I had rather bury them now.

I came down home three days ago, found things about as I left them. The negros are doing nothing, but ours are not doing that job alone[;] nearly all the negros around here are at it, some of them are getting so high in anticipation of their glorious freedom by the yankees I suppose, that they resist a whipping. Mrs Oliver's negro cut up when Langum went to whip him lately—

old Johny Driscol attempted to whip a hired negro, & he cursed the old man all to pieces, and walked off in the woods, and then sent the old man word if he would pledge his word not to whip he would come back and work for him, he sent him word to come home, he did so, & he never touched him. Old Mrs Driscol his wife told Bill Dodd this & he told me. Bill says a great many of the people are actually affraid to whip the negros, & I believe him. Uncle Mc undertook to whip Sam, the boy he has of mothers and he run from him, he put the dogs on his track, and caught him down at our field, he run through our yard twice to deceive the dogs. The negros say they have picked over all the cotton but one cut, put it in a rail pen, have it full, waist high when they get the cotton house done[;] if that time ever arrives, I will have it weighed before it is put in the house. Thornton & Sam were 4 days last week making 860 3ft boards to cover the house and Sam pretended to have cut the tree down, & sharpened the saw one evening before Thornton commenced with him[;] they were [at it] two days, all the hands but Joe hauling the logs. The negros say Joe would not haul the logs while Sam & Thornton were splitting the boards, & then would not help them haul because lifting was harder work than picking cotton. I was gone six nights, & not one of the negros would say that Joe stayed one night at home while I was gone. Bill Dodd says John's horses are rode all over the county at night says he knows it. I believe if I was to tell Rivers to whip one of the negros they would resist & it would make matters no better so I shall say nothing, and if they stop work entirely, I will try to feel thankful if they let me alone. I won't sleep with my doors open any more, & if they break open either door or window I'll have time to be better prepared for them & will fight till I die. Every body even the most sanguine believe the yankees will be here in three or four months, and every woman I meet says, "what will become of us when the yankees come." It is all folly to talk about saving negro's, for if you hide them they can run to the yankees. I don't think we have one who will stay with us. Dr Dickson says Bing Black[19] & himself will be richer than anybody after the yanks pass through[;] they will have so many boys to work for them.

Coleman has been riding nearly two weeks, and Dodd part of the time trying to get John a substitute. Dodd says they wont talk about Confederate money. Coleman left here this morning after a man that Jeff Haynie is also

---

19. Gavin Bingley Black (39) was a farmer living with his wife, Margaret (33), and ten children in 1860. He had personal and real property valued at $8,000. TX Census 1860.

after, he says he will go for $6,500 and Coleman went to Haynie's this morning to see him and give that price. I think he is trying to get a big sum out of Jeff for the militia and after that the man can go for Confederate service. I hope Jeff will have to hire a substitute for Confederate service, he is not 45 [and] that is all the way he will help the war. [T]hey say Dickson says he is willing for peace to come on any terms, is willing to go back into the union—would you have believed it? Babe took a notion & came home with me, to go to the meeting down here, we took Bill to take care of our horses, and went in Company with Mrs Collins & Dony—Dony Collins professed religion & joined the church. We will go to night again I reckon, Babe goes home tomorrow Aunt Cinda is going with her. I fear they won't be able to get John a substitute. Oh Will I fear you will never live to see the end of this war. If we would give all we have, I don't believe we could get a substitute. I tell you I have kept as still as a mouse, about that man your Pa wrote to you about. If you find you can't stand it you will be obliged to try and get one, & then maybe that man will come in if some body else don't find him, which I hope they wont. I tell you Will these hogs in the yard are a great pest. [T]hey have broke up all my setting hens, and don't look any better than they did before you left I think. Randle brings corn but I don't know whether he gives them as much as I told him—about 14 ears at night & 14 a morning—and Joe about 50 ears a day to the hogs outside. I had the Tan trough nailed up & filled with ooze. Mrs Hutcheson & Mrs Baker[20] stoped & dined at Red neck Brown's, on the way to the Depot lately, & told Babe that Violante is as big a fool as ever, put on more airs, played on the accordion & acted the fool generally, say she talks grandly of the Neblett's, thinks they are great folks, quite different to the way *my nice kin* estimate the Scott's. It is a fine thing she has a baby, if she dident have one I would feel fearful that she would disgrace the Nebletts by turning a Magruder fool. I will leave the ballance of this sheet to scribble on in the morning, if I get a letter from you to day or to night rather. Busick Post master has been out of office, and is now gone into service. He went down to Fanthorps and opened a most terrible battery of angry words on Sallie Basset because he thought or knew that Bassett was the cause, or instrumental in

20. In 1860 Issac (60) and Aurelia (56) Baker had personal and real property valued at $80,000. They had three children: Jessie (26), Carrie (18), and Susan (15). Mrs. Hutcheson probably refers to Laura Hutcheson (22, spelled Hutchinson in the 1860 census), who was living with her husband, J. W. (30), in 1860. TX Census 1860.

having him removed from office. Howard Burton & Dr Dickson keep the office now.

Friday 14th Aug. Sure enough I did get a letter last night at church. I feel much better about you this morning. Coleman stayed all night here last night no substitute for John yet that man wants $7500 now. Your second letter has not come to hand yet, so I don't know what you have done with your cotton. Somebody took the Lake Creek mail out the week that letter came, and no body can tell any thing about it. So write me again about it. Susan sent for the Sugar and got it home, & the woman sent Susan word she did not want the corn, but wanted 1.00 in confederate money. Susan says she wont take the sugar, I cant pay the money you know. The negro's have put up the logs of the house. I saw Mrs Oliver at church last night, all well with her. Write every week certain.

Harrisburg Texas
Aug 18th/63

Dear Lizzie

Yours of the 11th inst was recd a few days since. It is really astonishing how much pleasure it gives me to receive a letter from home and although there is no news related still the fact that all are well is sufficient to make the heart thrill with joy. There is a member of Capt. Dickie's Co here who says he left Orange yesterday week. He says John Scott was well & the Co well pleased with their situation. Two letters came to John after he left both of which I forwarded to him at Orange. We arrived here on the 16th and will remain here until 1st of Sept unless some unexpected order moves us. There has been considerable insubordination among the troops in Galveston lately. Col Lucketts Reg[21] recently from the Rio Grande were furnished it seems with corn meal with worms in it. They refused to drill unless flour was furnished. Debray ordered all the troops on the Island including Lucketts out to the parade ground. All supposed it was for General Inspection but when the troops arrived Lucketts men still not suspecting anything were ordered to stack their arms, which they did. Their guns were taken away and the parade dismissed to their respective quarters. Since then Cooks Reg have demanded furlough

---

21. Philip N. Luckett was the commander of the Third Texas Infantry Regiment, which was mustered into service in 1861. The regiment never left Texas. Wright and Simpson, *Texas in the War*, 19, 163.

and are in a state of insubordination have or did in one instance turn the guns of one of the Forts on the city declaring that they would fire on the town and troops if any attempt was made to disarm them.[22] Yesterday Lucketts Reg was sent from the Island and are near here now and Browns Battallion[23] sent down. This Co received orders also to go back to Galveston yesterday but the Bayou City being out of order the order was countermanded. I fear there will be some trouble if not bloodshed before the matter is settled. Gen Magruder passed here on the way to Galveston yesterday.

There is a great deal of demoralization in the Regiments here. From what I can hear such is not the case with the troops East of the Mississippi or those who have been in active service from Texas. I notice that you are quite despondend in your last letter and am sorry to see it. For my own part I have never lost hope even for a moment and moreover I do not think it probable that Texas will be invaded within the next six months by any force formidable enough to make head against the forces in Texas and moreover I think that within the next six months France will recognize our Independence & be followed soon by England & other powers. You ask what are you to do in case the yankees get to Grimes. This is like providing for a remote contingency but still one in the limits of possibility. In such a case all the advise [sic] I can give is to harness up your horses and have the wagon & oxen to help haul what provisions &c with all the wagons. The direction you go will have to be determined by the direction the yanks come from. I do not think an attempt will be made to subjugate Texas until East of the Mis[sissippi] is subjugated & at least until our great armies are whiped & dispersed. I do not anticipate any such direful result as this, and although the fall of Vicksburg was a sad reverse

22. On August 10, 1863, there was a mutiny of the Galveston garrison involving the Third Texas Infantry Regiment. Some of Colonel Joseph J. Cook's Artillery Regiment joined the mutiny the following day. The reasons given for the mutiny were the poor condition of the food and lack of furloughs. It is interesting to note that Will, although a private, seemed to have no trouble gaining access to sufficient and quality food. Despite Lizzie's complaints of poverty, the Nebletts obviously had enough to fare better than most. On the mutiny see U.S. War Department, *The War of the Rebellion: A Compilation of the Official Records of the Union and Confederate Armies* (Washington, D.C.: U.S. Government Printing Office, 1880–1901), series 1, vol. 26, 241–48. On the poor rations for the troops see Cotham, *Battle on the Bay,* 156, 162, 178.

23. Reuben R. Brown commanded the Twelfth Texas Cavalry Battalion. In late 1863 the battalion would be restructured into the Thirty-fifth Texas Cavalry Regiment. Wright and Simpson, *Texas in the War,* 121.

of fortune & the capture of Morgan[24] one of less magnitude still I do not think such things should alarm the country into inaction or submission. You ask me what should be done on the farm. I cannot well answer the question. I want the hogs taken care of, and the pork hogs kept growing so that when the mast[25] falls they will grow fast and fatter. I also wish that piece of new ground cleared up this month if possible. I suppose you have heard something of the bagging rope twine & salt which I was to get from Houston. I want the cotton hauled to the Gin & as soon as Ginned sent to [two words obliterated] of Houston who pay the Rail Road freight on the cotton while I am to pay the freight on the Bagging Rope Twine and salt. I also wish the cotton weighed and the weights kept so that I may know how much there is. As soon as the cotton is sold buy what you wish of flour and any other things. Calico is $4.00 per yard but it is best to buy & if I am where I can get it I will buy you some. Confederate money is going down fast & I believe as soon as the war ends it will be perfectly worthless and it may be so before then. Bonds may be worth something but there will be an effort made after the war to repudiate them unless they are in the hands of foreigners and the fear of a war prevents repudiating of such as are held by them. For this reason [the] money you get for the cotton had best be spent in paying debts contracted since the war and for such things as you wish. Have the seed saved from the cotton sent to McCune I shall want at least half of it for planting next year. The balance can be used for feeding the oxen this Winter & next Spring. I agreed to let McCune have a few bushels to plant (say 4 or 5 bus).

I am glad to hear that Bettie is getting well of her cholic. I hear that there is prevailing east of Lake Creek putrid soar throat or Diptheria[26] and has been quite fatal. I feel uneasy sometimes about our children on that account. Tell Mary to write me another letter when you write again. I expect you had better try and get old Keifer to come and curry your leather about the first of Sept.

24. John Hunt Morgan was well known for his harassing raids against the Union army. He was captured during a raid in Ohio on July 26, 1863. In April 1864 he escaped and was given command of the Department of Southwestern Virginia. Morgan was killed September 4, 1864, at Greenville, Tennessee. Wakelyn, *Biographical Dictionary of the Confederacy*, 325.

25. Mast refers to nuts that accumulate on the ground that were used to feed swine.

26. Diphtheria, commonly called putrid sore throat, is a highly infectious disease. It is characterized by the production of a toxin that forms a membrane in the throat and respiratory tract. The disease causes tissue damage in the affected areas and can cause asphyxiation. Today there is a vaccine for the disease.

You can get him to do so I expect for $10. or 12.00. Get him also to blacken the calf and coon skins. I expect you had better look out for some person to make your shoes and Marys & Walters. If you could get McDonald's negro to do so at $2 or 3.00 per day it will be about as cheap as you may expect, & you may have to pay $4 or 5.00 to get shoes for yourself made fit to wear. Perhaps you had better write to Mrs Mc Donald on the subject. I am in good health.

yours affectionately
Wm H Neblett

P.S. The following is used by the soldiers here for flux[27] very sucessfully. Tea spoon full of salt and Table spoon full of vinegar with a little water to be repeated after every operation.

At Home
Aug 18th 1863

Dear Will—

I went to see Susan yesterday as she is sick been suffering 10 or 12 days with Neuralgia[28] in her face & eye she is better now. About 4 oclock yesterday evening a cloud came up a great deal of wind and the best rain we have had in three months—it rained on till after sundown, so I was forced to stay all night. I rode old Sam & Mary & Polly[29] walked; did not complain of being tired left the three boys at home. Bettie squalled with the cholic, she grows fast they all say, but I yet have more pity than love for her & try to forget that she is my child. I always think of her as being your baby & not mine. Susan got a letter from John while I was there dated 9th Aug. She gave it to me to read. I never saw any one more anxious for anything than John is for a substitute. I read both of his letters writen since he went down the last time, & tis almost the only subject of his letters—seems to be so home sick, and altho he has been

27. Flux refers to diarrhea, a common complaint in military camps during the war. Also, the bloody flux was another name for dysentery, which is characterized by fever, cramps, and diarrhea with bloody mucous evacuations.

28. Neuralgia is an acute paroxysmal pain along a nerve or group of nerves. It is most common in the face, and its causes include infection, cold, or possibly shingles.

29. Polly was a young slave girl who primarily looked after the baby, Bettie. She belonged to Lizzie Neblett's brother, Garrett. After Garrett's will was read Lizzie was forced to give Polly up to her sister Sallie, to whom Garrett had bequeathed several of his slaves. NP.

married nearly twice as long as you have, is much more lover like in his letters than you are. He writes to her that he had not heard from her since he left home, and that he has read over one of her old letters five or six times as it is the only one he has with him from her. Now any body catch you reading over the most interesting bran[d] *new* letter five or six times? I found two points of resemblance where as I never thought there was any between John and myself. His great eagerness to accomplish an undertaking (get his substitute) and his fondness for his wife, which induces both of us to read over old letters when we cant get new ones. He writes his health is improving & thinks if he don't get his substitute soon he will grow fat and fit. He was at Orange, Orange Co where he wrote & thought they would remain there some time. Neither Coleman Susan nor Bill Dodd, all in active service have been able to find a sub yet. Susan has given up the hope of finding one, and mother sent word that me or Susan must write to John and tell him that he must go before the board of Physicians & be examined and get a discharge. I think I will write to him. I know I get no credit for the affection that I feel for different members of my family, yet I know that I have more real self sacrificing affection for them, than any one of them ever felt for me unless it was from dear Garrett, & you know I loved him better than all the others put together. Babe dislikes me, & Sallie too, & they are certainly striving both of them to injure me as much as possible in the eyes of every body—but I forgive them the injury they do me, & will feel content as long as I have a few friends [t]hat know me to be all I pretend to be, and am certain of your love & esteem, if you can not always award me your respect. I forfeit all claims to it sometimes I admit[,] when the evil in me gets so big that I must give vent to it. But thank God! I am not all evil, I have my angle [*sic*] side. But how egotistical, & how certain I am to always branch off on some theory of mine or utterance of my thoughts on different subjects, which I know is contrary to your opinion of what a letter should contain. You often complain of a want of *facts* to make your letters long[;] now this always surprises me, for I let my sentiments, or the *feelings*, heart, love, & every thing in general crowd out the *facts* I have to tell, & no doubt always weary you before you reach the *plain prose* of my letters, but dear Will pity & forgive my failings no matter how numerous, on account of the fervent & faithful affection I bear you.

When I reached home this morning I found your letter of date 3rd of Aug. I cannot make out the man's name you sold your cotton to and am rather mystified about what you got the man to advance, but suppose it was 300 or 400 lbs of salt tho' why you say he promised to send them to Navasota, I cant tell.

And then you say you promised to have the cotton at Navasota by the 1st of Sept at farthest, & yet don't tell me where I am to get the bagging & rope, nor when I am to send after it. I think you left some of your facts out that time—tho I guess you meant the man would send both bagging rope & the salt to Navasota. If I had rec'd your letter when it was due, I could have got the Gov wagons to haul it from Navasota for me, as they were hauling corn from mothers to the depot & coming up empty every day—they hauled mothers salt for nothing, but you did not tell me who to send to in Navasota, nor who the articles will be directed to. You spoke before you left home of getting a sow from Pa's when I send the wagon to the depot. I fear you cant get the cotton to the depot by first of Sept. I will do the best I can but if I send I would not know who to send to, & you must remember that I dont know the name of a single house in Navasota. That everlasting cotton house is done at last, a poor affair I think. I had the cotton taken out of the pen, weighed and put in the house[;] they have picked in all, 2876 pounds, picked one day 701 pounds the six hands, and yesterday 694 & stoped about 4 Oclock, by the rain. The cotton is opening up fast, quit flowering, wont make much the farmers say—they have picked the cotton over once, & a third over the second time.

Wednesday morn, Aug 19th—Just as I put up my writing yesterday evening Coleman stepped in—& from him I learned the name of the only ware house in Nav[asota]—Thomas & Brockway, and will write & see if the articles are there before I send, & as the Gov has to haul some more corn from Mothers, perhaps Coleman can have it hauled by them for me[;] he promised to try, & perhaps will go to the depot himself this week, & will see to it. He & Susan have Old Dowdy[30] in tow now, & he has promised to go for John's sub. They made him three offers & he is now deliberating which to take, is to let them know in a day or two. 200 head of cattle $7 per head, a note for $1400 bearing ten per cent interest or $5000 in Confederate money. I am afraid he will back out. John wrote Susan that he thinks there is much demoralization in Elmore's Regt, heard men say in Co (I) that they might lead them to battle but they would not fight—this knowledge makes me more fearful of our final success than any thing I have heard. If our soldiers won't fight, for God's sake try and get out of the army if it takes all you have and come to the rescue of your family. You are naturally so sanguine and let hope deceive you till it is too late to do any thing.

---

30. There is no mention of a Dowdy in the 1860 census.

Garrett Scott speaks of joining Branch's Co. (Cavalry)[31] Garrett is in a bad way now, having risings, the worst kind. He as good as told Uncle Mc some time ago, that he had a certain *bad disease* & now he is having risings.[32] An awful boy, no pride, (only in doing as bad as he can) & no shame about him. I took the old Clock down after I came home and cleaned it out myself and then put it up & it has been running ever since & keeps excellent time, I can tell by the sun at 12. It was mighty dirty, the oil was cankered by the brass, the strike weight broke, and I fixed a new cord on that, and now it goes finely & is a vast deal of company for me, and a great use in regulating my time & the negros also. I sleep now with my doors locked, & do not suffer with fear, for I would not care if they killed me, if they did not do worse, & yet leave me alive. Oh it is so lonely here and it is no pleasure for me to visit with this crying baby of yours. I wish I had more patience with her. I think you ought to pay me liberally for raising her. I don't charge for the others, but I have no claim to her. But you will never thank me, no body will, for raising her & what is worse than all, she will thank me less than any one if she reaches womanhood. I judge her by myself. I cannot thank any body for giving me a boon that inflicts misery on me. But I hope she will partake as much of your temperament as she does of your looks, & then perhaps she will think she is doing a glorious work, bringing children into the world. She sucks her thumb, you know she has been trying all her life to get her thumb into her mouth—she sucks it now night and day, and I don't care, so it stops her mouth. I hear that Amanda White is very low, I am not surprised for she was looking awful bad when I saw her—poor Amanda she is not long for this world—she ought to live, for she has always managed to extract much sweetness from life, and never repined at her lot. John seems to think he has a good many enemy in Co (I) particularly, Bradley, Polk, & some others I don't remember the names, took an active part in keeping out his substitute. John is quite mad about it.

31. Anthony Martin Branch was born in Virginia on July 16, 1823. Five years after graduating from Hampden-Sydney College in 1842, he came to Texas. A lawyer, he served as district attorney for the Seventh Judicial District and was elected to the Texas legislature in 1859 and to the Texas senate in 1861. In 1862 he resigned his senate seat and accepted a commission in the Confederate army. He was given command of Company A of the Twenty-first Texas Cavalry Regiment, which served primarily in Louisiana. After being elected to the Second Confederate Congress, Branch resigned from the army. He died in a yellow fever epidemic in 1867. Wright and Simpson, *Texas in the War*, 151.

32. Risings could refer to any of a number of skin eruptions, but Lizzie seems to be implying the cause is some form of venereal disease.

This rain will do a good deal of good but did not give us stock water in the branches, & the earth was so parched that it wont last long. I think the negros ought to soon get done picking cotton. During this long drouth two of our yard trees have died the large red oak by the Dairy and one the other side of it I am so sorry about. During the rain & storm the other day a limb on top of that dead tree by the kitchen chimney blew off & came near falling on Sarah, she was out by [the] chimney after something. Write often give me a few more of your thoughts mixed with the facts.

Lizzie

Harrisburg Texas
Aug 22nd/63
Mrs L S Neblett

Dear Lizzie

I wrote you last Monday and am now writing in advance of my stated time (reg on Mondays) for the purpose of saying that while engaged yesterday in collecting what the Gov owed for Randal's work I learned that a lot of fellows would come to Grimes next week for the purpose of collecting the run away negroes. I wish you would send Randal down to Pa's with directions for him to stay there until I write to Pa whether and when to send him. I may take him in camps to cook or I may if I cannot avoid it put him back to work in the place he came from. I collected forty four dollars for his work. I met Charley & Dick Van Horn in Houston yesterday. We were both in the act of leaving when we met & therefore did not have much time to learn the news up the country. I was pained to learn the death of our friend Dr Malloy. He was shot in the knee in some skirmish or fight in Ark. His leg was amputated and he died soon after. I wrote to Coleman yesterday in relation to the Bagging Rope & salt which I learned that day had been shiped to Navasota care of W S Thomas 295 lbs Salt 28 yds Bagging 30 lbs of Rope. I wrote to Coleman requesting him to haul it to your mother's when he sent the corn to Navasota and that if he did not send the waggons there soon to let you know it and for you to send for the articles immediately. As soon as you get the Bagging &c send it with the cotton to McCune's and direct the negroes to haul back seed. I must close as the mail will close by the time I can get this to the office.

yours affectionately
Wm H. Neblett

Harrisburg Texas
Aug 25th/63
Mrs L S Neblett

Dear Lizzie

Yours of the 18th & 19th inst came to hand yesterday. I am somewhat surprised to hear that John takes camp life so hard[;] if his health improves & he
can stand it he is better able to be from home than thousands of others. Camp
life is very disagreeable to most men of family, particularly when they arrive at
middle age, but we should recollect who we are contending for—for our families and their safety & liberty. Men of property should by all means remain if
they can do service. For the envy of many poor men is such that when men of
property get out the army that has the effect to demoralize them. The substitutes who have been received in the army so far as my knowledge extends are
almost entirely worthless. My eyes have been opened on this subject very
lately. We have had these desertions from this Co this week. One was a substitute considered before the best one in the Co. The others were not substitutes.
I heard yesterday that the Cos of this Reg (20th Reg Tx I) now at Orange &
Nebletts Bluff have been ordered back & am expecting to see John on his way
to Galveston every day. Bates Reg[33] has arrived from La & I hear that Youngs
Reg[34] is on its way to Texas. I do not understand what this withdrawal of
troops from La means unless an invasion of Texas is expected.

I feel very certain old man Dowdy will not be received as a substitute for
they have become very strict about whom is received.

The man to whom I sold the cotton is named Wynn but he was an agent
of Peel & Dumble of Houston. I am to pay the freight on the Bagging Rope &
salt and Peel & Dumble on the cotton from Navasota to Houston. I sold for
45cts & had the Bagging & Rope furnished. I wrote to you on this subject a
few days ago & also to Coleman. The articles were sent to W S Thomas of
Navasota.

I notice that you seldom mention the name of Rivers in your letters. Does
he not attend to the negroes. Do not let old Keifer take the hides home with
him to curry for I fear they may be stolen. If he will do it all he must do it

---

33. Joseph Bates commanded the Thirteenth Texas Infantry Regiment. The regiment spent
most of the war guarding the Texas coast between Galveston and Matagorda. Wright and Simpson, *Texas in the War*, 106.

34. William H. Young commanded the Ninth Texas Infantry Regiment. Ibid., 20, 97.

where it now is. If you cannot get him you will have to send it to Mussel. It is too far to send to Ashfords. If those hogs annoy you much turn them out, but do not let them die for something to eat.

I am sorry Lizzie that you cannot take my love for you on trust without frequent renewal of the pledge. I am sure I live up to the pledge or at least I think so. Tho' I am not vain enough to suppose I am perfect in that respect and know that sometimes I may have acted in such a way as to cast suspicion upon the strength of my affections. But it is not fair to judge me by exceptional acts produced from hasty and momentary anger nor is it fair to judge me by my natural style of writing by comparing mine with that of others. The language of sentiment is much stronger in some than others, but I hold the want of the language does not disprove the existance of that feeling which gives birth to sentiment. My mind I think is of the matter of fact & reflective cast and of course dictates the style of my letters.

We will leave this place about the 1st of Sept. We are in very good health. Some cases of Flux. Kiss the children for me—particularly my Bettie. Poor thing she has no parent but me.

> yours affectionately
> Wm H. Neblett

At Home
Aug 25th 1863

Dear Will—

Altho' I see no near prospect of sending this to the office I will begin my letter now and end it when I find a chance to send it to the office. We went to bed last night, suffering from the warmth of the weather, & I awoke this morning to find myself cold. The wind is blowing directly from the north and it is cold. The children look b[l]ue and Bettie is wrapped up in her cloak, & yet looks cold. I think it is the coldest weather I ever felt in Aug. It is cloudy too, no doubt it rained some where yesterday. The ground is thoroughly dry again no sign of the rain that fell here on the 17th. I fear we will make no potatoes, but if we have a good crop of Cushaws,[35] we can make out. I love them so much that I wont let the negros destroy them all like they did last year. The children are all very fond of them. Mary and Bob started to school

---

35. Cushaws are a type of winter squash.

yesterday 24th. I think Bob is going to learn fast. He would say his lesson over three times last night before he went to bed, (a lesson in the Ab ab's) and this morning the first thing I saw was Bob seated on the hearth by the fire studying his lesson—says he wishes he had gone to school long ago. He is going to try and catch up with Bob McClure,[36] who detests his book & wont learn. I am gratified to see Bob so studious, if he will only continue so. But I often fear that Bob will not be raised or [will] die in early manhood. Bob is the only child we have who pleases me in his disposition entirely, and I do feel more sympathy for him in all his little troubles, and love him better than any of the other children. A better disposed boy never lived. I think the other children are as smart as he is—Mary will always learn, but she don't suit me in other respects, and this little crying brat of yours will I fear be much less to my taste than Mary is. I don't know how she can be a good child. I don't fear any want of intellect, if we judge by the activity of my brain, but whether it will be a laudable kind of sense is another question. I'll bet you if there is any truth in Fowlers[37] theory that her causality or reasoning prowess will be larger than the other children but the organs that govern the feelings of the heart, I fear will enlist in a way you won't like. Poor little creature, I pity her from the depths of my heart, and most heartily deplore that she was ever created. I sin in my feelings towards that child I know I do—and to love her better I continually think of her as your baby & not mine, & thus strive to forget the terrible *nine months*, with their train of thoughts & feelings, and their excruciating termination. All the gold the world has ever coined, could not tempt me to go through with it again, exactly as it was, in every particular. I believe if my brain was not well ballanced I would have gone crazy—an end I used to sigh for, to rid me of the dark despairing, sinful goading thoughts, that haunted me day and night. You never awarded me the pity I deserved, it was more anger than pity you gave—but away with such thoughts it is certain they make me no happier, nor better, neither as they alter my case one single iota.

You say in your last letter of the 18th inst that you are sorry to see or know me to be so desponding about the war—it is not only about the war, but everything. I feel like a wrecked mariner clinging to a narrow plank, amid the turbulent waves, and not [a] remote speck in sight which might be mistaken for

36. Robert McClure was the son of Lizzie Neblett's aunt Lucinda Lane Nix McClure and Mark McClure.

37. Orson S. Fowler promoted phrenology in the United States. Phrenology was the study of the shape and bumps on the skull, which supposedly revealed character and mental capacity.

a boat of deliverance. No I am stranded, let the war end as it will, I am a doomed creature. I did feel hopeful, and like there was something worth living for, during the first week or so of your absence[;] now I wonder [how] I could in the face of all the difficulties I have to contend with, feel or think otherwise than very gloomy. I was sadly dispointed last Thursday when Dony Collins came back from town and brought no letter for me. I could have cryed if the fountain of tears was not dry. I was at Susan's on the Monday before, and she got a letter from John that day and Dony brought two letters from John to her, and [I] felt then that John loved Susan much more than you loved me. I had just read his loving letter to her too. I often feel that I don't deserve your love, yet I know & can say without flattering myself that I am more deserving of your love than Susan is of John's. Well I had to wait impatiently until sat night I sent up to get the mail sunday. Randal started sat night & reached there just as Warner[38] was ready to start down here with Susan's mine & Aunt Cinda's mail sent by Coleman. They reached here Sat night 12 Oclock, and woke Kate up, and handed in the papers & letters. I found one from you, of date 18th inst, and one to Coleman about the thing at Navasota. I was glad to hear from you, and to find you still hopeful amid all the difficulties & reversals. I do envy you your disposition.

I started Thornton to the Depot this morning, would have sent yesterday but the oxen had to be got up and the wagon run into the lake to tighten the tyres, all of them are loose & all have to be cut Thornton says. He thinks he can haul the cotton to the Gin with the wagon just as it is and after that job is through I'll send it up to mothers & have it fixed. The negros have got through picking over the cotton the second time, worked one day in the clearing, & Rivers sent me word that he would swap work with me, so I thought it best to send our five hands over to pick cotton for Hurst, and he will return the work in clearing. I don't think they were doing or would do much in the clearing alone, & Rivers don't go into our field upon an average once a week, and as he has our hands with his, I thought he would stay with them & see that they picked cotton & then see that they done good work in the clearing, and I droped him a note letting him know that I expected him to oversee them when they returned the work in the clearing. *Rivers is no count.* Sarah was with a negro girl of Mr Hursts a few nights ago, and her child is white, Mrs Hurst & all the negros said it was River's, & one old negro woman called out

38. Warner was a slave of Lizzie's mother, Sarah Scott.

to Rivers to "come in & see his fine daughter" he asked who was in there on finding out nobody but Sarah was there went in and said to Sarah, "let me see my fine daughter," which she took up & exibited to him, when he said "By God I must go to town & buy it a coat." Detestable puke! I feel like I never want to speak to him, no wonder he avoids decent ladies. I don't think either negro's or white people care any more for him than a dog. He has an other child at Hursts, four or five years old, born when he stayed with them in Fla. He was gone three days last week pretending to look for a beef, but instead of that went to town got drunk, got no beef. Mrs H would not begin to have him if she could get any body else.

I rec'ed a letter yesterday eve from Serena Jemigan, containing the sad news of Dr Malloy's death. He was wounded in the leg in one of the recent battles in Ark so badly that the leg had to be amputated, after it was cut off he died. I am truly sorry to hear of it, he was very kind to us in the sickness of Bob & Walter, and I have ever since held him in greatful remembrance. Poor fellow, I hope & believe that he is in Heaven. She writes that old man Pugh had $3000 in gold stolen from him recently that it was all he had, & no body to work for him, his sons all in the army, no more news of any consequence in her letter. Dick Van Horn stayed all night at mothers the 15th inst on his way to Houston trading, had a negro man for sale & something else, brought me seven flour sacks, all cut to pieces by the mice Aunt Cinda says, I havent seen them. What became of the other six is more than I'll ever know. Aunt Cinda was there when he came, & says he told mother a long string to tell me about your business, but she could not tell it all to me, but enough to know that he has not sold your cotton nor had it gined. I am going to try and go up to mothers friday evening, go by the school & take the children in, & stay until sunday evening. I'll finish this letter after reaching there & tell you what Van Horn said. I have kept an account of what cotton they have picked and it all now amounts to 5636 pounds. Mrs Hurst's cotton is turning out better than ours, the negros say it has opened more than ours, & more bowls on it. Marke Kennard[39] started to Orange with John's sub old Dowdy who is going for 200 head of cattle 50 cows 50 calves, 50 2 year olds & 50 yearlings, John can't furnish half. They tell me that they loose [*sic*] nearly or quite half of their calves every

---

39. Marcus L. Kennard (age 37, spelled Kinnard in the 1860 census) was a farmer with real and personal property valued at more than $32,000. He was married to Martha Helen E. Walker (24). TX Census 1860; Mullins, *Grimes County, Texas, Marriage Records.*

year, Mother and Coleman help out with what Susan lacks & Coleman took Dowdy before Dr Kerr and he thinks they will take him as a substitute.

Friday eve Aug 28th—My visit to mothers is I guess all cancelled on the hold. Bettie Scott & Mary Eliza Goodrich[40] came down to Jim Rogers wednesday evening, Bettie was at John's yesterday, & I think perhaps will be over here tomorrow, I don't like to stay home on her account but as she comes so seldom & knows that I know of her being down I had best stay. I had several jobs to perform at mothers get a slate for Mary and a Testament, have a rope made for old Sam and some other matters, but I will have to defer it 'till next friday. Well, I like to broke my neck getting Thornton off to the depot, sent him by Pa's to stay all night, and when he got there Pa told him that Mr Coleman had stayed there a few nights before & said he had sent the Bagging rope & salt to Anderson, so he came back to Anderson here then was gone to the Depot, had to wait till night for his return to get the Bagging &c and got home that night 5 Oclock almost day. Coleman did not send me word that he was going to the depot, nor any thing about it only the letter you wrote. Next day, I was going to make them load with the cotton for the Gin, & Thornton said one of Martins negro's said his master had just failed to get ginning done at McCune's Gin, so I thought it best to send & find out if yours could be ginned immediately. Mrs McCune sent me word that McCune was in Militia Camps (some one told me he drew clean) and nobody there to attend to it—so that stopped me from sending. She said that McCune told Coleman that he could not Gin your cotton. I don't know what to do now. I thought it was a settled thing that he was to Gin your cotton as soon as you sent it with the Bagging. I will try Dr Brown, and will send to McCune's again, she did not write & perhaps McCune was only gone to Camps that day to be back the next, I wrote him a note, but you know he would not trouble him self to send me any word about it when he comes home. If you had not promised to let the man have the cotton I believe I would not do another thing about it. If I send it to Alston's, he *will take so much toll,* I know there wont be five bales of it. I don't know what to do, and wish most heartily that you were at home to ride around & see about it & get it done.

I am so sick of trying to do a man's business when I am nothing but a poor contemptible piece of multiplying human flesh tied to the house by a crying

---

40. Mary Eliza Goodrich (28) was living in the household of Benjamin Briggs Goodrich (62) in 1860 and had personal and real property valued at $15,000. TX Census 1860.

young one, looked upon as belonging to a race of inferior beings as Swift[41] says scarcely a degree above a monkey & not half so diverting. God knows I wish I had been placed in my grave before I ever brought one of my sex in this world. Had I died then you might have loved & cherished my memory, now, you would be like Coleman, hunting a better monkey before I was dead six months—no I take that back I don't think you would make a fool of yourself about marrying at least. "A burnt child ought to dread the fire."[42] But I stop. Altho I have been all day long entertaining myself with a train of thought some thing like the above, yet I did not intend to entertain you in the same way. I have to day been thinking about you calling me a fool about the old cradle to rock, what I never wanted, & would never have had, if it had not been to pleasure you. It is not your way to say you are sorry for any thing you ever did or said. I don't ask you to compromise your dignity so much in my case, but if I am of an inferior order, I have as much sensibility of feeling as you have—but away, I don't like to think of it. I have a great mind to get Morphine & take it, see if I will not be happier. 'Twill make a woman forget her woe 'twill highten all her joy wont it? If it shortens my life, it will be an end most devoutly wished.

Nelia wrote me a note by Thornton & sent your saddle bags home. She says Mittie's children have had the Hooping cough[43] the baby three weeks, the boy 2 weeks, goes right hard with them. Nelia thought she had it once, but she has had it only a week, hoops good fashion now. According to your orders I still keep Randle here I have inquired of several & hear no talk of those fellows being about, & Mr Oliver who came over with Mrs O. the other evening said he did not think they were coming, so I will instruct Randle to leave for Pa's as soon as he hears any talk of them being about, but that wont do any good for they will take an other in his place I think, thinking that he had just dodged out of the way from them.

Dear Will—In spite of all difficulties I came to Mothers this morning.

41. Lizzie is referring to Jonathan Swift's "Letter to a Young Lady on Her Marriage," first printed in Swift's *Miscellanies,* vol. 2, 1727 ("I cannot conceive you to be Human Creatures, but a sort of Species hardly a degree above a Monkey; who has more diverting Tricks than any of you").

42. "Burnt child fire dredth" is a proverb of unknown origin. It appears in John Heywood's *Proverbes,* printed in 1546.

43. Whooping cough or pertussis is an infectious disease of the respiratory system. It is distinguished by coughing and noisy inhalations with a characteristic "whoop" sound. Severe cases can lead to pneumonia, convulsions, or brain damage. Today there is a vaccine for the disease.

Havent time to tell you the reasons that let me off. Mother had just finished reading your letter of 22nd when I came. Coleman tells me that McCune joined the Militia, to keep from being Conscripted I suppose, part of them are going to return home & stay awhile, & if it comes to his turn first to return that he will see about it and Gin your cotton if possible. Mother is going to town this evening to swear that she cant get an overseer & will thus retain C[oleman] and pay $500. No late news from John. You have seen the list of Causualitys in Hutchesons Co. Mrs Patrick's sore distressed about her only son Rudolf Beeker.[44] Poor fellows I fear there will not be one left to tell the tale of that brave tho' unfortunate Comp. Why did you not send me that little book about the ear? Send it first chance. My other ear is now seriously affected, cant hear much out of it when I first get up 'till about 8 or 9 Oclock it seems to burst open. In less than ten years if I live I expect to be without ears and teeth. My ears trouble me, the continual and roaring and deafness is truly distressing. Charley Van H is up here again, after Babe I guess tho' he pretends to be out in quest of corn & Bacon, don't tell who for. As you saw Van Horn I need not tell any thing he said. Sallie Bassett has been out here to see mother, to get board out here, I cant write you all she said, but mother asked her if she was to take her what would she do when I came here she said *"shut the door in her face" she never expected to speak to me.* Now it will be late in the day before she has the chance. I'll tell you more about it when I write again, am hurryed now to get this off to town. Mother would not take her to board.

Sat eve, Aug 29th 1863.

Pelican Spit
Sept 3rd/63
Mrs L S Neblett

Dear Lizzie

Yours of the 25th and 29th arrived yesterday evening. I have been deferring writing for several days in expectation of one from you & therefore for the first time since I have been here failed to write on Monday when here and Tuesday when at Harrisburg in order that my letters might always get to Anderson on Wednesday night with the Weekly paper mail from Houston. I concluded that

---

44. Rudolf Beeker (18, spelled Rudolph in the 1860 census) was the son of Augusta Patrick and the stepson of Dr. George M. Patrick. TX Census 1860.

you had no regular time for sending to the office & for that reason was not as particular about the time as I have been heretofore. I believe it does not give you as much pleasure to get letters from me as it does me to receive them from you. There may be several reasons for this and among them the fact that yours brings news of all the children besides of yourself while mine is only of myself. Besides this there is one other and that is my letters never have been satisfactory to you in expressions of sentiment. In one thing I claim a superiority and that is the virtue of forgiveness or rather perhaps of forgetfulness of foibles or failings in you which I have long since observed you never do. You also hold an oral expression of repentance indispensable. While I contend that acts at variance with any former acts of unkindness is [a] better indication of repent at unkind words than mere words. I believe I understand you but I know you do not and never have comprehended my character in some respects. Then there is another difference[:] you doubt and suspect when you are not positive in regard to me and my thoughts and actions whereas I test you by a milder standard. It seems strange to me that you still seem not to know me after so many years of matrimony. This is not the first time this thought has occurred to me. In regard to that one thing which gives you so much unhappyness you may make yourself easy. I think it not only possible but probable that we can live together and have no more children. I am willing to make sacrifices for your happiness or peace even if it results in unhappiness for me. But this is a subject better to talk of than to write about.

I am writing on board of the boat with a fiddle screaming in my ears. I have no other place to write now. On arriving here we found our old comfortable quarters occupied by three companys. We have therefore been compelled to sleep on board or on the wharf. To day we received tents and have been engaged this morning in [stretching] them. We miss our old quarters much and particularly do I miss and need a mattress. I want you to make me one and I will contrive to get it down within the next month by some one if I do not have a chance of coming home within that time, which I think very uncertain. One width of board is wide enough and four yards and a half will be enough to make a matress sufficiently long. A thin one made of cotton & shucks is what I want. I thought for some time I would get the one John had & would have done so while in Harrisburg but heard & in fact saw the order for the Cos at Orange & Nebletts Bluff to return to Galveston. I expect John back to the Island in a few days. I doubt much if he succeeds in getting his substitute received. In regard to the demoralization existing in Co I it is confined almost entirely to persons from the Sandy Creek settlement who I understand were

Unionist at first. Two of the deserters of whom I wrote you have returned. Our commanders here have snuffed danger in the distance or at least pretend to do so. Martial law goes into force over Galveston & vicinity on the 10th and familys are warned to leave & facility [is] offered by the Gov to do so.

Write me what you need & when I return to Harrisburg (on the 16th) I will get them. I noticed when in Houston that Brilliantine white was selling at $3.00 per yd & callico at $4. and 4.50 do you want a white Brilliantine dress. You had better take 50lbs of that sugar at John's for it is difficult to get less than a barrel in Houston & troublesome to do even that for most of it is put up in Hogs heads I hardly think it could be purchased by 50lbs at less than $1.00 there. I am glad to hear that the children have started to school and particularly that Bob likes his books. I thought he would not. I want to see the children as much as I do you. If nothing takes place to change the usual current of our course I hope to be at home in about six weeks from this time but do not permit myself to build to[o] much on this hope for fear of disappointment. I know every thing is wraped in uncertainty & mystery connected with military matters. The news of the occupation of Monroe La by six or seven thousand yankees induces me to believe the time not distant when they will attack this place or some other point in Southern Texas.[45]

The division that Robert is in will have to fight the yankees now in Monroe I expect. The cold weather you speak of was felt by us very seriously. I caught a cold & had a severe sore throat—had to have it cauterized—was sick with head aches for four or five days—in fact was not at myself until yesterday. I fear that in using the wagon without cutting the tyres on the hind wheels that they will break. If I were at home I would have it done the first thing. It should have been done when you sent after the salt. If the wheels get broken I do not know when you can get them mended. Tell Mary I will write to her in my next to you. I have some curiosity to know how your Mother received Sally B[assett] & what she said to her. I do not suppose we will know much. If you need any of the ingredients to make composition let me know I would like to get some. Mine is about out. I can get Ginger here at 50 cts a paper.

yours affectionately
Wm H. Neblett

45. There were Union forces operating near Monroe, Louisiana, between August 20 and August 28, 1863. The city itself was not captured. Long, *Civil War Day by Day*, 399.

Pelican Spit (Fort Jackson) Texas
Sept 7th/63
Mrs L S Neblett

Dear Lizzie

Altho' I have not rec'd any letter since yours of the 29th I permit myself to indulge the hope strongly that I will get one by Oliver who is expected this evening. He went to get recruits but I think he will fail in getting even one. Gen Magruders orders to the Militia Cavalry has no doubt caused consternation to the hearts of many of the Militia & indicates a disposition by Magruder to be prepared for the worst if it should come. For my own part I have seen nothing to lead me to the belief that we are in great danger of a formidable invasion. In fact it would not surprise me if the state escaped entirely this Fall & Winter. The Fort at this place is about completed—has the large guns mounted & ready & will receive two more. It has been christened Fort Jackson. We have one gun on the Bayou City every thing is progressing rapidly to a readiness to repell an attack. About half the Co now sleep & stand gard the Boat every night. Notwithstanding all this preparation I do not think there is any strong prospect of an immediate attack. We are in our tents & find them very hot in the day & quite cool in the night.

When I wrote to you last I stated that I expected John Scott in Galveston soon. That order has been countermanded & his Co will probably remain at Orange. A man by the name of Neel belonging to this Co who returned from Bill Dodds lately tells me that he thinks Dowdy will be received as a substitute & if so John may be at home before this. I cannot imagine why it is that John takes camp life so hard. He is certainly paying a large price but I expect he calculates that it will not be out his pocket. He is lucky in not getting his substitute in before the draft or he would have been compelled to go into the Militia that is if his sub was under fifty years of age. If McCune is not in the Militia Cavalry he will be at home enough to have the cotton ginned. I wish you would make Joe examine the box in the Buggy wheels & if they are loose send the Buggy to Joe Collins & get him to wedge and tighten them. If it is not done the wheels may get injured. Your Mothers boy Turn may do the job if you are up there. Have they commenced on the clearing yet? How are the hogs doing? and is there enough mast to fatten them.

If McCune does not gin the cotton you will have to get Alston to do so & in that event have it weighed as it is put in the wagon & instruct him to not mix the seed with other kinds of seed. Dr Brown told me he could not gin the cotton as his pick room was full of cotton.

I came to town since writing the above but have not time to write more. Oliver did not come to day & I have recd no letter.

yours affectionately
Wm H. Neblett

Fort Jackson Galveston Texas
Sept 15th/63
Mrs L S Neblett

Dear Lizzie

Altho' I wrote to you by Jack Oliver only a few days since I think it my duty to write you this soon on account of the threatening aspect of affairs when I last wrote you. Nothing of importance has transpired here since I last wrote you. At last accounts from Sabine Pass the Yankee vessells were not to be seen. A courier who passed here two days since says the beach is strewn with bacon dried apples candles &c from Sabine Pass 35 miles West. It is also said that the same sight may be seen near the mouth of the Brazos and that two horses & a dead Yankee was washed ashore near there. Every indication goes to prove that a naval engagement has occurred in the Gulf near here.[46] The Co that John was in did not reach Sabine Pass in time for the fight. I have heard nothing from him since then. He left his matress in Houston & gave me permission to get it but it is too large—wide. I was expecting his Co back every week & therefore did not get it.

I wrote to Peel & Dumble yesterday [to] inform the[m] why I did not have the cotton out to Navasota by the 1st of Sept & asked them if they still would receive it. I directed them to address me at Anderson in order that you may get it soon. If they decline to receive the cotton & it has not been sent to the Gin do not send it until you hear from me again for by not ginning it the Gov will be kept from pressing it. I suppose you have seen the call for 1/2 of the negroes between 16 and 50. I suppose they will not be kept long but there is no certainty in this. Do not send any volunteerilary. I suppose you have sent Joe to shell corn. Jack Oliver told me that he saw some of my hogs between

46. On September 8, 1863, Union ships attacked the fort at Sabine Pass. The Federals withdrew after one ship was compelled to surrender and two more were crippled.

the Gelmore field & Garretts creek. Have them taken care of[.] Bacon retails here at $1.50 pr lb Butter $1.50 lb dried peaches $2.00 pr quart. Coffee 50 a cup small chickens $1[.]25 to 1.50 a small pie $2.00 and every thing in proportion. I sent you by Jack Oliver one ball thread one thimble & not my get in change. I delayed writing this till very late in order to hear the news but have learned nothing. It is now growing so late I can hardly see to write & must close & start this to town early in the morning.

yours affectionately
Wm H Neblett

copy. Fort Jackson, Galveston Bay Texas[47]
Sept 19th 1863

Dear Lizzie:

Yours of the 11th and 12th bearing a post mark of the 17th was handed me this morning on landing at the wharf from the Bayou City. I came near never receiving it, and the last one I wrote you came equally in near being my last. But I will not speak in enigmas. Yesterday evening a portion of the guard started for the Bayou City, which had been compelled to leave the wharf on account of high winds, and roughness of the water. She lay at anchor about a half a mile off. The first boat load had but a few men in it, and arrived at the Bayou City after sunset half filled with water. It returned with one sailor at

---

47. This letter is a copy of one written from Will Neblett to Lizzie Neblett. The original is not in the collection. Lizzie Neblett wrote the following on the envelope of the copied letter: "This envelope contains a copy of a letter writen on Sept 19th 1863 by Wm H Neblett while he was located on Pelican Island near Galveston and serving with his Co. which was taken from Col Elmores Regt. for the purpose of guarding the Bayou City gun boat which was stationed in the gulf channel to prevent the Yankee gun boats from capturing Galveston City. This letter gives a history of the sinking of the small boat that carried the guard, from Pelican Island to the Bayou City, and the narrow escape they made from drowning on night of Sept 18th 1863. In the 49 years since the letter was writen, many of the words have faded and are so dim it is difficult to read the letter. This April 29th 1912, copied at Austin Texas. I gave the original letter to R[obert] S N[eblett]." Lizzie also wrote the following words at the top of the copied letter: "Copy of letter writen to me a few days after my husband Wm H Neblett had been in a sinking boat with the crew from Pelican Island who were going to the Gun Boat Bayou City anchored off Galveston Island as a guard, to prevent the Yankee gun boats slipping in, and taking Galveston City. This was Sept 19th 1863. April 29th 1912 now almost 49 years ago. The original letter I gave to R S N in May 1912. L. S. N."

the helm and one at the oars to the wharf just about dark. This time nine of our Co, which with the two sailors made eleven men got in, sinking her down within six inches of the top. The wind was blowing hard from the North and, the Bay so rough that it was difficult to get in the boat without falling down. In this condition we put off from the wharf and had not gotten fifty yards when waves commenced breaking over us and throwing at least half dozen buckets full of water each time. I saw at once she was going to sink and told the man at the helm to go back, but none of the rest said any thing and he did not notice me. None of the rest said a word and seemed not to see the danger. As soon as I found he would not go back, I untied the strings of the grey blanket you fixed for me (for I had it on to keep the spray from wetting me) and untied my shoes and commenced bailing the boat with a wool hat belonging to one of the soldiers. Two more were at the same thing with their shoes. The boat was now half full and we had got within one hundred yards of the Bayou City, when a large wave struck her and filled her, and she sunk like lead from under us and stood with one end straight up about eighteen inches high. Some of the men pitched into the water head foremost. I sat still and was let down in the water as the boat went from under me, and I seized an oar which some of the men had dropped in their fright. The next wave ran over me, and I recollect taking one swallow of salt water, [a]nd dashed me up against the end of the boat, which still floated. I siezed a rope with my left hand, and held the oar in my right, and soon learned to hold my breath and shut my mouth when a wave broke over us, which was about every minute.

Some one on the Bayou City saw our boat as she sunk, and in about ten minutes Captain Lubbuck[48] with two sailors picked up these men, who had very foolishly attempted to swim against the waves and a rapid tide to the Bayou City. Two of these men were so nearly drowned that they could not stand, altho' they had not been in the water more than ten minutes, these were carried to the boat and the small boat returned after more. We had by this time drifted a quarter of a mile. The small boat made its appearance a second time and halted about twenty steps off, when Capt Lubbock told us two or three times for us to come one at a time and be helped in, and that if more than one came to his boat, he would push him off with an oar, and we must stop coming when he said stop. I could have gone to the boat then, but the

---

48. Henry Lubbock, brother to the governor of Texas, commanded the *Bayou City*.

two strongest sailors could not swim. They happened to be seated in the end of the boat which floated, and held on to it from the beginning to the end, and kept the rest of us alarmed all the time lest they should loose their hold and seize some of us and drown us. The small boat had to come up and they got in leaving a young man named Brenan, and Fulton and myself. We had by this time got so far from the Bayou City that this load started for Pelican Island to land them there as nearest. When the boat left us we had been in the water more than an hour, but now there was but three of us, we held on very easily and I had learned to keep from strangling. I had by this time become very much chilled. I asked Fulton if he was cold and he replied that he was so chilled that he could not hold on much longer. I told him I was in the same fix. Young Brenan lay with his arms on the boat moaning at a most piteous rate and never sa[y]ing a word to either of us. The boat had been gone full half an hour and we had been expecting it back some time. I told Fulton that I expected the boat had missed us, as we were drifting rapidly up the channel, and we must halloo, or they never would find us in the dark and amid the high waves.

It was just at this time that I first felt alarmed. I saw that if the boat missed us or if she had sunk in carrying the last load, that we would drift up the channel in the dark, get gradually chilled and exhausted until we would be lost. I hallood as loud as I could, but my teeth chattered at such a rate, that I could not be heard amid the waters but a few steps. I told Fulton he must halloo to enable the boat to find us. He yelled out finely and when he would forget to halloo, I would remind him of it. I had now a good hold on the boat and had plenty of time to think of you and all the children. I recollect distinctly of thinking of all the children separately except Bettie. I do not recollect of thinking of her, perhaps because I have not been in the habit of doing so for as long a time as the others.[49] I wondered what would be the fate of you and [the] children in this war. I did not think of my own hereafter, but I had not lost all hope. Just as the ray of hope was getting very dim, Fulton saw the boat approaching us very rapidly. We got in by the assistance of the boatmen, for we were too much chilled to do so alone, or even to stand alone. We were rowed to the boat, and by the time we reached there our little boat was half filled with water. We learned afterwards that the boat in carrying the second

---

49. The following was added to the letter at a later date: "Lizzie as we call her now was then only four months old."

load was filled with water in landing and had to be bailed out before it came after us, and for that reason was so much longer coming than we expected.

Sept 21st—Yesterday I felt as well as I ever did in my life—did not drink as much water in our scrape as most did, a majority vomited up large quantities of water, while I was not affected in the slightest degree. It was nine Oclock when we reached the boat. To day my old back or spinal affection is upon me and I can hardly walk. As soon as I finish this I will have it rubed with peper and vinegar.

There were many ludicrous things happening while we were in the water, but I have already been too minute, and must drop it until I can see you. When that will be I do not permit myself to fix upon any definite period. A few days ago we had it reported here that the Yankees had landed near Sabine in large numbers, but since it has been ascertained that there are no Yankee vessels to be seen there except the old blockading squadron.[50]

You are right in not selling your Piano. Van Horn asked me the same thing when I saw him in Houston and I told him it was not for sale. My pen is very bad—send me two of those brass pens in your next letter.

There is no Yellow fever in Galveston but we have a good deal of mild cases of fever here and on the Boat, and some cases of flux but none have proven fatal. I can buy you some paper, but do not know how I can send it to you. I prefer greatly long letters even if I do not always write them myself. Paper is five dollars a quire in Galveston. What are you to do for calico dresses? I could buy you one with what money I have on hand, and have a few dollars left, but how am I to get it to you? It is worth from $4 to $7 dollars per yard I am told. In relation to the cotton I have nothing more to say in addition to what I said in my last. I expect from what you say that the deer are eating up the potato vines and if so I do not know what can be done to prevent it, unless you get Rivers to fire hunt for them a few times. If it rains you must have the vines raised, so they will not take root in the ground. The corn which has blown down should be leaned against other stalks, to keep it from rotting when it rains, but it would be best to do this soon *after* a rain. I do not know how I am to get the matrass here that you are making for me, but will try and do so some how before cold weather, if the Yankees do not make us march from here. If we have to march, [the] matrass will have to be dispensed with. What

50. This is most likely erroneous information stemming from the failed September 8 attack by Union vessels at Sabine Pass.

do you think is the matter with Walter that he falls off in flesh? I must send some of my summer clothes home the first chance.

> Yours affectionately
> Wm H Neblett
> {I gave the original letter to R S
> Neblett Corsicana in 1912.}

Pelican Spit Galveston Bay
Sept 24/63

Dear Lizzie

The arrival of Daniel Bookman[51] at our camps to day offers me an opportunity of sending you some money and you will find enclosed forty dollars which you can use in such manner as you see proper. But I think you had better at least buy one calico dress for I know you must need it badly and when the cotton is sold you can buy another & such other things as you desire. Mr Bookman tells me that Thigpen has calico & paper which he sells cheaper than can be had here or in Houston or Anderson. He says you can get calico at $4 or 5 per yard. Thigpen has his goods at Edmundsons near Red Top. I wrote to you on the 22nd and can not say more now for in the first place I am suffering with a head ache and my old back complaint as badly as I ever had it and can only creep about very cautiously.

I lost my blanket shoes & socks in my ship wreck scrape. My blanket (the one your Mother gave me and you fixed is the one I lost[)]. I drew from the Gov a spanish blanket in the place of the one I lost but those blankets are so narrow that I shall sell it or send it to your Mother in place of the mate to the one she gave me for they are much narrower than the one I lost and are not so warm—so narrow in fact that I cannot turn over without uncovering a portion of my back. I would like to have it fixed like the one I lost. It is so convenient and comfortable in standing guard in the wind & rain but I shall not need it before winter. I enclose to you five dollars more making forty five dollars in all which you will find in this. Get some paper with a portion of it. It is getting late and I must stop and have my spine rubed with vinegar and pepper. If I were able I would go to town early in the morning with Mr Bookman

---

51. In 1860 Daniel Bookman (age 50) was married to Susan (45) and was a farmer with personal and real property valued at $20,685. TX Census 1860.

and buy and send the ingredients for making Composition & would like to send home some of [my] summer clothing but understand he is troubled with too much already. He tells me that he has heard that his son Isaah Bookman[52] was killed in a skirmish with the enemy near Culpeper Va but does not believe the report. Kiss Bettie & the children for me. Just as I was signing my name to this yours of the 17th was handed me. I will reply to it in a few days. If you can manage to make that exchange (it is too far to haul cotton to your Ma's to gin in the place of the cotton she would swap). If you cannot get it ginned soon make the exchange with Coleman and send to Navasota immediately.

yours affectionately
Wm H. Neblett

Pelican Spit Galveston Bay Texas
Oct 5th/63
Mrs L S Neblett

Dear Lizzie

I have been sadly disappointed in not receiving a letter from you in the last few days. One was due day before yesterday. When I wrote you last a week ago to day I told you I anticipated an equinoxial storm. Sure enough it came that evening and night. I and some ten or twelve others moved out [of] our tents in the morning & took up quarters in the upper story of our old barracks but many remained until evening and were run from their tents by the waves running over the beach where the tents were. That night the water ran over the whole island from one to two feet deep. The house we were in shook like a reed from the wind. At one time if the wind had changed suddenly to the North it is probable every house and every human being would have been swept away into the Gulf. Many of us thought of Lost Island and the ill fated Nautilus and did not sleep until late in the night but after a while all fell asleep to be awakened occasionally by the shaking of the house. Our tents had to be removed to keep them from being swepted away by the water.

Last night a bearer of dispatches [came] from Sabine Pass. We did not see the dispatches but learned from the bearer that all our troops at Sabine Pass

---

52. There is some confusion over Isaah Bookman's name. He is listed in the 1850 census as Isaah. In the 1860 census there is a J. M. Bookman of the correct age who was killed September 20, 1863, at Chickamauga. Apparently Isaah Bookman was also called Bob.

except those in the forts had taken up the line of march towards La to meet Gen Taylor's[53] army which was falling back towards Texas followed by the Yankee army. If this news is true I suppose agents will be in the country soon to get half the negroes and if so I expect it would be best to let Sam and Joe go. They are the ones whom I would soonest expect to runaway & go to the Yankees and would probably be safer with the army than at home in case of an invasion. But send whom you please if the impressing officer comes but do not let them (the negroes) know it. Under the circumstances it would be best to gather the corn as soon as possible if the cotton is not wasting too much. In case of an invasion of Texas with a formidable army every thing will be thrown into confusion and it will therefore be difficult to have anything done. It would therefore be best to have shoes for yourself and all the children made as soon as you can. Do not make the mistake I did last year in taking their measures over their *bare feet* and consequently were too small. Bobs and Billys should be made out of something thicker than thin calf skin. Those two small calf skins should be saved for yours Marys and Walters shoes this Fall and next Spring. Have you ever heard how those two hides at Dr Browns are doing or when they will be ready. Did you ever get a large cow and calf up [that] ran at Joe Collin's mill. If she lost her calf this year as she did last, it will be best to make beef of her this Winter if she gets fat enough. She is not any account for milk.

The storm last monday came near ruining the Fort at this place. The water washed down about half the front and it will take 100 hands a month to repair it. It is not more than half as strong as it was before the storm. The forts on Galveston Island I understand were not seriously injured. You need not send the matrass or any clothing to me until I write you when and how to send. I shall need nothing in the way of clothing except a pr of pants this Winter and perhaps a vest. I shall try and send my summer clothing home by the first one that goes from this Co on sick furloughs. I have gotten over that attack of Rhumatism & stood guard night before last in the North wind without any ill effects. A few days ago I saw your Mothers negroes Wash and Hiram on board the steam boat Col Stell at this place. They appeared to be in fine health. Wash looked fatter than I ever saw him and both were well clothed. Hiram said in answer to my questions that he liked steam boating first rate. News

---

53. Richard Taylor commanded the District of West Louisiana. Long, *Civil War Day by Day*, 253.

came here last night that four Co of Elmores Regt and four Co of Cooks Regt have been ordered to Sabine. There are already four Co of this Reg there & if four more are ordered it will leave only two here which we suppose will be Stephensons & Bennetts. We will be apt to hear about it this evening on Dress parade if the news is true. Do not swap any more work with Rivers until he returns what he owes[.] I fear in case the negroes are impressed he will not be able to repay what is now due. I enclose an article signed "Private" written by me while at Harrisburg. I did not like the article after writing it & kept it some time before sending but was too lazy to rewrite. I also send an article to "Literary men and women" I shall not make an effort to respond. Perhaps you may. Under the present aspect of affairs all hope of seeing you and children is banished for a while and I fear it may be a long while at that. Even sick furloughs are rarely granted now. It is harder for those who are sanguine in temperament to yield up a cherished hope than those [who] are not so much so. Good bye & kiss the children for me. The news of the order of 4 Co of this & Cook Reg to go to Sabine Pass has been denied also of the movement of our army to La is also denied. Probably it is all unfounded. I recd yours of 27 yesterday eve just in time to write this & send it to the office. Hurry that cotton to Navasota as soon as possible. If you can exchange it for cotton already baled do so at once. I fear the Gov will commence impressing all the cotton & then Peel & Dumble will not receive it. If you could swap one of those new sides of leather for sole leather it would go much farther. I am sleeping with Bookman—and doing very well at present.

Yours affectionately
Wm H. Neblett

Galveston Bay Texas
Oct 13th/63
Mrs L S Neblett

Dear Lizzie

Yours of the 1st and 3rd inst was received several days since and I would have written before this but was taken with a fever last Friday night and to day is the first time I have been well enough for that effort. My fever was not very severe but was somewhat of a remittant character and I thought for a while that I would have Typhoid fever before it was through but was clear of it yesterday and today. I think I had poor medical treatment or I would have been well before. No doubt this will bring to mind your dream of my sickness and what is singular about it (you speak of my mouth being parched and dry) is the fact that during my sickness my tongue has been remarkably dry and coated but I fear I shall not have a chance of having Bettie in my arms soon. Now you know I do not believe in dreams unless it is after they are fulfilled[;] yours came nearly to pass or did in part. But when I come home and say that I am not going back I shall th[e]n think I have realized a a [*sic*] glorious dream. The peaches you sent have served me an excellent purpose I have used about a quart of them this spell of sickness.

When I recd yours stating that the cotton had been started to Peel & Dumble I wrote to Owen Cochran and requested him to draw the money from them & hold it subject to my or your order. In reply to my question he gives the following "Texas sugar sells at 50 cts by the hdds[54] & other sugar for 75 to $1 by bbl. A good article can be had at 90 cts. Mollasses $1.60 to $1.80 per bbl and not plentiful. (which is 4 to 4.50 pr gal) Bleached domestic $6 to 7 and calico $5 pr yd." If you cannot do better in Grimes you will have to get in Houston. I am writing in a very uncomfortable place and must therefore be short. I will write again in two or three days. Braggs victory[55] is very cheering news and makes some of the croakers hush for a while. Tell Mary I will write to her in a few days. She has improved greatly.

yours affectionately
Wm H. Neblett

At home Thursday eve
Oct 15/63

Dear Will,

Altho' I am as busy as I can be working on your blanket in order to get it fixed so I can try it on Coleman when I am at mothers sat, yet I must stop and write some on my weekly letter, else I won't get it off in due time, & in this matter I am punctillious, for I know what a depressing feeling a failure [to get] a letter brings to me, & I judge you by myself. I am anxiously looking for a letter from you now[;] it is now 10 days since your last that came to hand was

---

54. A hogshead was a barrel holding between 63 and 140 gallons.

55. This reference is to General Braxton Bragg's victory in the Battle of Chickamauga, which began September 18, 1863.

writen and your escapes from water come so often and so many other evils, [that my] fea[r] for you makes me anxious all the time. Oh! that ardent longing heart desires could move the ear of our Heavenly Father, and close this heart rendering war. Daily & hourly I repeat inwardly to my impatient sorrowful, & almost despairing spirit—you must wait, & you must bear whatsoever your Maker may inflict upon you—time you cannot speed, sorrow you cannot avert, & joy & peace you cannot claim, so pray for faith to hope and strength to bear whatever may be inflicted, but oh pray that the hand of Mercy deal tenderly with thee! I long so to see you, & the prospect is so gloomy for the realization of my wish, that I am ready to give up in despair at times, but then, I am determined to battle against this feeling in order to give you pleasure, as well as cheat myself of much unnessary pain. I am less selfish than I have been for many long months, at least I have been more serene in mind thoughtless of my past pains & trials, & viewed my lot with more cheerfulness in fact have striven to forget myself in thoughts of you, but it cannot last much longer, I feel the *old fiend,* my mortal enemy, the blues, creeping on, soon I will be in his power, & the cup he prepares will be all bitterness, & my distorted vision will recognize only clouds and darkness. Oh that I could shake off the spell he weaves! Tis some, nay great consolation, since I can believe that I have your sympathy during my miserable periods, & this knowledge is what has rendered me more cheerful for a longer period than usual. I thank you for your hopes that time may have the effect to make me more hopeful of the future, & cheerful of the present, yet I feel that this can never be—time hitherto has had the very opposite effect. There was a time when I did hope that each child was the last, & the prospect of a future, devoid of childbearing while it would be filled with your love & esteem, without any disatisfaction, did cheer my daily thoughts & feelings—*that is past never to return,* & yet I feel more certain, have no doubt upon my mind that I will ever have another child, yet the knowledge give me neither hope nor pleasure, for I know what the purchase will cost, yet I am determined—a life time of dull heavy heart misery, rather than an other nine months of the scorching Simoon, which would wither & destroy both my heart & intellect. Neither happiness nor cheerfulness of long duration is for me, & to my fate I submit myself, yet will I strive on your account to let my murmurings be heard as seldom as possible.

They did not have quite three loads of the white corn, and to day will haul the 9th load to the crib. I don't think they will finish hauling this week. They made a crossing on that ravine through the field opposite the potatoe bed, a very good crossing they say & haul three loads a day now. Nancy helps, while

Sam cards. I am looking every day for the Impressing officers to come here, mother sent hers, dident wait for the officer, but I am waiting to hear from you before I know what to do. I am going to try & have the Gable ends of the crib pegged on, as I think I can get lumber enough throwing about the yard, & if I don't take some precaution against thieves, & Joe's mule, I fear our bread will be out by Jan, & our horses, oxen & all dead poor. Pony ox is much worsted by his trip to the Depot, got his neck hurt, & worms in it don't use him now. Pat still here recruiting some. I reviewed the hogs on *dress parade* (ie at feeding time) and was gratified to see their improved looks, they seem to be thriving finely now for the last three weeks I have had them fed their full allowance at night ie fed them as much as they had both night & morning & gave it all at night. Mr Collins says he fears there will not be mast enough to put them even in a good thriving condition, before time to put them up, to fatten for killing. The old white sow's pigs I have under my eye, & have three or four ear's of corn boiled daily for them, to keep them from killing the mother—she still remains quite poor the pigs look finely. My patch of Rye is coming up finely & if the cows don't wean the calves I'll make some butter this winter, & perhaps get old Sam to looking a little better. I have got that cow up that was out with an unbranded calf.

Mage[56] gets a long very well with the shoes, makes a pair a day & praises the leather very much. I havent heard a word about those hides at Dr Brown's, will try and swap some of the upper leather for sole. Mother has sent her leather to Old man Mangum to curry, and I expect to get my Kipp skin soon to make the boys shoes. I have taken my largest thickest calf skin to Collins & he promises to make Mary's Walter's & my shoes next week, and agrees to take corn, at cash price $75. per bushel, and make my shoes at the old prices $1.80 or $2.00 for mine, Mary's & Walters less[.] I agreed to pay him in corn, but fear now I did wrong, but I can't tell 'till they gather all the corn. I know Joe has fed more corn to his mule than would pay for us all a pair of shoes a piece. I told him he had better sell his mule, can't get any one to trade yet he says. He & his trading propensity particularly in horseflesh is a great vexation—he will run about, & won't go on foot. Mrs Oliver spent a day with me this week, looks better & is in better health than she has been for some time, complains of her hard lot, negros mismanagement carelessness & idleness, which I echoed—tho' I tell you with a little vanity that I think I manage a

---

56. Mage or Major was a slave of Lizzie Neblett's mother, Sarah Scott.

little better than she does. The hogs by getting in her potato patch forced her to dig, & after she had banked them in the yard the hogs got in & ate nearly all she had up, only a few bushels left. If I get mine to the house I bet I save them if they don't break into the smokehouse. I fear more from 2 legged than 4 legged hogs. I expect we will make two or three cotton baskets full, & I am going to move into the field while they are digging. Mrs Hurst came over yesterday evening & payed Sarah for her services, three cases, $10 confederate money, & after she left Sarah let out, says she ought to have $50 in that money, that Mrs Hurst said if she had sent for a Dr, it would have cost her $100, and she ought to have half price, she has supreme contempt for con. money. I can't help laughing at her.

I have had to plant Turnips again the seed you saved for me did not come up, have set out my white shalots & some buttons of the red onion. I forgot to send Ma some of our white Shalots, & regret it so much.

I met Garrett & Susan at Aunt Cinda's monday, he said his business there was to clear up that Bettie Scott scrape, his talking about the Scott's, denied it all, or as good as denied it, & she said I told Bettie he was only in jest, just trying her—which Aunt Cinda says is not so, she never opened her mouth. She looks down, & badly—as Mrs Croom used to say this war had brought her to her milk. She was quite friendly with me. Says John has despaired of getting out & wrote in mighty low spirits, said he wrote [he'll] try & do nothing desperate, neither drink nor gamble. Poor John, I feel sorry for him when the yoke presses *so hard*, and despair shakes him by the hand. God knows I am glad as you are bound to serve, as duty & conscience demands it, that you don't take it so hard. John's health it is true may be worse than yours, but it is my opinion that his mind, his earnest & ever present desire to get out [of] service affects his health some. I feel for him *but not her*, uncharitable tho' it be. I asked her about saying that John had writen two letter to you which you failed to notice, said he wrote her to that effect, & asked her to write to him about you as he could not hear from you. I don't believe that John ever wrote that, she wanted to flatter me a little bit. Kit Hall[57] is creating quite a stir in the neighborhood just now, has returned from La, bringing several mules with him, fine saddle &c, and since his return has bought (five) 5 negros, Carry al,

---

57. Kit Hall is listed in the 1860 census as C. C. Hawl (or perhaps Haul). He was 20 years old and living with his stepfather, M. L Waid (50), and mother, M. A. Waid (40). TX Census 1860.

and two of the finest kind of mules. [People] think he must have visited the valley of Diamonds we read of in the Arabian nights,[58] or has found Aladin's lamp, or something else magical or wonderful has turned up in his path. People shake their heads, & many think that blood may be upon his hands or thief writen on his heart. He went with Bill Loggins,[59] returned without him, says Loggins went on in to Miss. Henry White has been whipped twice within the last six weeks. The first time by Arington, about a calf sucking his cow with White brand on it, Henry resented the insinuation, & Arrington slapped his jaws good, he did not resent the blows, in the least. The next time Oney knocked him down, jumped on him kicked & stamped him, bruising him up mightly. I don't know what that was about, but White did not resent the blows, just threw up hands & cried out "will you let a man be murdered before your eyes," none of the crowd gazing on interfered but Coleman who succeeded in getting Oney off him.

Amanda White still lingers, don't think she can live through the winter. Bad news of my piano comes from all sides. Wm Terrell sent me word by Thonton that if I did not have it moved it would be ruined, don't know how he heard, and Dr Edwards who has made two trips up the country for flour sent me word by Joe that he was in C[orsicana], and saw the box & that the house was now used to store away *salt* & my piano would be ruined if it was not moved. I fear it will never benefit me or mine, in fact I never expect to set eyes on, but will write immediately to Mrs Henderson to have it moved to her house, unboxed & set up. Edwards said if his wagon had come through C[orsicana] he would have brought it down for me, as his wagon came back empty. He sells his flour at $50 per hundred. I recd a letter from Mollie White a few days since. Old man Hays has sold out & gone. From her letter I learn that Dr Malloy died a prisoner. His watch finger ring and the likeness of a young lady were taken from him before he died. I let mother and Babe carry Walter home with them, & I miss the little fellow so much. He continues to talk so much about you, I have felt more for you since Walter left me, for I think oftener of how much you must want to see the children and my baby I love her better, every day. I cant withstand her intelligence & winning little ways. I hardly ever clasp her in my arms that I don't think of how much you

---

58. Lizzie Neblett is referring to the popular *Arabian Nights* or *The Thousand and One Nights*, a collection of stories written in Arabic and dating to at least the tenth century.

59. William Loggins (age 33) was a farmer living with his wife, Julia (24), and daughter in 1860. His personal and real property was valued at $14,000. TX Census 1860.

must want to see her, and how much I wish you could see her now, your love for our children is not as strong as mine, but is more uniform.

Sunday Oct 18, Dear Will, I came up to mothers Friday eve, and on the road heard news! news! John Nix has got home! Reached here 16th came up on the Galery between midnight & day, knocked, when mother says, who is it "some one who wants to talk a little while to you" he replied—who are you mother asked, when Babe began to caper round in the room, & says mother it is John Nix, she knew his voice, & mother says well if it is you John go round to the door by the chimney as it is unlocked & John went round & was let in. His arm is stiff, & his fingers drawn, cant cut up his food, has been quite sick since he was wounded & mother says looks badly. I havent seen him brought no war news, more than you will see in the papers & they copied from Va papers he brought through. Says all the prisoners taken at Gettysburge have been heard of but John Green, fear he is dead. I could not help crying when I heard he had come. I did not weep because he had come, but because my poor dear brother who went with him came not, & never would come to gladen our hearts, on this earth. Oh my dearest brother, time only teaches me how dear thou weret to my soul, and what a blessing I lost, when death claimed thee. Had his fall been different I could grow reconciled with time, but as it is, his death will remain as a thorn in my heart, rankling until the day of my death. Dear dear Garrett misfortune early marked you as her own, and tho' you deserved the highest and best upon the earth, like our Savior *you receive only the bitter dregs!*

Dr Johnson[60] sent me word that he was ready to do some plugging for me so yesterday I left the baby & went to his house, and he plugged one of my front teeth, found the other plugged & the best plug in my mouth he said. The one he plugged was a large cavity & he made a good job of it I think. He says there is a good deal of work to do in my mouth one tooth so far gone now cant be saved, but I dont know whether to have any more done or not. I told him I had just as well pay as I went & asked his price & he said $30—I reckon I will give up the idea of getting me one or two dresses, and put the money in my mouth. I can make out some way, & must get my homespun wove, think I'll try Gravy. I am used to self denial, in dressing at least, & it won't hurt me. I learned on reaching mothers that poor Amanda White was buried the day I

---

60. The 1860 census lists J. E. Johnston (age 27) as a dentist married to Sallie (20) with personal and real property valued at $2,200. TX Census 1860.

began my letter. She is out of trouble, at rest, tho' she clung to life to the very last, & talked of living even in the jaws of death. Thank God I don't think it will be hard for me to die. Sallie has left Fanthorps gone to Cauthon's to be confined. Babe says she has fallen out with her, quarrels at her every time she sees her, because she (Babe) has not made her a number of little things for her expected baby, & she thought Babe was going to do so much for her. Babe thinks now since she quarrels at her before company that she said more of the things about me & mother than she ever believed she did before. Babe says she aint going to see her any more untill after all is over. They say Sallie cry's insessantly has almost despaired of Bassett reaching here before she is sick. Her trouble don't seem to have humbled her any yet. Babe says they all told her (Sallie) in town that if she did not come out to see mother, they would drop her & in order to elevate herself she came.

Dr Carter speaks in Anderson tomorrow, & I have a sly notion of staying & going to hear him, as it is said to be fine medicine for the depressed in spirits about this war, to listen to his speeches—and then, I want to kill two birds with one stone. While I was at Johnson's yesterday I sent Jim with our buggy to old Christian's shop, to see what work our buggy needed, as I could tell nothing about it, & had no one to tell me. He told Jim it was needing repair badly & ought not to be used 'till it was fixed. One of the wheels needed fixing so bad, he wedged the boxing himself—the last time I was at mothers before this I sent it to the shop for Jack to make claw for old Sam's singletree,[61] for Turn to wedge the boxing in the front wheels. I suppose it came undone. Christian says the spring behind is broken don't know what I'll do about that. The drouth this summer has been quite a trying time on it, & the old thing is going down hill fast, but to be ready for the Yankees, and to be able to smell the air away from my own dull, lonely fireplace occasionally I must have it fixed, tho no doubt Christian will charge me a big sum and if he can do the work on the buggy tomorrow, I'll stay & go to the speaking & have the work done, & I missed my letter from you last week & do hope so much that Teusday's mail will bring me one. I feel so anxious to get a letter of late date from you, yours are six & seven days old when they reach here, & some nearly two weeks old. Oh, 'tis so trying to my patience. I have sent Jim to town to find out whether Christian can do the work on the buggy tomorrow.

61. A singletree is a horizontal crossbar to which the harness of a draft animal is fastened, which is then hitched to the vehicle.

Christian can do some of the most urgent work today so I will go to the speaking and have what can be done attended to. Babe & Mary go with me—will have the baby at Betties.

Oct 19th 1863

Galveston Texas Oct 22/63
Mrs L S Neblett

Dear Lizzie

When I wrote to you a few days since I forgot to say to you that I wished you to send that matrass as soon as you can [f]or Bookman with whom I have been sleeping is expecting his old bed fellow Parson Wilson who has been at home for several months on sick furlough.

If the Gov agent has not already taken the quota of our negroes[,] by sending one to me[,] that one being here in the army will be counted as in the service of the Gov. Bookmans wife brought him one and as they had but two men it prevented the Gov from getting any. She started forth the negro after Mooring (the agent) came to her for the negro. But if these impressing officers have got what they are going to take you can send the matras to Navasota and direct Thomas & Brockway to send it to me by express to Galveston. Mark my name with thread. Co I 20 Reg and also on a card my name Co I 20 Reg Galveston Texas and say on the card [page torn] and the express agent will send it through without further trouble. I do not need a negro but rather than the Gov shall have two I will take one and if I choose I can send him back as soon as I please. Your Ma's boys Dave Ted & Turn are on the steamer Lone Star so Hiram told me yesterday. He says Wash was at the Hospital in Houston—was not sick much so Hiram said. I have not been very well since I wrote you last. My liver has been deranged and I have had several very severe head aches with loss of appetite. To day I feel better and hope I will now continue to improve. Do not send any clothing in the matras you can send me a small hand towel in the matras. Mine is completely worn out and I cannot get any thing in Gal suitable for the purpose. I must hasten to close this in time to get it off. I have not heard of the cotton sent Peel & Dumble tho Owen Cochran promised to write me as soon as it arrived and he draws the proceeds.

Yours affectionately
Wm H. Neblett

Galveston Texas
Oct 24th/63
Mrs L S Neblett

Dear Lizzie

I wrote you a few lines two or three days ago and since then have rec'd a letter from Owen Cochran enclosing [a] statement of the account of sales of the cotton sold Peel & Dumble which I enclose to you for safe keeping and settlement with Coleman for the cotton exchanged & Peel & Dumble you will see holds in their hands 8 pr cent of the value of the cotton upon the grounds that it is liab[l]e for the tax unless a voucher is sent from the Assessor & Col[lector] of Grimes showing that the amt of taxes has been paid. I have written to them to day requesting them to retain the amt of the tax in their hands until I can send them the necessary voucher. I understood from one of your letters that you had given it in to the Ass & Col in Grimes and it may be necessary now for you to pay the tax and get Coleman to get a voucher to send to Peel & Dumble to enable them to have the cotton released or the money paid back. I wrote to Peel & Dumble to write to me at Anderson and inform me exactly what kind of a voucher would be required. When you get that you will know how to proceed in the matter.

For the last two days we have had a severe Norther—quite stormy weather here but since our shipwreck the guard has not ventured out as we had been doing before. It is quite cold to day and my hands feel quite stiff and cold. There is no comfortable place to be found here except around a pine wood fire and in the smoke. Night before last the rain kept me up most of the night and wet most every thing in our tents. I feel no ill effect from it now, though last night I suffered some with Asthma.

If you get this before you send the matras & towel you can send the blanket also. The pants you can send by Pres Carrington who is now at home on sick furlough & who will be back I suppose in a month or so. I rec'd yours of the 19th yesterday was glad to hear of John Nixes arrival. If he is so badly crippled as you understand he will now have to qualify himself to make a living by some other mode besides manual labor.

If you have to send a negro to work the fortifications I expect Joe will be the best chance. He can take better care of himself than Randle.

yours affectionately
Wm H. Neblett

At Home
Oct 25th 1863
W H Neblett

Dear Will,

More fortunate than usual, two letters from you fell to my share last week, one Teusday & one Thursday. I was not surprised to learn of your sickness for I expected it—so often have my dreams boded some thing that they now have undue weight with me when they are vivid. I forgot to ask you if an ill man did not share your sick bed for in my dream a sick man did & was in the front & when I approached he sat up that I might lean over and kiss you. Now don't smile for if you don't mind I'll convince you some day that my dreams where they relate to those whom I love dearly are often prophetic, the past in many instances has taught me this belief. Just as I reached this point in my letter Aunt Cinda, Uncle Mc and John Nix rode up, so away went all my writing for the day and I promised myself so much pleasure in writing to you to day, as I feel hurried and uneasy when I seat myself to write a long letter during or on any other day than Sunday—and I am particularly anxious to hurry myself now to get Joe started to you with your matrass and clothes as soon as possible. The impressing officers have not paid me a visit yet. I send you Joe because I know he is smart enough to carry what I wish to send safely if he will only do it. He will stay all night at Pa's the first night, and will direct him to stay all night in Houston at Mrs Cochran's, my only fear is his getting the things to you safely from Galveston to Pelican Spit, but I reckon he will manage some how. Sam [is] still living up with his foot, and I would not be surprised if he was not in the house all winter with it[;] if he were able to travel I would send him.

I am glad Will that you are satisfied with my letters and find them a source of interest and pleasure, & I feel thankful that I have the natural capacity & education to devote to your service, and I often feel ashamed of having found fault either in my heart or through my letters of what you write me. I believe you love me better & more devoutly than most men love their wives, and no doubt miss the comforts of home more than the majority of men. Sometimes when I am very much depressed, in an ill humor with fate for placing me in the position & sphere I occupy in life, when I find the flower that has sprung up in my path from my birth up, but has a thorn that pierced deeper than all the combined roses were worth—in times & moments like these, I have shed many tears over what I tortured myself by calling & believing your coldness and want of sympathy—but I always condemned myself for being the unintending cause—and like Job cursed the hour of my birth. But, I have times when the spirit that ruleth the hour deals more kindly more leniently with me, when sun beams cross my path, and birds sing for me, then I see you in your true light, & am thankful for having such a good husband[;] this is my thankful mood, the other is my unthankful distorted and self torturing mood—alas, for me, for you & for all those at all dependent upon me for any degree of happiness that the latter mood greatly predominates. I believe you know me better than any one else does, & on account of the good you find in me forgive the many faults. I am thankful that I can believe so. I know that you feel that I love you deeply & you know that my love is not put on & off at pleasure. As to this war spoiling me, I think not[;] most gladly would I give up what little & poor management I do with the out door farm work. Yet if God wills that you return, I fear I'll fret you even more than I used to by wanting restrictions & penalties put upon some of our negros more than others, in payment of the manner in which they now treat me, & Joe & Sam are two I will long remember, & Tom is one I never want to have anything to do with. Since Bill has been at mothers I send him to do jobs, have sent him twice & he has torn the black leather off the sheep skin tacked on the seat of yr saddle & lost it & I never thought 'till to night that the saddle Joe rides is yours, else I would have had it long since. He keeps it hid out round the field, ready to use at any time. I vow Joe shall never keep a horse on the place after this, while I pretend to be chief of affairs. I told him he had to get rid of the mule as soon as I found out he had it but that done no good. I told him yesterday that I was going to send him to you this week, so I reckon he will get somebody to keep his mule, for fear he will have to come back, & will then want the mule again.

Our horses look badly, & every time Uncle Mc sees them he asks me what makes them look so poor. Truth is they are not attended to, I am busiest at the times they should be fed, & can't go every time, nor think every time to send somebody to see after it, so it goes, but thank God the war can't last always, and from the inmost depths of my heart I pray hourly that when the end shall come that you will return to us, & that you will long be in the midst of your family even if I be under the soil. The idea of your never returning is so terrible that I never entertain it longer than a moment at a time. I put it far from me, but then I think even so I did about my poor dear brother, & hundreds of times pictured to myself how I should meet him when he returned alas, he returned not, & now I picture how I shall meet him in that Better Land—will that hope too fail? I know tis bad doing without your presence, that the wheel in out door affairs has almost ceased to turn, but I miss you most round the fire side, at morning noon, at night—& tho' sadness often oppresses me, and tears unbiden are shed, yet I feel & know that you are doing your duty, & I glory in the spirit of patriotism that binds you to your post, and enables you to leave the endearments of home and family, to aid in the achievement of our national independence—and altho' I think my trials are hard, yet I know your[s] are harder, but let us hope that the end is not far distant and that with us God will deal mercifully, that you will return safely, and the perfect fruition of that return will compensate for much that we have both suffered. Oh that I knew you would return what a mountain load of anxiety would be removed, what joy would I feel. But I shut my eyes upon that dim uncertain future, & gather up my energies for the present while I live from the past, & am happy or sad just as the flower that morning calls be sweet or obnoxious. I know Will you want to see me & the children very much, yet think how much better we are situated then thousands of others at home and in regard to each other. You are in the state where we can hear from each other every week, and as yet you have suffered nothing in comparison with our Va or Ky Regts, and I pray God you never may! Altho' life has never been very dear to me, yet I want to live, & see the end of this war if you are to return. What joy will be the portion of some, & what sorrow and desolation will fill the bosoms of others because their loved ones will return no more on earth. But you are a man whose thoughts dwell most upon the future (the only part of time upon which we have no claim) and no doubt all that I have been writing to night has passed through your brain many times, & you have thought many times with bounding heart of the time when you will be ordered to march home under the banner of peace, to remain always!

The negros finished gathering corn, the 7th day. We had, including the white corn, just nineteen loads, & I estimated the corn we have fed away to the hogs as one load, which would make two loads to the Gov which I have place[d] in a pen, & if Joe & his mule leaves it may stay there until I get ready to haul it to the depot. Thornton says River's said if I did not make Joe remove his mule, that he would feed all the Gov corn away that he had seen places around the field where Joe had fed his mule. Martin says he will kill Joe if he ever catches him on his place, & several others have been trying to catch him, but he manages to elude them all. I estimate our corn crop at 500 bushels, 25 bu[shels] a load—50 goes to the Gov 31 to mother and 4 bu to Collins borrowed before the corn was hard enough to shell, that will leave us with 415 bu on hand. Susan and Uncle Mc have bought B[agging] & rope and are ginning out some cotton to get the seed to feed on this winter, & mother is going to do the same. Susan will sell the cotton she Baled out. Coleman told me he had no idea that McCune even Gin[ned] that cotton I swaped with him this winter as he is not at home. I see no chance to get cotton seed for our oxen this winter—like you I fear our cotton will get mixed with Mrs Hursts or be stolen but cant help myself[;] if Rivers is any account he will see to it. Coleman has made an overwhelming crop of cotton, more than was ever raised upon the place before in one year. 250 acres in cotton & they say at least a hundred b[a]les now in the field and a large new cotton house filled, and another cotton house building, he can't begin to save the cotton—don't know what Coleman was thinking about, unless he wanted to grow very rich while the other men were off fighting. I had that division fence run, and our oxen and old Sam & Ranger put in the old field, where they have fine crab grass pa[s]ture, and will do finely. I sent Rivers word that he must turn our oxen out, but have failed to inquire about it, & expect he has them now hauling corn[;] none of our negros would speak to me about it, they never speak to me about anything that may be going on wrong altho' they may know what I want done, and I never had so much on my mind in my life—spinning & having weaving done, patching & mending, a hundred things demanding my immediate attention. And my little untimely babe who is a perfect little sensitive plant physically and mentally and requires so much of my time & attention, and I can't neglect her—and then the thinking of the out door affairs, the oxen the calves, the cows the hogs, if they require any attention I must see to it, no general reporter, what I find out is by accident. All these things press heavily on my mind, and in the characteristic language of a weaver when the threads all get crossed & tangled, I say with Dicken's weaver "its all a muddle,"[62] & I tell you my mind feels mighty muddled sometimes. But as Dr McAnnelly used to say, I try to take it easy along. Don't you *muddle* your brains with it, one of us is enough, & I don't fear that we will any us either starve or freeze to death. We had a big frost and a little ice here the night of the 23rd and two nights since have had frost. The children say the Potatoe vines, cotton &c all killed, I have not seen them myself, but I felt the cold & got up every morning a heap colder than I went to bed. The baby gets up nearly every morning 5 Oclock, & I make Kate heat me an iron, put it to my feet, & she makes a good fire and takes up Bettie and I take an other nap. I dread the cold this winter I

---

62. Charles Dickens, *Hard Times*, book 3, chapter 6 (1864).

always suffer so much, but thank goodness I'll not have the cramp[63] this winter.

Now let me tell you a little about John Nix. He seems to be *mighty down,* I think he is a cripple for life—the leaders or muscle that moved his three fingers, (all except his fore finger) were cut in two, and the wound has healed up and they have grown fast to the bone, and his wrist is crooked, & his fingers [have] no strength and the leaders all too short, and his fingers cup in, cant straighten them good, his whole arm is perished away and his shoulder is much smaller than the other one is. His wound had gangrene[64] in it, and a large piece sloughed out, the wound is all below the elbow. He is thin in flesh, had quite a bad spell after he was wounded. He got a sixty days furlough & came as far [as] they would give furloughs to Meridian Miss, and there showed his furlough and asked for transportation on to Tex, two other wounded soldiers were with him, they had late Va papers so they copied their papers & gave them transportation, and so, from place to place they acted & got transportation home. He was nearly a month coming. I think the wounded men with [him] were strangers to us. I don't think he will ever go back. He says that man Mays that came with Bob, from Va, went back to Richmond to get a discharge & he left him in the Hospital, won't discharge him nor furlough him, him [*sic*] home & John don't talk much, don't seem to be much glad to get home, nor much sorry that he is a cripple, just seems *apathetic.* He has spent two days with me now, & I learned nothing much from him but what little there is I'll tell you. In the first place, he seems to know less than any body about poor Garrett's death. He never asked Charley Floyd any thing and he tells a few things he *thinks* Davis said but it has been so long ago he wont be certain. He don't know whether any letters went to the Regt for Garrett or not after his death, but is certain he got no letter out of the office at Richmond for Garrett except the one he sent by Bob. (this is the only thing he is certain of about Garrett.[)] (But the clock warns me that it is now 12 Oclock at night and I must finish this subject tomorrow night. I took a cup of coffee to night & feel as wide awake as you please but I must go to sleep else I'll not be fit for work tomorrow, so Good night & God bless you!)

---

63. Lizzie most likely was breast-feeding her baby and, therefore, was not expecting to menstruate during that time.

64. Gangrene is the decay of body tissue caused by an insufficient blood supply, commonly seen in disease or injury. In the days before antibiotics the only treatment was amputation of the affected part.

(Night has again come, another weary harassing day has passed into eternity, and the war is one day near its close, but oh! are *you* one day nearer home? God grant it's all I can pray! I have drank my cup of coffee and will now take up the broken threads of my story and proceed.) What seems strange to me, John seems to know more about the death of all the others in Hutcheson's Co than Garrett, seems to have inquired more into others death than Garrett's, about his, can tell absolutely nothing—seems to have been perfectly unconcerned. I asked him in my letter you know to talk to Charley Floyd, & write me what he said & thought to inquire about letters going to the Regt for G—— after his death, well he says he never heard Charley say anything about the search for poor Garretts body & never asked about the letters, he heard Charley say that he got a letter from me, & he thought he answered it. Oh Will how could John be so *unconcerned* when Garrett had been such a good friend to him. Oh God! is there no disinterested friendship upon earth? And Garrett, poor dear good, humane, feeling heart, to meet such an awful end, to have left no friend no true, feeling heart, to have searched out & eased his dying hour. In my anguish I often think "my God why didst thou forsake him!"[65] But, I hope God was near him, & in his death anguish did support him. John says G—— did not reach the Regt the night after the Gains farm fight, and the next morn, he was sent to the battle field to help remove some cannon we took & there he saw Garrett for the first time after the fight, helping *the wounded* which he had volunteered to do, & no doubt after every battle, when others were talking their rest, he was a voluntary help to the wounded and dying. John says (& 'tis all the praise he gives) that Garrett was as brave a man as ever went to Va, and was liked by the whole Co, if he had an enemy he did not know it—but alas, it was the most of it interested friendship.

Mark Womack,[66] John thinks did run, but says he fought bravely in the Gettysburge battle. Mark is *exceedingly unpopular*. Garrett disliked him very much, & did have an open breach with him. G—— took a dram, & was a little merry from its effects, & Mark pretended that he believed he was drunk (it was on the cars going to Va) and he undertook to take care of G, & would take hold of him, telling G—— he was drunk & would fall off the cars. G—— repeatedly told him to let him alone. (G was shooting at Aligators as the cars

65. Any of a number of Bible passages including Ps. 22:1 and Matt. 27:46.

66. Mark Womack was the brother of Susan Womack Scott. In 1860 he was 18 years old and living with his father and mother, Abe (62) and Elizabeth (51). TX Census 1860.

passed by them) and at last he gave Mark a lick over the head with his pistol, when he left him. G—— afterwards told Mark he had a great mind to have put a ball through him that day, & M turned off saying nothing. John thinks Bassett can't get home. N[oah] Bassett[67] is only Agent not [Adjutant] of the 4th Texas. He say G told him after B became Capt of Co G—that he intended to get a transfer to another Co don't know [page torn] did not. A few days after John reached here, Aunt Cinda went up to mothers and asked her to give Garrett's clothes, shirts &c to John, as he had only the shirt he wore home, & one shirt. Mother told her, G——s shirts & fine clothes were locked up in his trunk & she could not open that, she replied if she couldent she did not know who could. Mother gave her a new shirt that poor Walter left (& I suppose on account of the association Garrett would never wear), and one of Pa's which was almost new, is all she gave her. Mother says John manifested too little interest & concern about Garrett for her to ever give him what he left here, & I feel like mother. John says Jessie B[aker][68] hasent one particle of energy, that Hutch provided for him & shared with him to the last, & that he has no smartness, no intellect about him, after John told his tale, Babe said to me that he was a fool, & that was why they all were courting so hard for him, that they knew he hadent the energy nor sense to court for himself. She seems to be out of the notion now. I think Sallie B—— is mad with her because she let her drop when she took up with the Bakers, & Sallie fears that Noah's prospects are somewhat slim, unless she can keep Babe under *her thumb*. So it goes, I am not of them, nor with them, my only brother my only true blood relation is now in Heaven.

Now a few words upon our particular friend over the creek. She still cuts *didoes*[69]—she and her lovely son have a lively jolly time of it. Shannon hasent made up his Co yet & Garrett has been home some time on furlough he says. He is the most consumate fool, & the biggest puppy I know of, altogether a nice young man. He got to cutting up the other boys bridles the other day to make him a good one, Elliott[70] rebelled at it, & Garrett whipped him, & Susan pounced upon Garrett and whipped him all over the yard with the bri-

67. Noah Bassett was Robert Bassett's brother. In 1860 he was a 21-year-old clerk with personal property valued at $500. TX Census 1860.

68. In 1860 Jessie Baker (26) was living with his father, Issac (60), and mother, Aurelia (56). The family had real and personal property valued at $80,000. TX Census 1860.

69. Didoes are pranks or capers.

70. William Elliott (age 8 in 1860) was the son of John and Susan Scott. TX Census 1860.

dle reins & then drove him off. He went to town, where John Nix saw him *drunk,* sick as a dog—so he did not stay drunk long, told John he spent 25 dollars for whiskey—he was staying there at his Grandma Womack's,[71] & as he is now at home again I suppose his Grandma drove away[.] [H]e told John that if it had been any body but his mother he would have taken the reins away from her, and stamped her all over the yard. I expect the next thing will be that he will beat her, almost to death. I don't pity either her or John. I permited Joe to ask Abe[72] & Elliott to help him get that wild bunch of cattle in some field so as to kill one and she said no she had to send Elliott to town to day—a paltry excuse—and I have had two of her cows penned here at different times, & sent her word (by stopping a hand) to send for them or the worms would eat them up, one they saved, the other they got the hide of. But I would do the same again. Joe penned some beeves in Mrs Wades field to day sent Tom back to me and I wrote a note asking Uncle Mc to ride over to the field, & shoot the beef, he sent Tom back to tell Thornton to bring on the wagon, & I thought the beef was shot, & hurried the wagon off post haste with Randle & the knives & to night they all came back with out the beef. Joe says he got right close to the beef, (twas not a wild one) and he got as close as he wanted to be and missed, Joe says he saw a little hair fly off his head but could find no blood, & the beef then left for parts unknown, & of course cant be got again, & Joe says he is very fat and a very fine 4 yr old. Will I think Uncle Mc is exactly like the negros coon dog. I have tried him for every thing else, & now two failures where he had such good chances to hit, proves to me that he an't good at shooting, tho he pretends to be a fine shot. I'll try & get Rivers to go tomorrow, hope he will have better luck. On asking Thornton, I found it as I suspected, Rivers still working our oxen, I made Thornton get them up, & had them drove to the cane, when I did the others they went back, & he says Rivers told him when I sent him word about them that he wouldent use them any more then he could help, that he had only three yoke beside them, so he has gathered all his corn with them, & Thornton never said a word to me about what Rivers said nor what he was doing, until I thought to inquire—just so they all do me. I have given Thornton another talk about the oxen, & will have them put in the field with our other oxen as soon as this

---

71. Elizabeth C. Womack (51) was the mother of Susan Womack Scott. Her husband, Abe (62), was a farmer with personal and real property valued at $45,340. TX Census 1860.

72. Abraham Scott (10) was the son of John and Susan Scott. TX Census 1860.

beef business is over with. Thornton understood well enough that I did not want Rivers to use the oxen but you see he dident care, & as I did not ask, he would never speak.

Oct 27th Teusday night—The 3 yr old beef was killed to day by River's. Joe could not find that cow that run at the mill 'till they were coming home with the beef, he says she is very fat, & don't think she will have a calf this winter. I expect when we eat up the one we have, it would be best to kill her, counting all our killing hogs, we will have 18, but two of those Zuber hogs are so thin now that they won't do to kill 'till late, if they do then & all our meat will be small this year. Our pigs look fine, have 17 come since the 1st of Apr, all weaned & six left of those that got poisoned in the field. I am going to put Thornton over the hogs & oxen both and make the others help him, and as soon as I can lend them my *presence* I'll have our potatoes dug & banked in the smoke house, and the hogs then turned in the field. We have 14 middlings of meat now, but some are small, but I think they would last us fully three months. Now hadent I better kill that cow, and save my bacon for next year? And then had I better try and tan some more leather, have about enough leather left to make 4 pr shoes, I saw Mage cut all the shoes but 2 pr, which Sarah saw him do while I was at Carter's speaking & having the buggy fixed, so I reckon he did not steal much. I expect they will all be bare footed by Christmas as I let them take the shoes as they were made & they know 'tis all they will get. I have got a half hide from Dr Brown's, but you know we sent two there, did we not? When I get the other side, I guess I'll have to risk it with Old Keifer. (as Dr B lets him take some of his home to work) They owe us an untaned hide at the mill Tan yard dont they? Collins has made my shoes, but they don't fit well, & I am going to let Mrs Tom Collins[73] take them & he will make me another pr out of her calf skin, which he says is equally if not better than mine. He will make Walters & Mary's soon. When they sent that Kidd skin of mine from mothers, they found it & all mothers leather not half tanned, so Mangum kept my skin & mothers calf skins & put them in his vats. I will make Mage make the boys some shoes out of that goat skin. Mary's lasted very well you know. Bill still at mothers & as soon as they get done the cotton house up there Mage will return here—make the boys shoes, make some ox yokes (*short yokes* to use in the wagon, as we have only one good yoke) and then fix up the gable ends of our crib, & I'll put a lock on it.

73. In 1860 Thomas (30), a farmer, and Mary (19) Collins had personal property valued at $4,000 and had a year-old daughter, Clara. TX Census 1860.

I was very sorry to see in the Tri weekly News that Poor Bob Bookman was killed in those recent battles, 20th Sept,[74] only a few days over a year from Garrett's death. Poor fellow, I shall ever hold him in greatful remembrance for his promptness and kindness in answering my letter to him about poor Garrett. I see too that Tobe Riggs was killed. I haven't succeeded in getting any paper yet, but will soon I think. Mrs Hutcheson has promised to let me have some Legal paper, left by Mr H, and I have sent by Mrs Oliver to the Dutch store for some when she goes—this I am writing on is so bad I fear you will not be able to read it all I can hardly write on it. Jim Scott bought me a ½ Brl of Sugar in Houston last week, gave 70 cts per lb. When Mrs Oliver sends her bale of cotton to the depot to sell to get money to pay her taxes, I'll get her wagon to bring my sugar from Anderson where it is. What about our Taxes, how much will it be? [A]nd did I give in all I ought to have given in to Frank Briggance?

Wednesday night. Joe told Bob to day that he thought that cow at the mill would have a calf in two months, and understood him to say she would not have a calf this winter when I talked to him. I sent him to Sim Thomases this morning to get one of our cows that Joe saw with his cattle sunday—one he has been telling me about for a month, & that he missed her out of her range, & knew she had a calf. She is only marked in Jim's mark not branded, but make Joe tell you all about it, & how he done about Mr Gray's cow, and the trick he served McCune. Thomas is a grand rascal, and wont go into service. People still talk about Kit Hall, & old Mr Gray was here a little while this evening looking for a mule, and asked me if Bill Loggins had ever returned or been heard [of], & said some thought that Hall killed him & took his money, thinking that no one would ever suppose he did it, from his coming back here so boldly. If Bill Loggins has ever been heard from since Kit returned I don't know it. He has offered old Dowdy $6,000 to go as a substitute for him, has bought two or three more negros bought plank, & is putting up cabins on his mothers place for the negroes to live in. Some supposed he was an agent for some man, but he would not build cabins if he was, and Mrs Wade[75] as good as says they are Kits negroes. There is something black at the bottom [of] the

---

74. The Battle of Chickamauga.

75. In the 1860 census M. A. Waid (age 40) was married to a farmer, M. L. Waid (51), who had personal and real property valued at $5,770. There were five children living with the couple with the last name of Hawl or Haul, including C. C. Hawl or Kit Hall. TX Census 1860.

affair I fear, & I think as poor a man as he has always been known to be should be arrested upon suspicion when they take the sudden rise he has.

Now a few words about the children. Mary is learning fast applys herself closely, is very ambitious. She is up before light of morning studying & has never been punished in any form at school—stands at the head of her class. Bob too learns fast, is studious & ambitious and a favorite with Mrs Buckley. A negro or some one broke open a desk at school, which held all the children's copy books and, stole all the blank paper out of them, stole some once before but not all, so Mrs B told them it was no use to bring paper there to be stolen, & Mary has quit writing but I am going to make her a copy book and let her bring it home every night. She had just taken a start in writing when she had to quit. Bob understands more about pronunciation now [than] Bob Mc-L[ure] does. Billy shall I speak of him? I never like to think of him—he grows worse all the time, is so hateful, such a mean, bad child, and you can't appeal to his feelings, he is too flinty to care for any thing, & stubborn as ever. I can't get him to do any thing unless I get the cowhide in hand, & I am too busy, and try to put thoughts of him far from me, and make Lee[76] do little errands & let Billy alone, spoiling him I know, but I am by Billy like I am by Tom, if there is any body else to call on I let them alone[;] tis too hard work [and] ruffles my feelings too much to get any thing out of them. I paddled Billy to night for imposing on Walter, which he does constantly, hitting him when ever he pleases & without provocation. I am determined I wont stand this from him, if I have to whip him every day. Alas, he will be a thorn in my heart as long as he lives & I cant feel towards him as I do the other children. He will make me sup sorrow. Walter is a high tempered fractious little fellow, rather hard to manage sometimes, but I never fear but he will turn out all right—his cup is so much better than Billy's. Walters health is better than it was some time ago. He talkes about you, very often. (Billy is the only one of the children who never speaks of you voluntarily) The other day at table he began his favorite questions. "Ma who gave you these spoons, knives &c," & at last he says "well Ma who gave you these boys?["] (looking at Bob & Billy & himself) I replied that your Pa *bought them, but I paid for them* which answer, tho' beyond his comprehension, satisfied him as you had something to do with it—that was in our true answer—& tho' Billy cost me less at his birth, I still

---

76. Levi or Lee was the son of Thornton and Nancy, two of the Nebletts' slaves. He was born on July 23, 1857. LND.

paid infinitely too dear for my whistle. I know it is wrong & unfortunate for me to feel so, but children have lost their charm for me, & in the sober hour of reflection I regret that I ever had a child. And now the baby your little one, must I portray her? I believe my writing often makes you want to see her worse, so here after I had better not write of her. As each day develops what I suppose will be her disposition, I love her, & sympathize with her more—now that word sympathize seems misplaced, but 'tis not. The most sensitive feelings you ever knew in a baby, if she is hurt a little, she seems to treasure the unkindness long after the hurt has ceased to smart and sobs so *piteously* at intervals, that I can hardly help crying with her, as she lays her little head upon my shoulder—I think of how heart broken I felt & what hours of anguish I passed before she came into the world. Alas I fear, she is too sensitive to ever be happy & that she has inherited my gloomy despairing disposition. I can only hope that she will grow out of it. Mother says she cry's just like I did when I was a baby. Polly let her fall about a month ago, & she sobbed about it two or three hours, at intervals, & yet it made no bruised place, her feelings were so hurt that even Billy's flinty heart was touched, & every where I walked with her, (for I won't let any body else have her when her feelings are hurt) Walter & Billy followed, & tried all the means they could employ to make her forget her distress, which she would do for a little while even smile, but her woe would return & she would sob again. I call her my little sensitive plant, a precious little darling she has become to me, I am always attracted to people who betray depth of soul, and feeling.

I am schooling my heart not to expect you for many long months yet, & I often think of how weary the time will be, but then I murmur not, if you can only keep well and return to me safely after the war. I believe it is as hard for you as 'tis for me, perhaps harder, as you are fonder of the society of our children then I am. Bear it as well as you can, & make up your mind to stay months yet before you get home even on a furlough. I *was* delighted with Carter's speech. I wish I could see you to talk with you about it, the hits he made &c, my letter is spun out now to such a length I fear you will grow tired this time of reading. When I get to writing to you I never know when to stop. I have every thing packed up for Joe to start tomorrow, except the butter, which I will do in the morning. The last butter I made is white butter, it got too warm by the fire, but I send it on top so as to be used up first. We all quit eating butter so as to save as much as possible to send to you. I send you an old vest of yours, fixed up as good as I can, which I have surnamed "*silver sides*," in honor of its patches. I regret that I can't send you a better one, and that I have no new socks to send. God knows I would like to do more better for you than I do, but I do my best. Not *complaining*, but my baby has been & is yet more trouble than any three of my other babes were up to her age. True she don't require much now as she did when she had the colic, but still more than the others did by far, & that is one thing you know I never do, neglect my baby's. *My hands, brain & heart are all full.* In your vest pocket I put some Composition Powders, sent you all I have but a little saved for Bettie's use. Don't give out but [a] few of yr peaches at a time, I know you relish them so when you are sick I want you to keep some on hand all the time for sickness. Mrs Oliver sends some socks for Mr O which you will find among your things. Put the rope that comes round your matrass away in your trunk you may need it again. I thought of sending you a quilt, but John Nix thinks what I send with what you have down there will be as much as you will want to take care of, if you want more, let me know and I'll send you a quilt. Write me how you like your matrass if your pants fit, and how the *blanket cloak* does. I had to guess at a part of it. I have sent Randal to mothers to night so as to get a letter from you tomorrow, (if there is one in the mail) before I start Joe, thinking you may write for something I havent sent you. I hope I'll get a letter. Write as soon as Joe gets to you as I will feel anxious to hear.

Oct 29th Randal has brought me yr letter of Oct 24th enclosing act of sale of cotton, also one from Peel & Dumble, which I understand & will get Coleman to pay the Tax & get Briggance voucher, when they say they can get the money back in due time. I got a little note from Hattie which I enclose to let you see what news it contains & will write to Frank to bring me some calico, for self & Mary, some domestic & flannel. I have no money to send you know, but can pay him when I get the things. I feel so sorry for Sterling. Old Christian did part of the work on the buggy when I went to town that day, have since found out that the front axeltree is broken, allmost in two, in the middle. Next time I go up I'll send it in to him again. I would like to have some of that money to pay some debts here, pay taxes &c, and if I see a chance will write to [O]wen & get some. Write me what to do. I fear when you read this *very long* letter you will think 'tis a great waste of paper, but I have writen it at night so no waste of time. Good bye.

> Your loving wife,
> Lizzie S. Neblett

4

Working for Negroes and Children

November 4, 1863–December 25, 1863

At home, Wednesday night
Nov 4th 1863
W. H. Neblett

Dear Will

After drinking a pleasant cup of coffee, & lighting a star candle, I have spread this sheet of paper before me, and began my weekly letter to you. I have been strongly tempted to defer writing several days to hear from you & to glean more news than I now possess, but recollecting how pleasant it is for the expected letter to arrive in its proper time, I have turned aside from the temptation. Oh Will, there are times when my heart is too full to find utterance either thro' pen or tongue, & I often feel that it is a fortunate thing for you that 'tis so. I so often wish that you had the inclination & felt the desire to communicate your thoughts & feelings to me, that you found it a pleasant task to write to me, & could write your letters in peace & quietness with the sweet & harmonious music of your heart in full & perfect tune, vibrating through every thought you penned. I know dear Will, that in your love & sympathy I am secure, yet it maketh such pleasant music in my heart to receive a word of commendation and an assurance that I am remembered by you day & night, that I often in my isolated & lonely condition actually pine & thirst for it. I know you never praise even those you love. I never remember your praising me in words but few times in your life, & tho' flattery is my abomination, yet heart felt praise from one I love admire & respect is very greatful to my soul. Our children (save Billy) resemble me in this particular & for that reason, I intend to strive never to with hold praise & approbation where it is due. Now these things you never think of, & altho' you care much less for praise than I do, you are never left to desire it from me, for 'tis so much the spontaneous offering of my heart to your merits, which I have studied as a book that it springs to my pen & is transcribed almost before I am aware of it. I have sometimes wondered if you ever had moments when your heart seemed warmer & more enthusiastic than usual, and you have felt like saying or writing to me in this wise. "Lizzie you have been a good faithful wife to me, having faults, tis true, yet faults which are so softened by your virtues & good qualities that one almost forgets them & in the possession of your love & respect, I feel that I have much to be thankful for—in a word that you are no ordinary woman." Now I know you smile & perhaps think you have a very romantic wife at least, but tis no more, nor half so much praise as I have thought felt & expressed for you thousands of times, yet never has my ear drank in such words or sentiments from your tongue or pen, & this night I could not conscientiously say that I believed you thought me any worthier of love & respect than the generality of women.

But let us return to something more interesting, but before we leave this subject let me say that I have learned more wisdom as regards your actions & expressions towards me. I never expect now any outpouring of feeling any enthusiastic outbreak of love or admiration, any expression which would show that my virtues have been studied, or my acts of love & remembrance pondered on. If any such feelings ever sweep across your soul, they will ever be as a sealed book to me and, I have almost taught my heart to pine not for such things, & I now thankfully & unmurmingly read your letters striving to put all selfishness far from me, remembering only what concerneth thee & thy welfare, & how I can promote both your happiness & comfort. And this has strengthened & comforted me. I say to my heart, ["]be still he loveth thee, accept thankfully the share & portion he giveth and study to deserve a larger share & it will come, even if you never receive evidence of it." I never knew until recently that there was so much selfishness in my heart. But I have perhaps tired you sufficiently for this time. I pass to other things. It requires greater self control than I can command, to write you a letter (when I have time & leisure a head of me) without telling you of my secret feelings of the war, the discord & contentions that fills my bosom, but you assure me that I neither disgust nor tire, for which I am thankful.

A most terrible & painful tragedy has been acted only a few miles from me this evening, but I have tried not to allow my thoughts to dwell upon it. The most horrible affair I ever knew of my own personal knowledge. Kit Hall was hung this evening about a mile from John Scott's. The startling developments of the last few days have horrified & aroused the whole community. The women left alone have been affraid to sleep—for a wonder I have remained comparatively calm. I will relate the story as fully as I can, but am not in possession of all the facts, having seen no one but Aunt Cinda Uncle Mc & John Nix. You remember I wrote to you of Kit Hall's sudden rise, what people surmised &c, well a little sooner than we expected justice has over taken him, & a little nearer home than we dreamed of was the horrible & cold blooded murder perpetuated by him. About a month ago he (Kit Hall) met two negro traders speculators for the first time as I understand it in Anderson. He bought of them one negro, paying $2500, and wanted more, but could not pay the money then, they were on their way to Houston, but bargained the negroes (8 in number I think) to Kit, who promised them that he would meet them in Red Top on their return & pay for the whole lot—the two men, Col Hoit and Mr Boone both from eastern Tex, one Cherokee Co, the other I dont remember the Co, told Kit to take the negroes home with him, & loaned him the cary all & mules to take them, while they pursued their way to Houston in a buggy with one mule attached. Kit met them according to promise in Red Top, couldent pay the money then, but if they would go with him to Huntsville he had a cousin there who would loan him the money & he would pay them there. For some cause he did not go with them but promised to meet them there at a stated time—which he did, and then told them that he left one of the negroes very sick & that he would not buy the sick negro unless they returned from Huntsville with him to his mothers & looked at the sick negro, & agreed upon some terms, the men suspecting no evil, returned with him—but as he [Kit] went on to Huntsville he stopped at Mrs Rogers & borrowed her gun. The men were both invalides one Col Hoit a large man weighing over 200 lbs, & crippled with the gout, the other man baring fever not well at all. He led them on 'till within a mile of Rogers, John Scotts off the road in the pine woods, he shot both of the men, one with a shot gun the other a pistol, both in the back, & there he burried them, borrowing a shovel from Mrs Rogers to do it with. Came home & had been home three weeks, buying lumber, building cabins & fixing round preparatory to starting off to his Co again.

In the mean while the wives of these two men became uneasy & alarmed at their protracted stay, as they were to be gone only 12 days when they left home, and they each got a Bro in law to start out to hunt them, giving them a description of the harness on the mule, & the buggy & the clothing of the two men, and they knowing the rout they came, got on track of them & lost the track with them returning with Kit Hall, who they found out had the negroes—they kept their own counsel, one stayed all night as a traveller at Mrs Wades & recognized Boone's coat from his wifes description of it on Kit Hall's person, they went on to Montgomery where they ferreted out the buggy & identified it by the Harness & cushiones, which one of the wives had made out of some cloth, a piece of which she showed them, and patched the reins which were old with cloth. The buggy had been repainted, and Kit Hall had it done claiming the buggy as his—they returned with the Sheriff of Montgy Co, & Walker Co and some others surrounded Mrs Wades house before day light and took him prisoner, & marched him to the Penitentiary, sending the negroes to Montg jail. He had on when arrested, Boones coat, vest, and his boots with his name "Boone' in them which Kit tried after he was taken to convert into Boot. The whole neighborhood of men then turned out to search for the bodies of the murdered men—and after a search of two & a half day's found the grave, within a mile of John Scott's & Mrs Rogers, 300 yds off from any road, they tracked the buggy by the skinned places on the little bushes & the wheel tracks occasionally, and right where the tracks ceased they found a large quantity of blood, & just 180 yds from that place, in the bottom of a ravine, they found the grave, no sign of any drag on the ground, consequently they say he must have had help to carry that large man that distance. Boone was in his stocking feet & the coat Kit was wearing was one he had in the buggy[. Boone] had a fever that day & was wearing a linen coat, which they found with Col Hoits coat [that] he was shot in[. The coats were] out of the grave, some distance from the grave, a little brush thrown on them. The linen coat [was] very bloody as if he had wiped out the buggy with it. It was just three weeks to a day from the time the murder was done 'till the grave was found. They suppose others were implicated & suspicion points to Geo Alston[1] a confession was expected from Hall to day who, I hear thro' Jack Oliver was hung on the spot where he killed the men. They tried to have a trial before a Magistrate in Huntsville but failed as the state, so Uncle Mc said, had no witnesses and they did not wait any farther but just brought him back & hung him. I cant tell you all the little minutia but 'tis the plainest case you ever heard.

---

1. In 1850 George W. Alston was 11 years old and living with Nathaniel (40) and Winford (36) Alston. There is no record of him or his family in the 1860 census. TX Census 1850.

A more exasperated community you never saw. It has broken up the school. Dr Browns & Jeff Haynie's children have the whooping cough, & the Alston's & Hall children have stopped, which thins out the school so she [Mrs. Buckley, the schoolteacher] quit, & her feelings were so worked upon, she got Mrs Brown to go to the school house with her, the morning after the bodies were found—she was affraid to go alone. I am sorry the school has ended—our children were learning so fast. Mrs Wade poor woman is almost if not quite crazy. Hall satisfied his mother & Alston by telling them that his Cousin near Huntsville (who is a wealthy man, & is winding up his Bro in laws estate who was wealthy & has a large quantity of money in his hands) loaned him the money, & he was to have it untill after the war some year, without interest, & they say they believed him. He had forged Bill's of sale for the negroes not in his hand writing they say, one true bill of sale for the negro he bought of them at Fanthops tavern—from the place where the buggy wheels stopped & the murder was done, all traces of the buggy tracks cease for a considerable distance & sudde[n]ly appear in the road—which makes them think the buggy was carried that far & put down again. ('twas a light concern without a top) I am anxious to hear if he made a confession.[2]

Alex Coleman, is fixing to be off for the wars in less than a month, John Nix tells me that mother told him she thought he was needed worse in the service than she needed him, & so he is fixing to be off—I suppose mothers patience became exhausted as he grew less account to her every day more so since he got courting in his head. They say it hurts him mighty bad, is very much crest fallen. I wrote to mother to get him to attend to that certificate from Briggance & asked him to enclose it in a letter I wrote to Peel & Dumble. I told them P&D to hand the money to Owen when they got it back. I must try & get some of that money to pay mother & Jim for the Sugar, & some other debts. Have finished banking my potatoes to day—fixed them up very snugly in the smoke house—tried to make it rat proof under neath by placing boards down, banked seed in there too—made 55 bushels eating size and 10 bushels of seed, with some four or five bus of cut & bruised potatoes left out in baskets for present use—5 bushels I put up for the Gov. They are larger potatoes than we made last year, & more of them, plenty with careful

---

2. On lynch law and southern society see Edward Ayers, *Vengeance and Justice: Crime and Punishment in the Nineteenth Century American South* (New York: Oxford University Press, 1984); Wyatt-Brown, *Southern Honor*, 435–93.

use of them to last till late next spring & they won't steal them this time unless they break open the smoke house. But it is now 12 Oclock, & I must stop—the baby has been up once since I have been writing & is stirring again—so good night, I have had more dreams which I must tell you tomorrow.

Nov 6th Friday morn "Tomorrow" came & past, & yet I wrote not, & last night I would not for prudence sake write as my eyes have been a little sore ever since I wrote so many nights running to you before Joe left & for fear that I would get past sewing for the children I did not write last night. My work rests heavy on my mind, & the day is gone before I have done any thing. Polly is too small to do anything for the baby but hold her & consequently my attention to the baby takes up so much time. Hearing of the trouble, the inexpressible anguish Mrs Wade's child has brought upon her, makes me look at my children & wonder if all my care, solicitude & labor for my children will be rewarded by any one of them in like manner, and having no natural desire for children, having always been so bothered with sewing for them, that I never had time to feel proud of them & that they were treasures to me, & now I feel like I had much rather die & leave them than run the risk of ever having a disgraced child to mourn to my grave. God deliver me from such a fate! Billy is enough now to mourn over. I feel weighed down, crushed to the earth with sorrowful feelings & bitter repinings as I think of the past and what might have been, but for your sake I'll try & still these feelings & bother you not with my unavailing regrets.

I went over to Aunt Cinda's yesterday eve to hear Kit Hall's confession. In the first place he implicated no one, says he did it all by himself. I give you now a part of what he said after he became convinced that he would be hung, which was done by the mob on the spot he killed the men, & the knot was fixed by some Dr who placed it so he could with great effort get his breath as he hung, & thus his death agonies were prolonged & agrivated in a most fearful degree. I cant commend this course, which I fear had a deleterious effect upon the hearts of the spectators, & there was a crowd of little *boys there*—every one of John's boys, except little Jim—and Garrett the very mention of whom makes my heart ache, was what they call *gentlemanly drunk,* swearing round that he knew old Alston was his accomplice & ought to be hung by him, & doing & saying a thousand disgusting & fiendish things, because his old enemy had proven himself a thief & a murderer, & Justice had over taken him. Oh what a dark spot in the heart does such conduct betray, to gloat over the misfortunes of an enemy or tread on a fallen foe. He wanted to go to the dungeon in the Penitentiary & curse Hall, & was prevented. He followed him every where, and yesterday after his body had been carried to his mother & shrouded, & lay in her room, he followed him there to gaze upon the anguish of his frantic mother & sisters, whom he calls his enemys. Oh Will he is a hardened boy, destitute of feelings or respect, a *blot* upon the name of Scott. And Susan; exalted in the same manner, & as revelation after revelation was made known thro his confession & she heard it, she would clap her hands and cry out "*I told you so!*" She had a great deal of company men stoping & eating & sleeping there during the time, the search &c was going on and when they went to leave after it was all over, one of the men said "well Mrs Scott how much have we damaged you, what do we owe, nothing sir" she replied "I would give that much any time to have Kit Hall caught" said in an exalting manner. Kit Hall selected Garret & gave him a little advise [*sic*] in particular. He said Garret I have been your enemy but all such feelings are now dead I wish you well, & just look at me & take warning, & whenever you are tempted to do wrong think of me. I have often heard it remarked of you "that boy will be hung," and I want you to change your ways, and be a better boy." Garrett said "who did you ever hear say so? none but your clicque, & I have no ways to mend & never expect to alter." Kit was very penitent before he died, prayed with *fervor*—yet, poor fellow I do not think he felt the full weight of his crime, & consequently could not have repented in a manner acceptable with God. He said that he raised the Gun several times to shoot before he did & his heart would fail him & that was why he killed them so near home he put if off as long as he could. He shot Boone first, and he fell out the buggy & he exclaimed "God have mercy Col Hoit I have killed Mr Boone, what shall we do," Col Hoit said, why we must do the best we can, Kit says you just get out Col, and take the mule & turn it around and I think I can get him in the buggy myself, and before he reached the mule, he shot Hoit, when Hoit turned round & said for God sake Hall, don't shoot me again and he then shot him through the top of his head—and he says he killed them in [the] road, & not where they found that blood, (which tale is not believed) and that he put them in the buggy & hauled them to the ravine & robbed them down, where he left them till next day when he borrowed the shovel from Mrs Rogers, & buried them & standing there looking at the spot the grave he dug he said Gent[le-man] I have done much hard work in my life but I done the hardest I ever done in my life right there it liked to have killed me. Says he only got about $4000 from the men, and that he stole $2100 from Bill Loggins didn't kill him, tho' he was strongly tempted to kill some man who came back with [him] & was there at his hanging. Several men sent money by Bill Loggins to make purchases for *them*, & he said he took some out of each pile, so that it would not be missed soon, & remarked that was a cute trick, and a man present who sent money by Loggins said did you get any of mine, when Kit smiled & said yes I damaged you a little. He did not destroy any of the traces of things the men had, hid the hat, the boots of Boone, (which he did not have on 'twas said) a saddle valise, papers pocket book, &c &c all about in different places, some right close to John's, some down below Uncle Mc's, the pocketbook & papers, took the head of the walking cane home with him which was silver & Boones blanket & pistol. He whispered to his mother to burn that blanket when he was arrested which she did, & told his sister Ann to hide the things in his trunk which she did, but brought them in when they went after them. They say that he has not accounted for a good deal of money that Hoit & Boone are believed to have, independent of the 2100 he got from Loggins—says he stole a gun from a poor soldier in La, but killed no one then. That he crippled the mule in shooting the men, & then took him off behind his mothers field & shot him. They found all the things where he said he hid them, every thing just as he said. He says he copied the bills of sale from the one true & good one he had, and altered his hand writing.

Many are not satisfied with his tale still believe he had help & an accomplice, and as George Alston is now off on a speculating tour as people suppose, he is regarded very suspiciously tho' Kit said George had nothing to do with & knew nothing of it that he was a good honest boy. I reckon he tells the truth, for if any one had helped him it seems to me, they would have put all the articles belonging to the dead men, buggy and all, and burnt them up. Poor Mrs Wade is I verily believe, insane, she lays and repeats poetry awhile, and then commences screaming, seems to be almost entirely bereft of reason. Oh how I pity her, from the depths of my soul. Tho' she may not have raised her son right, yet is she to be deeply pitied. He requested Uncle Mc to tell his mother not to have his body placed by his father, that his father was a good man, & he did not want to disgrace his grave so she had him buried in her garden at home. He hung nearly all night. Alston had him cut down & carried him to his mother, just before day. The Alston family are also in great distress & feel the disgrace keenly. Alston is trying to sell out & leave, & some talk of old Sandlin buying from him.

I saw Jim at Aunt Cindas yesterday & he said it was 90 cts he gave for the sugar, I made Bettie's figures out [to be] 70. He got 200 pounds, & says he has put up about 72 pounds for me, which I will take, tho' tis a little more than I want but if the Yankees don't run us off, it will last me a long long time.

Jim uses more Sugar than any small family I ever knew. He got 72 pounds in peach time & I judge from what he said that is all gone, as he has put my sugar in that barrell. He says he don't know why mother dismissed Coleman & thinks it a bad move on her part, which I think too. I know something about it. I could not begin to write you how our negros do all the little things, what eye servants they all are. And none but Sarah will report one single thing to me, what she finds out she comes & tells. I find that Thornton is very little better than the others, but I find him & Bill the most trust worthy about doing any jobs out of my sight. I *find I must think continually for them,* & when they know & see a thing that ought to be done, they never do it, & never say a word 'till I see it, or think of it & call up some one about it, & then I hear the tale. "Yes I knowd it ought to be done, but I dident know you wanted it done cause you never said any thing about it," & that makes me so mad I can't help myself. Bob is my reporter now, I send him to find out about things, & he does it, most willingly. I don't allow my self to think of what I will do next year. Uncle Mc would *be worse than nobody.* I never saw such a crowd in one house, as there is over there. John Nix arm is improving some, but will always be crooked. Jane has writen that she will be here before Christmas. Uncle Mc has not made near corn enough, can't fatten any meat to sell, & no mast to fatten it for him. I have our hogs in the field now, to get the good of the potatoe patch, corn &c. Rivers never turned out one of those oxen till a few days ago. I could not get him as he had him at the Wassen place. He will never get another ox from me if I can help it. He is now paying back my work, & don't stay with the hands, visits them once a day, & I know they are not working, but I can't help it. I would like to get that cleared up, & all broke up & fenced in before christmas & a part of the rails are to split & from what Thornton tells me, there is not near enough split to make that pasture. A part of the cotton near those cedar trees needs picking now, but I thought it best to put all hands in the clearing while River's was pretending to over see them. 4 of Mrs Hurst men are working here, the other part of her hands picking cotton.

I expect there is a letter at town for me, but I sent to the office three time last week, & twice the week before, & am waiting for some one else to send this week. I wrote once for Burton to send me my mail, and not to send me the Lake creek mail, & he sent it, & then I had to send it around. I am going to try and get my mail by itself no body brings mine. I believe Susan instructs her boys to leave my mail. And as long as Susan & I will send to town Uncle Mc don't trouble himself to go only when he feels like it, & of course his son Bob is too small to go by himself, & 'tis a pity to make him go unless he wants to, so it goes, "every man for himself & the devil take the hind most."[3] I am going up to mother in a few days, & *take a little rest,* try to leave all my trouble about the negroes & farm behind me. I must have the buggy fixed and go before Dr Partick & file my petition for some more cloth, in order to get it early next spring as it takes several months to get it you know—& if I can sum up courage enough will have some teeth extracted, old decayed ones, even if I don't have any plugging done. Frank Perry had left before my note reached there, & Nelia writes she can't promise any thing from him until he returns as they don't know what he will bring & that Ma only sent for negros clothes. I know if you had been going I would have writen to Mittie & the others to send in there [*sic*] bills if they wanted any thing done. You know how Bettie acted with what Jim bought & tho Babe sent a bill she got nothing hardly, which was Bettie's fault—as I said before, "every man & woman for his & herself, &c." Well if this ant a selfish world, I don't know, & if people don't forget favors sooner they do a good dinner I'll give up.

I could write you three times as much as I have written & then not be to the middle of what I want to say, but I stop for the present. I forgot to send Mary's letter in the one I wrote by Joe, & send it now. I am quite anxious to know whether Joe reached you with what I sent all safe. Oliver writes that he expects you & him will be home soon, as they will begin to furlough the men soon. Oliver being an officer no doubt will get to come, but build not hopes up on coming yourself, for all furloughs will be stopped as soon as the officers all get home. Never mind I believe in the old saying "every dog has his day"[4] & tho yours may be a long time coming, perhaps it will be all the brighter when it does come but I shall long for it & dream of it many a time before it comes. I dreamed of your coming the other night very unexpectedly, but I think you only felt badly had the headache, or was going to have it. I wish I had your last letter. It seems like it has been a year since I saw you Will. Oh the time has passed so slowly & it seems so long. Good bye, John Nix will carry this to town. All well at Mr Olivers I saw Jack this morn. You see my old journal is going a piece at a time. John Scott hadent heard from his last papers when he wrote last. I don't expect he will get old Dowdy in at last.

Yours affectionately,
Lizzie S Neblett

3. Samuel Butler, *Hudibras,* part 1, canto 2 (1663).
4. John Heywood, *Proverbes* (1549).

Nov 6th Friday night. After I finished my letter, Wm Oliver sent the bucket, clothes & letter you sent by Warren. I often wonder if you feel as glad to get a letter from me as I do one from you, and as soon as the children find out I have a letter from you they flock around and all ask, what does Pa say? When is he coming home? read me some of the letter—did he say any thing about little sisy? and I have to say go away, go away and I'll tell you what he said when I finish reading it. They form many imaginary pictures of what they will do when you come, they fully expect that some one will run against a tree & butt their head, & they wonder who you want to see the worst, who you will speak to first, what you will say when you see little sister, & a thousand other things, which makes me feel figity as you say. Oh that you could come, but I don't allow myself to build any hopes, 'tis so bad to be disappointed. You see I have already banked my potatoes in the smoke house, but as the dirt was dug up hunting the rats, and our meat dripped so little, & the smoke house so new, I dont think what little salt is in the earth will hurt them, and then they were pretty well covered with dry fodder before the dirt was put on, so I think I will let them stand, till I find they are rotting. I intended having dirt put on that came from out side the house, but the day they were Banked it was raining & could not get dry dirt out side, but I don't think they will rot. Sam missed his stolen share this year. Sarah dug & guarded the patch, six hands including Kate dug them in two days. I think they worked well. Old Sam carded,[5] & Mary was down there when he was carding & heard him say "I wish my foot was well about this time." Polly says "why Uncle Sam,["] & he said "nary word." Mary says she knows it was because he wanted to steal some of the potatos, he had a few vines which I had dug for him & he made about 2 washpan's full. I fear you was not pleased with "Silver sides" made you send it back. You always had an aversion for patches, but I thought it was fixed up so neatly and I gave the old vest such a musical name "silver sides" that I thought it would please you as well as it did the children, who all wondered to see silver sides return. I too have thought of John Nix as an overseer, but thought I would not be hasty in the matter would wait & see his motions. If I can get old Myers[6] no doubt it would be best, for I tell you these negroes

---

5. Cards were wire-toothed brushes that were used to disentangle fibers (i.e., cotton, wool) prior to spinning.

6. Presumably L. M. Myers, listed in the 1860 census as a 44-year-old farmer with personal and real property valued at $1,400. He was married to Mary (41) and had four children living with him in 1860. TX Census 1860.

need a strict overseer. Walter was delighted with the candy and was just this moment smacking his mouth, like he was dreaming of eating candy. Bettie is very well pleased with the taste also. Mrs Oliver put in her application for the three bolt of cloth she got recently way last spring. She keeps an application in all the time, has got cloth three times this year from the Penitentiary & sold old Myers some this time for going after it, which I don't see how she can do consistently with the oath they made me take. She says she is in fine health now, is as well as she ever was in her life. I reckon the men do wonder what I can have to write so much about but they don't know me.

Sure enough you did have the headache worse than usual as I thought my dream foreboded. I am a stronger believer in dreams than I was before.

Dear Will—In great haste I write this slip to say that John Nix failed to go to Town as expected, and I failed to send mother word that I could not go up to her house on friday so yesterday morn, I met her on the road coming down to see what was the matter—and in the eve John & all the family came up, so their is now a crowd of us here. All well. Mother after she was talked to by Jim, told Coleman to stay as Jim thought she could not get along without him was endangering herself & Babe &c, so Coleman is perfectly delighted, walks on stilts of delight & accommodation to Jim especially [as] either Jim or Coleman are going to carry out some cotton to Mexico Town, & get some things for mother & Jim, maybe I'll get a callico dress now. I have fixed Bettie up pretty snugly out of the old flannel about the house, am astonished at the out fit myself, and am vastly pleased with myself that I have done so well out of the material I had. "Necessity is the Mother of invention."[7] I wish you could see the little darling. Could write much more but havent time will write again in a few days. L S N monday morn, Nov 9th

At Mothers,
Friday Nov 13th/63
W.H. Neblett

Dear Will,

I went to town yesterday, hoping so earnestly that I would find a letter there from you, but was doomed to meet with disappointment. If I did not

7. The origin is unknown, but the adage can be found in Richard Franck, *Northern Memoirs* (1694); William Wycherley, *Love in a Wood,* act 3, scene 3 (1671); and George Farquhar, *The Twin Rivals,* act 1 (1703).

have your letters to look forward to, what should I do? I never knew, or never felt, so forcibly before you were called into service, how utterly dependent I am on you for what little pleasure & enjoyment of life that falls to my lot. You are the center of all my thoughts your idea your approval or disapproval, the main spring of all my acts, and were you lost to me forever, what would my life be worth—a tree striped forever of its verdu[r]e, a river with its fountain dry, its waters gone. When I think that such a fate may overtake me; children & mother are all forgotten (I have neither brothers nor sisters, nor friends) and an involuntary prayer accends that reason may be dethroned if such a fate awaits me, but oh the anguish that must intervene before reason deserts her throne. But why do I borrow trouble of the future, surely the present has evil enough. I do feel so weary of life sometimes, its duties, its trials, its sorrows, all press so heavily upon me, that I wish only for the quietude of the grave.

But no doubt you have your trials, tho' in a different form from mine, but you should be thankful that you can bear yours better than I can mine. Our children trouble me greatly, both time & mind in a continual stretch for them, and every moment should be filled with work & when this is neglected a reproach is left upon my mind, & even when I will indulge in my chief and almost only pleasure of writing long letters to you, I feel that [the] sentimental & the gloomy part ought to have remained unwriten, & that time been filled with work, & I often feel that in reading such portions you have thought that my time had better have been empl[o]yed in manual labor for the good of my family, & while I submisively acknowledge the justice of such thoughts, the flood gates of bitterness are opened, & I mentally exclaim ["]why were so many children given to me", & then follows a train of self accusation in which self respect is often wounded, and the well of bitterness & unceasing & unavailing regrets is so agitated that I do not get over it for days, in fact it is ever present & with it too the feeling that I may some day see the time when the memory of such thoughts will stab me to the heart. I once felt differently about children & I sigh that that time has past, & then the labor I had to perform was one of love, & did not crush me, like the labor of duty— but my last child was the feather that broke the cam[el]'s back, I will never *recover* from it. My good sense teaches me to feel ashamed of these feelings & thoughts, but does not teach me to discard them, & to you only do I tell them, just as they are. But I stop the subject, tears blind me and this choking sensation in my throat warns me to go no farther.

The school has closed down in our neighborhood and now is the time I

have looked forward to, as the period when I could visit Ma & Hattie, before
[it is] time to kill our meat, the corn & cotton gathered, the potatoes
housed, &c, but the children are not ready & with my cross baby, when I work
hard all day, at night I can hardly see what I have done. Tis usel[ess] to try to
hire help, every one so busy getting cloth wove & made up for winter, & I can
not travel about to see who could help me, so I don't try & have given up the
hope of ever getting down to Pa's again while I live—true I should not care.
Ma I know would find some pleasure in the company of your children, but she
has other grand children near her, and as to me, none of them care much
whether they ever see me. You know Mittie could come to see me any time in
her carry all but as Frank says she is too proud to go in that, & her desire to
see me is not strong else pride would not over come it. I should not care about
these things, but my heart is not entirely crusted over with indifference, hence
I fret over such things. I came up last sunday as you know, so I cant tell you
what the negroes are doing, but left some of them picking out what little cotton was open, & the rest clearing. Mother wants John Nix to stay with her,
sleep in the house and report to her Colemans movements &c & is going to
pay him for doing so if he will stay which is not a settled thing as yet. He has
to go to Houston the 19th inst to have his furlough extended, & he don't
know how that will end—his arm is improving both in strength & flesh, tho'
I don't think he will ever be able to straighten it—he cant hold a gun to chest
yet, & may never be able to do so, still our Gov is so pushed for men they may
give him some position to fill where shooting is not demanded, he thinks it
will be likely that he will have to go into service again before the war ends.
When I return home I will go over to Mrs Oliver & see if there is any chance
to get Meyers to attend to our farm also—but Will, I fear the[y] cant make
another crop with the plows we have now, & where are the new ones to come
from. I have spoken to Coleman to go & see the plows & see what he thinks
about it, & have been trying to find out if there is any chance for me to get
any iron or plows by mothers, Jim's & Colemans wagons going to Brownsville,
but can't find out, I asked Jim, & he laughed & said I must see mother about
that, which was as good as saying I need not expect any favors from him. I
talked to Coleman, & he could tell nothing. Susan Scott is going to send her
mule wagon & two bales & pay half of the expenses of that wagon, & get
farming utensils with the cotton. I heard a rumor in town yesterday which I
was told came in the papers also that Brownsville was in ashes, if so that trip

is knocked in the head.[8] Jim pretends to be fixing to farm next year & says he is going to move on Lake Creek. I shall not believe this till I see him move. He is not certain that he can keep out of service. His sub went in as 42 I think tho' he says he is over 45. Jim went to him recently at Valasco, but don't know the result of his trip, as Jim tells so little & seems so crusty when questioned— but Coleman says if he was in Jim's place he would pay the man $1000 to swear he was over 45, but I hope Jim has a truer idea of what would be up-right & creditable than to propose such a measure to any man. Bettie makes Jim worse than he naturally is, & if he goes into service it will be like pulling his eye teeth. She says she just wants to die when Jim starts if he does have to go, & a thousand other things. Jim & Dr Dickson are the most desponding men we have any where around here. Nothing Jim says has any effect on me, seems to have the effect to renew my hope for I do think his views are per[v]erted & unsound—he is too hopeless tho' loyal enough, his patriotism seems dead.

I went to town yesterday hoping to put a letter in the first place, & then get my teeth & the old buggy worked on. Dr Johnson was not at home, negro dident know when he would be at home, & Christian only did part of the work, mended the axel tree, have to send it again—& I expect all of Johnson's gold will be gone the next time I come in, but I feel like giving up every thing & folding my hands, and gazing on the wreck of nature and hope. Mother has had my lindsy[9] wove must go back home sunday & put out Joes clothes and have them made, to send by Olivers negro. I wish I had your socks [k]nit to send, but, havent. I ate dinner on yesterday with Laura Hutcheson.[10] She is a mystery to me. She lost her sister Mrs Ed Florester some 10 days ago with diptheria, and she is as cheerful & lively now as I ever saw her, talks with-out the slightest sign of emotion of her death, her last words, & all the little minutia attending her sickness & burial. Talks of Hutcheson with as much

8. Union general Nathaniel Banks did gain a foothold in Texas in early November 1863. He occupied Brazos Island and areas around Brownsville and Point Isabel. Long, *Civil War Day by Day*, 431.

9. Linsey or linsey-woolsey was a coarse fabric made of linen and wool or cotton and wool.

10. In 1860 Laura Hutcheson (age 22, spelled Hutchinson in the 1860 census) was living with her husband, J. W. (30) Hutcheson, a lawyer with personal and real property valued at $4,200. He was also the captain of Company G of the Fourth Texas Infantry Regiment. He died at the Battle of Gaines Mill. TX Census 1860; Allen, *Saga of Anderson*, 155–56.

unconcern as I can, & do & does not pay as much reverence to his virtues, his generosity & magnamosity of heart, as I do. Is in favor of marrying, what we were made for, to bear children &c, tho' she never had but one, thanks be to preventives I think. I cant write all I think but if I could see you I could I think give you right interesting talk with her for the subject. Babe still intoxicated with the Bakers—tells them every thing that any body says to her about Jessie, & yet says Jessie never said any thing to her about love or marriage in his life, & she don't know that he wants to. Babe has a very *shallow heart.* I don't say one word to her in the way of advice about any thing nor never shall. She dislikes me more & more *but we never clash,* I never let on. She quit going to see Sallie some time ago because Sallie quarreled with her, about giving her up for the Bakers, & not doing anything for her expected baby—which by the way arrived in this world on yesterday while we were at Laura's—don't know what sort of a time she had, but Laura sent over after dinner to hear how she was, as she knew what was going on, & found it all over, & Sallie told the negro to tell me that she done better than I did. I don't know whether she meant had a better time or that she done better because she has a boy.[11] I feel glad that it is over with on her account, but I am sorry that Bassett & I both claim kin with the same object. He has not yet come. I w[e]nt to Dr Patricks two days ago and took the oath to procure cloth and asked Dr Partick to enclose the same to Col Rogers of Huntsville to get the cloth for me, who does such things on commission. I find Mrs Patrick as much grieved as any one I ever saw in my life. I find her a very superior woman—a refined heart and a cultivated brain. Poor mothers her heart was bound up in her child—& now he is no more—& tho' she feels all the bitterness of intense grief yet she says she would not have loved him less for worlds. I will go to see Mary Haynie a little while this evening. The girls all laugh & make fun of her, because she is an old maid, and is old fashioned in her dress & notions—what fools, her friendship & association would be an honor to any of them. I stop now to get ready to go.

Sat morn, Nov 14th. Jim was here after I finished the [above], & says the Fed[erals] have Brownsville so the trip is knocked in the head, to day the men meet at town to see about raising a Co. to go to Brownsville, and I must send this by Coleman to the office.

---

11. This child would die before 1870. Sallie and Robert Bassett had only one child who lived to maturity, Belle Bassett Blackley. TX Census 1870.

Have sent to the office, Smith hasent yet returned, hope he will bring a letter for me. Aunt Cinda rec'ed a letter from Bob Teel a few days since, he has a position as cotton agent, and something to do with the stage line at Corpus Christi, & has moved his family there. Jim Scott is in trouble about his mule teams & wagons. Impressing officers [are] here now after mules & wagons. Havent been to mothers yet. Jim says his *Sub* told him he would swear that he was over 45 if he would pay him 100 dollars in specie, which he did not have with him, else he would have done it. Jim says if he don't swear that [he] is over 45, it will cost him about 12 thousand dollars, as he is determined not to go in himself, & if the Legislature prohibits Sub, compelling all men to go in themselves, that he will emigrate, leave the county. The women folks have stirred up quite a muss on Lake Creek, about Mrs Magee (the mid wife) & McCune, cant write it now, but every woman is liable to be talked about, it seems the state of society is coming to an *awful pass.* I forgot to tell you that there has been a little whispering out about Uncle Mc not taking the right steps about Kit Hall, & he is awful wrathy. I'll tell you more when I have time. Do write often, Coleman waits, Good bye.

Affectionately
Lizzie S. Neblett

Nov 14th Sat Evening—Just as I was going to seal my letter & back it, I thought of your writing that it was probable that the Co might go up to Harrisburge with the Bayou City for repairs—so I did not send by Coleman [am] waiting to see if Smith would not bring me a letter from you, which he did, saying not a word of Harrisburge, & now my letter wont get to the office 'till monday. You seem to be further from [me] in this last letter than usual, but I don't murmur, you are well, & I will try & reconcile myself to your absence, tho' I sometimes fear I will never see you again. Oh I feel that it would be such a consolation to have you with me, for a week or two if no longer—there is so much I long to say to you, that I can not write in a satisfactory manner, and so much I would like to hear from you, tho you never feel like you want to talk to me. But I did not commence this slip to write of my feelings, but it is so natural for such thought to take the place of more material & useful ones that I write as they come.

That little sow you speak of in your last, happened to some accident I suppose & lost her pigs, all died, came too soon, & I don't think she is worth $10. I wrote to Nelia some time ago that if Pa was well supplied with hogs, been

more fortunate than we were, I would like to get that sow he promised you &
Nelia says I can get the sow, & the pair of geese, when I send. This sow you
speak of is small. It is unfortunate that your advise [*sic*] about what I ought to
do always comes after I have acted, I have both stock & pork hogs in the field,
except that original hog, he runs over at Hursts place & is so bad about fighting I don't care if he never stays at home. I will try & sell your hat for you,
tho' I fear it will be a bad business. I think I will put up our pork hogs when
I go home. Coleman tells me (& I havent the law to consult) that the Gov
allows everyone 100 bu of corn, & the 10th after that goes to the Gov, if so I
will have only 40 bu to pay as my tax, & he says I can haul that down to Navasota at one load while the road is good, as it is now, & that the Gov allows
pay per mile, over the 8 miles you haul—& they are now rec[eiving] in the
ears & Brown has hauled to the depot, & every body else seem to be doing
the same, so I think I had better send mine too right away & be done with it.
Since Joe left[,] Thornton has found that barrow that runs at Hursts & was
missing, both he & the young sow so wild [he] can't toll them, I will kill them
both. I havent figured up the weights of the cotton been so busy, but will let
you know in my next letter. I will speak to Coleman about hauling the cotton
up here, &c.

Sunday morn Nov 15th Mary Haynie came in & I had to stop yesterday
eve, & last night Bill Dodd stayed with us & from him I learned a more satisfactory account of the murder of Boone & Hoit than I have yet learned. You
are out of the excitement, hence dont take the interest in it I do, such things
always had great interest for me. Dodd is firmly of the opinion that Hall lied,
says he had help & many little circumstances put together tend to convince
me that he is right, & tho' he did not say, I think he believes the Alston family
are the helpers. He says he believes the men will return & sift the matter
deeper. The men say they sent a negro, monday morn before the search began,
to Uncle Mc to ask his help in the search, & he was gone, which is true he
went up to Huntsville he says because he wanted to hear the trial, but they
had no trial, but he really went because Mrs Wade begged him to go & bring
her news from Kit [and] see what they done with him &c. [S]o when they
sent for him to help search for the dead men, he was gone—and Will I fear
he will get him self many enemies for he tries to convince (in his negro fashion & of course never succeeds) every body that Alston nor no one else had a
hand in it, that Kit told the truth about where he had hid all the things & his
little stealing scrapes, he *must have told all the truth* but the wounds on the
dead mens bodys showed he lied about how he shot them, & he lied about the

place where he killed them, and seemed all the time he was talking to prefer telling of his stealing, & other unimportant things rather than talk of the murdering of the men—he certainly had help. I wish you could hear Bill Dodd talk about [it], he is so in earnest, has searched so deeply into the matter & thought so much about it, and tells so much of what happened at the hanging &c. Altho' it is an awful thing yet, to hear him tell some of it, it was so supremely ridiculous I could not help laughing heartily. Bill made my heart flutter faster than it has done in some time, by telling of some man from your Co coming home last week, & telling some one of his neighbors that the boat was going up to Harrisburge, & the Co with it, & that the boys were going to stampede, come home by the flocks. For a few minutes I felt so glad but then I knew it might all be false, the boat had not come up when the man left. I was very anxious to get your letter, writen last monday 9th hoping you would say the boat was at Harrisburge but you never said one word, oh well we cant help it, & if I never see you more that can't be altered, but oh, that I could stop this accursed war! I won't write about this for I won't make you nor myself feel any better. I go home this evening don't know when I will leave home again. My children are such a pest, that I feel like I ought never to leave home with them & I get more loth to do so, all the time. Children are any thing but a pleasure & treasure to me. Sometimes I get along very well with the baby, & then again she is nothing but a trial & cross to me.

At Home Teusday night
Nov 17 1863

Dear Will—

I lay down after supper to night and took a nap, arose and drank a cup of coffee, then provided myself with pen ink & paper, and then commence a letter to you, but I feel very weary, tired and without energy. I have had a sick baby all day, just sick enough to be very cross & fretful, and her crying & fretting has worn me out, I cant do anything when I hear it, I forget all I know, & it does seem this baby tries me more than all the others put together did. Her coming was so out of place and season, & I feel it so sensibly yet, & that makes the matter worse. If I was raising her for anything but an inheritance of woe, even if her life is most favored, I might for her future good stand the evil of the present, but when imagination pictures a future more blest than mine, I think of the times when like me, she will murmur, "oh that I had died in infancy," and tho' no doubt I would miss her more than any child I have, yet I

don't think I would grieve after her & wish her back. She is the most sensitive
little thing to cold, & a bad cold seems to hurt her so much [that of] every
change she takes cold in spite of all my precaution, & I spare no pains to prevent it— for the last week, she has had a cold which uses her a little worse than
common, had had the sore eyes with it, one sore at a time, and last night &
yesterday she had a fever—had a fever nearly all night last night, is clear to
night. She hasent been well of a cold since the cool weather set in this fall—
notwithstanding all she grows fast & is right plump & fat. Her hand & foot
is larger than Bettie's baby's, in fact, she is larger than Bettie's baby every
way & almost as tall, and Bettie's child is seven months the oldest, & is walking & talking some. I sometimes think you will never see this baby, but you
would soon forget that you ever had such a child, for altho' she troubled me
so before & since her birth she never impressed herself upon your memory in
a favorable way, but poor little creature she was born to misfortune. I did not
begin my letter thinking to write so much about her, and must hasten on to
more important things. I must write all I can to night, for she won't let me
write nor sew tomorrow.

I came [by] Mrs Oliver's yesterday as I came home from Mothers, & saw
old man (tho' he looks mighty young) Meyers there, and asked him about it
tending to our negroes, he don't seem to be at all anxious to do it, but I rather
insisted & this morning he came over to see the land, &c, and says he will
attend to the farm next year, beginning now, for $400 confederate money
which he estimates as 80 dollars good money, or specie, and he can't spend
but a half a day with our negroes every other day or three times a week. He
will attend to Mrs Roger's Mrs Oliver's and our farm. Susan Scott he says
[was] very anxious to get him also, but I think he don't want to go there, if I
agree to take him upon the terms he proposes. He says he will be perfectly
willing to stop when the crop is made, if you or I think it best & that the
negros can gather it themselves, & he be paid at the rate of 400$ a year. I made
no bargain with him, but told him I would write to you immediately & hear
what you say. I think myself, it would be better to pay him that. Mrs Rogers &
Mrs Oliver agree to cultivate his crop between them & each pay him 200$ in
addition, & he says they have 3 hands a piece, while I will have about five at
least, he thinks the Gov will take one from me. He will be right tight on the
negroes I think, but they need it, they have never feared Rivers one single bit.
Meyers will lay down the law and enforce it. I will not let him treat the negroes cruelly, nor abuse them, & don't think he will have to whip but one or
two before the others will take the hint. He says I must have all the plows

fixed up right away and they must go to breaking up the new land, which is nearly burnt off & ready for the plows, & the negros tell me all the plows have to be sent to the shop, & I think all have to be stocked—two are mothers, never been brought home, I am going to have them gathered up tomorrow, & when he comes back as he said he would on Thursday I will let him look at them see what [he] says.

Major is here now making ox yokes; & after that will stock the plows. I can keep him three weeks if I want to as Bill stayed three weeks over the time. Mage was shoe making down here. Old Sam will turn out tomorrow, and walk about on his foot & harden it, he can burn brush & do other work in the clearing. I think I shall send my 40 bushels of Gov corn to the depot this week, & send the plows to the shop, either mothers or Christians & get those two from Mothers when he returns & bring my sugar from town [that] Mrs Olivers wagon failed to do, and get that sow & geese from Ma's. I'll try and fix this all up, dont know how I will come out. There is no chance to get that cotton ginned at mothers, they will use up all the bagging they have, & have the lint room full of ginned cotton, & then not have as many seed as they want for the stock, & there is no chance to get it ginned at McCunes. I'll have to give up trying to get the seed I reckon. I added up the weights of the cotton picked this year to day, I make it out 12612 pounds, about 8 bales. Mrs Rogers made with her three hands this year, 13000 bu of corn, and 9 bales of cotton, beside cultivating Myers crop, & he made over 400 bu corn, & some cotton I think, but old Sam says Mrs Rogers worked 4 hands this year, but that is good cropping I think. Meyers don't want part of the crop, says he will make as much as he wants at home, & would be troubled about taking care & dividing the crop, &c. Thornton has begun putting up the meat hogs, the baby has been too sick & cross all day for me to leave her, & go to the field and see about it, & when he came to report about it, she was screaming so I could not hear a word he said, & I drove him off—so I don't now know whether he tolled any in the pen or not. Meyers says the oxen look in very good order except the old ones, they are thin yet, that field is yet a very good pasture for them he says, & there is plenty of water in there you know.

Mrs Oliver showed me a part of Mr O's letter to her by Warren & I judge from that she has been letting on to him that she believed him guilty of something wrong, & he deny's any such thing only makes social calls on the ladies when he goes in city, & has almost quit that, but speaks of expecting to visit a mighty nice lady by the name of Mrs Samuels. He writes to her that I write you books instead of letters & considers what I can find to write so much about, thinks I must write a heap of love to you. Warren told Mrs O that Joe did not like to stay in camps much & that you had been sick & was very cross, & he expected you would whip Joe before he got back, but I did not believe that, I know you—and how unreasonable & unseasonable your anger sometimes is, & how you grumble & threaten, but never whip. Mrs O has heard, but don't know how true it is that your Regt was ordered to La, & she hurried the negro back, & I did not get to send Joe's clothes, nor a letter by him as I was not at home when he started. John Nix starts to the Depot to-morrow on his way to Houston where he has to go to get his furlough extended. I sent by him for six hundred dollars of that money. I never heard such a hue & cry about taxes in my life, every body seems put to there [sic] wits end to get money enough to pay all the taxes. You have never writen me any thing about how much we will have to pay &c. I must stop for to night one of my eyes is quite sore, & the candle & writing makes it worse, but it is my only chance to write. I'll try & finish this tomorrow and send it to the office, & hope I will get a letter from you, I hope & believe that you will not be ordered off to La. Oliver writes about coming home all the time, but he is an officer & may come, but poor privates like you have to stay. I expect the baby will be walking & talking before you see her, if you ever see her again—but I won't write nor think about this it unnerves me.

Wednesday Nov 18th—Dear Will—I did not sleep last night till after 12 Oclock, when I took the baby up found her with another fever, & I felt so uneasy about her I could not go to sleep for some time. She seems better this morning, but is still feverish, her eyes are better. I have just been to look at our meat hogs, Thornton has 16 up besides the three wild hogs, which are in a pen to themselves & look better than the most of the others. There is some of those Zuber hogs that look so poor now that I think I had better turn them out, & not try to fatten them. I think there is 18 will do to fatten & kill. The largest bunch of Mrs Olivers hogs are missing been hunting over a week & are still hunting. Mrs Hurst tells me six of her killing hogs are missing. Thornton got his hand badly cut by one of those wild hogs this morning, he threw his head around, and his tusk run in the back of his hand, & cut a place 2 inches long and seems to be right deep. He came to me scared almost to death, said the hog had cut one of the strings of his finger in two, & I reckon he thought he was going to bleed to death, as it was bleeding profusely. I took two stiches through the flesh, and tied it, to bring the cut together, it was the hardest sewing I ever done, & he seemed to suffer a good deal. I then put sugar & spit turpentine on it. I am affraid it will make him stop work, tho' it is his left hand. Susan started 5 bales of cotton to Navasota this week, cotton has fallen since the news reached here of the fall of Brownsville. I sent to Navasota by John Nix for one quire of paper. Mrs Oliver got one quire & let me have half, and Laura Hutcheson let me have 10 sheets of Legal paper. I carried her 4 pounds of butter. I asked mother about that butter your mess wanted & she had let Charly Van Horn have all she had to spare, just a few days before, at one dollar per pound—she don't make enough now for her own use. When John returns to Galveston, old Dowdy is going to go down & take his place, & let John come home for awhile, he says the Capt says he could do that. Oh Will you don't know how long it seems since I saw you—it seems at least a year to me and it is not quite 4 months yet. Some men can get home others have to stay all the time. Chester Carter's at home again, no doubt with a 60 day furlough. If I did not have a baby I would venture on a visit to you, I believe, but I never think of such a thing with her—but next fall if you are within reach of me & we are all alive I will visit you. Some folks, Dr Foster for one says this war will last 30 yrs, if so all my boy's will have to do there share of fighting in it after you are dead & gone.

My paper is out, but my subject being inexhaustible, necessity is all that compells me to stop writing. Write immediately so I will know what to do about old Meyers. Mother wants John Nix. Jim wants him to go with his wagon up the Country after flour will give him part of the profits so there is no chance for me to get him & all kinds are looking out now for an overseer, so all will be soon engaged. Mrs Hurst don't know yet whether she will rent Bassetts place, & if she does don't know whether she will keep Rivers or not. The baby is very fretful and feverish I feel uneasy about her but don't know what to do. My patience energy and life seems almost worn out. I never felt more spiritless in my life. Be sure and write me word about those plows at mothers did you send them up & what did you intend them for. Break new land or to use in old land?

> yours affectionately
> Lizzie S Neblett

Pelican Spit Galveston Texas
Nov 22nd/63
Mrs L S Neblett

Dear Lizzie

Another Sunday has come and it finds me seated to hold communion in thought with thee and thine. Things way on in the same uninterrupted course leaving us here as mere spectators of that great drama of the war with now and then some stirring report of our going into active service but so far it has all been mere idle rumor. To day a report comes that 1500 yankees have captured about 200 militia at Corpus Christi after considerable fighting and if 5000 would land on the West end of Galveston Island the place would be captured for I do not think 2000 men can be had on the Island.[12]

Last Tuesday I wrote to you by Dr Foster and gave him an order to draw all the money in Owen Cochrans hands except twenty dollars, which I wished sent to me. Have you got it. You asked me some time ago about our taxes. Our taxes this year (that is the property) is about the same [as] it was last year except that house that was burnt in Corsicana and and [sic] Nancys baby. I do not know what the difference will be in valuation. That is a matter for the Assessor and Collector and you to determine. You need not put yourself to the trouble to see Mrs Oliver about Myers overseeing for us next year for I learn from Oliver that he is now employed to oversee for him & Mrs Rogers. If you cannot get John Nix you will have to get Rivers again. I think he will do very well if you will go over to Mrs Hursts and talk to him occasionally. He is very easily flattered by any little attention I noticed. Half or quarter of an overseer is better than none. If the Yankees do not run us from this place soon I can get what ever we need for the plows. In fact I wrote to Coleman a few days ago to ascertain what one could be sold for in Grimes with the intention of buying some on speculation. I think there is enough old iron—old plows and coulters[13] &c to fix up enough plows to make a crop with. Make the negroes gather up all the old iron about and put it in the smoke house. You report not having my socks done. Now you are giving yourself more uneasiness about my welfare than I deserve. I can get along through the winter I think with the two old ones pairs I have. You have excited my curiosity very much by your allusion to Mrs Magee and Mrs McCune. Are the women at home get to acting as badly as the men. I heard a few days ago of a young lady—a Miss Cappleman on the Bedias who has had a negro child and that the people have hung the negro in front of the house & close by.

You are right about that sow of Collins if she has lost her pigs. She is not worth more than five dollars & I would not wish to buy if she did run with

12. On November 16, 1863, Union general Nathaniel Banks occupied Corpus Christi. Long, *Civil War Day by Day*, 434.

13. A coulter plow had a blade or wheel fastened to the beam of the plow, which made vertical cuts in the soil ahead of the plowshare.

our hog. That hog should be spayed and it would be best to get John's Frank to spay him right off even if it kills him. It will not do to keep him among the sows.

Our trip to Harrisburg has blown over and all reasonable hope of any of us getting home for an indefinite time in the near future, for the Bayou City has gone to Galveston for repairs and the steamer Diana is here for us to man and guard. I never permitted myself to hope much by that means to get to see you soon, and as much as it would make my heart leap for joy to see you and the children once more, so slender was the hope that I have resigned it without a struggle tho not without a feeling akin to the blues. I hope to see you notwithstanding within the next six months, but I have not been from home but four months and six months seems an age and close on the confines of eternity when I look at it ahead. Oliver and I were talking this morning of the hardship it places middle aged men of family under to be confined in camps for years when they should be at home to assist their familys & instruct their children. Oliver is in excellent health. I do not think he is much of a rake—probably as much so as the majority of men. At any rate he seldom goes to Galveston, and very seldom stays all night. I have been having the flux in a mild form for eight or ten days—not been confined to my bed—have not eat any meat for a week and am now about well. I enclose a letter to Rivers which upon reading will explain itself. Tell Mary I will answer her letter the next time. That beef hide which Dr Brown got to tan last March was taken to his house by his boy who goes to mill I sent it by him. The hide had Jim Scotts Brand on it. The beef was 3½ years old.

Your affectionately
Wm H. Neblett

Galveston Texas Nov 23rd/63
Mrs L S Neblett

Dear Lizzie

Yours of the 17th and 19th was recd late this evening and having finished reading it hasten to answer in regard to the employing of Myers. I wrote to you yesterday and stated that I did not think it worth the trouble to see Myers because I had understood that he was employed by Oliver & Mrs Rogers. He will have his hands full to attend to three farms besides his own but I suppose he can do so in such a manner as to make it a good deal better than no overseer at all. If you can get him upon the terms you speak of ($400.00 in confederate money with the understanding that if after the crop is made that he can quit & make the proper deductions) hire him at once. But is there not some danger that Oliver or Mrs Rogers may not be willing to let him do so as it will cut them out of a portion of his services. In regards to those plows at your mothers I know nothing except that the negroes told me last July that some of the plows were at your mothers for Jack to repair. I suppose they are the ones the negroes told you of. There are two large coulters and a big foot coulter which might be used in repairing and also some old pieces of wagon tyre to lay plows under the house or in the smoke house. If you can have three plows repaired without using the coulters I would prefer it as they would do for new plows, & I will try and get some iron to make the shears of here. You need not send Joes clothes to him until I write for them. I let him have an old pr—he can make out until Christmas at least. You make me feel uneasy about Bettie—poor child I fear she has a hard time of it. If she only knew what thoughts you entertain of her and her destiny she would be miserable. Sometimes I fear she will die before I ever get to see her again. You are mistaken on supposing I did not think as much of her as the other children, for I do and if I were allowed the privilege of nursing and fondling her I might love her best. You merely give her your sympathy, she should have at least my love. I believe I am well again—went to drill to day. You should notice & see that those hogs you put up do not fight each other. Different gangs are apt to do so and then should be put in different pens. We have heard nothing of going to La or elsewhere. DeBrays Reg has gone west I suppose.

Yours affectionately
Wm H Neblett

At Home
Monday night 9 Oclock Nov 23rd 1863
W H Neblett

Dear Will—

As I will have oportunity of sending this to the office tomorrow by Mr Rivers, I concluded to write you a hurried letter. I have my coffee put on the fire, to take an invigorating cup when drowsiness begins to creep upon me. What should I do without a little coffee on occasions like the present, & what an amount of trash you would miss. The day is too full of noise, & work, for me to write a letter in peace, but when night comes on, and the children are all asleep, even the unquiet spirit of this war baby is at rest, then I can write to you & then most forcibly comes over me the longing to see you once more, but I curb this desire as much a possible. I often try to imagine exactly how you look. The children talk insesantly of your coming, and tell what they would do if the[y] should look out & see you at the gate. Dr Foster tells Mrs Oliver that Macgruder says he will not furlough the men before next summer, & if any of the[m] get sick they will have to remain in the hospital even if they die. Mrs Oliver was here this evening and told me what Oliver wrote of your health, & then sent the letter to me to read by a passing chance, & so I have to night read three pages of Olivers letter to her writen before Warren returned & part after he returned. Don't tell him I read it. She sent it to me to see the particular clause he wrote about your health as I had heard of it through Myers who heard her read that portion of the letter. He says you make a good soldier when you are able, but that you don't stand soldiering well, & is affraid he will have to loose [*sic*] you, tho hopes not. Now I don't know whether he means he thinks you will die (for that it seems is the only outlet from service) or that you will get a discharge, this has made me feel very sad & depressed. I think less than I ever did about the future—imagination always pictures the dark sides, & I draw back horror struck at what may be. Oh what is life worth when a continual dread hangs suspended over you ready to descend at any moment. Life is a poor boon at best, & mine has seemed always to me such a poor gift that I have perhaps sinned in ingratitude, to my parents & my God. But you don't want to hear this, & I dont want to think about it & won't try to bother you with my trials, you have your share I know yet don't try in a selfish way to lay them on my shoulders also, as I do mine upon you.

But let us talk about things that touch the present tangible objects. Meyers has been here three or four times, says he will come 'till I hear from you, & if you don't like his price no harm will be done, he is going on the same way at Mrs Olivers. He has wrought a great change here, & at Mrs O's so she says. The second time he came here he whiped Bill Tom & Randal for idling away their time, I did not tell him that they had been idle either, & the next time he came which was last Saturday, he undertook old Sam & had quite a scrape with him.[14] He whiped him for slight provocation, but the secret of it lay here—old Sam talked to Mrs Olivers Bill, & Bill told Jack, & then Myers

---

14. On the whipping of slaves see Genovese, *Roll, Jordan, Roll*, 63–67, 619–20.

heard the story he told Bill, that Myers should not whip him, no white man should, that he would stay in the woods all the year & do no good—so I think Meyers whiped him as much or more to let him know that he would whip him than anything else. Mary with her indiscretion repeated to Sam what she heard me say to Meyers, when he asked if I thought he would have any difficulty in managing the negroes. I told him I thought not unless it was Sam, that he might try to run, & not submit to a whipping. When Mary repeated this to him he said to Bob & her Your Ma was right I will run, he shant whip me. But Meyers heard the tale at Mrs Olivers & that was enough. When he told Sam to come to come to [sic] him (he was on the waggon at the time with his arm full of stakes he had been using in laying the fence worm[15][)] he sat still saying he had done nothing to be whipped for, he threatened to knock him off before he would move, & then he got down & moved away from him instead of to him, he [Meyers] told him to stop & he would not, he then shot at him not aiming to hit him of course missed him, & his pistol was only loaded with shot. Sam took down the turn row, & Randal & Tom after him, & Meyers also, for he did not stop for the shooting & when they would get up close enough to him Sam would turn on them with one of the stakes (which he held on to defend himself the whole round) & tell them if they layed hands on him he would kill them, & Meyers says he could not get near enough to him to knock him down with the butt end of his whip as he feared he would knock him over with the stake—so they both stood with their weapons drawn, & Rivers who saw the first of it but did not follow them down the turn row, was called by Meyers to come to them & bring his gun, & Rivers went, & told Sam if he did not come back he would shoot him & he then turned, & they marched back up to the bars, & Myers whipped him, give him bad whipping too, worse than he intended, he admited after he came to the house.

Just at this moment Dr Foster rode up, & Meyers told him what had happened, & he began to ask if he complained of colic symptoms, &c, & it alarmed me, so I asked Foster to please walk down to the cabin & see what he thought of him. He went down, said he had a pretty bad whipping, but no danger of dying, but I had better have some peper tea made & give him, & he told them not to give him any water 'till reaction took place which directions were followed. I have not yet seen him & tho' I pity the poor wretch I don't

---

15. A worm fence was a series of rails stacked on one another at an angle.

want him to know it. Sarah came with such doleful tales to day, and I began giving him pills yesterday to move his bowels,[16] & they failed to operate readily & Sarah said he complained of a pain in his ribs more than any thing else, that I got uneasy about it, & so sent this evening for Dr Foster, to see if he had sustained any internal injury. Myers said he threw & hit him but hit him in the back with [a] stick as large as his wrist. Dr Fosters says none of his ribs are broke & the soreness proceeds from the whipping, no internal injury & tho he is whipped pretty bad, he came off well, as he made fight at Myers, & Myers could have killed & the law not touch him. Says he has seen negroes whipped worse than he is, & that he does not seem at all humbled by the whipping, & says he thinks from the way Sam talks, he wont do any good under Myers, has a spite at him. He reffered Dr F to Mr Rivers who he says saw it all, but Rivers says he did not see it all, as he did not follow them when they left the clearing where it happened. Truth is Rivers said to Hursts negros that it was a "damed shame the way Sam was whipped," & they were so anxious for me to see Rivers & ask about it that they told Rivers I wanted to see him, & so he come this morning. Jack O was at Hursts & heard the negro tell him I wanted to see him, which was a lie I never sent for him.[17] Kate said to me that Mr Rivers said he would tell me all about it, & that it was a d——— shame. I told her to hold her mouth, that I did not want Rivers to tell me any thing[,] that I knew Meyers would not have whipped him if he had not deserved it, & that it was a wonder he left life in him. They don't want him here all down [on] him—but I tell you somebody must take them in hand, they grow worse all the time. I could not begin to write you how idle & trifling they were, & how little they minded me, Thornton Sam, & all were alike. I tell you they move at an other rate now. He says he has no idea he will have any more trouble with them if he stays a whole year, says he lets them know what he is when he first starts, & then has no more trouble. He whipped Mrs O's Bill & old Min a day or two after he began there, neither of them resisted. I am sorry he whipped Sam so, but I suppose there was no help for it. Dr F says he thinks he will stay there in the cabin three weeks perhaps pretending to be awful bad off & that he puts on a heap now, & he thinks if Meyers should go to whip him he would run again, but I will not let Meyers know

16. Most likely Lizzie is referring to a laxative. Laxatives and purgatives were the primary medicines of the day and were used for almost all diseases or medical problems.

17. On slaves playing one white person off another see Genovese, *Roll, Jordan, Roll,* 609–21.

that Foster said this for fear he will take unnessary occasion to try him. Mrs O says that Meyers says that our land is as good again as hers & Mrs Rogers, told me that there was not better land in the Co than this—he laughs at the crop we made this year. Mrs Rogers made twice as much as was ever made on her place any previous year, & tended his crops also, & he made 500 bu corn on his place.

I reckon & fear that we have lost those two hogs that run over at Hursts, the sow & Barrow, I counted so certain on them that I wrote you that we had up 20 I think including them in my count, but when I sent over to have them caught with the dogs they were missing, havent been seen in over two weeks now, Thornton has hunted all day to day, can hear nothing of them. They are gone I think. Mrs Oliver hasent found her big gang of 50 or 60 killing hogs yet, offered me 10 of them if I would have them found. Wish Joe was here I would send him out to hunt ours & hers at the same time. Thornton is such a fool he cant remember ear mark, flesh mark nor nothing. I am going to have that barren cow killed in a few days, she is [torn page], & they tell me [she will] not have a calf soon. Dr Foster brought me $869.55. Owen sent you 20, and paid Joe C[ollins] to carry him to Galveston. Uncle Mc said he could go to Galveston for 5 dol half price, baggage would cost nothing & to carry his provision along, so I told Joe that as he owed me 5 dol, I would not give him any but to use that in paying his way, so when he gets to Houston he gets 6 dol from Owen—one of Joe's rascally tricks—you see Peel & D. have not paid that 81.95 cts I think Tax on the cotton to Owen. I fear we will loose that. Rivers has not paid all of our work back yet, they are splitting rails & Meyers says they will or ought to split almost enough to fence in that Elm flat beside the end strings of the clearing, which is about ready to run the plows now. Mage is stocking them, have all been to the shop at mothers had that horse plow changed into a Cary plow & hunted up old Iron, enough to lay three others, which gives us 4 turning plows but Meyers says he is affraid they will break in the clearing, & wants you to get two new Cary plows made [if] you can. Things have turned up so I could not send to the depot dont know when I will now. Had to get all the staple to the ox yokes mended. No further developments in the Hall tragedy. Mrs Wade has never been arrested they had a warrant for old Alston but he proved he was in Huntsville at the time, so they never touched him. All well at Mrs Olivers. I wish I had time to write more. The baby is as well as usual, now had the fever two days & nights. Write often. Good bye. Bassett reached home this week.

Lizzie N.

At Home
Wednesday Nov. 25th/63

Dear Will,

Altho' I wrote only two days since, yet I am not satisfied with what I wrote, & I doubt not it was not satisfactory to you on the subject of Sam & his whipping. I have been & am yet considerably troubled about the old rascal. He had a chill after he was whipped that day, & and [*sic*] I thought it best to give him pills for fear he would have more chills, & his bowels turned so torpid, & he complained so much so Sarah said of internal soreness that I thought it best to call in a Dr, so sent for Foster who said he was doing very well, as the medicine began to opperate after I sent for the Dr. just at night. I wrote you what Dr F said, he thinks he is not at all humbled, & would run if Meyers went to whip him again. Rivers acted very wrong to talk in the manner he did, & is what has made Sam worse, if he thought Meyers was too severe & even unreasonable he should under no consideration have let the negroes know it. Dr F said Sam refered him to Mr Rivers. Rivers did not know of Sams boasting that no white man should whip him particularly Meyers. Meyers told me h[e] was sorry he whipped him so severely, that he lost his temper [at] Sam striking at him, & when he spoke to him & told him to get down off the wagon Sam said to him that "no body could please him no way" which he said made him mad.

This morning Sarah having a chance to speake to me alone revealed the following. She says she went down to Nancy's house where Sam is last night & when she reached the fence she heard him talking & she stopped & listened, & then came back to the kitchen without going in, so none of them knew she overheard the conversation. She says Sam was talking to Mage & Thornton, and said he never intended to work a day under Meyers while he lived, that as soon as he got well enough he was going to leave & stay out 'till you come home—& that he believes that I had him whipped, told Meyers to whip & she tried to persuade him differently told him no body could make her believe that, that if I had wanted him whipped I would have come out & told him plainly that I intended to have him whipped that I never went behind the stump [to] do any thing, I was not that sort of a woman, she knew me too well for that & she says mothers negro Ann sent Sam word by Major "that that notion of his (Sam's) would not do, no, no, no, I was too bold in what I do for that, that she knew me too well, &c," now from this I judge that more than likely he has been vowing vengence, or revenge upon me, as he seems to think I told Meyers to whip. I some how cant feel affraid of him touching me, yet 'tis best to risk nothing in that way. She says Mage advised him to come to me before he left, & tell me he would not work under Meyers[,] & Sam said he would, but I don't believe that he thought of doing such a thing. Now I am going to send for Coleman & get his advise [*sic*] & assistance, something must be done soon, & I must be very quiet about it, or he will start before he gets ready, & if he should get a chance to run away, he would make his way to the Yanks, or else lay out in the woods all the year, perhaps do all sorts of devilment & be killed at last. He is a very mean negro, & his example & talk have a bad influence upon our other negros. Joe Collins was here yesterday & he says he told Meyers to watch Sam, & that he believed Sam would fight him. Since he & John Collins had that difficulty with that negro he looks out for such things & he said he told Myers that he ought to come down on them at first, let them know that he would whip, & would have work done, else he would do none of us any good in farming, as he could not stay much with any of them—he told him this before he whipped Sam. Mrs Oliver told me that old Mrs Hurst told her that Rivers would whip her negros & tell them "I would not have whipped you, but your old Mistress kept such a fuss I had to do it to please her" now you may judge what his whipping are worth. He told me this morning that he saw Bassett in town yesterday, he is advertising his place down here for rent will stay here till Feb[ruar]y, that he is wearing his coat sleeve off that rounded shoulder. Meyers was here this morning called on Sam, & I asked him how Sam talked—says he talks mighty polite, says he is doing very well & will soon be able to work. You see the deceitful old dog how he talks. I did not tell him what Sarah nor Dr Foster told me, as I had rather trust Colemans judgment than his in this case. I know Coleman best. M thinks he humbled Sam completely, said this morn that he did not think he would have to strike Sam another lick this year, that Sam told him while he was whipping him that they could live together always after this with out any difficulty.

Having heard that the cotton cards for Soldiers wives were in A[nderson] I got Rivers to go for Mrs Oliver & I, but he says Dr P[atrick] told him they would not be here before 10 or 12 days. I must get two pr if I can do so at $10. He came in a few moments this morn to return me the money I sent by him for the cards. I gave him some of your inferior caps & he is to divide deer meat with me. He killed one to day & will send me some. He kills a great many deer, but was out of caps & could not buy any. I let him have 10 or 12 upon the terms stated.

At Home
Sunday Nov 29th 1863
W H Neblett

Dear Will,

My hand is so cold this morning that I don't know whether I can make my writing intelligible or not but I will try. We are having a long way the coldest weather we have had this winter, it has been freezing all morning, & it seemed to me it it [*sic*] was exceedingly cold last night. I know I awoke last night and thought of you & your unpleasant situation, even if you are well, which I feared was not the case until I could not sleep. I know I was cold, but I consoled myself by remembering how warm you were naturally compared to my frog like nature, & hoped that you were even more comfortable than I was. I put Walter at my feet now, & he is highly pleased to get to sleep in my bed once more. The baby is warmer natured than Walter, but is as wakeful as a cat, & forces me to rest nearly, sometimes quite all night on the same side & every morning by day light sometimes at 4 oclock, she forces me to rise with her & dress her then I leave her in Kate's & Polly's hands & I go back to bed & sleep 'till day light, sun up, & often after sun up. She is now six months old & has been more trouble to me than the other 4 had been up to her age, all put together. She is so sensitive to cold I cant trust them to dress her in the morning, & if I don't dress her, she takes violent cold, & is then so much more trouble that I find it the cheapest way to take all possible care of her. Never a day passes away that I do not wish that she had never been born, tis awful for me to think of raising her to fulfill woman's destiny, marry & bring forth. I know I had rather bury one of my daughters than see them marry even the highest in [the] land if I knew they would entertain the same feelings about child bearing & children that I do & was at the same time compelled to have them. But I'll try & finish such thoughts, I cant alter my case now, but regrets & images of what might have been will force themselves upon me. I have no one but myself to blame, hence the bitter enmity I feel for myself. There was a time when I wondered what feelings Pa entertained for his children, he always seemed so strange, I no longer wonder I know—& each year I grow more like him, in feeling & opinion, & altho he he [*sic*] is past all earthly suffering, is at rest, yet the perfect knowledge, taught me through my own self knowledge, of what he suffered mentally upon many subjects draws from me tears of sympathy. Poor Pa, he was not comprehended.

Bill has just come back with your letter writen last sunday. I am glad to learn that you were at that time about well of the Flux. I have been feeling more uneasiness than common about you, since your letter by Dr Foster was read. Oh Will, I do want to see you, worse than I ever did before in my life, & I think & feel sometimes that I can't stand it, but I know I must. Oh this cruel war, when will it end? and will you return to me? are questions that arise each hour of my life & are always unanswered. If you stay there six months longer I will wean the baby at 9 or ten months and go down there to see you, only one thing makes me hesitate. I think you sometimes forget that you have a baby. Poor little thing tho' she says, in her glee, Pa Pa Pa, she don't know what the word means. She will watch my mouth very attentively while I say Pa Pa to her, & then she will fix hers & begin Pa Pa Pa. She is a fat little thing but not hardy, a very tender plant. The children just asked me if you said any thing about little sister. I said no, well, they said, I believe Pa has forgotten he has a baby.

I see from your letter that you had not rec'ed the letter I wrote to you about what Meyers proposed to attend to our farm for. I wish I knew so I could tell the old fellow what to depend on but it seems to me he must have made up his mind to go on with our farm any how, no matter whether you liked his price or not—he said all the time that if you did not like his price, there was no harm done, & that he would come in 'till I heard what you said. He is a very accommodating [sort] of a fellow, & I think is a much better chance than Rivers if he does not come but three times a week. He says, since looking at our land, he had just as soon have part of the crop as the $400, & he told Mrs O if confederate money goes up he will knock off some of his price, he esti- mates it at 5 for one. Uncle Mc and Aunt Cinda are down on him. Uncle Mc will set up & tell how much affraid of negros Meyers is, & how deficient in judgment he is, & how he would have acted with old Sam &c &c. I think he fully calculated that our negros would work his old crab grass field next year— and he would set around the house, chew tobacco & go to see how Mrs Wade was coming on, & do me nor the Negros no earthly good. He would be worse than nobody. The last work he has done was fixing Susan's wagon body's, for which she hauled & gathered his corn & he had done nothing from the time he made those Looms til then. I have no kind of patience with him. I wrote to you about John Nix going to Houston to get his furlough extended. He has returned, so I am told, but Macgruder did not extend his furlough, but gave him 'till the 3rd of next month, Dec, to report himself at the Hospital at Chappel Hill, from which place he hopes to get a furlough back home. I have a right bad case of Flux on hand [with] the little negro Lee. He was bad off before I knew anything about it, I have him in the room where the boys sleep by the fire, and he is just like a baby, so you may guess what a time we have of it. I fear some of the children will take it from him, but I am bound to have him in the house or he will die, & there is a continual stench about him, being larger he is worse than a baby. I think he is some better, it is almost impossible to do any thing with him by the hands of his fool mother, & I have used my hands up so now that they are painful to me, so chafed. I rather doctor any disease I ever saw than the Flux.

I sent for Coleman as I wrote you I would, & he went down and talked to Sam & told me he thought Sam would go to work under Meyers, that he promised him he would &c. Coleman had a long talk with him, & he tried to show Sam the error he had been guilty of, he said at last that he knew he did wrong when he run, & that he would let Meyers whip him one more time, & if he gave him such a beating next time, he would never let him whip him again, Coleman promised Sam to talk to Meyers & tell him how he ought to treat him, & told him if he would only be humble & submissive that Meyers would never whip him so again, that I would not allow it, &c. So we concluded to just let Sam alone. Coleman seems to have faith in what he says. I don't know how it will turn out. Coleman says he harped upon Rivers mightily, & he censures Rivers very much for taking Sams part as he did. I don't feel affraid of Sam hurting me, & to tell the truth I would not care, if he would only murder me. Rivers is nearly done paying back our work, & he thinks when they finish paying back that we will have rails enough split to fence in that elm flat pasture, they have fenced in the clearing and that is all ready to start the plows. I don't think River's understood you to want the pasture as large as your last letter indicates, so we may want some rails now to make it that large—he has had 4 hands & some says 5 hands making rails here for two weeks; 125 rails a piece, & some of them 150 I think. I don't know whether Bro Jim is going to move down or not, but that is very doubtful. I will keep your note to Rivers until I hear what you say about Myers. You see, the negros of Hurst will have something over 7000 rails split when they get done, & I cautioned both Rivers & Meyers, and Hursts negros to use timber that would do for boards, tho' I said nothing about Gin timbers & they have split them as near the line where the fence will run as they could get too [*sic*] I saw this myself.

Major will finish stocking the last plow tomorrow. Have 4 Cary's or turning plows, two sweeps & two shovels. The 4 Carys have been to mothers shop, I hunted up enough old iron on the place to have them all laid again, which is done tolerable well so Meyers says & some of the bars had to be laid again.

He says he is affraid that the roots in the new land will break the plows. I failed to get my corn to the depot in time to be rec'ed in the car, so now I will have to shell and sack it. They will rec[eive] no more in the car after the first of Dec. Thornton's hand has been & is yet right sore, so that he can do nothing but drive the wagon, & I was affraid to start him to the depot, for fear something would happen, & he can not yoke the oxen with one hand—when my neighbors near me get a sheller, I will get it from them. I havent got my sugar from Jim's yet, Mrs O's wagon didn't bring it, & Meyers told Susan's Frank to bring it from Jim's but I reckon he was instructed by his mistress to do no favors. I am anxious to get that sow from Pa's if we had got her last winter, we would now have some pigs from her. Those two hogs that run at Hursts place I have just given up Thornton looked all day one day, without hearing any thing of them—somebody has taken them. I never heard such an universal complaint of missing hogs in my life. I think Sim Thomas drove ours off when he got his, not with a view to steal them but because it was a trouble to separate them from his, with which they run. I have the shotes belonging to the sow that died over there, & will keep them up 'till I have all of our pigs marked & altered. We have a young cow been milking all summer, that got a lick with an ax last sunday from some vile negro, I reckon, and cut her by the back bone near the tail, clear into the hollow. I had the place sewed up, but she is now full of worms. I fear it will kill her—she has her first calf & is very gentle, good conditioned cow, as the old farmers say. I keep her in my rye patch where I can watch her & have her doctored.

Monday Nov 30th—Night forced me to stop, & my eyes hurt me so I would not attempt writing last night. I think after this spell I can have our pigs & calves marked & altered with safety. I hate loosing [*sic*] those two meat hogs, & some I have up are so thin that it will take quantity of corn to fatten them. I intend to have that cow killed this week she seems to be very fat. Meyers says we will either have to build a division fence between our field & Jim's or fix up Jim's part of the fence, else the stock will get into our new field, also there is rails enough split the negros tell me in the bottom below the field to run that division fence, what do you say to having it put up when plowing can't be done? Myers tells me that Alston says I can get one & perhaps two loads of seed to feed our oxen on, & I will have them hauled home as soon as they finish putting up the new ground fence, which they are doing to day, staking & riders also. Well if you conclude not to have Meyers I will be under many obligations to him & must offer him pay for his attention to the hands, so far. Rivers never would come about, has been here twice since Meyers set in, the first time Mrs Hurst sent him to bring Sarah 9 *dollars in gold & silver,* in payment for her services, & now she is satisfied, the next time is when them negros told him I sent for him, they were so anxious for me to hear his tale about Sam's whipping. John Nix told mother *(but you must keep this secret that John told it)* that Bassett talked to him after he went back to Va, & left Sallie here, said that he would make mother smoke for the way she had treated & intended treating Sallie, that he just considered it robbing her of at least $20,000 cutting her off in her will, as she designed doing, & not paying the hire she ought while she had Sallie's negros. He is a glorious fellow, I reckon he will try & force the opening of Garrett's will this winter, he is so anxious to get all he can. I haven't heard much more about Mrs Magee and McCune. I think that was all smoke & no fire. Ann Garner (Parnal use to be) started it because McCune showed Mrs Magee some attention at church & went & stayed all night at her house to get an ox that came to her cow pen at night. Mrs McCune said she did not believe one word of it, & would stand by Mrs Magee to the last. Dr Dickson advised Mrs Magee who is his sister you know to trace the tales up, and bring the matter up in church, which I heard she was going to do, but never heard the result.

You did not hear the whole of that negro story—-Two of those girls sisters on the Bedias, had negro babys by the same negro[;] one, a year or two since & one recently & they hired a negro to bury them alive at least he buried them alive, & he has been hung also, and while the hanging of the two negros was going on all the white family took occasion to leave, but I heard they had them all, was going to hang the two that brought forth, & the old woman, & another girl would be sent to the Penitentiary. A part of this is no doubt false. The excitement about Kit Hall is fast dying away, tho' many believe that Alston knew of the murder & Mrs Wade also. Alston's friends tell him (so I heard) that he must feret out all these slanderous tales about his hog stealing &c, & prove them false, else they will drop him, & he threatens to sew [*sic*] some folk for slander, & some pro[p]hesy that there will be a suit brought against Susan & Garrett. Garrett just swears he knows all he says is true & can prove it &c. Some three or four men came after Sim Thomas & Henry Hill recently & marched them off giving them only five minutes to get ready in. They say Sim was scared almost to death, saying "gentleman what do you reckon they will do with me," when one answered saying "D——m you they'll shoot you." Henry Hill reared & pitched they say, but the pointed guns made him march. Susan talks of going to see John soon, leaving all her children at home, but Garrett who will be her escort. She says John says she must go to him, that he has important business, & will trust it in no hands but hers. I suppose he must want to fix up his will, or matters of business fearing he may never return I havent seen her lately. Lee is some better to day. I never want another case of Flux. The baby is six months old can set alone, & say Pa Pa Pa! But has no teeth yet, is more backward in teething than any of the others. Oh how I dread her teething this summer.

Teusday Dec 1st—Garrett has just sent me over a note from Jack Wilson requesting me to send him my war Tax to Anderson to day & urges it upon me, as to day is his last day for collecting. He writes that it is $80. eighty dollars—says he will send the receipt by the person who brings the money. I must start Bill with it immediately, don't like to trust it in his hands but there is no other way to do it. Coleman may not be at home & Rivers is gone today. Lee is still improving, think now he will get well, thought it doubtful for awhile. I had one of my vivid dreams about you this morning after day light. You don't comprehend my theory of dreams, I don't believe that any prophetic power is given us in our sleeping hours, any more than when we are awake, but, I believe, there is a kind of magnetic influence exerted by one mind over another where there is love & sympathy existing between the two minds, & thus we are often warned as it were, when any thing presses on the mind of the loved one—and I think when you feel badly, threatened with sickness, or actually sick you think more about me, & long more for my presence than when you are well, hence, your mind exerts an influence over my mind when it is in a pasive state, (& more easily operated on than when awake & filled with conflicting thoughts & feelings) hence I have vivid dreams of you when you are sick. This is only a part of my theory haven't time to explain myself fully even if I could do so. But don't this seem as probable as that the magnetic needle always points to the north, & other magnetic truths? Meyers has just come in & says he will start two plows to day & Rivers hands finish work here today—the 4 hands have split 150 rails a piece, every day for 12 days. Do write often & long letters—all well at Mrs Olivers on sunday.

yours affectionately
Lizzie

Pelican Spit Galveston Texas
Nov 30th/63
Mrs L S Neblett

Dear Lizzie

Yesterday and day before (saturday and sunday) were the days I generally select to write to you as we have no drilling then but it was so cold that I found it impossible. Our mess had just finished a shanty constructed of old pieces of wreck and made a chimny of brick and bats just in the nick of time to save us from the severe Norther. The house is intended for a kitchen and to sit in by the fire for we still sleep in the tents and I am surprised to find them as comfortable in a Norther as they are. I was lucky enough to escape guard duty on these two cold nights as it did not quite reach me but I will go on to night, but the weather is moderate fast to day and will not be very cold to night. Yours of the 23rd reached me on the 27th. I was not much surprised at the row between Myers and Sam for I recollect that Coleman & Sterling both had them with him, I judge they will get along hereafter. I was in town last Friday and saw John Scott who looks as well as I ever saw him. I think he has about given up the idea of getting a sub though he did not say so. He had a a [*sic*] great deal to say about the Hall tragedy and was talking about it when I went in. He says that Kit Hall confessed to killing two beeves of his since he purchased those negroes. I expect it will turn out that the beeves were some of those I bought of Jim Scott, and were intended for oxen. They ran near McClures.

I expect that you had better notice Thorntons hand and make him use his fingers to prevent them from getting stiff. Did you get that Ginger Cloves and Cinnamon I sent by Dr Foster. The morning Dr F left here he went in a boat with some of this Co and I gave Babus two dollars & a half to get 50 cts of Cloves 50 cts of cinnamon and $1.50 of Ginger. He said he got them & gave to Dr F. I was told these articles were worth 50 cts pr oz. This will enable you to make up a good lot of Composition. That you sent me has been of great benefit to me while I had the flux. I wish you would have old Pat fed enough to keep him alive this Winter. I heard Oliver say some time ago that he was going to have some of his cotton ginned at Browns. Could you not do the same with that Coleman cotton by furnishing the bagging that was intended for it. We will have to get seed at least from some place to plant. Tell Myers I want the old land and all East of the turn row in the new ground (except the potato patch and what is taken in this Winter) in corn and all West of the turn row in the New ground with what is taken in this Winter or Fall in cotton which will give about 50 acres in corn & 40 or 50 in cotton, and if I were in your place I would have him to plant about ten acres of the corn with that white corn, and also some of that white Corsicana corn. You ought to save that white corn & not let the negroes have it, as it stands the weevils better than the yellow corn.

I saw some of the Navarro militia in Galveston last Friday (Jason Thompson and Jimmy Jones) and I think Fielder at a distance they are staying in Galveston. The militia are coming into Galveston every day and it is supposed that they may take our places & we take the field out West or some where. John Scott introduced me to Trevanninen Teel when I was in Galveston. He is Major of artillery but his command is in La in Taylors army. He thinks Bob has been taken by the Yankees at Brownsville or Corpus Christi. I do not recollect which place now. I found him quite agreeable. He remarked when I was introduced that the name was so familiar that it seemed that he was already acquainted with me. He is staying in Galveston & will remain there he says several weeks. I have stood this spell of cold weather without ever feeling unwell. I notice that Oliver is suffering with a bad cold but not hard up. He is a very healthy man. Mrs Samuels whom you mention is the wife of Lt Samuels of this Co. She is undoubtedly an excellent lady and Samuels is one of my best friends here. He is a lawyer and a long way the most intelligent man in the company. I was a little surprised at what you wrote regarding what you read in Olivers letter. About my health. My health has been bad for six weeks past but my sickness has not been of a dangerous character. You know I frequently at home get in bad health for a week or two with all the care I can take of myself.

I was very glad to hear of Bettie getting well. I feared she was about to have an attack of pneumonia. I would like very much to to [*sic*] see Bettie, I have almost forgotten how she looks. I noticed in the Telegraph of the 25th that the impressment law[18] authorises the taking of negroes only where the owner has more than three between the ages of 17 and 50. Under this none of ours will be liable for I do not believe Randal or Bill are 17 yrs of age. If you cannot get paper in Grimes I will buy you some and send by first chance. Such as I am writing on cost me $3.00 a quire about a month ago. I[t] may be higher now, perhaps as high as 4 or $5. John Scott says he fears McClure has impared himself very much in the way he acted in the Hall tragedy. He says he is accused of being the medium of communication between Kit and his mother while Kit was in jail. Nelia writes to me that if I wear flannel shirts that she will knit me two as soon as she can get the thread. If you can have some

---

18. The Confederate Impressment Act of March 26, 1863, allowed the army to impress slaves to work on fortifications. There was some variation from state to state, but generally slaveowners were paid $30 a month for the use of each slave. No more than one-fifth of a single planter's slaves could be taken; each state had additional exemptions. Many slave owners resented the law because it took away from their labor force. Also, the government often did not pay on time, kept slaves for longer than agreed upon, and often returned them in poor condition.

spun & send to her I would like it, for by that means I will save my coats for next year.

Yours truly
Wm H. Neblett

Galveston Texas Dec 1st/63
Mrs L S Neblett

Dear Lizzie

Yours of the 25th reached me last night too late to get it in the mail this morning. The contents of your letter relative to Sam has given much cause for thought and no little trouble I hardly know what course to pursue with the old scoundrel, unless I were there. I have been thinking it would be a good plan to handcuff him & send him to work on the fortifications on Galveston Island. I believe there is a pr of handcuffs in the closet. Or in case he is not sent there perhaps you might make some arrangement to put him under Coleman. If John Nix stays at your mothers she would hardly object to this. I care very little which of these measures is adopted. I expect to send Joe home by Christmas and if Sam is put to work on the fortifications there will be enough left to cultivate the land. But you must excercise your own judgment and do what you think best. If he was fed on bread & water for a while and whiped several times it might do him some good. If he should run away I would send after Coleman & his dogs without delay.

Tell Sarah to tell him I say that if he takes advantage of me while I am away to run away that I shall not forget it soon. Sometimes I have thought that what you have been told by the negroes was intended to scare you into turning Myers off. I may be mistaken in this supposition. If he ever comes to you and tells you he will run away if Myers stays send at once for Coleman & his dogs or have him taken in custody if he has to be killed in doing so.

Rivers acted like a trifling fool in talking as he did.

I think you made a good bargain in getting venison as cheap as Rivers proposes. I would let all of those caps in the paper box go on those terms and one third of the other box and throw in half the buck shot to be run up into lead bullets to hunt and half of the powder also. If you could get one or two deer skins it would be well for they make very good leather.

I wrote and mailed a letter yesterday and it had not passed out of my hands to the office but a few minutes when I recd your[s] of the 25th to which this is answer or at least as much of an answer as I can give.

Yours affectionately
Wm H. Neblett

P.S. Tell Sarah to twist me up some of her tobacco to send to me by Johns Jack who will be up in a few days. If it was sprinkled or moistened (after all the sand was washed off) with water sweetened with honey if you have any and then twist and dry it so that it would not mould it would be much better. But you must count it & send me word or Jack will steal it. Let Sarah have ¼ of an acre again next year to raise tobacco as she did this year.

At Home in the woods alone & gloomy
Sunday Dec 6th 1863
W H Neblett

Dear Will

You have an idea of my mood from the date of this, but for your sake, I'll try & restrain the gloomy outpouring as much as possible. You have heard my complaints my bitter repinings, my distaste for life, its cares & burdens, which seem made for me, mixed with but a slender portion of its joys and luxurious ease until I know you dread to read or hear a repetition of the same. From my cradle up[,] my path has been any thing but a smooth one, & tho' compared with some whom I know, a casual observer would say that I have been blessed, but they had a fund of hope, cheerfulness & elasticity in their nature, which enabled them to gather from their apparently forlorn condition more real enjoyment & pleasure than I have from mine, but I will spare you this for my case is beyond remedy, & I should think only of endeavoring to support my fate with fortitude, & a hope that the end is not far distant, when I will indeed rest quietly in the grave.

I feel more worn out to day than common & this will account for my being a little more desponding then usual. I have been doctoring & working with Lee faithfully now for over a week, one night set up nearly all night, & for the last three nights a good part of the time, & he is still having bloody discharged mixed with mucus.[19] Friday his disease took a change & I thought he was

---

19. On slave health see Todd L. Savitt, *Medicine and Slavery: The Diseases and Health Care of Blacks in Antebellum Virginia* (Urbana: University of Illinois Press, 1978).

going to get well, but that night the disease returned, tho' not so violent as at first. I hope I shall never have another case of Flux or whatever it is. I hear many doubts of his recovery, for I think the disease is assuming a Thyphoid form & he will probably have that fever. I have sent for no doctor nor don't intend to. I fear all or part of the children will take the disease. I moved the boys out of the room, & try to keep the children out [of] the room where he is as much as possible. I never had such a time with any thing before. He lay on his pallet, & had nearly all his evacuations in the bed without saying a word which kept up a stench all the time. I have him bathed every morning in ley water & clean clothes put on him. He was taken sick the day the norther blew up & she [Nancy] asked for something to give him, saying he "had a running off his bowells." I gave her peper & spice to make tea, & thought no more about it, & the next morning she came & woke me up saying he had been having bloody opperating all night & it was all over his bed, & she knew nothing of it till she got up in the morning. I found out he had been up & down all night, lay down of the hearth the fire almost out, & it was *bitter cold*, & Mage says he got up & covered him up himself & they called Nancy several times & as she did not awake they let her alone. As soon as I could get a fire made in that room that morning I had him brought up & found him so cold, numb & prostrated that I could find no pulse. I put mustard to his wrists & ankles hot rocks around him, & commenced giving him stimulating injections. His getting so cold is why he has been so hard to cure. If my baby takes the disease I don't know what I shall do. I thought of trying your remedy of salt & vinegar but have no vinegar. I am trying Beach's remedy, called Neutralizing mixture composed of Rhubarb, soda, pepermint leaves pulverized & cinnamon bark equal parts of each, steeped in hot water, & given every two or three hours,[20] I think it checked the disease once but it returned again—as soon as he gets well or dies I am going up to mothers, & perhaps the change of air will prevent the children taking it.

Susan came over to see me one evening last week, & was remarkably friendly. She is so bitter against Mrs Wade, says she knows she must have known all about the murder of Boone & Hoit, and tells things that she says

---

20. Wooster Beach (1794–1868) wrote a medical advice book titled *The Family Physician*, which was in its seventeenth edition in 1857. The rhubarb in the neutralizing mixture would have acted as a laxative, and the soda (presumably sodium bicarbonate) would have worked on excessive stomach acidity. The peppermint and cinnamon were probably for taste, although they may have been added as sedatives or digestive aids.

different men said to her, which looks like they suspected that Uncle Mc was knowing to the murder also, but I don't believe she ever heard the things she tells—she says Mr McClure is doing his best to clear up matters for "Mr Alston & Miss Wade" the calling of the names she mimics him. He is strongly for Alston & Mrs Wade it is true, & I don't myself believe that Alston knew any thing about it, & tho' Mrs W may have felt uneasy & fearful that Kit had done something wrong, yet I don't believe she knew he had murdered the men, or intended it. But Uncle Mc is not going to desert Mrs Wade. Aunt Cinda has not been there but once since Kit was hung went there on business & only stayed a few minutes. I don't know whether she is going to quit going there or not. John Nix saw Bro John in Houston & says he is the most home sick man he has seen in a long time, asked him ten thousand questions about Susan & all the children, & Susan says he has been writing to her & begging like it was for his life for her to come down to Galveston & see him, says he can't stand it, she must come &c, but she says her children are all so bad off for clothes she cant go 'till she weaves cloth & makes them some, & then she says she [is] affraid to go, she might get into deeper trouble & she has as much as she can stand up under now—if John was sick, she would not hesitate to start at a moments warning, & trust to providence to take care of the children 'till she returned, but she wanted no farther increase of family 'till the war was over at least. God know[s] I cant blame her, if I was like her, I had rather meet a woods full of Bare than meet you after a long absence, when I feared the love I have you would over come the awful dread I have of a certain thing, not over come it either, but make me willing for your sake to risk a certain event happening. Even as it stands now I dread to see you, tho' I love you better far than I do my own life. I fear always in thinking of it, that you will love me less—but I try not to trouble myself on this subject, I may never behold you again, it seems already to me like you have been gone at least a year, & I now think of your return like I did poor dear Garrett's as a very uncertain event.

I dreamed of you once since I wrote last, rather a vivid dream. The first dream was very vivid and actually made me feel happier next day. I saw you so plainly, your coming gave me such a joyful surprise, & you set down at the foot of our bed & I seated myself in your lap, put my hands on each of your cheeks & gazed at you, & you said "why you look blooming as a rose," & I kissed you, & the kiss was so vivid I think I must have kissed the baby. You said you could only stay with me one day. I then started to get the baby to bring her to you, & awoke. As soon as I woke I feared you had the headache, or was sick in some way & had been thinking of me more intently than common. While John Nix was gone to Houston, I dreamed that Magruder would not extend his furlough, & that he would have to leave home again, go into service I thought. The next day I went over to Aunt Cindas expecting to see John, & found her feeling very anxious about him as he had over stayed his time there several days. I told her my dream & I declare I had never thought of his not getting his furlough extended, thought it more than probable that he would be discharged. Now I put no faith nor attach no significance to dreams like that, but vivid life like dreams of one I love, & one whom I believe loves me will make an impression on me. I want to hear from you so much. Your letter of the 23rd Nov, was re'cd last Wednesday & it will be two weeks tomorrow since it was written. I cant see why it is your letters are so long reaching me. Susan has got two letters from John by mail, & one by Jack since John returned to Galveston & all of them were writen since your last letter to me. If I could get your letters immediately after they are writen I would feel better satisfied, but when I get a letter it is usually so old that I think "well I don't know what may have happened since this was writen." Aunt Cinda tells me that Bassett has bought a place in town, with a piece of land attached, house with eight rooms, she could not tell what place it was, but he gave only $2000 for it & is going to fix Sallie up for housekeeping—will keep old Henry & Nancy & Lou, & hire out the rest, is going to get a loom, wheels &c, & Sallie is going to weave herself & make lots of cloth—big *spouting* ain't it? I hoped before Jack got here that you would write by him, & now I would like to send this by him but don't know when he will return. He brought up vessels from Mrs Cochran to get Lard & butter in, & Mother regrets so much that she let Charley Van Horn have all she had to spare.

They get on tolerably well plowing havent broken any plow yet. Sam is stirring around now but says his foot is not yet well enough to follow the plow. I never said a word to him about his scrape till yesterday morning, he came up to tell me that Myers had told him to go to plowing, but his foot was not well enough. I told him not to plow then. He talks mighty fine & almost committed himself in talking about his whipping, his thinking I had told Myers to whip him that evening, he almost said he had made his threats about what he would do to me, but better thoughts came over him, he knew you was gone, he had already lost so much time & you charged him when you left to take care of things make the boys work & to do the best he could for me, that I would not stay at home all the time and as he was the oldest on the place you expected much from him, & so now he was going to stay not going to lay out in the woods, but going to do his work faithfully, & be of as much service to me as he could. I could not help feeling sorry for the old fellow to save my life, he talked so humbly, & seemed so hurt that I should have had him whipped so. I told him [I] did not have him whipped & indeed was astonished when I heard the fuss at the field. Old Myers did wrong to whip or attempt to do it, before he had done any thing to deserve a whipping. You wrote me that he had considerable experience as an overseer, but I am satisfied that you were misinformed, he is no doubt a splendid farmer, & knows exactly how much work a negro ought to do, but he know[s] nothing about the management of them—he don't treat them as moral beings but manages by brute force. I gave him a talking about whipping them, & told him I did not want my negros whipped severely, did not want their skin cut, they say he will do just as you want him. Sam pretends like he is very much affraid of him, & I know Thornton & Bill are. Tom ain't affraid of the devil, I don't think Randal is much scared. I know they work better than they have since you left. I told Sam, if he would do his work faithfully, be humble & submissive to Myers that I would insure that he would not get another lick, & if he would act so I would see to it that Myers should not give him any other such a whipping. He made all sorts of promises, & I told him I would look to him to see that these negro boys did their work, & attended to the hogs, &c, & that if any thing went wrong on the place I would expect him to report to me. He made the boys rope our sick cow this morning put worm medicine in her, stopped it up & tied her so she could not lick the place, & he said the worms would die. I feel sorry for the poor cow, but think she will die.

Major has made Bob's & Billys shoes, they are full large for them, but do very well. Collins hasent made those shoes for me yet, & I am nearer barefooted than I ever remember being since I was a child. He came here nearly two weeks ago to borrow my wagon (you see I have learned to say *my*) to move to another mill, we were using it, & I did not let him have it, & told him I was almost barefooted & wished he would make my shoes as soon as possible, he told me he would make them the first thing after he moved, & send them to me—he went from here over to Susans to borrow her wagon, & there cut out shoes for her, Sallie Hattie, Nettie & Jim,[21] & promised to make & send them to her last Sat—& he may have done it and he has had the leather to make Mary's & Walters shoes & promised to have them done a month &

---

21. Sallie, Hattie, Nettie, and Jim were four of the eleven children of John and Susan Scott.

more ago. Mary says she reckons she will get hers next Spring. Mary & Walter have old shoes they wear. I reckon I will have to make me some cloth shoes & just give up shoes leather & all. I thought Collins was a man of his word before. Our hogs are fattening right fast, but two or three of them are quite small, but I reckon we will have to kill all that will begin to do. Thornton took an other hunt for those two pork hogs that run over at Hursts, but dident find them. I have no idea we will ever hear of them. I had that cow that run at the mill killed and after she was killed found out she would have had a calf this spring, if I had know[n] that I would not have had her killed. Myers said if it was his cow & he wanted beef he would kill her. She was very fat, makes nice beef. I hope we will save it all. The Plows were repaired without using the coulters & Myers says he wishes you would get enough iron to make two new turning plows.

Monday Morn, Dec 7th. Instead of seating myself to work this morning, I take my pen to tell you a few news items that I have thought of & if I don't transcribe them may fade from my mind, & I must have my letter ready to send to the office at a moments warning. First I will tell you that Lee is about on a stand still, he has a badly coated tongue as I ever saw, but I think I see signs of its clearing off, tho' he has a slight cough now, & I fear his lungs are becoming involved. I give him the 3rd pr of Lobelia, through the day & night, he is greatly emaciated. I have nursed him closely, & done as much for him as if he was my own child, but have not of course felt the anxiety about him that I would one of my own. I would send for a doctor, but dont believe he would be of any benefit to him, I have used all kind of remedies on him, one of the worst cases the hardest for medicine to act upon I ever saw. I am so anxious for him to get well so I can leave for a while, before any of my children take his disease. Aunt Cinda told me when she was here Sat that Mrs Squire Graves had sent word to Uncle Mc that she wanted to see him, wanted to get him to attend to her business, oversee for her, he hasent been to see her yet. I know if she will give him a fair price, & accommodate him with a house for his family that he will leave the place he is now. Aunt Cinda is so tired of living on Susan's place. If Uncle Mc had been saving, & sold his cotton when it brought a good price he would have had enough to buy him a small place in the county some where, but instead of that his money is all gone, principally for the good of his belly, & his debts are all unpaid & will remain so till the end of time, only corn enough to fatten his own pork, what he wants for his family & no money to buy corn to fatten pork to sell, but *he is* happy *as a lord*—rides about at his leisure, no doors to his east room yet, the chimney nearly fallen down, the well going to ruin, two buckets in it, & rope thread been laying in the house for three months waiting for him to make a rope, before the well buckets can be got out the well—no bars to his horse lot yet, every thing going to rack, & there he sets, smokes his pipe, stuffs himself & goes to "Miss Wade" while all of "*heins*" business takes care of itself. He has only paid mother 50 dollars & that is all she will get, for he is out of money now. If I had such a husband I would go into fits I know.

Jim Rogers reached home a few days ago, just wanted one day of being gone 18 months, only think of that, he comes back on sick furlough, has *scrofula*,[22] rose once & was lanced on the side of his neck, his head is shaved all over they tell me—his furlough is for 60 days. Did I ever write to you about John Black[23] shooting himself just below the knee, about an inch between the place where the ball went in & where it came out, & when the doctor went to see him, & made some remark about the wound, Black said "yes 'tis a very nice little furlough wound" & every one thinks he shot himself on purpose but done it so nicely that it will give him a stiff knee & save him from further service in the war.

A negro boy of Ben Goodriche's[24] the only negro he had, the mulato boy Charles, run away just before that severe spell of cold weather a week since and was found dead in some body's gin, they suppose he got so chilled he went in there, but froze to death after he reached the Gin house. Thornton started to plowing this morning have three plows running now, Randal Bill & Thornton.

Teusday eve Dec 8th—John's Jack starts tomorrow I hear but I am affraid to send this letter by him, for I don't think Susan would hesitate to unseal & read it, & she could do it without leaving any sign on the letter. Uncle Mc was here this morning & I have got him to go to town tomorrow & get me a pair of cotton cards. Mrs Oliver was kind enough to come over this morn to bring me two letters from you & to let me know the cards had come to town as she got her pair yesterday & they were going like hot cakes—11 dollars is the price—Garrett passed by her house yesterday on his way to town & she gave

---

22. Scrofula is a form of tuberculosis affecting the lymph nodes, especially those of the neck.

23. In 1860 John S. Black (age 27) was a bar keeper with personal and real property valued at $6,500. His wife is listed as P. A. (22); they had two children. TX Census 1860.

24. In 1860 Ben Goodrich was a 21-year-old lawyer living with his father and mother, Benjamin Briggs (62) and Serena (53) Goodrich. His sister Bettie married Lizzie's brother James Lane Scott. TX Census 1860.

him him [*sic*] 20 dollars it being the smallest change she had & asked him to get her cards, & last night he reached her house so drunk he could hardly walk, but brought her cards safely for a wonder. The nine dollars he had left of her money he told her he bought whiskey with it, & brought a bottle with him containing a little whiskey. Mrs O says he just yelled like a wild indian & lay down on the floor by the fire in her room, & when she tried to get him up to go to bed in the other room, he swore he would not get up, & she told him she would make the negros come in and take him up, & finally prevailed upon him to get up, & *stagger off to bed*—and this morning he was as bold faced & as undaunted as ever—no shame about him. I don't know how Mrs O stands him, he goes there a great deal—don't tell John any thing about this[.] Mrs O dont want it known that she told it. He told her this morning that he was 140 dollars in debt & no money to pay it with, she puts her nine dollars down as lost, but says she would not say a word to his mother about it for double or thrible that amount. He swares when he goes into service that he is coming home when he wants to, he is told that he will then be considered a deserter & treated as such, & be a disgrace to his family & he say he don't care. Oh Will, he makes my heart ache, he will certainly disgrace himself, & probably reflect dishonor on all his relatives as Kit Hall has done. Don't believe all the tales you will probably here John tell about the Kit Hall Tradegy, for Susan tells manifold lies about it & will no doubt write many to John. I never heard, & don't believe Kit told whose beeves he killed, & she says he told Garrett that he had singled him out as his next victim, which Garrett denys as does others I have talked to—and about Uncle Mc. I have never heard any one but her or those she talked to censure him about the Hall affair. He went to Huntsville to hear the trial, & when she Mrs Wade found out he was going to Huntsville, Mrs Wade asked him to tell her when he returned all he knew about it let it be good or bad & this was said in presence of Aunt Cinda, & she heard all that was said—she sent him no word. I heard Bill Dodd say that, tho' he was a poor man, he would give $100 if Uncle Mc had not went to Hunts. Susan as you know [is] awful bitter against Mrs Wade & Alston, & is very mad because Aunt Cinda & Uncle Mc don't fall out with them also.

Garrett brought your letters to me, & the tax receipt from Jack Wilson to Mrs Olivers last night and she brought them over this morning, & Jim Driscol came with her, just full filling my dream I had last night & told to Mary this morning—that I got two letters from you & that Jim Driscol brought them. I was so glad to get your letters, I never grumble at the contents, length nor nothing now. I am very fearful that your Regt & Co will have to leave Galves-

ton now be supplanted by the militia—& if you go off, no telling when if ever
I will see you. Oliver writes that he expects to come home before or by Christmas. I told Mrs O to write to him if he came home without you, I intended
to have him *mobbed*—for he really deserves no more priviledges than you if he
is an officer. Sam is moving round yet, but I am at a loss to determine whether
he is only waiting to get perfectly well in his foot, or intends doing me so[me]
damage when he has quieted my fears, but I some how don't fear him. He is
very *deceitful* you know. Bill broke his plow to day in the new land, & has gone
with it to mothers this eve. Myers says he fears the new land will use up all
our plow's. I think Lee is on the mend, but tis very slow, I put mustard on his
chest last night & to day to make the skin sore, his bowels are blistered.[25] He
continues to pass mucus & blood, but not often, & some of the opperations
are bilious. I keep up the Rhubarb mixture, which acts mildly on the bowels—he don't cough so often since I applied the mustard. Myers told me to
day that a lady near Red Top died a few days ago with Flux. Dr Foster brought
me the cloves, Ginger & cinnamon, & I will make it up & send you some, by
the first chance. I got a half quire of paper, like the piece I am writing on,
from Mrs Oliver & she gave $4 at the Depot. I sent by John Nix for a quire
which he left at mothers for me, that with what I got from Mrs Hutcheson &
Mrs Oliver will supply me for awhile. Susan & I have had it up & down about
the calf skin that Mr Mangum dressed for me out of mothers Tan Vat—& she
had told several lies about it, she got mine & I got one of hers—but the tale
aint worth telling by letters. Oh I have so many many things I want to talk to
you about. I like the children try to imagine often, how happy I would be if
you should open the door and walk in. Oh what would I not give to see you.
I am so glad you did not have to stand guard those bitter cold nights.

John Nix got a letter from Jane saying that they did not reach Corpus
Christi before they heard of the Yanks close proximity & turned their course
to Sam Lane's & from there would return to San Antonio, so Bob is not captured. The baby is *just screaming* so I I [sic] will stop. I sent a little bag with
29 twists of tobacco in it for Jack to take you. I was affraid to let this letter
pass thro' Susan's hands. I think the twists that have been pressed will do very

---

25. Hot mustard plasters were often applied to irritate and blister the skin over an affected
area. The blisters would then be broken and the pus released. The belief was that one could coun-
teract an internal disease by the emission of the harmful matter through external means.

well & of course judge only from the looks. Buck Barry married a widow with one child three months after his wife died.

yours with much love
Lizzie S Neblett

Galveston
December 6/63
Mrs L S Neblett

Dear Lizzie

Yours of the 29th Nov & 1st of Dec was recd last evening and it like all other comes to cheer me with tidings of yourself and children. You and the children have had such good health and I may say good luck for being exempted from any serious misfortune that I some times almost fear to open your letters lest it bring bad news. From what you say of Bettie I fear she has inherited one of my constitutional defects we being so prone to take cold and one of yours in exhibiting such depth or morbidness of feeling. I certainly should like above all the children to see her & study her character. She is such a stranger to me that my curiosity is very strong on the subject. I can now realize the feeling of a parent to see his child when it has grown up out of his sight. I am sorry that you still distress yourself because she happened to be a girl and as such liable to the pains and cares of womanhood. I do not blame you for your sympathy but you must recollect all women do not look upon their lots in the same light that you do and Bettie may be able to extract as much of happiness as falls to the lot of most women and more than you have ever done. I notice that you do not receive all of my letters or if you do that they do not arrive in there [*sic*] regular order. It seems to me that it has been about two weeks since I wrote to you to accept of Myers terms for overseeing. Your letter on the subject arrived one day & was answered the next. If he prefers a part of the crop let him have it but I believe I would rather that he would take the $400.00 dollars for the reason that if he got a part of the crop he might be inclined to keep the hands in the field to the sacrifice of the stock of cattle hogs and other interests out the field.

You ask me if I did not enlarge the pasture beyond what was intended at first? Yes. Upon reflection I thought it best to do so as by that means the lake near the old field which holds water till late in the summer would be included.

It is the lake the negroes catch fish [in] by muddying. It was to get water that I thought it best to extend it. However if the rails are split in such places as to cause too much work in hauling let it alone, but if not have it made as I last wrote to Rivers for I intended next year to clear up and break up a portion of that elm flat as far at least as it has been deadened and if the pasture is not extended as I wrote to Rivers the pasture would have to be enlarged. I wish you would find out and write me word what that tax was for that Wilson wrote to you about. I expect it would be best to have that cotton tax fixed up and write to Peel & Dumble to pay the money to Owen Cochran. It would be best not to neglect it longer. I came over to Galveston last Thursday to do some writing for the Co and expected to send a bunch of envelops by Jack but he had started the day before. John told him he was going to let him go sometime in the week. I would have come over earlier but waited to draw a pr of pants, shoes and flannel shirt. I drew a red flannel shirt & bought one for six dollars, and concluded not to wear them if I can get those which Nelia promised to knit but send them to you for yourself and Bettie. They are made of fine red flannel but would not wear as well as knit shirts. I have been staying with John since I came over—brought my rations and some blankets and since I came over have been writing as a clerk in the office of the Adjutant General and have a promise of a detail for that business. If it were Spring or Summer I would not have it but as it will enable me to protect myself in the Winter I would like to get it. If I get the detail I will get $3.00 pr day besides $11.00 pr month but will have to board & clothe myself. I have not looked around to see what I can get boarding at but from what I have heard it will take nearly all I get to board me. I am glad you have got that trouble with old Sam over. I was afraid he would cause you much uneasiness and alarm if he ran away. I hear it rumored the Yankees have the mouth of the Brazos and I understand that all the negroes on the Island were [hurried] to Morgans Point.[26] This looks as if an [attack] was expected at this place soon. If I hear any thing more before mailing this I will write more. I must go now to the Spit and have no time to write more now.

Yours affectionately
Wm H. Neblett

26. On November 30, 1863, Union general Banks landed at Saluria on Matagorda Island.

At Home
Sunday Dec 13th/63
W H Neblett

Dear Will—

An other sabath finds me pen in hand, to communicate a small portion of the turning thoughts of my brain, and a portion of the fulness of my heart and its ardent longing to see and speak with you face to face, oh what satisfaction would even a few days of your company afford me. I never write to you without feeling the longing[,] for the pen is such a slow medium of communication, and I always desire to say so much more than I have time to write that invariably end my letters dissatisfied. Now I don't believe you ever feel thus, for when with me, you never felt much desire to tell me any news you heard, or exchange opinions with me, or tell your thoughts. I have often thought as you say that your thoughts went on improfitable errands and that you omited so many little things for me, & my pleasure, which I have often attributed to a want of affection for me, but I now persuade myself that it is only your abstracted mental condition that is at fault & not your heart. You perhaps know nothing of the deep anguish awakened in the bosom of one, loving with the entire capacity of an ardent & feeling heart, when they imagine that all the wealth of the heart has been & is lavished upon one who appreciates it not, & retains not one tenth of the love. Such moments I have passed, but I hope for better things in the future. You never felt proud of me, as some men do of their wives, you never studied my wishes, & sought to give me pleasant surprises by little attentions which would have been very grat[e]ful to my heart, but I attribute this as I said before to your mind & not your heart, & tho' I wish you were differently cons[t]ituted, yet I love you all the same, & cherish no discontent, nor unkind feeling for you, for I am aware that I have many faults, & that your kindness to me is perhaps more than I deserve.

Well I have Lee on [my] hands yet, and no nearer well or not much than he was last Sunday. I am almost worn out with him and last Thursday night I felt certain that he could not live, and his disease seemed so strange to me, & I had no experience in any such diseases, that, for the safety of my own children I thought it best to send for a Dr, & see what he called the disease, & how it should be treated. I sent for Foster but told Tom if he could not get Foster to get Brown, and, as Foster was not at home, he brought Brown. I questioned him closely as you know I can do, & he is a non *commital Dr,* but

I made him give his opinion, & asked as many questions as I wanted to. I never had or saw such a case before, and I do hope & pray that none of us will take his disease. Brown says he cant call it any thing but Flux, but a very violent & bad case, caused I think from his getting so cold the night the disease developed itself. After I sent for the Dr, he took a change for the better, commenced passing bile, produced by the pills I gave him the night I despaired entirely of him, his pulse grew better immediately, & when the Dr came he said he thought he would get well with close nursing &c. What seems astonishing is that he never seemed to suffer any pain, no straining, and he would lay & sleep and all his evacuations would come in the bed, without waking him. I have taken every precaution to prevent its spreading, have the vesel emptied away off & dirt thrown over it, his clothes & bed changed often & keep the children out of the room as much as possible, but if any one takes it it will be me for I have spared neither hands nor nose. Nance is the biggest fool & devil I ever met, my patience is exhausted with her, & I have tried to keep Sarah's hands out of the mess as much as possible as she had to cook. But every night she has laid by him, & wakes if he makes any noise, while it is a job for all hands to get Nance awake. She is wore out too & said the other day to Sarah that she wished he was dead, manifests no feeling for him & he wont talk to her but calls on Sarah for something every time he sees her. The last three nights I havent had my clothes off, the first night I did not sleep an hour the whole night, since then I tax my mind with the hour I want to wake, & can come with in a few minutes of it. Dr B[rown] says he hasent Typhoid fever yet but may have it. He gave me some grey mercury & Dovers powders to give to him told me to check his bowels with Laudnum[27] after he had had three [bilious] opperations. I had been using starch & laudnum injections, but did not use enough he said. I have been trying one a day to check his bowels, & hope now I have succeeded, tho he was up after day light this morning. He has 20 drops of Laudnum now in his stomach, and nearly a tea spoon full in an injection, I have gradually increased the dose till I have got to

27. Mercury was often given as a laxative or cathartic. The purging and salivation associated with the use of mercury were considered signs that the drug was working. Mercury is a cumulative poison, and repeated use leads to destruction of tissue, hemorrhaging, liver and kidney damage, and gastrointestinal problems. Dover's Powder was a well-known drug developed by a British physician, Dr. Thomas Dover (1660–1742). The powder contained ipecac and opium and was used for pain and to induce vomiting and perspiration. Laudanum was a tincture of opium commonly used for pain relief.

that. He seems right strong to day & has eaten some soup & rice, the first food he has taken in three days. If it was not for the humanity of the thing I had much rather have let him lay in his mothers house & died than to run the risk of myself & all the children taking it, by having him in the house & nursing him as I have done. I have had a great deal of trouble with him, more than he is worth. I had such a time in learning him to walk you know. I wish I had a good sensible negro in Nance's place. Her children are not worth the trouble of raising them. If she had got up and attended to Lee that cold night, he would have been well now and Thornton is as bad as her, neither care any more for their children than if they were pigs.

Yesterday I had quite a crowd of visitors. Aunt Cinda Uncle Mc John Nix Mr Coleman & Bro Jim, & then Myers ate dinner here. Jim & Coleman came down the day before, and were waiting for Old Dowdy to get back to John's, as Coleman engaged him as a Sub for Jim some time ago, and they heard thro' Susan that Dowdy said he was going for Harve Briggance.[28] Susan is violently opposed to his going for Jim, and said some time ago that she would feed Dowdy & his horse a whole year for nothing if it would keep him from going as a Sub for Jim Scott, who was strong and able to go in service, & she wanted him to go. Jim wants to engage Dowdy in case his other Sub swears he is under 45. Oh Susan is so mad, & Dowdy is affraid [of] her, told John Nix that he would go for Jim Scott but he was affraid that Mrs Scott would never forgive him if he did. Jim & Coleman stayed all night last night at John's, & old Dowdy was there, came yesterday. I dont know how they made it, I would not be surprised if Susan did not let out on Jim. *She is [an] awful woman,* you have no idea how she cuts up. She seems to be mad at the whole world because John could not get a Sub in, and upon his family in particular does she pour out her wrath, & spend her time in abusing & telling lies upon them. The eve she spent here with me gave her room to tell several lies upon me, that I have heard of. Says I wrote her a most insulting note about the Calf skin that was in dispute, & that she wrote me a scorcher. I was not nor havent been mad about the skin, & never thought of writing any thing insulting to her, & she was quite civil in her notes to me—"and after all "she said", the evening she came here I had the assurance to ask her to knit sock for Neblett" as grand a lie as she ever told[.] I had as soon go to the man in the moon to knit socks

---

28. Harvey Briggance (age 40) was a farmer with personal and real property valued at $38,550 in 1860. His brother Frank was the district clerk. TX Census 1860.

as ask her. And her son Garrett will surely come to some bad end. Aunt Cinda saw him the day after he went to town for Mrs Oliver & got drunk, & she says if he wasent drunk that day she is no judge. A few days ago, Aunt Cinda was over there & Susan had her two little negros busy & Garrett ordered them to make him a fire, she told them to do what she had them at, & after awhile he caught one of them in the house & commenced whipping her, & she screamed & screamed until Susan arose, and said I can't help it if you all are here, (Aunt Cinda Uncle Mc Jim Rogers & Dowdy were there) I must go and whip Garrett, she started with a leather strap, Aunt Cinda says, she don't know whether she whipped him or not, but there was an awful fuss raised in the room and the little negro came kiting out—and after a while, he [Garrett] caught the other one in the yard whipped her the same way. She [Susan] sent by him recently to Red Top to get her some shoe thread & pipes, gave him ten dollars & he met some one on the way with an old fiddle with no bow, & [no] strings to it, gave the $10 for it & came back home. No trust no dependence to be placed in him, not as much as in a negro, and all the money he can get he buys whiskey with & gets drunk. His mother bought a five shooter for him gave $100 for it, & he now wears that at home & every where belted around him, & he begged Mrs Rogers out of a box of caps, pretending he wanted them to hunt deer, & he has shot the whole box away at a tree in the yard at home, & caps so scarce & high—he is either a fool, devil, or crazy a little of all perhaps. Jim laughed heartily at the scrape Susan and I have had about the Calf skin, she got mine through mistake, & was for hanging on to it, whether or no, & to prove to all that it had her brand on it, she sent to Lancaster's for it & called in Uncle Mc to see her brand on it, & the L. S. did show on the blackened side, & he turned it over on the grain side & showed her very plainly L. S—then she snorted, and she had a great mind to cut her own throat for being such a fool &c &c. Uncle Mc says it got her down worse than any thing he ever saw. She is more terrible than an army with banners.

I am rejoiced to hear that you are likely to get a position or detail as a clerk in Adjutant General's office—as it will save you from the bullets, as well as the weather, guard duty &c. They all say you will be lucky and do well if you will take it. I thought all details would be called in, in case of battle, but John Nix says not, that your services as Clerk would be needed as much then as ever. Jim John Nix Coleman & all thought you would do well to get it. Jim never fails to ask me, "what does Bill Neblett think of the war now?" I always tell him you are still hopeful & he laughs. I am affraid that Jim & John, if they live thro' this war will have it thrown up to them their eagerness for substitutes. Coleman told me to tell you that he had asked a great many about the iron & nobody wanted to buy any, & you had better get some sheet iron to make sweeps, and the shears of the plows & the bar iron to make the bars of the plows. He says no body wants to buy because every body is fixing to run from the Yankees, and dont want any thing they cant move. The ordinance department has been moved to Anderson from Houston, and it has scared the town folks into fits almost, for they think the Yanks will aim to take that the first thing. They use the Redtop school house for the magazine, & the court house for something else. I see in the news a notice of a call for the people to rally to the defense of Houston that the enemy were in a few days march of the city.[29] Some how I dont feel alarmed about the Yanks coming. Jim asked me again what I was going to do when the Yankees come. I told him I would wait till they get a little nearer before I determine upon my course of action, & if they do come, I expect no help for any body & if I cant help myself I'll be in a bad fix. Myers says he wishes you would get enough iron to make two turning plows, they broke three plows in breaking up the new ground which they finished yesterday. Myers bestows more attention on our negros than I expected he would, Garrett found out he came here last week two days running, and he let out about it, 'twas not fair to come here that often. Coleman told him he reckoned Myers knew his own business. Susan tried to get him before I did & he refused her—she now says he lies she did not say any thing to him 'till after he undertook here, at Mrs Olivers & Rogers and that she would not have a man who had three farms to attend to, & that she was only making fun of him when she spoke to him, that Myers should not whip one of her negros, they (the negros) would not let him—Garrett accuses mother of taking his mothers calf skins she says she sent five or six up there, & now wont claim the one I had first & sent her. Coleman says he never saw but one that belonged to her and if she sent more the negros did not bring them up there. I wish I knew how Jim old Dowdy and Susan made it about the Sub. John wrote to her two months and more ago, to turn old Dowdy off[;] there was no chance to get him in, but she has been holding on to him, because she found out by some means that Jim wanted him.

I have a faint hope that if you get that detail that you will stand a better chance to get a furlough to come home, Jim Collin's is detailed to work in [a] cabinet shop & he comes home every three months. I can well imagine your

29. The Union army did land on Matagorda Island, but did not reach Houston.

desire and curiosity to see our baby (I cant call her Bettie) I don't think I could hardly stand to leave the children and not see them for five months unless I was situated like you are [and] couldent help myself. The baby dont look so much like Bob as she did at first, Jim and John's little Sallie Bug says she looks more like me than any of the other children—she is a fat little thing, large enough to her age, she sets alone well now and is trying to crawl some, but the crossest thing you ever saw, and she will scream by the hour & not shed a tear but if any of them hurt her feelings, she sobs and the tears roll down her cheeks. Billy is a bad fellow yet, & I fear will make a churlish, unloved, and hateful man if he lives. He has a fashion of scratching the children with his finger nails, and their faces bear the marks of his nails nearly all the time. I whipped him yesterday, & I do it well when I begin. He runs from me every time & I have to make them catch him for me. He loves the baby better than I ever saw him love any thing. I asked them all one day which one of my children did they think loved me the best, and they all thought Bob did, Bob was not at home, was staying with Henry Scott,[30] & I reckon he does love us both better than the others do, tho' Mary loves you very much and has been looking so anxiously for a letter from you in answer to her last. She tells me to write you that she wants you to answer her letter. Uncle Mc got me a good pair of cotton cards for $11 and some postage stamps. I dont know what his visit to Mrs Graves resulted in, but I reckon he won't go, for he told me to tell you to get him enough iron to make him a couple of sweeps. Coleman says ready made iron sells at $3 per pound which makes a plow cost $60 without the stock.

Sunday night. I must write a little to you to night, & try and get my letter as near finished as possible so if a chance offers of sending to the office I can fix it up in a few minutes. I can't send to the office now without stopping a plow for when it is good weather I hate to stop a plow & send upon uncertainty. Sam came to me Sat and asked me to please write you to dun Mr Olivers Warren for him, that Warren owed him $10 & promised that he would give the money to you to send in your letter to me. Mr Myers promised me that he would come soon, and superintend the pig marking and the calves. I must have a pen made and get up all our unmarked shotes, we have 17 unmarked as near as I can make it out, we may have more. Thornton is a mighty big fool about learning the number of stock the color &c he don't try to learn

---

30. Henry Scott (age 5 in 1860) was the son of John and Susan Scott. TX Census 1860.

any thing himself & don't remember it any longer than you are telling him. My two missing hogs I have entirely despaired of getting. Our sick cow has all the worms out of that sore place, but [the wound] stands open, I don't see how it will grow together. Browns old hog negro man was here to day & Bob heard him telling the negros how many hogs they had up—117. Killed 20 & they averaged over 200 lbs, says Dr B—just rides around and begs people to come & look at his hogs, he says our missing hogs have never been with his. Sim Thomas drove them out of the range, or some body else came and got them.

Teusday morn, Dec 15th Yesterday evening, Mother and Babe came down & spent the night with me, & have gone to day to Susan's & Aunt Cindas. Mother is taking all the calf skins for Susan to select hers. She has been so mad about the skins, & says Mr Scott wrote to her to buy her leather, and let what she has been cheated out of go. Mother says all the folks up her way are planning what they will do when the Yankees come, and she thinks of digging a hole under old Turn's cabin & burying her valuables, she cant make up her mind to leave her house, tho' Jim advised her to leave it & try & escape with her negros. Jim is firmly of the opinion that slavery will be extinct before this war closes, so many will be killed so many die, & go to the yankee states. One of mothers old Miss[issippi] acquaintances staid all night recently with her, & told her so much of the Yanks doings in and around Raymond that mother is much excited. This lady is a widow, & she was here on a visit when the raid in her neighborhood in Miss was made, & she lost all of her negros but two invalid ones, and her father Daniel Thomas lost all his but one negro woman, his yard was the Yankee Gen Headquarters & the battle in Raymond[31] was fought on his plantation, took all their silver ware, broke up all their dishes, took all their provisions, destroyed all their furniture, & those two old people, who were very wealthy & lived in style, have now only one negro woman to wait upon them, and the empty house over their head. Her father was lying at the point of death when this plundering happened, & they did spare the furniture in his room.

Bettie Scott & Jim are fixing all their plans to move, & Bettie like old Mrs Hale wears the breeches & carrys the money with her, mother says, a pile of

---

31. The Battle of Raymond occurred on May 12, 1863. Toward the start of the Vicksburg campaign, Confederate general John Gregg attacked Union general John Logan at Raymond, Mississippi. The skirmish ended with the Confederates' withdrawal. *Official Records*, series 1, vol. 24, 704–48.

confederate money as big as a large dictionary & some bags of Silver I think, & she takes both that and the pistol under her charge. Mother is worst outed with her than she ever was before, she gave mother a lecture about the way in which she had raised her family, & she intended to raise hers to be affectionate to her & to one another, & every minute or two it was "come here Jimmy & Kiss your Ma, now Kiss your sister" that is her plan for making them affectionate. Now some how my faith in the belief that the Yankees will never molest me has never been shaken, & I don't feel alarmed and shall form no plans 'till they get nearer me than they are at present. Jim took old Dowdy off from Susan in triumph, & now he has him holding on 'till he finds out whether he will want him or not, & mother says he is ashamed to keep him at his own house 'till he finds out whether he will want him or not, & Coleman is keeping him [I] think. How much more to be admired is my own precious brother Garretts noble brave & patriotic conduct than either Jim's or John's. Jim is much worse than John.

I don't know what Jim is to give Dowdy. Mother says Lee hasent the Flux, that he is just like Mack was. Some of [his] symptoms are very favorable this morning, he has no fever, I gave him Quinine yesterday & to day am giving him my tonic pills,[32] but this morning he has began to pass blood again has no pain, no straining. I never saw any ones tongue clean off faster than his has done since Sunday. I quit the Laudnum yesterday, after giving him nearly one vial full of Laudnum, & I now believe if I had continued the stimulating remedies he would not have had a return of the bloody operations. I think if he don't get well or mend, in that particular I[']ll be like Nance, wish him dead. Nance is complaining of her belly but the prompt treatment I have given her I hope will arrest it. Mrs Oliver sent this morning to grind her sausage meat, all well there, I think I shall wait 'till after Christmas to kill most of my meat, as it is so small.

I wish Will you would try and get me some Rhubarb, and some Lobelia seed if you can, don't get much of either and send them to me by the first chance. Well Lee has had 4 bloody discharges, three almost entirely blood, looks in lump like old dead blood. I am affraid he will get back as low as ever. I am sorry now I sent for Brown for I did have the disease checked, he had ceased to pass blood for several days, & had tapered off on pure matter it seemed to me which mother says was favorable. Steeping him in Laudnum for three days & stopping the stimulating remedies has caused him to fall back.

---

32. Tonics contained a variety of ingredients, but one common ingredient was quinine.

My patience is almost exhausted. The men company I had Saturday say you must think the war will close in 1864 from the amount of cotton you want to plant next year. Coleman says he is not going to plant any next year. I could write much more but must stop and send this over to John's for mother to take home with her & send to the office. I'll write to Peel & Dumble again about that money. When I sent that certificate I wrote them to pay the 81 dollars to Owen Cochran—tho' I did not write to Owen to apply for it. I shall have to write to both I expect. I wish you had got me a calico dress like Oliver got for Mrs O, gave $50 tis good callico & dark enough. He sent it by Warren. I have no hopes now of getting a dress. Dr Kerr has callico in town selling for $10 per yard, but I live in the woods where no body will see me, & if I can only get my home spun wool I'll be fixed. In haste.

> yours affectionately
> Lizzie
> If you want me to change your address
> you must write to me.

Galveston
Dec 14th/63
Mrs L S Neblett

Dear Lizzie

I have been expecting a letter for several days and when I fail to get one at its expected time I then realize the feeling of one who is so situated that months role away with a continual anxiety and expectation of hearing from home. Last Saturday Jack arrived on the cars a few minutes after I had left for Pelican Split to get my trunk & mattrass. John overtook me before the boat left—gave me a letter for Oliver & said I had a package & short note attached but no letter. I returned yesterday with my trunk & mattrass and put them in the room where John & Graves sleep and will remain there awhile. I commenced boarding yesterday with an old dutch woman & her daughter—a young grass widow.[33] Another one of the clerks boards there also. We have to pay $1.50 per day each of us or $45.00 per month each. I was detailed on the

---

33. The term "grass widow" had various meanings. It could refer to a woman who was divorced, separated, or whose husband was temporarily absent. Other possibilities include a discarded mistress or the mother of an illegitimate child.

4th as one of the clerks in the Adjutant Generals Office here. We do not have much to do—probably not more than three hours work a day, but we have to remain in the office about eight awaiting for business comes in. We have a very comfortable room & good fire. So you see I am doing remarkably well just now but still I do not like the business much & would not have the place if it were in the Spring or Summer. But my ill health this Fall & the cold bleak situation of Pelican Spit impells me to accept and hold on as long as I can. Tho' I am liable to be ordered back to my Co in case it marches. All detailed men are liable to this except in a few cases.

John Scott told me last night that Susan stated in her letter that Lee was in great danger of dying, but upon looking at your note attached to the tobacco I found that the note was written only one day before Susans letter, I am and have been for some time uneasy lest some of the children take the flux from him. You ought to keep him in another room by the fire & not in the room where you & the children stay.

Sarah sent a much larger quantity of tobacco than I expected or wanted at one time. I tryed some of it this morning and found it very good home made tobacco better in fact than can be bought here for $3.00 a pkg of manufactured.

The cars have just arrived and I feel certain of getting a letter just as soon as the mail is distributed. The Post Office is kept in one room of this building (the Custom house) and I will step in there in a few minutes. John Scott looks in good health but still complains of something like rhumatism in his knees & legs. I will tell you a good joke on John. A few evenings since he was strolling about the suburbs of town trying to find an old stove. He met a lot of little boys eight or ten years old & asked them where he could find an old stove. They pointed to an out house close by and told him there were three there. He went in the house walked over several rooms & suddenly came in one where he found two whores of the lowest kind. They had nothing there but a mattrass. John told them what he was after & they told him there were no stoves there. The idea of these little rascals knowing any thing about whores & terming them stoves shows how early the vices of the world are known to boys raised in the city.

I have just returned from the PO—find no letter when I was so certain of getting one. You state in your note by Jack that you have just written and he has now been here two days and your letter not yet come. This is vexatious. I have no doubt there are many rumors up the country of the Yankees &c. There is no doubt an army near Matagorda but how many I have never yet learned.[34] Several days ago there was great apprehensions entertained here that an attack would be made on this place either by land force from the West end of the Island or by the Gunboats but things are now quiet. Three or four days ago an order was issued from this office ordering all the women and children & non-combatants away. A few have gone but nine tenths will remain. The place is liable to be attacked any day. In yours of the 29th you ask if it would not be best to run that division fence between Jims & our field I think it would. There are 1100 rails split in the bottom near by & and [*sic*] Sandlen had as many or more split for the same purpose. Jim ou[gh]t to make half the fence or pay for having it done. I think those pigs you speak of loosing [*sic*] are in the Basset field after the waste corn but Sim Thomas may have them. They were not marked. In yours of the 29th you speak of coming down to see me & weaning the baby. Now I will tell you and I want you to recollect it. Don't you come without that baby. I want to see the little chap very much and all of the children. I will mail this without waiting longer for yours & if it requires answering soon I will write again. When you kill the hogs I would let them hang up all night then next morning cut the feet off and the head and weigh and keep the weights so that you will know how much to let the Gov have. The paws of the hogs might be weighed but not the head. If something of this is not done the govt will get ⅓ instead of one tenth of [the] small hogs. The Gov gets 60 lbs of bacon for every 1000 lbs pork. In salting I would use some coarse & some fine salt and let the brine run off to keep it from souring.

yours affectionately
Wm H Neblett

Galveston Texas
Dec 17th/63
Mrs L S Neblett

Dear Lizzie

Yours of the 9th was delayed and did not reach me until Teusday. I was somewhat uneasy before your letter arrived and it has made me more so. I suppose by this time Lee is either much better or dead, but my principal cause for

34. On November 30, 1863, Union troops gained control of Fort Esperanza in Matagorda Bay. Long, *Civil War Day by Day*, 441.

alarm is for the children. I think Flux is contagious or what is nearly the same thing epidemic. I have no doubt you have had a dreadful time with Lee and can well sympathise with you in advance if you should have a case among the children. Coit Fisher the Surgeon of Elmores Regt has had so much practice in such cases that I went around to get his treatment which I enclose to you for such physician as you may choose to call in if you have another case. I had heard that he had great success in such cases. He told me that he had never lost a case. He considered it easily managed in its early stage but says it cannot be entirely cured in a few days. I do not consider Flux very contagious I think it somewhat so or if it is not that it is epidemic. Here in camps we have ceased to regard it as dangerous though it is sometimes quite severe and when it is severe it takes a good while to get over it. I think at least one third of the men in Co (I) have had it since I joined the Co and there has not been a death from it. I will write to you in a few days I am going around tomorrow morning to be vaccinated.[35] I understand there are 70 or 80 cases of small pox in Houston and have no doubt it will soon be here. I have no recent news from the Yankees but what you will see in the papers before this reaches you. I wish you would write oftener even if you do not have the time to write as long letters as usual.

Your affectionately
Wm H Neblett

At Home
Sunday Dec 20th 1863
Wm H Neblett

Dear Will,

Here I am still nursing this sick negro, over three weeks now since I brought him in the house, but I think now he is getting well. I never was as near worn out with any thing in my life as I have been with him. And never found out till he began to get well what was the matter with him. I sent again for Dr Foster to come and tell me what was the matter, for I never could be-

---

35. In 1796 British physician Edward Jenner developed a vaccination against smallpox, a disease characterized by high fever and severe skin eruptions. Scabs from a person infected with cowpox, a milder form of smallpox, were introduced into a healthy person by means of cuts made on the skin (usually the arm). If successful, the cowpox provided immunity against smallpox.

lieve that it was the Flux, & from close watching had found out that his liver was the seat of his disease,[36] but where the blood came from was what I could not determine, & I could find no case similar in Beach, & I had no other medical work, & tho' I had begun & determined to keep the liver acting all the time if I could, for I found whenever his liver was acting the blood ceased to come—yet I wanted some body to tell me what was the matter. Dr Foster came & from what I told him & from examination he says it is Hemorage of the liver, & a very rare thing, never knew but two case before this. His liver is greatly enlarged. When I applied mustard to his bowels I made the plaster large enough to cover the region of the liver also. His tongue now [clear] and much inflamation of the bowels. He has been clear of fever now for several days & the Hemorage is gradually diminishing, so he has very little now. I keep him under the the [*sic*] influence of my Bundle's pills all the time, & a few days ago gave him three very minute doses of [word illegible]. I think now he will get well & I feel I will. I know it is a contagious disease. Oh you have no idea what [a] pill I have had with him & his mammy & her children, for I have had to have all of them in the house, & you know she never has learned any of them any thing & they are all like hogs, worse than dogs. And now after all my trouble with Lee if Nance & Thornton take a notion to go with the Yanks they will pitch all their children with the first creek they come to [instead] of parking them.

I was disappointed last Friday in not getting a letter from you. Susan sent to the office & I sent over there that night to see if I had any thing & she only sent the News. I sometimes think she gets my letters reads them—then returns them to the office. I never like for your letters to pass thro' her hands & I never send one of mine there to go to the office. I sent Bill to mothers last night with instructions to go to the office this morning, & be back by dinner— Perhaps he will bring a letter. We have had some fine weather for Killing hogs but I have killed none yet, but thanks to my neighbors, I am supplied with bones and sausage meat. Mrs Oliver sent me some, Susan sent some when she sent her sausage meat over to be ground on my cutter, and Aunt Cinda sent me some. Mrs Oliver is an excellent neighbor any have had, she looks for Mr Oliver about Christmas, that is next weeks, but I indulge in no such false hopes. Every day I ask myself shall I ever see Will again but, I am making up

36. In the nineteenth century many believed that a particular organ or body system was responsible for an illness. The liver was thought to be the culprit of a variety of ailments.

[my] mind to receive & submit to my fate, what ever be in store for me. I have no bright prospects, no hopes in the future to be blasted, for I dwell less than ever on the thoughts of the future. I think God must have intended me as the expiator of the sins of my forefathers for the two or three generations past, and that my trouble will end only with my life—& since it only agravates the matter to kick against the thorns, I am learning to come like a whipped dog, but oh what well of bitterness my heart contains & its waters never rest. My sex has always troubled me, but if my life could be like some womens I know of[,] it would seem more endurable, some seem to have an easy time of it, & tho' they bear children the drudgery the wear & tear of life is lifted from their shoulders and pleasures & privledges given them that I have never known but, I am in a complaining mood and will stop, for no complaint that I ever entered bettered my condition. Sallie Kennard[37] is a woman who has slept on down and been fed with a silver spoon all her life. The finest & best taste have always clothed her & her children and her thoughts have not been taxed with the working servants, and friends have waited faithfully upon her and her mind like her body has been free from care—true we may suppose that her heart has ached, that her eyes have shed many tears since this war began for her husband has been gone now nearly two years, has endured a multitude of hardships & anguish privations, but when we look at her and view her grandeure and style we cant' help thinking that [it] is not deep. She sent to Mexico last summer for a mantle which cost her $300, the finest kind of a thing the fringe of which touched the floor when she had it on, and she bought a new bonnet from Mrs Hazerton, gave $60 & all her other parts of dress correspond with the mantle & bonnet. Now how can she feel like dressing when she [despairs] of her husband, whose life may cut off any moment. I heard several say that she was the finest dressed lady—at her sisters burial & Bettie was wicked enough to say that she saw her adjusting her laces & ribbons while they were standing round poor Amanda's open grave. But if it was her husbands burial she would not forget to fix herself as fine as possible & bask in the glass before she started to the grave. She has never made any sacrifices. Don't think I want to dress fine like her, nor to lead a lazy & indolent [life] as she does but I would like time to draw an occasional long breath and in the past I would like to have had occasionally dress enough to wear into the society that education and nature fitted me for.[38]

37. Sallie Noble Kennard was Lizzie Neblett's childhood friend.

38. The rest of this page of the letter has been omitted because its poor condition left too many gaps to be coherent. The transcription is picked up again on the following page.

Monday Dec 21st. Dear Will, Myers came this morning and marked & spayed the shotes. Bob has his little sow pig untouched, & I told Bill to tell Myers to leave an other, but Billy tells me he left only Bob's. You gave me no instructions on this subject, so I have to depend on my own judgement. It is my private opinion Will that you think very little about home affairs, and I always have to act before I can find out what you say or think but so far, my views have coincided with yours. Myers says he hauled rails from both sides of the line to fix that diversion fence and it has been built and they have torn down that old fence next to the bottom, and are now fixing it up—it was rotting down. I spoke to Jim about helping to build that fence, & he laughed & said it was his advise [*sic*] for every man to fix his own fence—our crop would have been endangered if the fence had not been built. I have concluded to send Randle to the breastworks, will send him to Mr Coleman and ask him to get a receipt for him. You wrote me some time ago that you would send Joe home christmas, but havent mentioned it lately & I don't know what you have Joe doing or any thing about it. If I told you as little about what we are doing at home, our plans &c, as you tell me, you would lie very much in the dark as to our movements. You never seemed to think any knowledge you had was worth the trouble of imparting to me. I sometimes have a very strong notion of doing as I am done by.

You never told me through & by whose influence you were fortunate enough to get your present office. I think the cause & it is an old long standing one, of your not being more communicative to me is that you never care nor think of giving me pleasure by imparting little items which may be interesting to me—but my lecture is long enough. I am convinced that I think of you, your pleasure, interests and welfare, 40 times where you think of me once— but you were born for good luck, while I inherited a stray dog's fate—but may be in the next world we will be even, if I do retain my sex in that world. I had rather Joe would go, & if I knew he was coming christmas I could know better how to act. Randle & Bill are both 17 yrs old—so you see, some of them will have to go. Randle is well fixed now, a new pr woolen pants, new shirt and a splendid new coat. I have been very busy lately cutting out & basting the negros clothes will finish all tomorrow. The Lindsey Mother wove for me is the best kind. Lee is mending fast, got up last night and went to the back of the room & ate a tin bucket full of soup & meat, & Nancy found him just as he was finishing and woke me up, and I gave him lobelia and emptied his stomach right away, his feet hands & face are all swollen, badly. Coleman has just sent me a note warning me to send one hand immediately to Anderson. They pressed Mrs Hursts team & wagon to day to haul a load of lumber to the Gun factory going up near town, Myers saw wagon loads of powder, cannon balls & Bomb shells going to Anderson—yesterday. We begin to feel like the war is getting closer to us.

Galveston

Dec 22nd 1863

Dear Lizzie

Yours of the 13 & 15th was rec'd to day—it is just a week old I cannot imagine why your letters are so long coming. Yesterday was my regular time for writing and did not write for the reason that I wanted to get one from you first. I have written you three letters and this is the fourth since I have been in here. Two of them were short. There is a good deal of uneasiness here about the Yankees. A few of the citizens have moved and in fact few but those who are too poor to leave are left. I think it is the intention of Gen Magruder to prepare the place for a siege from what I have heard of the provisions &c sent down lately. This gives us some uneasiness for fear that we may be cut off and starved after a long time into a surrender. A few days ago an order was issued to drive all the cattle off the Island except a few milch cows and the Gov. beeves. This looks as if it was thought that the Yankees might land on the West end of the Island. I fear we have not enough troops here to defend the place against a strong force, though the place may be reinforced. Tho the defeat of our army a[t] Look out Mountain has had a very demoralizing effect on the soldiers—great many now despair—another victory may cheer them up.[39] I think it the most disastrous affair of the war—not even excepting the fall of Vicksburg. If we do not retrieve our loss there soon the Yankees will be able to spare enough troops to overrun Texas this winter & spring, but I do not look for it for some time yet if such a fate even does overtake us.

I believe I wrote to you that I had been detailed as one of the clerks in the [Adjutant] Gen[eral]'s Office here of Col Rainey[40] who commands the forces

---

39. The Battle of Lookout Mountain, Tennessee, took place November 24, 1863. With this Union victory, and the victory at Missionary Ridge the next day, the Union army gained control of Chattanooga and surrounding areas. Long, *Civil War Day by Day,* 438.

40. Alexis Theodore Rainey was born June 5, 1822, in Alabama. In 1854 he moved to Palestine, Texas, and was a lawyer and state senator. During the Civil War Rainey raised Company H of Hood's Brigade (First Texas Infantry). He was wounded at Gaines Mill, and after his recovery was given command of Galveston Island. Rainey died in May 1891. Sid S. Johnson, *Texans Who Wore the Gray* (Tyler, Tex.: n.p., 1907).

here. There are three of us and in case of a fight probably at least two of us will go back to our Cos. This is only a surmise on my part and I have already told John Scott that if I could not get back to my Co I should join the Co he is in. There is a prospect for John to get into the Signal Corps. There are several details to be made for that Dept and instructions were given by Col Rainey to detail them out the militia, but I saw the officer who was to select the details and told him of John & about his inability to do full service as a soldier and afterwards sent John to him. John saw him and ascertained that there was great difficulty in processing spy glasses and last Sunday while we were dining with Shackelford he got a promise of an excellent one Shackelford had. By this means he will I think get a detail. It is a better place than I have and not likely result in going back to his Co again under any circumstances. In the letter before your last you speak of Johns being home sick or rather you say John Nix says so. I have never been able to see much evidence of it. He is in low spirits about the result of the war but this is very common. I know he cannot want to see his wife and children more than I do, and I cannot see why he should do so as much. However there is no accounting for the tast[e] or affection of people. I frequently indulge my self in the luxury of calling up yours and the childrens faces. It is a poor luxury compared with the reality, but adds something to the pleasure of memory. Your last tells me that Bettie could crawl struck me with surprise. I left her a little helpless babe that could not move its body. My heart yearns to see that child. I have no mental image of her face and it confuses my memory of any one not to be able to recall their faces. I expect neither Walter nor Bettie would approach me now any more than they would a stranger.

Joe will start home tomorrow. He has been hired to a man at Lynchburg and I will clear about $50 pr month for him. If there was not so much danger of the Yankees taking this place & capturing every thing on the Island in case of a siege I would have him sent down here and may do so if things get better. I was surprised to hear that you had not got your shoes made. You ought not to put it off. I wish I could have sent you a dress by Olivers boy but it was impossible for I did not have half enough money to buy one. Why did you not get John Nix to buy some for you. You have never told me what you could & what you could not buy nor the prices of things in Grimes. You need not postpone buying any thing for every thing is rising in price and the money going down to nothing. I hear of its selling Houston twenty for one for gold & silver. I think it would be a good plan for you to buy from the negroes all the calf and yearling skins you can & pay five to six or eight dollars a piece. Calf skins tanned are worth $1000.00 per doz in Houston or $80.00 each. The next time you send a wagon to Pa's send after some Indian peach seed Ma promised me. I want them planted (after they have been buried a while) where the potatoes were in the new ground. How are the potatoes keeping.

yours affectionately
Wm H Neblett

At Home
Christmas night, 1863
W H Neblett

Dear Will,

I have concluded to tax my eyes with a little scribbling to you to night, altho I fear my eyes will be made worse. Altho' the Almanac proclaims this day to be christmas, yet, there is no external nor internal sign of a holiday or rejoicing in my heart. I remember what a long weary year has already passed, and yet no sign of the war closing, and I have asked myself many times to day where & what will I be next christmas? I have been alone all day with the children. Mary went up to mothers yesterday in the ox wagon as I sent Thornton down to Pa's and to get my sugar from Jim's, & Sarah wanted to go down with him, and Mary was on her head to get to her Grandma Scott's because Sallie Bug and Kate McClure[41] are there—so they both went in the wagon. Mary carried 7½ doz of eggs, she has been gathering for three weeks past, to sell & get money to buy her a calico dress. Mother promised to let Bob carry them to town & sell them for her. I sent Ma some white Shallots and a bottle of wine—but this little trash don't interest you, you never tell me any little thing and are going to do likewise after this—but this one must be filled with scandal, and is intended as a warning to you. Susan Scott you are aware is & has been very mad at me, and all of John's family in particular & every body in general. She has worked John up almost to her pitch of frenzy if we judge by his letters. He is I suppose mighty mad about the leather, at me also. She wrote him all about the notes that passed between us about the calf skins, my cutting one which was not mine, & then sending it & my skin to her to cut one of her childrens shoes out of my skin. John wrote to her to take the skin I cut first & to cut a pair out of my skin, to take all she could get & hold on to it, that I was trying

---

41. Kate McClure (age 5 in the 1860 census) was the daughter of Lucinda Lane Nix McClure, Lizzie Neblett's aunt, and Mark McClure. TX Census 1860.

my best to injure her all I could—she would not cut my skin, nor have the one I cut first, and would have none that mother carried down to her. She cut loose on mother that day—told her that Mr Scott said that she got more of that Keifer taned leather than she had hides, that none of the scapulage was deducted from hers—and when she told mother that John said this, mother said "well if I knew John said that I would never have any thing to do with him again,["] & began to cry which will do for her to exult over as long as she lives. Abe John and Coleman divided the leather, & mother took what they gave her & said nothing about it, & knew nothing about it—but John wrote just what Susan said for both Aunt Cinda & John Nix read the letter. He told her to have no more partnership with them, that his children had to go barefooted while others wore his leather, & for her to send her leather to Brown's tan yard—and for her to tell them what he said, he wanted them to know it. I suppose them includes me. He wrote for her to "Keep on asking for that *blanket*" that astonished me, for I fully thought you had given John one of your blankets in place of [that] his mother gave him. You never tell me any thing you do or think, so I thought altho you had never mentioned it in your letters, that that blanket affair was fixed up & thought perhaps Jack brought the blanket home, as it was Garrett who wanted the blanket. For God sake, give John a blanket, I could send her over one of my bed blankets, but am affraid I would insult her thereby & she would come over & cow hide me. She told mother I wrote her a very insulting note about the calf skin, & said in the note that I *knew* all the time that the first skin I had was hers, & she says "if she knew all the time why in devil dident she say so at first." [S]he lied I said I thought it was hers, from a mark that Coleman showed me on the skin. She gave it to mother good fashioned, said Mr Scott had always said harder things of his family than she ever did. John writes to her every little thing he hears or knows, don't mind the trouble it is to think up the little items, and write them down for her gratification, and your name mingles in a heap of it, told her you had hired out Joe, been staying with him, &c and she read to aunt Cinda that he wrote back that you gave him the note I wrote by Jack to read and I said you would get a share of John's good things.

Now let me tell you John Scott has no more use for you than a wagon for the fifth wheel, every thing he can pick out of you is written back for his beautiful wife to handle & shake her *sides over* laughing. She dispises you & me, & so does John, but he cloaks his with a smiling face, so as to find out all he can from you to make fun for *his dearest*. Now I think if you have any independence about you, you will move your bedding from John's quarters and hear after let John Scott alone. Almost every word you say is writen back here. Aunt Cinda would not tell me all nor the worst I know & tried to make me promise not to write what she did tell me, but you are my husband & even if you don't love me, & feel no pride for me, yet I don't want you ridiculed by John Scott let your superior do that, all this makes me remember the ridicule he heaped upon you the day we were married. Your lite eyes and red head, & being the sort of a man to let a wife starve &c. I don't want you to have any [talk] with John, for then Aunt Cinda my informant would be brought into the matter, & she did not want to make a fuss, but only to let me know how things were going on. If John wont take the blanket leave it on his bed, and if you have any respect for me or your self let John Scott pass with as few words as possible. He even wrote to her about your asking him if he raised Honey at home. Susan sent him a bottle, & seemed to insinuate that you thought mother sent John the honey, & you did not like it—but he said he was going to save the Honey for his own tooth. Aunt Cinda thinks the reason John & Susan are so down on me & you is because John knows that mother thinks more of you than she does of his lovely wife, & fears that she thinks more of me than she does of him. Mrs Oliver was at Susan's recently & tells me that Susan took text on me that day & carried me high & low all day, but would not tell me but few things she said, & they were lies. John writes back a heap of things that Oliver tells him, & Susan boiling over about some of that. He wrote her that Oliver told that it was reported that Garrett had the bad complaint, and she [said] she "just wrote to Mr Scott if Garrett had it, he caught it from Mr Oliver." [A]nd the black hearted wretch Garrett insinuates that she is not the right sort of a woman.

My eyes hurt me so I must stop. I havent read more than two pages at night since Joe left here and I havent read two hours in the day time since, putting what I have read together. I cant read at night without my [torn page] eyes so sore that I cant sew next day, and I havent time in [the] day time, and every Sunday has been devoted to writing to [you], spinning out long letters with stuff you would not give [torn page] to hear. Susan knows five times as much about you your movements, plans, thoughts & ideas than I do. John don't mind the trouble of communicating news—but I would not let her know unless she know by having unsealed & read some of your letters that you do not tell me any thing to save her life. Garret said a [torn page] time ago in lessing you to Mr Oliver for being a coward that you did not care any thing [for] me, he said you hardly ever wrote, which you know is a lie. I reckon Susan told him you wrote me nothing, no love no news—but I don't care what the devils says, & just write me any kind of letter you please, and [as] long as you can write that you are well & as comfortably situated [as you] are at present I will be thankful. I hope you havent been [more] communicative to John than you ever were to me, yet I think you told him many things that I have writen, but, for my sake, if you have any love or respect for me, don't after this tell him any [thing] I write even when you know that it would be news to him.

Night Dec 26th I have been so busy all day long that I did not have [time] to write, and so must tax my eyes again. I must write you a little [torn page] the Bassett said—the 23rd inst, Bassett & Sallie & her baby went to mothers to get her bed & bedding together with other things she had there. [John] Nix was there at the time and came by here and told me all I know. John happened to be out in the lane when Bassett drove up, Sallie got out took her baby and went in the house, while Bassett was taking his horse out of the buggy & hitching him—as he paused in the job he saw negro Jim sitting on the wood pile gazing with astonishment, and he said to him, "What in the devil are you doing there Jim, if you dont look out I'll *wallop* you like damnation, I am boss of this place" John Nix heard this, & as soon as Jim got a chance he went and told mother and of course she was mad. He then walked on in the front way John went in the back way, he pushed upon the hall door and walked in, and Babe asked him into mothers room. Mother was as busy as could be getting up Sallie's things and never noticed him, Sallie [torn page] the baby. Sallie then went into every room about the house looking for her books, and he followed her, John says making all kinds of fool comments, about pocketing every thing he saw. Treated mother by [torn page] there just like she was some old negro wench. John says he knew mother was alone & unprotected, is why he acted so. They got their things and left. Mother made him give her a receipt for all he got. I stepped into the dining room just now and the wind blew the sheet into the fire, but I cant write it over and have a great mind to burn up all I have writen. I have the worst pen in the world to [write] with and am entirely out of time, I am tired in a thousand ways almost beyond endurance. I have been here now alone for six weeks, was at Aunt Cindas a little while over a month ago, have gone through a great deal that was immensely disagreeable in nursing Lee, and this time had no one to display my attention to, as you once said, I can not afford to nurse home folks, as I could not make a display [torn page]. I have worked hard all the time, notwithstanding there was four or five nights that I never pulled my clothes off, and did not sleep more then two hours each night—And who have I been working for negros and children, not more than fifteen minutes work for myself, & that done last night and now my wardrobe puts me more in mind of some indigent free negros, than any thing I can think of. I have worked [less] for myself than any one, ever since I have been married, yet you have accused me of being very selfish. One thing I must say right here, and forever after hold my peace, you never have recognized my merits (and I know with all my faults I have some good) and you never will, until I am placed under the ground, where my head aches to rest this minute. But I am nothing but a poor weak contemptible woman, who misfortune marked for her own, the hour I first breathed. You are sick of this I know so I'll end it.

Sunday Dec 27th I looked for Sarah & Thornton back last night but they did not come, a norther attended with rain blew up yesterday evening which I suppose prevented them reaching home last night. If it still continues cold I will have 9 or 10 hogs killed tomorrow, and have all the bone taken out, pork is too high & scarce to risk it with the bone in. Myers & Jack Oliver called in this morning. Myers thought I was not at home & he came over to give directions about killing hogs tomorrow. He tells me that Henry Hill is dead. He was vacinated and his arm was so bad they sent him to the Hospital at Chappel Hill where he died from his arm mortifying, and it is said that the man from whose arm the vacine matter was taken to vacinate—Hill died in the same way and his wife brought the blanket home he died on, tho' the Dr told her that his disease might be contagious—Jack says his Pa wrote in his last letter that he was coming home christmas so she is looking for him now. You wrote in your last, of the 17th inst that you were going to be vacinated next morning but I know you will be careful about getting the matter from a healthy subject so I don't make myself uneasy about it.

It has been ten days now since I heard from you. One of Susan negros came by here yesterday morning on his way to the office & I loaned him the saddle Joe rode, and he promised to return by here, & bring my mail but he did not come, & has not yet come. I wish you would give Susan the devil in one of your letters, so if she gets the reading of that she will be paid for her trouble. I was so mad when Aunt Cinda was telling me about John's letters & Susans talk, that I forgot to ask her when when [*sic*] John said Joe was coming home or what you were getting for him when he was hired &c. You said in one of your letters that you had moved your matrass and trunk to the room that John & Graves occupied. I suppose perhaps you bunk with John as Bassett said, I don't know that any thing I have said or can say will have any effect upon you in causing you to change your quarters, and your acts towards John, but I felt that I was doing towards you as I would be done by. I believe John hates you, & writes many things home, which his wife turns into ridicule and is no doubt writen for her to handle in the way she does. He just as good as accused mother of stealing his leather, & wants *them* to *know* what he says— and my God, if he talks or writes so about his mother, and cherishes animosity for her, who will he spare? [torn page] if you do nothing else let me entreat you to offer and force [him] to take a blanket. I'll send you another, and explain the [torn page] to him how you happened to apply for the blanket, and as he had never said a word about wanting it mother supposed he had no use for it. He wanted the blanket for Garrett, & he has to go into the service the 7th Jan, as he will then be 18 yrs old.

I am getting the thread ready to send to Nelia to knit your undershirts but never mind about sending your flannel shirts you drew to me and the baby. The baby can go through this winter with what she has, and I'll shivver no worse this winter than I have always done, and perhaps we will be beyond the reach of cold next winter. I hope I may be. I havent paid any debts with that money yet because I havent been off the place since I got it—yes, Uncle Mc sent your note over here by John Nix and I paid him 38 dollars, it was 36 dollars with five months interest. Lee has been up now a week, but mends very slowly still passes a little blood occasionally, and is as ravenous as a wolf, is still bloated, feet hands & face, tho' not so much as he was a week ago—perhaps he will get well. I keep him in the house yet make Nance sleep by him. All the children are very healthy now. Walter is as fat as a pig, he talks about you some, but not as much as [he] did. Mary will write to you as soon as she comes home. I have no idea that you would know the baby, she has changed so. She is not pretty, but I hope will make a large woman—if she has to be a slave, let her shoulders be broad, & her mussels [*sic*] strong so she can stand up under it better. Her fate is to raise children for some man, who will perhaps think it delightful work for her, but I hope a more merciful fate awaits her—that she will die, ere her wifehood begins.

Dec 28th In the morning I will go to mother and I write a few words to night, & will send my letter to the office as soon as I get there. Sarah and Thornton brought me 2 pr geese from Ma, one pr of them to Mary and a nice sow shote to Bob and two sows to me, Berkshire breed. Ma sent the children some flour and Pecan's and Rinders all of which delighted them beyond measure. Mrs Oliver gave Bob a sow shote a week ago, half Guinia Jack says. One of the sows that Myers spayed has died. I reckon you have heard that Jess died at Sabine Pass about six weeks or two months ago, and two weeks ago Jim reached home one day, and died the next that is two men Pa has in the Gov service.[42] Ma is about as usual she says she dont hear from you often—was glad

---

42. Jess and Jim were presumably two slaves owned by Robert Neblett.

to hear of your comfortable position. Sterling is faring badly in the Indian Territory. Sarah says Ma said she wanted to see me and the children so bad it made her sick. Poor dear Ma, I ought to go to see her—even if the others do treat me a little shabby by not visiting me when they can if they would. Yet Ma cant come, if it was not for her I would never try to go there again. I love her very much and she has always been so kind to me. They killed the hogs to day had the head & feet cut off and the largest weighed 120 pounds. Killed 10—Myers came and superintended the killing here and at Mrs Olivers. Hattie says that Ma had rec[eived] two letter from you which were of great consolation to her. They have rec[eived] two letters from Sterling since the fights in Ark, he writes that they had very hard times when they were doing so much fighting like to have starved to death. He came through without a scratch. I examined the baby's mouth good to day, & to my astonishment found one corner of a jaw tooth through and an other very much swollen—this is one cause of her delicate health, but not the sole cause—her tongue is coated all the time, & I fear she is going to have a sore mouth now. She sweated as much as ever last night. I will get some Elixer of vitr[i]ol,[43] which Eastman recomends as a tonic, for night sweats &c—poor little darling, I pity her so much. I looked in the negro baby's mouth to day also, found him with three jaw teeth through entirely, & the other nearly through, & all his front teeth, and he is now as fat as a pig, never has hurt him one single bit. How I wish my precious little darling could be as fortunate as the poor African baby. She looks now like Walter did when he got to running about after his severe spell. I hope you will be able to come home this summer, next month any how. I fear she won't live through the summer. I can do very little work, & I wont neglect her, under no consideration. I can't think you are much attached to her, & when she is gone, & you return, you will not miss her, but I will miss her, ever & always. It is going to rain again, is thundering & a dark cloud, oh we will have so much sickness after this. Sarah is sick now but not much I think, she has got so she is sick for several days every week or two.

Thornton's Bee Hive has swarmed twice and he is now fixing to hive the second swarm. Lake Creek is swimming about every other day, it is raining now. The old farmers' all say if it continues to rain much more it will injure the corn, already too much.

Yours with eternal love
L S Neblett

---

43. Elixir of vitriol contained zinc sulfate, sometimes called white vitriol, which acts as an emetic and astringent.

Will and Lizzie Scott Neblett, 1871
Courtesy Center for American History, University of Texas at Austin

Lizzie Neblett, seated at left, with unidentified group, n.d.
Courtesy Center for American History, University of Texas at Austin

Lizzie Neblett, n.d.
Courtesy Center for American History,
University of Texas at Austin

Lizzie and Will's first child, Mary Caroline, ca. 1863
Courtesy Center for American History,
University of Texas at Austin

Lizzie and Will's son Robert Scott, n.d.
Courtesy Center for American History,
University of Texas at Austin

Lizzie and Will's daughter Elizabeth "Bettie," ca. 1868
Courtesy Center for American History,
University of Texas at Austin

Lizzie and Will's youngest child, Grace, 1887
Courtesy Center for American History,
University of Texas at Austin

Will Neblett's boyhood home

Courtesy Texas State Library and Archives Commission

5

No Sympathy from the Curious World

January 2, 1864–February 12, 1864

Galveston Texas
Jany 2nd/64
Mrs L S Neblett

Dear Lizzie

Another year has passed and we are now launched upon another destined no doubt to be the most important in our lives. What the future holds in store for us we can only guess and hope and fear. Many others in Texas no doubt are staring their mental eye in the vane hope to catch a glympse of the hidden hand of fate as she spins or clips the tender threads of life. But is there any one brave or rash enough to ask the devine foresight to see the future of himself or of those near and dear to him as life itself in its youthful vigar. The future at any time has always held in ambush many causes of dread to me, but in times like these, one must be peculiarly stated or indifferent not to be impressed. These thoughts have been revolving in my mind since yesterday morning and do not qualify me to enter into the scenes of merriment to be had even here by a little effort and a good deal of money. But I have passed them by un-heeded and have gotten over Christmas & new Years day without any thing to distinguish them from ordinary days. Last night I took supper with John and got a better supper by far than I would have done at my boarding house. They had an excellent supper in fact—fresh pork, butter, hunney, biscuit &c. Yesterday was very cold—said to be as cold as was ever known in this place. I got through it very well but could not help thinking about the boys on Pelican Spit and Robert on the Alchafalia La and Sterling in the Indian Territory. I suppose you had hogs killed and cannot now help thinking of the spare ribs sausages &c for we do not get any meat at our house except beef and it is getting very poor. So you need not be surprised to have a letter before long for a supply of fresh pork sausages &c if things do not continue to look too threatening here.

Last night I could not help thinking of you and Bettie and Walter in your warm bed piled up together and afraid to straighten your limbs for the cold. Poor Bettie—she is almost an ideal being with me. I want to see you and the children worse than I ever did in my life. If Oliver gets home soon he will surprise me for things are closed up so close that it [is] almost an impossibility to get off the Island. If I hold on to this position until spring I have some hopes that I may get a chance to pay you a short visit. But the difficulties of getting of[f] were never so insurmountable as at present, on account of strict orders from Gen Magruder stoping all details on business off or furloughs sick or well. I suppose you have been expecting Joe for some time. The rascal should have started on the 23 of Dec but on the 28 I recd a note from the man he was hired to stating that Joe said they were conscripting negros in Grimes and that he wanted me to hire him to the same man again. I saw the man that day (28) and he told me that he told him to start home on the 23 but that Joe pretended that a horse had kicked & hurt him, but he would not let him see the place—that he laid and went to making baskets. Landone (the man he was hired to) was to pay Joe $4 to pay his passage on the Central R Road. When Joe gets home make him pay $2 pr day for the time he lost (giving him three or four days for Christmas) but not his Christmas and three days in coming home. He is the greatest rascal I ever saw. Tell Myers not to let him keep that mule or horse—make him sell him immediately to some one out the neighborhood. I got fifty dollars for his hire a few days ago. If you have not got a supply of paper at least three or four quires do not delay purchasing immediately even if you have to send a negro after it alone. I do not suppose you can get it for less than $6 or $8 a quire in Anderson. Four weeks ago it could be bought here for five. None is to be had now & I understand it is worth $12 in Houston. You had better send for $23 worth and get it be that great or small in quantity and any thing else that you must have[;] it would be best for you to buy it at once for every thing is going up or what is the same thing the money is going down fast—very fast. I owe old Keifer 10 with 18 mos interest making it now 11.50 pay him and any or all other debts you can. I wrote to you once on this subject but you have never mentioned the matter in any of your letters. I also wrote to you about sending Nelia some yarn to knit me some under shirts but have never mentioned the subject to me so I must conclude you read my letters very car[e]lessly or forget what is in them very soon. I think you had better buy yourself a calico dress even if you have to pay eight or ten dollars a yard. I think I will be able to buy you one as soon as I get my pay that is if the price does not go up too fast. It was worth seven dollars last week. I was surprised when you wrote me that you had not got your shoes. I see that you are inclined to neglect yourself more than I did altho your own wants were perpetually reminding you of them while I did not have any such reminders to jog my memory, for it was my memory and not my heart that was at fault.

Sunday Jany 3rd 1864—I have been expecting a letter from you for two days. Your last was dated Dec 21st twelve days ago. If you write once a week I should have got one five days ago. I think I have a right to complain of neglect if your letters did not miscarry or were not delayed. You wrote to me that you had gotten one pr of cards—why did you not get two—a pr of woolen and a pr of cotton cards. You had better do so without delay. I saw Lewes Haynie a few days ago. He is Capt of a militia Co from Navarro Co. I learned from him the particulars relating to the death of Doct Malloy. He says Malloy commanded a squadron of horse in Col Basse's Reg[1]—that they were rival suitors for the hand of a young lady. Col Bass remarked upon the eve of an expected battle that he would put Malloy in a place hot enough for him next day, and did accordingly next day order him to support a Battery with his squadron and under no circumstances to fall back. Haynie says the Indian portion of the army were soon drove back and soon after all the rest of our army also except Malloys squadron and the Battery which were soon entirely surrounded, that Malloys command had to cut their way out & in doing so lost many in killed & wounded and prisoners and he was shot in the knee and died from the effect of amputation. Haynie says Malloys bro[ther]s will kill Bass. According to this Malloy was murdered in the most atrocious manner.

There is no change in the aspect of military affairs here. An attack may be made on the place any day or night. I read a command to day from Gen M[agruder] to Col Rainey ordering the guards to be doubled &c and other things to be so arranged as to be ready at any moment for an attack. Greens Division[2]

---

1. Thomas Coke Bass commanded the Twentieth Texas Cavalry Regiment, which served in Texas, Arkansas, and the Indian Territory. Wright and Simpson, *Texas in the War*, 26, 118.

2. On January 1, 1863, Thomas Green had charge of the ground forces at Galveston. He was made brigadier general May 20, 1863. He commanded a brigade made from the Fourth, Fifth, and Seventh Texas Cavalry Regiments and spent much of the war in Louisiana. He was killed in

will soon be at Va Pt to assist in the defence of this place. Still we can see no indication of an attack. I understand Greens Division is in Houston now— that in consequence of fears of them by the merchants and shop keepers all the shops & stores are closed in Houston. If the soldiers ever get half a chance they will sack Houston on account of the speculators & extortioners in the place. This is a bad state of affairs but the place almost deserves the fate.

What are you doing about the schooling of the children. This next to your safety is the one nearest to my heart. If I should die or be killed I wish you to recollect this as a dying request. I have suffered with Neuralgia and light fevers from vaccination for five or six days since I wrote to you last, but am feeling quite well yesterday and to day. I have gotten rid of the cough which I had for so long while on Pelican Island. Tell Mary I send her the leaf of paper to write to me on—Jany 4th

Yours affectionately
Wm H Neblett

At Mothers
Jan 3rd 1864 Sunday
W H Neblett

Dear Will,

Your Christmas letter reached me on New years day just one week old, and that is a quick trip compared to some I get. I can't tell where the fault lies but think it is the office at Anderson. There is quite a difference in our Christmas letters, & the manner in which we spent the day. I read aloud to the children your history of how you spent the day and when I finished, Bob said, "why Pa had a better christmas than we had.["] Mine was a gloomy bitter & dissatisfied spirit that bore me company & entertained me all day long, and far into the night, and the same spirit still occupies his seat—and this morning I debated within myself shall I write or shall I not? and if it was not that by writing I hear from you, I feel like I would never dip pen in ink to you 'till I felt like I could write a calm reasonable letter, but God only knows if that time will ever arrive, it seems impossible now. I know you derive very little pleasure from reading what I write when I feel as I do at present, but if I should cease writing

the Battle at Blair's Landing, Louisiana, April 12, 1864. Tom Green County, Texas, is named for him. Ibid., 6, 78–79.

you would think some of the children were dangerously sick, and for that reason I I [*sic*] continue the doleful strain, better that perhaps than be kept in uneasiness & suspense about the welfare of your children. You need feel no uneasiness about me, for sickness and death, like sleep shuns the miserable, and I expect to live many a year yet, in the service of my family & tho' the service is a coercive one, yet I will be faithful and conscientious in its discharge.

I came up here the 29th ult,[3] and the next day it began to turn cold & sleet and we have had a very severe spell of cold weather, seven or eight of mothers large hogs froze to death, & I don't know how many pigs, & some sheep. The children were more comfortable here than they would have been at home, for that is an awful cold house, but they were running out all the time in the cold, all, even the baby & she was so bundled up she did not feel the cold much. I fear that the negros did not feed any thing at home, and that our hogs & pigs froze to death, and I felt some fear of Nance letting her children freeze, she has let them treat her bed clothes in such a manner that they are almost rotten & worn out. If it was not for my children I would not care what became of the negros, and most heartily do I constantly wish that I had no one in the world to care for but myself, no child I mean. I never expect you to come home alive, out of the service, for the termination of the war is remote, five or six years perhaps longer in my estimation, and you can't live through it all & so I view my situation in this way. I am the unwilling mother of five little helpless and dependent children—that they are here, in this world is not their fault while it is my duty to provide, to educate, both brain and heart, and fit them to take their place in the world as useful & good citizens. It takes money to do this, hence I must take care of what I have, & strive to make everything count. I must be independent. I must make a support. If the Yankees invade & over run Texas my negros will be lost, and then all will depend upon my exertions, and how shall I meet the emergency? If my education was better, I might by getting a lucrative position in some high school, do very well but my education is not sufficient for that, and it will be a good many years before my smallest children can dispense with my constant care, unless I do like Madam Beck in Villette[4] hire a nurse, but I'll dismiss this like I do my plans of action

3. Ult. is the abbreviation for ultimo, meaning in or of the previous month.

4. In Charlotte Brontë's Villette (1853), the English heroine Lucy Snow is a governess in France for Madame Beck's children, freeing her employer to make her living running a school for other people's children.

if the Yankees visit me, I'll wait till things get a little nearer before I fix up all the minutia of action.

So you were amused at my saying you were born for good luck, but you cant find when and where the luck happened. In the first place, Nature formed you in her hopeful sunny mood, that was the first stroke of good luck, then you had a remarkably tender loving, patient & forbearing mother, who sprung to meet your wishes ere you expressed them. True in your youth, many of the advantages of education were denied you, owing to the force of circumstances that your parents could not well help, but your heart has not famished for food for a loving kindness has attended you from your youth up. Of your married life I forbear to speak, let your heart, and your judgment tell you that tale— and now view mine mentally from my youth up, and say if it hasent been more like some poor stray dogs fate than any thing you can liken it to. Would to God that I could forget myself entirely, and live for my children alone, could forget that I have any physical or spiritual wants, that all selfishness was dried up in both heart & brain. You say in one of your letters that if Galveston is attacked you will go in John's Co if you cannot get to your own. This seems foolish to me, you did not (and it is well known) seek your present position to shield yourself from yankee bullets, but, on account of your bad health, and now if your office will shield you from the storm of battle why not accept the advantage? I honor patriotism and bravery a brave—a patriotic deed calls forth my praise and admiration, but Will, could I praise and admire your act when there was no emergency for it, and may result in your death? If you were a young man, without a family the case would be different, but you may do your country more service by shielding yourself as far as it is honorable, and thus save your life, to devote it to the proper culture of your sons in making them upright & useful members of society. God knows I wish you could raise & educate the children, and I could be allowed the delightful privilege of dying.

Coleman tells me that he had the power of detailing 10 negros to wait in the Hospital at Brenham he says, and he put Randal in that detail. Randle told me before he left that he had been vacinated by mother, before we owned him, I reckon that is so but he may meet many other contagious diseases in the Hospital. As to Joe I don't know what has become of him. He had not come home when I left the 29th & you wrote that he would start home the 23rd. I have heard nothing of him yet. I suppose he has been conscripted or has gone to mexico or the yankees, and I reckon it will be be [*sic*] many a day before we find out what has become of him. Seward lost in his trip to Mexico 75 yoke of oxen, and the best negro he had, took his mule and went over into Mexico, but he says he dident loose [*sic*] money by the trip, he landed 200 bales of cotton in an English ware house in Mexico, he was fixing the last account I had of him to go into service, had been sworn in. He promised nearly every body over here to bring things for them from Brownsville, but the people in Washington Co swept all he brought—he did not promise me anything so I am not disappointed. I have been forced to wear the shoes Colins made & brought me, tho' they don't fit at all, I was to let Mary Collins have them as they fit her exactly and and [*sic*] I don't suppose he has commenced Mary's or Walters yet, if he lived nearer I would go there and get my leather and try and get somebody to make them. Mrs Oliver & Susan Scott sent and got their leather—Collins promises are worth no more than a negros. Dr Johnson moved to Grimes prairie after he sold out to Bassett[.] Dr Mosely[5] died near two months ago.

Lish Womack[6] got up a little party at Mike Kennards, and Coleman went with Babe & Mittie Womack,[7] and was the gayest of the gay the butt of all their jokes, &c. He is one of the big[gest] fools you have seen, crazy to get married. If mother could get along without him I would be highly delighted to see him shoulder his gun & march, is always reporting some big tale against the south, to work mother up, & I know he believes when he tells it that it is false but he don't say so. McCune has reached home wounded, by the accidental discharge of a cannon a piece of shell struck him on the neck, & came near cutting that large arte[r]y which would have killed him, his wife went after him and brought him home. Jack Montgomey was powder burnt on the neck, none killed that I have heard of. I was surprised at what you write in your last about offering John one of your blankets. I think Aunt Cinda read Johns letter in which he said to "Keep on asking for the blanket" she sometimes reads his letters to Aunt C[inda] & makes them as she goes I think. But I want you to insist on his taking the blanket, and leave it on his bed if he won't take it and if I were in your place I would move my bed to some other place than where John stays, for I tell you he has no good will for you, tho' he hides it under a smiling face. I know how he talked about you to me when he knew we would

5. In 1860 Dr. Miles Mosley (age 28) was a dentist married to Lucinda (18) with personal and real property valued at $3,500. TX Census 1860.

6. In 1860 Elisha Womack was 16 and living with his father and mother, Abe and Elizabeth Womack. He was the brother of Susan Womack Scott, Lizzie's sister-in-law. TX Census 1860.

7. Mittie Womack was the sister of Susan Womack Scott. She was 21 years old and living with her father and mother, Abe and Elizabeth Womack, in 1860. TX Census 1860.

be married that night. He thinks you are a fool. I think John is deceitful, he will spare you face, but to his dearest wife, he spreads himself. Aunt Cinda says she never saw such letters as he writes, just as close and fine as he can write it, & then crosses it—he tells it all, & advises how to conduct her troubles with the Scott family. Pity he don't tell her how to manage *his lovely son* ain't it? I don't think I shall ever darken Johns doors again. I never forget, when any body injures me by word thought or act, and altho' I have forgiven you, (tho' the forgiveness was was [*sic*] unsought, & uncared for) yet I can't forget the little cutting and taunting remarks you have made—you have noticed this trait of mine I know, and always say that you show me more kindness than I do you because you forget these things—now the trouble is this: if we don't care much for the person we don't care much for the opinion, & let it be good or bad we soon forget it. When we were first married I could talk back to you when you were mad, now & for many years I cant speak, my heart comes up in my throat & chokes utterance—you know this, & you know that I seek never to hurt your feelings—but you dont want to hear this.

Our potatoes are keeping tolerably well a few rotten ones among them. I am affraid the seed bank froze this cold spell, for I noticed that the top was wet from a leak in the roof that I did not know of & intended having the seed bank covered with a hide before I left & forgot it so I expect a good part of them froze. Babe has been sick now for two days with a bad cold, came near having Pneumonia. Babe is not near so friendly nor carried away with the Baker family as she was. They have dropped her after finding out that they could not marry her to Jessie and have Mary Fanthorp[8] now in tow. And she does not think half as much of Sallie & Bassett as she did 12 months ago. Sallie gathered up closely, and remembered a little book she wrote Mary's name in & said "presented by her aunt Sallie" & told Babe she remembered writing it, but did not intend it, and wanted her to get it for her. Babe says Sallie says she never gave any body any thing that she did not wake up in the night & wish she had it back, always felt so sorry she had given it away. She never gave me 10 cts worth of any thing in her life to be sorry for.

Mother wants Garrets will opened, says she has given up all hopes of his return and she don't want to take care of his negros any longer. She don't know how to proceed about it and wanted me to write you & for you to talk

8. In 1860 Mary Fanthorp was 15 years old and living with her father, Henry Fanthorp, a hotel keeper, and mother, Rachel Fanthorp. TX Census 1860.

to John about it, but I told her no I would write to John by her request &
enclose the note in your letter & if he & his sweet one don't like the manner &
matter of what I say they can dislike it. I know he will enclose the note to her
for her to pick something out of it. I have all the notes that passed between us
about the leather, she wrote back on the back of mine, & so I have them all,
mother pocketed the "devilish insulting one" she gave her to read when she
went to see her about the leather, & now I have them all—& if John returns
from the wars, I'll get him to read them.

They all say up here that the baby has changed very much since you saw
her. Her head is shaped more like Hogan's (your fellow boarder) than any one
I know of, tho' I reckon she will be smarter, but fool women are the happiest.
She will certainly have auburn hair, & the bluest eyes, & the most active little
thing you ever saw. She took *jumping lessons* at such an early period that she
excells in the act. She takes Babe for me when she sees us a part, and crys for
her to take her but when we are together she knows which is her Ma. I wish
you could see your children even if you don't want to see me.

I was provoked beyond measure at Walter this morning. I was combing my
hair & had my tucking comb in my lap, he was by me and unknown to me
took the comb, and straddled on a chair round, and broke out two teeth in the
middle, 'tis now almost worthless. I took it from him before he broke it, & he
stole it out of my lap again. It suited my hair better than any comb I ever had,
the teeth were so long & it was such a strong one I would not have taken 50
dollars in Con[federate] money for it. I told you I whipped him good, & I
wished a little stronger than usual that I never had been cursed with children.
I tolerate them less & less—they have been the bane of my life & will be so
'till I die, here to fore I have lived in dread of more coming—now, I live in
horror of what I have. I'll never have another, & I'll stick as close to that as a
mason ever did to his oath. I rec'ed a letter from Owen the same day I did
yours. He writes that Peel & Dumble have promised to pay him that money &
he writes that salt is 75 cts per lb. Thornton said that Wm Terrell was gone
for salt when he was down there. I have the thread ready to send Nelia to knit
your undershirts & will send it while I am up here. Dont Pa have bad luck
with his negros, lost the two he sent to the breastworks, Jess & Jim.

One of Hoage's negro's, a black smith, took the small pox from a soldier,
who stopped to have his horse shod—and Jim Brown Dr Brown's son, was
boarding there going to school, and has now come back home, & Dr Brown
has vaccinated him, but it seems to me it would be too late after being exposed
to it to vaccinate. Hoague lives at Huntsville you remember seeing the daugh-

ter at Dr Brown's. If it dont spread at Huntsville I am going up there to get some cloth soon—that is the only way to get cloth is to go after it and insist upon having it. I am very fearful that the small pox will spread here, and some of our negos will bring [it] here. I forgot to tell you that Coleman is certainly off for the war's at last—finds he will have to go in the 2nd division of militia & has joined the regular service—is trying to raise a comp[any], don't believe in going in as high private—is going to send his children to his sister. I know it nearly kills him.

Affectionately
Lizzie S Neblett

At mothers
Jan 9th 1864 Saturday
W H Neblett,

Dear Will,

I have just [left] all the folks down stairs, and came up to our old room to write, or begin to write my weekly letter to you. You see I am still at mothers, held here by the cold weather, which has been one continual spell of the coldest kind of weather, now for 10 days, and no sign of much moderation yet—it looks like I wont get home soon, and my children have done worse than they ever did before, & in addition to my flock, Sallie Bug & Kate have been here all the time. Bob & Billy have scorched their pants into holes behind, for 10 inches up the legs, their knees & seat are out. Bob's shoe, burnt clear through the sole, Billy's worn into three or four holes, no caps no hats, no drawers, in fact nearly naked while I am in rags, & Mary & Walter nearly as bad. I try to shut my eyes to it all, but the work I have on hands, the doleful talks of *subjugation* being over run by the invading foe, and the idea that you are lost to me forever on this earth, almost turns my brain. I often pause in my sad & distracting thoughts and in heart felt misery exclaim "why did I not die in my infancy." Oh God! How dark does the future seem! If it was not for the conscientious regard I have for the duty I owe my children I would give up, & in calmness await the coming stroke, but the children's interest & welfare lie sore upon my heart. I have given up all hopes of the better time coming, & am powerless to do any thing. I have made up [my] mind to meet the struggle alone I have no male friend on whom I can call, Jim Scott has Bettie & his children & the whole of the Goodrich family to attend to when the Yankees come—but the truth is this, I don't think now I will leave home at all. And when I view my children I think I'll never leave Lake Creek with them again, they are such torments. Why were they given to me? When I reckon time by the mental pain & conflicts I have had, it seems I have lived a 100 yrs 50 of which it seems have passed since I saw you. What has my life been worth? & what is yet in store for me? But, I'll stop I only make you feel sad. If it was not for my baby I would go to you in my rags, & see you once more, but I can never get my consent to visit you with this child, a little harmless innocent babe, but she filled my measure of trouble to the brim, and I'll remain at home with her & the rest. You have never asked me to come, 'tis true but if you had there is too many if's in the way. You said in your last, of the 4th inst read two days ago, that our childrens schooling next to their safety lay nearest your heart & you wanted me to remember this if you should die or be killed as as [*sic*] a dying request. This clause in your letter made me feel very badly, you so rarely speak of dying that it made me think you probably had some presentiment of death. The education of our children, and the proper cultivation of their hearts, is now the chief end & aim of my life, and if you die, or get killed, rest assured that so far as is in my power, their education shall be attended to. If I do nothing else for them I shall try & educate them well.

Bro Jim & Bettie are down stairs, been here since yesterday. Jim has come out to get Garrets will to file in the Clerks office and says he will act as executor of the will. Uncle Mc told us last week that Bassett told him none of the family had been to him about Garrett's will and if they dident do something about it soon he intended taking it in his hands, right here let me tell you what Babe heard him say, & told to Bettie who told Jim & he told me to day. Bassett says that when he was having that settlement with John—that you were pretending to write a will or or [*sic*] something and that you had one eye locked towards him and therefore he took occasion to give you several rubs. I asked Babe about it & she said yes he said so, I told her it was all lost upon you, & he would have to repeat it. You complained in your last that my letters were too far apart to be weekly unless they were detained upon the road, & that I never mentioned the paying of our debts, or the sending & preparing of the yarn for your under shirts, you concluded that I either did not read your letters carefully or forget what is in them very soon. Now you do me injustice, and I must say so. I write regularly, let what will happen, and read your letters carefully, and have been trying my best to get the yarn ready to send Nelia, which I did do to day, and Will you forget how closely I was confined to home while Lee was sick, nearly two months I did not leave, only for a few hours twice, so I could not pay debts, neither can I seek out calico, domestic shoes and other things necessary to my comfort, so I neglect myself because there is no help for it—if I had no little children I could get on my horse & ride around and help myself, but this little helpless, unfortunate babe, cursed like its mother with the female sex, ties me stronger than a cable to home—but thank God she is my last hobbling string, the rope is used up. I never was a good amiable woman, always had too much of the evil, but I am worse than I ever was before, and if you cease entirely to love me I can not wonder at it, & should not murmur, but one thing is certain, I am true to your interest & welfare, and am ready to work for you any & all the time. Some how I have given up all hopes of ever seeing you again & do indeed feel almost like I am a widow. I expect no help nor assistance from any one[.] I tried to day to get Jim to promise to get me some paper from Howard Burton in town who expects to get paper shortly but I found from the way he talked he did not want to be troubled with it so I gave that up. I don't know how I will get paper. I must have it, true I write now no letters but to you, & they are very little satisfaction but as long as you desire such, I will continue to write. Last night Mary Haynie stayed with us, I love to hear her talk, & can't help feeling attached to her—she is very desponding in regard to the final close of this war, fears the worst.

As we were eating dinner to day Aunt Cinda and Uncle Mc rode up, and have just been telling us of their trip over to John's to see Garrett leave for the wars—it farely makes the blood curdle in my veins. Susan and Garrett had the biggest kind of a fuss that morning in the first place he whipped three or four negros severely, and she tried her best to stop him, hung on to his coat tail, & he pulled her all over the house, and then he called her a fool about some shoes, and she told him she would try to knock him down if he repeated it, which he did several times & she took a little chair to him; and he shoved her against the table and she made at him again and he pushed her down sprawling on the floor, & she rose, and he downed her again, three times, and if Uncle Mc & Aunt Cinda & John Nix had not been there to have held him off, I expect he would have almost ruined her. My God is it not awful? He has gone to Hempstead now, but tis supposed will return as he left his clothes, he joined a Cadet Company of Cavalry. What will become of him? In two months he has spent three hundred dollars & has nothing to show for it. I expect he was drunk the morning he left.

I am feeling very badly and very uneasy this evening, Uncle Mc says he & John heard the firing of cannon yesterday & the day before in the direction of

Galveston, & I fear a battle has been going on down there. My God how I dread a battle there—the thought almost paralizes both mind and body. But Will, fear prayers nor hope cannot avert the doom if you are to die in battle, and let me beg of you to try and prepare yourself & hold yourself in readiness to meet death, and your God, as a man and a christian. I have never set you a good example, but do not think of that, and try and be prepared. Oh God, Will I can't write of this my heart is too full. I looked at Jim with his children and my poor little ones gazing at him nurse his children, and I looked at them thought of their fate if they became fatherless, and it made them seem nearer & dearer to me. The negro who carried Nelia the yarn has just returned with a note from Pa as Nelia was not at home. Pa tells me to be more hopeful that we will whip the Yanks yet. I suppose they are all well, have heard recently from Sterling & Robert, were doing better than we have reason to hope.

I havent heard from Joe yet but think it probable he hasent started I expect you had better keep him. It is warmer this morning but is misting rain, & looks very threatening. I am anxious to go home, but last night Walter had a fever & is still feverish from a very bad cold, and the Baby is half sick with a cold, so I am affraid to start home. I feel very anxious about home affairs. I have bought a calico dress from negro Lize tis one I gave her several years ago is good & pretty calico, and as good as new, gave her 35 dol[lar]s. I feel very proud of it am making up my damask window curtains like Aunt Cindas, so I'll soon be fixed nicely. Jim will move to Lake Creek this week will buy negros & plant wheat. He will not go back into the army unless compelled says if Congress passes the law to compell men with subs to go back he is going to Mexico & trade. He proved his man's age to be 52 yrs so that let him out, and let old Dowdy loose, he is going for Harve Briggance if he can get in. Uncle Mc is waiting for this as he goes to town this morn. I have paid mother your two notes and what I owe her and paid Jim 60 dollars for the sugar. John wrote to Susan that you offered him choice of your blankets but he would not take it & that he told you that his only reason for wanting the blanket was to keep her from working so hard to make Jim & Garrett blankets but still he tells her to keep on asking for it to devil us I suppose. Monday morn, Jan 11 1864

Galveston
Jany 11th 1864
Mrs L S Neblett

Dear Lizzie

Yours of the 1st was recd several days since and a few days after yours of the 25th. So it seems you were writing to me at the same moment that I was to you, and the same thing occurred on the 1st. Yours of the 1st is distressingly gloomy with many sharp cuts and flings at me. I suppose [you] were out of humor generally with the blues super added and took the occasion to remember and remind me of my faul[t]s failings and imbecility generally. I believe you feel that you sacrificed yourself some what if not entirely in marrying me and that you remind me of how you have discharged your duty as a wife (which I have never denied or doubted) in connexion with the faults you find in me. It seems you never have forgotten any of them & while you claim credit for it and you discredit me for forgetting your[s] I have no doubt I could remember yours if I wished to do so but I do not and never desired to carry in my heart anything which I could pluck out, and remove as a barrier to perfect love and confidence between us, and I cannot think your love uncontaminated while you treasure up in such perfect security all my faults and guard them from slipping your memory by frequent repetitions verbally and in writing. I know you claim all the feeling and give me credit for none and upon this ground justify yourself. There are some very great differences between us and most of them in your favor, but not all. I believe a gloomy melancholy feeling sets you to writing or talking and puts you out of sorts with every body and thing and me in particular as the author of your unhappiness. While with me it has directly the contrary effect. It silences me, makes me sad, and draws me closer to you and my children, and makes me think rather of acts of kindness than of any other. However your own unhappy temperament inflicts ten times greater injury to your own peace of mind than the manifestations of it does to me, although you have and always have had my sympathy for your misfortune.

I carried the note to John Scott you sent and handed it to him while a number of persons were sitting around a stove in his room. I watched him as he read it. He first looked at the signature then read it over slowly and after finishing it, remarked that that matter had been put off so long that he expected the time had past. (He alluded to the will) I told him no, that I thought that law related only to nuncupative (or unwritten) wills. He said perhaps so. I told him I had not looked at the law in two years. He then remarked that the uncertainty of the death for so long a time might prevent it from being barred. Here the conversation droped and I went to my boarding house for supper. He wanted me to come around after supper, but I told him it was too dark and muddy. He wants me to come around to supper &c or to sit a while almost every time I meet him. I have not been back since. He was here yesterday and stayed several hours in the office but I was bussy [*sic*] part of the time and nothing was said on the subject of the will. As he left he asked me when I would be around. He is fatter than I ever saw him. I looked at the law and found that delay in prooving up the will does not effect it, but the law requires that the executor shall prove up the will within thirty days or in case the executor fails that the devisees (heirs under the will) can do so. As none have applied the lapse of the thirty days will not prevent your Ma from prooving up the will. I moved my sleeping quarters to the house in which the office is near three weeks ago, altho I had a pressing invitation from John to stay. I also changed my boarding house a day or two since. I have been suspecting that the young widow was not all right from what I had seen of her & several men who came there, but a few days ago a woman splendidly dressed in black silk and fine jewelry with a young girl about 16 took dinner there. They left the table before the rest did to go to the depot and some of us asked the question who they were, and were informed that one was Mrs Hawkerson and the other—I cannot recollect her name. Mrs H is a woman famous in Galveston for keeping a sort of private aristocratic whore house a short distance out town. I was surprised at this discovery and particularly at the elegance of her manners and it at once made up my mind to quit the place. I settled up night before last and drew my rations and commenced at a new house yesterday. Mr Smith the chief clerk selected the place and so far we are much pleased. This time our land lady is an American. The law expired allowing us $3.00 per day on the 1st of Jany but there was some doubt about it and we did not have the matter settled until the 9th. Now we get soldiers rations, clothing, $11.00 per month & 25 cts extra. We have to pay $3.00 per week for cooking our rations of beef corn bread & a little flour. There is a little talk (secretly) that Rainey will be superceeded soon & if so we will loose [*sic*] our places. One of the clerks quits to day dissatisfied with the pay. It is by no means a very desirable place except to keep one out the weather. If John Scott has been writing to Susan about me as you think, and I suspect you know more than you told me, he is certainly very deceitful. For since I have been staying here he has been more friendly that he ever was before. I expect Susan distorts his expressions & makes them worse than they are. However I shall not be quite so unsuspecting as I have been. Dont speak of the reason why we changed our boarding house where Susan can get it, for she will make some thing out of it. I have not told John, and will not. You are mistaken in thinking that I might tell John more than I do you. I have been very cautious in talking to him since I learned that he writes every thing to his wife for I knew she would distort what was said. If I do not tell you much then I tell others nothing in comparison. I do not see how it is that I fill for six pages and still tell you nothing as you say. I may not write on the subject you wish but it seems to me I wrote something about every thing. You complain of Jane Teels letters in the same manner, but I think mine has more news than hers.

It seems to me strange that John should write such things as that I had asked him "if he raised the honey at home". I never thought of such a thing as you think he intended to insinuate. I knew he had hives and the question was intended to find out whether he raised it or Graves for they both had things brought down by Jack. I went by there one evening to swap a pr of pants, I had drawers which were too large, with a man by the name of Jeters who is in Johns mess. They were eating supper and John invited me to eat with them. I did so. I would have overlooked the honey for there was not more than two spoonfuls in it but John as I was about finishing passed the cup to me and I took about a teaspoonful of it. I have [been] in most of the stores here (or rather shops) but cannot find a tortois comb. I have purchased a piece of Boiler Iron from John Harris and wrote to him to send it to Navasota care of Thomas & Brockway. He let me have it at 75 pr lb if I wanted it for my own use, but said it was worth $1.50 in Houston. I do not know what it will weigh but I suppose about 100 lbs. I will have to give him an order on Peel & Dumble for the money. Paper cannot be had here but I found an opportunity of buying a blank book for $8. and got it. It has about three or more quires of paper in it and will send it with some clothing &c by Express to Navasota to the care of Thomas & Brockway & write to Pa to take them home.

Oliver was here a few days ago—says he would be back to day to stay several days—will board at the same house I do & we will sleep together. He understands Susan very well from what I have heard him say. I [do] not now recollect any words as it has been several months since I have heard him say any thing of her. He has the most contemptible opinion of Garret, and seems to blame Susan and John both but her most for G conduct. Tell Myers I would like to plant an acre of tobacco this year. I understand Hearst has a good kind of seed. I expect it would be best to plant it on old land. I will not want to use it all myself but it will make more money to the acre than any thing else if properly handled.

A day or two since I sent by Bookmans boy a lot of old iron rods which I picked up on Pelican Spit. Bookman was gathering some & I did the same & put them in his box. He will take them home and some time when it is convenient you can send and get them. They will weigh about fifty pounds. I am sorry you were so unfortunate as not to get your shoes to fit. A neat shoe for a lady is worth fifty dollars here, but if I had the leather I could get them made for fifteen or twenty dollars.

Jany 12th. The reason why [I] did not give John that blanket before this is as follows. Before I came over hear [*sic*] I offered him the blanket & he said he had sent up after one and did not want any more as he did not have time to stop Jack from bringing two from home. When I started from Pelican a young man quite a boy saw that I had plenty asked me to lend him one & I did so. But since I came over I offered to let John have one & he agreed to accept it & when Oliver comes over he will bring it & I will certainly give it to him. I told him I would let him have the one I got from his mother but there was too much cloth & work put in it.

Yours affectionately
Wm H Neblett

At Home
Jan 13th 1864 Wednesday
W H Neblett,

Dear Will,

I have determined to send to the Post Office tomorrow and cannot let the opportunity slip without writing to you. You certainly forgot (when you thought my letters were not writen weekly) that the Post office was not at my door, and that I never knew when I began a letter how I would get it to the office, unless I was going to send myself. I have almost concluded to send to the office every Thursday if I do have to stop a hand. I don't expect to have the negros long & better use them all I can. Susan Scott is independent she has three boys and a negro who cant do much in the farm, and she says she don't thank any body for bringing her mail, and she hasen't brought any thing for me in a long time, if she does she sends it back to the office for ma to get. I only guess at her sending my letters back.

I came home yesterday morning, found things better than I feared none of our hogs froze, but some of the potatoes did, tho I hope I can pick out enough small ones out of my eating bank to make up for the loss in my seed. I tell you I have very little interest in the future, which was always uncertain, but is more so than usual now & if it was not for the diversion from gloomy thoughts that the planning for the future affords me, I would give up, & lie down in despair. My children too are a great incentive to keep me going and doing. Acting the widow is no pleasant thing, but I could not find it sufficantly unpleasant as to force me to marry again. Walter had three fevers, but is now going about, tho' he has a severe cold. The baby is almost sick with a cold, and she is still sneezing. She is very much like you about taking cold. I am more careful with her than any baby I ever had, & yet she is seldom well of a cold. Her birth was one of the greatest misfortunes that ever befell me, and no doubt she will marry in time & oft bitterly repent the hour of her birth if she lives to be a married woman.

No doubt you often think as I do that your children's greatest misfortune is in having such an unwilling mother, and if my conscientiousness & sound judgment of right and wrong were less than they are you might have cause to fear for their present & future welfare, so far as it rests in my power. But I feel that a large development of these two faculties will enable me to be a better mother to my children, than many a one who is more fond & proud of her children.

I fear that our meat will be very short this year. I found when I reached home that Myers had made the negros kill all of our hogs, they were all weighed without the head & feet, and the 14 hogs just made 1815 pounds. Last year our pork, weighed with the head & feet on came to 2,950 pounds. I have 12 old middlings & we have killed two beeves, & have some dry beef yet on hand. Myers marked the two sows & Bob's pig that Pa sent me. He sent unmarked sows. I'll have them turned out to night when the other hogs come up. Myers has hauled the load of cotton seed and gives the oxen cotton seed & corn mixed, 5 ears to each ox. He says we are bound to feed the oxen some [of] our corn until the grass puts up. I think we can get along without buying any corn. I find the 800 dollars is going fast. I have paid out 516 dollars and have 352.50 cts left. I only paid the principal of your two notes to mother, one note for $100, the other for $50. I calculated the interest but am so poor in calculation I feared to risk myself, and want you to calculate it & send me the process so I can settle with mother. I left the notes in her hand 'till I pay the interest, there is 20 months, or 1 yr & 8 mo interest on the $100 note, and just 12 mo on the $50 note. I paid mother all I owe her, but the interest mentioned. I will pay old Keifer what you owe him, & then I am going to stop until I pay the taxes yet to come—paid taxes last year, 143 dol, 65 dol for the state & county tax & $50 war tax. I thought of paying Susan money for the cotton we have spun up, but I fear it will leave me with too little money to meet the tax payment. I have been thinking of getting Alston to Gin some of this years cotton for me, enough to repay Susan, and have enough for spinning this year, and then we will have the seed to plant if you still intend planting cotton this year. What do you think of this plan? I am anxious to pay Susan. I want to feel that I owe her nothing, and hereafter it will be a great force of circumstances which will compel me to ask a favor at her hands. I hear that the Penitentiary will let no more cloth go for negros and only 3 yds to each white member of the soldiers families, so we must make more cloth than we did last year. I intend having you a coat wove on the piece of cloth I shall spin for mine & Mary's dresses. As soon as Nelia knits your shirts I will send them by the first chance. I sent you some socks two pair, by Mr Clements. I hope you will get them—wear the flannel shirts you drew 'till you get the ones Nelia will knit and then you can will the old ones to the baby if you want to. I used to think of the baby as your baby all the time, I now think of her as a little fatherless one, for it don't seem to me she has a father, you were with her so short a time. I have just examined my potatoes & am glad to find that the cold weather injured them very little.

Jim & Bettie both thought that Finley wrote Garrett's will, & argued from that that Bassett knew exactly what it contains. But from the hand writing on the back I judge Hutcheson wrote it, & John Nix says if H—— did write it, Bassett knows all about it from him, but I don't think Hutcheson would divulge a secret of honor, as he must have regarded that. If Garrett did leave the largest portion to his sisters, Jim says Bassett will attend to it, to get his share, and neither Babe nor I have any one to represent us. I am inclined now to think that Sallies portion will be larger than any one else, mother says he seemed to think so much of Sallie just before he left, & said he intended to devote himself to her, as she had acted so well in discarding Bassett. It will seem hard to see Bassett enjoying poor Garrett's property, when I think of his acknowledged treatment of him, and my belief of the actual treatment. I rec'ed a note from Sallie which I will copy and send to you. Babe is some what disappointed in her, tells many little things now. Sallie is mad at Babe, and Babe now sees her as the most penurious grasping stingy girl or woman to be started any where. I am not disappointed in her, she has no gratitude, no generosity, in fact no heart nor soul. Jim told me (I did not ask him where he got it but suppose Babe told Bettie) that Babe said she hated me, and that Sallie and Bassett were perfect lady & gentleman compared to me and you, and after I told Aunt Cinda what Jim told me she said Susan told her that same tale & we suppose that Babe told Mary Scott the same tale. Aint it awful? I told Jim it made no difference to me what Babe said, I di[d]ent care. I have become some what stubborn in the matter, they want to run me off & for spite I am going to stay & will stick to mother through thick & thin because I believe it to be my duty, and not through the motives Susan ascribes to me, to get mother to will me most. I never expect mother to make a will, and if she were to, I have no idea my portion would be any greater than John Jim's and Babe's. Babe Susan John, and Sallie seem to fear some such thing and have all combined against me—if the world at large believes, or judges me, by my kin folks opinion they must think I am the devil. I feel greatly mortified when I think it all over, but won't condescend to talk to other people about it. I am forced to think there is something wrong in the family, and I often ask myself haven't I the taint also, & perhaps you can see it, while I fail to discover it. God knows I strive to be above any thing mean or low. My standard is high and so help me God, I'll come as near up to it as possible.

I send by request of Sam some money he got from Warren—give Warren this & tell him to send other money, this wont pass.

Affectionately yours
Lizzie S. Neblett

Copy of Sallie's note

"Mrs L S Neblett. You have several books of mine I believe. I would like for you to send them to me. You have my "Moss Side" and a little blue book of poetry for children that I know of, and you may have some of my Lady's books or other books. Send them to the Post Office as soon as you can, and I will get them there. The little poetry book I remember writing Mary's name in it intending to give it to her, but never did. You will also please send me something to pay me for the calico dress you took of mine, and if you have any of my handkerchiefs you will please send them along too, as I am very much in need of handkerchiefs. Sallie Bassett." Aint that a grand note, it was put in an envelope and directed by Bassett. Mother says he made her write it but Babe says no, she done it with her own accord. Babe says that when she started home with three or four pieces of music that Bassett brought her that Sallie said "now I would be ashamed to take that music when you have treated me so bad, and have so many of my things at home using them," and Bassett said "oh hush Sallie let Babe have the music, you don't treat your sisters and brothers like I always treated mine." [S]o Babe brought the music away. Now to explain the note, Babe told me that Sallie wanted the books I had of hers, & I forgot to take them to her when I went up last, and the calico dress she speaks of was an old dress she gave negro Julia before she left mothers and mother would not let the negro have it and gave it to me and I fool like used it in making me a sack, it was old & wore out directly, now she wants pay for it. I sent all her Lady's books home last year, you carried them, I have "Moss Side["] & two Vol of Irving's works. I had two of her handkerchiefs, one she left at our house, & one old Kiefer found & brought to me. I used the handkerchiefs a few times before she returned from Va, and one of those times was the day of her return when I went to Nelia's from Wm Runnels burial & left the handkerchief then & Nelia had it washed & sent to her, telling her I left it there & that was pie for her to harp on you know. The other I took to Babe, before my baby was born, & a piece of Gingham Sallie gave me & told her to take them to Sallie, she told her of the Gingham but kept the handkerchief & has been using it ever since, said Sallie had plenty & she would not give it to her. My God what kind of a woman is she. She forgets that we boarded her 8 mo[nths] for nothing, that I helped her do all her work, my needles & thread and all I had was used by her as her own. That I made her several presents, and to come to a more recent date, I sent out Sarah and Kate & had her Squaw vine gathered when her good friend Aunt Cinda failed to get it for her, and then sent her Raspeberry leaves & Composition when I heard she said she would give anything for some. But I don't regret anything I have done for her & if she was in a pinch I would help her again. I did nothing more than my duty & deserve no credit, but do deserve a little better treatment at her hands. I don't know how I will pay her for the dress, but must pay her something, it is the only thing of hers I ever used in my life, and she never done a half hours work for me in her life and never gave me 10cts worth.

Jim says if mother does get friendly with Bassett, he will move off, tells mother that a great many people say that Bassett will get all she has. Mother says I don't know how he could do that "why weedle in with you & wrap you round his little finger" Jim replied and that made mother a little mad. Jim has his faults[,] is very selfish & no accommodation about [him] and is over bearing but is the best member of mothers family now left. Dear good Garrett, his loss can never be forgotten by me. A nobler kinder better man never lived. My tears often flow when I think of his mysterious death, and my heart yearns for him. Dear good brother, tho' I loved you devotedly, yet I did not love and appreciate you as you deserved. Oh I would give worlds if I had them, to have him back with me. I feel that I have no brother nor sister upon earth—what will become of me if this cruel war takes you from me. My God! the thought is too painful to dwell upon.

Myers started 4 plows yesterday, got all the field cleared up. Joe has not yet come home, I fear he has run away. Oliver has written home that he would come home the last of this month. I [have] a very slender hope of ever seeing you again, nearly six mo[nths] since I saw you. Mrs Buckley will open her school again in Feby, & I will start Mary & Bob. I have good news to write you of Billy, there is a great improvement in him, so much so that both mother & Aunt Cinda noticed it. I have had to whip him sever[e]ly several times, been a good while since I whipped him. Mary says she will write in my next letter. Ma sent me 15 Indian peach seed, and I have buried them. Lee looks about as well as he ever did. You can & will have a use for all the money you can get, so don't think of buying me a dress.

Affectionately yours
Lizzie S Neblett

At Home
Friday night Jan 15th 1864
Wm H Neblett,

Dear Will,

I am writing my third letter since I rec'd one from you. I sent to the office Thursday thinking I would be sure to get a letter, & was as usual disappointed. I can't see why it is that Susan can get letters direct from John, & I cant from you. Aunt Cinda was here this evening, and said that Susan came to her house two days ago, and told her of the note I wrote for mother to John about Garretts will. Aunt Cinda told the contents verbatim, and I know Susan told her, for no one read that note but mother, and I told no one, so John either sent her the note or copied it. The last letter I got from you you had not rec'd the 1st letter I sent to the office after I went to mothers and I wrote two others while there, the 2nd one contained the note to John. Susan said she wished to God Garrett had willed all his property to mother, for at her death there would be an equal division, & as it was she did not expect such a thing, & Mr Scott said if it was not an equal division, he intended to protest the will. Jim came over this morning and told me the will had been opened, as it was not known who the executor was, it was opened to find out Mother was as I expected. Jim told me after he got up to leave and I dident have time to ask any questions before he was gone, but as I understood it, I'll tell you. 1st he left Ellen (Mary's nurse you remember) & her family to Aunt Cinda & her heirs,

(Ellen now has a baby) to Babe he left Mele and her family three children one six yrs one 4 yrs and an infant, to Sallie Bob & his family in number 8, and that leaves me without a nurse for this cross, crying baby, to Jim Mack and $1000, to John (& here I am not positive) Warner and some money dont know how much, dident understand Jim, and now to me, what do you think he left? his land, and to mother the ballance of his property, his mules, plows, and his crop. I suppose 30 bales of cotton, 29 loads of corn, which was sold for that lumber you know. Mother's share amounts to more than two negros. I am satisfied if Garrett wished it so but the land will never benefit me any even if we have peace upon honorable terms. Mother will never be willing for it to be sold, even if any one would be willing to buy it situated in the midst of hers as it is, and she will never be willing to buy it, so it will lay there & we will pay taxes on it & perhaps 50 yrs hence some of our children may be some what benefited by it. It has always been our fortune to never have our property in an available form. If I had of had money in the beginning of this long & bloody war, I would not now be so destitute, & now I have a little, and it takes a bushel of it to buy anything—but the fact is I have given up, stuck fast in the mud and never expect to get out. I expect Bassett will burst wide open now, he has so many negros, 17 in all, & Babe has 16, and my number is 11. Garrett never valued Bob and his family as much, & that is why he did not alter his will I reckon after her marriage, he thought if he was killed & it went into force, it wouldent be much. Every body is already talking about what a fool he is, he can't talk five minutes to any body they tell me without having something about his negros in it. He wanted to hire Ben to Uncle Mc he pretended, but asked him about $4 or $5 hundred dollars, he wanted to take pork for the hire, at 8ct, & hire Ben at confederate rates. Uncle Mc is down on him now, can see a few of his faults now. I sent Sallie's books to her on Thursday, but dident nor don't expect to dip pen in ink to her—and have a great notion to never notice her request to pay for the old calico dress, just leave it for her to do like John does about the blanket. Will if you never return I cant live here, I will be between two fires, Susan & John on one side, and Bassett & Sallie on the other.

Jim dident seem at all disturbed about Garretts will—tell me what you think about it when you write. Bill broke his plow and carried it to mothers shop this morning, and says Joe is there, will be here to night or in the morning, traveled all the way up on foot, & in the night, to keep from being conscripted on the road—he wont be here long before they will have him. Coleman wrote me not to send Sam, as he would not be received as a sound negro (on account of his being ruptured[9]), so Joe will have to go when they come for him. I send Bill to mothers to night and will go to the office in the morning and if I dont get a letter I wont know what to think—unless you are sick & cant write.

Sat Jan 16th I shall leave that 81 dollars in Owen's hands for you to get when you need or want it. You can buy the iron with it. Myers says they are not going to plant a seed of cotton at Mrs Rogers or Mrs Olivers, if we dont plant cotton they cant press our negros next year if we have any next year.

It will be two weeks tomorrow since your last letter that I have rec'd was writen. Havent heard from you since I wrote to you about the blanket & that has been nearly three weeks ago. We will be all ready to plant corn before I can get a reply to this. Myers wants to know so he can alter the cotton rows if you plant corn on the west of the west row. I mentioned about Jim Coleman & Myers wondering at your notion for planting so much cotton, but you never replied to that, and never mentioned the iron for the plows after I wrote what Coleman said. You never talked to me about your business thoughts nor plans, so I cant expect you to write what you never talked. I wish I could hold my tongue or write without exposing my whole heart—but I can't alter myself if I could I would have done it long ago. Sat Jan 16th 1864

Jany 17th 1864[10]

This is your birth day and a most beautiful day it is—clear and warm and balmy as a May day. The most pleasant one of the month. I hope it is indication of your future. To day fourteen years ago I was here and you at your Pa's a young maiden seventeen years of age seeing things in the rosy light of youth. I do not believe you have realized half your hopes of happiness in married life—not that I doubt your love or devotion. I have been much happier than you, and to you I must give most of the credit. If I knew how to render you as happy for the next fourteen as I have been for the last I do not think a more willing heart could be found or one more devoted to a wifes welfare. I hope to have the chance of doing so.

In passing the house I boarded at while here in 1850 I could not help [feel] sad. In place of the neat comfortable house filled with happy faces, there

---

9. "Ruptured" meant having a hernia.

10. Lizzie added the following words to the top of this letter: "He lived just 7 years after this was writen the half of the 14 yrs he hoped to live with me."

stands the same house dilapidated in appearance dirty and filled with soldiers not one of whom I know. I have not seen but one or two persons in the place among the many I then knew—"some at the bridal and some at the tomb." Among all these changes my affections have undergone the least. I loved you then dearly and time had added a bond of esteem and respect for the many self sacrifices you have made for me, and my comfort and happiness, and rendered that a part of my nature which might fourteen years ago been changed.

But if time has not passed happily with you, it cannot be denied that in looking back it seems to have passed very rapidly. I was startled when I counted it up. Fourteen years is a long time I hope you may be as happy the next as I have been with you for the last. The time does not seem to favor the realization of it, but still I hope it with faith and a resolution that I will contribute my efforts to its accomplishment.

Yours affectionately
Wm H. Neblett
Galveston

Jany 17th 1864
Mrs L S Neblett

Dear Lizzie

I expected a letter from you yesterday and again to day, but was doomed to disappointment. It is now twelve [days since] the last one I read was written. You certainly do not write as often as I do. I never fail one a week and generally on Sunday or Monday, and yours have generally arrived on Fridays & Saturdays. I am alone to night in the office—have my bed there. The other clerks sleep over at my boarding house & the other with his Co. So you see I have a quiet time of it. This is a new arrangement somewhat though I have been sleeping in an adjoining room for a month or more, where there were several others staying. I have been reading the History of England—that portion of it relative to the reyhn of Charles the 1st and Oliver Cromwell. I regarded it as apropo to the events transpiring at this time in North America. But the present uncertain state of every thing destroys the pleasure to be derived from such a source because it is continually bringing to mind a comparison between the same fanaticism then rampant among the Puritans of that day and almost the same fanaticism among the same Puritans now waging war against the South. They succeded then,—seized the reigns of Government but prooving themselves inconsistent, hypocritical and incompetent, lost their power on the death of Cromwell & the old order of things were reestablished. I cannot help thinking of Lincoln when I seen the name Cromwell, & think there are many points of resemblance.

But enough of this—I carried the blanket Ma sent me—a very good white bed blanket over to John a few days ago and laid it on his bed, and told him I had brought the blanket I told I would bring & the reason why I had not done so earlier. He said he did not need it and did not want it. I told him that when I mentioned the subject last I understood him to say he would take it. He said I must have misunderstood him. I then asked if Garret would not need blankets. He said Garret also had enough. I then told him that if he would give me as much wool as was in the one got from your Ma that he could have that. He said all he hated about it was that they had to use up the wool he had in making blankets in place of clothes. He appeared to be in perfect humor about the matter, though I do not *know* whether he was or not. The blanket I offered him was a much better one than that you sent me. When I went to leave he called my attention to the blanket again (as he saw I was going to leave it) & asked me to come around after supper. He had eaten his supper but I had not.

Jany 18th To day John came to the office for me to go around to dinner at Shackelfords. I told him I could not go for dinner. He then proposed to go to night & take supper but I told him I thought it would be dark & rainey & that I thought we could not go to night. He said he would wait till night if I would go. To which I replied that I did not think we could go on account of the weather. He then went off. I am this minute in order that you may see how he acts towards me. He has never said a word to me about Garrets property, tho I expect he will when he gets a good chance. In fact we have never been alone since I gave him your note. You said some time ago that Myers thought there would not be enough corn. If it is not more than half grown their ought to be enough. Has more than half the corn been used? I expect another yoke of oxen had best be broken. However this may be left with Myers. When you have potato seed beded recollect to put them where there be no shade. I did not do this last year & it caused the plants to come up late. Have you got any calf or cow hides? What did you do about that side of leather Dr Brown owes? and what do you expect to do about tanning this year? What debts have you paid. I expect these are as many questions as you will find it convenient to answer at one time. I believe I asked you what you were doing about sending the children to school? Sometimes I think of writing something to you and cannot recollect whether I had written any certain thing or merely thought of doing it. I believe I told you I had changed my boarding house. I like the change very much. We draw rations now and get clothing & $11.00 per month & 25 cts extra per day. Two of us board by furnishing our rations & paying five dollars per week, which is $1.50 per month more than we get. It is probable that the law allowing three dollars per day & 11 pr month in place of rations & clothing will be passed again by Congress. I regret it expired so soon for I wanted to buy Mary & the Baby some calico but I will not have money enough after buying yours to do so. In a few days I will send some of my clothes by Express to Pa's together with the dress I will buy for you. I have lately drawn some clothing—did so because the position I occupy afforded the opportunity of doing it in advance of the time, & I availed myself of it for fear there would be none on hand when the regular time came. I think I will have enough winter pants to do me next winter and so I will not need them I send home for safe keeping for we may leave here sometime in a hurry.

Jany 19th To day I recd yours of the 9th & 13th both mailed the same day. I have been expecting one for several days and would not finish this until this morning. I have nothing more to add, in the way of news. There appears to be no more prospect of an attack on this place than there did a month ago, and I and every one here ceases to think about it, although every precaution has been taken in expectation of it. So you need give yourself no uneasiness about me I fully expect to see you once more and to live the balance of my days with you and the children after the war is over. Of course I do not know this, but I feel it, and hope you may do so too. I do not believe we will be subjugated or that any great portion of the State overrun by the Yankees. If Southern men would not give up until they were whiped we never can be subjugated.

You speak of making me some cloth for a coat when you have the piece for your & Marys dress woven. Now I want to make a suggestion. If you can consistently have the filling made of blue and white cotton carded together it would be the very thing and of the grey uniform color. You mention in your last that you had sent me two prs of socks by Clements. I have not seen him & had no intelligence of the socks, though he is over on Pelican & I have no doubt he has them safe. I wrote to him a few minutes since. They came in time for my old ones are out at the heels & toes & I was going to write to you for some for they cannot be bought here now, though I understand they have been selling at $8. pr pr. That affair of Garret & Susans is perfectly shocking, one of the most disgraceful things I ever heard of.

I recd a letter from John Harris stating that he had shiped that piece of

Boiler iron to Navasota for me. It weighs 90 lbs & comes to $65.50. I will
write to Pa to take care of it. You are right in stop paying out any more money.
I have not time to write more at present. I will calculate that interest on the
top of this page.

Your affectionately
Wm H. Neblett

At Home
Teusday Jan 19th/64
W H Neblett,

Dear Will,

Yours of the 11th and 12th came to me on sunday the 17th I find that you
must have delayed writing longer than usual nine days passed between your
last letters that have come to me. You are rather severe on me in your last, and
don't do me full justice. I admit that I am much oftener in the wrong than you
are, from the fact that I can't suspend my jud[g]ement & allow my feelings to
influence me entirely too much. I knew when I was writing these letters at
which you very justly complain, that I should defer writing until I could do it
in a better frame of mind, but I did not know whether that time would soon
arrive. I said all this to you in my letter. You misconstrued me in several particulars, but it does no good to justify myself. There are times when the veil is
lifted from my eyes and I imagine that I can see myself as others see me—and
I pledge you my word, that I do not fall in love with myself, when such views
are held up. You are more generous than I am, better and happier than I ever
hope to be, and I intended no sharp cut or fling at you when I contrasted your
life & mine, did not intend you to think that I was well satisfied at the manner
in which I have discharged my duty as a wife, or that I thought you should be
satisfied. I have always thought, & think I have so expressed myself to you, a
woman with a more hopeful [disposition] and less morbidly sensitive than I
am would have made you a better wife & rendered you a happier man than
you have been, & no doubt the greatest misfortune of your life has been your
marriage. But while I have not heightened all your joys or increased your happiness, I hope & trust that I have been no thorn in your side. True I have often
thought that had I my present knowledge I would never have married, because
having the views, and feelings, about raising children that I have unfits me in
some measure for the duty I owe both them and you. Had I remained unmar-

ried I would perhaps have been equally unhappy as I am as a wife and mother, but in that case no one would have been the sufferer but myself. As it is I have no doubt but several of my children have inherited my unhappy disposition, and I fear my conduct influenced by my unfortunate views of marriage & children will cause my children to love and respect me less than I deserve. I know and feel all this, and yet I fear it is beyond my power to reform. I have always thought and so expressed myself to you before, that my marriage was a fortunate thing for me—for if I had not married you no doubt I would have married some one else, and of your treatment I could never justly complain. You have been kinder and more indulgent to me and my faults than one man out of a hundred would probably have been, and it has been very foolish in me to desire your praise as I have, and longed to hear you say what your acts spoke for you, but I'll try and reform in some measure, and display a little more common sense than I have here to fore. The things I remember against you, at times when I am feeling particularly miserable and every thing that ever happened to me the least unpleasant arises before me, are not your faults as you term them but only some hard thing, some "sharp cut or fling" as you say that you in a fretted mind have said to me, and the memory returns, in spite of me, to sting me as keenly as it did when first spoken—only one of the methods that memory has of inflicting pain, and tho' it may be unjust to you, it inflicts more pain upon myself than injustice to you[.] I should feel thankful that you have been so uniformly kind and lenient, when you have the power to act indifferent. I am very sorry that there has been a jar between us, for I never expect to see you again and I shall always blame myself for giving you pain, abusing our last months of intercourse, when I should think only of you and your pleasure & comfort. The past I cannot recall, but in the future I [will] try and act differently. You say in yours last that you will try and buy me another dress in a day or two. I am in hopes you won't succeed, for two or three reasons which I will tell you. I have made up that green damask curtain dress, and bought a new calico from Lize, which I will make when I get time, so don't feel [I am] in that poverty stricken condition my letters perhaps led you to believe, and I would always feel ashamed when I looked at the dress, and thought of what induced you to buy the dress for me. I had rather you would keep the money and supply your wants. I did not intend my allusions to [the] utter scarcity of my wardrobe as hints to you to buy me a dress, if I had wanted you to do so I would not have hesitated to have asked you. It was my own fault that I had not exerted myself more to get me some dresses, but I have been so situated that I could not leave home and could not go, nor send in quest of calico, or any thing else I need—and this very knowledge has fretted me so much, but I intend to try and make the most of things & cease to fret at what I can't help. My whole life has been a grand mistake.

You need not think of getting me a tortois comb, I have the one Hattie sent me two years ago. Tho' I am still using the one Walter broke so badly. I have been over to Jim's one evening since they moved, & dident fancy myself very well treated, don't think I'll trouble them often. Bettie [is] perfectly disgusting, & Jim the most obedient husband I ever saw. Bettie has converted him into a waiting maid and nurse, and he performs well, in every capacity. She sits in her rocking chair, and orders him about, & seems to exert her mind only in finding something for him to do. He understands perfectly the mystery of her drawers and trunks, and can get anything she wants. You were always so clumsy at such things, that his handy talent astonishes me. I did not find out, correctly, what John's portion in Garrett's will was till a few days ago, and find that he left Warner to Mother, and to John what money is left after paying his debts, and a 1000 dols to Jim. I don't know what amount of money Garrett had but don't think John will get 1000 dols, and if there is any chance to protest the will he is going to do it. His conversation with you, & what Susan said proves it to my mind. I remember now that John never liked Garrett, and I think Garrett was disgusted at the way John acted in the division of Pa's estate, in claiming the $700 advancement, and the inventory he made out and swore to of the things he had rec'd, a good many little things he left out you know. None of them (I've seen none but Jim) have said anything about the unequal portions. I am satisfied with my portion, tho' it may never do me any good, don't expect it to. The land is worth more than the share of any of the others is it not? I don't think Garrett showed much favoritism in giving Bob's family to Sallie. I would not begin to give the land for twice such a family of diseased negros. I am very sorry to have to give up Polly. I like her better than any little negro I ever had about me, & have just got her in good train. I really feel attached to her, and she loves the baby so much, and the baby loves her. I have got a little negro girl (not so large as Polly about as large as she was when I first took her) from Mrs Oliver, for her vituals & clothes, it is quite an accommodation to me. I have to give Polly up the last of the month, & then I'll get the one from Mrs Olivers. I am glad that Garrett remembered Aunt Cinda, her health is worse than it has been for several years, & Uncle Mc failed to hire a woman—or any body to wait upon him. I fear he will take the big head as bad as Bassett at the idea of having a negro. Susan told Bettie that she was going to dismiss him as an overseer as soon as he displeased her. I am affraid that you will loose [*sic*] your clothes by sending them to Thomas & Brockway. Thomas is an old sot, & don't half attend to his business. I'll try and get the iron as soon as possible from the depot & will send Joe some Teusday after the rods at Brockman's.

Wednesday Jan 20th Jim's wagon goes to town to day and I will send this to the office by Sandy. I fear I won't hear from you soon as you are a little mad at me, but when you think the matter all over I hope you will not blame me as much as at the first glance.

Galveston
Jany 20th/64

Dear Lizzie

Yours of the 16th arrived this evening and somewhat alarmed me. I was not expecting one for four or five days and when it was placed in my hands I thought some misfortune had befallen you or some of the children and was the cause of your writing. It turned out to be a very agreeable surprise. I am astonished that you have not got my letters. You say it is near three weeks since you have got a letter from me. I always write one every week. I suppose they will come to hand after awhile. It was not longer than yesterday since I mailed one to you. This morning I started by Express a bundle enclosed in an old shirt made into a bag the following articles, 1 pr of shoes I drew from the Govmt, 1 pr of pants I drew from the Govmt, 1 pr of pants which you sent me by Joe which I wore about six weeks. 2 Red Flannel shirts one of which I bough[t] and one I drew from the Govmt, which you can use for yourself or Bettie as you choose, 1 pr of drawers got from the Govmt last summer, 1 Blowse or jacket got from the Gov a few days ago which you can use in making yourself a sack if you think it will answer for that purpose. 9 yds of calico for yourself, it cost $67.50 or $7.50 per yard. I had recd $50 for Joe's hire and could spare the money, 110 envelops (very poor things) I got the paper & had them cut for one fourth and it was badly done. One Blank book and a lot of scraps of paper upon which you can perpetrate as many interesting notes to me as you please provided you page them. ½ lb of candy, about one pound of lead which I hope will enable you to get some venison. A package of my letters which you wrote, and must take care of. Two small pieces of soap. The blank book contains paper equivalent to three quires but you will have to cut it out and fold as note paper. The freight by Express to Navasota cost $2.50. I wrote to Pa and Ma of it and the Boiler iron sent several days ago to [the] same place and requested that both be taken to their house. I could not get any other kind of iron. Perhaps you may be able to exchange some of it for some bar iron. I regret very much that I could not spare the money to buy Mary a calico dress. I may be able to do so after a while. How many yds will it take for a dress? And how much for Bettie.

I am sorry that I could not send all the children some little thing but every article is so high that it looks like extravagance to use any thing except air and water. I will agree to change my directions about planting so much cotton this fall. Plant the land taken in this Winter (about 8 or 10 acres I suppose) and twenty acres more in cotton—the balance in corn potatoes &c. If we were [housing] near enough to the Rail Road to haul corn I would not plant cotton, but it is too far to haul corn & if a good crop is made it could not be sold at home, and we will have to have some money to get along on and some to pay Taxes with. I would also like to plant some cotton between the corn when it is laid by. I took a walk this evening to find a vaccine scab to send you—saw Dr Fisher and got the promise of a part of one he expected to get off the arm of a child tomorrow morning. He told me that the small pox was in Brenham and the town of Washington. I saved the scab off my arm but do not have much confidence its being good altho it (or something else) gave me light fevers for several days. Dr Fisher said he would not like to depend on it. By the way, Dr F says he never heard of such a thing as hemorrage from the Liver as Dr Foster said was Lee's case.

And now Garrets will has been opened I wish he could have been spared. He was the only one of the family that had any liking for you or me. [A]lthough I think Jim is a tolerable good fellow but Garret was the only one to whose disinterestedness, generosity and sense of justice I would expect to assist you in case of my death. And you know I have always thought more of him than any of the family. It has indeed always been our luck to have our property in such a form as not to do us any good but in this case of the land you get from Garret I think it the best thing that could have happened. I think Garret gave it to you because he thought you would not use it to annoy your Mother for he did not know if Sallie & Babe would marry. I think it is an evidence of his kindness & love he had for his mother.

As it is and considering the situation of the country it is probably as valuable and much the safest property you could have. *Entre nous* after a while I think the place can be exchanged with your Mother for her Quinn p[l]ace & part of the Bowen place and we can sell the Lake Creek place & get out [of] that Susan cursed place, but I would not say anything about this and if you do not to use my name. The land you get from Garret was worth before the war $20 pr acre & will be again when things assume their proper value I consider you have the most valuable share. You will recollect what I wrote you John said about the will being out of date or rather that it had been put "off so long that the time had passed[.]" From what you write what Susan [is] saying John would contest the will & I suppose he must have had an idea of that sort. It will not do him any good. I expect if you had been at your Mothers when Garret made his will you would have been accused of influencing him in his will. It seems none of your brothers or sisters except Garret ever understood or appreciated [your] character. I cannot understand why it is. It is natural that you should feel mortified but I would if in your place counteract such a feeling by the consciousness of the rectitude of my (your) intentions. This is the best you can do but is very unpleasant particularly to one of your sensitive and mor-bid feeling to be cut off from the affections of those whose kindred ties should have made them your friends instead of enemies. I never have know[n] any one to discard without cause the friendship of their brothers or sisters but have been made to repent it some day.

Well we can live without their friendship thank Heaven. But do nothing to justify their bad opinion, and a clear conscience will support you. Perhaps some day they may know you through others and learn to appreciate your character. As regards [to] that fellow Basset I think he will proove himself an unprincipled fool yet. I told you all he said (all that I heard him say for I was writing a deed for land Pa sold to Maddox at the time) and did finish it & went out long before he and John got through.

It is now getting near ten Oclock. I have written this far since supper and will reserve the balance of this sheet for tomorrow night, for I will not be able to get that scab [in] time enough for the mail. Perhaps you would like to know what I have to do in the Office. Well I write orders sometimes, endorse and file papers, and copy orders, and direct and send out papers, &c I have the courier service under my charge exclusively and it is my business to No the dispatches coming from one department to or through another—make a rec-ord of the No & address & send with the papers a record also. Couriers who travel on horseback or on the cars carry these dispatches. We have quite an aristocratic set here in point of birth, though I have seen no disagreeable result from it. Capt Tyler the AA Gen'l is the nephew of President Tyler and Mr Smith the principal clerk is the nephew of the present Gov of Va. They are both poor. Smith has clerked in Washington city, Richmond and was Re-corder in Houston. He is a man of better education and mind than Tyler or

even Col Rainey who commands all the troops on the Island, although he occupies an obscure position and is like my self a private in the army and a lawyer
also though he has not practiced long. We sometimes amuse ourselves by criti-
cisms on our superiors in rank. The other one J C Scott is I am satisfied some
kin to you. His father is from Ga. He puts me in mind of Jim in some
things & Garret in others. I like him very much. He lives near Waverly—has
some property & is a very clear headed young fellow about 23 yrs old. He has
quit clerking & is going into the Navy. Quite a wild goose chase—he starts
for Red River tomorrow. I never expect to see him again—he is sitting near
me now reading a novel. It is after ten Oclock—so good by—I wish I could
give you a good night kiss. I recollect we did not take a parting kiss when last
we parted. I have thought of it often & regreted it. Good bye—Kiss the children for me. Do not think me pathetic because I think I am in danger, for I
do not think I am in any greater than I was a month ago and besides I fully
expect to see you again. But if I should die Lizzie without ever seeing you
again I expect to think of you and Ma as the best and most devoted of wives
and mothers. But Good bye, i[t] seems hard for me to quit to night. Teach
the children to love and remember me—it does any one good to love some
body, and makes them better.

Jany 21st at night. I went around to day but could not find Dr Fisher until
to night after supper. He said the woman who promised him a scab has given
it away & he could only get arm matter on a cloth. He also gave me a part of
a scab from the arm of a boy. Perhaps it would be best to not mix them. I have
labeled them so that you can distinguish them & also the scab from my arm.
He says the best plan to vaccinate is to mix the scab in water to the consistency
of cream & and [sic] then check a place on the arm thus [cross hatched mark
on paper] so as to make it bleed a little and then smear the matter on & keep
the sleeves up until it dries. He did mine that way. The man to whom Joe was
hired paid me five dollars for Joes work after Christmas up to the 1st when he
left. He says he cut 5 cords of wood in the time. He says there was so much
water on the country that his wife thought it best not to start him through
it—that his wife paid him $4.00 to pay his way home—that Joe made a good
many baskets in the time for which he got three dollars a piece. He did not
want to pay me anything for the time as he said his board was worth the five
cords of wood he chopped but I insisted and he paid me five dollars. You speak
of there being more of our negroes impressed. I would not send any more but
let them impress Joe if the[y] will impress. They have no right to impress any
more for the Gov now has one fourth of our able backed negro men between

the ages of 18 and 50. Such is the purport of a late order issued by Gen Magruder, as you will see in the papers. If the Galveston News has stoped let me know & I will have it sent to you.

This evening the news came from Gen M[agruder] that a large force of the enemy was approaching the *coast* of Texas and an order was issued requiring great vigilance on the part of men & officers &c.[11] No one seems to regard it as much. Three thousand more troops will be at Va Point tomorrow to assist in the defense of the place which will make about 5500 in all to defend the place. I do not consider it by any means certain that this place will be the point of attack. They may go to Matagorda or Velasco or Sabine Pass, and it [is] just as probable that either of these places will be attacked as here & probably more so for this is the strongest place on the coast.

yours affectionately
Wm H. Neblett

At Home
Jan 21st/64 Thursday night
W H Neblett—

Dear Will—

I have such awful news to tell you that I don't know how to tell it. A most terrible calamity has befallen mother, and Babe. Last night, her house and all it contained was burned to ashes. Poor mother went over to Mrs Womacks in her night gown, and barefooted, out of a sick bed been spitting blood. Oh Will it is terrible terrible, Saved the Bureau, (which contained her notes papers money &c) two chairs and her two carriages,—which Jim hauled out into the prairie, every thing else was consumed, dident even save a dress nor a pr of shoes. Babe saved a few clothes. Elliott stayed at Colemans last night and came home to day and told the news. I was at Aunt Cinda's this evening and heard it. Coleman was at a party at Lindley's,[12] and when the Cabin negros reached there it was almost burned up. Elliott says the fire originated in the parlor, and when Babe attempted to find the parlor key she could not tell

---

11. The concern over an attack on the coast of Texas may have stemmed from a Union bombardment at Caney Bayou, Texas, on January 8–9. Long, *Civil War Day by Day,* 454.

12. In 1860 John Lindley (age 30) was a farmer married to Eliza A. (35), with personal and real property valued at $7,150. TX Census 1860.

where she had put it. But I am going up in the morning and hunt mother up and see what she is going to do, and if I can't help her. I have no clothes to divide none of mine would fit her, I'll lend Babe some 'till she can get more. I'll find out the true statement and write after I find mother. She was with Mrs Haynie & Mary this morning. If this calamity had happened at any other time it would not have been so bad, now, money can't replace what is burned. Mother has nothing, no wheels, no loom, no cards, none of the things belonging to a loom, no clothes no bed, bed clothing nor nothing, saved a little meat. Kitchen negro cabin, smoke house, chicken house, part of the yard fence, and all save her two carriage houses, and she had the carriages run off some distance. I believe it was set on fire. Some of the negros recently stole 5 bolts of her penitentiary cloth out of her store room, she had Lize whipped about it, and I think the stealing scrape led to the burning down the house.

I fear it will almost kill mother being sick any how, & going over to Mrs Womacks out a warm bed, in her night clothes & bare footed, and the trouble altogether will I fear kill her. My God is it not awful oh Will I wish you was here to do something for her. I feel so much as if it was myself, the burning of our house was nothing to it.[13] I feel almost as bad as if mother was dead. Poor mother she will never get over it. My scotch plaid dress I [got] from Michall six years ago, and my new gingham, three nice colars, all I had, my best underskirt, were at mothers, and Mary's sunday clothes, all burned up. I kept those dresses to wear when up there, and I wanted to visit. My worsted dress I carried up Christmas. I never thought of mothers house being burned she was always so careful about fire—it must have been set on fire. Oh I cant realize it is burned up.

Sat night At Mrs Haynies Jan 23rd 1864 Dear Will, I came up yesterday, came to Mrs Haynie's expecting to find mother sick in bed, but she has left, and gone over to the old home place, so I drove on over there (Aunt Cinda John Nix & Mary Scott came up also) and there in sight of the old chimney's we met mother and Babe in her carriage. Mother was sick ought to have been in bed but she would be up & going. Oh I do fear so much for her & Babe, but I am rejoiced to be able to tell you that she bears it wonderfully better than I had any idea she could, said it was awful, but not so bad as death, that if she

---

13. The reader will remember that the Nebletts' Corsicana home, which was rented out, had burned to the ground in 1862. Lizzie was bitter about the loss and felt the slaves had done nothing to put out the fire. On slaves and arson, see Genovese, *Roll, Jordan, Roll*, 613–15.

could have saved Garrett or bring him back by burning her house & all it contained she would have gladly applied the torch herself. First let me tell you all I know of its probable origin. There had been a little fire in the parlor that day but Babe went to the hearth after dark to examine the fire & there was nothing but some coals, and it was about half after 10 Oclock when the fire broke out or was discovered by mother. She was sick went to bed early, took a nap, & awoke as it was her time to awake, when she heard a popping noise, & a big light, she sprung out of bed called Babe, & said what a big torch that must be, she then went & opened the parlor door, and the room was in a blaze, had a bucket of water thrown on, found it was too late to put it out, & she run out the back hall door & round into her room, & screamed for help to move her Beaureu out, after finding she could not get the top drawer out, couldent break the lock, & so the only plan to save her papers was to get the Bureau out, which she & Lize moved out on the galery & she so weak she could hardly walk, and after she got it on the ground the negros left her, & she made Tillis & Smith help her off with it, after the slab fell off, Babe, poor thing started to the stair step room to save some of her clothes, & mother called to her & told her not to go she would be burned, she turned then opened the wardrobe, got some things in her arms, and run off & never went back, & after mother got her beaureau safe, she could find Babe no where, & thought for several minutes that she was in the flames, had tried to get her clothes & it was great relief to find that Babe was safe, in the grab Babe made, she got my dress & the most of Mary's clothes & that fine shawl of hers she bought from Bob, & a bonnet for mother, & on one of the two chairs that were saved mother happened to have one of her homespun dresses. Lish Womack left the party at Lindley's thinking it was his mothers house burning, & after he came, some ¼ of an hour, Coleman came, but it was too late, the house was all falling in. Jim saved the feather bed & mattress on the trundle bed & a little clothing for it. The negros reached there time enough to save all the meat out the smoke house. [Jim] stayed all night at Mrs Goodrichs[14] with Bettie the night of the burning & went over next day to the place & there saw mother—she told him she had a good carriage sheet which she could cut up & make her some clothes, he said "no I wouldent do that Bettie can help you to some things"

14. Serena Goodrich (age 53 in 1860) was the mother of Bettie Goodrich Scott, Lizzie's sister-in-law. Her husband, B. B. Goodrich (62), was a farmer with personal and real property valued at $40,000. TX Census 1860.

but of course Bettie never said any thing and never will, & she has quantities of things put away to show her *greediness,* she has 13 or 16 pounds of black & white flax, and won't let Jim sell any of it, says she will sew it up before the war ends, this I heard her say with my own ears, & Jim very graciously gave me one skein.

The day after the burning, Jim talked of going to Houston and mother wanted him to get pay from some Quarter M[aster] at Houston for the corn Owney bought for the Gov, & to collect the interest on the money deposited with Sorley[;] Bettie stopped at Coleman's gate in her buggy while Jim went in to get the papers from mother. (Her Bureau was there) and mother was talking to him, consulting what to do, and he did not come quick enough to suit Bettie & she sent a little negro three separate times to him saying "Mas Jim Miss Bettie says come out." She dident want him to talk to mother or be any satisfaction to her. So neither Jim nor Coleman made a single move to find out any thing about the house being burnt, no wonder mother regrets and mourns Garrett's loss, he was the only true son she ever had. Aunt Cinda told me since I returned that Susan says Coleman told her that it was a very strange thing that Sallie got all her things out of the house, and Garretts will was out also, & then the house be burnt. Susan, tho she don't rejoice over the misfortune, says mother had more useless no count plunder about her then any one she ever knew, was so close & stingy that she knew there were preserves burnt in that house that mother brought with her from Miss[issippi], that I must go up, and sail around at the depot, I was so affraid mother would spend a dollar & I know nothing about it, that their was no more use in my going to the depot, than there was in my making a stink." Aunt Cinda says she gets worse & worse about me, farely *foams* at the mouth when she gets to talking, and Aunt Cinda says this hatred has been in her heart all the time but she never let it out so plain before. Tells what M[ary] Scott and she said when they found we were going to move down here—that they both said they knew I was coming down to rule mother, & when be in with her, to get what she had, wanted to be near so as to watch her, see how she spent her money &c. Will, John Scott is one of the most *deceitful* men that God ever made. You know Sallie is full of it, & John is her twin bro. He talked to Uncle Mc at Sabine pass, laid bare the whole family matter, told him the family did not like Susan, particularly me, & I was using my dislike for [her] in predudicing mother against her. Aunt Cinda would not tell all he said, but he was down on me in particular, said I never liked him, was doing all I could against him also. Garrett was at the party at Lindley the night the house was burned, and says they all went and looked at it, then went back to their fun, some sayying oh "she will sell tomatoes enough in two years to get another house & furniture"—& Susan laughed heartily over it. My God Will, what will become of us all. I expect Susan to burn me out, or poison me, & if she don't Bassett will.

Mothers life is no longer any pleasure to her, for she thinks if she ever gets fixed again that Bassett will burn her out again or he will do some other devilment to her. I wrote to you I believe that John Nix told mother that Bassett told him in Va that mother intended disinheriting Sallie, and he just considered it cheating him out of $20,000 and that he intended to devil her as long as he lived. John told mother this soon after he came back, & I think I wrote it to you, but don't mention this, for it would make John's evening for a life time. Babe says that Bassett told her that he was about to get another negro, a free negro in town about to choose him for a master, now you know how he got him. Babe don't dream that mother or I or any body suspect Bassett of putting Ben up to do the burning. She knows we suspect Ben, but no more. Sallie wrote Babe a note (when she sent to her, for clothes to change in) saying her home was open to her and had plenty of house room for mother also, if she would accept it, but Babe must come & live with her. Who knows that Bassett did not think that would be killing two birds with one stone, spiting mother, and forcing Babe to live with Sallie. I awfully fear that Babe will be dissatisfied at that old house, & never want to stay at home. Mother says she cant think of building & fixing up permanently until peace is established, and I think that old house can be made tolerably comfortable by working on it. I am going to lend mother a feather bed and matrass and bed clothes, and any thing I can spare. I don't know what I shall do about clothing the children & negros, it is such a difficult matter to get weaving done, & of course mother can't help me now. Susan rejoices over this, Aunt Cinda says, she has been mad all the time about mother weaving for me, Aunt Cinda told her I paid her in spin thread & she [said] that was all in her eye, she knew better than that. Mr Scott talked about my going up to mothers, and Aunt Cinda must help me make your clothes before you went into the militia, this winter a year ago, and mother must pay Aunt Cinda for helping me. Oh Will you have no idea of what a devil Susan is, I can't write you one tenth of what I know. And her imp, her counterpart, second self, Garrett, continues his mad car[e]er, like to have been shot a few days ago, and has been warned by a certain neighborhood on Sandy Creek that if he ever comes in that neighborhood again, they will take him up & tie him to a black jack & horse whip him. Jim Rogers, as a friend of his Pa's talked to him, & told him not to go in that neighborhood again. He killed some woman's dog she had tied to the corner of her house, shot him dead where he was tied & scared the woman nearly to death, shot an other mans dog in his yard because he barked at him, cursed, yelled, and said he did it to bring on a difficulty with Bob Williamson the owner of the dog. Oh I cant tell you how bad he acts. His Capt[ain], a drunken sot named Scofield, gave him authority to get stray horses, and Garrett, Pat Black, and some other fellow were on Sandy creek getting stray horses & insulting people.

Mother sent me word to day that I must send Polly up tomorrow & the will had been fixed up, probated, & she expected Bassett would be after his negros tomorrow. I feel bad at the idea of giving up Polly I know I'll miss her so much. The Baby loves her, & she is such a good nurse. I'll be almost broke up when she leaves. Aunt Cinda says Coleman told Susan the strait of the will, & said he did not think there would be $300 left after Jim got his $1000 & Garretts debts were paid. She says Mr Scott will blow that up sky high. But we will wait 'till we see it done before we call Mr Scott a Sampson. The idea of my share being more valuable than the others maddens her almost beyond herself. Aunt Cinda says she is wearing herself out, looking wretchedly bad, like she can't live long, is never well, [spends] a good part of her time in bed. Aunt Cinda says she heard Garrett let out severely on his Pa, before Old Dowdy and Uncle Mc. He said his Pa was one of the most deceitful men that God ever made, that he has seen people come in that he knew his Pa hated, and he would meet them friendly as a brother, and as soon as they were gone, he would commence abusing them. Susan who heard all he said, remarked that he would not talk so if his Pa was at home—he said "I swear to God it is so." Bettie Scott is mad at mother, and I reckon Susan will talk her over, about me and mother. Aunt Cinda says Bettie is inclined to think from Susan's tale that John was defrauded in the division of Pa's estate. I was not treated with common politeness the evening I went to Jim's. I was never treated so before. As badly as Mrs Cawthon treated me. I had [an] early dinner, & got to Jims before they *dined* and they both got up & went to dinner & never asked me if I had been to dinner, if I would not have some more nor nothing noticed me no more than if I had been a free negro, or an old squaw. Just as Jim was finishing his dinner he turned round to me, & said have you been to dinner, I said yes, & if I had not been I would not have ate there.

Bettie was so mad at mother when she was there last that she would not tell her good bye when she left. If it was not for mother I would urge you to leave, go thousands of miles from all the kin I have, but there is not one of them that will stand by mother, in any and all emergency's, and in her old age, & after raising a large family she might to have one at least to stay by her & do any thing in their power for her happiness & comfort. I don't want any larger share than the others of her property God knows no such notions influences me, if so, I would hate myself. I am a parent, & I hope & pray to God that I may raise my children to love and respect me, with as little selfishness mixed in it as I feel for my mother. But they can't make me desert her. I believe my society is a comfort & pleasure to her and so long as I think so, I will stay by her, and do all I can for her comfort & happiness, & the consciousness of the purity and honesty of my motives will sustain me. Babe and Sallie have injured me more than any 40 enemies I ever had. Aunt Cinda says Susan will talk & tell things about me, & she will say "for God sake Susan, who told that tale" and she will say in an exultant manner, "why *her own sister said so*." Babe is now in distress, and I have & will do all in my power to help her, all I can spare, all the sewing I can do shall be done for her. She is my sister and I would not harm a hair of her head. I have told no one but Aunt Cinda of the littleness disclosed in Sallie's note, asking pay for the old Calico dress, & I will not. Jim wants to go to Houston to buy negros, but is affraid of being conscripted. He is going to disgrace himself I am affraid, run off to mexico to avoid the service. He is up now at Mr Goodriches, on his way to Houston, [I] expect. I read your letter containing the vaccine matter last Sunday & vacinated the baby myself & Walter, and mine came nearer taking than any of them & mine is not good. I vacinated again yesterday with some matter I got from Dr Kerr before your letter came. I hope one or both will take.

I have a chance to send this to the office, and must close. I was disappointed in not getting a letter from you yesterday, hope I'll get one tomorrow.

You see I have made good use of your slips of paper, hope you wont get tired reading. Myers says he will get through bedding up all the land in 10 days or less time. You had better burn the slips up containing the private matters mentioned in them, some one might get hold of them.

Galveston
Jany 27th/64 At night

Dear Lizzie

Yours of the 21 & 23 was rec'd this evening. Last Sunday night I went over to Johns quarters (for I had not been there for a week before) and Graves told me that Parson Glass told him that evening that your Ma's house was burned down & every thing in it except the Bureau & papers. John came in soon after—had been to the office to see me—told me the same thing, but did not know more. Monday evening he recd a letter from Coleman giving us the particulars. Monday night he came to the office and we consulted about his getting a furlough upon that ground that night—next morning had it approved by his Capt, by Elmore, by Col Cook [commanding] the Post & saw Col Rainey who took it to get Magruder to grant it (he happened to be in town and no one else can grant a furlough) Rainey told John he would try Magruder again as he did not seem to wish to talk about it then. John came around to the office this morning to wait for Rainey to come in—found him & he took the application. I saw John this evening & told him Magruder was to leave town this evening & he had better see R & M immediately. He went found R who told him he had no opportunity of presenting it to M & M was gone. So the chance of his getting a furlough is remote. I advised John to get R's approval and send direct to M at or near Velasco as a private letter and not through Gen Slaughter[15] the regular channel who always rejects and sends back to this office—every day applications go from here—(I have the curiosity to read them before putting them in envelop[e]s) and every day they come back disapproved by Slaughter. I think John will do as I advised & send up in the morning.

The news of the burning of your Ma's house affected me a great deal more than the burning of ours. I feel very sorry for her to have such a calamity to happen in her old age & at such a time. I felt very anxious to hear how she would bear up under it & was very glad to hear from you that she was full of resolution & energy, still, I did all I could to help John get a furlough to come to her assistance & if John had not applied I would have done so. I hope he may yet get it though I know he will attend to his business more than he does hers. But still it is his right first to come & it would be impossible for us both to come. He gave me a letter from Susan to read about the burning of the house which is two pages in length & is about as yours. He recd it this evening. She says his mother wants him to assist her very much. She says she is too sick to go & see her—had sent Mary [Scott] to offer as-

15. James Edwin Slaughter made brigadier general March 8, 1862. In April 1863 he became General Magruder's chief of artillery and was given command of the East Subdistrict of Texas. Wakelyn, *Biographical Dictionary of the Confederacy*, 387.

sistance—I expect John would like to be up there when that will is probated & if he wishes to *contest* it (not protest is as you say) but he has never
mentioned the subject to me since I gave him your note. Is not this singular.
He has had ample opportunity for he has been at the office every day or
night for three days past & we were by ourselves most of the time. I have
delayed writing to you several days longer than usual because I expected a
letter from you about the burning of your Ma's house. John said night before
last to me if I did not expect to have some trouble with Jim & I told him no.
He then asked if I did not see any grounds for it I told him no (but I thought
he was hunting about the will) He said from what Susan wrote him that Jim
had said that Jim *was going to take the cattle back*. I told him Jim could not
take them back for it was a sale, & that I did not pay for [the cattle] because
I thought it was unfair to insist upon his taking confederate money but that
if he wanted part back I could not object for it was an accommodation to me
to get them, altho they were for sale to any body & if he had sold them to
any one else he would have been paid in confederate money. Have you heard
anything of it? Jim must have strange notions of law & justice both. You
have not written any thing about the farm lately. I am at a loss to form an
opinion as to the origin of the burning of your Ma's house but am inclined
to think it was done intentionally. Susan seems to think so too. Coleman
hinted at Bill's bro who belongs to Basset. I cant think of his name now.
The disappearance of the silver ware indicates to my mind that white persons were at th[e] head of it. Was not S[allie] & B[assett] lucky in getting
their things away in time.

There is at our boarding house the wife of Mr Smith one of the clerks. He
has a little boy named Walter who puts me in mind of our Walter. I mentioned to S[mith] about a boy 4 years old & the only other married boarder
said he had one four years old named Walter. Is not this a strange coincidence
as poor Amanda used to say, I see children every day on the streets but never
without thinking of our Bettie poor thing is a child of my imagination & if it
were possible I would like to have her likeness. It is getting late & I must say
good bye. Paper cannot be purchased here & am told not in Houston I use
Gov paper while here. Have a little of my own. I send a sheet for Mary to
write to me on.

                              Yours affectionately
                              Wm H. Neblett

At Home,
Sunday 31st January 1864
W H Neblett

Dear Will

I fear you are feeling uneasy about mother and our children, as I know this letter will not reach you at the expected time, I will have to trust to chances to get it to the office. I sent a letter to the office last sunday telling you of mothers sad misfortune, and her sickness & my intention to stay by her and aid her all I could. I told you in that letter I believe, that I went to Anderson that day, and succeeded in buying her three pr cards, two pr wool, & one pr cotton cards, for $50. Dr Patrick let me have two pr for $17. We tried in vain to get into Cawthon's[16] store, & were told that Cawthon always came home from his farm to dinner so in order to catch him, Mary Haynie & I went over to his house, about 1 Oclock, and Babe went to Sallie's to get her to help her about a dress pattern she saved in one of the Bureau drawers. When we reached Cawthon's house, we were met at the door, & asked into the parlor—treated with politeness but no cordiality. I stated my business & that I had been told that I would find him there at home at dinner time, but he was not there did-ent come to his dinner, and if she would send for him she dident think he would leave his farm. We heard the dishes rattling, saw some men pass out the door going up town, we supposed they had just finished their dinner, but we were not asked one word about dinner, and after asking her if she could not spare mother and Babe a few yds of something she had put away for her own use, as it seemed almost impossible to buy anything in the stores, & they were left without a change of garments, & a few yds would be a help. She said she dident have enough for herself, that Mr Cawthon had been receiving goods all the time & she had failed to put any thing away. That her mother Mrs Womack was burned out last summer and lost every thing she had, but her bacon & meat, & some beds, & they had given her all her mother now had, & all she could spare, had kept no account of what they had given her mother. Well we di[d]ent stay longer than 15 or 20 minutes and left, & ate a cold biscuit Mary had in her pocket. Since visiting Mrs Cawthon we have found out that her mother saved nearly every thing she had in the house except

16. E. W. Cawthon (age 54, spelled Cauthon in 1860 census) was a merchant living with his wife, Aurelia (34), with real and personal property valued at $99,000. TX Census 1860.

her bed steads & some other furniture. She had help, & her kitchen caught first—so that was one lie she told, and before I went there I was well aware that one of the shed rooms of her house was packed full of goods, so there was two lies, the good, zealous christian told. Cawthon sent mother word as soon as he heard of her being burnt out to come & stay at his house as long as she pleased.

We paid Mrs Buffington a visit, also. Babe heard her tell Sallie Bassett last fall that she would let her have something for her baby clothes, that Mrs Buffington had laid in enough goods to last her five or six years if the war lasted that long. So we went to her to see if she could not spare a few yds, so as to get a change of clothes for mother and Babe, but she good christian soul, said she hadent enough for herself so the world goes. This war had developed more selfishness than I ever thought the world contained & I always thought it bad enough. We were forced to go back to Mrs Haynie with only the three pr cards. On Monday evening we went down to Mr Fields on our way to Miligan depot but after reaching Field's we learned we were on a cold track for goods, and that some more goods had been acquired in Navasota, so Teusday morn we started to Navasota. Mary Haynie myself baby & Polly in Mrs Haynie's carriage & horses and Mrs Womack's driver. Mittie Womack & Babe in mothers carriage & Jim driving. We reached Navasota about 11 Oclock, & found more goods than we expected, & much better than any I have seen from mexico. They came from Eagle Pass. Mitchel and Smith sent 50 bales cotton & got goods, & notwithstanding the high prices they are going like hot cakes. We bought good bleached domestic 47 yds at $10 pr yd good calico at $10, muslin $9, other things in proportion, spent for mother and Babe $1,424.50cts or something near that, and I tell you when it was put together it did not look and was not more than $50 would have bought [before] we left Corsicana. Babe was better satisfied after we bought these goods, but was sorry after she left that she did not buy all he had. It goes very hard with Babe loosing her clothes & Piano she thought more of dressing than any thing else you know, and had such a supply of clothes on hand.

While we were there in Navasota, the cars came in, a new sight to me & Babe. We had quite a laughable scene in the street. Jims mules scared at the whistle, and he took them out of the carriage, with dispatch. Bettie jumped, Mary Haynie clapped her hands & started to run to her mothers horses, to get them out of the carriage. I was standing gazing as you know I can, when somebody said "is this Mrs Neblett," & I turned & saw Charley Van Horn who had come up on the cars, and shortly after Pa stepped in the Post office where we were. I bought 10g of Rhubarb (expressly for Bettie while she is teething) & gave $10 for it, two boxes of McLane's pills $3 per box—that was all I spent. That night we went to Pa's stayed all night & started home next morning after breakfast. While in the Post office, Pa got your letter to himself & Ma, and one from Robert the 14th Jan, he was well when he wrote, fared very well during that cold weather about Christmas, they were in a little town on Red River I think & were in houses during the cold weather. They have also heard from Sterling he was in the Indian nation, & on a Raid when the cold caught them the rations gave out, had to eat parched corn, and stood round the fire three days & nights during that excessive cold spell. He has not suffered with the Rheumatism, but has a spell of the sick headache regularly once a week. I did not stay long enough at Pa's to glean much family news, saw no one but Ma & Nelia—but I learned that Violante has bought her a buggy at last, gave $300 & Ma says that William Terrell has given her $1100 since Sterling left. I suppose Sterling gave Terrell his money or got him to sell something for him. I don't know how it is. Ma & Pa are mightily out with Violante. Pa tried to keep her from buying the buggy & says he reckon's he insulted her so, she will never pardon him. Ma looks as well as usual, stirred around more than I have seen her do for a long time, & next morning left her sewing.

I sent around to Thomas & Brockway's while I was in Navasota & got the bundle of clothing you sent and brought it home with me, the Iron is still there. I had to pay one dollar ware house charge on the bundle. I found every thing safe that you mentioned in your letter. The calico will make up very nicely. I have now two new calico dresses, and can make out for some time yet. I lost in the burning of mothers house my new gingham you bought at Cawthon's and the only nice underskirt I had to wear with a muslin dress, lost the thread mother had colored blue for me, & Mary's dress, and 10 yrds I had colored for the boys pants, & some other little things I left there. Babe saved my plaid dress, Mary's Gingham & one of her underskirts & pr of stockings. Babe only made one grab in the wardrobe, & run off & turned her back on the burning house, & screamed as loud as she could, she might have saved many things, if she had not been so scared. Jim saved the bed and matrass on the trundle bed the worst bed mother had in her house. Oh Will you don't know how the burning of mothers house troubles me. I awake in the night, and tis the first thing I think of—her being without a shelter, and so perfectly destitute as she is. She had so much and such valuable things in her house— more than any one I know of any where. Such a total destruction I never heard

of—not even the family bible saved, all the relicks of poor Garrett Walter &
Pa, all burned. The burning of our house did not begin to hurt me like this—
and my grief springs not from a selfish motive—for I always thought it highly
probable that mother would out live me, and God knows I never thought of
any thing she has as being mine in the future. Mother bears it wonderfully and
the knowledge she has of the world naming no sympathy for her, moves her
to bear it better. Mrs Black[17] started to see her last sunday & we met her when
the house was burned, and she said by way of consoling mother "why you are
plenty able to loose [*sic*] it and have more clothes now than I have" & mother
then said "yes I am able to loose [*sic*] it and if I have health & a pr of cards I
can spin & weave me a dress as quick as any woman in the Co, & I'll do it."
She meets with no sympathy from the curious world. What she had she
worked for—it was not given her.

I went to town to day on business for mother, saw Mrs Cawthon and she
says that Dick Trillis has silver spoons that has stood two fires and retain their
form entirely yet—now what seems strange mothers havent been found, nor
the melted particles, & Bro Jim was there very early next morning, having
stayed at Mrs Goodriches, & when mother reached there from Mrs Womacks,
the ashes were so hot couldent put your hand to them, she went where the safe
stood [and] made them take sticks & search, couldent find any thing & since
the ashes grew cold, have searched. Now this makes us think the spoons were
taken before the house was burned, and perhaps many other things, if we only
knew it, & if we could be satisfied that the spoons were taken before, it would
be convincing in my mind that the house was set on fire—and to day Coleman
told mother that he found a place in the rye field, on the west of the house,
where a horse was tied, when he stood & trampled his track indicated that his
feet had been recently trimmed, or his shoes were old so the nails did not show,
and the shoe track was without a heel, tracked them to the fence, where the
plum trees were thickest & there he must have got over, & was going towards
the house. Coleman has the measure of the man's track & horse track.

Nearly every one seems to think it must have been set on fire. Will mother
has concluded to have the old house fixed up, & made so she can live in it, &
Colemans new crib turned into a smoke house, and go to house keeping again
as soon as possible, I can lend her a feather bed & matrass & some bed clothes,

17. Margaret Black (age 33 in 1860) was married to Gavin B. Black, a farmer with personal
property valued at $8,000. TX Census 1860.

and other things she will need & all I can do for her shall be done. She has been a kind good mother to me, helped me in many a strait. I succeeded in getting her a pr of cotton cards & a pr of wool cards from the county supply, also a pr wool cards from Ben Davis. The county cards cost her 19, the ones from Davis 33, the 3 pr costing $50—and Mrs Womack & Mittie divided with mother & Babe a little domestic. Neither of them have a change of undergarments. I have loaned to Babe so has Sallie but mother cant wear our's you know. John Nix has half way promised to stay with mother. Mother is fixing up her wagon to send a load of cotton to Huntsville to get cloth, they give 25 cts for cotton, & pay you half in cotton goods, at $2.80 per yard, & the other half in con[federate] money. I don't know what I shall do for cloth. Mother had my weaving done you know, & it is such a hard matter to get weaving done, soldiers families can't be supplied any more at the Penitentiary. So much cloth is gone to the Co & it is then distributed like the cards. I fear my share will be nothing. I don't know what I will do. John Nix will go for mother to Huntsville.

I got some vaccine matter from Dr Kerr to day says it is fresh & from a healthy subject. There has been one death at Huntsville, the first case, Hogues negro, & a good m[an]y other cases in town. If Jim Brown takes it we will be close to it. I read your letter in town to day writen the 17th 18th and 19th. Its perusal has done me more good than any thing I ever read from your pen. I feel greatful and thankful for all the kindness and affection expressed in your letter. I made a mental note of my birth day, but would not write on the subject because I felt so dissatisfied at the manner in which I have been writing to you recently. I have been so selfish & egotistical, and foolish. I would not blame you, to cease loving me entirely. I hope & pray [to] God Will, that you may come out of this cruel war, and live many years with me & the children and if you do return to us, I feel than I ought to be happier than I have ever been, for I will feel like the dead has been restored to life. Oh may God grant you safe return! Mr Mooring told me to day upon inquiring for mother, that Mr & Mrs Searcy who are the living witnesses to Garrett's will, would be in town next week and process the will, & after it is probated mother will make her oath and fix up the matter. I fear John will try to tear the thing up, for he will be as good as cut out, the land is I believe 320 acres, at $30 silver pieces before the war, it would be $9600, the largest share. Susan I guess wrote John what I wrote you first, as Aunt Cinda told her that I so understood it, and she exclaimed "yes I thought so,["] & Jim said if any body got a share it would be me—that I had got it all, the land was more than all their property put together. She will snort when she hears the worth of it.

I have not yet sent for the rods of iron you sent in Bookman's box, but will send soon. Myers says he got some blacksmith in Navasota to look at the boiler iron you sent, & the smith said that it would make the wings of six Cary plows. I don't think I'll have any turning plows made now. Myers says the plows we have will he thinks finish bedding up the land, and planting; and that the crop will be cultivated with sweeps, & this boiler iron will make sweeps, so I'll have them made & defer the turning plows awhile. Thornton has a b[arrel] of tar he wants to sell, & I will let him take the horses, & get Bro Jim's small wagon, and carry his tar to Pa's & get the iron, he will go next sunday & return monday. We have some sweeps you got from Sandlin, but they are too small somebody said. We will plant 30 acres in cotton Myers says, if we don't have a wet spring there won't be much danger of any body making too much corn, this has been a remarkably dry winter so far. Dr Brown sent me a half hide first, and after christmas he sent about a third of a hide full of holes, and not good leather, so I have made up my mind to tan my own leather. I have two hides, & the one they owe us at the tan yard, have bought one coon skin, cant buy any calf skins mother has promised me one. I got Myers to speak to Ferrel the tanner, & he has promised to lime my hides for me, and fix them ready to put in the tan bark. I'll have my bark gathered, & perhaps I can get it ground. I have tried to buy calf skins, & coon skins. You ask about the school. Mrs Buckley says she will teach again if she can get 25 pupils, & speaks of beginning next month. I hope she will, I am anxious for the children to be going to school. Bob cried when he found out I had been to the depot and saw the cars, he thinks I'll never go now because my curiosity is satisfied. Mary quarreled because Polly saw the cars, the town &c, and she was left at Mrs Haynies to wait on Walter. Poor children I wish I could take them to Pa's and from there to the depot. If the lead you send dont bring me more venison than the caps did it won't be much. Rivers never sent me but that piece of fawn I wrote you about. I'll try him again & will try & get a couple of hides to tan. My little sow, the pig that was saved of the Terrell sow, now has pigs, six in number and I have had brought [them] over here, & will try to keep her where I can have an eye to her welfare. I think she will have as many pigs as we can take care of this spring.

How the [money] went, &
$80.00 War tax.
　38.00 to Uncle Mc for borrowed money
　　4.00 to Mrs Oliver for paper.

150.00 to mother, two notes.

10.00 for salt to mother.

35.00 for wool from mother

60.00 to Jim for Sugar.

63.00 for State & Co Tax (mother paid this last spring & I paid her)

35.00 to Lize for calico dress.

31.00 for wool cards.

11.00 for cotton cards

16.00 for medicine

21.66 interest on the two notes

 10.00 to old Keifer.

564.66

20.00 I gave Meyers to buy paper, half a quire of my paper was burned up. I have more now than I need, since I got the blank book you sent.

You see how the money has gone, and that note to Jeff Haynie not yet paid. I wish you could sell the cotton we have on hand get bagging & rope for it I am so anxious to pay that cotton we owe Susan, & I have to keep sending to her gin for cotton to spin. Do try and sell it & I will do my best to get it ginned[;] if the Yanks come near us we will have to burn it. I was so sorry I could not buy six yds of nice pink calico I saw at the depot, for Mary & the baby, and 5 yds of domestic to make me an underskirt, and the 11 yds would have cost me $110. Billy says "tell Pa I say Howdy a hundred times," he has improved his ways so much, and I feel so glad of it. Bob says howdy too, and you must send him a cake in your next letter. Mary says write her a long letter. Walter is now a sleep, but if awake would say send him some candy. Poor little sister, as we all call her, cant say any thing don't know that she has a Pa. She grows fast, they all thought her like you at Pa's, & pronounced her good looking. She was 8 months old the day I was there—she has no teeth yet. She is a perfect little rowdy. I think if I knew you would be at home in a month, I would be so glad I couldent sleep. Oh I do want to see you so much. I never wanted to see any one so badly. I am feeling more anxious than usual about you since I heard of that fleet lying off the coast at Galveston their landing at the mouth of caney and Powder Horn.[18] May God protect you, is my hours prayers.

18. A Union bombardment did occur at the mouth of Caney Bayou, Texas, January 8–9. Long, *Civil War Day by Day,* 454.

Mother was very kindly treated at Mrs Womacks & is now wearing Lish's shoes. He lent her his shoes when he found her out on the ground in her stocking feet & she wore them over to Mrs Ws. Mother is much better to day than she was yesterday. I'll go [to] town tomorrow and when I am not so bussied I'll answer your questions about the money payed out [for] my leather &c. I hope mother will be well soon. She is eager to fix up and go to housekeeping again. Oh she bears her loss with so much fortitude considering her being sick & every thing. I left Bettie to day [with] Mary all day & she was a very good baby. Oh I do want you to see her and all the children so much. She has no teeth yet. I saw Frank at Nelia Kerr's to day says they are all well at his house, Hatties and at Pas. Ma has been up town to church lately & it dident make her sick. They are all asleep and I must stop. I'll write again in a few days. Coleman leaves for the wars in a few weeks. My eyes hurt me so I can hardly see must stop. Good bye and may God watch over, protect & bless you is my hourly & nightly prayer.

> Yours affectionately
> Lizzie S. Neblett

Galveston
Feb 2nd 1864

Dear Lizzie

I expected a letter from you to day and did not get it. John Scott came in to day and told me that if he did not get a furlough on account of the burning of his mothers house that the Capt would give him and one other person from his Co a detail for ten days to get meat for the different members of the Co. I understand all the Cos are to detail two men for that purpose. So it seems he is in luck. I have been looking for a chance to get a detail but without success. I still have a hope of doing so but cannot see my way, though I will continue trying until I succeed. If I had known that John had a chance of getting the detail that he will get I should have made an effort while Magruder was here to come home on account of your Ma's misfortune. But I did not know it until today & Magruder left yesterday, & if John fails on his written application it would be useless for me to try. I recd the socks (two prs) to day you sent by Clements. Oliver brought them from the Spit & gave them to John Scott who gave them to me. They are knit of fine wool I noticed. You spoke of knitting me some cotton socks—I do not think I shall need them next summer & if I need them at [all] it will be late in the season & so you had better turn your attention to the more pressing wants of yourself and children. John tells me that he will remain at home five or six days & have some one to go around the neighborhood to get the meat. I wish you would send by him about 50 lbs of pork (this winters pork and bacon). I also wish you to send my hat—the one I have is almost unfit to wear. I expect it would be best for him to wear it over his hat. I would like to exchange it for a darker & lower one if it is not too much soiled before it gets here. He has promised to bring it if he can. This would be a good opportunity to send you & the children something but my money is so scarce that I will be nearly if not quite out by the time I get pay again, but I can get along & do not intend this as a hint for you to send me any. I shall go back to my company as soon [as] the winter breaks & would do so before if I did not hope to get a detail of some kind before I leave. It does seem a long time since I saw you, and if I knew that I would be unable to see you in as long time ahead as it has been I would feel miserable but I cannot give up the hope even under the most gloomy prospect. There does not seem to exist that universal apprehension of an attack here or near Matagorda that there was a month since. The Yankees are really not strong enough to risk a fight and are awaiting reinforcements as they are weak and are merely threatening Texas to draw our forces from other points which they wish to capture.

I was somewhat amused at your allusion to the grass widow & what you wrote that Oliver said. He was in town today but did not come around. I think in fact know the place I am boarding at now will not turn out as the other did. They are very respectable and intelligent people. However there is no one but the lady & her daughter about ten years of age. Her husband is in the army near Velasco & her other daughter 18 or 20 yrs old [is] at Brenham on a visit—quite a dashing girl—good looking and intelligent I understand.

About a week ago Scott (the clerk) and I went around to see the grass widow late one evening. I thought when I left there that she was mad with me but was not certain. So when I went around I noticed and when we left she invited Scott to come again but not to me. I called his attention to it I do not know what she fell out with me about. There are about five thousand soldiers here and at Va Point 5 miles off.

Feb 3 I did not think last night that John would get off to day but he is on the cars & will be off in a few minutes. But I have nothing of importance to say so good bye.

Yours affectionately
Wm H N

At Home
Saturday evening Feby 6th 1864
W H Neblett

Dear Will,

John Scott arrived home Thursday night 11 Oclock, and on Friday I went over to Aunt Cinda's, & in the evening John sent your letter by him, and that white blanket I suppose that you let him have, and a blue blouse, and some turned envelopes—over to Aunt Cinda's to me. I am pretty certain that the blanket is the one Ma sent you, tis white with black stripe at the ends. I brought it home with me. Uncle Mc went over to see John that morning, and Mittie Womack said that he & Susan had gone off into the woods to talk I suppose, he set there an hour & a half & left without seeing him. Oh what tales, what terrible tales she will relate. Aunt Cinda says she is almost a skeleton has fretted herself nearly to death. They say that John's portion in Garretts will hurts her worse than any thing they ever saw. She told Aunt Cinda this week a grand secret—she said, "I tell you there is juggling going on about that will, they are fixing it up not to let Bassett have those negros." Aunt Cinda says, "how what do you mean?" ["]Why Lizzie wrote to Neblett (& he cant keep anything lets his guts to Mr Scott) that Jim was going to administer on Garrett's estate & that the will was nothing." Just one of her lies to find out what Aunt Cinda knew & if there was any chance to do anything. I tried to find out from Uncle Mc all that John told to him at the Pass. He says John told him that I was opposed to mother's helping him get a sub that I wanted mother to help you get one—that I disliked him & Susan & was doing all I could against them both—that because I knew that mother had said that the child who treated her best, she would leave the most to at her death, I was doing my best to get on her good side, &c &c[.]" My God Will, did you ever know such folks, because I act towards mother as a child should, show her the respect & affection that all children owe their parents, they say I am working for what she has. Oh Will how it pains and mortifies me, to be so regarded by my relatives.

While I was at Aunt Cinda's Jim stopped in awhile on his return from a sale in Montgomery Co. He told me that Bassett said publicly in town before Bing Black, Lindly and several others that he was glad mothers house was burned down, that it would have done for the heirs to squabble over. You know he did not expect a share in that, as Mother had said she intended disinheriting Sallie. I felt certain that he was glad of it, but thought he would not have the boldness to express it publickly. But he is very revengful by nature, and enjoyed the idea of being revenged so much, that the passion gets the upperhand of his policy & desire to be popular. I expect to suffer at his hands for I have said & done more to excite his desire to be revenged than even poor dear Garrett did, and how dearly he paid for it, & now mother['s] troubles have begun anew. Aunt Cinda and Uncle Mc both heard Jim say he believed he would take the cattle back, if it was agreeable all around, and asked Uncle Mc if the beef we had killed would not pay us for the trouble we have had with the cattle. Jim has never said anything to me about the matter. Let me tell you how Jim treated mother about that business with Sorley & the pay for the Gov corn Oney bought. I wrote you about mother asking him to do this for her when he thought of going the day after mothers house was burned, well he did not go then, but went last week to Houston & mother sent him word to come & see her before he went, & do that business for her—he never went near her, & hasent been to see her since he got his wagon off to Huntsville for cloth. You know he tried to buy Coleman's bacon & Lard to send to Huntsville, & was led near mother, in order to get that & to try and buy cotton from her to send for cloth. Oh Will, God forbid that my children should ever treat me so. Aunt Cinda says Susan declared before John came home that he should never do any thing for mother again. I don't know how mother can bear the treatment her children give her with the calmness & charity she does. Her heart excuses them, in every possible way and I do not call her attention to their want of interest in her affairs, & excuse the matter to her by saying that their wives are unwilling for them to do any thing for any body but them. Bettie & Jim spent an evening this week with Susan, so Aunt C[inda] said, she has not yet returned my visit, and after she has I will not be in a hurry to go again. John Nix says Babe is so much opposed to mothers moving into those old houses that she is almost if not quite in the notion of putting up a cheap temporary building where the old house stood. I am satisfied it would be the best plan for several reasons, they could not have the benefit of the fruit at the old place, and mother['s] garden spot is paled in you know, & at the old place she would only have a fence round the garden spot, all her fowls would have to be moved to attend to their setting & hatching. In fact I don't see how she can get away from that place. But it would require some one to superintend, & direct Turn & Mage, to build her a house, and who can & will do it. John Nix seems to be willing to do all he can, & has done much more for her in her present distress than Jim has.

Oh how I wish I could see you to talk all day & night to you, this writing is such an unsatisfactory method of communicating thoughts & knowledge. I have to day made an effort to get you home, it remains to be tried, before I can tell whether or not it will succeed. I have writen a letter to Gen Magruder asking for a furlough in mothers name, to come home and asist her, and have endorsed it with a note to Mr Oliver, asking him to forward it to Magruder if he thinks it will do any good, I wrote him to place the matter before you. He will show you the letter & note to him,—and if you do get to come home on that ground I want you to do all & every thing you can for mother. She needs help about her papers, should have a settlement with Coleman before he leaves, which will be the 1st of March, and she wants her papers fixed up as Babes guardian, no returns were made last year and various other matters need attention, beside the fixing up to live again. If you do get to come I know they will be down on me worse than ever. I don't want any one to find out, save those to whom it is necessary to communicate the fact that I wish to Magruder. Mother gave me no authority to use her name, but I know she wants help, but like me, she deemed it impossible for you or John to get furloughs on any grounds home, she never mentioned wanting John nor you to come home. I don't build but a slender hope upon the trial for a furlough to assist mother. God knows I want you to help mother, but I fear there is much selfishness in wanting you to come so bad. I do long to see you so much, it seems like it has been years since I saw you. Don't give up trying to come, for if you don't try you certainly never will come.

When the children heard that their Uncle John had come they all wore long faces, and said "I wish Pa could come." "I don't believe Pa's time to come home ever will come[.]" They are nearly done bedding up the land, will begin to plant the last of this month. Everybody nearly had bedded out potatoes but me. Myers ordered that done to day, but I was too busy to day to leave the house, & I knew if some body was not there to watch Sam & perhaps all of them [they] would take the seed & bed for themselves, so I will get Myers to see to it Monday. Thornton is fixing to take his Tar to Pa's get the iron, and take the sweeps & bull tongue to the shop to sharpen. Bob was ready to go with him this morning, but Ranger could not be found, & I learned for the first time that he went off with some horses three days ago. So he looked until late & then went to Jims, & borrowed his wagon & a mule, & will go tomorrow—but I don't think I'll let Bob go, his face is bruised up so badly, & swollen. Billy threw a stick & cut a gash in his cheek, & grained his whole cheek, Billy was mad, & allways aims at the face when he is mad. Bob & Mary now have scars on their faces made by Billy's finger nails that they will carry to their graves. I whipped him good about hurting Bob—the first time he has been whipped in a good while. The Baby nor Walter, nor the little negros vacination did not take, my own is still sore. I have my new nurse from Mrs Oliver—she does badly yet, & never will do as well as Polly did. I fear my trouble with this baby will never end. Send a special message for each one of the children it delights them so to get a message, and a bean like the one you sent in your shoe, or a shell with their names on it would please them so much as if it cost $20. The baby has been playing with the bean but tis now lost. I fear for good.

Galveston
Feb 8th 1864

Dear Lizzie

Yours of the 31st of Jany was recd a few days ago. It is a very long and interesting letter, though there are many things you recite of a dark & humiliating character. I do feel for your Mother, but Lizzie do not encourage her to suspect future injuries. It would kill her or any one of her age to live under the fear of danger from the source you and she suspects. It will do no good to do so except to be somewhat on the alert. If things ever develop themselves it would be right and the duty of any one to move in the matter. I think Coleman & Jim have neglected their duty in not making some effort to investigate the affair. A negroe's evidence is good against a negro in the courts. I think by being cautious in procuring the evidence the guilt of the negro Ben may yet be brought to light through their evidence. It will not be too late for a year to put the guilty party on his trial.

I think you permit yourself to be annoyed too much at the treatment you have received from your kins folks. It is enough to mortify any one and I sympathise with you but you must learn to regard them as really of little kin to you and make up your mind to treat them with indifference, if not contempt. It may be hard to do this at first but you can learn to do so. You are singular in some respects. After Babe has treated you as badly as she has you permit yourself to be enlisted & troubled at her distress for loosing [*sic*] her fine class. [None would] have given you any of them if you were naked and you speak of helping her sew, when you know she will never thank you for it, but wound your feelings in some way for the deed. Now I do not believe in the doctrine of doing good for evil or of evil for evil for such a cause would in the former event cause the good people [to] work for the bad. They should be let alone and by that means be made to see & suffer the consequences of their own acts.

How much sewing did she ever do for you, when you were pushed to death with work. I believe in the doctrine "not to cast pearls before swine."[19] Select good people for acts of kindness & social intercourse & [do] not try to make selfish people good friends by good acts. Your mother should have all your sympathy & assistance but Babe none. Now it is the nature of selfish people to suspect all acts of kindness to be prompted by selfish or interested motives, & I have no doubt you will be suspected by your bro & sisters on any acts of kindness to your Mother. It is hard to have ones good intentions suspected of bad motives, but nevertheless it cannot be helped & must be borne. But I must stop I have no doubt you think I am on quite a sermonizing vein to night.

On the 4th I wrote to you by John Scott, and requested you to send me by him 50 lbs of bacon. If he does not appear *very* willing to bring it do not send it. I can do without it and hope to be able to come after it. I also sent by him two packs of grape cutting twelve or fifteen in each—one of El Paso grape & the other of white Marsaillaise (French) grape, said to be very rare & fine. I wish you could get one or two of each kind grafted. Could you not make some of the negroes do it? I told John he might have a part of them. I think it best to plant them in the new ground field near the potato patch. I do not suppose your Mother would take any interest in such things right now. I also sent by John the blanket Ma sent me. The one I offered him I thought you might need it in dividing things with your Ma, or to give her in place of the one she let me have. There were a few envelop[e]s I *suppose* about 20, and a blue shirt which you might use for Walter rolled up in the blanket.

I send some Havana tobacco seed (fine for smoking) I would like to raise a little of it. The negroes might have the balance of the young plants. They could make a great deal of money by it, for cigars made of it are worth 50 cts apiece here.

I enclose you an old countersign to show you how such things are done up. I do not recollect who wrote it that day.

It seems to me you might get Brown to gin enough cotton to pay John and what you would spin this year. It would not have to be bailed. What was ever done with the cotton raised the first year. What has Coleman done with the bagging & rope. I do not think to sacrifice, & if it could be done I think there is more danger of the money becoming perfectly worthless than of the Yankees burning us getting it. There seems to prevail but little apprehension here of

19. Matt. 7:6.

the Yankees doing much in Texas this year. The Militia will all start home on the 15, but will reorganize for six months longer. Whether they will remain at home until an emergency or not I do not yet know. There was a false alarm to day of the Yankees landing on the West end of the Island, but it turned out to be only four Yankees & they soon went to their boat. I recd a letter from Nelia on the same day of yours of the 31st. She asks when she shall send the shirts she will soon finish. I wrote to her that I would tell you to tell John to call at Thomas & Brockway & get them, but it is getting so late I hardly know whether to have them brought down or not. Tell Sarah if she has any more tobacco to save me some. I am nearly out. I had about ⅓ of what she sent stolen. I like that dry kind better than that which was pressed—it is not so strong. In fact I have got so now that I had rather use it than the rotten tobacco to be had in the stores at $7 & 8 a plug. I expect Bettie S[cott] & Susan will get very thick for a while—the bond being a jealousy & envy of you, in regard to Garrets will & your Mother but won't they have a time when they do split in talking about each other. Keep as clear of them as possible consistent with common civility.

I was disappointed in not getting a letter from you to day.

Yours affectionately
Wm H Neblett

At Home
Friday evening Feby 12th 1864
W H Neblett

Dear Will,

I write a few days in advance of my usual time because I will have a chance of sending this up to the office tomorrow. You have no doubt read my [letter] to Oliver enclosing one to Magruder making an effort to get you a furlough. Altho I don't allow myself to hope much from that yet, I can't banish all hope, and find myself continually whispering to myself what I will do & say "when Will comes home," and to the children I say ["]when your Pa comes home." I have thought many times that I should never see you again, now, I cant help indulging in a little hope, guard against it as I will. I know if you dont come it will not be your fault, & that you will be the sufferer also, which knowledge (tho to do so betrays a selfish feeling) gives me some consolation.

Tis now night, and while writing the above day lines I was interrupted three times, once to attend to the baby, once by the tanner Ferrell[20] coming in, of whose business more anon, and last by the children en masse, calling on me to redeem a promise made a month ago to make them sweet cakes out of some of the flour that Ma sent them, so I put by the writing and have just finished baking the cakes and eating my supper. It has been so long since I have baked any cakes for them that I could not help smiling at their chat about it. Bob & Billy said it seemed like we were going to move, & I was making cake to eat on the road. Mary felt like she was going to hear good news which remark made Bob think that Mr Ferrell's question if you were not coming home soon? an ominous one—he wondered why Mr Ferrell asked such a question. Bob is the only one into the secret of my writing to Gen Magruder. Walter said nothing but made the cakes disappear rapidly, and little Sister was munching away on hers, like a little squirrel. They all had quite a jubilee over her at dinner, it was just discovered that she had a tooth. Tis an under tooth, & I think all of the others cut their upper teeth first. She is a perfect little rowdy, and is a very good child during the day, but when night comes on, no one can do any thing with her but me. This little negro is not half as good a nurse as Polly. I never hated to give up a negro so much in my life as I did to see Polly go. All these little trials I have with this baby puts me always in a bad humor with myself for the first thought that comes up is, if I had not been the biggest fool in the world that child would never have been here to molest me as she does, and from that, thought runs riot, & I run crazy it may be for a whole day but perhaps only a few hours. Poor little innocent, it is not her fault, but if she lives to be my age, how often will her aching heart prompt her lips to say "would that I had died in infancy."

Mr Ferrell called by this evening to see if I would let him have some red oak timber to get bark for tanning. I would give him no answer 'till I hear from you. He is to get some from Dr Foster, who lets him take the bark off the rail trees, for cutting the timber ready to split the rails—he proposes to do the same here if we want the rails. We are too busy now to think of doing any thing about the pasture, and will be for some time to come unless it rains, so they can't plow. Myers says Joe told him that that little lake you spoke of fencing in, will be dry in ten days if it don't rain before that time. Ferrell says he is willing to do any thing almost to get bark, when it can be peeled. He will

---

20. Possibly W. H. Ferrell (age 29), who was a laborer living with Ann Randle (37) and her children. He had personal property valued at $40. TX Census 1860.

let me know when he is ready to lime my hides, & I am to let him know about the bark, when I hear from you. Myers will commence planting the first of next week—two weeks earlier than we planted last year. This negro Joe has not sold his mule yet, it runs at the back of our field and I expect will eat a big hole in the Gov corn, which the squirrels will have to answer for—says he can't sell him. I told him I would have him killed if he did not sell him out of the neighborhood and now I will not give him much longer to get rid of him. He went over to Bro Jims (so Jim told me) one night over a week ago to borrow a mule from him to ride to Red Top. I don't think Jim would let him have one. Aunt Cinda & Uncle Mc came over last sunday, & after they came mother & Babe drove up. Mother & Babe staid all night, and all hands told me that I ought to go to see John, that it might be the last time I could see him, &c &c. I never like to act stubborn, & am always willing to do my duty, so far as I recognize it. [I went] over to John's next day with mother Babe & Aunt Cinda. Susan was as friendly as usual, saw no difference in John. I did not ask him many questions about you—he laughed heartily at what you said to him, just as he was leaving—that if you had known he had the chance of the detail you would have tried to get a furlough upon the ground of mothers misfortune, that you said, "them fellows over there think that I am in such a hell of a good place, that they would not give me a detail nor furlough upon any condition." John made no offer to assist or advise mother in any way even, said to Uncle Mc in mothers presence that he wanted John Nix to ride around for him, and get up the meat when he must have known that John Nix was the only one she had to send around & do things for her.

Sat morn 13th My eyes pained me, so I stopped here last night, I think my eyes are like Pa's were for a great number of years before he died. I fear so at least. I asked John about taking your hat say[s] he cant take it, unless I can fix it up & put it in with the meat, it would be a nice hat when it reached you woul[d] it not? says he will take the meat you want. Nelia has sent your under-shirts home, but it is now so late in the winter that I hardly know whether to send them to you or not, for if I were in your place I would not put them on this winter. Susan was very cold to mother. Johns boys were here yesterday & said their Pa was going round after the meat himself—he will start back on the 17th he says. It is very evident that he don't feel in the humor of assisting mother any. Susan has made her brags to Aunt Cinda several times since John went into service that mother would open her eyes if she were to show her some documents that were [a]bout her house. Aunt did not ask what it was, but I think 'tis the account he has kept against mother for the business he has

done for her, and at her death it may cover half of her estate. I have no confidence in John. I found a little more from mother about Jims anger. He & Bettie are both mad—when Jim was there just before the house was burned he &
mother had a little settlement & he brought up that old interest quarrel, wanting her to pay interest on the money she had a few weeks after the negros she
bought from Jim came on her place, and she wanted him to pay interest on a
thousand dollar note she held against him. I cant tell it all with the pen, but
they both Jim & Bet were mad. Jim then said, "When did you ever charge
Elizabeth for a pound of butter?" and laughed heartily at her for saying I owed
her corn & would pay it back, "do you suppose she will ever pay that back,"
he said no, and Coleman says, ["]she has got corn from here every year since
they moved down from Corsicana" and Susan says Bettie said to her, "she did
not know what she would do when I took Caroline (her nurse) that she knew
I would as soon as I sent Polly home.["] They all seem to think that I can do
any thing with mother, & that my disposition will prompt me to ride rough
shod over them. I have never done it yet. Jim is mad at me because he thinks
mother likes me best & does more for me. I have been to mothers a great deal
it is true & mother has been kind to me, but they forget that there was years
of my life that I did not have the privilege of going to see mother when I felt
like it. They cast me off because they think mother is partial to me, & for the
same reason, they desert her. Now if I am to sever her children from her—I
will stick closer to her, they are all mad at her, & will not do one thing for her.
I will bend myself in her service—they are not mad because they think I have
the greatest share of her love, but simply because they fear I'll get the largest
share of her *property*—is it not awful.

Jim nor Bettie have not been over to see me yet, & they may take their time
for it, & I'll do the same in returning the visit. Jim bought furniture for himself
in Houston, cup & saucers, dishes &c the very things he must have known
that mother wanted. And when he left for Houston, he did not even know
whether mother & Babe had a change of clothes, & never went to offer to buy
for them in Houston if they wanted him to. Mother cries over his treatment.
She sent him word by John Nix to be certain to go & see her before he went
to H—as she wanted him to attend to some business in H for her. Will, it
sometimes comes into my mind that you may think I exaggerate things about
my family, it seems so strange & difficult to believe some things I write, the
conduct of mothers children to her seems so unnatural, and because I show
her the respect & affection that nature planted in my bosom, they cry out
against me, & say "she wants what mother has." If you are fortunate enough

to get home on the ground of aiding mother, & my letter to M[agruder] is at all instrumental in getting you off, & they find it out, they will all be so mad at me that I fear they will be ready to mob both of us. Susan crys down my smartness, Jim always hooted at it, which makes me know that he recognizes it, fact is they know I am as smart by nature as any of them & better educated—but I'll let it pass, & do my duty, just as conscience dictates, and leave the rest with God. I have had a great deal to fret, annoy, & distress me since you left, but unlike Susan I batten on, I am fleshier than I ever was before in my life[. I] weighed at the depot 108—105 is the highest I ever weighed before, Nelia was amazed to see me looking so fleshy. She is so fat she is a sight. Ma had the headache last sunday, a bad spell. I am going to send up to mothers tomorrow to get that ox of ours that is up there, cant do without him, or some other one. Old Parmer got crippled last Sunday some how (it was Toms day to attend to them)—I think he hurt him, and old Lamb is almost on the lift, has been sick, hollow horn or something else. I think Myers ought to have broken some young oxen, but he did not want to hinder time with them if it could be avoided, but the heaviest of the plowing is now over. Mrs Buckley proposes in her article of agreement to commence her school next monday. I fear she has failed she wanted 20 or 25 pupils. Susan was going to send out when she saw the paper with Mrs Wade [with] 2 schollars subscribed[;] she drew back, wont send to a school where the Hall children go. And Mary Scott says she wont go, because Ann Hall is going to go. Garrett, surnamed the Devil, has gone at last, Scoffield's Co have to report some where the 15th of this month. I rec'd a letter this morning from Dr W Sanders inquiring about some notes, & he talks like he wants to pay them if Confederate money will be taken. I don't know any thing about the notes, but have this plan to make if the notes are not for too large a sum, & they are yours, take confederate money, for tho' it is worth nothing, I have never had too much of it yet. This cotton debt I owe Susan troubles me, and I really havent enough money to spare to pay the debt, and I cant get any cotton ginned. I enclose Sanders letter to you, & you can answer it.

If our negros do not do better than they have done since we owned them, we will be worse off next year than this, they have never made a living since we had them. If their meat, clothes & any doctors bills had to be paid out of what they made they would not be able to do it, & have never done it since we had them, & I am awful tired of them. Ten thousand times I have wished you had listened to me & sold them all but what we wanted to wait on us, years ago. I don't say much about them, but they are a great trouble to me—a perfect vexation. I am going to buy another wheel, & make Kate spin—Uncle Mc is going to make a Loom, and Aunt Cinda will help me, & I will do her weaving, I will have to do this or let the black devils go naked. Frank Briggance made me a visit a few days ago, and made me pay 19 dollars tax on live stock, I gave in 36 head of stock cattle, three horses, (not used in the farm) one mare & colt. I believe that was all. He took my corn in fodder tithe, & says I am to deliver it in 60 days, or pay a forfeit, but don't suppose they will compell me to haul it until a depot is established. I expect Joes mule will eat about half of it up by that time, he keeps the mule in Bro Jim's field, near the brickyard. I don't think I can stand his mule much longer. I asked Myers to shoot the mule, but he don't want to do it & I don't know how I'll get it done unless I get Myers to load the gun and I will make Thornton do the shooting—he told me he wanted to keep the mule to go to see his wife at Corsicana Christmas. I saw Rivers, & divided powder & caps with him, but he has sent in nothing yet, and Myers says he will start into service tomorrow. Dr Brown would not give him a discharge on account of his leg. I hear Rivers went to see him, & give him a straight talk, says he'll get a Dr and a gentleman to examine him in Houston, & thinks he will be discharged. Brown discharges those he wants to hunt with Rivers says. Finch went back to his command, & was discharged & is not at Dr B-s, so is A Brown.

I will start Mary & Bob to school next monday as the school commences then. I will make them walk only when the weather is bad. I dont think she will have a full school so many have fallen out with her. I saw Old Mr Mangum on his way to Huntsville with a load of Gov leather, and he says if I can't get Ferrell to curry our leather, that he will do it for nothing if I will send it to him at Ashfords—says a wagon could go down one day & he could have the leather ready time enough for him to come back next day. Don't you think some of the thick leather will have to be curried down, and used for upper leather. I think you said the most of the hides would make sole leather. Mangum said he could make the thickest part of the hide do for upper leather. Don't we owe John 18 pounds of salt I want to pay that as soon as we get our salt. Susan sent & got 2 barrels of sugar from that woman, & she wrote her she did not want the corn could get it nearer home, but wants 25 ct in specie or $1.00 in paper. I hear that sugar can be bought at the Depot for 75 cts, don't know how true it is. Susan has used some out of one of the barrels which she will pay the woman her price for & is not a first rate article of sugar. I don't see how they get through with so much sugar at John's, you know when they get sugar last fall it is all out now & they don't use coffee. I have one big lump left of my sugar, & when that is gone I guess I'll do without. I won't go in debt for my luxuries, if I do think the Yankees will strip me of every thing soon. I bought two calf skins [from] a negro to day, seem to be very good hides gave him $5 a piece. Jim says he did not buy negros in Houston says he would not give 75 cts for a negro now, bought furniture, bedstead chairs, &c gave at the rate of $20 for 1 dollar in silver. I have divided caps & powder with Rivers, he had plenty of lead. He says the reason he never sent me any more meat was because the caps I gave him got wet, & he could not shoot any more, he promised me two skins also. They gave him $8 for the skins at the Tan yard. John had his likeness taken at Galveston & sent it home. Aunt Cinda says 'tis very good. Why don't you have yours taken for me & the children? Do have it taken. I fear we are going to have a job to find Ranger again. I told Bill to night if he did not find him tomorrow I would have him whipped for not telling me when he failed to come up. I have a heap of trouble with the negros yet, but not as much as I did before Myers came here.

Joe has not sold that old mule yet. I will not wait much longer before I will have him knocked in the head. Mrs Buckley wants to open her school the 15 of this month. I subscribed 2 schollars. I have planted no garden seed yet. I wish you were at home to plant my garden, or help me do it. I am going to fix & get a loom and weave my own cloth. Aunt Cinda is going to show me how & help me. I am forced to do this, & must get an other wheel & make Kate spin. Do sell that cotton, my money will be out before the tax payment comes I fear. I spend as little as possible.

affectionately yours
Lizzie S Neblett[21]

21. Will Neblett returned home for a few days at the end of February.

6

A Bare Living & a Grave

February 27, 1864–April 27, 1864

At Home
Sat evening Feby 27th 1864
W H Neblett

Dear Will,

Tomorrow is my day for writing, but I fear I will have company tomorrow & cant write, so I write this evening. I have just returned from a fish fry at the Scott Lake, they call it a fish fry but there was no fish caught to be fried. Finch was the originator of the party. Mrs Buckley sent me an invitation by Mary. I found a pretty good crowd for war times. I made the acquaintance of George Alston, he seemed very chatty & lively, says he will start on monday for the wars, is ashamed to stay out any longer. He has a substitute you know. When Joe reached Pa's the day you left, it was too late to reach mothers for dinner so we had an early dinner and I got to mothers some time before night & told Joe to come on home, & I would drive myself the next day—but he stayed all night I think & did not reach home until after sun up some time. That is the way the rascal minds me. I am going to get Jack Oliver to kill his old mule, he seems so attached to Jim's field I think Joe must lead him in there. The next day I came home & mother came down to Aunt Cinda's to get her to help her make harness for weaving and, she took the baby the most of the way in her carriage, and she cried almost all the way, & the tears dropped off her cheeks, and she has cried almost incessantly ever since, is better when I am away than when I am at home. I have sent Mrs Olivers little negro home, & have one of mothers, not so large nor so old, but is better nurse, I can keep her two or three years. Oh this baby is such a sore trial to me, she won't let me work, and my work is so much needed. If I dident have her to trouble me I could soon make up what little cloth I have. I would not let my work trouble me when you were at home, but now it does, I have had the blues awfully since you left, and expect to have them worse.

The baby's cold is not much better yet, and she has a bad cough & cry's when she coughs like it hurt her. Walter has a bad cold also has had two fevers at night, & rests badly every night—Bob stayed up all day the day you left, but was sick at the stomach & threw up coming to mothers, & did not get out of bed next day till nearly dinner time but has been going to school since, and I think now will get well without medicine. When I stopped at mothers I mentioned to Babe Nelia's visit to Pa, & said that there was quite a number of young ladys near Pa's now, & spoke of Dr Foster teaching, & then said that Nelia was an old sweet heart of Fosters [who] came to Texas to see her. And Babe said yes she had heard all about it, that Bettie Scott told her a great deal about how folks were talking about Nelia Kerr. That Mary Demoret[1] told Sallie Bassett that Mrs Kerr told her, that she loved her Bro better than she did Dr Kerr, and cried when she was talking to her—and Bettie of course, always knew she dident love Dr K, said she heard Mary Demoret plaguing Nelia about Foster, and that Nelia would laugh & blush, & seemed to be pleased to be plagued about Foster—tho' she heard her say that she intended to make Mary Demoret mad if she did not quit it, but Bettie said after that Mary come to town spent almost all her time at Nelias & that Nelia exerted herself to entertain her. I fear Nelia will be talked about a great deal, she is acting *very imprudently.* I did not tell Babe anything that I knew, & tried to soothe the matter over as much as possible. Susan sent for Aunt Cinda one day this week, & drove all the children out of the house, & then gave her *"bankings"* and Aunt C gave her as good as she sent, you never heard the like, she as good as told Aunt she wanted her to leave the place she is living on, & Aunt says if they had not planted a crop, & it is too late to go any where else & make a crop, she would have her place. Susan is run mad. I cant write all she said & done. The negros will nearly finish planting this evening. Myers examined our potatoe seed again yesterday says he found none rotten. Uncle Mc says almost all I let him have, have rotted. Rivers brought me a deer a few days since, I

1. In 1860 Mary Demoret (spelled Demerrit in the census) was 13 years old and living with M. H. Demerrit (age 40), a farmer with personal and real property valued at $37,000. TX Census 1860.

have his hide also. I feel anxious to hear from you & if your cold is well. I have been feeling badly & have now two fever blisters on my mouth. I must stop, for the piteous wailing of this cross sick baby distresses me so I can't write in any peace. I can hardly realize that you have been home, it seems like a dream. Write punctually & pray for the war to end. Mothers box sent by express has come to hand at last. Write me what Smith said about your staying over our time, how he liked the wine &C. Good bye.

affectionately
Lizze S N

Teusday night March 1st My letter was writen Sat, and I thought then that I would have a chance of sending it to the office before now, but we have had such a rainy spell of weather that every body has been housed up. It was misting rain all day sunday, and sunday night began in earnest, and rained all day long yesterday and nearly all night long last night, a cold, chilling rain, which has made the stock suffer so much, and will be the cause of many a poor one dying. Last night I could not help thinking of the poor cattle. Before I went to bed I could hear the little pigs in the rye patch squealing, & I made the negros fix a shelter for them & the sow, had old Sam [the] horse put under the buggy shelter, tho I trembled for both his safety & the buggy's. I thought of the poor soldier's, and felt so thankful that the poor soldier in whose fate I am most interested was fixed even more comfortably than I was, and thought of my poor bro Garrett who is beyond the reach of both cold & rain— infinitely better off than I am. Yesterday evening, old Lamb [the] ox died, he was very poor & sick, & find since his death that he has been unable to get up without help for two or three weeks. I find from what Joe says that the blame according to what he *thinks* rest on Myers about the oxen being so poor, worked so hard &c &c. I fear more of the oxen will die, Ratler looks very bad, so does the Dunn one Rivers worked. I went to the ox lot to night & looked at them. I will get the one from Mrs Oliver, & try and save the lives of Ratler & the dunn one. Last night a poor little calf came almost to our gate, & lay down & died, found it this morning. Tis the calf of the Heifer that had that cut with the ax, it did not seem to be very poor, but was weak, I reckon, & thin & was chilled through with the rain & cold. I feel so sorry it died, it was so gentle, the children say it came up and eat shucks with the oxen in the lot, almost every night. I fear its mother died also. Myers says after this spell the woods will be full of dead cows & calves. There was ice this morning & he fears the ground will freeze to night & kill the sprouted grain in the ground. I planted my garden, last week. Had a fine chance of white schallotts, set out more than we had last year, by a good deal. Myers says he has tried all around here to get cotton seed to plant and get any and the only chance now is to try mother & if she cant let us have any to send a load of cotton to Pa's and bring back a load of seed, & go some other time after the ginned cotton. I hate this, for it will be hard on the oxen to do so much hauling.

Galveston
Feb 28th/64
Mrs L S Neblett

Dear Lizzie

I find myself once more at the old place but I believe more dissatisfied than before I left. For I cannot now look forward to be at home for some time— probably four or six months, and am thus robed of the pleasure of hoping to be at home soon. I felt thus way as soon as I got to the cars the morning I left, and could not help comparing my feelings there with what they were when I went up. I found every thing here as I left—no complaint about my staying two days over the time. But I am more dissatisfied at the office than when I left, and will go back to my Company in two or four weeks. I despise Tyler, he is such a swell headed fool and treats persons who come to the office with such rudeness if they are not of a superior rank that it is disgusting. I cannot complain of any personal act towards me for I have as little as possible to do with him. All of the clerks despise him.

I have been regretting ever since I left that I did not bring the children to Navasota that morning to see the cars. I might have done so very easily for I got there half an hour before they arrived. Bob looked disappointed when I left him, I thought once of taking him behind me but thought he was not well enough to go out in the cold so early. I have felt a little uneasy too about Bob & Bettie since I left, as well as about Ma's & Nelia's arms.[2] I have got no letter from you since I returned but expect one in a day or two. Oliver is with me to night this far on his way home to recruit for the Company. He will stay 15 or 20 days he says. I would like to send the children some little thing but

2. Will was probably referring to his anxiety about the effect of vaccination on his mother and sister.

have barely money enough to pay my board up to this time but will draw some in a few days. Things are very dull here every one has ceased to expect an attack on this place or any thing like a formidable invasion of the state earlier than Fall if then. I saw John to day for the first time since I arrived. His Co has gone out to Fort Magruder on the East end of the Island about 2½ miles from this place. He did not stay long nor have much to say. As I have but little to say & a bad chance to say well [with] that I will stop. good night.

yours affectionately
Wm H. Neblett[3]

At Home
Sat morning March 12th 1864

Dear Will,

Altho this is a work day, I feel better satisfied with my weeks work than usual, hence, don't feel so much like I was eating forbidden fruit in writing to you by the light of a working day. I borrowed Mrs Hurst clock reel two days ago, and reeled up about sixty yards of thread, and I feel tired & sore from the work—in fact, don't feel as well as usual, owing no doubt to my dissipation on Thursday night. There was a big party (one of these party's that are all the fashion now) at old man Alston's and they sent me an invitation, & Aunt Cinda came over & persuaded me to go, & my curiosity also prompted me to go & see how the party's were conducted, so I went. I took Bill with me, went early & stopped at Bettie's and went with the crowd from there. I found Babe, (who came down in a buggy with Mary Fanthorp from Lizzie Kennards wedding, and dinner at Jeff Haynie's) the two Goodrich girls, Serena Rogers,[4] and Mary Eliza Goodrich. The house was full at Alston's, had two fiddles, and dancing, and a nice supper, but I was soon satisfied with looking on. All the old married men & ladies around were there Oliver was skipping around the young girls and dancing & enjoying himself generally. George Alston is still at home. I expected Babe to come home with me when I went, but she came down in a buggy with Mary Fan, & it was too dark to drive through the bot-

---

3. The next letter in the collection has been omitted because of water-stain damage. The letter was from Lizzie Neblett to Will Neblett and was dated March 7, 1864.

4. In 1860 Serena Rogers was 23 and lived with Benjamin Briggs and Serena Goodrich with her two children. Her real and personal property was valued at $7,500. TX Census 1860.

tom, so I got Uncle Mc to come home with me. He got a lamp from Alston, and by the light of it I reached home—found the baby sleeping and had been a good child. I got cold coming home, and I suppose that accounts for my bad feelings. Walter had a very high fever for a day & night, three days ago, and had symptoms of spasms, but soon grew quiet after I began cooling his head with a wet cloth. I gave him two of McLane's pills in two doses, and after his fever left gave him a large dose of Quinine, and he has had no return of it. I think cold was the cause of it. The baby still has a cold, but is better of it, poor little thing she has never been clear of a cold this winter. She is not quite so cross as when you saw her. I have whipped her several times.

The negros plowed two days this week, & it rained a heavy rain and stopped them for the remainder of the week. Joe & Bill have been out hunting cattle. They got up that little cow that Uncle Mc was telling you about being so bad to come up to her calf, & it died last year, & he thought this year also, but was mistaken, she has a very fat, fine calf, and we have her up, and Bro Jim has got up old Red head. He has had Sandy & Mack out hunting a great deal for cows, over this side of the creek, and has not said one word to me about wanting to milk some of our cows. He acts just like they were his, and will take all the cows, as fast as they have calves, if he can get them. I cant send as often as he does, because I will have to select times when they can't work in the field, well let him go I can live without the cows, but I will get all I can, and never say a word to him. He is awful mad at mother just now be-cause she sold some cotton to a man recently and did not send him word she would let him have the cotton. Susan promised to let him have her cotton & then said she would not do it until she wrote to Mr Scott & she knew he would sell it to him, that Jim treated John so bad in not trying to get him a Sub when he wanted one. I think Susan will ruin her family before she quits, the negros are almost ready to give up & leave her. Frank talked to Uncle Mc said he did not see how they could stand it till Mas John came home. That she went into the field last week, and cursed all the negros in it about the stand of corn—cursed equal to any man Frank ever heard, whipped the one that dropped the corn awfully and said she would be damned if she dident have every d—— negro on the place whipped about the stand of corn—cursed Uncle Mc also, and used the most vulgar language you ever heard to Frank about Uncle Mc & Mrs Wade. Bro Jim & Uncle Mc says her stand of corn is a[s] good as they ever saw. She talked to Uncle Mc in the most vulgar style about Febe's child. Will Mrs Croom was nothing to her. She is the blackest hearted woman I ever knew—& Jim says he believes that John is worse on his family than she is, & backs her in all she says & does. She swears to Uncle Mc that she won't take cotton for the cotton I have used out of her Gin—but if she dont she won't take any thing for I won't pay her money & John agreed to take cotton.

I paid Carley[5] my Tax a few evenings since, it was $158.25 cts. I did not give in that land willed to me by Garret, but told him about it & he said he would see mother & fix it. The tax collector of Montgomery Co told Uncle Mc that Susan gave in only 15 negros last year three less than they have, & did not give in half of her land, and valued it at $2 per acre I think, but the present Tax man says he will get her this year. Old Mangum stole leather to please her last year, told Uncle Mc & Aunt that he had taken Mrs Scotts leather which was very inferior & had given her good leather for it that he could use her leather in the place of good & answer very well. But Susan did not hear his tale, & she showed both the good leather & the bad, & said she bought the good leather from Mangum. He is working to her hand all the time. He meets Ann Rogers at Susan's & she tries to please the old man, in many ways. I don't believe that Mangum is strictly honest.

Sam & Thornton split rails three days this week, they have all gone to plowing this morning. Yesterday evening Tom came in, came round to the door, and began to beg—said he thought it was something to run away, but he has found out that it is nothing, and will never try it again. I told him to go to Mr Myers & talk to him, & he went off & told the children that I said Mr Myers should not whip. I told Myers what Joe say's and he said he only said to Joe & Tom that he would whip them if they broke their plow—never said a word about giving him 500. Tom is telling his tale said the same Myers said. Joe only wants an excuse to run away & if he gets off it will be as he says, a while before any body sees him. Joe got up another young ox, the first one he got up worked very gentle will make a fine ox. He branded the yearling & 2 yr old at Uncle Mc & tried to brand & alter that young Bull over the creek, but he fought so they could do nothing with him. I think the little calf I wrote you about dying is the only one of ours that has died this winter. Many of our cows we milked last year will not have calves at all or will be late this summer. I fear we will have to do without butter this year. I haven't heard from Pa's since you left & fear that Ma's & Nelia's arms are not well yet. Mrs Brown

5. William Carley was elected assesor and collector of taxes of Anderson in 1858 and re-elected in 1862. Allen, *Saga of Anderson,* 141.

told me that there is only one case on their place that has the appearance of getting well, & they have all been vaccinated over seven weeks, have burnt the places a number of times with caustic, it does no good.[6] Pa burnt Ma's & Nelia's the morning I left there. Mary Haynies arm is not yet well, been lanced three times. The peach seed I planted have come up very well, hardly a single one missed coming. I planted the 15 Indian peach seed a few days ago, I hope they will come up well. I have a lot of little pigs in my Rye patch now. Billy's sow has 10, and that Collins sow 9. They tell me that sow ought to be ours for we raised her with our hogs from a pig, so Joe says.

The old white sow has pigs but I haven't seen her & don't know how many she has. I am longing for a letter from you, but can't send to the office 'till this evening or rather in the morning from mother. Every day I wish so earnestly that you were at home. Oh how anxious I am for this year to roll around, but if the war party predominates at the north, & there is a prospect of an other 4 yrs war, what shall I do. I think I'll give up if that is the case. If a chance for coming home to stay two or three weeks comes, how I pray that you can get that detail in time.

affectionately
Lizzie S. N

Galveston
March 12th 1864

Dear Lizzie

Is almost a month since I left home and I have recd but one letter written since I returned. I felt certain of getting one yesterday & to day. The last I recd was dated 24th Feb just seventeen days ago. What is the matter? I sometimes think you are sick. I suppose you have seen Oliver since his return home & if so you are better posted in affairs here than if I were with you. For he sees & hears every thing & can tell it without an effort all in a string. With me it comes by piece meal. But he has one fault. He tells a great deal of unreliable news in such a way that it looks reliable. I like him & consider him a friend but this is one fault. I think he is a warm friend but I know he is a very bitter enemy with very strong prejudices. Since he left and only a few days ago

---

6. Caustic probably refers to sodium hydroxide or potassium hydroxide, also called lye. It was used in the manufacture of soaps, dyes, bleaches, and other chemicals.

there came very near being a great run or almost a mutiny among the troops on the Island occasioned by the poor beef which had been issued to them for a month past. A ball was given by the ladies of Galveston on the 9th in [the] home of Col Sulakowski, the Engineer in charge of the building of the fortifications here. He was about to start to France with his family (I expect not to return soon if ever[)]. The soldiers took offense at the revelry & carousal and concocted a plot to make a raid on the delicacies at the table in order to break it up. Soldiers from Elmores Cooks Hobbys[7] & Terrells Regmts[8] were concerned to the number of several hundred. But the secret leaked out & got to the ears of Col Rainey who commands these four Regtms about six hours before the ball was to come off. A Co of cavalry was ordered to guard the house. After Supper (in town) pistols & guns could be heard in various directions indicating a preparation to carry out the plot. Magruder Gen Majors[9] Rainey & Cook became alarmed & had an order for a Battalion to be sent out to protect the place. They also were preparing to get Majors Brigade at Va Point. In the mean time several hundred of the soldiers had collected at the market house & Col Cook Gen Major & Magruder found out where they were & all went there and made speeches—made excuses for the bad rations & Gen Magruder promised them furloughs soon. The crowd dispersed & thus it ended. It came very near being a very serious affair. I understand that the Cavalry Co sent the soldiers word to come on that they would not fire on them. The soldiers at Va Pt I hear were anxious that the ball should be broken up. So there was nothing to restrain them but a sense of propriety or a disinclination to go into such rash measures if it could be avoided. However the ball came off and was largely attended by officers and all the silly women in Galveston & many in Houston who believe that gold lace makes the man and this includes nearly the whole sex. A fellow who is clerking in this office by the name of Gameson found out the plot & told Rainey of it. I knew nothing of it as usual of such things but if I had I would not have acted the spy. I think the poor devil thought he would get a ticket to the ball by telling, but he did

---

7. Alfred Marmaduke Hobby commanded the Eighth Texas Infantry Regiment. Wright and Simpson, *Texas in the War*, 163.

8. Alexander Watkins Terrell commanded Terrell's Texas Cavalry Regiment, which served primarily in Texas and Louisiana. Ibid., 93–94.

9. James Patrick Major made brigadier general July 21, 1863. He commanded a Texas cavalry brigade under General Richard Taylor. Boatner, *The Civil War Dictionary*, 503.

not.[10] But enough of this I am sure you are tired of it. You cannot say I did not tell you the particulars. Nine men deserted from Pelican Spit last night from Co E & D Cooks Regt & went to the blockaders it is supposed. I enclose you ten dollars which I wish you would give to Oliver to buy me some tobacco & bring when he returns.

March 15th I with held this for the purpose of learning whether Elmores Regt would go to La or not for an order has come to Gen Magruder to send all the troops to Shreveport or Alexandria leaving this Garrison to its minimum number. I saw that there was an effort being made to get Elmores Regt off because it is the largest Reg here. I have no idea now that this Reg will go for Majors Brigade commenced leaving yesterday for La and Terrells Reg is under orders also which will leave at this place Cooks Elmores & Hobbys—just as fine as can be got along with.

I have been suffering very much yesterday & last night and to day with neuralgia in my head—was in bed yesterday half of the day. I have not been well for a week. I have recd no letters from you since about the first of March. What is the matter I feel uneasy about you—some times [I] think you are sick or that the horses have run away with the buggy & crippled you. John S[cott] told me he had got a letter of the 9th from home.

Do not mention the name of the young man who told of the soldiers plot to break up the ball—for it might cause him to be injured by the soldiers. I must close to get this in the office.

yours affectionately
Wm H. Neblett

Galveston
Mar 18th/64

Dear Lizzie

Yours of the 7th & 12th both reached me three days ago. I had been to feel very uneasy for fear that something had happened to you. I noticed that they were both mailed on the 15th. There has been a general stir among military matters here for the last ten days. The last Reg of Majors Brigade leaves to-

---

10. An attempted mutiny did occur in Galveston to protest officers' privileges, poor food, and a ball given to honor General Magruder. Cotham, *Battle on the Bay*, 162; Wright and Simpson, *Texas in the War*, 143.

morrow leaving Hobbys Cooks & Elmores here Pyrons expected here in a few days. Military affairs look threatening in La. Elmores Reg will hardly go unless militia troops take its place. Last night a steamer ran the blockade at this place loaded with shoes blankets iron ammunition & She is four days from Havannah and is the first steamer that has run in here since the blockade. I fear the cold weather a few days ago has injured the corn gardens &c. Did Myers get a good stand of corn. I expect it would be best to let Myers have one seventh of the crop in place of the $400.00 and one seventh is enough for you know he is engaged only one third of his time at our place—in fact less. From what I have seen Congress has or will require all the money in circulation to be put into bonds by a certain time and if such is the case money will be scarce & every thing cheap that is raised in the country.[11] If Myers thinks of this he might refuse to change. Speak to him on the subject. I have had a very good pr of shoes made of the leather I brought down. I believe I never told you of changing my boarding house. I did so on the 1st of March because the price of board was raised to about $80.00 pr month. I am now boarding at a Dutch house—a rough place & rough fare at $50 pr month. Three clerks besides myself are boarding there. I do not like it much but do not know how to better myself. I lost all the bacon I brought down. I got McCray whom I fell in with at Navasota with meat for Co (I) to put it with his & leave it at the commisary here. He did so and I saw it there twice—had my name on it. I had no place to leave it at & thought that as safe a place a[s] could be found. I went around a few days ago & missing it inquired about it & was told that a man came there and said he wanted a sack of meat McCray left there & got it. The man who gave it to him did not know his name. I think it must have been some one from Co (I) because no one knew of McCray leaving a sack of bacon there unless some one might have heard me when I first went & inquired there.

John Scott came here to day & took dinner with me. He said very little about home matters. He said Susan wrote to him that Dr Brown had a surprise party at Mrs Womacks and had the Alstons there which made Mrs Womack mad. He told me Jim had a contract with the Govmt in which he is to buy & haul cotton to Eagle pass & sell & let the Govmt have one half of the proceeds for Gov bonds. So it seems he may be able to keep out the army. I

11. Effective April 1, 1864, the Confederate congress passed a 33 percent tax on money, which made it preferable to purchase bonds.

can hardly believe John wrote that I did not get here until Thursday, for I got here on Teusday & think I told him so. I wonder how your Ma is going to fix that estate matter up with him. She will have to give him up his notes to the amount of what is coming to him & get his receipt for them as if for money. John could send the proper receipt to Susan & then your Ma could give her up the notes & take the receipt. She had better fix it up at once, for there is no certainty where a soldier will be a month ahead.

I fear from what you say that you will have more pigs than you can feed this spring & summer, but if you have to raise that sow & pigs of Collins, you had better buy her if you can get her cheap.

You mentioned the hope of my getting a furlough. An order for furloughing men reached this office the 9th the night the soldiers threatened to break up the ball. The next morning the order was suspended that is withheld and has been so up to this time. It was to this effect. A furlough at the rate of one man to every fifteen[,] long enough to stay at home ten days—to be granted to such as had not been at home in six months on furlough or *detail* or absent without leave. So you see it cut me out entirely at least for six months from the time I was at home, but I will try & get home sooner than that. I think furloughs are withheld now because so many troops are ordered off & to give furloughs to those remaining before the others get off would produce great dissatisfaction among those going to La.

Sunday night 9 O clock 20th March. I have just returned from supping at Shackelfords. John came by this evening according to agreement & we went there together. Had a good supper—biscuit have butter & coffee which I relished finely. Shackelford was & has been sick for several weeks with Rheumatism Mrs S was also sick. We spent our stay in Shackelfords room. I have just gotten back & John gone to Fort Magruder 1½ miles off. Last night for the first time I went to the theater to hear "Camille" played & did not get back till 10½. I found the playing as good as I expected for third rate actors. But apropos of these diversions I must say that while I am glad to hear that you have had some also I am sorry that you had to make your debut at the Alstons. I have not changed my opinions of them though their desperate efforts at reinstating themselves may succeed with some. John told me about the frolic up there & at Alstons particularly & remarked casually that "Lizzie" was there. I told him that you had written to me about it. He says Calvin Rizzle chose Geo[rge] A[lston] as one of his waiters but that Mary Fan[thorp] & Lizzie Montgomery refused to stand with him. How is this, of course Susan told him so.

I wish you would speak to Oliver and see if he can bring my hat down without too much trouble.

I wish you would enclose to me that letter of introduction to Gen Magruder by Gray. I sent it to you with some of yours last fall by Jack Oliver. I may possibly use it in some way. I enclose to you a piece of smutty rhymes as a sample of what the soldiers sometimes have among them. I believe the women will be as badly demoralized by the war as the men. A rich thing occurred in the office a few days ago. Col Rainey brought in an application for a furlough in which the applicant stated among other things that he had not been home in eighteen months and at the same time—that his wife would soon be confined. There was considerable laugh & the application refused. Now dont you think that cup of coffee & hearty supper at Shackelfords has made me garrulous. But what have I to write about to interest you. You have a great advantage in procuring material for your letters over me[,] home affairs & the children afford an endless theme of interest to me. Elmores Reg just did escape a trip to La I understand. Good bye,—I wish I could could [*sic*] say so with a kiss—but not go.

Mar 22, No letter from you yet. I fear this morning that the cold to night will kill the corn so that it will have to be planted over. If all of our corn has to be planted over do not plant a seed of cotton except in the new ground.

yours affectionately
Wm H Neblett

At Home
Friday March 18th 1864

Dear Will,

I can't refrain from beginning my weekly letter any longer was strongly tempted to begin yesterday evening, and to keep from it, I got on old Sam & traveled over to Aunt Cinda's. I had a fit of the blues, felt most miserable & tho' the circumstances that made my unhappiness have not altered, yet I do not feel quite so unhappy to day about the general state of my affairs. Oh my life does seem so weary, so monotonous, so lonely, so cheerless that one with my natural bias for gloom & despondency couldent help being unhappy the greater part of the time. I have tried to battle with this feeling, & have visited more the last month than usual, I forget myself & my woes for the day that I visit, but with the next rising sun they again present themselves. Two nights ago the 16th we had a heavy frost, and ice all day, and I walked down into the field & garden to see what the prospect was, found my beans killed and the corn dead, but it may come out as it is so young[,] saw our poor oxen, who have my heart felt pity, almost reeling in the plow, came back by the crib, the corn very low, came on to the house, found those of my little pigs I had in the Rye patch when you were at home, dead, came in the house, set down over a double hand full of coals, and cried—all I could do yet, something that I have not permitted myself to do, for several months before. I thought of the negros, to be clothed and fed, the crop yet to make, the oxen so poor, no corn, and to cup the climax, the black wretches trying all they can it seems to me to agrivate me, taking no interest, having no care about the future, neglecting their duty &c—and if we do have to plant the corn over it will be so much worse on the oxen.

If the war don't end this year, or the early part of next, I don't think I can stand a farm life an other year. I don't know how I can stand it, if our prospects for peace do not brighten this summer, the prospect of an other four years war, will almost kill me. But let me hope that something will happen to brighten my life. I am getting mighty tired of this old fool Myers, and if I can do any better I wont have him any longer than this year.[12] He is sadly deficient in sense & judgement, and is cruel, and devoid of mercy. He whipped Sam unmercifully, but I could say nothing in that case, but the other day, he bucked Tom, and give him the worst sort of a whipping, cut his back all to pieces so Sarah and the children say. I dident examine myself. There were several poleating circumstances in Tom's favor, his youth, and his first offense of the kind, his coming in himself in a few days, and his humility when he went to whip him, he dident consider any of these things, and then whipped him with his whip, when I told him after he whipped Sam that I did not want the negros back cut, and not to whip on the naked skin when he used his whip. I intend to give him a piece of my mind next time I see him, havent seen him since I found out how badly he whipped Tom. And an other thing I intend to have stopped his shooting at the negros, it is all fudge. He shot at Tom when he ran—and asked me at the mill if I wanted the negros ruled, said he could do it, but expected he would have to kill one or two of them. I told him if he

---

12. On similar problems with overseers see Joan Cashin, " 'Since the War Broke Out': The Marriage of Kate and William McLure," in *Divided Houses*, Clinton and Silber, eds., 200–212. William K. Scarborough, *The Overseer: Plantation Management in the Old South* (Baton Rouge: Louisiana State University Press, 1966).

could not get along without it he could shoot at their legs, but I did not want any of them killed, the old fool with great pomp went to Jim Rogers borrowed his gun, & said "Mrs Neblett said just shoot her negros down, so he did not quite kill them was all she asked," & here he has been packing his gun for our negros. He has acted the fool so largely that I shall feel like shooting him down if he shoots at another one of the negros. He don't approach them right when he goes to whip them, and there is no need of his shooting at all. Madam Susan got hold of what Myers said about my telling him to shoot, and last Sunday she gave Joe a talking about it, said to Joe that Mr Oliver said he dident care what Mrs N said, but he dident have to shoot one of his negros, and she said no man [would] shoot her negros, & a good deal more about it, trying to create a feeling of dissatisfaction among our negros, at my course towards them & if she could would cause them all to run away, and cut up awfully. Her negros are almost ready to leave her now. Frank tells Uncle Mc that he don't know what in the name of the lord they will do if Mas John don't come home soon.

They will finish bedding up the new ground this week, and this evening Sarah Nancy, Kate and Thornton will load the wagon with cotton, and tomorrow Thornton will take the load up to mothers and get a load of seed back, to commence planting cotton on monday. Mother has to have her gin repaired to Gin some cotton for herself & when she gins hers will Gin mine. I will get two or three yoke of oxen from Mr Oliver to haul the cotton to mothers, they are done using their oxen in the farm this year, and they are fat now. I have at last learned to tell fat oxen & when they are very poor. I cant tell what made my little pigs die unless it was eating so much green rye, & getting no milk and no slop, for the sows whipped them off when the slop was poured in. I have the remaining three put up in a pen, & will slop them, & not let them on the rye, nor to their mother. Jim's Red head cow got her calf out some how, & last sunday John's Henry and negro Spence drove her up here, and we now milk her. I will churn this evening, how I wish you were here to eat of the butter with me. I got a letter last sunday from you as I hoped and expected and was amused at Tylers remark to Smith about your being very Lazy, you could never brag much on your great industry but I never thought you a lazy man, but I fear you will be some what so, if you have the good fortune to out live the war and come home, it will go hard with the most of the men, to go to work after living such an idle life for so long a time. You ask if Garett left me his land or mentioned the tract. He only said "my land 320 acres," which is the place by mothers and I will not be [entitled] to his portion of the undivided land. I will get a certified copy of the will, as a [title] to the land. I don't know how mother & John will arrange it about the money. Susan told Mrs Oliver that there was a screw loose in that will and that Mr Scott would tear that all up when he came out of the war. I don't know whether John is cherishing any such an idea or not, but if he can do so, he will I am sure, but I don't think he can do any thing.

I am surprised that your visit seems the same to you as it does to me, like a dream. I have had many dreams that seem as distinct as your visit does now to my memory. You troubled yourself about my old bed curtain dress, & that surprised me, for I had been grieving myself that I wore that dress while you were at home, not that I thought you would reproach yourself or feel mortified that I had to wear such a dress, but simply because I had an other that looked better, and I ought to have tried to leave a pleasant picture of myself upon your memory for you may never see me again, and I don't like to be associated in your mind with that old dress as I find I am. Yes I was so sorry after you were gone that I wore that old dress, if you did catch me with it on, but while you were at home I was so glad that I did not think of my appearance. I never cared much for dress, so if I havent dressed fine since my marriage, it has not hurt me to dress plainly. I did not dress much when I was a girl. A few times in my life I have regreted that my wardrobe was not nicer, when I have wished to visit those who dressed finely, but I never thought of it being your fault, and I knew that you never allowed yourself a fine suit. I could have bought me anything I wanted, but I never was disposed to run in debt and would never cause you trouble in that way. We have been unfortunate, our negros have been a draw back, but by strict economy on our part have managed so far to pay our debts & supply our necessities without sacrificing any property to do so—but after this war, (and here I draw a long sigh) and you return, we will both dress a little better, if we have to sell a negro to do it. I don't know a more disagreeable feeling than to blush at ones appearance, and I have said to myself many times since this war, that if I live to see peace, I will certainly have me plenty of neat calico dresses if I go no higher. Bet Scott has made me feel worse than any one else about my dressing. She has plenty, and fine ones at that, & she thinks it is only stinginess on both my part & yours that I don't, or did not have more clothes before the war—but I don't care for her opinion, let her go. Since I began this I have been to the cotton house & weighed the cotton as they put it in, weighed 1,600 pounds. I saw old Parmer while I was gone, and he is as lame as when you were here, the old fellow cant work any more this crop I reckon. I am going to try & get a couple of mules from Jim S[cott] to plant the cotton & let the oxen rest.

Sunday March 20th 1864

Dear Will, I have wandered around the place like a lost spirit seeing nothing to cheer the mind or gladden the heart, have been in the act three different times of taking the pen & paper to write to you, and then I would reflect that I had the blues most awfully and tho in my heart I blame you not, yet I feared if I indulged myself by giving free expression to all I thought & felt you would think that I was blaming you in [my] censure & thus excite your anger instead of your sympathy & so I was enabled to desist, until the fury of the storm has passed over. You with your hopeful disposition cannot conceive of the wretchedness of my feelings, John Pation,[13] nor the worst case of despondency on record never felt worse, more hopeless, and more like committing suicide than I do. The strongest plea not to do it is the idea of the punishment hereafter. If I did not believe in the bible, I would end this continual warfare, and do both you and myself a service by leaving this world, but I know I am full of sin, & might not better my condition by death, from my own hands at least. Life is short they tell me, and if I live the length of a natural life, yet I have already lived out half of it. The springtime, the freshness, the bloom of life has gone—and what freshness what bloom did it have for me? My life has never been much pleasure to me. A few months at a time I can remember, when I felt hopeful & contented if not proud of my children, and anticipated enjoyment & pleasure in the future, but such feelings had just had time to creep into my bosom, and make glad my heart when I have sunk again into the deepest despair by finding myself pregnant. The last time the gloom & despair were deeper than ever before, and I will never get over it and if I ever have cause to believe myself in the same fix again I shall certainly do something desperate.

Above all things I regret that I have lost all pride in the children, and view them more as a curse than a blessing, and this last one has been enough to vex the patience of a saint, and then the bitterness of having given birth to one of my sex to suffer, be humiliated, and to bear in hopeless misery the fate that her kind, loving and obliging heart led her into. Oh this is worse than ten

13. In 1860 J. J. A. Pation (age 27) was a high school teacher living in Grimes County with personal and real property valued at $4,000. TX Census 1860.

thousand deaths, & there is no hope no remedy for it, and I think I commit no sin, and display anything but selfishness when I say that it would be a relief to know that my daughters lives were ended, now in their youth & infancy while they are free from guilt or sin—but I have said all this again and again to you, yet there seems to be something in my heart & brain continually urging a repetition of the same old story. Oh how I hate myself, and yet I commiserate my woes & my misfortunes, so much that I am continually thinking of them & grieving over the irremediable past and the hidden future that is no doubt filled with vials of wrath ready to descend upon [my] head. Oh that I had died in infancy! and this wish comes up every week of my life, and some weeks it remains with me day & night. I believe you love me, notwithstanding all my faults [I] have more faith in your affection than I ever had before, I believe, but still feel that you are loving me upon false grounds. You speak of my self sacrifices, I admit, my life has been full of such, but don't make a virtue of what was a necessity. Woman was made for such things, and when she tries to evade them is only kicking against the thorns. True some women's "lives are cast in shady places" compared with others, but that is their good fortune, & because such has not been my fate, does not make me more worthy of your love. You have had your troubles no doubt but being less selfish than I, you have not sought to bother me with them. But of one thing I am sure, if the love of woman ever deserves a return, mine does. I have loved you long & faithfully & were I to live a thousand years, it would be the one love of my life. I never loved but one girl with my whole heart & her place was never filled, and the memory of that love haunts me still. I never loved but one Bro fervently, and the memory of that will go with me to the grave, and I have never loved man as I do you, and should you die first none could ever fill your place in my heart or in my home and I believe that you feel this to be true. I'll tell you one thing that is fast becoming a conviction in my mind, I think if I live ten or fifteen years longer, that I will be crazy—if I don't it will be because my brain is well ballanced—don't think I am crazy now not a bit of it I assure you, if I do write like a crazy woman.

Yesterday evening I put on my new calico dress you sent me, and Mary fixed up and we went to see Mrs Brown & Buckley, but unfortunately found them gone to Oakland church, came back by Mrs Olivers found her busy weaving & glad to stop. She had a good piece of news to tell me if true. Mr Mooring told Oliver that he had recd a letter from his son Pat, saying that Stephensons Co would be disbanded & sent home for 50 or 60 days some time in May, and the ship, the Gun boat would then be repaired. Oliver thinks it may be true tho he said he had rec[eived] a letter from the Capt a few days ago & he did not mention the subject. I am affraid to believe it, fear there is no such good luck in store. While I was at Mrs O's Bob came full tilt after me, saying that "Miss Ellen Van Horn"[14] was at our house. I found her on the trundle bed, sick as usual, and last night it took me Kate & Sarah to wait upon her. She had a bowel affection must have a poultice composition tea made twice, thickened milk, feet bathed, and numerous other things done, & if it had been me I would have managed to wait upon myself. A fine thing I reckon that God made me healthy for He certainly never made me for a Queen or to be waited upon. Van H expected to find you at home, is anxious to see you about your business, is going to buy your place, town place. He spoke of going to Galveston to see you. Ellen is going with him this time if he don't go to see you, will write you from Houston. They told me that Charly Lockhart is dead. Was found dead in his bed one morning when they went to wake him up for breakfast—he was at his farm & alone. Col H[enderson] has been at home some time, but says he will return soon—says Col Henderson rubs his hands together & says, "we *had several very pleasant little fights,*" just like him aint it? Van H complains of your not answering his questions as asked in his letters to you, thinks you perhaps did not get his letters. Hood will start into service again soon—and Dr. Croom threatens to leave Mrs Croom—she grows worse & worse & revived her old hatred of Lavenia who stayed with Ellen three months until the Pillow place was vacated & then Hood moved there— while Lavenia stayed with Ellen, Ellen was under Croom's treatment, and I guess Mrs C's jealousy became aroused & she went to Van H's and threw brick bats, sticks & rocks at the house, blasting Lavenia all the time, & they locked the door on her, & Jemigan came over and pushed her out of the gate and held it, she threatening to knock him down all the time. Croom told Ellen he would leave her if she ever cut up again. He moved his office up on the square, & she went at night, broke the glass & sash all to pieces tried to get in to destroy his medicine but failed he then declared he would leave her, but he has been hen pecked so long that he can never hold his head up long enough to take any decided step about anything.

All the wheat on that town place was killed not a sprig left, dont know how

14. Ellen Van Horn (age 22 in 1860) was the wife of Richard A. Van Horn (30), a printer from Corsicana who published the paper *Navarro Express.* Will Neblett had served a time as the paper's editor. TX Census 1860.

the River creek place is. Halburts house is not burned. Mrs Henderson moved my Piano down to her house a few weeks ago, and sent for the key to unlock it to see the amount of damage done to it, as they think the mice have been in the piano itself and if so have cut all the leather or cloth of the hammers, and it will make no sound. I am so sorry that you left that hole in the box. I did not know it until long after we moved down here when you told me. The want of money has cost us more trouble & double expense than any folks in the world I reckon. If you had been supplied with money you would have had a new box made & packed it right, now if the Piano is utterly ruined it will probably cost $100 in specie to have it fixed. If it had not been Pa's gift I would have sold it long ago, even yet, before I will be harassed out of my life about wanting a little money to buy necessities with & appear decent I'll sell it, that is if any body will buy it in its present fix which is doubtful—and if it [is] as badly damaged as I think, I never expect to have spare money enough to fix it, and I won't borrow from mother. I am so tired of people thinking & telling me that we are rich I don't know what to do, and I know of no poor, hard working people who have had a harder scuffle to keep their heads out of water than we have, pay so much taxes & never have any money—land, and a few mean lazy negros for whom I have to work, with both mind & body, harder than they will ever work for me, & deny myself and children all the luxuries & pleasures of life, and still keep in debt, & never enough money to do any good. I have regreted so often since this war that I did not sell my watch, and supplied myself with some domestic & calico before I left C[orsi-cana]. I desired so much to go to Youngers Store, & ransacked my mind to see if I could not fall upon some plan to get a little money I thought of my watch, but it being a gift from Pa, made me loath to part with it, and now, when such feelings yield to a pressing demand for more useful things, both the Piano and watch [are] reproaches to me—they are the only two articles of ornament, and not strictly necessities that I ever had, and no doubt will be the last, for if you live to come out of this war, and we gain our independence, I will never live to see times grow so I can indulge my taste or fancy. No the actual and pressing necessities of life are all I ever expect in this world, and if we are conquered I shall not even have them, and in addition to this I will have a large share of other kind of troubles to bear. If I could purchase a life of 80 years with 25 cts confederate money I would spurn the offer—like poor Burns "I backward cast my eye, on prospects drear, And forward tho' I cannot see I guess & fear"[15] and such a life is not worth buying at any price.

15. From the Scottish poet Robert Burns's "To a Mouse" (1786).

March 23rd. Van H told me that Mrs Miller, who has only one daughter, & is wealthy wants to rent my Piano for the use of her daughter, says she will take good care of it and pay for the use. Perhaps I can sell it to her, if the damage done it by the mice can be repaired. The material for fixing it may not be in the Confederacy. I was very foolish about a Piano after we were married, and wanted one so much to practice on. I was late getting the one from Pa's, then moved & had to leave it, and after I got it at Corsicana, I then had three children to torment and occupy my time, and I lost all my taste & fondness for music—since that time I have thought, I had better keep it for Mary's use, that if I sold it, & spent the money, we would never have money enough to spare to buy an other one for her—now, I feel like I could spend the money so as to benefit me & Mary more than the Piano would ever do. I don't care if she never learns a note. Poor devil of a woman has no business knowing any thing in the way of accomplishments, her life business is to bear & nurse children, & it is time labor & money thrown away, to try and give her accomplishments fit for the parlor & a life of ease & enjoyment. So you need not be surprised [if] you hear of the sale of my Piano soon.

They would have commenced planting the corn over last monday but it commenced raining before they reached the field, and rained so much that it has been too wet to plow 'till to day the 23rd. Myers thinks that the old field and a part of the new ground will have to be planted over, maybe all of it, can tell by the time the old ground is planted over. I pity the oxen. Two of them have the hollow horn, had their horns bored to day. I expect they will both die that is the way Old Lamb commenced. If old Lincoln is reelected or any other president with the prospect of an other 4 yrs war, you may give your negros away if you wont hire them [out], and I'll move into the white settlements, and work with my hands, as hard as I can, but my mind will rest. I feel like I could not take care of them an other year longer. Every body is planting over, but every body hasent the poor team that we have to do it with, and the next thing to no corn in the crib & no money to buy more with. I try to quit thinking about what I cant help, and am learning to feel like I don't care how soon the negros oxen, children & myself all go to the devil. I thought last Spring that I was hopeless enough, and felt weary enough of life, but I am much more so this Spring. I am not trying and don't [intend to] try to raise a quantity of chicken for the negros to sell for me. I have heretofore loved to raise chickens & worked hard to do so, but I have fought against difficulties in this as in every thing else I ever undertook. I have never had a new house since I have been married, God fixed me to have children in pain & sorrow, and I have fulfilled His law, and havent had much else fixed for me. All this I could forget, or cease to mourn over, if the prospect ahead of me was not darker, if any thing, than the past. I cant hope there is not the smallest foundation to build a hope upon and I often think and fear that self destruction, suicide will be my fate, that is a cowardly death, and I fear meets with perhaps a just punishment hereafter. Lord if I was made a woman why were such rebelious, such wicked feelings given to me why cant I feel & think like a poor weak inferior slave should. God gave me life, but in my case He did not "temper the wind to the shorn lamb."[16] No I cling to the old idea I must be the expiator of the sins of my forefathers generations ago—and they must have been a very wicked set, judging from my punishments already, and the end is not yet. But I know you are tired, sick of this long string that does not benefit me any, perhaps excites more anger than pity in your mind, but I am too unhappy to care much now.

March 23rd continued—With an effort I break off my miserable lamentations and will write now for your pleasure, & perhaps may manage to repay you for the time spent reading my miserable letter. Billy has been sick with a bile [boil] near the small of his back ever since I wrote you before. I think now that is what gave him fevers, and made his head ache so badly, but I did not find out for several days that he had a bile coming. He has very little patience in his affliction and won't let a poultice stay on long enough to do any good. I don't know what I will do about opening it, he won't let me touch it— monday night he cried, the best part of the night, first with his bile, then his legs, then his head, then his chin, & then his arms. I never saw any one in such a fix. It may have been neuralgia. He has to sleep on his stomach, and cant sit down. I picked it a little with a needle this morning, & have just looked at it and squeezed it, and it ran a good deal of matter. I know I am mighty tired of him & his bile. When his head was hurting so bad that night, he thought of every thing he ever saw you do for the head ache, & at last said, "Ma make me a palet by the fire, and put a chair at the head & a pillow on it, & let me get on it, Pa does that way and it always cured his head, right quick" it was as much as I could do to persuade him to stay in bed. Yesterday morning quite early Mr Oliver stopped here on his return from the mill, and chatted an hour or so with me, & said that perhaps he and Mrs O would come over & spend a day with me this week. He expects to start the 28th or 29th and as I want to go to Mothers Friday next I thought I would finish this sheet and send it to the office saturday morning, and it ought to reach you several

16. Laurence Sterne, "Maria," in *A Sentimental Journey through France and Italy* (1768).

days before he will reach camp. In your last you say you had not heard from me in 17 days & thought sometimes that the buggy had upset & crippled me. I could not help wishing when I read that, [that] the buggy had upset, & broke my neck, leaving the children unhurt. I have writen every week & cant imagine what detained my letters, unless John Nix forgot to send the letter I sent by him to the office. It always frets me when you imagine any evil has happened to me, for I long so for a telling misfortune to take away my life, that it frets me that it never happens, that I never get dangerously sick, never have been hurt in any way & never could hurt myself when I wanted to, and tried so hard. Walter took up a notion that Mr O was you and called him Pa all the time he stayed here, asked for his knife, and hung around him like it was you. I could not make him believe that it was not you. He is like Mary I guess cant remember faces, there is not the slightest resemblance between him.

Sat morning March 26th Dear Will, I intended writing to you yesterday morn but Aunt Cinda & Uncle Mc came in early, and I could not write & after dinner I came up to mothers. Wednesday morning [it] rained in torrents, and next day they split rails, and yesterday eve commenced again plowing up & planting corn in the old sandy field. Myers thinks a good deal of the new ground will not have to be planted over, but cant tell positively until he gets through planting the old field—if our team was good I would not mind it half so bad. Mother don't have to plant over. The corn was not killed near so bad up here as on Lake Creek. Since I wrote the 23rd Old Parmer died, two pigs and one shote, which last Joe says choked to death. I think he got cotton seed perhaps. I tell you it is gloomy times. They still talk of more tax to pay, on negro's on farming tools & every thing, if so I can't pay without money, they say you will have to pay about $1.25 on negros now. I have about 100 dollars left—and I know I have not spent any foolishly, or for luxuries. I don't know what is to become of me. Babe wants my Piano badly and I may sell it to her if mother is willing for her to buy, but I don't feel like spending it on the nasty mean negros, and won't do it. I wish I did not have but two or three enough to make bread for the children, and wait upon me & them. Do for God sake make some arrangements before the next year comes, to dispose of them some way.

Billy is suffering with his bile yet—the rest of the little torments are well. I have many things to write you, but havent time, and fear I won't have time after I reach home to write by Oliver, or he will start the 28th or 29th. I am about to start Bob to the Post office, and must close. Susan has disolved partnership with Uncle Mc, I can't tell you all but will write as soon as I go home, & send by mail if cant by Oliver

Your[s] with love
Lizzie S Neblett

Galveston
Mar 27th/64

Dear Lizzie

It is a natural selfishness of human nature and particularly of sick human nature to become garrulous of self. Therefore let me unburden myself in that respect as quickly as possible before proceeding to other more important or interesting things. Last Thursday I had a violent attack of flux which continued all day & did not check up until ten at night although I commenced taking medicine at twelve that day. Was very sick and perfectly prostrated by bed time suffering the most sickening pains. Sent for Dr Fisher but before he came the medicine began to operate & the bloody mucous discharge had almost ceased. He gave me dose of morphine. I rested well that night. Been troubled with pain in head and bowels with billious operations all the time. Yesterday had fever & severe head ache and had to repeat the medicine I first took. Slept little last night, but the medicine bringing billious operations this morning. I feel very well—free of fever and headache. I think the flux is entirely arrested & I may not have to take any more medicine. For the last three days I have been living on rice—a very small quantity at that but it is very well I use it in small quantities for I had to give $2.50 for one pound. This is written very badly but it is not caused by sickness for I am lying on my bed on my back and therefore cannot write steadily.

John S[cott] has called in twice since I have been sick. Yesterday I was surprised at the ungainly figure of Tom Walker protruding in my door with John. He was after his negro. He looked around at my splendid room & good bed & remarked he thought I was doing well. I told him I thought it as beautiful as a whited sepulcher and quite as cheerful. To explain[,] since my sickness I moved up stairs in a vacant room in one corner where it is silent as the grave except when the echo of foot steps from out rooms creeps through with hollow muffled tread. Walker staid about an hour told me that there [are] eight cases of small pox at Mr Forresters who you know lives two miles of Pa's. I only slept three hours last night by the town clock which sleeplessness was very convenient for I did not finish taking the medicine in broken doses until two O clock and I had to give it to myself. So you see "all things for the best" though retrospective glances are the only ones that see sickness in that light. I believe I thought enough to make a respectable look in self last night. I thought of a great many things or thoughts I would write you, but cant recall them to day. Just before day I dreamed of seeing you so vividly in *dishabille* (in your night gown) sitting up in the bed in the act of getting out, one foot and leg bare up to the knee. I thought I admired your foot so much, and perhaps this was not singular. For I always thought you had the prettiest foot & waist I ever saw. I had rather put my arms around you than any one I ever saw. & so I thought in my dreaming of you about a week since. But I expect you will think this rather romantic for a sick man. Well speaking of feet puts me in mind of shoes. I recollect that you have a nice pr of sewed shoes which riped of the soles. If you send them down by Oliver I will have them repaired?

You recollect that I told you in one of my letters that Congress would do something with the confed[erate] money which would effect it greatly. And so it has, I learn it fell in a few days in Houston to 30 for one & since 50 for one & that most of the stores are closed. I was surprised when you told me that your Mother had been selling cotton. I thought she had more Confederate money than she wanted to keep. She could have sold a part of her bonds for confederate money. I do not believe bonds or money will be worth any thing when our independence is achieved. I think she might sell some cotton for gold & silver and if she does I will ascertain. If you can procure my stock pea seed do so & plant in the new ground bottom. It will do to fatten hogs on or any thing else. I left word that the fence around Jims field adjoining ours should be kept up so as to keep cattle & horses out. If this is done it will afford very good pasture & there is a never failing spring in it which will save great trouble in watering. I think like you about Myers—he is a fool & cruel almost as a beast. But I think you pursue bad policy in concealing from the negroes that you condemn his cruelty. They will cease to hope for any protection from you & you will loose [*sic*] your influence over them. What he does wrong I would condemn—openly—what they do wrong I would likewise. Pursue your own course with him & if he gets mad & quits let him do so & get Rivers to assist you—but dont have an Irish quarrel, act discreetly & with dignity and if need be dismiss him by a note under my direction & authority. He should not be carrying to you for the negroes. They think he is afraid of them. You misunderstood my expression of regrets at seeing you in that old curtain calico dress. It was not because of its effect on me but because it made me feel sad that your wardrobe was so scant. Well I hope & think the war will end in the course of twelve months. I think Bankruptcy will force that on the North unless they gain greater victories than they have heretofore. This seems to be a general opinion. And I notice that some of the Northern papers regard Bankruptcy as to be the arbiter of the quarrel & Harbinger of peace. I am not surprised that you feel lonely out there in the woods. Cant you get Mary H[aynie] to visit you often. She is the most intelligent woman I know of & your best company. I forgot to ask Walker yesterday about her arm but thought of it before he had been gone five minutes. I have not yet heard from Ma's & Nelia's arms, I sent Ma some Oleanders[17] a few days ago.

Tell Joe that I say if he does not sell the mule out the neighborhood that I intend to kill it as soon as I come home & that will not be long off. And I will if it is not done before. How are your potatoe seed doing.

Mar 28th/64 Tom Walker has just called—will start back in few minutes. So I stop & will write again in a few days to let you know I am getting along.

At Home
Monday evening March 28th 1864
Dear Will,

As I came home yesterday evening from mothers I went by Mr Olivers to find out when he would start for camps, so that I would be ready with my letter. He says he will start wednesday and in order to give myself plenty of time to write in I commence this evening. I brought a bucket of butter from mothers to send to you—you will find it the nicest and sweetest butter you ever eat. I find it so at least. Mothers cows run on the rye at night & the calves in the day. I fear we won't make butter enough to do us this summer. Bettie sent Sandy after that "Red head" cow last week, and Kate had a little quarrel with him about the cow—told him that "Miss Lizzie ought not to let them take Red Head, that she was the best cow we had["]—and Sandy said, it was their cow that Miss Bettie said, you had never paid for the cattle consequently they are not ours. If Jim wants to, he may send and take every cow we have in the pen, but if he don't intend for us to have them I don't like to be at the trouble of getting them up for him. If John finds out that mother let me have the butter for you he will be mad. I expect Susan will find it out from the negros and I don't care. She told Uncle Mc that I created more excitement at

---

17. Oleander is an attractive, flowering evergreen shrub. It is also poisonous.

Alston's party than any one else—that I went there with negro Bill & went home with him. He told her she was mistaken, he went home with me, I expect she wrote John the same tale only fixed up in a more vulgar manner. She told Uncle Mc that I had raised a great stink since I came in to this neighborhood, but he did not ask her how, nor about what. You say you are sorry that I had to make my debut at Alson's—I am not sorry that I went and you forget that "beggars must not be choosers" it was the only invitation I got to any of the frolic's, and I went finding as good people as I am there. Old Alston & his sons may be thieves, perhaps worse, but the female portion of the family all nice ladylike people, and I have never heard any thing against them, but I have no idea of cultivating their acquaintance. No my debut, and my final farewell, my exit, were made the same night. Mother Babe & I went up to the Dutch store, saturday mother bought some few articles a beautiful calico dress, for $250 for one thing. I spent Mary's egg money for her got her 3 yds of pink muslin at $12 per yd, can make her a dress short sleeves & low neck. She is delighted with it. Mary will be very fond of dress, and will no doubt shed many a tear, because she will have to go without a great deal that her taste & fancy will desire. Fact is if we don't make more money than we have ever done, I don't see how we will dress and educate her & the other children, we cant do it. I know how bad it is, to desire to go into company and forced to stay at home for the want of proper apparel. I never desire much to have fine dressing, yet still I have stinted myself woefully all my life. Pa's anger was a restraint before marriage, & since my marriage your or rather our poverty, and a feeling that I always had that if you did not desire to see me dress, I should not dress for other people. If I could recall the past I would act differently. I would spend a little more on my self than I did. But that is past, and if I haven't a black silk to be burried in I have a white dress which will look well enough for me.

When we returned from the Dutch store we found Ellen Van Horn and Charley at mothers just from Houston. Dick came up as far as Navasota, & returned to H[ouston]. A part of his business down was to get his papers fixed up for a final exemption. Dr Oldham signed a final exemption, but when ordered to report & showed his papers was told that he ought to have the whole board of Dr's names on the paper. I forgot to ask Ellen if he got it fixed, but I judge not from the fact that she said he spoke of going into business at Houston & I expect it is the printer's business & there keep out of service. Ellen looks very badly—yet I had rather have her health than my good health & a house full of children, and if we should live together in peace &

your sort of love, an other five. But you know I will kill myself and run the risk of going to the devil before that ever happens. I don't think I am perfectly sound now in one respect, and another accident requiring certain drugs and a course of gymnastics would fix me for life, if it did not send me to another world. But it is worse than folly to write talk or think upon this subject[.] I have made up my mind to live & die without an other child let it cost what it may, and have dug a grave, and buried there the hope of ever being any thing but a poor miserable wretch, to whom God shows but little mercy in preserving from the grave. But over this grave of hope I sit & think and shed many tears. I found it hard to give up all hope of happiness, and it seems to me, if I could only look back upon a period of time wherein I was happy, I could bear it better but to bury the hope, without ever tasting of its fruits is bitter indeed.

While I was at mothers Friday night, I walked out in the hall of the old house, and the floor was flooded with moonlight, and the same old trees that knew my childhood, and maidenhood, made fantastic figures upon the floor, and with mighty force the past rushed back upon me. Time and distance were anhilated, and I felt as I did when we stood then lover and maiden, hand clasped in hand, & hearts warmly devoted, looking forward to the time when we should be husband & wife, and our days filled with happiness. Oh no cloud darked my prospective sky, children pain, poverty, toil, was all forgotten, and I thought only of being always with you & striving to do all in my power for your happiness. I asked myself where were all my hopes, framed in this spot upon many a moonlight night, years ago, with you standing by my side. Some few I realized, but the last wreck of those hopes were buried fifteen months ago, and the place & scene reserected them and it was like looking upon the face of the beloved dead. But of one thing I am glad—you have been happier than I, you have realized some of your dreams. You desired children no doubt, you have had them cheap, they never cost you a single pain, & so far have never caused you a single heart ache. You found me worse than you expected, but a better wife than some men have. A very selfish one it is true—but I am the more to be pitied, for I am an unwilling slave, made so by nature, yet designed to be a slave.

Yet I have struggled with my bonds, been alternately filled with hope and despair until the warfare has exhausted me, and I again unlike woman generally, have given up all hopes of happiness at the price I have had to pay for it, and between two evils have tried to choose the smallest. But I am swayed not entirely by selfish feelings in my decision.

By the same mail that brought your last letter I rec[eived] one from Jane

[Teel]—she writes of herself more cheerfully than she used to do, and tries to persuade me that I ought to be happy, and makes me so envious by telling me that her baby Julie is almost six years old. My God why is it that every body who has tried preventives that I know of have succeeded but me—and they did not desire success half as ardently as I did, they did not hate children as I do, & yet they succeeded and I never delayed the matter but a few months, by the devilish things. Oh how often have I wished that I had died when Mary was born, I was better prepared then for death than I have ever been since, and how much suffering, both physical & mental would I have escaped. You would have forgotten me long ago, and have perhaps a much better, and no doubt a happier wife than you now have.

Bob Teel is a clerk in Coopwoods establishment, Coopwood is a Gov contractor for Lead, & has also a whole sale establishment in San Antonio.

Teusday march 29th. We have to send out tithe corn to Lindley's near mothers, & they want it now. Mr Oliver's wagon is not in running order so they take their corn in our wagon and had to make two loads, and will return this eve when I will send & get their oxen, & bring the wagon home & tomorrow send mine. I gave mine in a[t] 40 bu[shels], and put one big load of corn & one small load in the pen not allowing myself the 100 bu[shels],— Myers says he don't think there is near 40 bu[shels] in the pen, & by rights I ought to have 10 bu[shels] out of the pen. He says he has been told that if the corn don't hold out for what it is given in for, it has to be made up, if ours falls short, as I expect it will, it will near about scrape the crib to make it up. Joe's old mule has got fat on the Gov corn I reckon, the mule is fat, & runs now in the Gilmore field. I thought sometime ago I would never live on the place with Joe's mule or horse, but I find that necessity compells me to do many things I rebel at, when they first present themselves. The negros care no more for me than if I was an old free darkey—and I get so mad sometimes that I think I don't care if Myers beats the last one of them to death. I cant stay with them an other year alone, & next year we wont have any thing to farm with. We have 32 pigs marked—the old white & the spotted sow have 11 between them—very fine looking pigs. I reckon they are all that will be raised. We have no corn to feed to them. Sometimes I think I don't care, but I do care, yet I cant help myself. Myers says he will have to plant over about 80 rows in this new bottom field will finish tomorrow I reckon. Mother cant Gin my cotton her pick room is wedged full, in order to get seed to plant—but she says I can get her oxen to haul it down to Pa's which I will try and do next week, by sending Sarah in the field to plant cotton seed & let Thornton go.

Susan declare[d] that she won't take cotton from me, I'll have to pay her the money but I'll see her in Halifax first, and when I get clear of her & John I will stay clear. I asked John Nix about Calvin R asking Geor[ge] Alston as a waiter, & the girls refusing to stand with him. He says he knows that to be a lie, he was never asked to be a waiter. She told Uncle Mc that she thought it advisable to disolve partnership, that as Aunt was mad [at] her, she was affraid people would say they were too intimate, & ruin her character. I would not be surprised if she dont try to start some tale on me, about having Myers to attend to our farm—but no body pays any attention to what she says. Garrett is still at home. They tell me that his arm is very bad. The worst case of this poisonous matter in the neighborhood. His system was in a bad fix to receive it, which make his worse I reckon. Mary was telling me of Elisha Womack's sad misfortune last night, she heard it at school. He was thrown from a horse (early yesterday morning I think) near Jeff Haynie's, and his piece of arm broken near the shoulder, and one of his ribs broken. Mary said the children said Dr B[rown] said the ballance of his arm would have to be taken off. Poor Lish he is truly unfortunate. Abe Womack[18] has a detail for tanning, & so will be at home all the time—and I hear that George Alston has a detail for the same business & is going in with Old Keifer. Oliver told me that Abe told him that he was trying to get a detail for Jno Scott to work in the saddle shop at Anderson that belongs to the ordinance department. Susan is on her head about it. She did sell her cotton to Bro Jim, but was forced to sell to get money for taxes &c. Garrett came back in debt to Coleman $300. This last Tax law will rake us, you will have to sell your cotton to pay it with. Bassett failed to raise either a Co or a Battalion, and has accepted a position under Barnes as Quarter Master of the Militia *I think* but don't know whether he will be permitted to do so. Myers says he told him that he wished there wasent a negro this side of Africa, that they were more agrivation than profit. He has grown tired of the beauties mighty quick hasent he? Mother has done nothing farther with her business as Garrets executrix. Susan has never said a word to her neither has John. Susan told Mrs Oliver soon after John was here that there was a screw loose in that will and that Mr Scott would blow that sky high when he came home out of service. Mother don't seem inclined to push matters, as I would do, & have the thing settled up.

18. In 1860 Abe Womack Jr. (age 30) was a farmer living with his wife, Adaline (26), and two children. His real and personal property was valued at $7,000. TX Census 1860.

Billy's bile is well at last, it was a blood bile, & he suffered awfully with it.

Collins has made Mary's shoes at last. I wrote to him, & urged the matter up—and told him of his sow & pigs & offered $5.00 for her, which he accepted. One of the calf skins I bought was injured by being on the ground in the smoke house. I have hides enough or will have before the crop is made to establish a tan yard of my own. Mother's house is framed, & they are working on it. Mr Taylor worked there last week. John Nix has sent a petition to some one for a detail to act as mothers overseer, & she is to give him what she did Coleman. I have the good news to tell you that this bad baby of mine is a better child than she has ever been—she crawls very fast now, & climbs up by everything, will soon walk—was the proudest little thing you ever saw the first time she pulled up by the Lounge, she made many efforts before she succeeded, & after she got up, turned around, & looked at me & laughed like she was well pleased at her feat, & wanted me to see her. She is a very sensible child she had the comb this morning, and tried to pull my head down to her to comb my hair, tries to put my night cap on my head at night, and even notices when I put on a new dress, and she grows prettier I think. She has five or six teeth nearly through, one is partly through, and it don't seem to hurt her at all, is better in her bowels then she was two months ago—how glad I will be if she cuts all her teeth as easily. How I sigh and think what is it when we sum up all her little tricks, her evidence of sense, and expansion of brain, when she is only a poor miserable wretch of a female, doomed to bear children suffer, and if like me in her disposition, doomed to go to hell at last. I declare it would be a relief to me to know she and Mary were both dead. I havent the heart to stimulate Mary to apply herself to her books, or learn anything, the idea of her fate here after if she lives to marry spoils every thing with me. Better [to] be a fool than educated. "Where ignorance is bliss 'tis folly to be wise."[19] I reckon you think I am worse than usual on a certain subject, being a woman &c. The risk I ran when you were at home will account for it. I wish to God the law and the heart of man would sanction the killing of a wife when she gets to entertain the idea's and feelings I do on childbearing. It is has been the rock on which I have shipwrecked all my happiness.

Oliver says he will take your hat to you, I was in hopes you would get a hat like his. I am going to take it to Aunt Cindas & get her & John Nix who is there now to show me how to cut it down. I am affraid I will spoil it if I under-

---

19. Thomas Gray, "Ode on a Distant Prospect of Eton College" (1742).

take it by myself. I have given up all hopes of seeing you under six or seven months. The bucket I send you has 112 pounds of butter in it and I will be mad if you let any one steal that. Oliver promises to take care of it for you until you leave the office. I am so sorry to hear of your loosing [*sic*] your meat—if I have a good chance I will send you some more. Oliver says you can share theirs, the Co's meat as long as it lasts. Van H[orn] brought down a note on account for $100 dollars, from Kerr I think, which he will take in Con[federate] money, but I could not pay it, & I know you cant so it will have to run along.

I wish we could pay our debts, all of them. He paid 700 dollars for you and wants your place for that I think but he wrote to you I reckon from Houston. Our mare has a colt, and the negros at mothers say it looks like it is a fine colt, you did not tell me whether to send her again or not to Brown's—the colt is three or four days old—neither of mothers mares she sent have or are going to have a colt. Coleman made a bargain, no colt no pay. The horses at mothers are running on the rye field and are getting fat. We have Dick down here to hunt cattle on, & the children ride him to school in bad weather, & through the mud, but will send him back to eat rye soon.

I believe I have told you all the news and must close and go to Aunt Cinda's with your hat, and return early and send the butter and this letter over to Mr Olivers to night as he will start about 12 Ocl[ock] to night to reach the depot in time. Aaron Shannon is dead—died some time ago. The soldiers are stealing a good many horses as they pass through on their way to La. Has Nelia writen to you yet. I havent heard from them since you left. I fear their arms are not well yet. Mary Haynie's is not yet well. I send as you request the letter to Gen Magruder. I hope it may be of service to you in getting you home on a long stay at least. I have got the iron from Bookman's, expect it to be of much use to me. Good bye, and forgive every thing I have said amiss. Barnes has been dethroned and is now [a] *private* may be conscripted. All the militia have been put into Con[federate] service—Bassett is put out again but he'll not stay out long.

yours with eternal love,
Lizzie S Neblett

Galveston
Apr 4th/64

Dear Lizzie

Last Friday Oliver arrived bringing my hat, your letter and a bucket of butter. The latter was not broken far at all and I feel that you deprived yourself of it. It is certainly the best butter I ever ate. It came in very good time for I was fast getting up from a spell of sickness and could have found nothing more to my taste. I will see to it that it is not stolen. My sickness of flux left me with a cough & pain in chest and considerable debility. To day is the first that I have attended to any business. I should like very much to be at home until I could recruit my strength if for no longer. But I do not think I should wish to do so when as it seems to leave you with fresh material to feed your thoughts of melancholy and trouble. Your last letter makes me feel sad whenever I think of home, and if I were to start there to day I would feel rather sad whenever I thought of you and your unhappiness. You say you do not like children and that ours is a cause of unhappiness. Now I do not believe all of this for I am not willing to believe that mere philanthropy has caused you to attend to the children so devotedly in sickness & health. However they may suggest ideas which touch you in tender points and by this rob you of the pleasure you might otherwise feel.

Oliver did not stop with me more than half an hour before leaving for Pelican. You are giving yourself unnecessary trouble about our taxes. I will meet that by sale of some land at public auction in Houston. I believe I had rather do this than sell the cotton. The land I expect to sell is not much account but as good as Confederate money, which I regard as worthless except for taxes. You should not think of selling your piano to any one. We will get it down time enough for a house if the Yankees do not destroy it.

What do you mean by saying that you "ran such a narrow risk["] when I was at home last. Have you come unwell? You write as if you were pregnant again or rather you could not appear to be more distressed if you were.

You ask me if I have heard from Pa's since I left. I got a letter from Nelia on the 25th. She says her & Ma's arm are nearly well but they suffered a good deal. I heard day before yesterday that Pa's Gin House was burned. A man who came down on the train heard it from a passenger who came from the town of Washington. It must have occurred between the 25th & 29 & Oliver I think would have heard it & if he did he would have told me. So I do not much believe it. Nelia wrote that Sterling had been home two weeks on furlough, I had just started back.

Send the mare to Browns again. You can write a note in my name & say that I send her to be put by the insurance as she was last year. Make Bill take her down some Saturday evening so that he can return Sunday night.

Now about those cattle I do not wish you to give away to Bettie & let her have the cows. They are legally and rightfully ours. If Jim had sold them to any one else he would have been compelled to take confederate money contrary to his wishes. Jim never expected me to pay him in gold & silver while the war lasted & he did not wish Confederate money & if the cattle had all died it would have been my loss & not his.

I thought I would go back to the Co by this time but my health will not permit me to do so before the 1st of May. It is growing too late in the evening to write more now. I will finish in the morning.

Apr 6th I did not have an opportunity to finish this yesterday in time for the mail.

Corn is worth $20.00 per bus[hel] here. If I could get 50 bushels at $5.00 pr bushel in Grimes it would it would [sic] clear me about $600.00 or about enough to pay our taxes. I wonder if your Ma has any for sale at $5.00 per bushel. I think I can get sacks here by borrowing. I am not well yet yesterday I had a Diarrhea which with the piles[20] caused me to take opium & I was quite sick all day—feel much better to day. I suppose you have heard that a Yankee cavalry raid took Edgars Battery of light Arty, on the Sabine 120 above the mouth.[21] I would not be surprised if some of these raids do not penetrate Texas a considerable distance this Spring.

yours affectionately
Wm H. Neblett

At Home
Teusday April 5th 1864

Dear Will—

I will have a chance of sending to the office Thursday through Mrs Tom Collins, & for fear that I will be prevented from writing tomorrow I commence to day. Mrs Collins sends to the office three times a week, sent to day, and I am in hopes I will hear from you, for I am feeling quite uneasy about you, since I read your letter by Tom Walker. I have been dreading the spring months on account of your liability to get sick, have a spell of fever, or something during those months. I hope you are now well of the flux and that your Spring sickness is over with—but I fear you will have another spell this sum-

20. "Piles" was a common name for hemorrhoids.
21. William Edgar commanded the First Texas Battery in Colonel Thomas N. Waul's legion. The battery was captured March 21, 1864, at Henderson's Hill, Louisiana. Wright and Simpson, *Texas in the War*, 132.

mer. I have a right bad case on hand now. Bill has been sick now nearly a week—first had violent pain in his head over his eyes, which settled in one eye & it swelled up, so he could not see out of it, had it poulticed & it is now nearly well, he spits blood, & complains of great soreness & pain over the region of his right lung. I have applied my ear to his chest & can detect no rattling nor wheezing so I think the inflamation is in the living membranes of the chest. I am applying mustard giving peper, horse mint tea & black or Virginia snake root[22] & keep his bowells moving. Have given him a little Colomel.[23] He is scared to death, thinks he is going to die, & wants some thing done for him all the time. I don't feel alarmed about him, but truth is I don't care much.

I have lost all interest in the negro race—& if it was not for humanity's sake, I would let them all die as they got sick to be rid of them. Every day strengthens my determination not to live with them an other year if the war continues if there is any earth[l]y chance to avoid it.

Nance is now out dropping cotton seed in Bill's place, and Sarah got along so slowly spinning I was talking to her about it while in there this morning & she complained of the cards, & to see I set down & tried to card in them, & find they are ruined, and, as I suspected, Nance has been carding her children's heads in them, and has pulled the teeth almost straight. She knew I had a new pair, & did not care. I have been trying to get a wheel from Old Coody,[24] which he had promised me (before you were home) that I should certainly have it the 1st day of Apr by paying 12 dollars. I sent & got no wheel, but this sweet tale. He was out of corn, or rather he wanted corn, & if I would give him 10 bu[shels] corn he would let me have a wheel in two weeks, but if [I] did not let him have corn, he would be compelled to let those have wheels who could give corn. Now you know the 10 bu[shels] of corn would bring about 50 dollars in this money—and in times of peace, McCune says it would have brought right now $1.50 per bu[shel]—and wheels were $5.00 then. McCune (at whose house I was yesterday eve) says he heard Coody say he would fix the people by working for corn, or other produce, & thus save himself from

22. Horsemint is an herb that induces the expulsion of gas from the stomach and intestines and causes redness of the skin. Black snakeroot was used most likely as an expectorant.

23. Calomel or chloride of mercury was a common medicine of the day and was used as a cathartic or laxative.

24. In 1860 B. S. Coody (age 37) was a farmer married to E. S. Coody (30). He had personal and real property valued at $1,520. TX Census 1860.

the low prices in Con[federate] money that he is bound to charge soldiers family. I am going to write him a note, and insist upon having the wheel according to his promise for money & insinuate that it would be perhaps better or more congenial to his taste to take that, than the $11 per month privates pay—and if he don't let me have it I intend to feret out his plan of operation to avoid the confederate money from soldiers families, and will write you, & feel obliged if you will report him, & make him shoulder his musket as that old dutchman said. We are trying hard to get in a piece of cloth for dresses for Aunt Cinda me Kate & Mary & we will need another wheel then, to fill quills &c, and I have come to the conclusion which has been forced on me, I will have to spin or weave one or the other myself, and have been doubly anxious to get a wheel, to find out which I can stand to do best, spin or weave. So I heard that Coleman had a wheel at Mrs McCune's that she did not use, & went yesterday eve to see if I could not borrow it until I can get me one but failed, she was using it, came by Mrs Hurst & tried there, but had no success. The fix I find the cards in, & knowing the cause of it has disconcerted all my plans, they are very little better than the old cards I brought from Corsicana. I don't feel mad only grieved. Can hardly keep from crying about it. To think I have to clothe & feed them, and they care no more for the difficulties in the way than they care for me, and no body can tell where our next cards will come from. She asked me once for the old cotton cards to comb her head in, & I refused telling her I would have to make rope through them, & save my good cards for cloth making—& have always preached to them of the high prices & the great scarcity of cards, to get them to take good care of them—but she knew I had a new pair in the house, and she thought I would make out some how to get more, & to clothe them.

To show you how Joe treats me. We have a mule of Jim's laying off with, have had him about two weeks, have been compelled to still keep mothers oxen also, it is necessary to keep the mule tied & gave up old Sams Rope to plow him with, & ordered Joes rope put on Sam, was told that Joe said it was broken all to pieces which I believe to be a lie. He knew I had a new grass rope in the house, & he did not want his rope used—since then I wanted to go to Aunts to fix your hat sent for Joes bridle & Nance said she heard Joe say he was going to hide his bridle, so I rode a blind bridle. The children had one bridle at school, & they were plowing with the other one. But like the sheep before the slaughter I am dumb. I get mad when I talk to them, & that only affords them merriment, so I submit in weakness never saying one word. It used to rouse my anger, such conduct as the negros now have, but now, feeling my entire inability to help myself I only feel like crying when things get too bad.

I find McCune is banking on the idea of that Co (I) being disbanded, & to come home on 30 days furlough, but being less hopeful I dont plume myself on any such an idea. The boat may be repaired, but there are many places beside home to be sent to. Coleman wont leave 'till 1st of May, is acting as recruiting officer, & has got a number so McCune says. Thornton went down to Pa's last Sat night, and returned with very bad news. Brought a note from Nelia but like her she did not mention one word about it—all I know is what Thornton tells. Last week Pa's Gin house, and all it contained was burned down. He had 15 bales which baled up, and the Gin house, pick room and a cotton house, which was near the Gin all full—it happened in the night, and suspicion rests on Sterling's Willis. They took him up & whipped him, but he denies knowing any thing about it. Pa sent for Negro dogs that night, & put on the track & they went right to Willis' house where he was, did this twice—of course some one set it on fire. Thornton says Pa has two or three other cotton houses full, but I dont know, I intended sending my cotton down this week, so it just missed the burning. Sterling has been home, two weeks ago on a short furlough. Nelia says looks better than she ever saw him, which I am glad to hear. Robert was 35 miles of Alexandria on the 19th March the last news they had of him was well, & like to have been captured by the Yanks. Went to Alexandria to carry some prisoners, when he returned Walkers division[25] had retreated, & the Yanks were pursuing he could see the dust caused by the division six miles off, & made for it in a round about way, at double quick time, & got to the rear of the division just in time. They caught several of the straglers.

Nelia says Ma's & her arms are well at last tho' she says nothing done any good but one application of mercurial ointment and she took enough [Blue] mass to kill a horse, tho' Ma did not take so much. As usual Ma was sick with the headache. She had received the Oleanders you sent. I do have such an admiration for your mother's character Will, and I know I love her well, even as Ruth did Naomi—& believe I would act the same part to her that Ruth did

---

25. After being promoted to major general November 8, 1862, John G. Walker commanded a division (made up primarily of the Fourteenth, Sixteenth, Seventeenth, Eighteenth, and Nineteenth Texas Infantry Regiments) in the Trans-Mississippi Department. This unit saw action at Mansfield, Louisiana, on April 8, 1864, and Pleasant Hill, Louisiana, on April 9, 1864. Wright and Simpson, *Texas in the War,* 164.

to her mother in law, under the same circumstances—tho' in a great many
other particulars I am far from being at all like the lovable character of Ruth.[26]
But I do bank largely upon the warmth the durability strength & unselfishness
of my affections, and when this is said, 'tis all the good that can be said of me,
all that is to be admired, by a refined judge. Yet in this even I fall far short of
your Ma's devotion, her great charity and extreme unselfishness. I never knew
a human being who could compete with her in this particular. She is all that
woman should be, a perfect type of what God intended a true woman to be,
and tho' I despise my calling & rebell at it most furiously, I can and do admire
the character of a true, patient, loving and faithful wife and mother. Nature
made me out of coarser clay than many women were moulded from, and at
her door do I lay the blame. But I intend no sentimentality in this, for the
pressure of circumstances makes me feel usually very prosaic.

I am going by Mrs Olivers this evening & she promised to go to George
Lancasters[27] with me. I go to try and get Mary another pr of shoes made, &
the pair you wrote of repaired, if possible. Mary won't wear the ones Collins
made to school, saving them for sunday wear. Poor child, she is getting old
enough to feel her poor outfit, and she gets mightily put out, more grieved
than angry tho' else I would not pity her. She is too large to go barefooted, if
I can help it, so I will try & get Lancaster to make her a pr out of the skin,
like yours you have had made. Uncle Mc promised to make me a cast for her
foot (he has made several) three weeks ago, but I cant wait for that it may be
three months coming. If I had a cast I could get Major to make her a pr that
would do very well. I must write a little about the children, as I believe it gives
you pleasure to hear from them. Mary & Bob are learning very well Mary in
particular. I never knew a more studious child. She urges Bob to study goes
over his lessons with him, and is as much gratified as Bob if he gets [a]head
in his class. He is now in the First reader, and spells by heart, is in a class with
Emmet Haynie, and Mary is with Attie Haynie.[28] Those Haynie children are
very smart, precocious, & ambitious. Billy was highly pleased with the letter
you wrote to him & Bob. He manifests much greater interest in you & your

26. A reference to the story of Ruth in the Old Testament.

27. George Lancaster (age 30 in 1860) was a farmer living with his wife, Harriet (30), with
personal and real property valued at $950. TX Census 1860.

28. In 1860 Emmett (age 4) and Diranthea (age 5) Haynie lived with their parents, Thomas J.
and Euny J. Haynie. Thomas J. Haynie was the brother of Lizzie Neblett's good friend Mary
Haynie. TX Census 1860.

welfare then formerly. I think I will start him to school this fall. Walter is as much a trouble as ever, he has been a greater pest to me than ever Billy or Bob were at his age, and lastly the little cross hussy. She is notwithstanding her being so unwelcome, before & after her birth, the only object that can beguile a smile from me in my gloomiest times. I can't resist her bright cunning look and her winning ways and at such times I clasp her to my heart with as fond feelings as I ever did any of them. Poor darling she can't help being here. She stands alone sometimes now, & her teeth don't hurt her yet. No doubt those who notice your letters think you have a very voluminous correspondent, but they don't know how selfish a one, for I tell you all my troubles & annoyances, which may have a tendency to disturb you, & yet do no good, only in a selfish way relieves me a little, but when you think thus, look on the other side, and view mentally your five children & ask yourself if some body did not forget self a few times for your pleasure. Would to God that pleasure had not borne living fruit. I am feeling very uneasy and anxious about you—for if I have despaired of happiness with you God knows I don't want you [to] die, or to suffer.

Wednesday April 6th While I think of it let me tell you the remainder of the news from Pa's as Thornton tells it. Both Pa's buggy and the wreck of his old carriage were burned up at the Gin—and Nelia writes that Mr Wm Forester has had nine cases of small pox [the] last one [a] negro woman with it. Both Mrs & Miss Forester have had it—they entertain great fear of its spreading. I went to Lancasters yesterday eve, & he won't promise to do the work under two weeks. If I could get a cast I would hire Major to make her a pr at night out of the piece of Goat skin I have. I came back by Mrs Hurst hoping to find a letter there from you, was disappointed but found my paper, and a letter from Mollie Graham. She got her Pa to go immediately for that old Piano, & she has it at her house—for which I am now very sorry, because he did not conform to my terms. She said nothing about his making a new box & of course he did not, & will not now, what the rats have left of it will go now— and even old confederate money is better than nothing I could buy me a sack of coffee with it. I presented so many difficulties, in way of her getting it, that I did not think she could get her Pa to go for it. It being locked, and one of the strings to be mended, & it tuned and a box made before it could be moved—but she has it. I told Van Horn if she sent not to let her have it. But Van H was not there when she sent of course. She sent one dollar to pay postage on the key. It has troubled me so much that I think now only of selling it but don't know what price to put on it. I would take a pair of large young mules for it, and if I never have a carriage they will do for the negros to ride. She writes that the music and cover are badly cut by the mice, & they have gnawed around the edges of the piano, the damage inside of course she cant tell. I have writen a note to Mr A Brown, asking as a favor for him to buy from the servants some tobacco for you. Have no doubt told you how scarce the article is. I will get you some if possible & send it by the first chance. You have so little pleasure & enjoyment of any kind that I am willing to exert my self to gratify your taste for the nauseous weed, tho' think my exertion to obtain & your devotion to the weed, are both worthier of a better cause. If it was not injurious I should not say a word.

Babe wrote to me that mother was grieved to death about her taxes, and I know Babe is grieved to death about her dressing. She is almost if not quite crazy on that subject—and it annoys mother very much. They will get through planting cotton this week, and will probably get [done] Saturday. Joe and old Myers had an encounter the day I sent Joe for the wheel. I got a yoke of oxen from Mrs Oliver and her wagon and sent Kate & Nance both to the field. Myers said Joe could have brought the wheel on old Sam [the] horse and said he would hurry on to Mrs Olivers & make him leave the wagon & bring the wheel on his shoulder home—he met him in the woods this side of Mrs O's told him to walk faster which he said Joe dident mind, & he got down & told him to pull off his coat he was going to whip him, Joe told him he had not done any thing to be whipped for & walked on, he told him to stop but he kept on & turned out the road, told him to get back in the road & Joe told him no he was coming home, & was coming through the woods. Says he left Myers standing in the road. Myers told about the same Joe did, & added he was surprised for he thought he would pull of[f] his coat, & take the whipping. Joe came & told me all about it, the next time Myers came I told him not to whip Joe, as long as he done his work well, & that he must not shoot at him, that he might run away & we might never get him, & if he never done me any good he might my children. So he has not touched him nor said any thing to him. You see what a fool he is. He wants to leave when the crop is made, and I think I'll tell him to go, I think he will take a part of the crop in payment. It is true the negros won't make that pasture unless there is some one to make them, but I can't help it. That fence of Jims which joins ours is so badly rotten that it [is] impossible to keep the stock out without putting many new rails on it, so Myers says, he has had it fixed up several times, but the stock soon break it down—so we will have to use our part only as a pasture & drive to water—or learn the oxen to live without water, the latter will be the negros plan I know. I have given out all idea of fixing the yard fence, have given up entirely—never felt so hopeless on all subjects and so little like resisting the difficulties in the way in my life. I cant live with the negros another year.

Bill is mending slowly he has been quite dangerous & is not out of danger yet. Billy is complaining to night of the head ache, and is fevered. There is something the matter with his Gums, I fear it is the disease I had two years ago. Walter had no return of fever. I suppose it was cold that caused it. The baby has a fresh cold, taken during this cool weather, was feverish two days & nights with it, and the worst baby I know of or ever saw. I havent whipped her in a week or so. Aunt Cinda asked me if I wrote you about my whipping her, and was some what surprised that you did not schold me a little for it in your letter, but, I thought, you know how bad she was & did not blame me, tho' you might pity her. I fear she will always be cross & fretful, and is fated to live a most miserable life. I learned from Jack Oliver to day that his Pa will stay at home two weeks longer, he says he has got 12 recruits, among them McCune and John Roan. Oh I wish you could have come home to stay a month. If you can get a furlough after you go to your Co I would do so, and that won't prevent your coming in the summer on detail will it? The spring is very late, the red oak trees are blooming, the buds of the post oak's have just commenced swelling, a great many show no sign of life yet. The freeze did not seem to hurt my little peach trees. I will send this up by Thornton when he goes with the cotton in the morning and send to the office when I hope to get a letter from you. Mary will answer your letter soon, she & Bob are learning very well. Mrs Buckley has a full school now. Sarah has the finest quantity of tobacco plants up, has enough to plant our whole field. I intend for her to plant a big patch this year, for your benefit[.] Uncle Mc bought $5 worth of Sarah, & could not chew that, & bought 1 lb of Dr Brown's negros at $6, and it is so strong it makes him sick. He thinks as I do also, that Dr B lets his negros sell his tobacco for him, he getting all the money. Joe said Mr B weighed what he got from the negro for you. Write me all the little minutia of your life your thoughts feelings &c. I fear I tell you too many of my thoughts & feelings—Good bye,

> your affectionately
> Lizzie S Neblett

Galveston
Apr 11th/64

Dear Lizzie

I have been anxiously expecting a letter for two days & to day it came. It is just ten days since yours by Oliver came and it seems much longer than that.

I began to look forward two or three days in advance of the time for receiving it & it does seem long before it comes. You cannot take that interest in mine that I do in your letters for mine can have but little of interest, as I am here by my self as it were while you & the children & every thing else touching on pecuniary interest are subjects of interests to me. For this reason I often feel at a loss what to write about until I commence, but once commenced I manage very easily to fill a sheet with something. I was surprised to hear that Molly Graham had your piano. I did not know that you had told her to get it. You write to me that you had a note in to do so. I hope you required a new piano box to be made so that when you send after it there will be that much made or saved rather. I thought you had sent the key up by Van Horn. If she does not seem impressed with the idea that she is to have a *new* box made and not the *old one repaired* I would try and make that impression on her mind very clearly. There will be no use in making the new box until you notify her of your desire to move it home. I think she will take as good care of it as any one. Do not think of selling it, and particularly for confederate money. I am a little (but not much) surprised that your Ma should be troubled about her taxes. She must have over a thousand dollars of interest due her on her bonds. Every thing is going up or rather Confederate money is going down fast. Coffee $20. pr lb, Bacon $2.00, Molasses $12 per gallon, sugar $3. to $5. per lb., corn meal $17. per bus[hel] (some time since) & more I expect now. If Coody does not let you have that wheel at the contract price let me know & I will try & have him ordered into service. If you had the corn 4 bushels would have been enough. But if he is not willing to take confederate money he should come in the army & take $11.00 per month. I saw Sim Thomas a few days ago. He belongs to Walkers Battery now here. He is trying to exchange with a fellow in Co (I). Now let me tell you how to direct a letter in ship shape.

W H N.
Co (I) 20th Regt Infantry
Galveston

Sim Thomas appears to be as good natured & smiling as ever. Oliver was here to day to get some furloughs signed—told me he had gotten a letter from home—had good stand of corn all well. He did not stay but a few minutes. Day before yesterday (9th) we heard by telegraph of the battle near Mansfield La on the 8th between our forces & the Yankees—that we had driven them back captured about 2000 prisoners 6 pieces of artillery—lost heavy on both sides. Since we hear very little of importance—no doubt another fight occurred next day—I feel anxious to hear from Robert.[29] He must have been in the fight. I feel more anxiety about Ma than Robert—she will get sick with anxiety about him. I expect it was a terrible battle against great odds. Raw troops always fight desperately or cowardly—one extreme or the other. I have been feeling very uneasy about the crops this year. These Northers must retard the growth of vegetation very much. I fear the wheat crop has been ruined by the cold, Flour is worth $2.50 per lb here. Tho the weather did not have any thing to do with the high prices. Tell Mary she owes me a letter. I am glad you are having her a pr of shoes to wear to school made. She is getting too large to go bare footed. She is growing up so fast it frightens me. Ten years more she will be grown. Does not the thought of it make you feel old. Well there is one thing certain We must convert some of our dead property such as land into some thing paying a quicker profit. I hope this war will not last more than through this year and then I can go about.

I am well and up again. Yesterday (sunday) John S[cott] & I took dinner at Shackelfords got a fine dinner among the articles were green pears. Shackelford was just up from a long spell of Rheumatism. He always appears to be very glad to see us. John goes out about once a week. I go about once a month. While writing the above an order by telegraph comes for 5 Co of Pyons Regt to proceed to Anderson Texas. For which purpose, I do not know. A raid may be feared on the Ordinance there or at Huntsville. Or it may be that they are wanted there to move to any point East or North. I hope you will try and get some pea seed. Do not let your potato crop suffer, plant all the ground by last of May if you have to water. It takes very little moisture to make them grow in Apr & first part of May. I heard that Pa's Gin house was burned & wrote to you about it, but did not place much credit in the report. I wrote to Nelia about it. I am expecting a letter every day from her. Two or three of the town negroes were detected here Saturday night trying to go to the Yankees. They were going to steal a boat. Two white men is said to have been at the head of the affair one of them has been identified. If McCune banks upon Co (I) being disbanded & sent home while the boat is being repaired he is bound to

29. The Battle of Mansfield, Louisiana, on April 8, 1864, drove the Federal advance on Shreveport back to Pleasant Hill. The following day another battle would be fought at Pleasant Hill, resulting in a Union victory. Will Neblett's brother Robert was a private in Company D of the Eighth Texas Infantry Regiment and was killed in the Battle of Pleasant Hill. Long, *Civil War Day by Day*, 482–83.

fail for he is banking on fictitious captial. There will be another boat to guard when the Bayou City is being repaired.

At Home
Wednesday April 13th/64

Dear kind, indulgent & forgiving Will,

Dont smile at my odd commencement for from my heart comes forth all those adjectives, which prefix your name. All this & more are you are to me; and when I read your letter of the 6th inst last Saturday at Mrs Jeff Haynie's, I felt my great inferiority in many things to yourself, & what I should be or strive to be to you. I am very selfish where my sorrow is concerned, & so wrapt do I become in my own grievances that I forget that I may by a selfish & useless indulgence of an expression of grief at least mar the peace & happiness of another who loves me well, perhaps better, for being the unintending cause of the most rebelious unhappiness I have ever known. You were sick when you read my letter by Oliver, and I know it did anything but cheer you—and have felt sorry as I always do after writing my most miserable letters to you. At the time I felt that my sorrow is greater then any ones and that I must impart it. I write too much from the dictates of the heart to be a pleasant correspondent to those who pity sympathize & love me, and I doubt not that I inflict more pain than pleasure upon you by writing. I may be ascribing to your nature more sympathy & impressibility than you really possess—for I remember that you tried before we were married, to teach me that I did not have the power of inflicting as much pain upon my lovers by harsh treatment as I fancied I had—but be that as it may I feel sorry that I cant write calmly, if not cheerfully even when I feel most miserable, for I know that it all does no good, the past is irremediable, & the future is full of uncertainty. But my feelings always discard reason & philosophy. When I am not grieved about my own causes for unhappiness I am grieved for your supposed woes in being united to a woman of so gloomy a disposition, one who is so bitterly opposed to childbearing, and finds so little comfort in the children for whom I have suffered so much. But you are more of a philosopher than I am, and must cast all distressing or sad thoughts of me far from you. I am really not worth your kindness & sympathy. You say you would like to be at home long enough to recruit your strength if no longer, but add you should not wish so, as it seems to leave me with fresh material for unhappiness. Now by this I know that you would not have made an effort to come home if you had thought it possible to do so—and this makes me think of the probable future if you should be fortunate enough to return from service. But no use to dwell on this & let us both hope that some merciful disaster will sweep me from your path if you are permitted to return to your home.

You ask me if I have been unwell? No I have not, but I have had some kind of a womb affection, and it distressed me so much, by fears that I might be pregnant. There has always seemed to be such a fatality attending me in that particular. I had symptoms like I had with my present babe, but I have recovered almost entirely from the womb affection, & the other symptoms have left, and my fears are quieted. I spent the day at Mrs Jeff Haynies on Sat and got little Jack Hurst to call by with my letters, as he came from the Post office. Since Bill has been sick she has brought my mail for me, I have furnished the horse to go on twice. She is very anxious to hear from her husband has been looking for him a long time, & there has been a rumor afloat that Story's Co[30] was captured in La, but she don't believe it now, tho' her last letter from Collins was dated 8th March.

Bill is getting well fast now, was in a critical situation for nearly a week, I had to blister his chest, his forehead & back of his neck, the blister is complained of more than any thing else now—on the 7th inst, we had quite a storm here. It came up in the evening and when it began to blow & rain it was as dark as night, I was looking every moment for the children from school but the rain came, the hail almost deafened me, & the wind blew like the trees would be almost uprooted, and I commenced crying, for I felt if the limbs of the trees did not blow down on them they would be frightened almost to death. In the midst of it Kate came rushing in, saying that Bill & all his bedclothes were getting wet, it was pouring down in the kitchen, I then made them set him in a chair, wrap him up & hold an umbrella over him, & Joe Sam & Thornton brought him in the house, where I had to fix up a bed, out of cotton, & a piece of bagging, and cover him with a blanket that kept dry & the ironing quilt. He was spitting blood, & scarcely able to hold himself up. I made some strong composition, & added lobelia, & made Kate give him tea all through the night when I would wake up, and he had no back set. I expect or think it was Pneumonia he had—as soon as I could have a horse caught I sent out to hunt the children up, found them at the negro cabins, at Sallies

30. A. D. Story was a captain in the regiment of O. Young, commander of the Eighth Texas Infantry.

place—just reached there as it began to rain, they made a fortunate escape. It blew off the top of a dead tree in the yard. Sarah was in the house with me & she made more fuss about the children than I did, she cried, and talked & wrung her hands, & Billy cried, & kept saying "Ma why don't you send after them" & it was hailing a while & then pouring down rain, & the wind blowing a gale. I could not help hoping all the time that they reached those cabins & stopped there. Mother & Babe came down sunday & said it was a worse storm up there in the prairie than here blew off the tops of several of Buck Walkers negro cabins.

The negros have finished planting cotton, are now breaking up & checking off the potatoe & Tobacco patches—when that is done will begin to run round the corn with the sweeps, I can't tell you whether it is a good stand of corn or not for I never thought to ask Myers. My garden looks badly I fear I won't raise any thing in it this year. No more of the oxen have died, but one of our calves have died, it was about two months old, had the scours.[31] I have not sent the hides to Ferrell yet, sent me word to send them next week. I fear he will be guilty of some yankee trick, I think I will go & see him & make my bargain about the pay & try & get my bark ground on his mill. I sent Coody a note, he wrote a polite one back, saying he had to pay so high for lumber, and "me & my family must starve," & his arm had rose, & he could not work for any body, & had not promised me a wheel for 12 dollars, he was to have the corn for the wheel he was to make for me, but he would try & have me a wheel done in 10 days for $15. He makes a better wheel than any one near here, & will try & get it for $15 from him. He is a grand old rascal, & old Myers says he will tell him next time he sees him of the lie he told about not promising me a wheel for $12. John Nix has got a detail for overseeing for Mother but she is now sorry for it, says he is too lazy to go to the field, has never been in the field but twice, & set in the house all day & laughs & talks with Babe, & goes to see Bettie Kelly. He told Babe if he got a detail for oversee for mother, that he was coming down to Lake Creek & get a walnut stock have it sawed up, & go to making furniture. Mother thinks he is in the notion of fixing to get married. Bettie Kelly takes his eye. He only rec'd the detail last week, & he may do better now, but you know he is naturally very lazy. Mother has plowed over nearly all her corn. Hers was not killed by frost. She will move in nine or ten days. She says she wont sell any more cotton & when she leaves

---

31. Scours referred to diarrhea in livestock.

the old house will have her cotton that is bagged up put away in the house. She would sell for specie but to whom & where could she sell?

John Kelly's son Frank who came out from Ft Delaware, & was afterwards captured near Richmond, is now at home on Parole, they thought him dead 'till he came home. I received a letter form [*sic*] Mrs Henderson last week, she writes that she has been in very bad health again this winter, took cold which settled in her lungs, & she has a cough, & fears she will die with consumption like her sister did. Col Henderson was in three fights during the raids made by Chalmers[32] in the north of Miss & Tenn. He had the promise of a silver medal from Gen Chalmers for his galantry at Collinsville, he acted on Chalmers staff. Her bad health has detained him here so long, but will go as soon as he can get across the Miss. She had to pay $5.00 to have the Piano moved to her house, says the cover is cut all to pieces & the out side disfigured in several places by the mice, & there is a hole where they could enter the inside if they chose but don't know how that is of course. I feel mad that I agreed to let Mollie G[raham] have it under any condition, for I know I'll never get a box made by him for it. I think I'll try & get Mrs Henderson to sell it for me for two good mules[,] for it will go down hill all the time & won't be worth moving when I will be able to send after it. It distresses me that it never did me any good, will never be any pleasure to Mary and now, it will do for mere acquaintances to bang on for their amusement, I had rather sell it for mules & let the Gov take them than to have it the way it is. I wish Pa had never bought or give me the Piano. But I reckon you are almost as tired of hearing or reading of the Piano, as you are of children & childbearing, and I will try & name the old Piano no more. Myers says (and he came up to dinner) that there is a very good stand of corn, and the Potatoe slips are coming up thick, they are making up some hills, & I have sent both Kate & Nance out to help. The next good season, we will try & set out half the patch.

One of my old Geese that Ma sent has hatched 8 goslings, the children are delighted & any other year I would be as much pleasured as they are, but I don't care any thing for goslings chickens nor nothing this spring. I feel like I don't care for any thing. The little pigs belonging to the three little sows continue to die, four have died since I put them up in a pen & have them

---

32. James Ronald Chalmers made brigadier general February 13, 1862. He commanded the military district of Mississippi and eastern Louisiana. Wakelyn, *Biographical Dictionary of the Confederacy,* 127.

slopped & corn boiled for them, & those with the sows look very poor. We don't get much more milk than the children can drink. If I had plenty [of] milk I could raise them without any trouble.

Little sister has a very bad cold again, was cross & wakeful last night & I had to get up to the fire with her, & bake her feet, until she went to sleep. Cold uses her up worse than any child I ever saw. Our old cat has kittens, & she is delighted with them—she improves rapidly, pushes a chair all over the house & clucks to it, can stand alone when she wants to, and her teeth are now through five at one time. She was so bad while you were at home that you were disgusted with her & never mention her now—but she don't care, for she don't know she has a father. Mary began a letter to you last week but did not have time to write it off. Mrs Buckley will not teach any more after this session is out, & I fear we will be without a teacher for some time. You have never told me a word about the boat being repaired &c.

affectionately
L S Neblett

Galveston
Apr 18th/64

Dear Lizzie

Last night while at church Dr Fisher approached and asked me if I have seen the list of killed and wounded. I at once knew what was coming. He told of the death of bro Robert, and Vol Womack[33] & Joe Stonum.[34] Poor Robert is dead I can hardly realize it. I find my self continually associating him and Garret together, for I liked Garret as much as him. I can recollect so distinctly when he was a baby then a child and a stripling, and I think I can realize the thoughts of a mother when death strikes down her child who even though grown never ceases to bring with his memory images of infancy and child-hood. While living I was not aware that I would have such feelings as I have at the death of Robert I find that like you my affections for my kindred is very strong.

---

33. Volney Womack was the brother of Susan Womack Scott. In 1860 he was 14 years old and living with his father and mother, Abe and Elizabeth Womack. TX Census 1860.

34. In 1860 Joseph Stonum (age 27) was a farmer who lived in Plantersville in Grimes County with his wife, Martha (age 22), and daughter. He had personal and real property valued at $40,000. TX Census 1860.

Robert might have made something of himself—he had a fine memory, excellent constitution and great energy. Poor Volnney, Rush Boggess[35] I suppose fell the same day. The Co seems to have suffered more severely than any other in the Regt. It was the Co that carried the flag & I suppose that was the cause. I notice that Ben Goodrich was wounded & nursing—I fear the death of Robert will very nearly kill Ma. I feel very uneasy for her, and Pa. Robert & Nelia you know were their babies and the death of Robert must hurt them very much. Pa is a very tender hearted man but is too proud to show his feelings much to any one except Ma. On the 8th the day of the fight I was in the street with a crowd awaiting the arrival of the train. It was a beautiful day and while standing listlessly there my attention was attracted by hearing a soldier remark, "I feel like there was a great battle being fought to day" No one made any remark but all looked serious and it proved true. As soon as I heard that the battle was fought I recollected the remarks[.] I am not given to having presentiments but when I heard of this battle I had less hope of Robert coming out than if I were going into one my self and when Dr Fisher told me of his death, I was surprised more that my fears should have been true than that he was among the killed. Or in other words the realization of my presentiment astonished me more than the death itself. I had written this far when the business of the office compelled me to stop, and in the mean time I have yours of the 13th. You cannot realize how much pleasure it gives me to receive a letter from home. I am anxious to hear from Ma. Nelia owes me a letter and should have answered before this this [*sic*] but it seems that when she should write she fails to do so.

I suppose you have recd a piece of calico (5 yds) I bought for Mary which I sent by Oliver. I could not well have done so but I sold four lbs of that butter your Ma sent me for ten dollars per lb. & by adding $20.00 bought the dress, $12.00 per yd. It is inferior calico I know. I am trying to get Randle home and if I do so I would like to collect up produce & have it sent to Houston. I think it would be more profitable than farming. That butter is the nicest I ever saw and that I have ever seen here [none] will compare with it, but I thought it nothing more than right that I should make that little sacrifice of my comfort. I would have divided with John but I knew if I ever mentioned the subject he would find out where it came from and make it another cause for getting mad

35. In 1860 Rush Boggess was 15 and living with his father, W. W. Boggess (age 52), a merchant with real property valued at $18,000. TX Census 1860.

at your ma & you and perhaps me too. You ask me in your last about the boat being repaired & I believe I told you that I did not think even if it was repaired that it would benefit Co (I) much. The Co may go to Harrisburg as it did last summer and get a chance to run away or get furloughs more easily but this is about all that can be reasonably expected. I hear a rumor from one of the boat hands that there is some talk of the Co or the crew going to Shreveport but do not believe it.

Since I wrote you last my health has been improving in some respects though I am annoyed with Piles and some thing like Bronchitis, pains or a tightness across the chest. I notice by your letters that you visit more than you formerly did and am glad to see it. I think you and I both should cultivate a more social feeling than we have done heretofore.

I wish you would tell Sarah or Myers to use plants from that Tobacco seed that she got from Pa. There is a great difference I am told in the kinds of tobacco—some much stronger than others. Graves told me that Hearst had year before last an excellent kind of chewing tobacco.

About a month ago a lot of letters came in by Flag of Truce & in reading them I found one from Frank Kelly to his mother which I forwarded & sometime ago I got one from his father enclosing one to Frank as well and it would have gone tomorrow by flag of truce but you tell me Frank K has gotten home. You speak of getting a letter from Mrs Henderson, & this reminds me of Nat Henderson. He is here in a Co in Hobby's Regt at this place. I forgot to write to you of him before. When I was sick he used to come around every night. He is with his Co across the Bay at Bolivar & came a few days ago & stayed all night with me. He does not look like Col H except in the eye. He married a sister of Tom H's first wife. He is in excellent health & fatter than I ever saw him. Gen Green & Majors both married cousins to the Hendersons. Tom Green you see is killed & his wifes brother Capt Chalmers—in the late battles in La. Green was probably the best Officer Texas has furnished & undoubtedly one of the very best men. He made a great contrast with the contemptible military fops to be seen every minute in this place. I will close for to night for last night the news of Roberts death kept me awake till midnight and every time I woke I would think of it the first thing.

Teusday Morn Apr 19th. We have a new commander here, in place of Rainey. Brig Genl Harris who once commanded the Brigade in which Story's Co was in now the commander of the brg. Rainey has an an [*sic*] inferior command. He does not deserve any. I wish Mary had sent her letter. I must close or I will not get this in time for the mail. I send Mary a good pen.

Yours truly
Wm H. Neblett

At Home
Tuesday night April 18th/64

Dear Will,

This evening late I read in the Tri weekly paper the distressing news of poor Roberts death. Oh Will I do feel so unhappy so miserable, and altho' I weep over poor Roberts untimely death yet, I grieve as much for poor dear Ma, I ask myself again & again How can Ma stand it & what will become of her. I know how you feel, and tho we are far separated yet I know that to night the same thoughts fill your brain and the same feelings thrill our hearts. We weep, and bitterly lament, poor dear Roberts death, & with the grief is mingled one almost as deep for poor dear Ma's anguish, and fears that she too will pass from us. Oh Will! Will this horrible war! will it never cease until every hearth stone in the C.S. is made desolate, and every heart filled with unutterable woe. I wish I could go down to see Ma, tho' I know I could give her no consolation, yet I feel so anxious about her, I feel like I want to go to her, & be with her. If I could do her any good, I would not hesitate one moment about going, but I know Hattie Nelia, & Mittie will be with her and that all that can be done to console or alleviate her suffering will be done. Mr Oliver whom I saw this morning told me that he saw Pa as he got off the cars at Navasota, & Pa told him if he would walk out to Frank's he would send him a horse to ride home, that he did so, & then went from Franks & ate supper with Pa, who told him that Ma had been quite sick, but was then some better, was in bed not able to be up. I feel almost certain that anxiety to hear and the agony of suspense was the cause of her sickness and now Oh God, what will she do? Almighty Father! strengthen and support her in this hour of heart rending grief. Oh God whisper comfort to her bleeding heart. Poor Robert, he loved Ma devotedly and I know if he was not killed instantly he thought of her in his dying moments with all the warmth of an affectionate heart. I feel for Pa too, it will grieve him so much, the hearts of old people become so bound up in their youngest children.

They tell me that Mrs Womack is greatly distressed about Vol. And Mrs Goodrich said before the news reached here that she had faith to believe that Ben was not hurt. Poor soul, her faith could not save him. I don't see why it was that Co (Storey's) suffered more than any other in the Regt. I will send down to Pa's sunday to see or hear how Ma is & will write you & send to the office next Teusday. I dread to hear from there. If you can get a furlough do try & do so, even if you do not come to see us—go and see Ma. Oh Will I fear so much that it will cause her death! I am very busy now, getting ready to get our dresses in to weave, & we need them so much, & my constant attention is needed just now, else I would send Mary & Bob to Aunt Cinda's to go to school with her children & would go down to Pa's, and if I hear any bad news from them will go any how. The children are all well except bad colds. Bill is yet in the house nursing his blister, but it is getting well fast. Nance & Kate are in the field yet. The grass & weeds are growing so fast in the field, but the corn grows as fast as the weeds. Myers says our corn is the best he has seen. He sent a large lot to mill Sat & did not grind it 'till this evening, & it comes back, greatly missing.

Jno Collins will move his mill this week & I tried to send in enough corn to last us a month, & by that time he will get his mill running again. He is going to move it some where near Holmes mill. I judge from what the negros say that the bags came back with three or four bu[shels] missing. I have no idea what I will do when the corn gives out. I went to mothers Sat, found a number of the negros sick, and she had just buried two. The little negro Bet that stayed in the house & Harriets baby, the age of nine. Bet had inf[l]amation of the brain I think, & Harriets baby was teething. She has several cases of the flux now.

Apr 20th Aunt Cinda has been here two days making our harness and she has seen Bet Scott lately & the cow subject was introduced and then Aunt Cinda said "how is it Bettie I thought Neblett bought Jim's Cows," well she says I dont call it buying when he paid no money and gave no note drawing interest and I am going to get as many of the cows as I want to milk and I don't care who milks the ballance—she says "I call it a poor sale, for him to pay $5 after the war in specie, and we have no note, and he getting all the increase & paying no interest & I'll have as many of the cows as I want or die." She told Aunt she understood that speck was a fine milch cow, & Sandy was watching her to get her up as soon as she had a calf. She has one now, & her bag is so full Aunt says it will spoil if she is not milked soon but she is too much trouble to drive for me to bring her home for Bet to send & take her out of our pen so I will let her alone. I dont expect to make any butter this summer. Why did you not give your note, or fix that matter up some way? I thought it best to write you about this, and you can act as you think best. But I won't contend with Bettie for the cows, & Jim lets her do as she pleases. Wednesday night April 20th.

Myers says Kate is mighty trifling in the field, he whipped her to day. Joe has sold his mule to Paul Hurst, the negro who went with Hurst—but I believe it is a sham sale, & Mr Collins has made Paul rue back. I think Joe is calculating to raise corn for his mule & I expect him to take all hands soon & build himself a stable. He has taken the stirrup leather off your Brier creek saddle & the girth to put his in riding order. I am determined not to live alone with them next year, I can't. I know tis no pleasure to hear of their doings so I have withheld a great deal of their doings. Apr 20th.

Myers says our new ground corn is knee high, says tis a splendid stand, and out grows anything he ever saw. Says he thought he was going to have the nicest kind of a piece of corn at Mrs Rogers but this beats it all to pieces. Says tho' it is very foul full of weeds & grass, and scares him. Bill got sick at a mighty bad time, & is slow recruiting but I think will be able to go to work next monday. Walter says you must get him some candy. Out of 25 pigs belonging to three sows, I have 9 left, & have them up in a pen and slop them. The White & spotted sow's are doing well with their 11 pigs but the pigs are wild, & Joe don't pay any attention to the hogs now, hasent called them in two mo[nths], tho I have told him I wanted it done & the white & spotted sows pigs bed & called up to gentle them. He thinks you are not coming under seven mo[nths], perhaps never. Bob says you must take care of your self & not get drowned nor let the Yankee's kill you if you can help it.

Mary says she would have writen last Sat but went to mothers, & is too busy during the week getting her lessons to write. Billy says he wants to see you, and you must come home tomorrow. I failed to get you any tobacco from Dr Brown's, and I can hear of none no where[,] will pick out the best Sarah has & have it twisted up for you.

Oliver brought Mary's dress & she is highly pleased with it.

At Pa's

Sat sun set April 23rd 1864

Dear Will,

You will perhaps be a little surprised to hear of my being here, but after I wrote you on wednesday that I would send down a note of inquiry as to the state of Ma's health &c. I felt so anxious to hear, & so uneasy about Ma that I determined to come myself, as being the most satisfactory plan to both you and myself. I came down yesterday evening & on reaching Pa's found no one at home, went on over to Hattie's, and from her learned that Ma was better & was over at Mitties, & as Mittie would have been crowded with my Baby & Mary, I concluded to stay all night at Hatties, & this morning went over to Mittie's to see Ma. I find her much more composed, & bearing her great affliction with more christian fortitude and patience than I had hoped or thought it possible. She is greatly grieved, and the wound will not close this side of her grave, & tho' she is as greatly grieved as ever Mrs Patrick was about her son, yet she does not display the rebelious feeling that Mrs Patrick did to me. Poor dear Ma, my sympathy is as much if not more strongly enlisted for her sufferings & her sorrow than any one I ever knew. The girls say she was more strongly attached to Robert than to any of her children, & since he went into service he seemed to be continually on her mind. You & Sterling had wives to think of your comfort & provide clothing and other things for your comfort and pleasure, but Robert was hers exclusively, her youngest son, and her heart was awake to all the fears known to a mother fearing that he might be led astray by bad company, and that his youth and thoughtlessness might lead him into dangers that maturity would have avoided. She had thread spun to weave him some clothes, and had so many plans laid out to give him comfort & pleasure. She has recently been suffering with a kidney affection, suffers dreadfully & Pa sent for both Dr Jameson & McIntosh & she has got a great deal better of that, but is in a very weak state. She has been suffering lately more severely & for a longer time with the sick headache, will grow better in the day & return with agrivated pain at night. Oh I do sympathize so much with her, & wish her physical sufferings at least could be cured.

The news of Roberts death reached Pa & Nelia monday night, & they with held it from her, but her fears were greatly alarmed by both Nelia & Pa's conduct, and she slept very little that night, & Pa said it seemed cruel to keep her in suspense, so he told her Teusday morn & she almost went into convulsions, they sent for Hattie & she says when she reached here, Ma looked like she would have spasms all the time. They had learned nothing but the newspaper account until I came down & told the girls the news Bro Jim gave me as have been writen back here by some of the boys. Joe Stonum & Robert were killed instantly. Joe's head was cut off by a shell & Robert was shot in the left side, near the heart. Vol Womack died that night on the battle field, where our wounded lay all night. Ben Goodrich had a flesh wound in the leg & was captured so understood Jim. I brought Mary & the baby with me, left the boys at mothers, I thought Ma might be very sick & their noise would disturb her. I made Bill ride Dick & had the mare down to Browns, but he wont take her. I drove myself—Ranger scares worse in harness than I ever knew him & if the harness was rotten I would feel affraid to drive him. I intend going back tomorrow. I left Old Sam sick, says he had a chill Thursday, I gave him broken doses of May apple,[36] & left some more of that, the bitter pills for Sarah to give him. Bill will go to work monday he has lost very nearly a month, quite a month, & now [with] Sam sick I feel very uneasy about the corn crop, it needs work so badly. We had a very heavy rain last night, could have done without it a week longer very well. I hope they set out plenty of Potatoe slips & Tobacco plants this evening at home. Ferrell sent me word to send my hides down to be limed next Sat. I will try & get my bark ground at Keifer's, as Ferrell wont let me grind on his mill. Keifer has been very sick, & lay there 8 days unable to wait upon him self, & some one happened to go there, & found him nearly dead, but at last accounts he was better. Mother is going to send her mares to Bill Dodd's, & if you say so I'll send Fanny also, upon the same terms that mother does, but I dont know what terms he offered her.

Pa told me to tell you that he would send you down some corn, bacon & eggs soon for your dutch landlady—how is it? Pa still clings to the notion that Willis burned his Gin house—his loss in cotton are not so great as [he] thought it was, lost only about 20 bales.

Pa so the girls tell me, was greatly grieved about Poor Bob's death, they all try to be cheerful before Ma. Nelia rec'd a letter from Robert writen the day before the fight he was greatly dissatisfied with Inf[antry] service, and was so anxious to get a transfer into Cavalry. He said in the letter that he had rather die the next day than serve in Inf[antry] six years. I think he was killed the first day.

Sunday morn before breakfast—I write early in order to finish my letter, so that I can mail it as I go through Town, and I must start early else I won't make mothers by dinner the roads are so heavy. It will be plenty wet to plant out slips & Tobacco plants tomorrow evening. Ranger ran away or followed a mare of Jim Collins & was gone several days, and Joe hunted him a day & a half but I don't know whether he was really hunting the horse or attending to his own business. Joe is doing very bad—it is his day now certainly, but

---

36. Mayapple was used as a laxative.

whether my day will ever arrive or not as far as he is concerned is exceedingly doubtful. When I speak to him, he cuts me up in the shortest kind of a style—& got the best end of the disputed saddle since Nance has been working out, she locks her house, so when I want to use the saddle, the girth is locked up in Nance's house. He says he don't ride his mule, & if he don't ride that why does he strip the saddle every time he rides it—he certainly rides something & I reckon tis our own horses. Since I got Ranger I have his head tied to his foot like I do old Sam & it is very convenient for Joe. I am more determined each day not to live alone with them next year. He never pretends to call the hogs or look after them at all altho' I have told him about it, & it makes me so mad when I speak to him & he answers in such short style that I don't speak to him when I can avoid it. Tom grows worse each day & he is getting to be such a devil that I fear he will try to insult Mary. I would not leave her there all day alone with the negros for nothing. A short time since I was passing by that old Giles house near the mill, & noticed two hens, and thought I knew one of them, & went back a few days after and found 4 of my old noted hens, stopped up in the house. That old negro who fought Collins & ran away and his wife stay there at night. I went on to the mill, and saw the negro woman, who said that our Tom sold her the hens—that night, Collins made the old negro man bring the hens home. Myers whipped Tom, & he owned it, but said the old negro persuaded him to do it telling him he would stand between him & all harm, & said he was nothing but a boy & did not know any better, & he thought Myers ought to go & whip that old negro too. I found out about a week ago that he has been cutting down the small trees between the house & the crib, & at the back of the garden place, for fire wood. Since Bill has been sick Tom got the wood for house & kitchen. I counted sixteen stumps where he had cut down the trees.

Ma is tolerable well this morning is free of the head ache. Pa's old wreck of a carriage was not burned up, but two buggys were, one with & one without a top. He has bought Ma a very good second handed buggy with a top at the depot for $1300, and Nelia drives her. She has been staying at Hatties & Mitties ever since she heard the news of poor Roberts death, until yesterday evening.

I doubt whether you can read this scrawl, but the pen don't write any better than a stick & it is the only chance. I have a great deal to tell you that I think would be interesting but havent room, nor time, & this pen frets me. I'll try and write again at the usual time. Wm Terrell is discharged again, he is fortunate, tho' he looks to be the healthiest stoutest man I know of. They have heard that Lou & Kenneth Demoret[37] came out of the battle safely. A good many of the grape cuttings you sent are living, don't know whether the Oleanders will live or not.

Affectionately,
Lizzie S Neblett

Galveston
Apr 25th/64

Dear Lizzie

Yours of the 18th reached me yesterday and I suppose mine of about same date has been recd by you. Yesterday was my regular time to write but I postponed it until to day on account of a severe head ache which I had all day. I like you fear the news of Roberts death will affect Ma very seriously I have been thinking for several days of writing to her on the subject but I am such an awkward hand at such things that for that reason I have deferred it till now. But I will write in a day or two and would also make an effort to go and see her but know it is useless to make the attempt. I think furloughs will be stopped soon on account of an apprehension of an attack on this place by an Iron clad fleet from Mobile. At any rate any rate [*sic*] details have been made or ordered to be made from the soldiers to work on the fortifications, and only three soldiers are allowed to leave the forts to come to town at a time.

For my own part I do not think that there is much danger of an attack. But if furloughs are stoped it will probably be a month before they are started again or even longer. For the authorities have always been very prompt to stop and very reluctant to start them. You ask me why it was that I did not give my note to Jim for the cattle. I bought the cattle from Jim at five dollars per head for cows & calves—yearlings & two year olds, the Price of the 3 at $12.00 4 and 5 years old was to be agreed upon by John Scott and myself. The Spring after I bought them was very dry & the cattle took to the bottom very early & before I could spare the time to get them up. (It is my recollection that Jim was to send Sandy to help gather them) I told Jim it was impossible to gather them all at once but that I would gather and brand and keep an account of the num-

---

37. Lewis (21) and Kenneth (14) Demoret (spelled Demerrit in the 1860 census) were the sons of Edgar (45) and Elisa (32) Demerrit. Both men lived with their parents. Lewis's occupation was listed as clerk. TX Census 1860.

ber and age—which I did as you will find in the bank. There were a good many unbranded yearlings and two years old which were unbranded and it was to Jims interest that I should brand for I was unwilling to take them upon the report of others unless I could find and brand them. Now you see it was impossible to to [*sic*] give a note until the number was fixed and I thought it was to Jims interest not to fix the number or give the note until all the cattle were gathered. I spoke to Jim of this last summer and told him the number I had branded and had up & he said that was about as many as he expected there was. I told him of several head more that I had heard of, that I would try & get up. I asked him if he was willing to take confederate money and he said no. I than told him it was a great deal of useless trouble to brand all the cattle over besides that the worms would kill many of them and asked him to let me have his brand to use on the stock which were unbranded and I would use my ear mark on those not marked. He agreed to this & I used his brand on many of the calves & with my ear mark.

We had a talk about the interest and I told him I was not willing to pay interest and count the increase after I bought them. He said it does not make much difference but that he wanted one or the other. I told him I preferred to pay the interest and not count the increase as it would be very troublesome to count the increase and deduct there from the number that might have died or been killed or were lost by straying. So you see the reason that influenced me and the understanding between Jim and me on the subject. You must not give up the brand I got from Jim unless Jim & I have another understanding on the subject. I will write to Jim to day or to morrow on the subject. Since writing the above I have written to Jim about the cattle[,] giving him my understanding of the contract and in doing so have copied what I wrote above (using the terms "you" in place of his name as above[)]. I did this because I wished you to knew what I said to him. I concluded by telling him if he wanted a part of the milch cows I would not object to his having part but that as he selected the best when he sold that he could not expect to select the best again. You have never told me what Jim is doing or whether he is at home but I suppose he is for it takes him a long time to do any thing.

I send you a recipe used here in flux cases with great success. It is what cured me, arresting the bloody mucus discharges in 5 hours. But it would have to be filled by a Dr or Apothecary.

I wish you would go to see Ma particularly if you hear that the news of Roberts death affects her health. It would be some consolation to be with her. She likes to have some one to talk to of her distresses. She is like you in that respect. For my part sorrow always silences me. It seems every paper I have got for the past week the first thing my eye rested upon was poor Roberts name. He is the next to the first in the long list of killed & wounded in Walkers Division, Wauls Brigade.[38]

What kind of a bargain did you make with Myers. If he only attends to the hands until the crop is made does he charge the same as if he attended to them until it was gathered. He ought of course to make some deductions in proportion to what he charges the others. Did you get a good stand of cotton and where did you get seed from. I have made an application to get Randle back—expect to hear from it in [a] few days, $30.00 is nothing now. A negro ought to be worth $200 a month. A shifty negro could clear ten dollars per day here. You ou[gh]t to have him in the crop for [if] you have to put Nance or Kate in the field you will not be able to make any cloth this year. A negro could make ten dollars in burning tar and that is almost two times as much as $30 per month. You need not send me any of Sarahs tobacco. It is too grain[y] to chew. I have much of what I got from her yet and cannot chew it. You must not give up to Bet and let her run over you, for that Goodrich set will do that if you let them, but are very easily stoped if they meet with any resolute person.

I have not heard from Pa's since the 25th of March—the date of Bob's last letter. Have been expecting one for two weeks. Kiss the children for me. I do not expect any of the children would know me in my grey jacket & pants which I drew last fall.

Yours affectionately
Wm H. Neblett

At Home
April 27th/64

Dear Will,

Altho' I am under promise to go to Aunt Cinda's this morning, yet I feel so much more like writing to you that I stay at home for that purpose. I am so tired & sleepy when night comes that I cannot write, I go to sleep with the pen in my hand. Nursing my babe is the cause of my sleepiness I reckon, but I am as sleepy headed as I am when I am pregnant, but I am determined to

---

38. Thomas Waul served under General Walker in the Red River campaign of 1864. Boatner, *The Civil War Dictionary,* 896–97.

make myself as easy on that score as possible, until I find out for certain. I have known many a woman have only 18 months between her children, mine was 9 mo old when you were at home. You never could seemingly comprehend how utterly wrecked the prospect of happiness was with me but perhaps you have slightly understood how miserable one could feel with the constant dread & fear of a calamity ten thousand times worse than death staring them in the face all the time. If not this fear, then ask yourself what? Determine yourself, you know there is but one sure & certain preventive. But it does no good to think or write on this subject. I have renounced all hopes of happiness in this life, yet I cannot at times help contrasting what has been & will be with what might have been. I pity you also for with such a woman you can not be as happy & contented as you might have been with another differently con-s[t]ituted—and for your sake I often wish that you had never seen me.

It rained very hard nearly all night the 22nd while I was at Pa's, and made the roads very heavy coming home. I started as soon as we had breakfast & reached mothers for late dinner & I had to drive myself, & I was so tired when I reached there that I concluded to wait till morning to come home & made Bob ride Dick, & Bill drove me. Bill was affraid to ride the mare, so he rode Dick & led her. Pa says her present colt is a very fine one. Bill Dodd's horse is a very good 4 year old & he told mother if you wished he would take your mare & hers, & I reckon a poor colt is better than none. I stopped at Browns a few minutes out of the rain. Violante & her mother were very friendly. Violante has changed a great deal in looks, is not at all handsome now, but her child is very good looking and looks like a monster beside mine and Will, it looks so much like you. I declare I could not keep my eyes off it, & felt like she had no business having a child that favored you so much. It looks more like you than any of ours do, I think. She said that Sterling said when he was at home that he felt right jealous because the child looked so much like you—he will have a red head also but I dont think it will be the kind of red your[s] is, will be like Brown's. Nelia had a letter from Sterling the 2nd of Apr, in which he said his command was going to Ark[ansas] and they think it probable that he was in a recent fight in Ark[ansas]. I don't think Sterling writes to Violante often, I have no doubt but that he loves his boy better than he does her.

At Fanthorps well I met Mr Boggess[39] & had a little chat with him. Says

---

39. In 1860 W. W. Boggess (52) was a merchant with real and personal property valued at $18,000. He was unmarried and living with his six children. TX Census 1860.

John Boggess[40] did not mention Roberts name in his letter, & that Rush was alive five days after the battle, he had telegraphed to Shreveport to find out from Dr Haynie if Rush was still alive, & was waiting to hear before he started to see him. At Bowens Creek I met Abe Womack and Lish, & Abe asked me if Ma was going to send after Roberts body [he] had understood so, & that he was going after Volney, & was anxious to find out if Pa was going to send so they could go together, & be of material assistance. I told him I did not hear the subject mentioned while I was there, so thought it untrue, that the newspaper report was all they had received. Vol's negro reached home Sunday, & reports that Robert, Joe Stonum, & Volney all fell in a space not larger than a house, & were all buried in the same grave & now they are going to get Vol out while they can distinguish one from the other, & will bring him home if possible if not bury him & mark the grave so they can return for him hereafter. Abe promised me that if Vol was in the middle he would dig a grave on each side & take Joe S. & Robert out, & leave Vol in the middle grave, & would mark Stonums & Roberts grave so they could be found. I fear that Stonum & Robert are side by side & will be left together. I was very anxious for Pa to know that Abe was going but did not have time to let him know as Abe said he was going to start that evening & take the negro back with him, to show the grave. Robert & Stonum were shot in the region of the heart & died instantly. Poor Bob, his death has left a void in Ma's heart that time can never fill. She thinks now that she can never take any interest in any thing again. I regret so much that some one of Pa's negros did not go with Abe & helped dig a grave for both Vol & Robert & put poor Robert away a little more decently than he is now. Poor fellow I guess his blanket was all they had to put him in. Vol's negro said that he left Rush Boggess alive, & he was 7 days on the road, but some letter from there stated that Dr Haynie thought his recovery very doubtful, he was wounded in the abdomen you know.

I wrote to you some time ago that John Nix got a detail to over see for mother. Well, Will you never saw any laziness & want of energy that surpassed him. He sets in the house from morning 'till night and reads, or pretends to read, novels and whenever mother leaves to attend to her sick negros or go to the garden & other places, he & Babe commence chatting and they keep it up 'till she steps in—and all their talk is "tom foolery." He told mother that old

---

40. In 1860 John Boggess was 16 and living with his father, W. W. Boggess. TX Census 1860.

Turn told him that Mittie W[omack] & several of the girls were setting their cap for him, but he had been thinking that there was a chance of his being his master—old Turn belongs to Babe you know. Mother is naturally very suspicious you know but she is greatly distressed now at the way Babe acts, her imprudent capers &c, & mother has remonstrated with her, but all in vain, Babe tells her that she will never act differently with John as long as he stays in the house. I can see nothing between them that betrays any love affair, but Mother says they act entirely different when I am about—but leaving that out, John is of no service to mother—he has not been to the field but two or three times, manifest no interest about what the negros are doing, & don't trouble himself to please mother about any thing, forgets all she asks him to do when he goes to town. I don't think she will keep him long. She could have secured old Nobles services, but 'tis now too late. John gets the dumps sometimes, and she will say nothing nor will he do any thing. He is fond of dress, & tries to fix up all the time. I can't believe that Babe is fool enough to fancy or encourage John, even if he is fool enough to think of her as any thing but a cousin. Mother thinks he told her & Babe what Turn said to him to see what she would say. I have never said a word to Babe, I never give her advice.

Myers told me yesterday that the negros were getting along tolerably well. Old Sam had a chill Thursday & did not go to work 'till monday evening, had no more chills, but was weak, and [had a] head ache. I let out about his staying in so long for one chill when I came home & he put out that evening. Joe keeps his saddle down in the field again & the children saw his mule tied down there—says he let Squire have the girth he took off your cattle saddle. Pa told me that he would ho[u]se our negros next year, and says he will swap me a hand for Joe now. I won't stay alone with them next year. They set out about half of the potatoe hills, but I notice that a good many have died they did not set them out well, left them suspended in the hole, & the root not touching the bottom—they know better but don't care—the corn has all been run around and are now plowing out the middles have a fine stand of cotton—this is excellent land, & Myers says it will make good land if it a[i]nt half cultivated. I wish I was a man, I would make mother earth give me more than a bare living & grave. Collins sent me word to send down & he would let me have what meal I thought missing and I sent & got 3 bu[shels]. I sent Bill out and got up two cows this morning, before Bet would find out they had calves, & now, if she sends over after them I am going to send the negros back & tell her, no one but her or Jim shall drive them out of the pen here. I feel so mad about the way she is acting that I don't know how I can visit her, she has never been [here] but once the day you came home. I have never been [there] one time. Jim & her drive by mothers often, but never turn their heads towards the house. I have met Jim & am always as friendly as ever with him.

Do write me, about what your trade was, about the cattle. Did you give a note, agree to pay interest, & you have the increase or how was it? Bob was not well at school yesterday took some pills last night, complaining this morning and ate no breakfast. Mary persuaded Billy to go with her this morning to school, he went rather reluctantly. Bob's tongue is very foul, no fever yet, but the liver pills are not acting well—his liver seems to be torpid. I must repeat the dose to night. Bob was healthier last year than he ever was before in his life. Old Turn's baby died with flux last week. Frances & Phillis have the flux but are better. My pig raising has turned out as badly as Joes, but I saved all the sows—out of 25 pigs there is now 4 alive, & they [are] very sorry looking ones—the blue sow that Mary claims had pigs while I was gone to Pa's she has none with her, lost them all I suppose, drowned perhaps, the two sows Pa sent me lost their pigs a long time ago. Perhaps we will have a lot of fall pigs. We have been so busy trying to get out of the grass that I have not sent to old Coody for that wheel yet. Oliver sent & borrowed Ranger to ride this week, hunting up recruits has gone to madison Co. We are now getting up barks roots &c to dye our thread with. Oh I get so out of patience making cloth, or trying to. I feel almost ready to give up sometimes. Hattie has wove one piece coarse cloth, & Mittie has a piece in the loom. I hatched out 15 goslings this year, but have only 9 now. I pay no attention to them. Am more apathetic than I ever was before in my life. I go to Aunts this eve to get some dye roots, & will add my name to night, if no more. Bob is about as he was this morning [with] no fever[,] will give him some more pills to night. I havent cured any peas yet, planted a few to day for table use.

affectionately
Lizzie S N

7

Pray That God May Grant Us Peace

May 2, 1864–July 3, 1864

Galveston
May 2nd/64

Dear Lizzie

I was fearing to day that because you wrote from Pas on the 23rd that you might not do so again at your regular time and was just about commencing this when yours of the 27th was handed me. You never have been so placed as to enable you to appreciate a "letter from home" and if ever you are I hope you may be as fortunate as I have been in having your longings satisfied. Yours of the 23rd and Nelias of the 24th were rec'd at the same time. I have never heard any thing after the news paper Report and what was contained in your letter about Roberts death.

I suppose there is very little to hear. Death on the battle field usually has but few attendant circumstances. I feel very anxious to hear from bro Sterling. He has probably been in one and perhaps two battles up to this time. But cavalry fighting is seldom as dangerous as infantry. Our arms appear to be victorious in every quarter. A few hours ago telegraphic dispatches say that we have captured 5000 Yanks, & 3000 negro soldiers near Vicksburg—the negro soldiers were all killed. Yesterday another dispatch says that Gen Hogan captured 2000 Yanks in Ark. I understand that Walkers Brigade the one in which Robert was has gone to Ark in pursuit of Gen Steele.[1] The Telegraph is up stairs

1. There were various skirmishes in Arkansas at the end of April as Federal troops under Frederick Steel began withdrawing from Camden, Arkansas.

and is very convenient to get the latest important news. You wanted to know "how about that corn for my Dutch land lady." I suppose you read my letter to Nelia, but if you did not I will say that when I first was there she acted so well & treated me so kindly that I tried to get the corn for her as a matter of charity. But I have since found out that she was unworthy of charity and I have consequently written to Pa not to send it. I came to the conclusion that she like almost all the Dutch here are not honest. I think she stole near half of my rations. It took all my wages last month to pay up. This month I have drawn rations from the Commissary and consequently will not get but about $18.00 per month but will have a chance of getting some clothing. Yesterday I changed my boarding house. This time I have a Northern woman for land lady. Her husband was captured near Charleston in attempting to run the blockade. She has not heard from him in 20 months—supposes he is in Fort Warren a prisoner. She has a daughter 12 or 14 and has no means—has a nice little house well furnished an[d] a good piano with a Melodean attachment, the first I ever saw. She has to do her own cooking and does it well. Speaking of cooking reminds me of telling you that I have lately learned to eat lettuce, and if you ever fix it up the same way I will guarantee that you will love it too. It is cut up and vinegar with sugar or good Molasses dissolved. I think it very nice and never fail to eat a saucerful of it. I do not suppose you have any lettuce. Did the frost kill the peaches & plums.

What you state about the removal of Vols remains by Abe makes me feel sad. If Ma should hear of it she would want Roberts brought home and if it were it would only reopen the wound in her heart when it arrives and her health is so precarious I do not think it would be prudent to risk the consequences on her.

I noted that you write as if you feared you were pregnant or might be so. I thought you said that you had some kind of a womb affection, but was getting well of it. Why did you not write more speciffically as to what was the matter. I recollect now since you spoke in your letter some time ago of having a womb affection that when I was at home, that you appeared to be swollen and I think I remarked at the time that you were getting fat. I hope it is genuine fat and not a disease and I am sure it is not pregnancy.

I am not surprised at what you write about John Nix you know I always thought him very lazy and would not be surprised if he did not court and marry Babe though I do not think she will have him. Your Ma pursues the wrong course with him—she should tell him of his duty as overseer &c. Has your Ma moved in the new house.

I understood that Jeff Haynie McCune and two or three others arrived here & went over to Pelican Spit a few days ago. I hear also that the Bayou City will soon go up the Bayou in fresh water for repairs—but have not heard what is to become of the Co. I suppose it will stay at Pelican. Now that Collins is about to move his mill it will be a good time for you to get refuse lumber to make your chicken house.

Why has not Mary written. A few days ago I took supper at McAlpins. Mrs McA told me she had lately recd a letter from M[ary] H[aynie] which stated that you & Babe & M Haynie had been talking of coming to G[alveston] but after talking it over the idea was abandoned. Mrs McA told me to say she would like to see you all. Mrs McA looks rather pale & appears to be in delicate health. They get their provisions from home & live very well. Her cousin a Miss Perry was staying with her.

yours affectionately
Wm H. Neblett

At Home
Teusday May 3rd 1864

Dear Will,

Altho' this is not my regular day for writing, and a lot of work for my fingers to do lies before me, yet the bright calm day with its sunshine & its shade & the knowledge that it is the anniversary of my departure from this place last year to mothers, to await there the coming of my present little one has made me desirous to communicate a few [of the] many thoughts that have flirted through my brain to day as I sat all alone dreaming of the past & fearing the future. I remember exactly how I felt 12 months ago, as I gazed around me & made a mute farewell to each familiar object and hoped with humility that the farewell might be eternal. I thought too, that ere an other year would roll around that the awful war would be closed, but I felt to[o] weary of life to live to see it. I live to see the anniversary of that day, but my feelings my hopes & wishes have not been made new, the same old mental darts crowd upon me, and sit as usual around hopes empty petal box her fount is dry "her lights are fled, her leaves dead,"[2] and a listless heavy apathetic feeling has taken

_____

2. From Thomas Moore's 1817 "Oft in the Stilly Night" ("Whose lights are fled/Whose garlands dead").

her place—and the war seems no nearer its close than it did 12 months ago. Oh if I could only hope, tho' each hope were hopes to die and it was fulfilled, my life would not be so cheerless, and I would have something to bring me up, infuse new life & render me cheerful at least. But to have no bright spot in the future to fix my gaze upon, to see only a barren waste, with a steep & rugged ascent up which I must toil, no matter how weary & desolate I feel, is dreadful and I try not to think of it, but moments will come when all this looms up before my mental vision & will not be shut out. To such as I am life is indeed a poor gift.

I believe there is a kind of rapport as it is termed in mesmerism between my mind & yours [I have] thought of it often, & watched closely to establish the truth of my belief, but you wrote so sparingly of your thoughts or feelings, that I dont gain much proof yet, I find it pleasant to indulge such a belief. I think you have the strongest will, and influence my mind more frequently than I do your[s]—reasoning from this belief I have concluded that you have felt much less desire since you were at home last to come home or see me & the children than you ever felt before, when absent from us.[3] I have felt this for some time, even when you were sick, I don't think you desired to be at home or with me. If you can remember or trace it back tell me if you did not desire more than usual to see me, & be with me last night the 2nd I don't care if you do think me foolish. I know I am but I am not so miserable when I am so foolish. I had a very distinct dream of you last night. I thought I was an eye witness to a battle, & gazing upon its ["]magnificently stand array." I became overwhelmed by emotion & wept aloud tho I knew that no one who was dear to me was in the battle, & while I wept you came & seated yourself by me, and put your arms around me & kissed me, just as you always do, and different from any one else that ever kissed me, & tho' you spoke not a word your silent sympathy was very consoling, and then you took my hand between yours & yours felt very hot to me it was so vivid that the memory of the kiss & the pressure of the hand has lingered with me all day.

But I guess you are tired of so much sentimentalism & so little sense.

Last Saturday evening 30th Apr we had a tremendous rain, it fell in floods, a washing rain. Sunday Lake Creek was level from bank to bank. Myers says it almost ruined Jim Rogers farm washed it so badly, dident hurt yours much. Sunday no one went round the field to see about the water gaps, & early Mon-

---

3. On mesmerism see McCandless, "Mesmerism and Phrenology," 199–230.

day morning the sun shining brightly & hotly in a perfectly cloudless sky, those tormenting negros of yours went to setting out potatoe slips before they fixed up the water gaps or any thing else. As soon as I found it out sent Kate post haste to tell them not to set out slips till late in the evening. Joe who always acts the gentleman first, had hilled up all the slips in one bed, & had planted part & Sam sent me word they wouldent die the ground was wet enough—and it was almost too wet to set out, & the sun hot enough to cook them all before night. I was so mad I sent Kate back & told them to pull every slip up that they had put out, & send them to me. I did not expect them to mind me, but they did, and I kept them sprinkled in the basket till evening & had them set out—the first planting nearly one ¼ of them died, they hung there in a hole, & no dirt touching the roots. Joe is without a riding horse again. Garrett sent by Rivers who belongs to scofield's Co, for the horse that Joe has been riding, he kept him tied down in the field, (his saddle, bridle & all hid out down there) & he got loose once, & walked over the corn—he will get an other one some where to ride, I think he is now too proud to ride his old mule. This season will set out all the hills which is about half of the po-tatoe patch, and if we don't have another season in 10 days more, I'll have what slips I can get out of the beds set out & watered. Sarah has a great many tobacco plants but has not put out a great many yet.

Our oxen continue poor & weak. Oliver says I can take his two yoke, which are fat now, and work them as long as I please. I sent over after them this morning but could not get them. Myers says they will do as much work in one day as one of our yoke will in three—says they are equal to the best mules. Myers says the bushes, the crab grass & weeds are scary in our field, and the team is so sorry that they get along so slowly plowing, the oxen give out & lay down. He has three plows running—tho sweeps is what he uses. Have had the old sweeps pointed with some of the iron I got from Bookmans, and the new ones were so thin that the points bent & turned in & had been to the shop once already—that boiler iron is too thin, & Jack says it won't do for the wings of Cary plows can't weld the base to them. I am making no calculation to farm next year. I have lost all hope of the war ending this year, and I have made up my mind *irrevocably* not to live alone with them next year. I am willing to live here, & take Thornton & Nance Bill, and Sarah—and the rest may go to the devil if they can't be hired out. I can put them out for their vituals & clothes, & have their taxes paid, and that is more than they do at home. And you need not make an effort to get Randal home for I will only have one more to feed & clothe, and if there was 40 hands to put in our little field, it would be kick & spur to cultivate it. Myers tried to scare Sam about the crop being so in the grass weeds & bushes, but Sam told him that they were more forward with the crop than they ever were before & don't seem at all uneasy or anxious to push ahead & Myers says if it has been worse here to fore than it is this year, he don't wonder that we never make corn to do us. I got cotton seed from mother and a few bushels from Mrs Rogers—have a fine stand—of course Myers agreed to deduct, if he left when the crop was made. I am to pay him at the rate of 400 dollars, or a part of the crop. I don't think there will be any difficulty about the pay. He says he will have to pay 40 dollars tax for each one of the places he oversees. He says he wont oversee next year. I am glad that you wrote to Jim about the cattle, tho' that will do no good. Bet sent after that Speck cow at Aunt Cinda's, had the dogs and all of Johns negro boys & Sandy & Mack & them couldent drive her, but caught the calf with the dogs, and carried it & put it in Jim's cow pen, & it got out before they caught the cow in the pen. Mack & Sandy have threat[e]ned Bill, to come over here and drive all the cows we have up over to their house, she has up 5 now, got one that runs round our field all the time, I sent Bob & Billy out to get her up, but Mack had got her a few evenings before. We have up 4 of our own and a little unmarked & unbranded cow that Bob drove up don't know whose she is. I make a little butter. I wish so much that I could send you an other bucket full by Oliver when he goes down. Jim Scott is fixing very slowly to get off to Mexico I don't think he will be ready under 2 months yet, for I think he calculates to lay by his corn before he starts.

Wednesday May 4th Aunt Cinda heard Bet almost swear to Jim that Susan her cook should not cultivate it. She leads him as much by the nose as ever Susan did John—and a closer, stingier young woman never was born. Uncle Mc had been repairing his wagons for him, has them all about fixed but he has to get traces yet, & numerous other things to do—& you know Jim is so slow. He wants Uncle Mc to drive one wagon to Mexico for him, will take Sandy & Mack, & has engaged fool Jim Mays. He went to Navasota with George Alston about 10 days ago & were both sworn into CS Service before they could get a detail to haul cotton. Alston expects a detail to haul cotton also. Yarborough has a detail to oversee for his son. Jeff Haynie failed to get his detail, & I hear has gone to Galveston to join Co I. Wm Terrell is still out & expects to remain out. Nelia is down on him about it, he is such a very healthy looking man that she seems to think his complaint is all fudge. He is no favorite with me. I like Frank Perry much the best. Frank has now the look of a drinking man & I hear takes a little too much sometimes. Mittie is very uneasy about her baby's lungs now, she seems very delicate, & the dregs of the Hooping cough cling to her yet—and althrough their sickness with the cough, they would bleed at the mouth when they would have a hard paroxism of coughing. Hatties children did not bleed so, nor none of the negros that had it. I fear they are born to fill an early grave. I feel sorry for Mittie she is such a devoted fond mother.

Bettie Scott is going to increase her family again and I am wicked & hard hearted enough to feel very little pity for her she says it don't hurt her.

One astonishing piece of news I must add. Jim Mays, that big fool that used to shout with Ben Jones, was married about 2 weeks ago, to a widow with two children named Johnson I think—is a sister of Jim Thomas' wife, and they say is about as big a fool as Jim Mays. Alston has been Jims guardian, and gave his consent for the license to be issued. Alston has a negro woman belonging to Mays. He has moved his wife down in one of those cabins in Jim Scott's yard & she is to remain there until Jim gets back from Mexico. What do you suppose their children will be, can they be any thing else but fools? and what will he do with a family. He carried her to church and he thought her so pretty and loved her so much that he got up and went to her & hugged & kissed her & she said "go away from here you nasty rascal, hugging & kissing me before all these folks" a glorious couple, but I think the marriage should have been prevented, for we have fools enough in the world now. Bob is not entirely well yet tho' he goes to school, stayed at home yesterday & Billy went with Mary. Bob is neater with his person than he was several months ago, never fails to wash his face & comb his hair before breakfast. I asked him why he did not part his hair to one side, & he said "why Ma Gen Magruder parts his hair in the middle" says he heard Charley Van H[orn] say so. Mr Oliver will go down in a week. How I wish you could stay at home a month. I hope to get a letter tomorrow from you.

affectionately
L S Neblett

Galveston
May 8th/64

Dear Lizzie

This is a lonely evening with me. As I have no where to go that would interest me I am in the Office by myself for it is Sunday and little or nothing to do to day. I feel so very lonely to day that it is akin to the blues. You know I seldom have that complaint. When I do it looks so strange that any one can take an interest in any thing. All familiar affairs appear so trivial and worthless and empty vanity. Do not think I have the blues now, for if I have it at all it is only a touch of it. It is lonelyness a yearning to see somebody that I care for—some human that I like & love wife children &c, to be at home to get away from the crowd of people who look which way you please may be seen standing sitting walking sauntering or riding. Just in my present frame of mind I look at these things as I would at a monotonous picture old, dingy, and covered with dust. In a word I should like to be at home very much. Now these feelings have no origin in my unpleasant circumstances or situation surrounding me. For on the contrary I am more pleasantly situated in the office and a boarding house than I have been since I left the Co. It is therefore that I realize those verses "the mind itself can make a hell of heaven or heaven of hell."[4] I take a strange fancy to look inwardly upon my mind and feelings when I am lonesome or have the blues and trying to find out the cause. As I have just said I am very pleasantly situated in regards to a boarding house. When I was looking around for a new boarding house I met a Capt Breidin who boarded with me at Mrs Heller last winter. He married a cousin of Frank Perry and appeared anxious for me to come to the house he was boarding at & I did so. [He was] boarding with a Mrs Jameson who has a daughter about 13 years old—but I recollect now that I told you of her &c. Well if it was not for being away from home or rather from my family whom I wish to see, I believe when I am pleasantly situated than any other time I should be as happy as a soldier could be but enough of this or I will fill my sheet with matters that you will probably say is not very interesting.

Several days ago I recd the articles I wrote to Ma about altho I wrote afterwards saying not to send anything but a few doz eggs and a ham. I got several pieces of bacon 5 bu[shels] of corn and two hundred & fifty eggs.

Sunday night. I had gotten this far when John sliped in on his return from Shackelfords and the remnant of the evening was spent on conversation. Well to return to the things sent, I kept a few doz eggs gave John two doz (did not let him know how many I had) & put the balance in the shop for sale—expect to get $2.00 or 3.00 per doz & if I want any I can use the money in buying. I sold the corn & have written to Pa that if they want any article which can not

---

4. John Milton, *Paradise Lost*, book 1.

be had in Navasota that I would use the money coming from sale of corn for that purpose. I expected to get a letter notifying me of the sending of the articles, but did not. They are a strange set about writing. I enclose Jim Scotts letter to me & my reply. I expected a little better of Jim but it seems he could not stand the temptation. I wish you would send me a copy of that list of cattle I made in that old book, I want to see what they come to and also to let John Scott value the 4 and 5 year olds. I expect the next thing Jim will say will be that he must have the increase counted and not the interest because the increase is more than the interest for counting the calves this year the stock has about doubled in number or nearly so and quite so in value unless cash down was demanded and nothing will bring now more than half its former value. Jim would not have thought of the cattle if he had not moved to Lake Creek. I saw Jeff Haynie a few days ago. He came here with the expectation of being transferred to Co (I) 20th Regt. He is about to fail & will have to rejoin his old Co. He is the most woe begone man I have seen in a long time—looks so dejected & care worn. I cannot help feeling sorry for him. He did not laugh once in half an hours talk & you know that is very unusual for him. Little Tom Rogers told me to day that Mary Eliza wrote to him that Noah Bassett had gotten back—discharged—Graves saw him & says he is fatter than he ever saw him. Parson Glass told me that R[obert] H. B[assett] told him that he had a notion to join Elmores Reg this Fall. You never have written to me what kind of a bargain you made with Myers—how long he is to stay—or what part of the crop he is to get. I suppose you have sent the mare to Dodds if you have not you had better do so at once.

May 9th From what you write me of Bob's health I fear he is studying too hard for a boy of his age. His mind has always been in advance of his body. See to this. I have come to the conclusion that a sound body is of more value than a sound mind. Bob is one of the best children I ever saw and it would make me very unhappy for him to have no health. Billy & Mary are tough and hearty I think Walter will be hearty often a while. Poor Bettie I fear she has inherited some of my infirmities. I would like to clasp the latter darling in my arms once again. I understand the Steamer Bayou City will soon start up the river for repairs—and it is reported that the Co will probably go to Houston & act as Provost Guard. If such proves to be the case it will give the boys a chance of running the blockade home as it is termed. At all events they seem to be pleased in the prospect. For my part I think Provost Guard duty is the meanest duty a soldier has to do. As I expect a letter from you this evening and shall be sorely disappointed if I do not get it, I will stop and finish when the mail is opened. We have a mail from Houston now only three time a week instead of a daily as formerly. If it were not for being separated from you & the children I could find means of having a pleasant time here. But this home feeling is a weakness of my family more so than any other I know of. But I must stop & await the mail.

The letter has come and I have just finished reading it with a kind of hasty joy such as a hungry child devours "good things." But I will read it again this evening and probably twice more before answering. I am not well—have had something like cholera morbus[5] all day—have only taken a cup of coffee altho my landlady very kindly sent me a nice dinner by one of the boarders—the leader of Col Hobby's band a very intelligent man who seems to like me as much as I like him. I tried Composition Powders but it did not ease the severe griping pains & I had to take two doses of pills before I got easy & am now walking about but feel feverish. I do not think I will have any more trouble. I enclose to you Jims letter & mine in reply. The law would give me the cattle if I chose to sue but I shall not. The longer I live the fewer honest men I believe there are. I suppose Bet S[cott] is the cause of it. John S[cott] thinks Ben G[oodrich] acted cowardly or he would not have been captured.

I will reply to yours when I write again. Kiss the children & tell Walter to kiss you for me. You need not send me any Bacon nor butter unless you wish it to sell. It is only worth six dollars per lb now.

yours affectionately
Wm H. Neblett

At Home
Monday May 9th 1864

Dear Will,

A few moments before dinner I happened to think that it was quite time for Mr Oliver to return, and it may be that he has gone, but I'll write & if he is gone I can mail this on my usual day. I have a pair of cotton socks that I intended sending by Oliver but if he has gone, I can send them by some one else, I hope before you need them. It rained almost the whole of Saturday & has been cloudy and misting rain, both yesterday and to day—everything is

---

5. "Cholera morbus" was a term for acute gastroenteritis, the symptoms of which included cramps, vomiting, and diarrhea.

growing fast grass weeds bushes & briars, and to one naturally despairing it is any thing but an enlivening sight to go through our farm, & see its present foul condition, & then cast your eyes on our poor but faithful oxen, almost staggering in the plow and then look at the black fat slick, greasy negros & think what they are. I don't go often I assure you & I seldom speak to the black devils. I think if they had attended to the oxen as they should while they were pretending to feed them, they would not be in their present fix—but it is all well with them. I got one yoke of oxen from Mr Oliver, but one was a very bad ox about breaking over fences, & he got out, & they both left—so we have only our own poor oxen. Uncle Mc offered to loan me his mare & mule, to work 'till he needed them again, but I have no corn to feed them on, & the oxen stagger along on grass. I can console myself in no way, but by inwardly resolving that this is my last farming year on so *grand a scale*—poor consolation, but my allowance of that commodity (consolation) has always been a very meager one, and is less palitable from the fact that I always have to administer the dose myself. You treat my manifold observations & resolutions upon my farming in the future in a very silent manner. I recognize the manner, and having felt the same treatment upon another subject nearer my heart, it causes very bitter unhappy & miserable thoughts to arise. Not that I care, much, but the manner makes me think of the seasons of woe through which I have past—how I wish I would bury those portions of the past in the sea of forgetfulness, and the next 12 years of my life (if I have to live that long) in the ocean of a happy lunacy—and now like an unreasonable fool because I can do neither of these things I am very miserable. Right here I pause and am led by reflection to wish that my letters to you were not such mirrors of my heart. Your letters betray very little of your heart, and your conversation is the same way, and I sometimes think it is an unfair bargain to write so fully & openly of my feelings and never to get a glimpse into your heart but we can neither of us change our nature, and I am well aware that by writing in a constrained manner I would punish myself more than I would you. Mr Oliver has just been here, & says he will start down on Thursday. He has more hope of a speedy peace resulting from our recent & many victories than the presidential election.[6] It is the general & almost universal opinion that the war will end this year, but I have less hope of it than I had of peace coming last year. For fear

---

6. Many southerners hoped that if the Confederate army could endure until the presidential election, a Peace Democrat would defeat Lincoln and negotiate peace with the South.

of disappointment I do not build upon the hope at all. My life seems so wrecked of happiness that I have for a long time felt that it mattered not which way nor how I pass my time—only this—not with a pasel of mean lazy trifling negros, whom I have to clothe feed, nurse & take care of, no matter how thievish, lazy & devilish they are—deliver me from this. I was disappointed by not getting a letter from you last Thursday, it reached me Sat. Mrs Collins sends to the office three times every week, & brings my mail also. I furnish a horse the most of the time. I don't know what I would have done if I had not met with such a good chance to send to the office. She feels very easy about Mr Collins because he was wagon master, & tho' he has recently been deprived of that office yet she thinks he will not be sent back to ranks. You certainly change your boarding houses often enough, and that mention of your present land lady's husband being a prisoner & not heard from in 20 months, made me think immediately of Garrett. I dreamed recently of his returning, & how elated I was, but poor dear Bro, the only true bro I ever had, you are I fear beyond recall, no matter how we wish to see you & be with you.

Don't seeing & hearing that womans Piano make you think of my rat box concern, up the country? I am having quite a time with sickness have one case at least on hands all the time. Sarah & Lee are sick now. Last week Ann my nurse was sick six days, & now the baby is not well—has some kind of a breaking out and the worst kind of a bowel affection, and had a little fever last night & is feverish to day. I bought $10 worth of Rhubarb in Navasota to make some Neutralizing mixture, which I am convinced would conduct her safely through her teething. But I have no receipt for making it, & mothers Beach is in ashes & mine as well be for I'll never see it, & so I can do nothing. Mrs Wilson has a book if I could send to her & get it & copy the receipt. My conduct & my words about my children do contradict each other—no mother ever felt more anxiety, or was more unwearied in her attention to her sick children than I am, & ever have been—and my babies especially weigh heavy on my heart, until they finished teething. I dread my baby more than I ever did any one of the others, and in looking forward to the end of this summer it seems an age.

I notice that you have ceased to mention any of the children in your letters for some time have inquired twice why Mary did not write—and this is an other reason why I think you are very well contented to remain away from home, and sometimes I think it is a very good thing that you are thus if we could both manage to make a living & have something ahead to educate & dress the children with, it would perhaps be better for us both to remain so,

about 12 years at least. I know it would be asking a great deal of you, to re-
nounce the comforts of home & the society of your children but if there could
be a comfortable & nice home for you & the children & some one to fill my
place as mother I would be willing to banish myself and be a wanderer upon
the face of the earth, earning my bread with toil, than to have an other child
or be harassed continually by fears that I was pregnant, or be treated with coldness and a want of affection by you, & yet be with you all the time. I think I
shall go crazy on this subject yet. It is mighty poor consolation you give in
yours of the 2nd about my being pregnant. You have no reason to be sure it is
not pregnancy that ails me, but I don't think so, if I did I would not be sitting
here this minute writing to you. If you could see me now you would not think
me so fat, I begin to feel the effects of nursing a yearling. I reckon you have
rec'd a letter from Jim on the cattle subject. He told Uncle Mc that he would
write, & you could have the cattle yet for the same prices agreed upon long
ago, only he must be paid now in specie or in cotton & he knows you have
neither of them now. Jim & Bet have acted mighty mean about the cattle I
think, & if Bet did make Jim act so, is no excuse for Jim. If I thought I had
the power to influence you to do a mean act, contrary to your sense of justice &
right, I would dispise you for your weakness. If they send over to get the cows
I have up I shall write Jim word that when he comes after them himself he
can get them, & then if he thinks his negro woman can't milk them all, he
will have to come over and take one of mine to do his milking.

Teusday morn 10th—I make near about as much butter as we can use now,
but if I had vegetables to season would not be enough. I had a weary time of
it last night with my baby—she was so hot I could not bear her feet to touch
me. Poor little thing, it will be a hard struggle for her to live through her teething, and when I think of what the future may hold in store for her I feel so
sad, & know that it would be much better for her to die now in her infancy,
but tis natural for the mothers heart to cling to her child & preserve it as long
as possible, no matter what fate may await it. I do want some of that Neautral-
izing mixture so badly—her bowels are so much disordered & no one can conceive the trouble a child with bowel affection is unless they have had the
nursing of one, & it all falls on me. John Nix spent last week at his mothers.
Mother has told him that she would have to pay too much to keep him, she
pretends like she believes that the law requiring such as Yarborough to pay 100
lbs of bacon 100 lbs beeff & a bond of $500 for each negro applies to her also.
I think it is only an excuse to be rid of him she is alarmed for fear that Babe &
he will take a notion to marry, & he is of no use to her on the farm. He prom-

ised to stay with the negros while they were at work on her house & did stay a good portion of the time the week Mr Taylor worked them, but after that did not go once in two or three days—just stayed in the house read a novel & chatted with Babe. She had two of Mrs Nelms hands who are pretty good carpenters hired but dismissed them long ago—was paying high & you know how slowly negros work by themselves. The work that remains to be done could be done in a week by two good hands, & she could move up, but I don't know what she intends doing. Her garden is up where the house was burned, and all her fruit is there, & her fine peach trees are fuller than they have been for four years, & the Plums are very plentiful have begun to ripen now. Aunt Cinda has been here to day and says that Bro Jim says he saw Mother last saturday & she says that Dr Patrick says he don't see how she can get out of paying the meat & giving bond for having John Nix detailed—if so I know mother is in trouble, I have no idea that John will stay with her—she is so out with him. Jim says that she is going to send a wagon load of cotton when he goes, & he promises to attend to it for her—she furnishes wagon team driver & cotton. Jim has not yet received his detail, & has been getting ready & acting upon a promise of one & is now in a most terrible hurry to get off this week, & says his crop may go to hell. He has been going to town some time expecting to receive his detail by mail, but had cut it yesterday.

I send my tithe meat to town with Mrs Collins & Mrs Hursts last Saturday. I weighed on my little brass scales 103 lbs & they sent me back a receipt for 94 lbs. I did not write what amount I sent. Wm Roe receives the meat—they have never assessed my meat yet, but I had such a good opportunity of sending it, I do so. I failed entirely to get a wheel from Coody, sent after it, & he was gone to Anderson so his wife told Joe to find out whether he would have to go to the war or not. Sent next day again & he said he could not tell whether he could make it [or] not as he had to go to Hemstead or Houston to find out whether he would have to go into service, & now if I find out any thing about it I must send again. I think I'll try Harbuck who does not make as good a wheel as Coody & asks about $30 for it, & then perhaps have to wait months before you get it. These detailed workmen play the devil. The baby is better to day than she was yesterday. The little thing looks much worsted already. I never know how much I love her until she gets sick. I don't believe you love her much, & are getting used to being away from both wife and children. If I knew whether you wanted your summer clothes I could send them by Mr Oliver, but will have a chance of sending by some one else. I have another sick negro to day Nances baby. Sarah is better—my medicine is almost out. They are plowing the cotton now, every one praises our corn, if we could only get it clean & if the team was good & the negros would work there would be nothing to prevent making a good crop. Ferrell has my hides liming now & I will try & get Mrs Oliver to go with me tomorrow to see if Old Keifer won't let me grind bark on his mill. I fear my tanning will be a failure. I must send this to Mr Oliver to night. When I forget about having children I want to see you so badly I can hardly stand it.

affectionately yours
L S Neblett

Galveston
May 17th/64

Dear Lizzie,

Yesterday was my regular time for writing to you but a severe Neuralgia I have been suffering with for the last three days without a moments ease day or night prevented me from doing so and as we have but three mails a week this will be two days behind. To day I am free of Neuralgia and well but quite weak. Your[s] of the 3rd and one by Oliver have been rec'd. I did not see Oliver. He gave the letter to John who gave it to me & said that Oliver had a pr of socks for me & would bring them over when he came to town. You never say any thing of Mrs Oliver now, have you fallen out.

Upon reading over yours of the 3rd I am reminded of your question "if I did not desire more than usual to see you last night" (2nd) I cannot recollect although I taxed my memory when I first recd your letter. But I think I did for the reason that I wrote to you that day and closed the letter late that evening. It is very difficult to recollect what one thinks of after a day or two passes. I know what I write about I think about afterwards and it [is] very probable that that night I thought of you and the children more than ordinarily, and wished to see you more than usual. You accuse me of not wishing to come home or rather of not desiring to see you. Now if you had accused me of not loving you I would deny it honestly and sincerely. But the other I do not think you could expect me to do otherwise for you admit that you would rather be a wanderer than that I should be with you and endanger you with pregnancy. Now do not think I do not or cannot appreciate or understand the acuteness of your painful feelings on that subject. I know that it goads you to the verge of insanity and that what can do or have such an effect must be

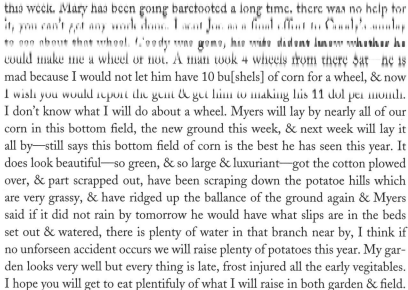

this week. Mary has been going barefooted a long time, there was no help for it, you can't get any work done. I went Joe on a final effort to Chealp's sunday to see about that wheel. Ceedy was gone, his wife dident know whether he could make me a wheel or not. A man took 4 wheels from there but he is mad because I would not let him have 10 bu[shels] of corn for a wheel, & now I wish you would report the gent & get him to making his 11 dol per month. I don't know what I will do about a wheel. Myers will lay by nearly all of our corn in this bottom field, the new ground this week, & next week will lay it all by—still says this bottom field of corn is the best he has seen this year. It does look beautiful—so green, & so large & luxuriant—got the cotton plowed over, & part scrapped out, have been scraping down the potatoe hills which are very grassy, & have ridged up the ballance of the ground again & Myers said if it did not rain by tomorrow he would have what slips are in the beds set out & watered, there is plenty of water in that branch near by, I think if no unforseen accident occurs we will raise plenty of potatoes this year. My garden looks very well but every thing is late, frost injured all the early vegitables. I hope you will get to eat plentifuly of what I will raise in both garden & field.

I tell you, your mind opperates upon mine as far distant as we are. I felt that you were longing to see home—me & the children. This constant & never ceasing horror I have of childbearing constantly obtrudes itself between me & my desire & longing to see & clasp you round the neck once more & thus my longing wears a curb. God who knows my heart, knows that no wife ever loved a husband more fondly or was ever more willing to make any kind of a reasonable sacrifice for his sake, but Will, I had rather live in perpetual banishment, than have an other child or live 12 yrs with the constant dread of such a disaster forever before me. Mary Haynie & Babe were both very anxious to go to G[alveston] some time ago, & Mary said if I would go she would, but I did not like the idea of spunging on Sarah McAlpine & beside if I voluntary entered the lions den, and got caught I would most certainly cut my throat. I know you think I have always been crazy enough on a certain subject, but I am a hundred times worse now. Bob's health is better now, & have nothing very good to say of Bob, he has changed greatly since he started to school & is still growing worse & is not hurting himself studying—don't do much of it, & has rebelled at school twice. She tried to make him set on the dunce stool once, & he told her he dident come to school to set on the dunce stool—she took hold of him to pull him on it, & he drew back his hand, shook his head, & entered into the pantomime of giving her a lick—she sent for a switch, & he then sung out the difficulty[,] the lesson was not in his book, so he could not study it. He has heard some of those bad boys too big for their pants talk & is imitating their talk. I am very sorry to see Bob act so, but evil communications will corrupt good manners. I want you to write to him, & I will make Mary read it to him, & try to enforce the idea that you are much hurt at hearing of his conduct, he don't mind me as well as he once did. Noah Bassett is not discharged, only transferred, to do indoor service on this side of the Miss river. If R[obert] H. B[assett] does enter your Co, I want you to get a transfer to an other. Well I know it must be getting late, & the fleas (of which there is a legion here) are nearly eating me up. I'll quit, & finish this sheet at mothers. Good night, how I wish I could hug & kiss you, before I close my eyes.

Wednesday eve—18th—I came up this morning to mothers safely. The baby had a fever last night & is still feverish, poor little darling she is suffering I must give her some purgative to night. Mother has a lot of sick negros on hand. Last sunday Frances, the diseased negro died, from that eating cancer or what ever it was, a great many bones came out of her face before she died. Mother is fixing up a wagon to send with Jim & six bales of cotton will lay it all out for cloth and bagging & rope. The Garvin family think that Ed Garvin is dead you saw his name in the list as dangerously wounded in the breast. Our mare is at Dodds staying there in his pasture. The Goodrich family have heard that Ben is accused of cowardice, & they ran round mightily, I think he acted cowardly, two men who were in the fight, one came to Anderson one to Montgomery, both tell the same tale that he got behind a stump & remained there 'till the yanks took him. John Nix has written to E R Smith for an other detail, mother feels greatly relieved that she is rid of him. If the baby gets worse & I think her in danger I'll let you know.

Affectionately,
L.S.N.

May 18th
[Will Neblett to Lizzie Neblett]

Ma is very uneasy about Sterling—says they have not heard from him in a long time. I suppose he is moving about in Ark so much that he cannot get time or material to write. Ma's letter was dated 13th and says that Dr McIntosh died yesterday (12) after illness of 16 days. He made a will and divides his property into four equal parts between his wife and three children. Pa was with him for 5 or 6 days and made himself sick sitting up with him. She says Roberts rings have been sent to her.

Ma's hand writing reminds me very much of Mary's. I think they are going to write the same kind of a hand. Tell Mary I will answer her letter next time I write. I suppose you assisted her in her last letter for I noted that the diction is good—better than I suppose she is capable of. I suppose you are having a plenty of vegetables now. There are plenty here in the market but are enormously high. I saw an old man here yesterday who raises strawberries for sale. I understood that he had sold $20,000 worth of berries off an acre. He told me he had gathered 200 bus[hels] from an acre.

You never have written to me what you thought of swaping Garrets place with your Ma and selling the Lake Creek place. The latter could not be sold during the war but the exchange with your mother might be made any time if she will agree to it. Do you think she will do it. I dislike the idea of moving again but if we conclude to do so the sooner the better for I am so tired [of] living on half fixed places and I suppose you have better cause to be so than I am. But I expect you think I am a little too early in scheming for the future. It is your nature to think of the past and ring the changes on those sad words it might have been, mine of what should be. I think it would take both our heads to make a wise one.

Galveston
May 22nd/64

Dear Lizzie

This is sunday evening and finds me alone in the office. Every body is gone or going in search of pleasure—some to ride some to walk and some to lurch. For my part having just returned from the telegraph office up stairs in search of news from Va I return to the office disappointed and painfully impressed with gloomy foreboding as to the result of the great struggle there between Grants and Lee's armies which is to have such an effect on lengthening or shortening this war.[7] It has been a fearful struggle for our army fighting against such odds. How many thousands now be cold and still in death—how many writhe in torture from ghastly wounds terrible to behold. How terrible

---

7. Beginning in May 1864 Robert E. Lee's and Ulysses S. Grant's armies clashed in a series of battles in Virginia. These battles were the Wilderness and Spotsylvania campaigns.

the stoutest heart must bleed when left to reflect undisturbed by exciting causes. I often think of an incident related by a captain of the 2nd Texas which goes to show how even a soldiers feelings are wrought upon by scenes of the battle field. He says a young man in his Co not more than eighteen at the battle of Shiloh fainted at the full sight of blood and he laid him down thinking that he had been shot. He says this young man fainted at the sight of blood in every battle but would soon recover and fight through the battle as bravely as the bravest, and never was known to falter from danger.

We have had nothing from Va since the 6th May altho there is Telegrapher communication all the way except three days travel across the Miss river. Not one half an hour passes but I think of this battle. This suspense and the unusual silence in this room makes me feel lonely and sad. I have been thinking of home and my desire to [be] with you and the children makes me feel still more gloomy. I expect a letter from you tomorrow and shall feel disappointed if I do not get it. I saw Oliver last Friday, he was well—gave me an idea that your crop was very promising—the corn particularly. Well I will stop and walk around town for exercise. I believe I have seen every house in the place in my evening walks. City scenery is very monotonous and I never have found a walk so uninteresting as are to me now in this place.

Monday 22 May. I have just finished yours of the 17 & 18th. It must have stayed at your Ma's several days for it was post marked 21st inst. And so you have confessed that you had rather not meet me, or in other words you had rather not under the circumstances see me now and perhaps any other time. I believe I can generally anticipate what you are gradually coming to before you are aware of it yourself. In this case I anticipated correctly, I suppose you will be sorry when the war or peace allows me to return. I am glad to hear that the children are well except Bettie. I think the hotness of her head arises from the inflamation of her bowels by sympathy. I would like to see her it seems to me that she must have improved very fast the last three months to be walking now. It is three months to day since I saw her. I was surprised at what you write me of Bob, but do not know that I should have been. He is getting large and old enough for us to expect some kind of devilment. I heard about a week ago that Parson Glass was going to be married to Mrs Hutcheson. Lt Samuels told me. He learned it through one of the Lewises here. Samuels ridiculed her & told me her relations here were bitterly opposed to it though he said this confidentially. Well I think I am a better judge of woman kind than you are though I must admit they sometimes go a little farther than I expected and are a good deal worse. But I do not mean to say that I have no confidence in womankind for I believe them better than mankind as a general thing. What are you going to do for a school when Mrs B[uckley] quits. I would like for the children to continue. What you write me about Ben G[oodrich] I heard a week ago from John S[cott]. I expect it is true and if so the blood of some of his Co is upon his hands for his Co suffered more than any other in the Reg. No news from the battles in Va—every body is expecting the worst. If any thing comes between this & morning I will write it. I am very well.

yours affectionately
Wm H. Neblett

May 23rd I went to Fort Magruder last evening with John & stayed all night and have just returned warm and a little tired for it is one and a half miles all the way through sand. John came in and is now in the office finishing his letter. He has been at it since day light. I suppose you have seen some of the rings he has made. Mit[tie] Womack sent him a piece of gilted pacha comb & he made several rings. He has one on now for Susan with a gold set inscribed with the initials of her name. It is really very pretty.

I am sorry to hear you speak of fleas at home. They are very bad here. Some nights between mosquitoes & fleas I do not sleep half the night. The fleas are insupportable at Fort Magruder but no mosquitoes. I would have written to Mary & Bob by this mail but my trip with John did not leave me time and I must close now or fail to get it on time.

yours affectionately
Wm H. Neblett

At Home
Teusday night May 24th 1864

Dear Will,

The 24th May, does it make any memories of the past with you? All day to day, the memory of 12 years ago has been with me, & I have viewed myself as I stood then, a maiden of 19 summers expecting more & building more upon the future than I ever have since. Upon the whole, I think I have no very just cause to murmur. My father & two Bro's were sleeping quietly & full of health within reach of my voice this time 12 yrs ago, and they are now numbered with the dead, and on my ear falls to night the regular & healthful breathing of five immortal souls who have sprung into existence since then. They have been dearly bought—gifts to me, & gifts forced upon me, yet I feel to night that I could cease to murmur at what has been, if I could only calculate with any degree of certainty upon what will be—but I know no doom that would horrify me so much, as to know, or believe that, 12 yrs to come would add 5 more children to my number. I had rather spend the remainder of my life even tho it were 35 yrs in the Penitentiary or in solitary confinement for the same length of time, either of which would be ten thousand times worse than death. Right here I think to myself "I do wish that this horrible bugbear of mine (childbearing) was not eternally thrusting itself before me,["] both in thoughts of the past, present, or future, and thus affording material for almost half I write to you. I know Will you are tired of it, and God knows my heart is worn to the very quick upon the subject, but like you, my memory of you is becoming more intimately associated with the idea of childbearing every day, and you have no idea how the fear of such a disaster clips the wings of my desire to see you, & be with you. I did not feel this in your absence heretofore, but now the age of my babe warns me that my time of danger has arrived.

You ask why have I lost all hope of our living together without any more children. I am naturally given to despondency and in this matter have had enough I think to clip the wings of the most hopeful. Have been trying to ward off this danger now 10 yrs, and had but three years between the two last, have never delayed the matter but a little over six months twice. Hope is dead, we can not live together without a constant fear & dread upon my mind, which would destroy all me peace, I believe you are willing to assist me, but I doubt all preventives in my case, & the one in which I have most faith would be quite if not utterly impossible to procure. I mean a syringe that will throw matter easily and with a great deal of force. The old thing I have would kill any body to use it a year even if it would prevent a mishap. I asked you last year to search out one, in fact, wanted you to try & exchange mine at the depot before I was caught the last time, but you seemed very indifferent on the subject, & I let it drop with a mental determination to stand on the safe side myself—but we can talk this matter over fully when we meet again, & if we never meet, there will be no use to agree upon any terms, but let me say right here that if you apply & get your wine detail this summer, dont start home without a good quantity of the pulverized Ergot,[8] and as good a syringe as you can find, Richardon's No 1 that I described to you long ago is the best I know of.

---

8. Ergot, a fungus that grows on grain, especially rye, causes contractions of the uterus. Some nineteenth-century doctors used it as an aid for hastening childbirth and for relieving postpartum hemorrhaging. The violent contractions caused by ergot, however, could cause ruptures, tears, fetal damage, or even death. It was a common belief that ergot induced abortion in the early stages

I returned home yesterday. When I wrote to you a week ago the babe had a fever she was not entirely clear of fever for six days—and Sat night I was very much alarmed about her, she had such a rattling in her throat (I now suppose) & she is always so restless when she has a fever that she would not let me apply my ear to her lungs. I did not sleep one third of the night for I thought she had Pneumonia, & that alarmed me so much—the next day mother & I began giving her Lobelia, which made her throw up a great deal of phlegm, & relieved her greatly, & that eve the fever went off. I gave her half a liver pill, for 4 successive nights, and her discharges were the most billious I ever saw from a baby. She is cool & moist now all the time, but is very fretful, & weak. I don't think her teeth had any thing to do with her sickness. I love her very much & I think her much more lovable now than when you saw her. The other children are well except bad colds, which nearly all of them have. I found Kate sick when I got home, & this evening Tom came in saying he was sick. I recd your letter in the legal envelope last Sat, & it had come unsealed, it contained six pages letter paper, but if that was the end of your letter you forgot or failed to sign your name. To day Jim Scott started with his waggons—5, Uncle Mc drove one & started half sick. Susan did let him have 5 bales at 60 cents, and Uncle Mc promised him 3 but Susan would not bale the cotton for him. She Susan tells it now that John has writen to her that he is completely disgusted with Elmores Regt & is going to try & get transfered, she told Myers the other day that John had writen to her that Elmores Regt was going to be disbanded soon. I don't believe the tale tho' John may have heard such a rumor & wrote it to Susan. Aunt Cinda told me to day that John was mad at you last year, about the way you treated him when he was sick over on the spit & when he went to leave he said he asked you to make Jack hunt up his things & help him off and you replied that you "dident care a damn about Jacks things" & said you would do nothing to assist him and blames you that he belongs to the Regt he does. I am glad he is not in the Co you belong to.

I came home by Mrs Olivers & gave her some plums. We have had no falling out, she is one of my best friends I think. She has made Seward come up or nearly so, to his promise about the articles he was to bring her from Browns-

---

of pregnancy. For more information on ergot and other forms of nineteenth-century birth control see Wertz, *Lying-In*, 65–66; Leavitt, *Brought to Bed*, 144–48; Brodie, *Contraception and Abortion*; Gordon, *Woman's Body, Woman's Right*, 49–71.

ville when she agreed to let him have the cotton. He has sent her two bolts of domestic 1 bolt of calico & 20 pounds of coffee & some other articles. I would be willing to give a good deal of cotton for as much as she has of cloth. Jim I think will accept your offer about the cattle. He asked mother if she would not let him have 4 bales & take the debt on me—said he had about 4 bales at my house. What do you think Mrs Oliver made me a present of 2 pounds of coffee, & said she had loaned Mrs Hurst 2 lbs which she would give me also when she returned it. I tried to make her take something but she would not hear to it. She is a very liberal hearted woman. That is all true about Mrs Hutcheson & Mr Glass but I cant tell whether she will have him now or not. I gathered my first mess of Peas this evening for tomorrow, & have had no beans yet, nothing in fact, and now it seems like the drouth has set in, the ground is all cracking open, & every thing seems suffering for rain. I reckon they will finish laying by the corn this week, & about finish scraping out the cotton. They replanted the potatoe hills, & set out four or five rows of ridges. I think he made the negros waste the slips by putting two in [every] hill, if he had not done that, our whole patch would now be set out. Mothers grape crop is fine, & has the only plums & peaches in the county—she will move up to her new house this week. I havent had the chance to notice for your crop of Mustang grapes, but hope there will be a fine crop and that you will come home, if you come on that detail you ought to come in about a month from this. It is so late that I must close for to night or else I cant work tomorrow. Aunt is getting over her hurt, but is not well yet by a good deal—she sent for Brown & he thinks one of her short ribs is broken. Tomorrow is our wedding day & I know almost that you won't forget it this time & will write some to me tomorrow. Good night, and may I give you one of your lingering kisses in your dreams of me to night.

May 25th The day is a bright cloudless one, and the sun seems hot enough to melt me. We are needing rain very much, and they need it much worse up about mothers. Myers says our corn is not suffering much yet. They have conscripted Ben Langham & Parson Sims, they ate dinner at mothers last night Thursday. Ben L. was awful mouthy, the Parson said not not [*sic*] a word. Myers told me to day that he read a letter from some one in La to Langford (the liar), and the letter stated that his mother was dead, & had left him 20 negros 4 good mules & a tract of good land. He says he is going to the land soon, will live there. I spent the day at Mrs Haynies on Sat, the baby seemed better that morning, & mother & I went over. Mary laughed about Jeff writing home so much about Jno Scott, told a good many things about him &

even went so far as to tell that he was then making a finger ring, while he was writing. I don't know whether John expresses his dissatisfaction about the Regt & Co to any one or not. Mary told me that it was reported before Dr McIntosh['s] death that his lady was as *"women wish to be who love their lords?"*[9] If my love was judged by that rule, it would be woefully deficient. She Mrs McI—is a very unpopular lady, she made a good many people mad while the Dr was sick by refusing their proffered aid about sitting up with the Dr. Nelia Kerr for one, I think she must be a fool with the big head. Like Bet Scott no doubt she thinks "money makes the man, and poverty *the fellow."*[10] She told Jno Nix that, and made him mad but he did not let on. I consider it a direct insult. Bet is one of the biggest fools I ever knew. It has been very warm all day, and many prophesy that we will have no more rain soon. Mrs Garvin has heard that Jno Terrell who has recently returned from Youngs Regt says that there is a some hope for Ed to recover. Ed Bowen has bought a furlough of 60 days, & is coming 1st part of June. Mrs Jim Collins has moved down to Harrisburge where her husband is at work in some kind of a shop. She is doing a bad business I think, for she will return with a baby in her arms or a prospect of one, and perhaps the war won't end for several years yet. I hope that the report of Lee whipping Grant is true—if Lee is whipped, it will add several years more to the length of the war.[11]

You misunderstand me about my farming next year. I am willing to stay here & would rather live here than in Anderson but I don't want all these negros to torment me, but we will talk it over when you come home. I don't want you [to] give out trying to get home this summer, you must come, I want to see you so much, and you can make up your mind to not endanger my safety, and I will be overjoyed to see you. Do come. I have never mentioned the land swap to mother. I have set my heart on that end for that reason delay saying any thing to her I fear she wont agree to it. She can not work this land as readily as she can that Quinn place, & you know mother is as eager to make now as when she first began her life. We both of us will talk it over with her when you come up. Now please Will try and come & stay at home as long as

9. John Home, *Douglas,* act 1, scene 1 (1756).

10. This expression may have derived from a line in Diogenes Laërtius's *Thales,* chapter 7, " 'Tis money makes the man; and he who's none/Is counted neither good nor honourable."

11. Lizzie is most likely referring to the Spotsylvania Campaign, which took place in Virginia toward the end of May 1864. With both sides sustaining heavy losses, Grant was unable to shake Confederate control of Spotsylvania. McPherson, *Battle Cry of Freedom,* 728–33.

you can. I don't think I'll ever wean my babe & that will help to ward off some danger. Good bye and may God watch over & bless you—is the prayer of one who loves you devotedly. Myers says that nearly half of the potatoe slips have died that were set out & watered last week. The sun is too hot, it seems awful warm & sultry to me.

L S Neblett

At Home
Sunday eve May 29th 1864

Dear Will,

I went to church this morning at the Gilmore school house returned, ate my dinner, read myself to sleep, and after a pleasant nap have awakened full of thoughts of you, and some items that your letters have recently contained which items were elicited by some of my not wise but strong expressions of feeling on a certain subject—and I feel like writing to you once again about the same thing, & if I thought I could perform the vow I would make one, having you for witness that I would never again trouble you on the same subject, but like all crazy people, I must & will talk of that which affects my mind temper heart & life most intimately. Will from you I could never keep a secret, have never an idea or opinion of any importance without feeling a strong desire to to [*sic*] tell you, & I have often thought, if I were to entertain an idea of murdering any one even yourself, I should certainly have to tell you of it, if the matter was delayed a single week. In your last of the 23rd inst read last Thursday, you say I confess that I had rather not meet you under the present circumstances now, & you add perhaps any other time—and say you can generally anticipate what I am gradually coming to before I am aware of it myself, and then say that "I suppose you will be sorry when the war or peace allows me to return." This clause drew tears to my eyes, for I knew by that you did not comprehend my feelings on this subject. My heart would be supremely selfish to frame such a wish, or feel sorrow at the close of the war. I sometimes think that I could in noble cause become a martyr, & your supposition suggested the idea that I could, if the welfare & peace of my country could be obtained then sacrifice myself upon the alter of childbearing, & feel that I was performing a noble work, which thoughts & feelings could sustain me in the pain & trials, as thoughts of God sustained the christian martyrs even at the burning of the stake—but nothing of the kind can effect the war or woe of my country, and this childbearing is only a private matter between you & I.

I have never doubted your desire to assist me, but alas! all our combined efforts have been a series of failures for 10 years, & I have grown more bitterly opposed each year until now it has become a matter of life & death to me—and tho' I admit that I fear to see & meet you, yet I feel that if I could banish you that the separation is & would be more acutely felt & wept over by me than by you. You are my all. My kindred have disappointed me, those who remain, and death has taken the dearest brother I ever had—my children are too small & young to be companions for many a long year, & to you all my thoughts & feelings turn, & if you are permitted to return to us, I feel that I would & could be as happy as any woman in the confederacy, with that horrible bug bear of mine removed. I would be willing to give up all the property I have upon earth freely, to be insured beyond a doubt that from this trouble I would hence forth be free—that I could live with you, in peace & love, undisturbed by such disasters or fears of such. I expect you often feel fretted & mad at me, that I feel so deeply on this subject, & when I think thus, I almost cry aloud for death. I can see no chance of happiness for me, therefore, I am ever ready to welcome death eagerly; it would be better for us both—time soon heals such wounds; (sooner it seems to me in cases of bereaved husbands & wives, than in any other) and you could marry again, & I know you could not marry an other woman with as strong feelings on this subject as I have. Oh how much better would it be if I could only die, & this longing for death is only an evidence of my love for you—better die than make you unhappy & discontented, & were you thus through my conduct, life would be worth nothing to me—but I can not hasten nor defer death, & it remains only for me to support the misery & trials of life as I best can. You have never thought on this subject as I have. You have always in thinking of it reasoned this to me & to yourself. A preventive can be used, there are infalible ones, & I am willing to do all I can to assist and I have no reason to believe, and strongly hope that no more accidents will occur—and then you let the subject drop. Never think of the past, & how every effort has been baffled for years, until hope has died in my breast, and now I want to beg of you not [to] think hard of me, that I said I had rather not meet you. If I did not love you devotedly I would not fear to meet you, but I fear that my affection & desire to please will get the better of my prudence & reason, & that I may thereby suffer immensely in both body & mind—but this life, the one I now lead in your absence is utterly devoid of pleasure, the highest pleasure I have is in reading & replying to your letters, and at times I long so ardently to see you, & talk with you, and be near you, that at such times I feel that I am willing to risk even pregnancy, provided I am armed with Ergot, and various other implements of or for safety.

You must try and come home this summer or fall, and assist me in making preparations for the next year. I build no hopes upon peace, and do not suffer myself to hope that you can return before the close of the war. Uncle Mc will leave John's place next year, & has as yet made no arrangements about getting another home. I have thought it would be as good a chance as I will have to get him to attend to the farm, provided there was a house for them to live in. I have mentioned this idea to no one, and am some what out of the notion on account of Bob McClure. He is an awful child. Last week, Aunt was over here several days putting in & starting our cloth, and Bob was not going to school, & came over with her two days. The first day he was hunting his old horse, & Aunt Cinda asked me to let Billy go with him, which I did. He spent the most of that day at the lake, tried to get Billy in, there were a lot of the school boys, & Johns boys there, & Henry Scott[12] got on old Crusader and made him swim in the lake, & Henry can't swim himself, & if he had fallen off might have drowned. The next day he came over, and Billy went with him to bring out Aunts horse out of the Gilmore's field & he put Lee up first and then in putting Billy up before Lee, pushed him clear over the horse, and the child fell on his arm in some way and strained it badly, he cant use it nor straighten it and it is swollen to twice its natural size. It is his left arm. I feel some uneasiness about it, he does not complain of it hurting him much. I have bound clay & vinegar to it, and keep wet bandages on it all the time, a little more & it would have been broken. Bob Mc curses like a trooper, & is very disgusting in his ways. I have learned in our Bob's case that "evil communications corrupt good manners,"[13] and I fear Bob Mc's influence so much that I don't think I can get my own consent to have him with my children—better loose [*sic*] all I have than have my boys ruined. While I was at mothers last Bob got mad at Billy and called him a "God damned liar" what do you think of that? he talks, so Mary says very largely at school about chewing tobacco, & has taken several chews, says he don't fear me, and when he gets on Dick [the] horse, or any other, he goes full tilt making them jump fences, &c. has no mercy on a horse. I have talked to him repeatedly about running his horse,

12. Henry Scott was the son of Lizzie Neblett's brother and sister-and-law, John and Susan Scott.

13. 1 Cor. 15:33.

and a whipping now hangs over him about cursing Billy. Bob's conduct has discouraged & mortified me more about our children than any thing that any of them ever did. He is the best child we have naturally, and if he is led astray so easily, what may we not expect of the others. I have taken occasion to mortify Bob about his conduct all the time, I want to make him feel it as keenly as possible, & feel that he looses [*sic*] something when he deserves my displeasure. He was complaining yesterday and to day of being sick, gave him some pills last night. I read a letter from Serena Jemigan last week—she wrote that poor Beaden Fielder had just died, he is the one who shot himself accidentally last fall he was confined to his bed for months. Fielder and his oldest son Curtis reached home before he was buried, but not before he died.

We were blessed with a splendid rain on the night of the 27th and the morning of the 28th inst. I think it will be almost the making of the corn crop, our corn was not suffering for rain, but my garden, potatoe vines &c was— have now about six ridges set out. If the potatoe crop does as well as the new vines we had last year we will have at least 200 bu[shels], so I feel easy about that crop. We will make as many potatoes as we want to eat I hope.

Monday morn May 30th/64 Dear Will, as I wrote 4 pages yesterday and will have an opportunity of sending to the office tomorrow I'll add a little more this morning and post it tomorrow instead of Thursday my usual day.

We have the first piece of cloth in the loom, and it is so fine that I won't undertake to weave it, or to put Sarah at it if I can do any better. We ought to have put in a coarse piece first, but Aunt Cinda & Kate were so much in need of dresses that I gave way to having the fine piece in first. I will go this evening and see Mrs Huddgins Old Man Leach's daughter, who is an excellent weaver, and will try and get her to come and weave the piece out. I will offer her any kind of produce that I have, or can make corn potatoes, or any thing I can spare. I hope I will be successful. I see in the last paper that Lee is reported victorious through Gen Sibley, but don't believe the great loss of the enemy. God knows I hope it is true that we are victorious & if so, I will have a small hope that peace will come within 12 monthes—in thinking of it I feel that I had rather die than live through an other 4 yrs war tho' I do not feel like submitting to Yankee rule. The baby is still improving, no more fevers, she is not so fretful now, I wish you could see her. Mary has distressed herself about your not mentioning her [the baby] since your visit home, and my accounting for your silence upon the ground that she was so cross while you were with her that you became disgusted and did not care any thing for her—now whenever the baby does anything smart or interesting, she says "now Ma look at her, don't you think Pa would love her if he could see her now?" Poor child, the time before & since her birth has been the darkest & gloomiest I ever knew, & I have suffered so much mental suffering during that time that in looking back at it it seems as long as the other portion of my married life. All the money in the Confederacy would not tempt me to go through with the same again. Mary said to me recently, "Ma if you could be again a little child, would you do it?" No I replied, I would not live my life over again for nothing upon earth. Why Ma she said, may be you would not marry again, if you could live your life over. I said, I would not if I could live it over with the experience I now I have. It surprised me to find that she had discovered the secret of my discontent, that I had children, and she knows enough to know that they almost universally follow marriage. I wish I could teach her to never marry—that is a much safer plan than to trust to frail and unfailing preventives.

I am reminded of what Aunt Cinda heard Bet say about our children, she was talking about your looks, when she threw herself back in her rocking chair, laughing heartily, and said "he is the funniest looking man I ever saw, has the longest sharpest face and a bald head, and the *softest look I ever saw. He looks so soft*, I don't believe he is a man." Aunt told her she thought you were good enough looking when she said "well you are easy pleased—all his children look exactly like him & they are the *ugliest* children I ever saw." I told the children what she said, Mary says she don't care, her saying it don't make it so. Bob says if she ever tells him so he will tell her he is as pretty as she is or her brothers. Don't you feel flattered by her high opinion of you. She is one of the biggest fools I ever knew, has less sound natural sense. I could tell you a great deal but tis not worth writing. (Just here Walter came along poping the cat with his whip & was so busy did not notice him, & he struck the ink bottle sitting in a chair by me, & over it went on the floor, spattering around for several yards, and tis all the ink I have, left about a tea spoonful.[)] Children may be some folks blessings but if they havent always been my curse, I can't see straight, I have committed more sin on their account than I fear God will ever pardon, have suffered more bodily & mental anguish than—1,000 men would in a whole life time. I love them after they come it is true, God planted the feeling in my bosom & I cant help that, but at all times I wish from the bottom of my heart that child had never been born to me. I ought not to let such things fret me, but can't help it. My thoughts have started now on my hatred of children's ways, the knowledge that they have been forced upon me, the torment they are, & so little satisfaction or pleasure, and I won't get over it for days—& before I would have an other one, I would be willing to try an other than an earthly hell. I'll stop for I am full of bitterness and can see & feel only my own misery & unavailing regrets.

Good bye
L.S.N.

Dear Lizzie—

Last night just before bed time I went into the Telegraph Office & learned from the operator in confidence (for the news was telegraphed to a paper here) that news had been received from Va up to 17 & 18. So far, Lee was victorious—but from what I understood the fighting was not considered over, and more may take place again, but we may now feel some what confident of success.[14] The Extra will be out but not in time for the mail which will be closed in a few minutes or I would send you one. Good bye dear Lizzie.

yours affectionately
Wm H. Neblett
May 31st/64

At Home
Sunday June 5th 1864

Dear Will,

With a weary sad heart, I seat myself this morning to write. The day is warm, & oppressive, and perhaps has opperated on my mind as a depressing medium. I grow so weary of life that at times I feel like I would not raise my arm to avert the most horrible death. But I won't write of this, yet I can't hope like you that a kinder fate awaits me in the future. I wish I could, the present the passing moments would at least be more supportable, for they would be sweetened with hope.

It is cloudy and has rained one shower this morning, & will rain again—we have already had too much rain by far, in the low places the corn has turned yellow, and haven't been able to plow any for 9 days, & cant plow before Teusday even if we have no more rain. Dident quite finish plowing the corn but it is laid by now, for with one of the rains last week we had a good deal of wind which blew down a great deal of corn, & any quantity of trees, at least 20 trees

14. The Spotsylvania campaign was being fought in Virginia at the time of the above dates.

in the new ground where the cotton is. It commenced raining 9 days ago, and hasn't missed but two or three days since without having a good shower. I think the sickness will come after this. Myers says he never saw as much rain fall at this season of the year before in his life, and he says he fears very much that our cotton will be entirely lost in the weeds and grass, if it is not plowed out this week, says they cant find the cotton rows—that comes of having poor weak ineffcent team—if your team had been good all the crop would have been laid by before this rain, but these poor oxen are an exellent excuse for the negros slow plowing. If I was a man or a widow & pretended to farm I would have [a] good strong team some mules & some oxen & then I would see to it that the negros did good plowing. Olivers three hands have cultivated as much or very near as much as our 5 constant hands, and Kate and Nancy thrown in for at least six weeks. This slow, creeping business, with the weeds & grass a long ways ahead all the time, and the oxen dying one by one makes me feel like every negro & ox & self included were on the crippled list no life no spirit about anything, but a dead drag all the time. I don't want to farm next year on so *grand a scale* unless I can get some one to come and attend all the time to the farm. Myers is getting mighty tired of attending to our negros, & wants to quit, but I will hold him on as long as I can, for I fear if he quits & they find out no one is coming to look after them that the jig will be up, & they won't gather what little they have made.

Well it is now after dinner and it is pouring down rain, & the darkest clouds hanging over head has set in for the ballance of the evening. I consider our cotton crop as lost, we are certainly like the lonely hero in Poe's Raven he "whom merciless disaster, followed fast & followed faster &c."[15] until I for one have have [*sic*] given up, & when I think of how necessary cloth domestic will soon be to my comfort, & no way to get, and this slow tedious method of spinning, and it will be a tight push to clothe the negros, & make pants for the boys, dresses for myself & Mary & my poor little baby. If Jim takes part of our cotton I would like to get the remainder baled, and try and sell it some way for the cloth, calico & domestic. I forgot to say that the cotton has been run around with the sweeps & scraped out, brought to a stand, but the weeds & grass grow so fast, that there is danger of loosing [*sic*] the rows, can't find them. Mrs Oliver sent over this morning to let me know that she had rec[eived] a letter from Oliver written on his way to La, in which he did not

---

15. From Edgar Allan Poe's poem "The Raven" (1845).

mention you but I hope & believe that you are still in the office. Oliver is so much like an Aligator that it may not hurt him to live this summer in a nasty La river, but I don't want you there. You did not say you had any idea of going with the Co, so I am not making myself unhappy about you. I rec[eived] your letter of the 29th on Thursday, & cant help coming to the conclusion that you have had touches of the blues several times recently which is unusual for you. Do pray don't cultivate the habit, & gloomy train of thought, for I am miserable enough for us both, don't want you to spoil your happiness & benefit me none. I couldent help smiling but it was a bitter smile when I read this clause "if I can come home I will do so with the intention of not endangering you" and I said to myself did Will ever *intend* to endanger me? but we wont write of this any more, & if I am to kill myself there is no use trying to avoid the doom.

I was trying for five or six days to go to Old man Leach's to get one of his daughters to come & weave out my piece of cloth, succeeded at last on friday—it rained every day so I could not go. One of them promised to come monday. I hope she will come. My pity was deeply excited on beholding the helpless condition of the old man's large family, all dependent on him, & he a poor weak frail old man with a broken cons[t]itution & no health. Has been sick nearly ever since you saw him while you were at home, yet seems cheerful & thinks he will make corn enough to bread them next year. The negros continue to set out potatoe slipes, will probably set out all the patch before the ground gets too dry, but Sam tells me that the deer have taken to the patch already, go in by big droves. Mary went home with Nelia Brown Friday night, sent for her yesterday eve, & she says they had sweet potatoes raised this year for dinner at Dr Browns yesterday, larger than her wrist she says. Now I must tell you some of my little & big troubles. In the first place let me tell my *heart trouble*. My baby has been sick again, had several fevers, which I broke with broken dose of Calomel, but she is now so weak & poor that the very fountain of pity is stirred to look at her. She seems nearly as poor as Walter was, but has more strength than he had, for she will exert herself and walk about the room, but is so feverish & fretful. I know the poor poor little thing feel[s] bad all the time, and her face is so white and apparently bloodless. I know she needs a tonic, but I have nothing to give her. She has had night sweats now for two nights and during the day when she goes to sleep, which is very debilitating you know. Poor little darling I don't expect she will see a single well day this summer even if she lives through it, which I think [is] very doubtful. It don't seem to be her teeth that is hurting her. I feel so uneasy about her that

I can't sleep well at night. I know it would be better, far better for her to die now in her infancy, pure & spotless as the angels, but 'tis natural for me to desire her to live because I love her, and never will conscience reproach me for neglect of my children's physical welfare. A delicate feeble teething infant is a weight upon my heart, and a stimulus to the brain, which is ever trying to think of something that might be beneficial. I am going to try bathing at night. I have been trying all day to think of the name of the tonic Croom gave us for Walter after his severe spell, & cant do it, tell me the name & I'll get a little from Brown & try it. She has lost her appetite, and depends entirely on the breast, when I left her all the eve last friday, she would not eat a mouthful all evening—how I wish summer was gone, & every day of my life I wish she was 2 yrs old, over her teething.

Now the next trouble is Billy's arm, I fear it will be stiff at the elbow, he keeps it crooked all the time but cant raise it to his mouth. I feel anxious about it, it seems to mend so slowly it has been done now 11 days, & is much swollen yet, & he can't use it—he can work his fingers and use his hand, but can't bend it at the elbow, that is where he complained when it was first done & tis much bruised about the elbow—now a minor trouble is that both of the old geese & one gander that Ma sent christmas died last week, seemed to have spasms, must have eaten some thing poisonous, that is a breaking up arrangement to my geese raising for the old goose Susan gave me never has done any thing. I grieve after my geese. Like some other things, it seems that I was never made to raise geese or cease to bear children—two things I have spread myself on & failed in both. Another vexation is the big wharf rats are catching all my young chickens, havent tried to poison them fearing nothing else will get it, & the Hawks are very bad also. To continue the vexations, I havent been able to get a wheel yet, have applied to Harbuck, and a wheel wright living by Jno Loggins, thinking out of two I may get one wheel. Myers says he heard that they have sent after Coody, I hope it is true. George Lancaster sent home the shoes he fixed for me yesterday which is not nicely done, and the pair he intended for Mary is a little too large [for] Walter, & not large enough for Billy. Sent word if they dident fit then to send him the measure & he would make her another pair. He kept them so long he lost the measure. I'll send the measure right off. I have no idea she will get them before cold weather. If I only had casts for the children & myself I would make Mage make our shoes, and not be deviled by these trifling sneaking detailed, cowardly shoe makers. You can't get any of them to do any thing for you, they won't work for me at least. I can't see how I will get shoes this winter for my self and the children. This other sneak at the mill, tanner Ferrell, come to borrow our wagon to go after lime nearly three weeks ago, & in order to get it, said he would have my hides limed & bated in about 10 days, to have my ooze ready by that time, which I did, & it has been nearly three weeks ago & so yesterday I went to the tan yard with Bob to see the Gent about it, & he said he couldent get lime until a few days ago, had just put my hides in, would let me know when to send for them &c. I fear I won't get it tanned [in] time to make the negros & childrens shoes, all this frets & worrys me, for I am very nervous any how nursing is such a drain on the nervous system. I have no confidence in any thing Ferrell says. How I wish I could be independent of all these detailed men. Joe Collins has a detail for running a mill. Dr Brown can get what he pleases out of any of these detailed men, they think it best to keep on the good side of him.

Monday eve, June 6th Dear Will, I must add a few more lines to my letter. I sent a note to Harbuck (by Jack Hurst who goes to school at Pine Grove, in sight of Harbucks) asking him to make me a wheel immediately, & to send word by Jack the price &c—& he sent word I could get one now by paying him in corn, meat or specie, did not send word how much corn or meat, but I know 'tis six dollars in specie. Aint he detailed to make wheels, & does it look fair that such as he is can stay at home & work only for specie, or something as good, while other men have to take 11 dollars in Confederate money per month, & be away from home & all its comforts & endearments, while their life & health are all the time exposed, & all sorts of hardships their lot. But necessity urges the soldiers wives to have wheels, & they pay any price to get them. I sent him word by John Nix this morning that I would give him six bushels of corn for a wheel, but if he asks ten I will have to give it, and after I get it, I wish you would report the game he is playing also. There is a big revival going on at Pine Grove among the Baptist have 25 & 30 mourners at one time, 9 have joined the church & the meeting continues with unabated interest. John Nix is a mourner or has professed. Aunt nor Jno won't tell what kind of a detail he has applied for. I rec[eived] a letter from Hattie last week in which she says that Ma had been sick came near having Pneumonia, but was better—that Ma wanted it, & Pa said he would bring Roberts remains home as soon as he can get a metalic coffin. Frank [Perry] has gone to San Antonio to carry cotton.

Wednesday June, 8th Dear Will, I sealed my letter monday night gave Bill directions to be off to town by day light, and went to sleep & was awakened about an hour afterwards by Sarah calling Kate to come out & catch the goslings that an awful rain was coming up, they caught them & got in the house, to night that I could cease to murmur at what has been, if I could only calculate with any degree of certainty upon what will be—but I know no doom that would horrify me so much, as to know, or believe that, 12 yrs to come would add 5 more children to my number. I had rather spend the remainder of my life even tho it were 35 yrs in the Penitentiary or in solitary confinement for the same length of time, either of which would be ten thousand times worse than death. Right here I think to myself "I do wish that this horrible bugbear of mine (childbearing) was not eternally thrusting itself before me,["] both in thoughts of the past, present, or future, and thus affording material for almost half I write to you. I know Will you are tired of it, and God knows my heart is worn to the very quick upon the subject, but like you, my memory of you is becoming more intimately associated with the idea of childbearing every day, and you have no idea how the fear of such a disaster clips the wings of my desire to see you, & be with you. I did not feel this in your absence heretofore, but now the age of my babe warns me that my time of danger has arrived.

You ask why have I lost all hope of our living together without any more children. I am naturally given to despondency and in this matter have had enough I think to clip the wings of the most hopeful. Have been trying to ward off this danger now 10 yrs, and had but three years between the two last, have never delayed the matter but a little over six months twice. Hope is dead, we can not live together without a constant fear & dread upon my mind, which would destroy all me peace, I believe you are willing to assist me, but I doubt all preventives in my case, & the one in which I have most faith would be quite if not utterly impossible to procure. I mean a syringe that will throw matter easily and with a great deal of force. The old thing I have would kill any body to use it a year even if it would prevent a mishap. I asked you last year to search out one, in fact, wanted you to try & exchange mine at the depot before I was caught the last time, but you seemed very indifferent on the subject, & I let it drop with a mental determination to stand on the safe side myself—but we can talk this matter over fully when we meet again, & if we never meet, there will be no use to agree upon any terms, but let me say right here that if you apply & get your wine detail this summer, dont start home without a good quantity of the pulverized Ergot,[8] and as good a syringe as you can find, Richardon's No 1 that I described to you long ago is the best I know of.

---

8. Ergot, a fungus that grows on grain, especially rye, causes contractions of the uterus. Some nineteenth-century doctors used it as an aid for hastening childbirth and for relieving postpartum hemorrhaging. The violent contractions caused by ergot, however, could cause ruptures, tears, fetal damage, or even death. It was a common belief that ergot induced abortion in the early stages

I returned home yesterday. When I wrote to you a week ago the babe had a fever she was not entirely clear of fever for six days—and Sat night I was very much alarmed about her, she had such a rattling in her throat (I now suppose) & she is always so restless when she has a fever that she would not let me apply my ear to her lungs. I did not sleep one third of the night for I thought she had Pneumonia, & that alarmed me so much—the next day mother & I began giving her Lobelia, which made her throw up a great deal of phlegm, & relieved her greatly, & that eve the fever went off. I gave her half a liver pill, for 4 successive nights, and her discharges were the most billious I ever saw from a baby. She is cool & moist now all the time, but is very fretful, & weak. I don't think her teeth had any thing to do with her sickness. I love her very much & I think her much more lovable now than when you saw her. The other children are well except bad colds, which nearly all of them have. I found Kate sick when I got home, & this evening Tom came in saying he was sick. I recd your letter in the legal envelope last Sat, & it had come unsealed, it contained six pages letter paper, but if that was the end of your letter you forgot or failed to sign your name. To day Jim Scott started with his waggons—5, Uncle Mc drove one & started half sick. Susan did let him have 5 bales at 60 cents, and Uncle Mc promised him 3 but Susan would not bale the cotton for him. She Susan tells it now that John has writen to her that he is completely disgusted with Elmores Regt & is going to try & get transfered, she told Myers the other day that John had writen to her that Elmores Regt was going to be disbanded soon. I don't believe the tale tho' John may have heard such a rumor & wrote it to Susan. Aunt Cinda told me to day that John was mad at you last year, about the way you treated him when he was sick over on the spit & when he went to leave he said he asked you to make Jack hunt up his things & help him off and you replied that you "dident care a damn about Jacks things" & said you would do nothing to assist him and blames you that he belongs to the Regt he does. I am glad he is not in the Co you belong to.

I came home by Mrs Olivers & gave her some plums. We have had no falling out, she is one of my best friends I think. She has made Seward come up or nearly so, to his promise about the articles he was to bring her from Browns-

---

of pregnancy. For more information on ergot and other forms of nineteenth-century birth control see Wertz, *Lying-In*, 65–66; Leavitt, *Brought to Bed*, 144–48; Brodie, *Contraception and Abortion*; Gordon, *Woman's Body, Woman's Right*, 49–71.

ville when she agreed to let him have the cotton. He has sent her two bolts of domestic 1 bolt of calico & 20 pounds of coffee & some other articles. I would be willing to give a good deal of cotton for as much as she has of cloth. Jim I think will accept your offer about the cattle. He asked mother if she would not let him have 4 bales & take the debt on me—said he had about 4 bales at my house. What do you think Mrs Oliver made me a present of 2 pounds of coffee, & said she had loaned Mrs Hurst 2 lbs which she would give me also when she returned it. I tried to make her take something but she would not hear to it. She is a very liberal hearted woman. That is all true about Mrs Hutcheson & Mr Glass but I cant tell whether she will have him now or not. I gathered my first mess of Peas this evening for tomorrow, & have had no beans yet, nothing in fact, and now it seems like the drouth has set in, the ground is all cracking open, & every thing seems suffering for rain. I reckon they will finish laying by the corn this week, & about finish scraping out the cotton. They replanted the potatoe hills, & set out four or five rows of ridges. I think he made the negros waste the slips by putting two in [every] hill, if he had not done that, our whole patch would now be set out. Mothers grape crop is fine, & has the only plums & peaches in the county—she will move up to her new house this week. I havent had the chance to notice for your crop of Mustang grapes, but hope there will be a fine crop and that you will come home, if you come on that detail you ought to come in about a month from this. It is so late that I must close for to night or else I cant work tomorrow. Aunt is getting over her hurt, but is not well yet by a good deal—she sent for Brown & he thinks one of her short ribs is broken. Tomorrow is our wedding day & I know almost that you won't forget it this time & will write some to me tomorrow. Good night, and may I give you one of your lingering kisses in your dreams of me to night.

May 25th The day is a bright cloudless one, and the sun seems hot enough to melt me. We are needing rain very much, and they need it much worse up about mothers. Myers says our corn is not suffering much yet. They have conscripted Ben Langham & Parson Sims, they ate dinner at mothers last night Thursday. Ben L. was awful mouthy, the Parson said not not [*sic*] a word. Myers told me to day that he read a letter from some one in La to Langford (the liar), and the letter stated that his mother was dead, & had left him 20 negros 4 good mules & a tract of good land. He says he is going to the land soon, will live there. I spent the day at Mrs Haynies on Sat, the baby seemed better that morning, & mother & I went over. Mary laughed about Jeff writing home so much about Jno Scott, told a good many things about him &

even went so far as to tell that he was then making a finger ring, while he was writing. I don't know whether John expresses his dissatisfaction about the Regt & Co to any one or not. Mary told me that it was reported before Dr McIntosh['s] death that his lady was as *"women wish to be who love their lords?"*[9] If my love was judged by that rule, it would be woefully deficient. She Mrs McI—is a very unpopular lady, she made a good many people mad while the Dr was sick by refusing their proffered aid about sitting up with the Dr. Nelia Kerr for one, I think she must be a fool with the big head. Like Bet Scott no doubt she thinks "money makes the man, and poverty *the fellow."*[10] She told Jno Nix that, and made him mad but he did not let on. I consider it a direct insult. Bet is one of the biggest fools I ever knew. It has been very warm all day, and many prophesy that we will have no more rain soon. Mrs Garvin has heard that Jno Terrell who has recently returned from Youngs Regt says that there is a some hope for Ed to recover. Ed Bowen has bought a furlough of 60 days, & is coming 1st part of June. Mrs Jim Collins has moved down to Harrisburge where her husband is at work in some kind of a shop. She is doing a bad business I think, for she will return with a baby in her arms or a prospect of one, and perhaps the war won't end for several years yet. I hope that the report of Lee whipping Grant is true—if Lee is whipped, it will add several years more to the length of the war.[11]

You misunderstand me about my farming next year. I am willing to stay here & would rather live here than in Anderson but I don't want all these negros to torment me, but we will talk it over when you come home. I don't want you [to] give out trying to get home this summer, you must come, I want to see you so much, and you can make up your mind to not endanger my safety, and I will be overjoyed to see you. Do come. I have never mentioned the land swap to mother. I have set my heart on that end for that reason delay saying any thing to her I fear she wont agree to it. She can not work this land as readily as she can that Quinn place, & you know mother is as eager to make now as when she first began her life. We both of us will talk it over with her when you come up. Now please Will try and come & stay at home as long as

9. John Home, *Douglas,* act 1, scene 1 (1756).

10. This expression may have derived from a line in Diogenes Laërtius's *Thales,* chapter 7, " 'Tis money makes the man; and he who's none/Is counted neither good nor honourable."

11. Lizzie is most likely referring to the Spotsylvania Campaign, which took place in Virginia toward the end of May 1864. With both sides sustaining heavy losses, Grant was unable to shake Confederate control of Spotsylvania. McPherson, *Battle Cry of Freedom,* 728–33.

you can. I don't think I'll ever wean my babe & that will help to ward off some danger. Good bye and may God watch over & bless you—is the prayer of one who loves you devotedly. Myers says that nearly half of the potatoe slips have died that were set out & watered last week. The sun is too hot, it seems awful warm & sultry to me.

L S Neblett

At Home
Sunday eve May 29th 1864

Dear Will,

I went to church this morning at the Gilmore school house returned, ate my dinner, read myself to sleep, and after a pleasant nap have awakened full of thoughts of you, and some items that your letters have recently contained which items were elicited by some of my not wise but strong expressions of feeling on a certain subject—and I feel like writing to you once again about the same thing, & if I thought I could perform the vow I would make one, having you for witness that I would never again trouble you on the same subject, but like all crazy people, I must & will talk of that which affects my mind temper heart & life most intimately. Will from you I could never keep a secret, have never an idea or opinion of any importance without feeling a strong desire to to [*sic*] tell you, & I have often thought, if I were to entertain an idea of murdering any one even yourself, I should certainly have to tell you of it, if the matter was delayed a single week. In your last of the 23rd inst read last Thursday, you say I confess that I had rather not meet you under the present circumstances now, & you add perhaps any other time—and say you can generally anticipate what I am gradually coming to before I am aware of it myself, and then say that "I suppose you will be sorry when the war or peace allows me to return." This clause drew tears to my eyes, for I knew by that you did not comprehend my feelings on this subject. My heart would be supremely selfish to frame such a wish, or feel sorrow at the close of the war. I sometimes think that I could in noble cause become a martyr, & your supposition suggested the idea that I could, if the welfare & peace of my country could be obtained then sacrifice myself upon the alter of childbearing, & feel that I was performing a noble work, which thoughts & feelings could sustain me in the pain & trials, as thoughts of God sustained the christian martyrs even at the burning of the stake—but nothing of the kind can effect the war or woe of my country, and this childbearing is only a private matter between you & I.

I have never doubted your desire to assist me, but alas! all our combined efforts have been a series of failures for 10 years, & I have grown more bitterly opposed each year until now it has become a matter of life & death to me—and tho' I admit that I fear to see & meet you, yet I feel that if I could banish you that the separation is & would be more acutely felt & wept over by me than by you. You are my all. My kindred have disappointed me, those who remain, and death has taken the dearest brother I ever had—my children are too small & young to be companions for many a long year, & to you all my thoughts & feelings turn, & if you are permitted to return to us, I feel that I would & could be as happy as any woman in the confederacy, with that horrible bug bear of mine removed. I would be willing to give up all the property I have upon earth freely, to be insured beyond a doubt that from this trouble I would hence forth be free—that I could live with you, in peace & love, undisturbed by such disasters or fears of such. I expect you often feel fretted & mad at me, that I feel so deeply on this subject, & when I think thus, I almost cry aloud for death. I can see no chance of happiness for me, therefore, I am ever ready to welcome death eagerly; it would be better for us both—time soon heals such wounds; (sooner it seems to me in cases of bereaved husbands & wives, than in any other) and you could marry again, & I know you could not marry an other woman with as strong feelings on this subject as I have. Oh how much better would it be if I could only die, & this longing for death is only an evidence of my love for you—better die than make you unhappy & discontented, & were you thus through my conduct, life would be worth nothing to me—but I can not hasten nor defer death, & it remains only for me to support the misery & trials of life as I best can. You have never thought on this subject as I have. You have always in thinking of it reasoned this to me & to yourself. A preventive can be used, there are infalible ones, & I am willing to do all I can to assist and I have no reason to believe, and strongly hope that no more accidents will occur—and then you let the subject drop. Never think of the past, & how every effort has been baffled for years, until hope has died in my breast, and now I want to beg of you not [to] think hard of me, that I said I had rather not meet you. If I did not love you devotedly I would not fear to meet you, but I fear that my affection & desire to please will get the better of my prudence & reason, & that I may thereby suffer immensely in both body & mind—but this life, the one I now lead in your absence is utterly devoid of pleasure, the highest pleasure I have is in reading & replying to your letters, and at times I long so ardently to see you, & talk with you, and be near you, that at such times I feel that I am willing to risk even pregnancy, provided I am armed with Ergot, and various other implements of or for safety.

You must try and come home this summer or fall, and assist me in making preparations for the next year. I build no hopes upon peace, and do not suffer myself to hope that you can return before the close of the war. Uncle Mc will leave John's place next year, & has as yet made no arrangements about getting another home. I have thought it would be as good a chance as I will have to get him to attend to the farm, provided there was a house for them to live in. I have mentioned this idea to no one, and am some what out of the notion on account of Bob McClure. He is an awful child. Last week, Aunt was over here several days putting in & starting our cloth, and Bob was not going to school, & came over with her two days. The first day he was hunting his old horse, & Aunt Cinda asked me to let Billy go with him, which I did. He spent the most of that day at the lake, tried to get Billy in, there were a lot of the school boys, & Johns boys there, & Henry Scott[12] got on old Crusader and made him swim in the lake, & Henry can't swim himself, & if he had fallen off might have drowned. The next day he came over, and Billy went with him to bring out Aunts horse out of the Gilmore's field & he put Lee up first and then in putting Billy up before Lee, pushed him clear over the horse, and the child fell on his arm in some way and strained it badly, he cant use it nor straighten it and it is swollen to twice its natural size. It is his left arm. I feel some uneasiness about it, he does not complain of it hurting him much. I have bound clay & vinegar to it, and keep wet bandages on it all the time, a little more & it would have been broken. Bob Mc curses like a trooper, & is very disgusting in his ways. I have learned in our Bob's case that "evil communications corrupt good manners,"[13] and I fear Bob Mc's influence so much that I don't think I can get my own consent to have him with my children—better loose [*sic*] all I have than have my boys ruined. While I was at mothers last Bob got mad at Billy and called him a "God damned liar" what do you think of that? he talks, so Mary says very largely at school about chewing tobacco, & has taken several chews, says he don't fear me, and when he gets on Dick [the] horse, or any other, he goes full tilt making them jump fences, &c. has no mercy on a horse. I have talked to him repeatedly about running his horse,

12. Henry Scott was the son of Lizzie Neblett's brother and sister-and-law, John and Susan Scott.

13. 1 Cor. 15:33.

and a whipping now hangs over him about cursing Billy. Bob's conduct has discouraged & mortified me more about our children than any thing that any of them ever did. He is the best child we have naturally, and if he is led astray so easily, what may we not expect of the others. I have taken occasion to mortify Bob about his conduct all the time, I want to make him feel it as keenly as possible, & feel that he looses [*sic*] something when he deserves my displeasure. He was complaining yesterday and to day of being sick, gave him some pills last night. I read a letter from Serena Jemigan last week—she wrote that poor Beaden Fielder had just died, he is the one who shot himself accidentally last fall he was confined to his bed for months. Fielder and his oldest son Curtis reached home before he was buried, but not before he died.

We were blessed with a splendid rain on the night of the 27th and the morning of the 28th inst. I think it will be almost the making of the corn crop, our corn was not suffering for rain, but my garden, potatoe vines &c was— have now about six ridges set out. If the potatoe crop does as well as the new vines we had last year we will have at least 200 bu[shels], so I feel easy about that crop. We will make as many potatoes as we want to eat I hope.

Monday morn May 30th/64 Dear Will, as I wrote 4 pages yesterday and will have an opportunity of sending to the office tomorrow I'll add a little more this morning and post it tomorrow instead of Thursday my usual day.

We have the first piece of cloth in the loom, and it is so fine that I won't undertake to weave it, or to put Sarah at it if I can do any better. We ought to have put in a coarse piece first, but Aunt Cinda & Kate were so much in need of dresses that I gave way to having the fine piece in first. I will go this evening and see Mrs Huddgins Old Man Leach's daughter, who is an excellent weaver, and will try and get her to come and weave the piece out. I will offer her any kind of produce that I have, or can make corn potatoes, or any thing I can spare. I hope I will be successful. I see in the last paper that Lee is reported victorious through Gen Sibley, but don't believe the great loss of the enemy. God knows I hope it is true that we are victorious & if so, I will have a small hope that peace will come within 12 monthes—in thinking of it I feel that I had rather die than live through an other 4 yrs war tho' I do not feel like submitting to Yankee rule. The baby is still improving, no more fevers, she is not so fretful now, I wish you could see her. Mary has distressed herself about your not mentioning her [the baby] since your visit home, and my accounting for your silence upon the ground that she was so cross while you were with her that you became disgusted and did not care any thing for her—now whenever the baby does anything smart or interesting, she says "now Ma look at her,

when the rain began to descend in torrents, which continued all night, every creek overflowed, & it seems to me the whole face of the earth covered with water, & yesterday it rained again, & today it is clouding up and thundering, will rain again this evening no doubt. I expect we will all die from sickness this summer—and I fear the corn will be ruined by too much rain. Myers says he will work the cotton out, if it takes him 'till fodder pulling time & this wet weather they are chopping at the weeds & grass in it on the highest parts. Yesterday they could do nothing it was so wet & boggy. Yesterday Tom Collins from Story's Co got home, I heard it just as I got in bed, & lay awake thinking of Mrs Collins' joy when she would hear it. She is at Pine Grove protracted meeting & they sent for her, but Garrett creek was away out of its banks & so they did not meet last night, I feel glad for her. She hasent seen him in near 16 months. Now her interest in the mails will be gone 'till he goes away again, so I will have to send to the office all the time after this. I know this will be two days behind the regular time, but I was affraid to start Bill & the creeks are up and it raining, so put it off 'till Thursday when I hope to get a letter from you.

Jno King has married a widow lady some where with 4 children. If Mrs Hutcheson is married I dont know it. Jim Scott did not throw away his crop, 25 or 30 acres of corn, but got Dr Brown to cultivate it for him, and he is to bring Brown six pair of cards for doings it. I don't know what I'll do for cards. I did not ask Jim to bring me a single thing. Bet is so mean & stingy that she don't want any body to have or get articles of use or comfort besides herself & she don't want Jim to bring any thing for any one but her. She is so perfectly hateful. She has something to say against every thing I do or have, my children are the ugliest she ever saw, & Walter looks ridiculous in pants—she don't intend to let Jimmy wear Pants till he is six yrs old—and it is perfect folly to permit & encourage such a young child as Mary to write & receive letters, & we are such fools to do it &c &c. I am glad to be able to write that the baby has improved perceptibly since monday, I hope she will recruit a little now, don't sweat as much, & ate some yesterday & to day. Mrs Buckley's school will end, in two weeks. I think I will start them to splitting rails tomorrow tis too sloppy to hoe or do any thing in the field, another hard rain coming— wont it never quit? Mrs Huddgins, can't get here for the creek, & my cloth wont never [get out of] the loom. Tis now pouring down rain. I will have to send Bill by Oakland church to avoid Garrett creek. We have had a tremendous rain this evening. Lake Creek was running over one end of the bridge yesterday. I don't think the creek was ever known to be higher. I can see no difference [in] Billy's arm. He don't complain of it.

At Home
Teusday June 14th 1864

Dear Will,

I write this to mail it when I send to the office tomorrow. I have felt very unhappy about you since I read yours of the 9th inst, on last Saturday, and I feel so anxious to hear from you that I will send to the office tomorrow hoping that you have writen to me, since the 9th I thought or feared you were sick when your letter failed to come at the usual time and I remembered that it was very near the time you were sick last year. You reached mothers last year on the 13th June. I have been hoping that you would try and would be successful to come home, and recruit your health, & perhaps get a detail also, so that you will not have to return soon. Oh Will I do long so to see you and when I know you are sick, and think of the dangers of your death, I do indeed feel very miserable. (Just as I reached here, Aunt Cinda stepped in, & I could write no more during the day, & intended drinking a cup of coffee after supper and writing then, but just before supper Babe rode up with little negro Smith, and so we chatted so late, I went to bed and have taken a good long nap of sleep and [am] up now writing in order that I may send you some little news when I send to the office tomorrow.[)]

The baby still continues very feeble, and had a fever all night & all day monday. I got Myers to sharpen my Gum lancet and I cut her Gums yesterday.[16] She looks badly, yet she walks about, and try's to play. I don't expect her to see a well day this summer even if she lives through it. Thornton is now in the house with the chills, has had two, and I stopped the third one with my homemade Quinine. I think he will go to work in an other day. It continued to rain until last Sunday and on that day the creek was all over the bottom, Joe says [it is] as high as it has been since we have been down here says that it would have swum a horse in one place where you want to run your pasture fence, when the water begins to dry up & the vegetable decomposition commences, then we will have the chills & fevers. I dread this summer so much,

16. Often in the nineteenth century any disease or ailment an infant had was attributed to teething. The problem, it was assumed, would be helped if the gums were scarified with a lance.

indeed the months that remain to finish out this year seem interminable. These negros are so harrassing to me, have become so trifling, that I long so much to be rid of them, or have some one with them constantly who will enforce commands, & make them earn a support. Bill has got to be so lazy & triffling & pays so little heed to what I say that I don't see how I can stand him. I would not live with them alone an other year for any thing. I can't nor won't undertake it. Myers says that he thinks the corn has been greatly injured, says he will try & get the cotton clean if possible and when he does that he must leave me—and when he does, I think they will all give up, & do nothing. Briggance was here yesterday & assessed my meat & cotton and took the income tax. I gave in the cotton as 5 bales, & will have to deliver to the Gov 250 pounds—my meat fell short 14 pounds, I have Roe's recpt for 94 lbs—it ought to be 108, I weighed 104 lbs, thinking that was my share, allowed myself 50 lbs & sent to town with Mrs Hurst & Collins. I told Briggance if they wanted the 14 lbs they must come after it that I did not intend to send them an other pound unless I was paid. He put down the two beeves I killed last year, and Nance Sarah Kate, which he made out 480 dollars, so I don't have to pay anything there as it does not reach $500. Mrs Huddgins hasent yet come to weave out my cloth, I expect I'll have to weave it out & if I dont make good cloth, I can't help it. The baby requires so much attention that I don't have time to do much. Oh I do wish & long so for you to be at home. I don't dare to indulge the hope that you will be at home next year, tho' nearly every body cry's out peace will certainly come, but I fear the wish is father to the thought, and they believe what they wish so earnestly. But I can most ardently pray that God may grant us peace, this year. They have set out all our potatoe patch but the rain has washed the hills down so it looks like they can't do much unless they are plowed & the hills pulled up which will be done as soon as it is dry enough if the vines are not too long by that time. Myers says the corn in the old field is firing up now, and the tobacco plants are dying & look like they had all been scalded with hot water. Ben Langham has got back home. Jeff Haynie is home on detail to burn coal. Old Coody hasent yet gone in to service. I sent to Harbuck to day and got a wheel am to pay him 12 bu[shels] of corn this fall for it. This fellow Ferrell hasent yet sent my hides. I think he is a grand liar, & a perfect Yankee. I fear I'll have no leather in time to make shoes this winter.

I must tell you Babe's business down here, which you must keep all to your self, in fact, I hope you don't "let out your guts to Mr Scott" these days. Last Sunday Yarborough carried her a letter asking her to be his wife, and she seems to be on the fence about her answer, which he is coming to receive next

Teusday.[17] The girls all make themselves fools about him & he is so rich, good looking & she hates to say no, & yet she don't love him, & don't you think she came down to get *my advise* [*sic*]—were you ever more astonished? I have spent no opinion as yet & don't know that I shall. I read his letter, which any school boy or girl of 13 yrs ought to blush to have writen. Such spelling & such composition. Babe laughs heartily at it. I don't like him, & would not sell myself to him for twice his sum of money. I hope she won't be fool enough to say yes—equippage & splendor dazzles Babe. Billy's arm is improving don't think now that it will be stiff. Oh that you were at home to night, where I could see and know how you are. I have been dreading this summer for you & the baby. She is constitutionally very much like you I think; her tongue is coated all over now. I hope you have writen to relieve my anxiety. Try to come home & recruit your health. I must end & go to bed again. May [God] take care of you, & save you, here & in eternity. Poor Ed Garvin died of his wound. John Nix has joined the Baptist church & been baptized. Aunt Cinda is greatly grieved about his joining that church some 13 or 20 were Baptized.

yours devotedly,
Lizzie S Neblett

At Home
Sunday June 19th 1864

Dear Will,

Your last letter of the 13th inst was read on last Thursday and its contents surprised me very much—while it at the same time relieved my anxiety greatly. It seems to me that there must be an unseen influence which opperates upon my mind, warning me when danger is near you. I fear that you withheld something when you wrote, & that it was not simple fever, but an inflamtory one, and I feared it was your lungs. I am glad now that you did not tell me the nature of your disease, and its remedy.[18] I would have felt so anxious & unhappy about the result, & even now, I fear that the one opperation will not effect a cure and if it does not, don't have it repeated until cool weather sets

---

17. J. Q. Yarbrough and Alice "Babe" Scott were married August 24, 1864. Mullins, *Grimes County, Texas, Marriage Records.*

18. Will received a pass to the hospital to be treated for hydrocele, which is the accumulation of serous fluids in the body cavity, especially the scrotal pouch.

in. You acted with discretion in not telling John Scott the truth, for it would certainly have been writen to Susan, and she would have derived great pleasure in circulating some outrageous lie about it, which in this case would no doubt have found believers, for man's nature in this particular is so well known that we never marvel, nor doubt much, when we hear of the best of men going astray. But if you had died, dear Will, and the tale you feared had reached my ears I would never have believed it, yet it would have grieved me greatly to have others thinks so, & tho unbelieved, your memory would have been linked with that vile passion, the unrestrained & unlawful exercise of which makes it a dark & hateful blot upon the nobility and divinity of man's nature. I always think of such men as being closely allied to the brute creation, & in my estima-tion they sink far below the dumb beasts—man was given reason & sense & when he makes a brute of himself deserves our greatest scorn & disapproval. In thinking this over, I am led as I have been thousands of times before to feel thankful that in the great lottery of marriage I drew the prize I did. The more I know (through the reports of married women) of the generality of men, the brighter does your worth appear. And when I hear some tales I involuntary think to myself "my God what would I do, if my husband was such a man?" I have unbounded confidence in your moral conduct & character, & my taste and pride on both gratified in your intellectual worth & attainments, & I know I am happier with you, tho' we are both poor, & have had to deny our-selves in many ways in order to keep what we have, & get along decently & comfortably, than I would have been united to [a] man of a coarse nature & deficient in mental culture, & perhaps sound sense & judgment, yet with an almost inexhaustible fund of money. Money don't make happiness all the time any more than money makes the man—yet it is good to have plenty of money, it removes many of the hardships of life, woman's in particular enables us to gratify our taste or inclinations, gives us comforts & luxuries, but there are things that wealth cannot buy—kindness, generosity, morality, truthfulness, and a host of other virtues inherent in the human mind over which wealth exercises no control.

These virtues you posses[s] and in my eye they are worth more than a mint of gold. You perhaps smile & wonder how this train of though[t] originated. I have been thinking of Babe's proposal, & its probable result, which will be in a wedding I think, and contrasting her probable position in life with mine, & I say it candidly I would not exchange you for a world of Yarboroughs, with their hundred negros, and piles of specie. Babe has no depth of feeling is fond of show, fine dressing, splendor and luxurious ease—all of which she expects to obtain by marriage with Col Yarborough. She has no taste for books or literature & is far from being a finished scholar & tho' she knows enough to see & laugh at his ludicrous blunders, yet his wealth covers a multitude of faults. I wish you could read his letter, I laughed heartily at it, so did Babe yet from the drift of her conversation I could see that she had made up her mind to accept him. One thing he said which I here repeat or quote verbtim. "I would have spoken to you on this subject before but I have bin affraid that I would have the *remoss* of concience to see you married to B[aker]" I can't remember all the misspelled words, nor the exact diction but the idea is truthfully rendered. Dont you think he has a very tender conscience, to suffer for others acts. I advised Babe, after her asking me several times what I thought about it, to give him no positive answer when he came to receive it next Teusday, & to wait & see if she could learn to love & respect him (after a careful inquiry into his habits & faults, sufficiently to live with him always, bear children for him, which last act all his wrath could not remove from her shoulders &c.[)] She said she thought mother was pleased with the idea, and no doubt she is, for wealth has almost as much power as knowledge. Babe has changed her mind in respect to me & my character since mothers house was burned so she told John, and from mother I have that she thinks I am very sensible, & have exellent judgment. She treats me with a show of respect & affection now. I don't admire Yarboroughs character he keeps whiskey all the time, & is under its influence slightly almost all the time is a boasting fellow, who believes his wealth covers all his faults—and tho he hasent vanity enough to think he has more sense, judgment & education than a few other men, yet he thinks his wealth raises him a head & shoulders above any man in this Co. Is a great brag. I think I could fancy him tho' sooner than Jessie Baker. I'll write you how the matter progresses. Don't *hint this to John,* keep it all to yourself. Altho' I would greatly prefer staying at home & writing the entire evening to you, yet I feel like I ought to go to see Mrs Collins this evening, & congratulate her upon her husbands getting home. I hear she rode a John Gilpin race home when she heard he had come. I have a thousand things to say to you, & shall be so busy next week I will not find time during the day, and will have to make a call upon Coffee to prop my eyes open, & infuse life into my brain, which is worn out with my body, & demands rest as loudly as my body does when night comes on. I have been weaving for two days past, that woman has disappointed me about coming to weave, & I have been trying it myself—tis very tedious, & the thread is so fine it keeps a continual breaking which disheartens me, & exhausts my small fund of patience. I hope she will come to-morrow—her child has been sick.

Monday eve 5 Oclock—Dear Will, I went over to see Mrs Collins yesterday eve, and made her husbands acquaintance, found him quite agreeable & sprightly in conversation, apparently quite intelligent. He speaks very highly of Robert. Bob he calls him, says he made a very fine soldier, & was very agreeable, & well liked in camps. Says there was few such boys as he was. Poor Robert, how sincerely I wish he had lived to return home. Dr Haynie said while he was at home this Spring that Roberts health had been bad & he tried to pursuade him to remain behind the Co, but he would march when he was totally unfit, & that he thought at the time that it would kill him. Mr Collins will start back to his command the 13th July, had a 40 days furlough. John Terrell has made application for a detail to work in the Pistol shop near Anderson, is now at home waiting over his time to hear from his application. Bob Bassett has a place in some Gov department at Marshall I think, is out as candidate for District Clerk, or Co Clerk, I am not sure which Old Man Watson & Jack Wilson his opponents. Bassett is determined to do no more field service—he staid in Va until he accomplished his design. Noah B[assett] is in the Gov department at Anderson doing some light duty. I have been weaving again to day, the thread seems to be so rotten that I can make no head way at it, and I am affraid that woman won't come, & if she don't I think I will have to burn it up to get rid of it, & put in a coarser piece that will weave without any trouble. Oh this scuffle to get something to eat & wear nearly wears my life out, and every day I ask myself how much longer will this state of affairs last, the idea of an other 4 years war makes my heart sick, and grow sick with the ideas that imagination conjures up, as being the probable result of any 4 yrs war. I don't believe that we will ever be conquered but the desolation that is now wide spread will be more extended, and I believe that in case of an other 4 yrs, it will close your life, & when you are gone, what will become of me? Life with its few charms would then be utterly darkened for me. But this is a very gloomy idea & I won't dwell on it. You say that I seem to avoid speaking of the mustang grape crop, no, you are mistaken if there was ever any thing relative to myself which I thought I should avoid mentioning I was always sure to recur to it again & again in writing or talking to you. I see no cause for avoiding the grape subject, for I want you to get that detail if possible, & if you will remember I have spoken of it several times, I have seen no mustang vines myself but from others I learn there is a fine crop—that crop seldom if ever fails, you know. I do hope you will make the effort and be successful. I long to see you so much and my fears on a certain point have become so quiet, & the desire to see you so much strengthened, that I forget the danger in thinking of the pleasure of having you at home. Now a little about the farm. It was just three weeks to the day that they were unable to plow a furough, the grass & weeds never stopped, & some portions of the cotton is covered knee high with crab grass, Myers has them plowing with sweeps, would use the Cary plows but ours are worn out—sent over & got one of Bro Jim's new Cary's this morning. I have Uncle Mc's mule, & one of Mrs Oliver's mules—it is so hot the oxen give out & lay down so much & I think we can spare the corn to feed the mules while we plow over the cotton. Bill is plowing Mrs Oliver's mule in the potatoe patch which we are now laying by. The rain washed the hills down to nothing and Myers says damaged us considerably a good deal of the corn has turned yellow where the water stood & will make little or nothing, & in our new ground, washed nearly all the plowed soil away from the corn roots. Sarah & Nance are both out in the potatoe patch, send Kate after dinner.

Jeff Haynie has had his quantity of coal reduced to 100 bu[shels] per week, & he will begin to burn now. The negros have all been finding Bee tree's & cutting them. Thornton's old Gum swarmed twice, & he gave me one swarm, to pay for time lost in attending to his, he & Sam do finely hiring them. Sarah has one gum, & Thornton three & two more trees to cut. Every body says they never knew the like of Bee trees in the woods before. The negros rove the woods Sunday's hunting Bee's. I wish you were at home, I think we could find some too. Bob & Billy want to go hunting there. My baby (I wish she did have a name) is much better than she was has been better ever since I cut her gums—the little thing has such winning ways that one of her parents at least cant help loving her. I think she will get along now 'till her next jaw teeth inflame the Gums badly which will be in two or three weeks. I went with the children to the Scott lake Sat eve, & put them all in the lake, Bob, Billy Walter & Mary, & never saw children enjoy themselves more than they did. Walter got a little frightened & did not stay in long. There is some talk of Finch taking the school when Mrs Buckly quits. I hope he will for he is a good strict teacher they say.

Teusday morn 21st June. John Nix has just called by to get Ranger to ride to town, as we are using their mule, and I must hasten & close this to send by him to town. John is half way engaged to Bettie Kelly Wm Kelly's daughter, so Babe says, & John tells her the old folks are very well pleased, *dont hint* this for it was given to me as a secret. All the negros are well just now. Sat Bill was sick—Thornton had only the two chills. That box of home made Quinine is worth $400 of this trash money. Thornton to whom I gave it pretty heavy says it made his head & ears roar, complained just like one does in taking large does of Quinine. Aunt Cinda & Kate are both sick & I must try & go over there this evening. Jim Scott was water bound at Colorado River, 7 of his mules got away which he soon recovered, & 2 of mothers & Nelson who is driving mothers wagon came home after them but they havent reached home & Bob went back with him to hunt them. That lying tanner Ferrell hasent got my hides ready yet. I wont have leather for negro shoes this winter. I feel so mad at him. I have got my wheel from Harbuck's, will pay 12 bu[shels] of corn this fall. I am going to Lancasters soon, & carry leather to make me a pair, and Walter, the baby and Mary. I must hasten up the tanning when I get the hides, to get some ready for the boys shoes. Bet Scott talks of killing a beef & no doubt she will, & of course it will spoil. I almost hate her. John waits & I must close tho I could write much more. Do try and come home soon.

your affectionate wife
Lizzie S Neblett

Va Point
June 19th/64

Dear Lizzie

This is sunday evening or at least after dinner, I concluded it probable you were if at home writing your weekly letter and knowing no better or pleasanter way of spending my super abundance of time here I thought of writing a part at least of my letter to you. I did not return last Friday as I expected but will tomorrow or Wednesday for I came about well. I suffered a good deal— became delirious in fact was on the eve of a billious fever when I had that operation performed.

If I knew you were engaged in a letter to me this instant it would add interest to my writing and would be the next thing to actual presence but as I have no great confidence in biology particularly at a great distance I do not suffer my self to feel what might be true. There has occurred some things between us to prove that there was a spiritual communication between us at times but such things are too difficult to prove. I have noticed that when we were together we found ourselves very frequently thinking of the same thing and this did look like mesmerism or biology or something akin to it.

I suppose from the terms upon which I can come home that you prescribe that if I cannot get the articles you do not want to see me or at least do not wish me to come home. I will try and get the articles you mention but doubt whether the Syring of the right kind can be had but I have no doubt the Ergot can. I could try in Galveston and if I start home will also in Houston. By this you will see that I am coming [on] home some of these times. If I had my choice I would prefer July in order to get peaches and roasting ears. I have not yet proposed that wine making detail but will when I return. If that fails I fear I will not get to see home until Fall if then for furloughs may be stopped by that time and if so I cannot expect to see you all until next Spring unless I find a detail of some kind. I will struggle hard before I yield to the idea of not coming home until next Spring. I have been at home four days in eleven months. The four days were so lost that they look like a small dim spot unremarkable to memorys eye. I wish to make that spot longer next time. Jim Scott never wrote to me what he would do about taking cotton for the cattle. Does he intend to hold on to the cows & calves he has up. When will he be back. But there is one thing certain when I pay him I will have a bill of sale in writing to the cattle any man that can be led and governed by as great a fool as his wife is, is not to be relied upon while under that compliance. None of that Goodrich family ever had the remotest idea of any honorable prospects. I believe I have said that often before. I know I have often thought it. I never knew any family like them.

June 20th If I were in Galveston this evening I would expect a letter from you but as it is I do not until in the morning. It has been very dry here this Spring—[very] brin[e]y now which reminds me to note that fact—a very important one to the soldiers for they are and have been using brackish water too bad for a cow to drink for a month past. I have been more fortunate.

I suppose you will soon have time from the crop to make some improvements on the place. I expect that cotton in your Mas gin house will have to be [word illegible] before Rivers commences picking if so it would be best to put it in the cotton house and raise the house fence or find logs higher. I would like to know what Jim intends doing first.

What has become of Coleman. Oliver told me that Garret had lost his office by a reorganization what has become of him. Have you heard from Randle lately. Tell Mary she owes me a letter. Wish the children could be down here to bathe in the bay. I took a very refreshing one this morning. The mosquitoes are so troublesome that I cannot write in any peace. If I did not have a bar[19] it would be impossible to sleep or live here. Your complaint of fleas is nothing to the mosquitoes here. I will go to Galveston on Wednesday (22)

Yours affectionately
Wm H N

Galveston
June 25th/64

Dear Lizzie

Yours of the 5th and 8th and post marked 11th did not reach me until the 20th & probably arrived in Galveston & lay there several days before it was sent to me at Va Pt. I am perfectly astonished at the rain you have been having every thing has been dried up here, cistern water almost out and only one good rain since Jan & that fell on the 20th. I fear the rains will produce sickness in Lake creek. John Scott says not. What you write me about Billy's arm has caused me great uneasiness. I was about to write to you the day I recd your letter of the 5th & say that his arm must be dislocated & that you must send immediately for a Doctor but recollected that I wrote you to that effect in my last & supposed that would certainly cause you to have his arm examined immediately & not risk the loss or crippling of him for life. I do not recollect the name of the tonic Dr Croom gave Walter. I expect teething is the exciting cause of Bettie's sickness & her weakness the cause of her night sweats. I think bathing would do her good & I would also give her wine well sweatened and weakened with water until she learns to [drink] it & then give it stronger. I was surprised to hear that she is so poor & weak. Your other letters did not say any thing of her being in such bad health.

I have just written to the Enrolling Officer at Houston about the conduct of Coody & Harbuck. I suggested that they be put in the service at least for a while so that they may enjoy the comfort of their detail if they get it again. You say the deer are eating the potato vines. Cant you get Rivers to fire hunt them a few times. If I can get to come home next month I will get him to go with me. I fear the tanning has been put off too late for heavy hides. About the Geese I can give no advice and just as little consolation. I suppose it was

19. A "bar" was the term for mosquito netting that formed a tent over a cot or bed.

the natural folly of a Goose to eat poison & the wisest thing they were capable of to die. You say in your last that you perceived a tinge of the blues in one or two of my last letters. Well I wish I could have the blues more frequently as a matter of revenge on you. You would not envy me so much & finding others unhappy besides yourself you would not be so unhappy yourself. You know misery loves company. The letter you speak of as bearing evidence of the blues was written while I was quite unwell—on the verge of a fever for a week—very billous and to this superadded the dangerously critical state of our armies in Va & Ga. On this later subject I feel uneasy yet, but not as much so as I did some time ago. I rec'd a letter from Nelia the day I rec'd your last. She informs me about the same things that you say Harriet wrote to you. She writes a very unsatisfactory letter—not near as good as Ma's. About the rats why dont you poison them—put it in the holes so that nothing else can get it. You should shoot the hawks and lay no claim to be a Southern war widow. About the spinning that makes me sick to think of the tedious & everlasting work to make cloth. I always hated to hear the sound of a spinning wheel. It always sounded like some mournful moaning—some Tantalus work—rolling up a rock & letting it roll back again—some non progressing everlasting job.[20] No one but the Fates should ever have been allowed to spin on a wheel. The sound positively makes me lonesome & gives me the blues. I will not live in a country where spinning wheels abound in peace times. I have been racking my brain for some time to devise some method of getting some cloth for you & the children as well. If I can come home I may do so. I will stop at Pa's (to my great scandle be it said) when I come & see if I can do any thing with him towards it. I have not heard from the Co (I) since it left. I expected it back by this time but it may stay much longer. If I had been well I should like to have gone with it. I do not think it will be sickly but the mosquitoes will be terrible. I do not see how a man can sleep a minute without a bar. I may be mistaken in this or both.

June 27th Monday Since writing the foregoing yours of the 14th has been received and greatly relieved my fears about the baby and Billy's arm though not entirely so particularly about Billy. I think now that the Baby will improve since she has cut those teeth.

---

20. Will Neblett is confusing two Greek myths. Tantalus was doomed to spend eternity thirsty and hungry, standing in water that always receded when he tried to drink and under branches of fruit he could never reach. Sisyphus was sentenced to forever roll uphill a heavy stone that always rolled down again.

I was greatly surprised at the prospect of Babes marriage. I had never had an intimation of it. But I was more surprised to hear that she had asked your advise [*sic*] on the subject. You did right not to give it. She only wants you to be come responsible for what she may [do or make] you the scape goat for what error she may commit. Have nothing to do with it or as little as possible. I do not suppose you know enough of the young man to form an opinion of him and this is a sufficient justification and excuse to evade advice. From what I have written you heretofore & I suppose you in receipt of them I hope you will make yourself entirely easy about me though I know you were greatly surprised at the malady. I am well of it I think as you may judge from the fact that last Saturday I walked out to the Gulf ³⁄₄ mile and had a fine bath in the serf which was very high. The walk together with swimming and jumping up to prevent the waves from running over me has made me so sore all over that I can hardly walk to day. I always think of Bob in my sport in the water. He would enjoy it finely. We had just had time to dress when two hacks came along full of ladies and among them were Mrs McAlpine & Miss Perry. The former has been very sick—looks badly. I will send this by Jack who starts home tomorrow. John talks of buying a furlough from a man in his Co. I expect he will have to pay 400 or 500 dollars in Confederate money.

Co (I) is expected here in ten days or two weeks. My friend Lt Samuels has been assigned to duty as Assistant Adjt Gen on Gen Magruders Staff & is in charge of the detail Bureau at Houston. After writing the first sheet of this letter I saw Coody. He has joined Co (I) and is now at Pelican Spit with about a dozen of the Co left there. They went as far as Houston on the way to join the Co in La but were ordered back. From this they suppose the Co will not remain long. I will not send the letter I wrote to the enrolling Officer. Harbuck is a very poor man & has a large & helpless family and unless he acts too badly he ought to remain. I am expecting a letter this evening from you. Did you ever intimate any thing to your Ma about exchanging land. If it comes convenient do so I would suppose your Ma would be willing to exchange some of her baled cotton with us for cotton in the seed as it will not be as liable to impressment as that which is baled. I will try Pa but expect the burning of his Gin leaves him very little if any that is baled. In my letter to Nelia I asked her to ascertain if I could not get Frank Perry to haul us a bale of cotton to San Antonio and invest the proceeds in calico & domestic for you. If he will do so I will try and get a bale from Pa or your Ma for that purpose. I see that it is worth 10 cts in San Antonio without any permit from the Govmt. If he will not charge more than three cents to haul it this would leave 35.00 in specie or enough to buy 50 or 60 yds of calico & domestic which would help you out very much. Calico is worth here from 50 cts to 100 per yard. Very good can be purchased at 75. I saw a blockade runner offering ordinary muslin at 60 cts per yd. News from Richmond looks gloomy and disheartening. But it is all Northern news & we must make allowances for that. The yankees say that they command the town of Petersburg often driving back our forces & capturing several thousand prisoners from Beauregard.[21] Petersburg is 20 miles South of Richmond. Whenever affairs look so gloomy I always I always [*sic*] think of you & the children. That picture is always in my future & the darker the time the plainer I see it.

> yours affectionately
> Wm H Neblett

I have just recd yours of the 19th which has given me much pleasure. I am sorry to hear that you have undertaken to weave. I think you have enough to do without undertaking that in your exhausted state. I do not like the idea of your weaving—it is mortifying to me. I wish you would stop it. I feel that I am somehow to blame for the necessity which has induced you to do so.

What aged man is Yarborough. You call him Col—he is not Col. Is he the man that has two fingers on each hand grown together. If he is I recollect him—was introduced once. I enclose you my transfer from the Hospital here to Va Pt. showing the disease. I must close as John S[cott] will be here in a minute to give this to Jack to carry.

> Tell Mary to kiss the Baby for me.
> Wm H. Neblett

At Mothers
sunday morn July 3rd/64

Dear Will—Your letter of the 27th was handed me by Jack, on Friday morning, the envelope *open at one end*. I said why how did this letter come open, Jack said, it got wet, & I said to him yes and Susan read every word of it, he said nothing to that. Now Will you have done it, dident let your guts

---

21. Union troops attacked Petersburg, Virginia, on June 15, 1864. The attack failed to capture the city, and the Union army settled in for a siege. The city finally fell April 3, 1865. Long, *Civil War Day by Day*, 522–25, 665.

out to John this time, but went to the madam herself to do it. Dident you know that I would not send a letter by Jack, & then to write and put anything in the letter that you would not be willing for the whole world to know, and send it so that it would go right into her hands. Don't you know if it had not been open that she would not hesitate one moment about opening it, which you know can be done, & it not detected. A woman who believes there is no God, Heaven nor hell, the bible a fable, and Jesus Christ a bastard—who is malicious & black hearted, prefering a lie to the truth at all times one who will and has perjured herself—would not hesitate to do any thing, particularly to find food to feed her bitter hatred. Oh Will, Will, why did you write by Jack won't you never comprehend her character, & John's, for he is almost as bad as she is, and I have talked to you so much about never writing a letter to me to pass through her hands particularly if it was from you, and then in this letter, every thing that I have felt desirous to keep a secret from her, was divulged. Stop now & think what you wrote, for she knows it all, & can & will build lies for years to come upon the foundation of that letter. In the first place, you sent her the evidence of your disease. Now wont she clap her hands & rejoice, for she will have one single thread of truth in the warp of which she will weave the blackest and most loathsome tales that any one ever listened to. True this tale will be principally on you, but Will your reputation is as dear to me as my own—in the next place you have told her of Babe's intended marriage, & she is the one Babe felt most anxious to keep it from. I havent told Babe that her affair was mentioned in your letter, & won't for it will only make her feel badly, & do no good—in the next place you mentioned the land swap with mother, another thing I did not want her to know. You speak of more things in this letter than you have in any letter in a long time, did indeed let all you know out to our particular friend. You say you don't like to hear of my weaving, &c, now Will, I would rather stay at home and weave hard six mo[nths] or a year, every day, than that you had sent that letter so that it would pass through Susans hands.

I was at mothers when Jack reached home came up the day before, and he says he started over to our house but heard before he reached there, that I was not at home & so kept the letter until the next day, & brought it by on his way to the Depot, for a trunk of things Jno sent up, his winter clothes I think. The letter being open, only saved her the trouble of unsealing it. True, she has but few to talk to—but the news of your complaint, & the cause she will assign will soon be on the whole neighborhood—and Jno will know that you told him a story, & will account for your telling me the truth, by thinking that I can be blinded by you, to believe that it was Hydrocele, when it was in reality the worst kind of venereal disease. But there is no use thinking or writing about it—but one thing let me beg and entreat of you, for God sake, write the next letter you send by anybody who will pass it through her hands before it reaches me for her eye, give her the devil generally, but don't mention your private home matters. I think you [should] do just the same way with John, have just as little caution & thought or suspicion in your intercourse with him, as you displayed in sending that letter by Jack. You know that I would not write by Jack to you, & you know how that single note I sent by him with the Tobacco was distorted, even by John. Jno Scott hasent the smallest particle of real, true friendship for you, makes you the butt of ridicule in his letters to his sweet wife, and to others, finds fault of you in every possible manner, and yet you treat Jno as you always did,—and it is his best fun to get you to go to camps with him, or spend several hours with him, to *pick you,* make you disgorge yourself so that he can write his lovely wife a spicy letter. I tell you Will, he is not to be relied upon—is *deceitful,* and not as honorable as he might be, for your dignity's sake, be as little with him as possible, and never touch on home matters in his hearing, but he won't want to pick you again for a long time your letter had so much in it, that her appetite will be glutted—but may be you were not full enough and he will try and find out something more on several points. Her reading this letter has troubled me more than any thing that has happened in a long time, I reckon 'tis the fulfillment of the feelings I had when writing my letter of the same date. I felt all the time I was writing that some one beside you would read that letter, and came very near suppressing any thing of a private nature. I had rather Susan had read my letter than to have read yours. I see that Jno must have told you Jack was going home & even called to get your letter to deliver it to Jack well knowing that he would get the benefit of all it contained. I spoke to mother this morning about the exchange of land, & she only said such a thing as that could not be fixed up until after the war, and I let it drop.

To my surprise, I found ripe June peaches when I came up to mothers. That large tree of soft juicy peaches in the corner of the garden, next to the smoke house, your favorite tree, is loaded, mother has all the limbs proped up, and the peaches have begun to ripen. Myers gave our negros holiday yesterday, and Thornton borrowed a mule from Aunt Cinda & came by here to carry a note from me to Hattie & Nelia, and I sent by him a basket of the nicest kind of peaches to Ma. Some off your tree as I call it, some June peaches, & two & the only ones ripe on one of mothers finest trees, they were as large as an ordinary sized Apple, and as red—they looked delicious. I hope Ma will be well enough to relish & eat them. I think of you when I see the peaches and wish you were here to enjoy them. The baby almost takes fits over a peach, & I have allowed her to eat as high as two soft peaches in a day, & can see no bad result. Biscuit & peaches are her glory. Her bowels are much disordered, & her lower jaw teeth are so near out that the skin looks white, or festered where the[y] are coming. I must lance them when I go home. She is yet very poor, but seems stronger than she was two weeks ago, hasent had a fever now in two weeks, except a day & night with cholera morbus. I was alarmed about her, and applied a mustard plaster to her bowels, & turpentine also & it relieved her. She came just now to my knees, and looked up in my face, & began her complaint I knew she wished some thing & took her up & went and offered her a piece of biscuit & she cast it from her & kept squealing, I found she had seen a peach & they would not give it to her, & she trotted in the next room to me, & made her complaint. I pealed her a ripe soft one and took the seed out, & gave it to her, & she trotted off perfectly satisfied. I have just taken an other look in her mouth, & find she has two jaw teeth almost entirely through, two more on the edge of the skin, & one front tooth through & the other nearly so. She has been cutting you see, 4 jaw & two front teeth all at the same time, enough to make her sick. Now a little of Babe's affair which I hope won't reach Susan's ears, through me in any way. She has said yes to Yarborough, tho' she says she don't know whether she loves him or not. She shows plainly by her talk & acts that 'tis his money and the style & position she hopes to gain which is inducing her to marry him. She says she loves to splurge as well as Sallie Kennard and Yarborough can afford to let her do it—& he is so fond of dress and show that he suits her exactly. She sent a note to Jim after he started to buy her a bonnet, & sent for a white [word illegible] dress, & as soon as she can make up some things after Jim's return, the wedding will be over. James Quincy Yarborough is a widower with one son, some 12 or 13 yrs old is a man about 36 yrs, & is not the man you spoke of in your letter, has no fingers grown together. He came from Ala[bama] here, has a good many negros, but the largest portion is his little boys left him by his mothers father. Mother wont object.

The negros at home finished plowing the cotton, and hoed out the worst portion of it, & finished the potatoe patch last week. Myers wants to borrow two mules this week and plow it over again, only run the two plows and have the others going over it with the hoes—he says it is small for this time in the year, but if we have seasons ought to make 20 bales. Says we may calculate with certainty upon making 1200 bushels of corn—tho the rain injured our best corn a good deal. I sent my bark to Keifers & had it ground and Friday Joe put the hides down in bark. Myers went to Keifer with the wagon, took Joe & Tom, & Mrs Oliver's mule to do the grinding. Myers is very accommodating & tho' he is deficient in judgment yet, for his good intentions, I like him. Mother is living very comfortably in her new house, and has an excellent crop of corn, and cotton looks tolerably well they say. Bet spent the day here, Friday, came up to attend the Barbecue at Anderson given to Capt Webbs Co, who are guarding the jail in Anderson. Bet says Jim only paid Susan for half of her cotton & she promised him to take the ballance right away & Bet says she went over to pay her as soon as Jim left, & she refuses to take the old issue, Bet wrote her a note that it would do for taxes & it would be no more trouble to fund what she owed her than to fund her own, & Susan wrote her a note saying "she dident have a cent to fund as her husband had never speculated"— and Bet says she knows she got Bill Dodd to take a thousand to Huntsville for her & fund it. I'm still over her about 1000 dollars. Everybody is on a strain or have been to fund money for taxes, I had none to fund. I only paid Mrs Buckly for six months tuition $99, paid her 3 for 2 her other patrons did so, & I would not kick up at it.

I think there is a big fuss brewing between Bet & Susan. I can see that Bet is mad now. Susan has come it over Jim about the cotton, he was to pay her 80 cts in the old issue tho' it was not so stipulated in the bond as old Shilock said—in fact they had no writings that I know of, & I don't know how Jim can get around paying in the new issue—but let them have it, I don't care. Bet has been believing (because she wanted to believe harm of me) all of Susan's tales about me, and now let her get a little taste of her. I think Billy's arm is about well, tho' he does not use it as well as he did before it was hurt, but will after a while I think—it was not dislocated as you feared. You keep writing about Rivers like he was at home, he was on the eve of leaving when you were at home in Feby and has been gone three or 4 months belongs to Terry's Regt.[22] The deer will have to eat the potatoe vines if they want to. Babe rec'd letters from Coleman & Garrett recently writen at Tyler. Coleman writes that his Co has been attached to Anderson Regt, don't speak of leaving there. Wants mother to let him have Little Bob, to buy up produce, & trade it off with the yankee prisoners for silver plate, jewelry watches &c, plunder stolen by them in La—as they gave nothing for it they part with their plunder for

---

22. More than likely D. S. Terry's Texas cavalry regiment. Wright and Simpson, *Texas in the War*, 30, 124.

very reduced prices. Mother has no notion of sending him Bob. Garrett writes a short letter no news in it, he says, father like "I think we have the poorest set of officers in the Confederacy."

Mrs McIntosh sent out her mother first to get her some peaches & fresh butter from mother wanted a peach if it was no bigger than her thumb. She is longing & makes an awful blow about it. I found her mother Mrs Godard a very intelligent woman, keen as a briar, and one of the best talkers I ever listened to. She disapproves of a woman accepting a step mothers place, & from her conversation you would judge that Dr McIntosh's children do not act right towards her, to hear Mrs Godard talk. I find that she lived in Raymond Miss—at the same time that Pa lived there & Jno Scott went to school with her boys by her first husband Buckholts—they are lawyers been living in Tex a good while you perhaps know them. Mrs McIntosh was a Godard—so she was not a Yankee school mistress as I always thought. Bet Scott says that she heard that Mrs McIntosh was going to sue for a larger portion than he willed her—she wants her marriage portion bequeathed to her by him before marriage, and a larger portion in his separate property. The property that came by his first wife he willed to be divided in three equal parts between his children, & *his property* in 4 parts. She sent a negro man for Peaches yesterday & I was so struck by his resemblance to Pa's Sigh that I asked him if he was kin to him, & he said he was Sigh's Bro. Mrs Hutcheson says she is ashamed of her scrape with Mr Glass tho' is glad she did not marry him, as she found out she did not love him, says she was too much carried away with the idea of an establishment in Galveston. I have heard that he rented a house & furnished it ready for her reception, invited a good many to go to church that night to see him marry &c. I hope you will get a detail to come home this month. You write that your friend Lt Samuels has c[h]arge of the Detail Bureau at Houston, & if you have to apply there, I hope you will be successful. If you cant comply with my orders, request or what you please about the preventives to come in your packet home—you may come home without, but must submit to my laws after reaching home, & you need not fear that they will not be made strict enough to ensure my safety. You had better feel a little unhappy, and even mad at me, than for me to suffer the uneasiness & distress that I do even fearing the disaster, and to have it happen would be ten thousand times worse than, then [*sic*] the most miserable death that history ever recorded— but I won't think on this, if I do much I will be certain to come to the conclusion that it would be better to never see you again—mind you, not better that you should be dead, for I can not bear the idea of living in this world without your being in it also. I sent our old clock over to for Mr Tom Collins to fix it so it will run before I left home, I hope he fix it so it will run. People says that Henry White and Mary Fanthorp will marry soon—he has been waiting on girls several months. I thought Thornton would come by on his way back, & I could write you how they were, but he has failed to call as I told him. Do try and come home time enough to get some peaches, & roasting ears. Sunday night July 3rd

Thornton came back last night says they are all well at Pas Nelia says Pa is not very well, Ma as well as usual.

> yours lovingly
> L S Neblett

Galveston
July 3rd/64

Dear Lizzie

Yours of the 26 & 27th was recd last Friday (the 2) I was writing a short note when it was placed on the table. I felt alarmed. It was three or four days in advance of the usual time and I was fearful that some misfortune had hastened it[s] departure. You may well believe that I was relieved when I found that your uneasiness for me was the cause of its early reception although regret that the failure of my letter to arrive in due time had caused you so much uneasiness. I thought at the time that you had forgotten that I could telegraph in an extremity to Pa at Navasota & have the message consigned to you in a half day from the time it started from here. I thought of this when I submitted to that operation.

I have now two of your touching & eloquent letters unanswered, and in the spirit and beauty I feel incapable of ever doing so. Do you know that I think you an extraordinary letter writer far above mediocrity and no doubt you could become so in other departments of litterature by practice. I hope some day you may be so situated as to do so to a greater advantage than you now have. I think you would be happier in the cultivation and exercise of your talents that you have been in being tied down to the cares and troubles of the last ten years. But nevertheless you can & should sketch an hour or two every day to improve & cultivate your [mind]. I do not think the affections of the wife need be dried up in the cultivation of the head. Most of men believe it has that effect but I do not see why it should have that effect on women when it does not on men. Some distinguished literary men as well as women have deformed intellects as well [as] hearts and perhaps this is the cause of the prevalent that the cultivation of the former in women is the cause of the latter. I do not fear that your intellect will ever deform your heart or make you forget your sense of duty to your family or dry up your affections. So far I believe I have without premeditation written you a lecture rather than a letter and if it is the first time I have ever said so it is by no means the first that I have thought it. I would feel a pride in your distinguishing yourself in literature. I believe many men are jealous or rather envious of talents in their wives and think the contrast warps them. It may [several words obliterated] I do not think the wings of those that can fly should be cliped to keep them from rising sometimes above those that cannot. For my own part I sometimes feel to a painful degree the truth that I have committed some great blunders and been guilty of some very fatal negligence in my own life for the last fifteen years. But how few are not pained & mortified by the ghost of misspent time. I am now a few years past the meridian of life and know that more of the working part of life yet remains. Or rather that portion of life yet remains in which might be put in practice what has heretofore been learned still I feel to a painful extent in my profession I have made a failure in my practice in the Dist. courts and altho' I have some consolation in feeling that such was not the case in the Supreme court where I have been twice as successful or indeed more so than common still I cannot help feeling that I never was [line obliterated] you, and I look now to that branch of the practice with loathing & and [*sic*] disgust. It always has been too much like a game of cards and you know I never had any taste or talent for that if indeed there is any talent required but rather a kind of *shrewdness* (which I believe means quick cunning)

Now I do not permit my self to be cast down but when I think of the past and look to the future I feel a degree of confusion and uncertainty very unpleasant and sometimes quite bewildering. Sometimes I ask myself the question if my whole life has not been a failure and altho I have been fortunate in the lottery of marriage and all my life have had the blessing of affectionate hearts in my parents & you, this only mortifies me the worse by being perhaps less discerning of it. It is not the "blues" which makes me think this for I do so with a calm sadness which the closest person I think could never detect. If I had a strong and robust a constitution as usually falls to man I might yet make some kind of a name. For I am now satisfied by close contact with the distinguished that such is the result more of physical powers of endurance than brain. But when I think of my uncertain health I feel quite despondent altho

I do not suffer my self to become miserable because I am unable to do what I might otherwise. Apropos of a name, I will here remark that I would have wished for you to come down and spend a short time much more ardently if I had not felt a kind of pride that you should not appear in a place as the wife of a private soldier where there is so much importance to military office. I think I have more philosophy on this subject than you and it sometimes makes my blood boil for a few minutes to see it although I cannot complain much personally and tho I know the vanity of much [is] really show & pomp. But I think I should feel it more for you than my self.

Just now an occurrence happened which as it has a little significance I will relate. While writing the third page of this Maj McClarty passed through the room & in returning stoped at the door and asked me if I was writing and what I was writing? I say why? He said you appear to be very intently engaged. I said said [sic] yes very intently and he walked off. He asked me a similar question once before. I was asked one by another if I did not correspond with the Gal[veston] News. I see that several have the opinion that I write frequently for the paper. I cannot imagine how this idea got out. I write sometimes a short article but have never told any one of it.

I have made an effort to get that detail for making wine but failed here. I have made an application to the chief Surgeon at Houston & requested Samuels to append a few words of recommendation. I expect to hear from it in a few days & if that fails I will try once more & if that fails I will try to get a leave of absence and if I fail in that I will try some thing else. I have set my head & heart upon coming home in July.

July 4th. I did not get any news by to days mail of my application for detail. I sometimes feel all my efforts will fail.

In looking over the above particularly the last three pages I had half a notion to destroy it but I believe I will let it go. This was my regular day for receiving your letters and more than a dozen times I have caught myself looking for a letter and sooner regreted that I got one on Friday as it deprived me of the pleasure on Monday. I have no doubt you have received some of my letters since the one was written that I received from you last. The rains I suppose will cause the worms to eat all the cotton up. I find so I look upon a little cotton as more important than you seem to do. In sending that bucket & bag by Jack, I through mistake sent my haversack also. I had placed it in with the bucket & forgot to take it out. Tell Mary that I am very glad to see that she is still working by her letters.

yours affectionately
Wm H. Neblett

Epilogue

In July 1864 Will received a transfer from Galveston to Houston for medical reasons. Apparently he spent most of the rest of the war at home, since the exchange of letters between Lizzie and Will stops after July 3, 1864. How the Nebletts fared in the postwar years is unclear, as there are few letters from this period in the Neblett collection. The value, however, of both their personal and real property dropped to $800 and $5,000, respectively, in 1870. In 1871, two months before Lizzie gave birth to her sixth and final child, Grace, Will Neblett died of pneumonia. His death left Lizzie to raise their children and manage their affairs alone.[1]

Unfortunately, few letters survive to indicate how Lizzie managed under such difficult circumstances. It is clear, though, that her circle of friends and family widened. From others' letters to Lizzie, and from the few extant ones written by her later in her life, we glimpse an older and much changed woman. Lizzie published essays in local newspapers and became involved in local affairs. By 1880 she had joined the Red Ribbon Temperance Society in Anderson, serving as secretary from 1880 to 1882. She also worked on a committee that prepared a temperance petition for presentation to state lawmakers. Besides maintaining a wide circle of correspondence, she regularly visited friends and family in the state. She even visited her sister Sally in Washington, D.C., and took a trip to Niagara Falls.

In light of Lizzie's earlier behavior toward her children, however, it is her relationship with them as adults that is most interesting. In a letter to a rela-

---

1. Military Records of William Neblett, Compiled Service Records; TX Census 1870.

tive, she apparently complained that her children treated her badly. The relative tried to comfort her: "Do not be too hard on them, I know your children love you dearly and have always felt proud of their mother."[2] Despite these reassurances it is clear there were problems in Lizzie's relationships with her children.

In a letter to Walter dated February 6, 1905, she lamented that she had not heard from him since May 1902. She called him a "wanderer" and said she often had trouble keeping up with his whereabouts. Their relationship deteriorated to the point that Lizzie contemplated throwing him off her land in Bell County because of his "gypsy" ways. In the same letter she wrote sadly about the condition of her family and the emptiness she felt at home since her children had left: "I no longer have a home. I own this house, farm and furniture with cattle horses &c, yet I am only a stray dog in my own house . . . the home feeling is gone. . . . I think we are all in rather a bad shape—I mean the whole family in the Neblett crowd."[3]

Even her relationship with Bob, her professed favorite, did not appear to develop into a close adult relationship. His letters to his mother centered around discussions of money, land, or other business ventures. Lizzie did visit Bob and his family occasionally, but he seemed absorbed by family troubles of his own. Around 1904 Lizzie attempted to comfort him in a letter filled with an optimism missing in her earlier years: "[Y]our way seems so dark, and full of insurmountable obstacles that prevent you from seeing the sunshine that lies beyond these mountain heights . . . your present trials become stepping stones to your higher enfoldment." She cautioned Bob that Mattie (Martha Conger Yeater), his wife, was experiencing "the change of life." She wrote that this was the time "when extreme nervousness, and want of mental poise so often prevail in a woman's life—She at times is *not responsible for her acts or words.*" She urged "kind charitable feeling" because she was sure that Mattie did not really believe what she was saying. Perhaps Lizzie saw some of her younger self in Mattie. She defended Mattie's "mental deformaties" and chastised Mattie's children for defaming "their mother with words of condemnation against her that ought never to pass their lips." Bob temporarily separated

2. Carri Perry to LN, March 10, 1889, NP.

3. LN to Walter Scott Neblett, February 6, 1905, NP. Walter never married and died May 5, 1957. NFB; Perkins, *Some Nebletts in America,* 109.

from Mattie. He left Corsicana, taking the children with him. Lizzie approved of his actions, stating that "she [Mattie] does not want you there to interfere."[4]

Of all her sons, perhaps it was Billy with whom she became closest. There appear to be more letters from Billy than from her other sons, and he seems to have kept an eye on her physical, not just financial, well being. Billy wrote to his sister Mary that the woman hired to help Lizzie "seems to be kind to Ma and she seems to feel more independent living in her own house." But it was her daughters, not sons, with whom Lizzie became closest. This closeness, unfortunately, did not prevent two of her three daughters from developing mental disorders, which may have stemmed from Lizzie's own earlier bouts of depression and abuse.[5]

Her youngest child, Grace, was born after the death of her father. During the 1890s, when Grace was in her twenties, she developed some sort of mental and physical illness. Lizzie cared for her unmarried daughter in her home and tried to cure her using spiritualism or "Mental Science." In 1894 she consulted a New Jersey spiritualist named Alvesta C. Scott Brown, who theorized that Grace was making herself ill and needed a stronger belief in God. Ironically, considering Lizzie's past admonishments to Will, Brown warned Lizzie not to give Grace too much sympathy for her condition. "Never sympathize with a falsity," she wrote. She suggested that Lizzie instead try the fashionable "rest cure": "Let her lie in bed all the time." She also suggested having Grace's horoscope cast. After "reading" the horoscope, Brown diagnosed Grace's "feelings of fear" as possibly caused by an "irregularity" of the womb and un- fulfilled sexual desires. Employing the popular idea that the state of women's reproductive organs determined their mental health, she advised, "Insanity is known to often arise from womb troubles. . . . She may have a conjestion of

<hr>

4. LN to Robert Scott Neblett [no date, probably latter part of 1904], NP. It is interesting to note that Lizzie's admonishments are reminiscent of the ones Will used to give her. Robert Scott became a lawyer like his father, was mayor of Corsicana from 1885 to 1888, and served a term as a Texas legislator in 1907. He died January 18, 1918. NFB; Perkins, *Some Nebletts in America*, 105–108.

5. William Teel Neblett to Mary Neblett Brown, January 17, 1916, NFB. William Neblett married Abigail Thomas and became a farmer and stock raiser. He died October 15, 1935. There are indications of a history of depression in Lizzie's family. She recorded in her memorial to Will that her father occasionally suffered from bouts of the "blues."

the womb arising from demands (natural and unconscious and unbridled) of the sexual nature not being met."[6]

Whether Lizzie took any of Brown's advice is unknown. Eventually, however, Grace was placed in an asylum in San Antonio. When Grace's physical health began to fade, Lizzie brought her home and nursed her until Grace's death in 1903. Lizzie would later write: "With a perfect knowledge that the life of one I loved more than my own life was slowly but surely ebbing away, yet I was so filled with devine love that for the good and pleasure and well being of my child I could put down self and think only of her."[7] Lizzie's words are reminiscent of the martyred air she often assumed as a young woman. She still appeared to use the illnesses of her children as a means to feeling selfless. After Grace's death Lizzie had a small cottage built, which she named Grace Cottage.

Lizzie and her oldest daughter, Mary, often corresponded, although their relationship obviously had its rough moments. Lizzie once wrote, "She wants to see me now and feels better towards me." Mary spent many years in a sanitarium with an undisclosed illness. Lizzie, however, believed that Mary's affliction was all in her mind. She eventually convinced Mary to leave the sanitarium and arranged for her to live in the home of her son Aubrey. Lizzie then wrote to a "doctor" whom she hoped would hypnotize Mary into a better frame of mind. Apparently, she saw nothing of herself in Mary when she noted that: "every little pain is magnified in her mind to an *awful suffering* that weakens her so she is set back a week in her efforts to throw off her *imaginary ailment*."[8]

---

6. Alvesta C. Scott Brown to LN, June 13, 1894; Alvesta C. Scott Brown to LN, June 29, 1894, NP. Included in the collection for the year 1914 is a list of books that Lizzie hoped to obtain that indicate her interest in spiritualism: *The Occultism in the Shakespeare Plays, Scientific Evidence of Future Life, Soul Power and Possibilities, The Hidden Side of Evolution,* and *Universal Brotherhood.* Also contained in the Neblett papers are several horoscopes that were cast for both Lizzie and Grace. On the "hysterical woman" see Carroll Smith-Rosenberg, "The Hysterical Woman: Sex Roles and Role Conflict in Nineteenth-Century America," in *Disorderly Conduct: Visions of Gender in Victorian America* (New York: Alfred A. Knopf, 1985), 197–216; and Charlotte Perkins Gilman's famous short story "The Yellow Wallpaper," found in numerous collections and anthologies.

7. LN to Lizzie Neblett Throop, February 4, 1904, NP.

8. LN to William Teel Neblett, July 31, 1908; LN to William Teel Neblett, August 18, 1908, NP. On February 12, 1873, Mary Neblett married Dr. James Tarry Brown. She apparently spent the last 30 years of her life as an invalid in the home of one or the other of her three living children. She died August 11, 1936. NFB; Perkins, *Some Nebletts in America*, 98–99.

Perhaps the greatest puzzle of Lizzie's life, however, was her relationship with Bettie (later called Lizzie). Among all the children, Bettie became her mother's closest confidante. Lizzie's collection of papers contains more letters from Bettie than from any of her other children. Lizzie visited friends and relatives often during her later years, but she went to Bettie's home with increasing regularity and for longer and longer periods of time, often to recuperate from illnesses. A niece once commented, "You are fortunate in having such a noble, kind loving daughter to watch over you and care for you." Perhaps Bettie's devoted care of her mother resulted from having been an unwanted child. Making herself indispensable to Lizzie as Lizzie grew old and infirm may have enabled her to feel truly "wanted" by her mother.[9]

In 1908, after Bettie became president of the Albert Sidney Johnson chapter of the United Daughters of the Confederacy (UDC), she asked Lizzie, as she often did, to write a speech for her to present to the UDC. The topic was to be the Confederate Veterans' Woman's Home, and Bettie advised her mother: "Don't have it too long and bring in something nice also about Tex [during] the confederacy and the work of the home." Lizzie seemed to have no qualms about helping to glorify what had been a terrible period of her life.[10]

Lizzie's personality seemed to undergo a transition in her later life. One friend praised her for her serenity and optimism: "I almost envy you your gentle cheerful disposition. You seem to me to always find the 'silver lining to a cloud.'" In another instance, Lizzie philosophically mused to a granddaughter, "It seems very strange yet when I think of you as a married woman. But this is the fate of the greater part of womankind, and if you have found a good kind husband and one that suits you, it will turn out for the best. In the ultimate all is for the best that comes into our lives." Perhaps the changes in Lizzie's outlook on life sprang from the fact that one of her fervent wishes had been fulfilled. Relieved of domestic responsibilities, she had become a wanderer upon the earth with no one to care for but herself.[11]

9. [Unknown] to Lizzie Neblett, March 7, 1915, NP. Lizzie "Bettie" Neblett married Benjamin Baden Throop; she died January 27, 1928. NP; Perkins, *Some Nebletts in America*, 110–111.

10. Lizzie Neblett Throop to LN, February 18, 1908. NP. On women's role in creating the "myth of the Lost Cause," see especially Whites, *Civil War as a Crisis in Gender.*

11. Laura E. Haynie to LN, July 24, 1904; LN to Conger Neblett, October 11, 1906, NP.

BIBLIOGRAPHY

UNPUBLISHED SOURCES

Manuscripts

Neblett (Elizabeth Scott) Papers, Center for American History, University of Texas at Austin. This collection contains letters to and from the Neblett family between the years 1848 and 1935, the Neblett family Bible, Lizzie Neblett's diary and her unpublished manuscript titled "A memoir of the Life, Death, and character of my dearly beloved husband William H. Neblett," along with various photographs, newspaper clippings, and miscellany collected by Lizzie Neblett.

John Newton Scott vertical file, Center for American History, University of Texas at Austin.

Robert Caldwell Neblett vertical file, Center for American History, University of Texas at Austin.

Public Documents and Records

Memorial: Judge R. S. Neblett. Texas: n.p., 1918.

Military Records of William Neblett, Company I, Twentieth Infantry (Elmore's Regiment), from Compiled Service Records of Confederate Soldiers Who Served in Organizations from the State of Texas, M323, roll 400, National Archives, Washington, D.C.

Mullins, Marion Day, copyist. *Grimes County, Texas, Marriage Records, 1848–1879.* N.p.,1962.

PUBLISHED SOURCES

Public Documents and Records

Federal Manuscript Census, Seventh Census, 1850, Texas.

Federal Manuscript Census, Eighth Census, 1860, Texas.

Federal Manuscript Census, Ninth Census, 1870, Texas.

U.S. Bureau of the Census. *Mortality Statistics of the Seventh Census of the United States, 1850.* Washington, D.C.: A. O. P. Nicholson, Printer, 1855.

U.S. War Department. *The War of the Rebellion: A Compilation of the Official Records of the Union and Confederate Armies.* 128 parts in 70 vols. Washington, D.C.: U.S. Government Printing Office, 1880–1901.

Books

Allen, Irene Taylor. *Saga of Anderson: The Proud Story of a Historic Texas Community.* New York: Greenwich Book Publishers, 1957.

Andrews, Gregg. *Insane Sisters: Or, the Price Paid for Challenging a Company Town.* Columbia: University of Missouri Press, 1999.

Ayers, Edward. *Vengeance and Justice: Crime and Punishment in the Nineteenth-Century American South.* New York: Oxford University Press, 1984.

Bleser, Carol, ed. *In Joy and in Sorrow: Women, Family, and Marriage in the Victorian South, 1830–1900.* New York: Oxford University Press, 1991.

Boatner, Mark Mayo, III. *The Civil War Dictionary.* New York: David McKay Company, 1959.

Brodie, Janet. *Contraception and Abortion in Nineteenth-Century America.* Ithaca, N.Y.: Cornell University Press, 1994.

Bynum, Victoria E. *Unruly Women: The Politics of Social and Sexual Control in the Old South.* Chapel Hill: University of North Carolina Press, 1992.

Cartwright, Gary. *Galveston: A History of the Island.* Fort Worth: Texas Christian University Press, 1991.

Casdorph, Paul D. *Prince John Magruder: His Life and Campaigns.* New York: John Wiley & Sons, 1996.

Cashin, Joan E. *A Family Venture: Men and Women on the Southern Frontier.* Baltimore: Johns Hopkins University Press, 1991.

Censer, Jane Turner. *North Carolina Planters and Their Children, 1800–1860.* Baton Rouge: Louisiana State University Press, 1984.

Clinton, Catherine. *The Plantation Mistress: Woman's World in the Old South.* New York: Pantheon Books, 1982.

Clinton, Catherine, and Nina Silber, eds. *Divided Houses: Gender and the Civil War.* New York: Oxford University Press, 1992.

Cotham, Edward T., Jr. *Battle on the Bay: The Civil War Struggle for Galveston.* Austin: University of Texas Press, 1998.

Faust, Drew Gilpin. *Mothers of Invention: Women of the Slaveholding South in the American Civil War.* Chapel Hill: University of North Carolina Press, 1996.

———. *Southern Stories: Slaveholders in Peace and War.* Columbia: University of Missouri Press, 1992.

Fowler, Gene, ed. *Mystic Healers and Medicine Shows: Blazing Trails to Wellness in the Old West and Beyond.* Santa Fe, N. Mex.: Ancient City Press, 1997.

Fox-Genovese, Elizabeth. *Within the Plantation Household: Black and White Women of the Old South.* Chapel Hill: University of North Carolina Press, 1988.

Friedman, Jean E. *The Enclosed Garden: Women and Community in the Evangelical South, 1830–1900.* Chapel Hill: University of North Carolina Press, 1985.

Gabriel, Mary. *Notorious Victoria: The Life of Victoria Woodhull, Uncensored.* Chapel Hill, N.C.: Algonquin Books of Chapel Hill, 1998.

Genovese, Eugene. *Roll, Jordan, Roll: The World the Slaves Made.* New York: Vintage Books, 1972.

Goldsmith, Barbara. *Other Powers: The Age of Suffrage, Spiritualism, and the Scandalous Victoria Woodhull.* New York, Alfred A. Knopf, 1998.

Gordon, Linda. *Woman's Body, Woman's Right: A Social History of Birth Control in America.* New York: Grossman Publishers, 1976.

Greenberg, Kenneth. *Honor and Slavery.* Princeton, N.J.: Princeton University Press, 1996.

Grimes County Historical Commission, comp. and ed. *History of Grimes County: Land of Heritage and Progress.* Navasota, Tex.: Grimes County Historical Commission, 1982.

Hassler, William W., ed. *The General to His Lady: The Civil War Letters of William Dorsey Pender to Fanny Pender.* Chapel Hill: University of North Carolina Press, 1988.

Johnson, Sid S. *Texans Who Wore the Gray.* (Tyler, Tex.: n.p., 1907).

Leavitt, Judith Walzer. *Brought to Bed: Childbearing in America, 1750–1950.* New York: Oxford University Press, 1986.

Long, E. B. *The Civil War Day by Day: An Almanac, 1861–1865.* Garden City, N.Y.: Doubleday, 1971.

Lowe, Richard G., and Randolph B. Campbell. *Planters and Plain Folk: Agriculture in Antebellum Texas.* Dallas, Tex.: Southern Methodist University Press, 1987.

McMillen, Sally G. *Motherhood in the Old South: Pregnancy, Childbirth, and Infant Rearing.* Baton Rouge: Louisiana State University Press, 1990.

McPherson, James M. *Battle Cry of Freedom: The Civil War Era.* New York: Ballantine Books, 1988.

Otto, John Solomon. *Southern Agriculture during the Civil War Era, 1860–1880.* Westport, Conn.: Greenwood Press, 1994.

Perkins, Dorothy Neblett. *Some Nebletts in America.* San Diego, Calif.: Neblett Press, 1994.

Pickrell, Annie Doom. *Pioneer Women in Texas.* Austin, Tex.: E. L. Steck Co., 1929.

Rable, George C. *Civil Wars: Women and the Crisis of Southern Nationalism.* Urbana: University of Illinois Press, 1989.

Red, Mrs. George Plunkett. *The Medicine Man in Texas.* Houston, Tex.: Standard Printing and Lithographing Co., 1930.

Reed, James. *From Private Vice to Public Virtue: The Birth Control Movement and American Society since 1830.* New York: Basic Books, 1978.

Rothman, Ellen K. *Hands and Hearts: A History of Courtship in America.* New York: Basic Books, Inc., 1984.

Savitt, Todd L. *Medicine and Slavery: The Diseases and Health Care of Blacks in Antebellum Virginia.* Urbana: University of Illinois Press, 1978.

Scarborough, William K. *The Overseer: Plantation Management in the Old South.* Baton Rouge: Louisiana State University Press, 1966.

Scott, Anne Firor. *The Southern Lady: From Pedestal to Politics, 1830–1930.* Chicago: University of Chicago Press, 1970.

Smith-Rosenberg, Carroll. *Disorderly Conduct: Visions of Gender in Victorian America.* New York: Alfred A. Knopf, 1985.

Stevenson, Brenda E. *Life in Black and White: Family and Community in the Slave South.* New York: Oxford University Press, 1996.

Stowe, Steven M. *Intimacy and Power in the Old South: Ritual in the Lives of the Planters.* Baltimore, Md.: John Hopkins University Press, 1987.

Wakelyn, Jon L. *Biographical Dictionary of the Confederacy.* With Advisory Editor Frank E. Vandiver. Westport, Conn.: Greenwood Press, 1977.

Wertz, Richard W., and Dorothy C. Wertz. *Lying-In: A History of Childbirth in America.* New Haven: Yale University Press, 1989.

Whites, Lee Ann. *The Civil War as a Crisis in Gender: Augusta, Georgia, 1860–1890.* Athens: University of Georgia Press, 1995.

Wright, Marcus J., comp., and Harold B. Simpson, ed. *Texas in the War, 1861–1865.* Hillsboro, Tex.: Hill Junior College Press, 1965.

Wyatt-Brown, Bertram. *Southern Honor: Ethics and Behavior in the Old South.* Oxford: Oxford University Press, 1982.

Articles:

McCandless, Peter. "Mesmerism and Phrenology in Antebellum Charleston: 'Enough of the Marvellous.'" *Journal of Southern History* 2008 (1992): 199–230.

Welter, Barbara. "The Cult of True Womanhood, 1820–1860." *American Quarterly* 18 (summer 1966): 151–74.

Index